computers in the medical office

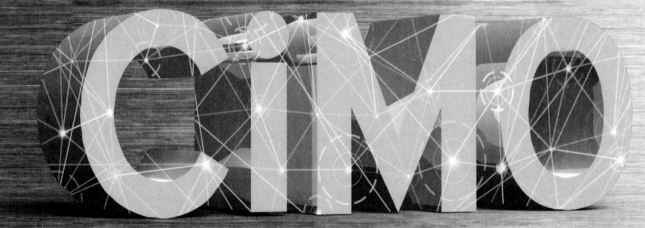

CiMo

SUSAN M. SANDERSON, CPEHR

Ninth Edition

Mc
Graw
Hill
Education

COMPUTERS IN THE MEDICAL OFFICE, NINTH EDITION

Published by McGraw-Hill Education, 2 Penn Plaza, New York, NY 10121. Copyright © 2016 by McGraw-Hill Education. All rights reserved. Printed in the United States of America. Previous editions © 2013, 2011, and 2009. No part of this publication may be reproduced or distributed in any form or by any means, or stored in a database or retrieval system, without the prior written consent of McGraw-Hill Education, including, but not limited to, in any network or other electronic storage or transmission, or broadcast for distance learning.

Some ancillaries, including electronic and print components, may not be available to customers outside the United States.

This book is printed on acid-free paper.

1 2 3 4 5 6 7 8 9 0 RMN/RMN 1 0 9 8 7 6 5

ISBN 978-0-07-783638-2
MHID 0-07-783638-3

Senior Vice President, Products & Markets: *Kurt L. Strand*
Vice President, General Manager, Products & Markets: *Marty Lange*
Vice President, Content Design & Delivery: *Kimberly Meriwether David*
Managing Director: *Chad Grall*
Executive Brand Manager: *William R. Lawrensen*
Director, Product Development: *Rose Koos*
Senior Product Developer: *Michelle L. Flomenhoft*
Executive Marketing Manager: *Roxan Kinsey*
Market Development Manager: *Kimberly Bauer*
Digital Product Analyst: *Katherine Ward*

Director, Content Design & Delivery: *Linda Avenarius*
Program Manager: *Angela R. FitzPatrick*
Content Project Managers: *Vicki Krug / Brent dela Cruz*
Buyer: *Laura M. Fuller*
Senior Design: *Srdjan Savanovic*
Content Licensing Specialists:
Lori Hancock / Lorraine Buczek
Cover Image: *©Magnilion / Getty images*
Compositor: *Lumina Datamatics, Inc.*
Printer: *R. R. Donnelley*

All credits appearing on page or at the end of the book are considered to be an extension of the copyright page.

Design Element
Puppet on Monitor: © frentusha/Getty RF.
CiMO logo: ©Magnilion / Getty images
CO1: © Tetra Images/INMAGINE.COM; CO2: © Getty RF; CO3: © McGraw-Hill Education. Rick Brady, photographer; CO4:
© Ingram Publishing RF; CO5: © Reza Estakhrian/Getty; CO6: © McGraw-Hill Education. Rick Brady, photographer;
CO7: © Reza Estakhrian/Getty; CO8: © Tom Grill/Getty; CO9: © Getty RF; CO10: © Jupiterimages/Getty RF; CO11, CO12:
© Getty RF; CO13: © Tetra Images/Getty RF; CO14: © Getty RF.

Medisoft® is a registered trademark of McKesson Corporation and/or one of its subsidiaries. Screenshots and material pertaining to Medisoft® Software used with permission of McKesson Corporation. © 2013 McKesson Corporation and/or one of its subsidiaries. All Rights Reserved.

The Medidata (student data file), illustrations, instructions, and exercises in Computers in the Medical Office are compatible with the Medisoft Advanced Version 19 Patient Accounting software available at the time of publication. Note that Medisoft Advanced Version 19 Patient Accounting software must be available to access the Medidata. It can be obtained by contacting your McGraw-Hill sales representative.

All brand or product names are trademarks or registered trademarks of their respective companies.

CPT five-digit codes, nomenclature, and other data are © 2015 American Medical Association. All Rights Reserved. No fee schedules, basic units relative values, or related listings are included in CPT. The AMA assumes no liability for the data contained herein.

CPT codes are based on CPT 2015.
ICD-10-CM codes are based on ICD-10-CM 2015.

All names, situations, and anecdotes are fictitious. They do not represent any person, event, or medical record.

Library of Congress Cataloging-in-Publication Data

Sanderson, Susan M.
    Computers in the medical office / Susan M. Sanderson, CPEHR.—Ninth edition.
      pages cm
    Includes index.
    ISBN 978-0-07-783638-2 (alk. paper)
    1. Medical offices—Automation. 2. MediSoft. I. Title.
    R864.S26 2016

  610.285—dc23

                                                                    2015010737

The Internet addresses listed in the text were accurate at the time of publication. The inclusion of a website does not indicate an endorsement by the authors or McGraw-Hill Education, and McGraw-Hill Education does not guarantee the accuracy of the information presented at these sites.

brief contents

CiMO contents

CiMO

CiMO

CiMO
preface

CiMO™: THE STEP-BY-STEP, HANDS-ON APPROACH

Welcome to the ninth edition of *Computers in the Medical Office (CiMO)!* This product introduces your students to the concepts and skills they will need for a successful career in medical office billing. Medical billers are in high demand, and theirs remains one of the ten fastest-growing allied health/health profession occupations. *CiMO* provides instruction on key tasks that students throughout the health professions curriculum, such as those studying medical assisting, health information management, and health information technology, will need to be competent and to move forward. Teaching this material to your students may be challenging because of the diverse student population that takes this course—some students may be very technology-savvy and move through the book quickly, while others may be computer novices and need more help. No matter what your students' skill levels are, *CiMO* gives not only the step-by-step instructions they need to learn, but also the "why" behind those steps.

CiMO is now available with McGraw-Hill Education's revolutionary adaptive learning technology, SmartBook®! You can study smarter, spending your valuable time on topics you don't know and less time on the topics you have already mastered. Succeed with Smart-Book . . . Join the learning revolution and achieve the success you deserve today!

Here's what you and your students can expect from *CiMO*:

- Coverage of Medisoft® Advanced Version 19 patient billing software, a full-featured software program, including screen captures showing how the concepts described in the book actually look in the medical billing software.

- Both a tutorial and a simulation of Medisoft, using a medical office setting, Family Care Center, and related patient data.

- Detailed, easy-to-understand explanations of concepts balanced by step-by-step, hands-on exercises, which can be completed using McGraw-Hill Connect® or the Medisoft software.

- The necessary building blocks for students to establish a strong skill set and gain confidence to attain the jobs they want.

- Realistic exercises, completed via simulations in Connect or by using Medisoft, that cover what students will see working in actual medical practices, no matter what software those practices might use.

- An understanding of the medical billing cycle and how completing the related tasks will positively affect the financial well-being of a medical practice.

ORGANIZATION OF *CiMO*, 9E

CiMO is divided into four parts:

Part	Coverage
1: Introduction to Computers in the Medical Office	Discusses the changes taking place in the field of healthcare. Covers the medical documentation and billing cycle and the role that computers play in that cycle. Also covers the use of health information technology, electronic health records, HIPAA, the HITECH Act, and the Patient Protection and Affordable Care Act.
2: Medisoft Advanced Training	Teaches the student how to start Medisoft; schedule appointments, enter patient information; work with cases; enter charges, payments, and adjustments; create claims; post insurance payments; create patient statements; create reports; and create collection letters. The sequence takes the student through Medisoft in a clear, concise manner. Each chapter includes a number of exercises that are to be done at the computer.
3: Applying Your Skills	Completes the learning process by requiring the student to perform a series of tasks using Medisoft. Each task is an application of knowledge required in the medical office.
4: Source Documents	Gives the student the data needed to complete the exercises. The patient information form, encounter form, and other forms are similar to those used in medical offices.

NEW TO THE NINTH EDITION!

The ninth edition of *CiMO* has been updated to reflect changes that have occurred in the healthcare field since the last edition, including the effects of the Affordable Care Act on physician practices and the billing specialist in particular. A greater number of Americans have health insurance, which means more office visits, especially for family care providers. Patients are responsible for a greater share of physician payments, requiring physician practices to collect at the time of service and carefully monitor overdue patient accounts. New physician payment models reward the quality of service provided, often measured by patient outcomes, rather than the quantity of services provided. While we introduced ICD-10-CM codes in the previous edition of CiMO, this edition we are adding back ICD-9-CM codes for those instructors who would like students to experience both sets of codes. An ICD mapping utility is also available in Medisoft Version 19, which is used in this new edition!

Key content changes include:

- Medisoft
  - Medisoft Version 19 is used for all databases and illustrations (screen captures).
  - ICD-9-CM and ICD-10-CM codes are included in the diagnosis code database.
  - Exercises now take place in 2018 and 2019.
  - Medisoft exercises can be completed using live software via CD-ROM or in simulated form via Connect.
- HIPAA/Federal Legislation-Related
  - Updated information on the effects of HITECH Act more than five years after its passage.
  - Coverage of the major provisions of the Affordable Care Act and its implications for physician practices.
  - Coverage of updates to HIPAA Privacy and Security Rules.
- Pedagogy
  - New "Be the Detective" feature. Video Cases with assessment questions are available in Connect to test students' critical thinking skills.
- Technology
  - Connect has been updated to reflect changes in the chapters and feedback from customers, including the new "Be the Detective" video cases.
  - *CiMO* is now available with SmartBook, an adaptive learning product.
- Chapter-by-Chapter
  - Chapter 1: New key terms: after-visit summary, audit, breach, bundled payments, business associate, electronic protected health information (ePHI), electronic remittance advice, fee-for-service, HIPAA Omnibus Rule, Notice of Privacy Practices, patient portal; revised introduction with less emphasis on rising medical costs and more emphasis on quality measures; updated content on the success of the HITECH Act and the number of physicians using electronic health records; new

content on the major provisions of the Affordable Care Act and how it affects physician practices; updated coverage of new models of healthcare including accountable care organizations, patient-centered medical homes, pay-for-performance, and bundled payments; additional coverage of how HITECH, ACA, and the HIPAA Omnibus Rule affected HIPAA rules; updated Notice of Privacy Practices; updated HIPAA enforcement, breaches, and monetary penalties.

- Chapter 2: Updated for Medisoft Version 19.

- Chapter 3: Updated Electronic Health Record Exchange feature to reflect new interface between Medisoft and Medisoft Clinical; now McKesson Practice Interface Center (MPIC) was Communication Manager.

- Chapter 4: Updated the Race, Ethnicity, and Language fields in the Patient/Guarantor dialog box; updated Electronic Health Record Exchange feature to reflect new interface between Medisoft and Medisoft Clinical; now McKesson Practice Interface Center (MPIC) was Communication Manager.

- Chapter 5: Added content to cover new fields in the Miscellaneous tab of the Case folder for completing boxes on the CMS-1500 (02/12) form; updated Electronic Health Record Exchange feature to reflect updated Unprocessed Transactions Edit screen.

- Chapter 6: Updated Electronic Health Record Exchange feature to reflect updated Unprocessed Transactions Edit screen.

- Chapter 7: Updated information on types of health plans to reflect changes in the health insurance market; updated chart showing enrollment in employer-sponsored health plans by type; updated to final version of CMS-1500 (02/12) form.

- Chapter 8: Updated practice fee schedule to accommodate new CPT codes.

- Chapter 9: Updated process of entering dates so when creating reports, dates are now entered without slashes.

- Chapter 10: New learning objective: Demonstrate how to create a payment plan and assign a patient account to a payment plan; new content on creating payment plans in Medisoft; new content on assigning a patient account to a payment plan; updated chart on medical bill problems or medical debt; new exercises 10-1 Creating a Patient Payment Plan and 10-2 Assigning a Patient Account to a Payment Plan.

- Chapters 11–14: Updated dates to 2018–2019

For a detailed transition guide between the eighth and ninth editions of *CiMO*, visit the Instructor Resources in Connect.

TO THE INSTRUCTOR

McGraw-Hill knows how much effort it takes to prepare for a new course. Through focus groups, symposia, reviews, and conversations with instructors like you, we have gathered information about what materials you need in order to facilitate successful courses. We are committed to providing you with high-quality, accurate instructor support.

USING MEDISOFT ADVANCED VERSION 19 WITH *CiMO*

CiMO features Medisoft Advanced Version 19 patient accounting software. Students who complete *CiMO* find that the concepts and activities in the textbook are general enough to cover most administrative software used by healthcare providers. McGraw-Hill has partnered with Medisoft from the very beginning, going back twenty years to when the software was DOS-based! The support you receive when you are using a McGraw-Hill text with Medisoft is second to none.

medisoft®

There are multiple options to complete the Medisoft exercises.

1. Students complete the exercises in live Medisoft. In this option, the Medisoft software is installed from a CD onto the computer and the Student Data File is downloaded from the book's website and installed onto the computer.

2. Students complete simulated versions of the exercises in Connect, McGraw-Hill's online assignment and assessment solution. No installations or downloads are needed with this option, and the Student Data File is built into the exercises.

For the CD option, your students will need the following:

- Minimum System Requirements

  - Pentium 4

  - 1.0 GHz (minimum) or higher processor

  - 500 MB available hard disk space

  - 1 GB RAM

  - 32-bit color display (minimum screen display of 1024 × 768)

  - Windows 7 Professional or Ultimate 32- or 64-bit

  - Windows 8 Professional 32- or 64-bit

- External storage device, such as a USB flash drive, for storing backup copies of the working database

- Medisoft Advanced Version 19 patient billing software

- Student patient data, available for download from www.mhhe.com/medisoft (More details on how to download the software can be found on the STOP pages between Chapters 1 and 2.)

Instructor's Software: Medisoft Advanced Version 19 CD-ROM

Instructors who use McGraw-Hill Medisoft-compatible titles in their courses may request a fully working version of Medisoft Advanced Version 19 software, which allows a school to place the live software on laboratory or classroom computers. Only one copy is needed per campus location. Your McGraw-Hill sales representative will help you obtain Medisoft for your campus.

Another option is the *Student At-Home Medisoft Advanced Version 19 CD* (1259671747, 9781259671746), a great option for online courses or students who wish to practice at home. Available individually or packaged with the textbook—it's up to you!

For the Connect option, your students will complete all of the Medisoft exercises from Chapters 2–14 in the online solution. Each exercise has the following modes for you to assign as desired:

- *Demo Mode*—watch a demonstration of the exercise.
- *Practice Mode*—try the exercise yourself with guidance.
- *Test Mode*—complete the exercise on your own.

For each Medisoft exercise, the same data are used for all of the modes in order to reinforce the skills being taught in that exercise. This is a proven learning methodology.

The Connect course for *CiMO*, 9e also contains all of the end-of-chapter exercises, as well as some simple interactives for each chapter and the new *Be the Detective* video cases.

Much more information on how to work with each of the Medisoft options, including detailed screenshots, can be found in the *McGraw-Hill Guides to Success* at www.mhhe.com/medisoft and in the Instructor Resources under the Library tab in Connect. One guide covers the following topics: software installation procedures for both the Instructor Edition and Student At-Home Edition of Medisoft; Student Data File installation procedures; use of flash drives; backup and restore processes; the other one focuses on Connect functionality as well as details on Demo, Practice, and Test Modes; both contain information on tips and frequently asked questions; instructor resources; and technical support.

DIGITAL RESOURCES

Knowing the importance of flexibility and digital learning, McGraw-Hill Education has created multiple assets to enhance the learning experience no matter what the class format: traditional, online, or hybrid. This product is designed with digital solutions to help instructors and students be successful.

Learn Without Limits: Connect

connect®

Connect is proven to deliver better results for students and instructors. Proven content integrates seamlessly with enhanced digital tools to create a personalized learning experience that drives efficient and effective learning by delivering precisely what they need, when they need it. With Connect, the educational possibilities are limitless.

The new release of Connect features a continually adaptive reading experience, integrated learning resources, a visual analytics dashboard, and anywhere/anytime mobile access that empower students so that your class-time is more engaging and effective.

Connect Is the Easiest Integrated Learning System to Use Technology can simplify everyday lives when the user's needs are placed at the forefront. Year after year, satisfied instructors continue using Connect for many reasons, but the most frequently cited reason: "It's easy-to-use." The latest release of Connect continues in this tradition by introducing complete mobile access, online and offline access, as well as an improved, streamlined user interface. When combined with Connect's flexible functionality, seamless systems integration and comprehensive training and support, it's no wonder that Connect remains the most frequently used and recommended integrated learning system.

- ✓ **Mobile [NEW]:** Students and instructors can now enjoy convenient anywhere/anytime access to Connect with a new mobile interface that's been designed for optimal use of tablet functionality. More than just a new way to access Connect, users can complete assignments, check progress, study and read material, with full use of SmartBook and Connect Insight®, Connect's new at-a-glance visual analytics dashboard.

- ✓ **User Interface Redesign [NEW]:** With a focus on clarity for users, a redesigned user interface features a seamless integration of learning tools, placing most important priorities in the forefront. Our redesign continues to put our users first—a hallmark of the Connect platform—and deliver a tool that fully engages students and solves real-world teaching and learning challenges.

- ✓ **Flexible:** Connect allows you to edit all existing content to match the way you teach the course. You can upload your own materials, including: Word documents, PowerPoint files, Excel spreadsheets, and web links. You can also share your own notes within our eBooks, record your lectures through Tegrity lecture capture, include bookmarks, incorporate news feeds and adjust assignment content within the platform.

- ✓ **LMS Integration:** Connect seamlessly integrates with every learning management system on the market today. Quickly access all course resources through a single login and simplify registration, assignments, and gradebook reporting for your students.

✓ **Service, Support & Training:** Connect customers receive comprehensive service, support, and training throughout every phase of partnership with us. Customers can access our Customer Experience Group at any time of day for immediate assistance, access the Digital Success Academy for on-demand training materials, and access the Connect Blog for tips on getting up and running quickly.

✓ Our Digital Faculty Consultants are a network of passionate educators, dedicated to advancing student learning through educational technologies, resources, and collaboration opportunities. This team of experienced Connect users is ready to help fellow peers achieve the greatest success using the platform, either 1:1 or in a group setting. In addition, help content is accessible directly within the Connect platform to make it easier to get the help you need when you need it most.

Connect Is an Efficient and Effective Learning Tool for Instructors and Students—With Connect, Users Get Better Results in Less Time Numerous effectiveness studies conducted since the first release of Connect tell the same story:

Students are more likely to stay in class and get better grades when using Connect. New visual analytics through Connect Insight now make it possible for instructors and students to get an instant perspective on what's happening in class with the tap of a finger. For those who want a more in-depth picture, powerful reporting capabilities within Connect make it easy for instructors to keep students on track and inspire them to succeed.

Learn more at **http://connect.mheducation.com**!

SMARTBOOK® *Learning at the speed of you: Smartbook*

Connect's Superior Adaptive Technology 'Fills the Knowledge Gap' and Empowers Students Outside of Class for a More Engaging and Interactive Experience in Class Connect builds student confidence outside of class with adaptive technology that pinpoints exactly what a student knows and what they don't, and then seamlessly offers up learning resources within the platform that are designed to have the greatest impact on that specific learning moment. With Smart-Book, reading is an interactive and dynamic experience in which content is tailor-made for each student. Built with the unique LearnSmart® adaptive technology, it focuses not only on addressing learning in the moment, but empowers students by helping them retain information over time, so that they are more prepared and engaged in class.

✓ **LearnSmart:** More than 2 million students have answered more than 1.3 billion questions in LearnSmart since 2009, making it the most widely used and intelligent adaptive study tool available on the market today. LearnSmart is proven to strengthen memory recall, keep students in class, and boost grades—students using LearnSmart are 13% more likely to pass their classes, and 35% less likely to dropout.

✓ **SmartBook [New Capabilities]:** SmartBook makes study time as productive and efficient as possible. It identifies and closes knowledge gaps through a continually adapting reading experience that provides personalized learning resources at the precise moment of need. This ensures that every minute spent with SmartBook is returned to the student as the most value-added minute possible. The result? More confidence, better grades, and greater success.

✓ **Adapts at the Learning Objective Level:** All material within any Connect product or capability (including SmartBook) has been tagged at the learning objective level. What this means is that the adaptive experience for students is intimately personalized in a very precise way. In addition, any analysis tools (Connect Insight and reports) are also able to present performance data by learning objective. Connect is the only integrated learning system that features this precise level of adaptive and analysis precision.

Go to **www.LearnSmartAdvantage.com** for more information!

Record and distribute your lectures for multiple viewing: My Lectures—Tegrity

Tegrity records and distributes your class lecture with just a click of a button. Students can view it anytime and anywhere via computer, iPod, or mobile device. It indexes as it records your Power-Point presentations and anything shown on your computer, so students can use keywords to find exactly what they want to study. Tegrity is available as an integrated feature of Connect and as a stand-alone product.

A single sign-on with Connect and your Blackboard course: McGraw-Hill Education and Blackboard—for a premium user experience

Blackboard, the web-based course management system, has partnered with McGraw-Hill Education to better allow students and faculty to use online materials and activities to complement face-to-face teaching. Blackboard features exciting social learning and teaching tools that foster active learning opportunities for students. You'll transform your closed-door classroom into communities where students remain connected to their educational experience 24 hours a day. This partnership allows you and your students access to Connect and McGraw-Hill Create™ right from within your Blackboard course—all with a single sign-on. Not only do you get single sign-on with Connect and Create, but you also get deep integration of McGraw-Hill Education content and content engines right in Blackboard. Whether you're choosing a book for your course or building Connect assignments, all the tools you need are right where you want them—inside Blackboard. Gradebooks are now seamless. When a student completes an integrated Connect assignment, the grade for that assignment automatically (and instantly) feeds into your Blackboard grade center. McGraw-Hill Education and Blackboard can now offer you easy access to industry leading technology and content, whether your campus hosts it or we do. Be sure to ask your local McGraw-Hill Education representative for details.

Still want a single sign-on solution and using another Learning Management System?

See how **McGraw-Hill Campus**® makes the grade by offering universal sign-on, automatic registration, gradebook synchronization, and open access to a multitude of learning resources—all in one place. MH Campus supports Active Directory, Angel, Blackboard, Canvas, Desire2Learn, eCollege, IMS, LDAP, Moodle, Moodlerooms, Sakai, Shibboleth, WebCT, BrainHoney, Campus Cruiser, and Jenzibar eRacer. Additionally, MH Campus can be easily connected with other authentication authorities and LMSs. Visit **http://mhcampus.mhhe.com/** to learn more.

Assemble a textbook organized the way you teach: McGraw-Hill Create

With Create, you can easily rearrange chapters, combine material from other content sources, and quickly upload content you have written, such as your course syllabus or teaching notes. Find the content you need in Create by searching through thousands of leading McGraw-Hill Education textbooks. Arrange your book to fit your teaching style. Create even allows you to personalize your book's appearance by selecting the cover and adding your name, school, and course information. Order a Create book and you'll receive a complimentary print review copy in 3 to 5 business days or a complimentary electronic review copy via e-mail in minutes. Go to **http://create.mheducation.com** today and register to experience how Create empowers you to teach *your* students *your* way.

Need help? Contact the McGraw-Hill Education Customer Experience Group (CXG)

Visit the CXG website at **www.mhhe.com/support**. Browse our FAQs (frequently asked questions) and product documentation and/or contact a CXG representative.

ADDITIONAL INSTRUCTORS' RESOURCES

You can rely on the following materials to help you and your students work through the material in the book, all of which are available in the Instructor Resources under the Library tab in Connect: (available only to instructors who are logged into Connect)

Supplement	Features
Instructor's Manual (organized by Learning Outcomes)	—Answer keys for all exercises —Documentation of steps and screenshots for Medisoft exercises
PowerPoint Presentations (organized by Learning Outcomes)	—Key terms —Key concepts
Electronic Testbank	—EZ Test Online (computerized) —Word version —Questions have tagging for Learning Outcomes, level of difficulty, level of Bloom's Taxonomy, topic, and the accrediting standards of ABHES, CAAHEP, and CAHIIM where appropriate
Tools to Plan Course	—Correlations of the Learning Outcomes to accrediting bodies such as CAHIIM, ABHES, and CAAHEP —Sample syllabi and lesson plans —Conversion guide for *CiMO, 8e* to *CiMO, 9e* —Asset map—a recap of the key instructor resources, as well as information on the content available through *Connect*
Medisoft Advanced Version 19 Tools	—Implementation Guides for Live and Simulated Medisoft —Technical support information —First day of class PowerPoint presentation —Installation videos and directions —Student Data File —Backup and restore videos, directions, and files for live Medisoft use. (The Medisoft backup files are an important resource if students make mistakes with their data and you want them to have the correct data to start the next chapter.) —Certificate of completion
Case Studies for use with Computers in the Medical Office, 9e *NOTE: The exercises in this book can be only completed with the live Medisoft software. They are not available in Connect.*	This book provides a capstone simulation using Medisoft Advanced Version 19. It offers students enhanced training that is meant to improve their qualifications for a variety of medical office jobs. Extensive hands-on practice with realistic source documents teaches students to input information, schedule appointments, and handle billing, reports, and other essential tasks. The book provides additional activities, including more complex activities for advanced students. On the website you will find: —Instructor's Manual with sample syllabi and answer keys —PowerPoint presentations —Conversion guides —Correlations to accrediting bodies —Asset Map —Information on how to load Student Data File for this book and *CiMO* at the same time

Want to learn more about this product? Attend one of our online webinars. To learn more about the webinars, please contact your McGraw-Hill sales representative. To find your McGraw-Hill representative, go to shop.mheducation.com and click "Find Your Learning Technology Representative" on the "CONTACT US" page.

about
the author

Susan M. Sanderson has authored all Windows-based editions of Computers in the Medical Office. She has also written *Case Studies for use with Computers in the Medical Office, Electronic Health Records for Allied Health Careers, and Practice Management and EHR: A Total Patient Encounter for Medisoft® Clinical.*

In her more than fifteen years' experience with Medisoft, Susan has participated in alpha and beta testing, worked with instructors to site-test materials, and provided technical support to McGraw-Hill customers.

In 2009, Susan earned her CPEHR (Certified Professional in Electronic Health Records) certification. In addition, she is a member of the Healthcare Information and Management Systems Society (HIMSS) and the eLearning Guild. Susan is a graduate of Drew University with further study at Columbia University.

CiMO
acknowledgments

Suggestions have been received from faculty and students throughout the country. This is vital feedback that is relied upon with each edition. Each person who has offered comments and suggestions has our thanks.

The efforts of many people are needed to develop and improve a product. Among these people are the reviewers and consultants who point out areas of concern, cite areas of strength, and make recommendations for change. In this regard, the following instructors provided feedback that was enormously helpful in preparing the ninth edition of *CiMO*.

SURVEYS

A number of instructors teaching in this course area participated in a survey to help guide the revision of the book and related materials.

Monika Bell, CMA
Monterey Peninsula College

Chantalle Blakesley-Boddie, BS, CMA
Lake Washington Institute of Technology

Amy L. Blochowiak, MBA, ACS, AIAA, AIRC, ARA, FLHC, FLMI, HCSA, HIA, HIPAA, MHP, PCS, SILA-F
Northeast Wisconsin Technical College

Jennifer K. Boles, MSN, RN
Cincinnati State Technical and Community College

Dr. Tammie Bolling, CBCS, CHI, CMAA, MOS, CEHRS, CHITS-TR
Pellissippi State Community College

Donna W. Brantley, CCS-P
Nash Community College

Sharon Breeding
Bluegrass Community and Technical College

Susan M. Bremer, MS, RHIA
Central Lakes College

Renae V. Brown, M.ED
Essex County College

Debra Charles, RHIA, CCS, CCS-A
Front Range Community College

Jean M. Chenu, MSEd
Genesee Community College

Amanda Davis-Smith, CPC, NCMA
Jefferson Community and Technical College

Denise J. DeDeaux, MBA
Fayetteville Technical Community College

Bobbi J Fields, CMA (AAMA), MPA, BS-HA
Moraine Park Technical College

Savanna Garrity, CPC, MPA
Madisonville Community College

Sheila Guillot, MSEd, CAP
Lamar State College-Port Arthur

Howard Gunning, MSEd, CMA (AAMA)
Southwestern Illinois College

Alice Kathryn Hansen, BS, CPC, REEGT
Bluegrass Community and Technical College

Lisa Huehns, MAEd
Lakeshore Technical College

Shalena Jarvis, RHIT, CCS
Hazard Community and Technical College

Diana Johnson, CMA (AAMA), RMA, RPT
Medical Professional Institute

NaTunya D. Johnson, EdS
Holmes Community College

Michelle Jubeck
Blackhawk Technical College

Jean M. Kindrick, MEd
Fox College

Keita Kornegay, BS
Wilson Community College

Marta Lopez, MD, LM, CPM, RMA, BMO
Miami Dade College

Barbara Marchelletta, CMA (AAMA),
RHIT, CPC, CPT
Beal College

Suzanne Mays, BS, MSH, MSIT
University of Phoenix

Tina Mazuch, MS, RHIA
Northeast Community College

Vonadean McFarland, BS
Salt Lake Community College

Revel Metzger, MAE
Elizabethtown Community & Technical
College

Jane O'Grady MSEd, RN, CMA, CPC
Northwestern CT Community College

Tatyana Pashnyak, M.Ed, CHIS-TR, COI
Bainbridge State College

Mitzi Poore, BS, MA
Surry Community College

Leslie Quinn, RMA
Eastern Florida State College

Kimberly K. Rash
Gateway Community & Technical College

Lisa Rocks, M.Ed
Allegany College of Maryland

Joni Schlatz, MS, RHIT
Central Community College

Karen K. Smith, M.Ed, RHIA, CPC
University of Arkansas for Medical
Sciences

Helen Spain, M.Ed
Wake Technical Community College

J. Ashleigh Spear, RN
Blue Ridge Community and Technical
College

Slavica Tumminelli, CPC, CGSC, CHI,
CBCS, CEHRS
Advantage Career Institute

Elizabeth Wanielista, M.Ed
Valencia College

Colette Washington, DME, MEd, CMA-R,
CPC, RHIA
Southeastern School of Health Sciences

Jodi Wijewickrama, RHIA
Haywood Community College

Dana Woods, CMA (AAMA)
Southwestern Illinois College

Bettie Wright, MBA, CMA (CCMA)
Umpqua Community College

LaQuinta S. Yates, M.Ed
Trident Technical College

Virginia V. York, MD
Ohio Business College

TECHNICAL EDITING/ACCURACY PANEL

A panel of instructors completed a technical edit and review of all of the content in the book page proofs to verify its accuracy, especially in relation to Medisoft.

Renae V. Brown, M.Ed
Essex County College

Jean M. Chenu, MSEd
Genesee Community College

Savanna Garrity, MPA, CPC
Madisonville Community College

Keita Kornegay, BS
Wilson Community College

Tatyana G. Pashnyak, MEd, CHIS-TR, COI
Bainbridge State College

Kimberly K. Rash
Gateway Community and Technical College

Lisa Rocks, M.Ed.
Allegany College of Maryland

DIGITAL PRODUCTS

Several instructors helped author and review the digital content for Connect, SmartBook, and more!

Monika Bell, CMA
Monterey Peninsula College

Chantalle Blakesley-Boddie, BS, CMA
Lake Washington Institute of Technology

Jennifer K. Boles MSN, RN
Cincinnati State Technical & Community College

Denise J. DeDeaux, MBA
Fayetteville Technical Community College

Amy Ensign, BHSA
Baker College of Clinton Township

Savanna Garrity, MPA, CPC
Madisonville Community College

Patricia Hamilton, BS
Pittsburgh Technical Institute

Judy Hurtt, MEd
East Central Community College

Tatyana Pashnyak, M.Ed, CHIS-TR, COI
Bainbridge State College

Shauna Phillips, RMA
Fortis College

Wendy Schmerse, CMRS
Southern California Health Institute

Karen K. Smith, M.Ed
University of Arkansas

Angela M.B. Oliva, BSHA
Heald College

Gina F. Umstetter, BA
Delta College of Arts & Technology

Deborah Zenzal, MS
Ameritech College

ACKNOWLEDGMENTS FROM THE AUTHOR

To the students and instructors who use this book, your feedback and suggestions have made *CiMO* a better learning tool for all.

I especially want to thank the editorial team at McGraw-Hill—Chad Grall, Bill Lawrensen, and Michelle Flomenhoft—for their enthusiastic support and their willingness to go the extra mile to take a successful book to the next level.

Hats off to the Customer Experience Group at McGraw-Hill for providing outstanding technical assistance to students and instructors. In addition, thank you to Katie Ward for her help on the digital front. The CDD staff was also outstanding; senior designer Srdj Savanovic created a terrific updated interior design and fantastic cover design, which was implemented through the production process by Vicki Krug, content project manager; Laura Fuller, buyer; Lori Hancock and Lorraine Buczek, content licensing specialists; and Brent dela Cruz, content project manager.

This book would not be in its ninth edition were it not for the tireless efforts of Roxan Kinsey, Executive Marketing Manager, who believed in *Computers in the Medical Office* and Medisoft from day one.

A big thanks also goes to Amy Blochowiak for her help on the Medisoft simulations!

Finally, I would like to thank Cynthia Newby of Chestnut Hill Enterprises, Inc., for providing wisdom and support throughout the years.

This book is truly the result of a group effort.

part 1

INTRODUCTION TO COMPUTERS IN THE MEDICAL OFFICE

Chapter 1:
Introduction to Health Information Technology and Medical Billing

INTRODUCTION TO HEALTH INFORMATION TECHNOLOGY AND MEDICAL BILLING

key terms

accountable care organization (ACO)

adjudication

Affordable Care Act (ACA)

after-visit summary (AVS)

audit

audit trail

breach

bundled payments

business associate

clearinghouse

coding

covered entity

Current Procedural Terminology (CPT®)

diagnosis

diagnosis code

documentation

electronic data interchange (EDI)

electronic health record (EHR)

electronic prescribing

electronic protected health information (ePHI)

learning outcomes

When you finish this chapter, you will be able to:

1.1 Explain the major changes taking place in the healthcare field.

1.2 Describe the functions of practice management programs.

1.3 Identify the core functions of electronic health record programs.

1.4 List the step in the medical documentation and billing cycle that occurs before a patient encounter.

1.5 List the steps in the medical documentation and billing cycle that occur during a patient encounter.

1.6 List the steps in the medical documentation and billing cycle that occur after a patient encounter.

1.7 Discuss how the HIPAA Privacy Rule and Security Rule protect patient health information.

1.1 THE CHANGING HEALTHCARE LANDSCAPE

key terms continued

In the United States, the healthcare system is in a period of ongoing upheaval, as government legislation changes the way individuals buy, access, and pay for medical care. Over the past decade, it became obvious that major reform was needed. Survey after survey reported that while the United States spends more than any other country on healthcare, it ranks below most other countries on quality and outcome measures. According to the Commonwealth Fund, the U.S. spent $8,508 per person on healthcare in 2011—more than twice the $3,406 the United Kingdom spent, which ranked first overall in quality. Despite spending more, the U.S. ranks last overall among 11 industrialized countries on measures of quality, efficiency, access to care, equity, and healthy lives (see Table 1-1).

Beginning in 2009, in an attempt to rein in spending and improve overall quality, the federal government—the largest payer for

TABLE 1-1	U.S. Healthcare Rankings
Category	**U.S. Ranking**
Healthy lives	The U.S. ranks last on infant mortality, last on deaths that were potentially preventable if the person had timely access to care, and next-to-last on healthy life expectancy at age 60.
Access to care	The U.S. ranks last on every measure of cost-related access to healthcare. Individuals are not receiving a recommended test, treatment, or follow-up care over one-third of the time because of cost.
Healthcare quality	The U.S. ranks near the top on providing effective care and patient-centered care, while it does not perform as well when it comes to providing safe or coordinated care.
Efficiency	The U.S ranks last, due to the amount of time spent on insurance administration, the lack of communication among healthcare providers, and duplicate medical tests performed by more than one provider.
Equity	The U.S. ranks last. Almost 40 percent of adults with below-average incomes reported a medical problem but did not visit a doctor because of costs. Individuals with lower incomes also had to wait longer to receive certain types of care, such as seeing a specialist.

[*Source:* K. Davis, K. Stremikis, C. Schoen, and D. Squires, *Mirror, Mirror on the Wall, 2014 Update: How the U.S. Health Care System Compares Internationally,* The Commonwealth Fund, June 2014.]

The key terms continued list:

electronic remittance advice (ERA)

encounter form

explanation of benefits (EOB)

fee-for-service

HCPCS

health information technology (HIT)

Health Information Technology for Economic and Clinical Health (HITECH) Act

Health Insurance Portability and Accountability Act of 1996 (HIPAA)

HIPAA Omnibus Rule

HIPAA Privacy Rule

HIPAA Security Rule

International Classification of Diseases, Ninth Revision, *Clinical Modification* (ICD-9-CM)

International Classification of Diseases, Tenth Revision, *Clinical Modification* (ICD-10-CM)

meaningful use

medical documentation and billing cycle

Notice of Privacy Practices

patient-centered medical home (PCMH)

patient information form

patient portal

practice management programs (PMP)

procedure

procedure code

protected health information (PHI)

remittance advice (RA)

revenue cycle management (RCM)

healthcare, with over 100 million beneficiaries—passed several major pieces of legislation designed to improve the healthcare system.

HITECH ACT

The same studies that revealed that the U.S. spent more and received less when it came to healthcare also found that U.S. physicians have problems receiving information in a timely manner, coordinating patient care with other providers, and managing the required administrative paperwork. While other countries had begun introducing technology in healthcare, the U.S. once again lagged behind. In 2009, 83 percent of U.S. physicians and 90 percent of hospitals were managing patient information on paper. It was commonplace to see rows upon rows of yellow folders lining the bookshelves or filing cabinets of a medical office. The information technology that had transformed other areas of life such as shopping, banking, and entertainment was not having the same impact on healthcare.

Health Information Technology for Economic and Clinical Health (HITECH) Act part of the American Recovery and Reinvestment Act of 2009 that provides financial incentives to physicians and hospitals to adopt EHRs and strengthens HIPAA privacy and security regulations.

health information technology (HIT) technology that is used to record, store, and manage patient healthcare information.

electronic health record (EHR) a computerized lifelong healthcare record for an individual that incorporates data from all providers who treat the individual.

meaningful use the utilization of certified EHR technology to improve quality, efficiency, and patient safety in the healthcare system.

Affordable Care Act (ACA) federal legislation passed in 2010 that includes a number of provisions designed to increase access to healthcare, improve the quality of healthcare, and explore new models of delivering and paying for healthcare.

To encourage the adoption of technology in healthcare, Congress passed the **Health Information Technology for Economic and Clinical Health (HITECH) Act**, part of the American Recovery and Reinvestment Act of 2009. The HITECH Act allocated billions of dollars to encourage physicians and hospitals to use health information technology to improve the quality and efficiency of care provided to patients. **Health information technology (HIT)** refers to the computer hardware, software, and networks that record, store, and manage health information.

Under the provisions of the act, physicians, hospitals, and other healthcare providers who adopt and use electronic health records are eligible for annual payments of up to $44,000 from Medicare and Medicaid. An **electronic health record (EHR)** is a computerized lifelong healthcare record for an individual that incorporates data from all sources that provide treatment. To receive payments, doctors and hospitals must show the systems are being used to improve patient care. **Meaningful use** is the utilization of certified EHR technology to improve quality, efficiency, and patient safety in the healthcare system. Beginning in 2015, providers who did not implement an electronic health record system received a reduction in Medicare reimbursement.

More than five years after its passage, the HITECH Act seems to have accomplished its major goal—increasing the use of HIT in healthcare. A study found that just over 80 percent of physicians and 97 percent of hospitals have EHRs that qualify for the government incentives.

AFFORDABLE CARE ACT

In 2010, the government passed the Patient Protection and Affordable Care Act—commonly referred to as the **Affordable Care Act (ACA)**.

The law was designed to increase access to healthcare, improve the quality of healthcare, and explore new models of delivering and paying for healthcare. This legislation significantly impacts everyone who uses or provides healthcare, including individuals, employers, health plans, and providers. While the scope of the changes are beyond this textbook, students must understand the basic provisions of the law and its effect on physician practices.

Major provisions of the ACA include:

- Expanding Medicaid to all non-Medicare eligible individuals under age 65 with incomes up to a certain level; optional on a state-by-state basis.
- Creating health insurance exchanges through which individuals who do not have access to public coverage or affordable employer coverage will be able to purchase insurance with premium and cost-sharing credits available to some people to make coverage more affordable.
- Requiring insurance companies to cover all applicants, including those with preexisting conditions with a minimum set of services, limit annual out-of-pocket expenses, and offer the same rates regardless of preexisting conditions or gender.
- Requiring most U.S. citizens and legal residents to obtain health insurance or pay a penalty.
- Requiring employers with 50 or more full-time employees to offer health coverage to employees or pay a penalty.
- Providing dependent coverage for children up to age 26 for all individual and group policies.
- Prohibiting health plans from placing lifetime limits on the dollar value of coverage and prohibit insurers from denying or canceling coverage except in cases of fraud.

IMPLICATIONS FOR PHYSICIAN PRACTICES

As the Affordable Care Act is implemented, physicians face a number of challenges, including an increase in individuals with insurance coverage, an increase in patients' financial responsibility for healthcare costs, and experimentation with new models of providing care and receiving payment.

More Patients

Millions of Americans who previously did not have health insurance are now insured. Some enrolled in the health insurance exchanges, while others are part of the ACA's expansion of Medicaid coverage. With more patients insured, providers, especially primary care providers, may see an increase in patient volume. Some practices may need to hire additional staff to handle the increase in volume.

More Coverage

Under the ACA, individual and small group health plans are required to cover 10 essential health benefits including maternity and newborn care, preventive and wellness services, chronic disease management; and pediatric services, including oral and vision care.

Patients Pay More

Health insurance exchange plans have relatively high out-of-pocket payments. Annual deductibles can reach $5,000 for individuals and $10,000 for families. As a result, physician practices will need to be vigilant about collecting patient payments at the time of service, rather than afterwards.

Changing Payment and Care Models

Both government payers and private health plans are experimenting with new payment and care models designed to change the way physicians, hospitals, and other providers are paid in order to provide higher quality care at lower costs. These models focus on encouraging the coordination of care among physicians, hospitals, and other providers and providing additional support to primary care practices.

fee-for-service a model of physician reimbursement in which payment is provided for specific, individual services provided to a patient.

The traditional **fee-for-service** model provides reimbursement for specific, individual services provided to a patient. The exact amount paid for services is negotiated between health plans and other payers and providers. The new models reward positive patient outcomes rather than the volume of procedures completed. Simply put, the emphasis of the new models is on paying for value, not volume. The most common new models include pay-for-performance, shared savings programs, and bundled payments. No one model is expected to replace the traditional fee-for-service. There is considerable overlap among the models, and many implementations combine some aspects of fee-for-service with some elements of the new models.

Pay-for-Performance

Pay-for-performance models compensate physicians for achieving defined and measurable goals related to care processes and outcomes, patient experience, resource use, and other factors. For a primary care provider, examples of goals include reducing hospital readmissions, prescribing generic rather than brand name drugs, and eliminating unnecessary diagnostic testing. The ability to track clinical data using an electronic health record program is essential to participation in a pay-for-performance program.

patient-centered medical home (PCMH) a model of primary care that provides comprehensive and timely care to patients, while emphasizing teamwork and patient involvement.

The **patient-centered medical home (PCMH)** is a pay-for-performance model of primary care that provides comprehensive and timely

Copyright ©2016 McGraw-Hill Education

TABLE 1-2	Core Features of a Patient-Centered Medical Home
Feature	**Description**
Patient Centered	Healthcare is viewed as a partnership among practitioners, patients, and their families. Patients have the education and support they need to make decisions and participate in their own care. Care decisions respect patients' wishes.
Comprehensive	Care is provided by a team of healthcare professionals, who collectively take responsibility for ongoing patient care, including preventive care, acute and chronic care, and end-of-life care.
Coordinated	Care is coordinated and integrated across the community's healthcare system, including specialists, hospitals, home health agencies, nursing homes, etc.
Quality and Safety	The healthcare team uses evidence-based medicine and clinical decision-support tools to ensure that patients and families make informed decisions about their health.
Access	Patient's waiting time for care is reduced, and access to care is expanded through features such as nontraditional office hours and the use of e-mail, patient portals, and other technology.

[*Source:* http://www.pcmh.ahrq.gov/page/defining-pcmh]

care to patients, while emphasizing teamwork and patient involvement. When primary care practices have the resources to better coordinate care, engage patients in their care plan, and provide appropriate, timely preventive care, many patients remain healthier and avoid hospitalization. Table 1-2 lists the core features of a PCMH.

Shared Savings

In the shared savings model, a group of providers—known as an **accountable care organization (ACO)**—share responsibility for managing the quality and cost of care provided to a group of patients. Such a group could include primary care physicians, specialists, hospitals, home healthcare providers, and others. The ACO contracts with a payer to provide care for a patient population and meet certain quality and cost benchmarks for that population over a set period of time. If the group provides care at a lower cost than the predetermined amount, it shares the savings with the payer. If the care costs exceed the amount, the group is responsible for the difference. By making this group of providers jointly accountable for the health of their patients, the program provides incentives to

accountable care organization (ACO) a network of doctors and hospitals that shares responsibility for managing the quality and cost of care provided to a group of patients.

coordinate care in a way that improves quality and saves money by avoiding unnecessary tests and procedures.

Bundled Payments

bundled payments a model of reimbursement in which single payments are made to multiple providers involved in an episode of care, creating a sense of shared accountability among providers.

Bundled payments, also known as episode payments, are single payments to multiple providers involved in an episode of care, creating a sense of shared accountability among providers. Payments are based on the expected costs for the episode of care, rather than for individual services provided. The episode may take place in multiple settings (inpatient, outpatient, etc.) over a period of time. Under this approach, providers have financial incentives to control the cost of the bundle. If the services can be delivered at a lower cost, the providers keep the savings. On the other hand, if services come in at a higher cost, perhaps because more care than expected had to be given, the group would also share in the losses.

1.2 FUNCTIONS OF PRACTICE MANAGEMENT PROGRAMS

practice management programs (PMP) software programs that automate many of the administrative and financial tasks in a medical practice.

To manage clinical and financial data, medical practices use two primary types of computer software: electronic health records record and store information about an individual's medical conditions, while **practice management programs (PMP)** manage the administrative and financial well-being of the practice. Practice management programs facilitate the day-to-day financial operations of a medical practice, from the time a patient makes an appointment until the time the account is fully paid. The PMP is used to complete many of the daily administrative and financial tasks of a medical practice, including:

- Verifying insurance eligibility and benefits.
- Organizing patient and payer information.
- Generating and transmitting insurance claims.
- Monitoring the status of claims.
- Recording payments from payers.
- Generating patients' statements, posting payments, and updating accounts.
- Managing collections activities.
- Creating financial and productivity reports.

CREATING AND TRANSMITTING CLAIMS

One of the most important functions of a PMP is to create and transmit healthcare claims. To accomplish this, the PMP collects information from its various databases and creates a claim file. A *database* is simply an organized collection of information. The PMP databases include information about the patient, the provider, the health plan,

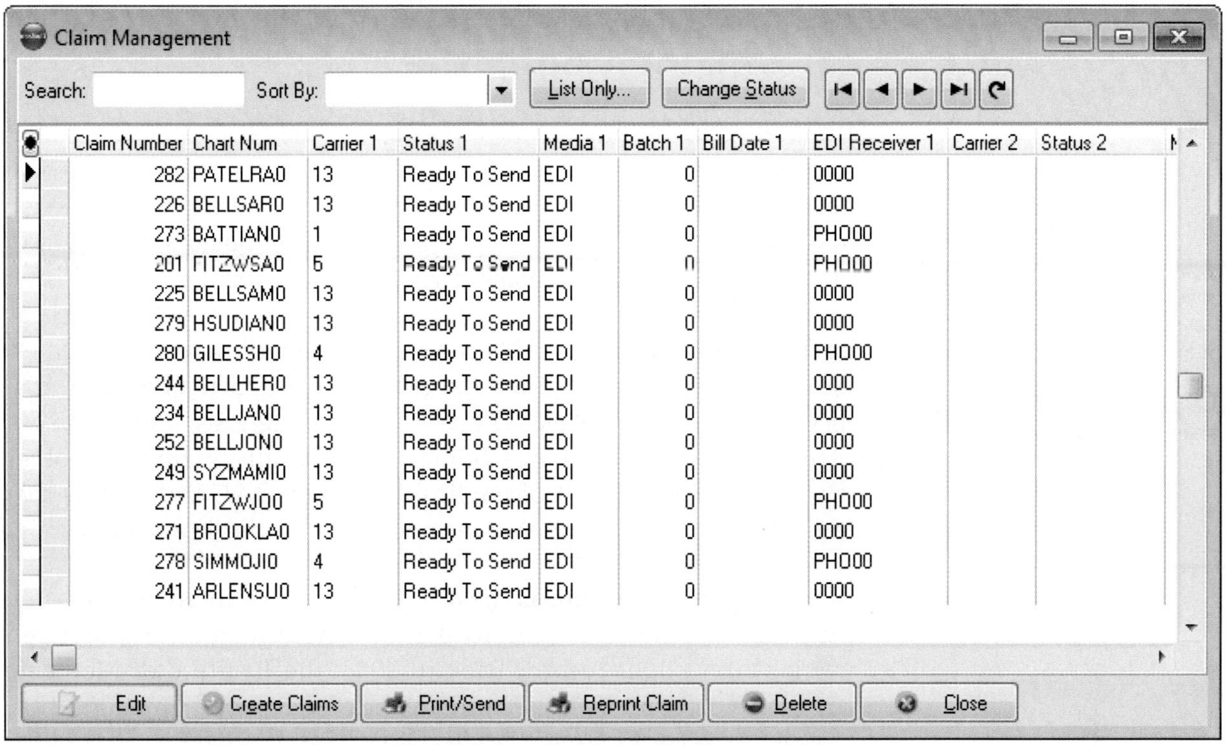

Figure 1-1 A screen from a practice management program showing claims ready to be sent

the facility, and more. In most cases, the claim file is sent to the insurance carrier electronically, using an Internet connection. The electronic transmission of the claim file replaces the previous method of processing claims, which required filling out paper claim forms and sending them in the mail. Since the PMP transmits claims electronically, physicians receive payment in less time than when performing the same tasks on paper. Figure 1-1 displays a claims screen from a PMP, with a batch of claims listed as "Ready to Send."

MONITORING CLAIM STATUS

Once the claim file has been transmitted to the health plan, the PMP is used to follow up on the status of claims. If the claim is not processed within the expected time frame, the PMP can send electronic messages to the health plan to find out the status of the claim. Monitoring claim status is necessary to ensure prompt payment of claims.

RECEIVING AND PROCESSING PAYMENTS

When the health plan has processed the claim, the PMP receives a document that lists the amount that has been paid on each claim as well as the reasons for nonpayment or partial payment. After careful review to determine whether the payments are as expected, the payment information is entered in the PMP and applied to each patient's account. The payment from the health plan is usually an electronic payment that is sent directly to the practice's bank account, although in some cases paper checks are still used.

1.3 FUNCTIONS OF ELECTRONIC HEALTH RECORD PROGRAMS

While practice management programs are the HIT applications that manage the financial operations of a medical practice, electronic health records are the HIT applications that store clinical data—the information about a patient's health entered by doctors, nurses, and other healthcare professionals. Every time a patient is treated by a healthcare provider, a record of the encounter, known as **documentation**, is made. This chronological medical record, or chart, includes information that the patient provides, such as medical history, as well as the physician's assessment, diagnosis, and treatment plan. Records also contain laboratory test results, X-rays and other diagnostic images, a list of medications prescribed, and reports that indicate the results of operations and other medical procedures.

documentation a record of healthcare encounters between the physician and the patient, created by the provider.

While paper and electronic health records serve many of the same purposes, the electronic record is much more than a computerized version of a paper record. Back in 2003, the Institute of Medicine suggested that an EHR should include eight core functions (*Key Capabilities of an Electronic Health Record System*, 2003):

1. Health information and data elements
2. Results management
3. Order management
4. Decision support
5. Electronic communication and connectivity
6. Patient support
7. Administrative support
8. Population reporting and management

While the exact words used to describe the information may differ slightly, these core functions are still relevant over a decade later. In fact, most of the current requirements for financial incentives under the meaningful use portion of the HITECH Act are contained within the Institute of Medicine categories.

HEALTH INFORMATION AND DATA ELEMENTS

An electronic health record must contain information about patients that enables healthcare providers to diagnose and treat injuries and illnesses. This includes demographic information about the patient, such as address and phone numbers, as well as clinical information about the patient's past and present health concerns, such as:

- Problem list
- Signs and symptoms
- Diagnoses

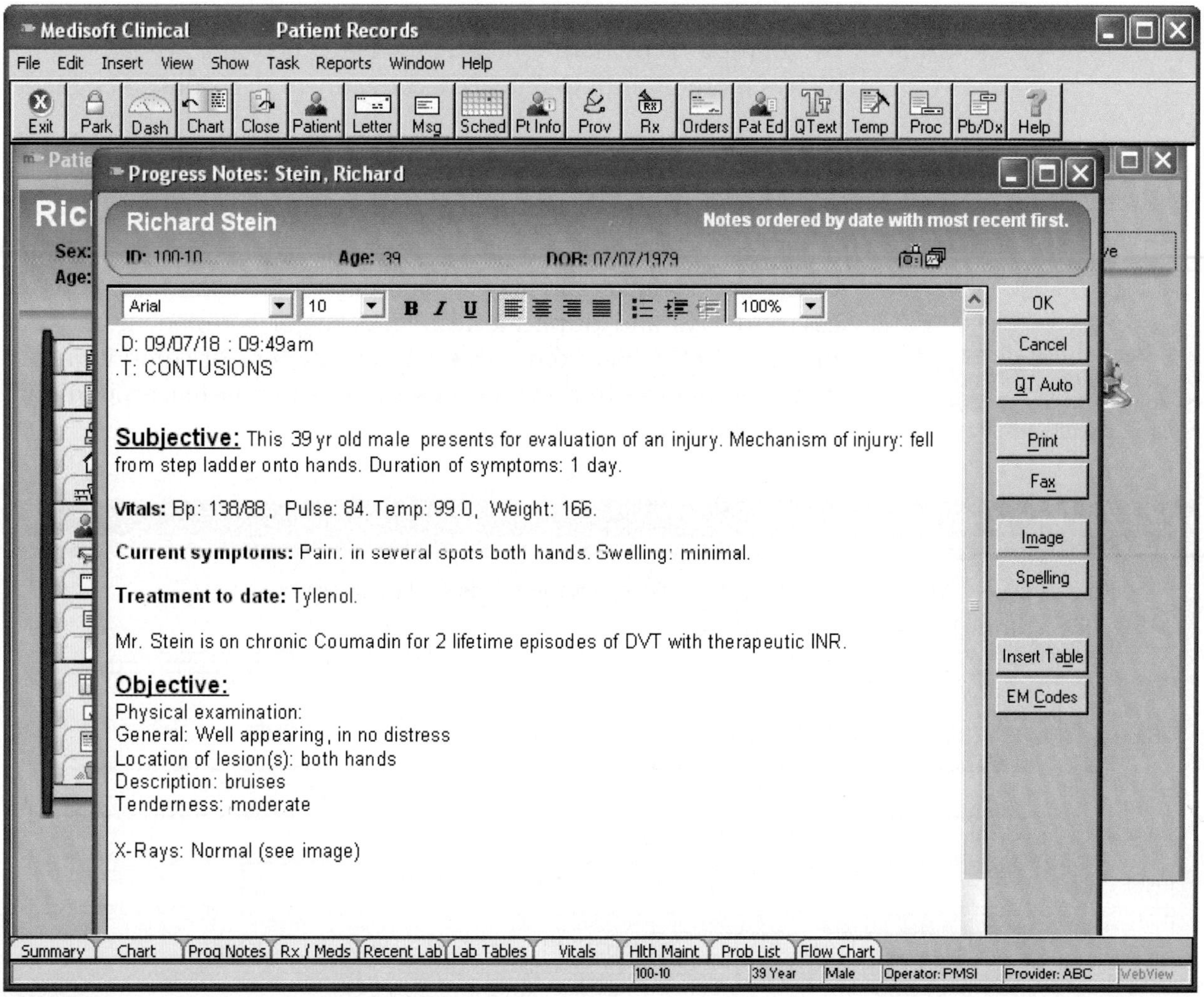

Medisoft Clinical — **Patient Records**

File Edit Insert View Show Task Reports Window Help

Exit | Park | Dash | Chart | Close | Patient | Letter | Msg | Sched | Pt Info | Prov | Rx | Orders | Pat Ed | QText | Temp | Proc | Pb/Dx | Help

Progress Notes: Stein, Richard

Richard Stein   Notes ordered by date with most recent first.

ID: 100-10   **Age:** 39   **DOB:** 07/07/1979

Arial ▼ 10 ▼ **B** *I* U |≡ ≡ ≡ ≡| := ≡ ≡ | 100% ▼

.D: 09/07/18 : 09:49am
.T: CONTUSIONS

Subjective: This 39 yr old male presents for evaluation of an injury. Mechanism of injury: fell from step ladder onto hands. Duration of symptoms: 1 day.

Vitals: Bp: 138/88, Pulse: 84. Temp: 99.0, Weight: 166.

Current symptoms: Pain. in several spots both hands. Swelling: minimal.

Treatment to date: Tylenol.

Mr. Stein is on chronic Coumadin for 2 lifetime episodes of DVT with therapeutic INR.

Objective:
Physical examination:
General: Well appearing, in no distress
Location of lesion(s): both hands
Description: bruises
Tenderness: moderate

X-Rays: Normal (see image)

Buttons (right side): OK · Cancel · QT Auto · Print · Fax · Image · Spelling · Insert Table · EM Codes

Summary | Chart | Prog Notes | Rx / Meds | Recent Lab | Lab Tables | Vitals | Hlth Maint | Prob List | Flow Chart

100-10   39 Year   Male   Operator: PMSI   Provider: ABC   WebView

Figure 1-2   Physician Progress Note in an Electronic Health Record

- Procedures
- Treatment plan
- Medication list
- Allergies
- Diagnostic test results
- Radiology results
- Health maintenance status
- Advance directives

Figure 1-2 shows a portion of a progress note in an EHR that lists symptoms, vital signs, and physical examination findings.

RESULTS MANAGEMENT

Providers must have access to current and past laboratory, radiology, and other test results performed by anyone involved in the treatment of the patient. These computerized results can be accessed by multiple providers when and where they are needed, which allows more prompt diagnosis and treatment decisions to be made.

ORDER MANAGEMENT

EHR programs must be able to send, receive, and store orders for medications, tests, and other services. Staff members in different offices and facilities can access the orders, which eliminates unnecessary delays and duplicate testing. A major component of order management is **electronic prescribing**—the use of computers and handheld devices to transmit prescriptions to pharmacies in digital format (see Figure 1-3).

electronic prescribing the use of computers and handheld devices to transmit prescriptions in digital format.

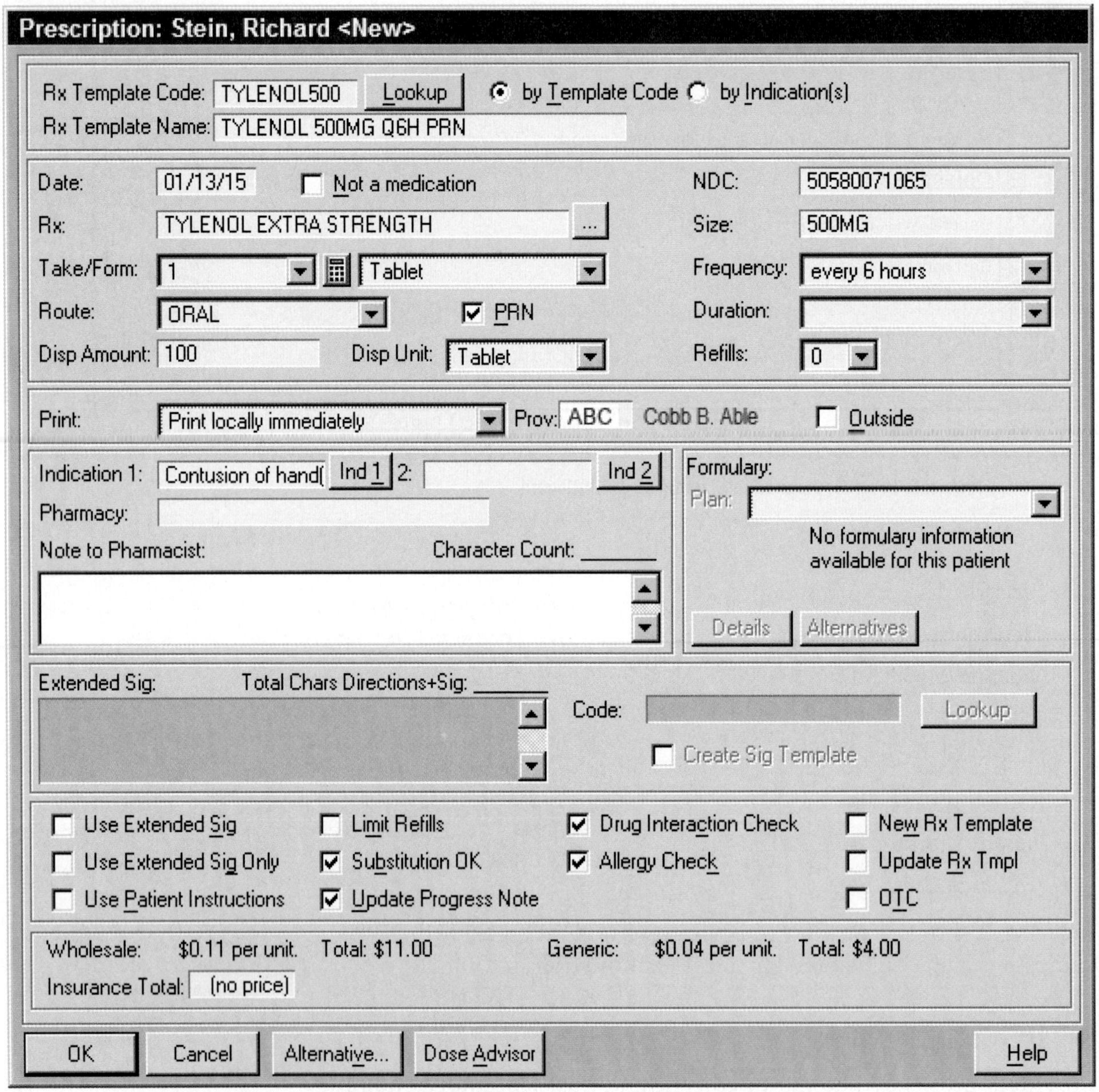

Figure 1-3 Electronic Prescribing in an Electronic Health Record

DECISION SUPPORT

As the practice of medicine becomes more complex, the amount of information available to physicians continues to grow. Hundreds of new studies are published on a daily basis. It is not possible for a physician to remember all this information or to be aware of all the latest, most effective treatments.

Electronic health records give a physician who is examining a patient immediate access to the latest clinical research on diagnosis and treatment. The physician can also view the latest information on medications, including suggested doses, common side effects, and possible interactions.

In addition, electronic record systems provide a variety of alerts and reminders that physicians can use to improve a patient's health. Physicians can, for example, see a list of all women over fifty years of age who have not had mammograms in the past year. If the physician chooses, these women will all receive letters reminding them that they are due for this preventive screening.

ELECTRONIC COMMUNICATION AND CONNECTIVITY

Today, a patient is typically treated by more than one provider in more than one facility. Physicians, nurses, medical assistants, referring doctors, testing facilities, and hospitals all need to communicate with one another to provide the safest and most effective care to patients. Insurance plans also need information from the health record to process claims for reimbursement. Using secure electronic messaging, EHRs facilitate communication with patients, providers, and health plans.

PATIENT SUPPORT

Electronic health records offer patients access to appropriate educational materials on health topics, instructions for preparing for common medical tests, and the ability to report on home monitoring and testing to their physician. In addition, patients are given a printed after-visit summary before they leave the office. An **after-visit summary (AVS)** is a communication tool that provides the patient with relevant and actionable information and instructions.

after-visit summary (AVS) a communication tool that provides the patient with relevant and actionable information and instructions.

In addition, many providers now offer patients access to a **patient portal**—a secure online website which provides patients with the ability to communicate with their provider and access their health information at any time. Providers also use secure electronic messaging to send patients reminders for preventive and follow-up care.

patient portal a secure online website which provides patients with the ability to communicate with their provider and access their health information at any time.

ADMINISTRATIVE PROCESSES

The administrative processes in a physician's office also benefit from the use of EHRs. While most physician practices already use computers for billing and scheduling, an EHR streamlines the processes. In an office that uses a PMP and an EHR, some administrative tasks may be performed in either program.

REPORTING AND POPULATION MANAGEMENT

Electronic health records generate reports that physician practices use to manage patients, track outcome indicators, and meet regulatory and accreditation requirements. In addition, EHRs produce reports that enable physicians to qualify for meaningful use incentives under the HITECH Act, as well as other programs that reward performance based on quality and patient outcomes.

Electronic health records also contain a wealth of information related to particular diseases and treatments. This information, as long as it does not include any patient's identity, can be used to advance medical knowledge through research. Electronic health records are used for reporting public health information, such as immunization status or cancer cases. Cancer cases are often reported to a cancer registry. A *registry* is a database of patients with specific diagnoses, conditions, or procedures. Registries are used to track patient progress and outcomes.

In addition, EHRs can assist in detecting threats to the health of the general population, such as bioterrorism or an outbreak of a new disease. For example, the immediate reporting of suspicious diseases to public health authorities may help identify a new influenza strain and prevent its spread.

1.4 THE MEDICAL DOCUMENTATION AND BILLING CYCLE: PRE-ENCOUNTER

The increased use of electronic health records in the physician practice has resulted in changes in office workflow. In a medical office, a workflow must be in place that provides medical care to patients and collects payment for these services. While a physician practice's main focus is to care for patients, to provide this care, the practice must be successful from a business perspective. Practices incur a number of expenses on a recurring basis, such as salaries, supplies, utilities, insurance, and equipment leasing. To meet its expenses, a practice needs a steady flow of income, known as revenue. This income comes from billing and collecting for services provided to patients. To maintain a regular *cash flow*—the movement of monies into or out of a business—specific tasks must be completed on a regular schedule before, during, and after a patient visit.

medical documentation and billing cycle a ten-step process that results in timely payment for medical services.

The **medical documentation and billing cycle** consists of ten steps that are required to maintain accurate patient records and

Medical Documentation and Billing Cycle

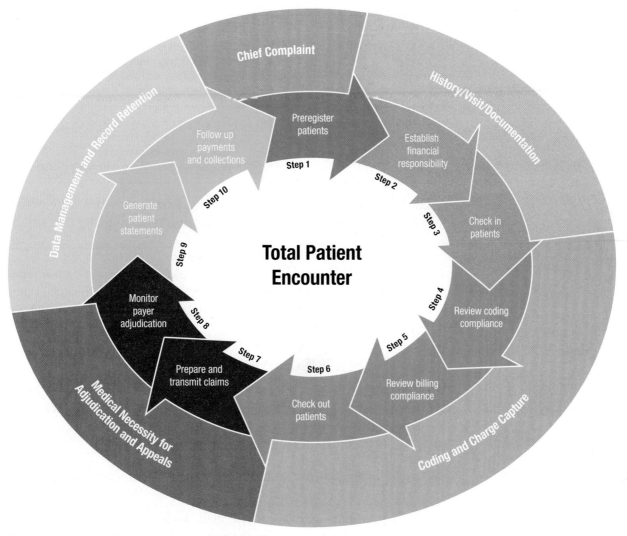

Figure 1-4 The Medical Documentation and Billing Cycle

to receive timely payment for services. This cycle is illustrated in Figure 1-4. The inner circle represents the billing cycle; the outer circle contains the medical documentation cycle. As you can see in the illustration, the two cycles are interrelated. For example, during Step 1, preregistration, a new patient phones for an appointment. Both billing and clinical information must be collected during the phone call. From a billing perspective, the office wants to know whether the patient has insurance that will cover some or all of the cost of the visit, or whether the patient will pay for the visit. From a health or medical perspective, the staff wants to know the reason the person needs to see the doctor, known as the chief complaint. As the medical documentation and billing cycle continues, so does the interaction between the two types of information.

TABLE 1-3	Steps in the Medical Documentation and Billing Cycle
Before the encounter	Step 1: Preregister patients
During the encounter	Step 2: Establish financial responsibility Step 3: Check in patients Step 4: Review coding compliance Step 5: Review billing compliance Step 6: Check out patients
After the encounter	Step 7: Prepare and transmit claims Step 8: Monitor payer adjudication Step 9: Generate patient statements Step 10: Follow up payments and collections

Table 1-3 lists the steps in the cycle, organized by when they occur: before the encounter, during the encounter, or after the encounter.

(*Note:* The steps in this cycle are based on an office using an electronic workflow—in other words, an integrated practice management program and electronic health record program. In offices that still use paper for one or more tasks in the workflow, the order of some steps may vary.)

STEP 1: PREREGISTER PATIENTS

The first step in the billing and reimbursement cycle is to gather information to preregister patients before their office visits. This information includes:

- The patient's name.
- The patient's contact information; at the minimum, address and phone number.
- The patient's reason for the visit, such as a medical complaint or a need for an immunization.
- Whether the patient is new to the practice.

The information is obtained over the telephone or via the Internet, if the practice has a website.

1.5 THE MEDICAL DOCUMENTATION AND BILLING CYCLE: ENCOUNTER

STEP 2: ESTABLISH FINANCIAL RESPONSIBILITY

Many patients are covered by some type of health plan. It is important to determine whether the patient has insurance and, if so, to obtain the identification number, plan name, and name of the person who is the policyholder. Once the insurance information is obtained, the patient's current eligibility and benefits can be verified with the payer. This may be completed before the patient arrives at the office, or it may be completed the day of the encounter; in any case, it should be completed before the patient is examined by the physician. If the patient does not have insurance, it is important to establish the patient's planned method of payment.

STEP 3: CHECK IN PATIENTS

When patients arrive in the office, they are asked to complete or update a **patient information form** that contains the personal, employment, and medical insurance data needed to collect payment for services. Most offices ask all patients to update this information periodically to ensure that it is current and accurate. This form, illustrated in Figure 1-5, becomes part of the patient's medical record and is updated when the patient reports a change, such as a new address or different medical insurance.

patient information form a form that includes a patient's personal, employment, and insurance data needed to complete an insurance claim.

The patient information form requires the patient's signature or the signature of a parent or guardian if the patient is a minor, mentally incapacitated, or incompetent. The signature also indicates that the patient accepts responsibility for payment of all charges not paid by the health plan and authorizes the release of information required to process an insurance claim. The signature also authorizes the health plan or government program to send payments directly to the provider rather than to the patient.

Verify Identity

During check-in, it is also common to photocopy or scan the patient's insurance identification card, front and back (see Figure 1-6), and a photo ID, such as a driver's license, to verify that the patient and the insured are in fact the same person.

Distribute Financial Policy and Privacy Policy

Whether they have insurance or not, all patients should be provided with a copy of the practice's financial policy. Patients covered by health plans must understand that they are responsible for payment of charges that are not paid by their health plans. The financial policy of a medical practice explains how the practice handles financial matters. Also at this time, patients must be given the practice's notice of privacy practices and a privacy authorization form.

Collect Time-of-Service Payments

Patient coinsurance or copayments, as required under the policy of the patient's health plan, may be paid during check-in or checkout, depending on the medical practice's procedures. In addition, if a patient owes a balance from a previous visit, this amount also may be collected. Most practices accept checks, cash, and debit and credit cards for payment, and offer payment plans to patients.

STEP 4: REVIEW CODING COMPLIANCE

Once check-in activities have been completed, the patient is escorted to an examination room where the provider evaluates the patient's

Patient

Last Name	First Name	MI	Sex __ M __ F	Date of Birth / /

Address	City	State	Zip

Home Ph # ( )	Cell Ph # ( )	Marital Status	Student Status

Race
__ American Indian or Alaska Native
__ Asian   __ Black or African American   __ White
__ Other   __ Native Hawaiian or Other Pacific Islander __ Declined

Ethnicity
__ Hispanic or   __ Non-Hispanic or
Latino   Latino
__ Declined

Language

SS#	E-mail	Allergies

Employment Status	Employer Name	Work Ph # ( )	Primary Insurance ID#

Employer Address	City	State	Zip

Referred By	Ph # of Referral ( )

Responsible Party (Complete this section if the person responsible for the bill is not the patient)

Last Name	First Name	MI	Sex __ M __ F	Date of Birth / /

Address	City	State	Zip	SS#

Relation to Patient __ Spouse __ Parent __ Other	Employer Name	Work Phone # ( )

Spouse, or Parent (if minor):	Home Phone # ( )

Insurance (If you have multiple coverage, supply information from both carriers)

Primary Carrier Name	Secondary Carrier Name
Name of the Insured (Name on ID Card)	Name of the Insured (Name on ID Card)
Patient's relationship to the insured __ Self __ Spouse __ Child	Patient's relationship to the insured __ Self __ Spouse __ Child
Insured ID #	Insured ID #
Group # or Company Name	Group # or Company Name
Insurance Address	Insurance Address

Phone #	Copay $	Phone #	Copay $
	Deductible $		Deductible $

Other Information

Is patient's condition related to:	Reason for visit:

__ Employment   __ Auto Accident (if yes, state in which accident occurred: ___)   __ Other Accident

Date of Accident: /   /   Date of First Symptom of Illness: /   /

Financial Agreement and Authorization for Treatment

I authorize treatment and agree to pay all fees and charges for the person named above. I agree to pay all charges shown by statements, promptly upon their presentation, unless credit arrangements are agreed upon in writing.

I authorize payment directly to FAMILY CARE CENTER of insurance benefits otherwise payable to me. I hereby authorize the release of any medical information necessary in order to process a claim for payment in my behalf.

Signed: _____   Date: _____

Figure 1-5 Patient Information Form

Your Health Insurance

PPO

Policy Number
345M678912

Group Number
345678A

Member Name
SAMUEL N. SAMPLE

Office Visit Copay: $25
Specialist: $25
Emergency Room: $100
Urgent Care: $50
Rx: $10/20/40

Network Coinsurance
In: 90%/10%
Out: 80%/20%

Emergency admissions require notification within 48
hours. Failure to comply may result in reduced benefits.

Customer Service: 1-800-555-1234, TDD: 1-800-555-5678
M–F, 8:00 a.m.–11:00 p.m. Eastern Standard Time

Provider Services: 1-800-555-8888, TDD: 1-800-555-7777
Submit Claims To:
PO Box 123
Any City, OH 60089-2222

This health plan is provided by Your Health Insurance. While coverage remains in force, members are
entitled to the benefits under the terms and conditions of the plan. This card is for identification only
and is not a guarantee of coverage. Deductibles and coinsurance may apply.

Figure 1-6 Sample Insurance Identification Card

condition, and develops a treatment plan. Each patient visit must
be carefully documented and must contain two very important
pieces of information—the **diagnosis**, which is the physician's
opinion of the nature of the patient's illness or injury, and the
procedures, which are the services performed. Without this information, the physician will not receive payment from a health plan.

When diagnoses and procedures are reported to health plans, code
numbers are used in place of descriptions. **Coding** is the process
of translating a description of a diagnosis or procedure into a standardized code. Standardization allows information to be shared
among physicians, office personnel, health plans, and so on, without losing the precise meaning.

The patient's primary complaint (the illness or condition that is the
reason for the visit) is assigned a **diagnosis code** from the International Classification of Diseases. Until October 1, 2015, these codes

diagnosis physician's opinion
of the nature of the patient's
illness or injury.

procedure medical treatment
provided by a physician or
other healthcare provider.

coding the process of translating a description of a diagnosis
or procedure into a standardized code.

diagnosis code a standardized
value that represents a
patient's illness, signs, and
symptoms.

were taken from the *International Classification of Diseases,* **Ninth Revision,** *Clinical Modification* **(ICD-9-CM)**. Since October 1, 2015, the *International Classification of Diseases,* **Tenth Revision,** *Clinical Modification* **(ICD-10-CM)** has been used for diagnosis coding.

Examples of ICD-10-CM Codes

G44.021	chronic cluster headache, intractable
J11.1	influenza with other respiratory manifestations

Implementation of ICD-10

While ICD-9 contains about 13,000 diagnosis codes, ICD-10 includes approximately 68,000 codes. Of course, no provider will need to learn all 68,000 codes. Nevertheless, physicians and other providers will need to document encounters in greater detail, or coders will be unable to translate the documentation into the appropriate ICD-10 code. The reward for documenting with detail and specificity will be more accurate coding, resulting in greater productivity and more accurate reimbursement. Without in-depth documentation, physicians will face more queries from coders, decreased productivity, and perhaps lower reimbursement for services.

In addition to increased demands on providers and staff, the transition to ICD-10 also requires a significant investment of time and money. The impact on productivity cannot be overemphasized; any staff member who determines, documents, records, or uses a diagnosis code will be affected.

Some of the major differences between ICD-9 and ICD-10 include:

- ICD-9 codes have three to five numeric digits, while ICD-10 codes contain three to seven alphanumeric digits.
- Increased specificity—such as exact disease names, causes, and locations.
- Coding injuries is more complicated.
- Documentation about the side of the body being treated will be required.

The ICD-10 system is more complex, and in many cases there is no simple mapping or translation from one code set to the other. For example, in ICD-9 there was one code for infectious mononucleosis; in ICD-10 there are ten (see Table 1-4).

Just as there are ICD-10 codes for specifying a patient's diagnosis, each procedure the physician performs is assigned a **procedure code** that stands for the particular service, treatment, or test. This code is selected from the **Current Procedural Terminology (CPT®)**. A large

ICD-9 Code	ICD-9 Description	ICD-10 Code	ICD-10 Description
075	Infectious mononucleosis	B27.8	Other infectious mononucleosis
		B27.80	Other infectious mononucleosis without complication
		B27.81	Other infectious mononucleosis with polyneuropathy
		B27.82	Other infectious mononucleosis with meningitis
		B27.89	Other infectious mononucleosis with other complication
		B27.9	Infectious mononucleosis, unspecified
		B27.90	Infectious mononucleosis, unspecified without complication
		B27.91	Infectious mononucleosis, unspecified with polyneuropathy
		B27.92	Infectious mononucleosis, unspecified with meningitis
		B27.99	Infectious mononucleosis, unspecified with other complication

TABLE 1-4   ICD-9 and ICD-10 Code Comparison

group of codes covers the physician's evaluation and management of a patient's condition during office visits or visits at other locations, such as nursing homes. Other codes cover groups of specific procedures, such as surgery, pathology, and radiology.

Examples of CPT Codes

99460   initial hospital or birthing center care, per day for evaluation and management of normal newborn infant

27130   total hip replacement

HCPCS codes (pronounced hick-picks) are used for supplies, equipment, and services not included in the CPT codes.

HCPCS codes used for supplies, equipment, and services not included in the CPT codes.

Examples of HCPCS Codes

E0114   crutches, underarm, other than wood, adjustable or fixed, pair, with pads, tips and handgrips

A0130   non-emergency transportation: wheel-chair van

The diagnosis and procedure codes are recorded on an **encounter form**, also known as a superbill (see Figure 1-7). Traditionally, the encounter form has been a paper form. Offices that use integrated

encounter form a list of the procedures and diagnoses for a patient's visit.

ENCOUNTER FORM

DATE _____ TIME _____

PATIENT NAME _____ CHART # _____

OFFICE VISITS - SYMPTOMATIC		
NEW		
99201	OF--New Patient Minimal	
99202	OF--New Patient Low	
99203	OF--New Patient Detailed	
99204	OF--New Patient Moderate	
99205	OF--New Patient High	
ESTABLISHED		
99211	OF--Established Patient Minimal	
99212	OF--Established Patient Low	
99213	OF--Established Patient Detailed	
99214	OF--Established Patient Moderate	
99215	OF--Established Patient High	
PREVENTIVE VISITS		
NEW		
99381	Under 1 Year	
99382	1 - 4 Years	
99383	5 - 11 Years	
99384	12 - 17 Years	
99385	18 - 39 Years	
99386	40 - 64 Years	
99387	65 Years & Up	
ESTABLISHED		
99391	Under 1 Year	
99392	1 - 4 Years	
99393	5 - 11 Years	
99394	12 - 17 Years	
99395	18 - 39 Years	
99396	40 - 64 Years	
99397	65 Years & Up	
PROCEDURES		
12011	Simple suture--face--local anes.	
29125	App. of short arm splint; static	
29425	Application of short leg cast, walking	
29540	Strapping, ankle	
50390	Aspiration of renal cyst by needle	
71010	Chest x-ray, single view, frontal	

PROCEDURES		
71020	Chest x-ray, two views, frontal & lateral	
71030	Chest x-ray, complete, four views	
73070	Elbow x-ray, AP & lateral views	
73090	Forearm x-ray, AP & lateral views	
73100	Wrist x-ray, AP & lateral views	
73510	Hip x-ray, complete, two views	
73600	Ankle x-ray, AP & lateral views	
LABORATORY		
80048	Basic metabolic panel	
80061	Lipid panel	
82270	Blood screening, occult; feces	
82947	Glucose screening--quantitative	
82951	Glucose tolerance test, three specimens	
83718	HDL cholesterol	
84478	Triglycerides test	
85007	Manual differential WBC	
85018	Hemoglobin	
85025	Complete CBC w/auto diff WBC	
85651	Erythrocyte sedimentation rate--non-auto	
86580	TB Mantoux test	
87040	Culture, bacterial; blood	
87076	Culture, anerobic isolate	
87077	Bacterial culture, aerobic isolate	
87086	Urine culture and colony count	
87430	Strep test	
87880	Direct streptococcus screen	
INJECTIONS AND OTHERS		
90471	Immunization administration	
90656	Influenza virus vaccine, 3+	
90662	Influenza virus vaccine, 65+	
90703	Tetanus injection	
96372	Injection	
92516	Facial nerve function studies	
93000	Electrocardiogram--ECG with interpretation	
93015	Treadmill stress test, with physician...	
96900	Ultraviolet light treatment	
99070	Supplies and materials provided	

FAMILY CARE CENTER
285 Stephenson Blvd.
Stephenson, OH 60089
614-555-0000

☐ DANA BANU, M.D.
☐ ROBERT BEACH, M.D.
☐ PATRICIA MCGRATH, M.D.

☐ JESSICA RUDNER, M.D.
☐ JOHN RUDNER, M.D.
☐ KATHERINE YAN, M.D.

NOTES

REFERRING PHYSICIAN	NPI	AUTHORIZATION #
DIAGNOSIS		
PAYMENT AMOUNT		

Figure 1-7 Encounter Form

EHR and PMPs use an electronic version of the form. Whether on paper or in electronic form, the codes on the encounter form must be recorded in the PMP, as they will be submitted to the health plan in the form of a claim.

STEP 5: REVIEW BILLING COMPLIANCE

To receive payment for services, medical practices bill numerous health plans and government payers. The provider's fees for services are listed on the medical practice's fee schedule. A *fee schedule* is a listing of standard charges for procedures. Each charge, or fee, is related to a specific procedure code. However, the fees listed on the master fee schedule are not necessarily the amount the provider will be paid. Instead, each of the health plans and government payers reimburses the practice according to its own negotiated or government-mandated fee schedule. Many providers enter into contracts with health plans that require a discount from standard fees. In addition, although there is a separate fee associated with each code, each code is not necessarily billable. Whether it can be billed depends on the payer's particular rules. Following these rules when preparing claims results in billing compliance.

STEP 6: CHECK OUT PATIENTS

Checkout is the last step that occurs while the patient is still in the office. The medical codes have been assigned and checked, and the amounts to be billed also have been verified according to the payers' rules. The charges for the visit are calculated, and payment for these types of charges is usually collected at the time of service:

- Previous balances
- Copayments or coinsurance
- Noncovered services
- Charges of nonparticipating providers
- Charges for self-pay patients
- Deductibles

A receipt is prepared for the payments made by the patients, and follow-up work is scheduled as ordered by the physician.

1.6 THE MEDICAL DOCUMENTATION AND BILLING CYCLE: POST-ENCOUNTER

STEP 7: PREPARE AND TRANSMIT CLAIMS

Physician practices use practice management programs to prepare and transmit claims. The claim must contain information about the patient, the procedures the provider performed while the patient was in the office, the patient's diagnosis, and the date and location of the encounter. Health plans also require basic information about the provider who is treating the patient, including the provider's name and identification number. Beyond the basic information requirements that are common to all payers, there are differences in what information is required on an insurance claim. A payer lists the required information in a provider's manual that is available to the medical office. Provider manuals are usually posted on the payers' websites.

When patient and transaction information have been entered in the PMP and checked for accuracy, the software is used to create insurance claims. Once created, claims are transmitted directly to a health plan, or to a clearinghouse. A **clearinghouse** is a company that receives electronic claims from medical practices and forwards the claims to the appropriate health plans (see Figure 1-8).

clearinghouse a company that receives electronic claims from medical practices and forwards the claims to the appropriate health plans.

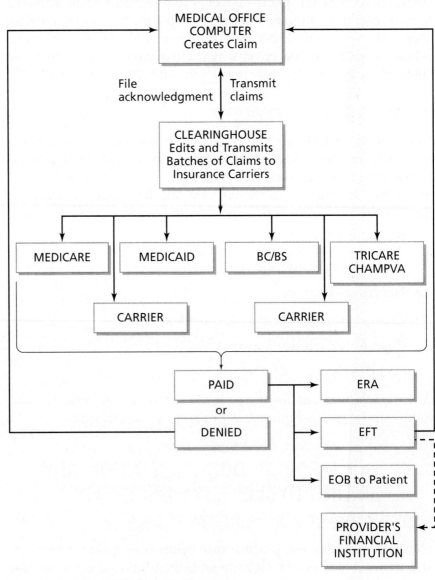

Figure 1-8   Claim Flow Using a Clearinghouse

When a clearinghouse receives a claim, it performs a series of reviews, known as *edits*, checking to see that all necessary information is included in the claim file. It checks for missing data and obvious errors, such as procedures performed on a date earlier than the patient's date of birth. After the basic edit is complete, a report is sent from the clearinghouse to the practice. This report lists problems that need to be corrected before the claim can be sent to the health plan. Ensuring "clean" claims before transmission greatly reduces the number of claim rejections and speeds payment. Once the claims are sent from the clearinghouse to the payer, another report is sent that lists whether each claim was accepted or rejected by the payer.

STEP 8: MONITOR PAYER ADJUDICATION

When the payer receives the claim, it goes through a series of steps designed to determine whether the claim should be paid, a process called **adjudication**. Claims may be paid in full, partially paid, or denied. When the payer has completed the adjudication process, a remittance advice is sent to the practice. The **remittance advice (RA)** lists the transactions included on the claims and the amount paid and, if appropriate, provides an explanation of why certain charges were not paid in full or were denied entirely (see Figure 1-9). An RA may be paper, or it may be electronic, in which case it is called an **electronic remittance advice (ERA)**. A copy of the RA, referred to as an **explanation of benefits (EOB)**, is sent to the patient.

Payments are usually made electronically; the payer transmits funds directly to the practice's bank account via a transmission called *electronic funds transfer (EFT)*. Electronic funds transfer improves the practice's cash flow by shortening the time it takes for the payment to be deposited into the practice's bank account.

Each RA must be carefully reviewed for accuracy by a member of the billing staff, such as a medical insurance specialist, before the payments are posted to the PMP. Each payment is compared against the claim to check that:

- All procedures that were listed on the claim also appear on the payment transaction.

- Any unpaid charges are explained.

- The codes on the payment transactions match those on the claim.

- The payment listed for each procedure is as expected.

If any discrepancies are found, a request for a review of the claim is filed with the payer. If no issues are discovered, the amount of the payment is recorded in the PMP. Depending on the rules of the health plan, the patient may be billed for an outstanding balance. In other circumstances, an adjustment is made and the patient is

adjudication a series of steps that determine whether a claim should be paid.

remittance advice (RA) a document that lists the amount that has been paid on each claim as well as the reasons for nonpayment or partial payment.

electronic remittance advice (ERA) an electronic document that lists patients, dates of service, charges, and the amount paid or denied by the insurance carrier.

explanation of benefits (EOB) paper document from a payer that shows how the amount of a benefit was determined.

EAST OHIO PPO
10 CENTRAL AVENUE
HALEVILLE, OH 60890-2222

PROVIDER REMITTANCE

FAMILY CARE CENTER
285 STEPHENSON BLVD.
STEPHENSON, OH 60089-1111

PAGE: 1 OF 1
DATE: 11/9/2018
ID NUMBER: 4679323

PROVIDER: PATRICIA MCGRATH, M.D.

PATIENT: BROOKS LAWANA   CLAIM: 234567890

FROM DATE	THRU DATE	PROC CODE	UNITS	AMOUNT BILLED	AMOUNT ALLOWED	DEDUCT	COPAY/ COINS	PROV PAID	REASON CODE
10/26/18	10/26/18	99212	1	54.00	48.60	.00	20.00	28.60	
10/26/18	10/26/18	73600	1	96.00	86.40	.00	.00	86.40	
	CLAIM TOTALS			150.00	135.00	.00	20.00	115.00	

PATIENT: HSU DIANE   CLAIM: 345678901

FROM DATE	THRU DATE	PROC CODE	UNITS	AMOUNT BILLED	AMOUNT ALLOWED	DEDUCT	COPAY/ COINS	PROV PAID	REASON CODE
10/26/18	10/26/18	99213	1	72.00	64.80	.00	20.00	44.80	
10/26/18	10/26/18	80048	1	50.00	45.00	.00	.00	45.00	
	CLAIM TOTALS			122.00	109.80	.00	20.00	89.80	

PROVIDER: DANA BANU, M.D.

PATIENT: PATEL RAJI   CLAIM: 567890123

FROM DATE	THRU DATE	PROC CODE	UNITS	AMOUNT BILLED	AMOUNT ALLOWED	DEDUCT	COPAY/ COINS	PROV PAID	REASON CODE
10/26/18	10/26/18	99212	1	54.00	48.60	.00	20.00	28.60	
	CLAIM TOTALS			54.00	48.60	.00	20.00	28.60	

PATIENT: SYZMANSKI MICHAEL   CLAIM: 678901234

FROM DATE	THRU DATE	PROC CODE	UNITS	AMOUNT BILLED	AMOUNT ALLOWED	DEDUCT	COPAY/ COINS	PROV PAID	REASON CODE
10/26/18	10/26/18	99212	1	54.00	48.60	.00	20.00	28.60	
	CLAIM TOTALS			54.00	48.60	.00	20.00	28.60	

PAYMENT SUMMARY		TOTAL ALL CLAIMS		EFT INFORMATION	
TOTAL AMOUNT PAID	262.00	AMOUNT CHARGED	380.00	NUMBER	4679323
PRIOR CREDIT BALANCE	.00	AMOUNT ALLOWED	342.00	DATE	11/9/18
CURRENT CREDIT DEFERRED	.00	DEDUCTIBLE	.00	AMOUNT	262.00
PRIOR CREDIT APPLIED	.00	COPAY	.00		
NEW CREDIT BALANCE	.00	COINSURANCE	80.00		
NET DISBURSED	262.00				

STATUS CODES:
A - APPROVED   AJ - ADJUSTMENT   IP - IN PROCESS   R - REJECTED   V - VOID

Figure 1-9 **Remittance Advice**

not billed. Occasionally, an overpayment may be received, and a refund check is issued by the medical practice.

STEP 9: GENERATE PATIENT STATEMENTS

If charges are billed to the patient, a statement is created and sent to the patient. The statement lists the services performed and the remaining balance that is the responsibility of the patient. Some practices send statements electronically, while others create and mail paper documents. Most medical practices have a regular schedule, referred to as a billing cycle, for sending statements to patients. For example, some practices bill half the patients on the fifteenth of the month and the other half on the thirtieth.

STEP 10: FOLLOW UP PAYMENTS AND COLLECTIONS

In a medical office, the billing staff regularly review reports that list the outstanding balances owed to the practice by insurance companies and by patients. These reports alert the staff to accounts that require action to collect the amount due. Overdue accounts require diligent follow-up to maintain the practice's cash flow. A collection process is often started when patient payments are later than permitted under the practice's financial policy. Insurance claims that are not paid in a timely manner also require follow-up to determine the reason for the nonpayment and to resubmit or appeal as appropriate. Managing the activities associated with a patient encounter to ensure that the provider receives full payment for services is known as **revenue cycle management (RCM)**.

revenue cycle management (RCM) managing the activities associated with a patient encounter to ensure that the provider receives full payment for services.

1.7 HIPAA, THEN AND NOW

To protect consumers' health, both the federal and state governments pass laws that affect the medical services offered to patients. To protect the privacy of patients' health information, additional laws cover the way healthcare plans and providers exchange information as they conduct business. In 1996, Congress passed the **Health Insurance Portability and Accountability Act of 1996 (HIPAA)**. The legislation was designed to:

Health Insurance Portability and Accountability Act of 1996 (HIPAA) federal act that set forth guidelines for standardizing the electronic data interchange of administrative and financial transactions, exposing fraud and abuse in government programs, and protecting the security and privacy of health information.

- Ensure the portability of insurance coverage when employees move from job to job.

- Increase accountability and decrease fraud and abuse in healthcare.

- Improve the efficiency of healthcare transactions and mandate standards for health information.

- Ensure the security and privacy of health information.

The passage of the HITECH Act in 2009 and the Affordable Care Act in 2010 brought major modifications to the original HIPAA rules and regulations. The healthcare environment was changing rapidly, as physicians and hospitals responded to the government's financial incentives to adopt and use electronic health records. Rules placed into effect in 1996 no longer seemed adequate to protect the large volume of health information that was increasingly sent over computer networks.

Recognizing that the existing HIPAA legislation would not adequately safeguard health information in this new electronic environment, the HITECH Act and the ACA included updated rules designed to protect health information. Finalized in 2013, the **HIPAA Omnibus Rule** made a number of significant changes to the privacy, security, and enforcement provisions of the original HIPAA legislation.

HIPAA Omnibus Rule
Legislation passed in 2013 that made significant changes to the privacy, security, and enforcement provisions of the original HIPAA legislation.

The original 1996 HIPAA law is divided into different sections that address unique aspects of healthcare reform. Title I deals with the portability of coverage. Of most concern to physician practices is Title II, Administrative Simplification, which focuses on mandating nationwide standards for health information and ensuring the security and privacy of the information. Administrative Simplification contains several sections, including:

- Electronic Transaction and Code Sets—The implementation of a national standard for transmitting health data electronically and using standard code sets to describe diseases, injuries and other health problems.

- Unique Identifiers—Assigning or using existing unique identifiers for providers, employers, and health plans.

- Privacy—Limiting the use or disclosure of certain health information to a minimum necessary standard and providing patients with certain rights.

- Security—Safeguarding the storage of, access to, and transmission of electronic patient information.

HIPAA ELECTRONIC TRANSACTION AND CODE SETS

HIPAA legislation seeks to reduce administrative costs and to minimize complexities in the healthcare industry by requiring the use of standardized electronic formats for the transmission of administrative and financial data. The HIPAA Electronic Transaction and Code Sets standards describe a particular electronic format that providers and health plans must use to send and receive healthcare transactions. The Centers for Medicare and Medicaid Services (CMS) is responsible for enforcing the Electronic Transaction and Code Sets standards.

Electronic Transactions

electronic data interchange (EDI) the exchange of routine business transactions from one computer to another using publicly available communications protocols.

The electronic transmission of data—called **electronic data interchange (EDI)**—involves sending information from computer to computer. In the past, many different EDI systems were used in healthcare, requiring a confusing array of software programs be used to decipher electronic messages. To address this situation, the HIPAA legislation standardized EDI formats and requires any covered entity working with electronic transactions to use the standard formats to send and receive data. The electronic formats are based on EDI standards called ASC X12, after the initials of the national committee that developed them (Accredited Standards Committee). There are also National Council for Prescription Drug Programs (NCPDP) standards used for some pharmacy transactions.

The original HIPAA regulations created standards for eight common transactions:

- Claims and encounter information
- Payment and remittance advice
- Claims status
- Eligibility
- Enrollment and disenrollment
- Referrals and authorizations
- Coordination of benefits
- Premium payment

The Affordable Care Act (ACA) added new requirements to these transaction standards, including more detailed operating rules for each type of transaction, and a new electronic transaction standard for electronic funds transfer (EFT). The ACA changes also require that health plans certify that they are in compliance with the standards and transaction rules or face penalties.

The standards commonly used by a physician practice, as well as the corresponding ASC X12 format, are listed in Table 1-5.

Most physician practices are required to use the HIPAA-standard electronic claim format called *X12-837 Health Care Claim*, or *837P* for short. This claim is called the professional claim because it is used to bill for a physician's services. A hospital's claim is called an institutional claim, and there are also HIPAA dental claims and drug claims. Exempt practices use the *CMS-1500 (02/12)* paper claim, which is the currently mandated paper claim form.

While health plans are now required to offer electronic funds transfer in the X12-835 format, providers are not required to accept electronic remittance advice or funds transfer. They may still use all paper, or a combination of paper and electronic. However, some health plans, such as Medicare, require that physicians accept electronic payment.

TABLE 1-5	HIPAA Standards and Electronic Formats
X12-270/271 **Health Care Eligibility Benefit Inquiry and Response**	Questions and answers about whether patients' health plans cover planned treatments and procedures
X12-276/277 **Health Care Claim Status Request and Response**	Questions and answers between providers— such as medical offices and hospitals—and payers about claims that are due to be paid
X12-278 **Health Care Services Review— Request for Review and Response**	Questions and answers between patients, or providers on their behalf, and managed care organizations for approval to see medical specialists
X12-835 **Claims Payment and Remittance Advice**	The payment and RA are sent from the payer to the provider; the payment may be sent electronically from the payer directly to the provider's bank
X12-837 **Health Care Claim or Encounter**	Data about the billing provider who requests payment, the patient, the diagnoses, and the procedures sent by a provider to a payer

Code Sets

In addition to standards for electronic transactions, the HIPAA Administrative Simplification legislation establishes standard medical code sets for use in healthcare transactions. The code sets include ICD-9 and ICD-10, CPT, HCPCS, National Drug Codes (NDC), and others.

Unique Identifiers

As part of the Administrative Simplification efforts, unique identifiers were proposed for the purpose of standardizing the identification numbers for providers, employers, health plans, and individuals to ensure future consistency and ease of use. Under the law, each healthcare provider was assigned a unique National Provider Identifier (NPI), which is a ten-position identifier consisting of all numbers. The numbers do not contain any information about healthcare providers, such as the state in which they practice or their provider type or specialization. The identifier for employers, known as the Standard Unique Employer Identifier, is the employer identification number (EIN) that has been assigned to that employer by the Internal Revenue Service. The proposed Health Plan Identifier (HPID) has not yet been implemented, and the identifier for individuals has been abandoned.

HIPAA PRIVACY REQUIREMENTS

As part of the Administrative Simplification provisions, the **HIPAA Privacy Rule** protects individually identifiable health information.

HIPAA Privacy Rule regulations for protecting individually identifiable information about a patient's health and payment for healthcare that is created or received by a healthcare provider.

Copyright ©2016 McGraw-Hill Education

Health information is information about a patient's past, present, or future physical or mental health; or payment for healthcare. If this information can be used to find out the person's identification, it is referred to as **protected health information (PHI)**. **Electronic protected health information (ePHI)** is any protected health information (PHI) that is created, stored, transmitted, or received electronically. Except for treatment, payment, and healthcare operations (TPO), the Privacy Rule limits the release of protected health information without the patient's consent.

The HIPAA Privacy Rule must be followed by all covered entities. A **covered entity (CE)** is a person or entity that furnishes, bills, or receives payment for healthcare in the normal course of business and conducts certain transactions in electronic form. Common examples of CEs include healthcare providers, health plans, and healthcare clearinghouses.

A **business associate (BA)** is an individual or entity that creates, receives, maintains, or transmits PHI on behalf of a covered entity; business associates may also include subcontractors of an entity. Examples of BAs include billing companies, data storage companies, claims processing, and data analysis organizations.

The rules mandate that a covered entity or business associate must:

- Adopt a set of privacy practices that are appropriate for its healthcare services.
- Notify patients about their privacy rights and how their information can be used or disclosed.
- Train employees so that they understand the privacy practices.
- Appoint a staff member to be the privacy official responsible for seeing that the privacy practices are adopted and followed.
- Secure patient records containing individually identifiable health information so that they are not readily available to those who do not need them.

The original HIPAA legislation focused on ensuring that providers and health plans protected patient's health information. Under the HIPAA Omnibus Rule, much of the Privacy Rule and all of the Security Rule now apply directly to business associates.

In addition, the definition of business associate has been expanded to include entities that create, receive, maintain, or transmit PHI on behalf of the business associate—in other words, the subcontractor of a business associate.

Under the HIPAA Privacy Rule, medical practices must have a written **Notice of Privacy Practices** (see Figure 1-10).

protected health information (PHI) information about a patient's health or payment for healthcare that can be used to identify the person.

electronic protected health information (ePHI) protected health information (PHI) that is created, stored, transmitted, or received electronically

covered entity a person or entity that furnishes, bills, or receives payment for healthcare in the normal course of business and conducts certain transactions in electronic form.

business associate an individual or entity that creates, receives, maintains, or transmits PHI on behalf of a covered entity; may also include subcontractors of an entity.

Notice of Privacy Practices a printed document given to patients that explains the medical office's use and disclosure of PHI.

Notice of Privacy Practices

This notice describes how medical information about you may be used and disclosed and how you can get access to this information. **Please review it carefully.**

Your Rights

When it comes to your health information, you have certain rights. This section explains your rights and some of our responsibilities to help you.

Get an electronic or paper copy of your medical record
- You can ask to see or get an electronic or paper copy of your medical record and other health information we have about you. Ask us how to do this.
- We will provide a copy or a summary of your health information, usually within 30 days of your request. We may charge a reasonable, cost-based fee.

Ask us to correct your medical record
- You can ask us to correct health information about you that you think is incorrect or incomplete. Ask us how to do this.
- We may say "no" to your request, but we'll tell you why in writing within 60 days.

Request confidential communications
- You can ask us to contact you in a specific way (for example, home or office phone) or to send mail to a different address.
- We will say "yes" to all reasonable requests.

Ask us to limit what we use or share
- You can ask us not to use or share certain health information for treatment, payment, or our operations. We are not required to agree to your request, and we may say "no" if it would affect your care.
- If you pay for a service or health care item out-of-pocket in full, you can ask us not to share that information for the purpose of payment or our operations with your health insurer. We will say "yes" unless a law requires us to share that information.

Get a list of those with whom we've shared information
- You can ask for a list (accounting) of the times we've shared your health information for six years prior to the date you ask, who we shared it with, and why.
- We will include all the disclosures except for those about treatment, payment, and health care operations, and certain other disclosures (such as any you asked us to make). We'll provide one accounting a year for free but will charge a reasonable, cost-based fee if you ask for another one within 12 months.

Get a copy of this privacy notice
- You can ask for a paper copy of this notice at any time, even if you have agreed to receive the notice electronically. We will provide you with a paper copy promptly.

Choose someone to act for you
- If you have given someone medical power of attorney or if someone is your legal guardian, that person can exercise your rights and make choices about your health information.
- We will make sure the person has this authority and can act for you before we take any action.

File a complaint if you feel your rights are violated
- You can complain if you feel we have violated your rights by contacting us using the information in this notice.

Figure 1-10   Notice of Privacy Practices

- You can file a complaint with the U.S. Department of Health and Human Services Office for Civil Rights by sending a letter to 200 Independence Avenue, S.W., Washington, D.C. 20201, calling 1-877-696-6775, or visiting **www.hhs.gov/ocr/privacy/hipaa/complaints/.**
- We will not retaliate against you for filing a complaint.

Your Choices

For certain health information, you can tell us your choices about what we share. If you have a clear preference for how we share your information in the situations described below, talk to us. Tell us what you want us to do, and we will follow your instructions.

In these cases, you have both the right and choice to tell us to:
- Share information with your family, close friends, or others involved in your care
- Share information in a disaster relief situation
- Include your information in a hospital directory

If you are not able to tell us your preference, for example if you are unconscious, we may go ahead and share your information if we believe it is in your best interest. We may also share your information when needed to lessen a serious and imminent threat to health or safety.

In these cases we never share your information unless you give us written permission:
- Marketing purposes
- Sale of your information
- Most sharing of psychotherapy notes

In the case of fundraising:
- We may contact you for fundraising efforts, but you can tell us not to contact you again.

Our Uses and Disclosures

How do we typically use or share your health information?

We typically use or share your health information in the following ways.

Treat you

We can use your health information and share it with other professionals who are treating you.
Example: A doctor treating you for an injury asks another doctor about your overall health condition.

Run our organization

We can use and share your health information to run our practice, improve your care, and contact you when necessary.
Example: We use health information about you to manage your treatment and services.

Bill for your services

We can use and share your health information to bill and get payment from health plans or other entities.
Example: We give information about you to your health insurance plan so it will pay for your services.

How else can we use or share your health information?

We are allowed or required to share your information in other ways – usually in ways that contribute to the public good, such as public health and research. We have to meet many conditions in the law before we can share your information for these purposes. For more information see: www.hhs.gov/ocr/privacy/hipaa/understanding/consumers/index.html.

Figure 1-10 (*continued*)

Help with public health and safety issues

We can share health information about you for certain situations such as:

- Preventing disease
- Helping with product recalls
- Reporting adverse reactions to medications
- Reporting suspected abuse, neglect, or domestic violence
- Preventing or reducing a serious threat to anyone's health or safety

Do research

We can use or share your information for health research.

Comply with the law

We will share information about you if state or federal laws require it, including with the Department of Health and Human Services if it wants to see that we're complying with federal privacy law.

Respond to organ and tissue donation requests

We can share health information about you with organ procurement organizations.

Work with a medical examiner or funeral director

We can share health information with a coroner, medical examiner, or funeral director when an individual dies.

Address workers' compensation, law enforcement, and other government requests

We can use or share health information about you:

- For workers' compensation claims
- For law enforcement purposes or with a law enforcement official
- With health oversight agencies for activities authorized by law
- For special government functions such as military, national security, and presidential protective services

Respond to lawsuits and legal actions

We can share health information about you in response to a court or administrative order, or in response to a subpoena.

Our Responsibilities

- We are required by law to maintain the privacy and security of your protected health information.
- We will let you know promptly if a breach occurs that may have compromised the privacy or security of your information.
- We must follow the duties and privacy practices described in this notice and give you a copy of it.
- We will not use or share your information other than as described here unless you tell us we can in writing. If you tell us we can, you may change your mind at any time. Let us know in writing if you change your mind.

For more information see: www.hhs.gov/ocr/privacy/hipaa/understanding/consumers/noticepp.html.

Changes to the Terms of this Notice

We can change the terms of this notice, and the changes will apply to all information we have about you. The new notice will be available upon request, in our office, and on our web site.

Figure 1-10 (*continued*)

This document describes the medical office's system for using and disclosing PHI. It also establishes the office's privacy complaint procedures, explains that disclosure is limited to the minimum necessary information, and discusses how consent for other types of information release is obtained.

The HIPAA Omnibus Rule required updates to the original Notice of Privacy Practices to advise individuals of several new privacy protections, including:

- A header statement such as "This notice describes how medical information about you may be used and disclosed and how you can get access to this information. Please review it carefully;"

- A statement describing when an authorization is needed for use or disclosure of health information;

- A statement that individuals will be notified following a breach;

- A statement addressing the restriction of psychotherapy notes from being shared (if applicable);

- A statement that the patient may opt out of fundraising communications;

- A statement addressing marketing, sale of health information and other uses that require patient's written authorization; and

- A statement that individuals who pay out-of-pocket in full for a healthcare service have the right to restrict disclosures of PHI to their health plan.

Medical practices are required to display the Notice of Privacy Practices in a prominent place in the office. The office must make a good-faith effort to obtain a patient's written acknowledgment of having received and read the Notice of Privacy Practices in the form of a signed Acknowledgment of Receipt of Notice of Privacy Practices (see Figure 1-11).

HIPAA SECURITY REQUIREMENTS

The **HIPAA Security Rule** outlines safeguards to protect the confidentiality, integrity, and availability of health information that is stored on a computer system or transmitted across computer networks, including the Internet. While the HIPAA Privacy Rule applies to all forms of protected health information, whether electronic, paper, or oral, the HIPAA Security Rule covers only PHI that is created, received, maintained, or transmitted in electronic form. The security standards are divided into three categories: administrative, physical, and technical safeguards.

Administrative safeguards are administrative policies and procedures designed to protect electronic health information. The management

HIPAA Security Rule
regulations outlining the minimum administrative, technical, and physical safeguards required to prevent unauthorized access to protected healthcare information.

Acknowledgment of Receipt of Privacy Practices Notice

PART A: The Patient.

Name: _____

Address: _____

Telephone: _____ E-mail: _____

Patient Number: _____ Social Security Number: _____

PART B: Acknowledgment of Receipt of Privacy Practices Notice.

I, _____ , acknowledge that I have received a Notice of Privacy Practices.

Signature: _____ Date: _____
If a personal representative signs this authorization on behalf of the individual, complete the following:

Personal Representative's Name: _____

Relationship to Individual: _____

PART C: Good-Faith Effort to Obtain Acknowledgment of Receipt.

Describe your good-faith effort to obtain the individual's signature on this form: _____

_____

_____

Describe the reason why the indvidual would not sign this form. _____

_____

_____

SIGNATURE.
I attest that the above information is correct.

Signature: _____ Date: _____

Print Name: _____ Title: _____
Include this acknowledgment of receipt in the individual's records.

Figure 1-11   Acknowledgment of Receipt of Privacy Practices Form

of security is assigned to one individual, who is required to conduct a risk assessment of the current level of data security. Once that assessment is complete, security policies and procedures are developed or modified to meet current needs. Security training is provided to educate staff members about the policies and to raise awareness of security and privacy issues.

Physical safeguards are the mechanisms required to protect electronic systems, equipment, and data from threats, environmental hazards, and unauthorized intrusion. Threats include computer hackers, disgruntled employees, and angry patients. Health information stored on computers can be at risk from physical threats and environmental hazards, such as unplanned system outages or floods. To protect data, medical practices create regular backups of computerized information on a daily basis. The backup files are stored at a remote physical location to minimize the likelihood of data loss in a large-scale disaster.

Technical safeguards are the automated processes used to protect data and control access to data. Access to information is granted on an as-needed basis. For example, the individual responsible for scheduling may not need access to billing data. Examples of technical safeguards include computer passwords, antivirus and firewall software, and secure transmission systems for sending patient data from one computer to another.

As an additional security measure, computer programs can keep track of data entry and create an **audit trail**—a report that shows who has accessed information and when. When new data are entered or existing data are changed, a log records the time and date of the entry as well as the name of the computer operator. The practice manager reviews the log on a regular basis to detect irregularities.

audit trail a report that traces who has accessed electronic information, when information was accessed, and whether any information was changed.

Enforcement and Breaches

The HIPAA Security Rule and the HIPAA Privacy Rule are enforced by the Office for Civil Rights (OCR). The acquisition, access, use, or disclosure of unsecured PHI in a manner not permitted under the HIPAA Privacy Rule is known as a **breach**. Examples of a breach include stolen or improperly accessed PHI, unauthorized viewing of PHI, and PHI sent to the wrong provider. PHI is considered "unsecured" if it is not encrypted to government standards.

breach the acquisition, access, use, or disclosure of unsecured PHI in a manner not permitted under the HIPAA Privacy Rule.

Under the HIPAA Omnibus Rule, the definition of breach has been expanded, and as a result, more unauthorized uses and disclosures of protected health information (PHI) must be reported. Previously, an incident was considered a breach only when it was found that the incident resulted in significant risk of harm to the individual. The updated definition presumes that any use or disclosure of PHI not allowed by HIPAA will harm an individual and is considered a breach, unless proven otherwise. The burden of proof has shifted; it is now up to the covered entity or business associate to prove that the disclosure was not a breach.

The HIPAA Breach Notification Rule requires HIPAA covered entities and their business associates to provide notification following a breach of unsecured protected health information. Notification must be provided to individuals, the Secretary of Health and Human Services, and if more than 500 individuals are affected, the media must be notified.

TABLE 1-6	Breach Violations and Monetary Penalties	
Violation Category	**Each Violation**	**Violation Cap**
Did not know	$100–$50,000	$1.5 million
Reasonable Cause	$1,000–$50,000	$1.5 million
Willful neglect/ corrected	$10,000–$50,000	$1.5 million
Willful neglect/ uncorrected	$50,000	$1.5 million

Enforcement and Penalties

The HITECH Act significantly strengthened HIPAA enforcement by instituting increased penalties for those entities that do not comply with the new Breach Notification regulations. The violation categories and monetary penalties are listed in Table 1-6.

audit a formal examination or review undertaken to determine whether a healthcare organization's staff members comply with regulations.

Under HITECH, the Office for Civil Rights is required to conduct audits to ensure compliance with HIPAA rules. Previously, audits were permissible but not required. An **audit** is a formal examination or review undertaken to determine whether a healthcare organization's staff members comply with regulations.

BE THE DETECTIVE!

If assigned by your instructor, complete the HealthCare.gov Video Case in Connect. Put your skills to use exploring the information available on the HealthCare.gov website and enhance your knowledge by comparing the plans offered in the health insurance marketplace.

LEARNING OUTCOME	CONCEPTS TO REVIEW
1.1 Explain the major changes taking place in the healthcare field.	– Healthcare costs are higher than in other countries, while the quality of healthcare lags behind. – Government legislation passed in recent years has changed the ways in which healthcare is accessed, provided, and paid for. – The Health Information Technology for Economic and Clinical Health (HITECH) Act allocated billions of dollars to be used to encourage physicians and hospitals to use health information technology to improve the quality and efficiency of care provided to patients. It also requires the government to develop standards for the electronic exchange of health information. – The Affordable Care Act (ACA) expands access to care and explores new models of delivering and paying for healthcare, rewarding providers who coordinate care, keep costs down, and provide quality care.
1.2 Describe the functions of practice management programs.	– Verifying insurance eligibility and benefits. – Organizing patient and payer information. – Generating and transmitting insurance claims. – Monitoring the status of claims. – Recording payments from payers. – Generating patients' statements, posting payments, and updating accounts. – Managing collections activities. – Creating financial and productivity reports.
1.3 Identify the core functions of electronic health record programs.	– Health information and data elements. – Results management. – Order management. – Decision support. – Electronic communication and connectivity. – Patient support. – Administrative support. – Population reporting and management.
1.4 List the step in the medical documentation and billing cycle that occurs before a patient encounter.	– Step 1: Preregister patients

LEARNING OUTCOME	CONCEPTS TO REVIEW
1.5 List the steps in the medical documentation and billing cycle that occur during a patient encounter.	– Step 2: Establish financial responsibility – Step 3: Check in patients – Step 4: Review coding compliance – Step 5: Review billing compliance – Step 6: Check out patients
1.6 List the steps in the medical documentation and billing cycle that occur after a patient encounter.	– Step 7: Prepare and transmit claims – Step 8: Monitor payer adjudication – Step 9: Generate patient statements – Step 10: Follow up payments and collections
1.7 Discuss how the HIPAA Privacy Rule and Security Rule protect patient health information.	– The HIPAA Privacy Rule regulates the use and disclosure of patients' protected health information (PHI). To release PHI for other than treatment, payment, or healthcare operations, an authorization must be signed by the patient. The authorization document must be in plain language and have a description of the information to be used, who can disclose it and for what purpose, who will receive it, an authorization date, and the patient's signature. – The HIPAA Security Rule requires covered entities to establish three types of safeguards to protect the confidentiality, integrity, and availability of electronic PHI: administrative safeguards (office policies and procedures designed to protect PHI); physical safeguards (mechanisms to protect electronic systems, equipment, and data from threats, environmental hazards, and unauthorized intrusion); and technical safeguards (the technology and related policies and procedures used to protect electronic data and control access to it, such as firewalls and antivirus software). – A breach is the acquisition, access, use, or disclosure of unsecured PHI in a manner not permitted under the HIPAA Privacy Rule. The HIPAA Breach Notification Rule requires HIPAA covered entities and their business associates to provide notification following a breach of unsecured protected health information. Under the HITECH Act, the Office for Civil Rights is required to conduct audits to ensure compliance with HIPAA rules.

USING TERMINOGY

Match the terms on the left with the definitions on the right.

1. *[LO 1.6]* adjudication
2. *[LO 1.6]* clearinghouse
3. *[LO 1.3]* documentation
4. *[LO 1.3]* electronic health record (EHR)
5. *[LO 1.5]* encounter form
6. *[LO 1.1]* fee-for-service
7. *[LO 1.1]* health information technology (HIT)
8. *[LO 1.1]* meaningful use
9. *[LO 1.4]* medical documentation and billing cycle
10. *[LO 1.1]* patient-centered medical home (PCMH)
11. *[LO 1.3]* patient portal
12. *[LO 1.2]* practice management program (PMP)
13. *[LO 1.7]* protected health information (PHI)
14. *[LO 1.6]* remittance advice (RA)
15. *[LO 1.6]* revenue cycle management (RCM)

a. A model of physician reimbursement in which payment is provided for specific, individual services provided to a patient.

b. An organization that receives claims from a provider, checks and prepares them for processing, and transmits them to insurance carriers in a standardized format.

c. A computerized lifelong healthcare record for an individual that incorporates data from all providers who treat the individual.

d. A document that lists the amount that has been paid on each claim as well as the reasons for nonpayment or partial payment.

e. A list of the procedures and diagnoses for a patient's visit.

f. The utilization of certified EHR technology to improve quality, efficiency, and patient safety in the healthcare system.

g. A ten-step process that results in timely payment for medical services.

h. Health information technology applications that facilitate the day-to-day financial operations of a medical practice.

i. Information about a patient's health or payment for healthcare that can be used to identify the person.

j. A model of primary care that provides comprehensive and timely care to patients, while emphasizing teamwork and patient involvement.

connect Enhance your learning by completing these exercises and more at http://connect.mheducation.com

k. Series of steps that determine whether a claim should be paid.

l. A record of healthcare encounters between the physician and the patient, created by the provider.

m. A secure online website which provides patients with the ability to communicate with their provider and access their health information at any time.

n. Technology that is used to record, store, and manage patient healthcare information.

o. The process of managing the activities associated with a patient encounter to ensure that the provider receives full payment for services.

CHECKING YOUR UNDERSTANDING

Choose the best answer.

16. *[LO 1.5]* A patient information form contains information such as name, address, employer, and

    a. a procedure code.

    b. insurance coverage information.

    c. charges for procedures performed.

17. *[LO 1.5]* Information about a patient's medical procedures that is needed to create an insurance claim is found on the

    a. remittance advice.

    b. encounter form.

    c. patient information form.

18. *[LO 1.3]* Electronic health records are used to record data such as physicians' reports of examinations, surgical procedures, tests results, and

    a. billing codes.

    b. X-rays.

    c. insurance claims.

19. *[LO 1.7]* Medical offices assign _____ to individuals who have access to computer data as a security measure.

    a. identification numbers

    b. private offices

    c. passwords

20. *[LO 1.1]* A network of doctors and hospitals that shares responsibility for managing the quality and cost of care provided to a group of patients is known as

    a. a health information organization.

    b. an accountable care organization.

    c. a health information network.

connect Enhance your learning by completing these exercises and more at http://connect.mheducation.com

21. *[LO 1.6]* Managing the activities associated with a patient's encounter to ensure that the provider receives full payment for services is known as

   a. electronic data interchange.

   b. accounting cycle.

   c. revenue cycle management.

22. *[LO 1.1]* The _____ allocated billions of dollars to encourage physicians and hospitals to adopt electronic health records.

   a. Affordable Care Act

   b. HITECH Act

   c. HIPAA Omnibus Rule

23. *[LO 1.2]* Practice management programs can be used to verify insurance eligibility, create and transmit insurance claims, and

   a. order lab tests.

   b. create reports.

   c. record vital signs.

24. *[LO 1.4]* During preregistration, it is important to obtain the patient's name and contact information, the reason for the visit, and

   a. whether the patient is new to the practice.

   b. the names and ages of all household members.

   c. the medical history of the patient's immediate family.

25. *[LO 1.6]* Claims are subjected to a series of reviews, or _____, before being transmitted to a payer.

   a. status reports

   b. adjudications

   c. edits

APPLYING YOUR KNOWLEDGE

26. *[LO 1.3, 1.5, 1.6]* Why does a medical insurance specialist need to learn about electronic health records?

27. *[LO 1.1–1.3]* Now that you understand the functions of practice management programs and electronic health records, explain why many in the healthcare field believe these programs can trim costs and improve quality.

28. *[LO 1.4–1.6]* Figure 1-4 illustrates the medical documentation and billing cycle. Some of the steps in the cycle, such as Step 2, Establish Financial Responsibility, focus more on billing activities. Explain how Step 4 includes a focus on both billing and clinical functions.

29. *[LO 1.5]* Why is it important to verify a patient's insurance before the office visit?

30. *[LO 1.5]* Why is it necessary to collect payments from patients during check-in?

 connect Enhance your learning by completing these exercises and more at http://connect.mheducation.com

STOP

STOP! Before you proceed on your CiMO adventure, read these important tips. You need to make sure you have access to Medisoft Advanced Version 19 and the related "CiMO9e" Student Data file!

With this 9th edition of CiMO, there are multiple options to access Medisoft. Students, please be sure to check with your instructor for the option you will use in your class.

Option 1: Install the Medisoft Program from a CD and Download the Student Data File.

The Student Data File contains the medical practice, physicians, and patients required to complete the exercises in Chapters 2–14.

a) If you are using a computer at your school [Instructor Edition CD]

Medisoft will most likely already be installed on the computer, so you don't need to install the program. You do still need to download and install the Student Data File (see page 45).

b) If you are working on your own computer [Student At-Home Edition CD]

You will need to purchase the Student At-Home Medisoft CD and install the program on your computer. You also need to download and install the Student Data File (see page 45).

Option 2: Complete the Exercises Through Connect ![connect] connect

Connect is McGraw-Hill's online assignment and assessment solution. No installation or downloads are needed with this option! In this option, the Student Data File is built into the Medisoft exercises in Connect.

To use this option, students will need to make sure they are registered into their instructor's section in Connect.

Be sure to download a copy of the "McGraw-Hill Guide to Success" for the option you are using to complete the Medisoft exercises from the website at www.mhhe.com/medisoft for much more detail on the items mentioned on these pages.

> *NEED HELP?*
>
> Contact McGraw-Hill's Customer Experience Group (CXG). Visit the CXG website at www.mhhe.com/support. Browse our FAQs (Frequently Asked Questions) and product documentation, and/or contact a CXG representative.

Instructions for Option 1: Install the Medisoft Program from a CD and Download the Student Data File.

a) If you are using a computer at your school [Instructor Edition CD]

STEP 1: Determine whether Medisoft Advanced Version 19 is installed on your school's computer. (If it is already installed, skip to Step 3.) To find out if it is installed:

1. Click the Start button, select All Programs, and look for the Medisoft folder. If you find a Medisoft folder, click Medisoft Advanced to launch the program. Once the program is open, determine which version of Medisoft is installed. Click Help on the menu bar and then click About Medisoft. Look in the window that appears, which lists the version number of the program.

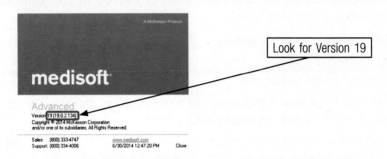

Look for Version 19

2. If you see Version 19, skip to Step 3.

STEP 2: Install Medisoft Version 19 if it is not already on your school computer.
Students, please check with your instructor before proceeding.

1. To install the software from the CD, go to the "Guide" at www.mhhe.com/medisoft for instructions.

STEP 3: Check to see if the "CiMO9e" Student Data File is installed. To find out if it is installed:

1. Start Medisoft Advanced Version 19 by double-clicking the desktop icon. Look at the title bar that contains the words "Medisoft Advanced." If the "CiMO9e" Student Data File has already been installed, you should see the "CiMO9e" to the right of "Medisoft Advanced".

Medisoft Advanced 19 - CiMO9e   Look for CiMO9e

2. If you see CiMO9e, close the program and go to Chapter 2! If not, proceed to Step 4.

STEP 4: Install the "CiMO9e" Student Data File if your computer does not have it.

1. Go to www.mhhe.com/medisoft and click on the appropriate page.
2. Look at the relevant chapter in the "Guide" to walk you through downloading the zip file to your computer with the Student Data File installer.
3. **Warning:** Make sure you do not have the Medisoft program open on your computer when you install the Student Data File.

b) If you are working on your own computer [Student At-Home Edition CD]
To purchase a copy of this optional version, check with your instructor first.

STEP 1: To install the software from the CD, go to the "Guide" at www.mhhe.com/medisoft for instructions.

STEP 2: To install the "CiMO9e" Student Data File, refer back to Step 4.

CiMO

Instructions for Option 2: Complete the Exercises Through Connect ▮ connect.

STEP 1: Make sure you have your Connect access code, either through the card that came with your book or via online.

STEP 2: Get the specific URL for this Connect course from your instructor and register yourself in that section.

STEP 3: Read the relevant chapters of the "McGraw-Hill Guide to Success for Medisoft Simulations" to make sure your settings are ready to complete the exercises and to get an understanding of how the different modes of the simulated exercises work. The different modes are:

- Demo Mode—watch a demonstration of the exercise. .
- Practice Mode—try the exercise yourself with guidance.
- Test Mode—complete the exercise on your own.

Remember, no downloading or installation of files is needed with this option. This refers to both the Medisoft software and the Student Data File, which are already part of Connect.

NOTE: Some steps in the simulated exercises in Connect may differ from what is listed for the exercises in the text, so be sure to refer to the steps listed in Demo and Practice Modes for guidance.

> *NEED HELP?*
>
> Contact McGraw-Hill's Customer Experience Group (CXG). Visit the CXG website at www.mhhe.com/support. Browse our FAQs (Frequently Asked Questions), product documentation, and/or contact a CXG representative.

part 2

MEDISOFT ADVANCED TRAINING

chapter 2

INTRODUCTION TO MEDISOFT

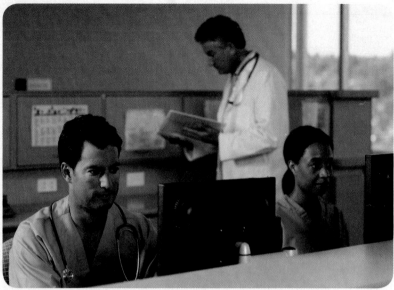

learning outcomes

When you finish this chapter, you will be able to:

2.1 List the six databases Medisoft uses to store information.

2.2 List the menus in Medisoft.

2.3 Explain the function of the Medisoft toolbar.

2.4 Explain how to enter, edit, save, and delete data in Medisoft.

2.5 Describe how to change the Medisoft Program Date.

2.6 Discuss two types of help available in Medisoft.

2.7 Explain how to create and restore backup files in Medisoft.

2.8 Describe the functions of the file maintenance utilities in Medisoft.

2.9 Describe the Medisoft security features used to ensure compliance with HIPAA and HITECH regulations.

what you need to know

To use this chapter, you need to know how to:

- Start your computer.
- Use the keyboard and mouse.
- Use Microsoft Windows 7 or 8.

Medisoft® is a practice management program (PMP). The program uses information about patients, providers, insurance carriers, procedures, and diagnoses to bill insurance carriers and patients for healthcare services. Medisoft also contains a built-in scheduling application called Office Hours. The Medisoft program is widely used by medical practices throughout the United States. It is typically used to accomplish the following daily work in a medical practice:

- Enter information on new patients and change information on established patients as needed.
- Enter transactions, such as charges, to patients' accounts.
- Submit insurance claims to payers.
- Record payments and adjustments from patients and insurance companies.
- Print walkout statements and remainder statements for patients.
- Monitor collections activities.
- Print standard reports and create custom reports.
- Schedule appointments.

This chapter focuses on the menus and functions of Medisoft. The menus and functions of Office Hours will be described in Chapter 3. Many of the general working concepts used in operating Medisoft are similar to those in other practice management programs. Thus, you should be able to transfer many skills taught in this text/workbook to other programs.

2.1 THE MEDISOFT DATABASES

Information entered into Medisoft is stored in databases. A **database** is a collection of related pieces of information. Medisoft stores six major types of data:

database a collection of related bits of information.

1. **Provider data** The provider database has information about the physicians as well as the practice, such as name, address, phone number, and tax and provider identification numbers.

2. **Patient data** Data from each patient information form is stored in the patient database, including the patient's chart number, name, address, phone number, e-mail address, birth date, Social Security number, gender, marital status, and employer.

3. **Insurance carriers** The insurance carrier database contains the name, address, and other data about each insurance carrier used by patients, such as the type of plan. Usually, this database also contains information on each carrier's electronic claim submission requirements.

4. **Diagnosis codes** The diagnosis code database contains the *International Classification of Diseases*, Tenth Revision, *Clinical*

Modification (ICD-10-CM) codes that indicate the reason a service is provided. This code set replaced the previous set, ICD-9-CM, on October 1, 2015. The codes entered in this database are those most frequently used by the practice. The practice's encounter form or superbill often serves as a source document when the Medisoft system is first set up.

5. **Procedure codes** The procedure code database contains the data needed to create charges. The *Current Procedural Terminology* (CPT) codes most often used by the practice are selected for this database. The practice's encounter form is often a good source document for the codes. Other claim data elements, such as the charge for each procedure, are also stored in the procedure code database.

6. **Transactions** The transaction database stores information about each patient's visits, diagnoses, and procedures, as well as received and outstanding payments. Transactions in the form of charges, payments, and adjustments are also stored in the transaction database.

Within Medisoft, each database is linked, or related, to each of the others by having at least one fact in common. For example, information entered in the patient database is shared with the transaction database, linking the two. Information is entered only once; Medisoft selects the data from each database as needed.

Before a medical office begins using Medisoft, basic information about the practice and its patients must be entered in the computer. The author has created a database—the Student Data File—that you will use to complete the exercises in this book. Check with your instructor to determine whether the Student Data File has already been loaded on your computer. If your instructor has not already loaded the data, go to the website at www.mhhe.com/medisoft, and download the Student Data File. You will need to load the database before you do the exercises in this chapter.

2.2 THE MEDISOFT MENUS

Medisoft offers choices of actions through a series of menus. Commands are issued by clicking options on the menus or by clicking shortcut buttons on the toolbar. The menu bar lists the names of the menus in Medisoft: File, Edit, Activities, Lists, Reports, Tools, Window, and Help (see Figure 2-1). Beneath each menu name is a pull-down menu with one or more options.

FILE MENU

The File menu is used to open an existing practice or create a new practice. It is also used to back up data and restore data, set program

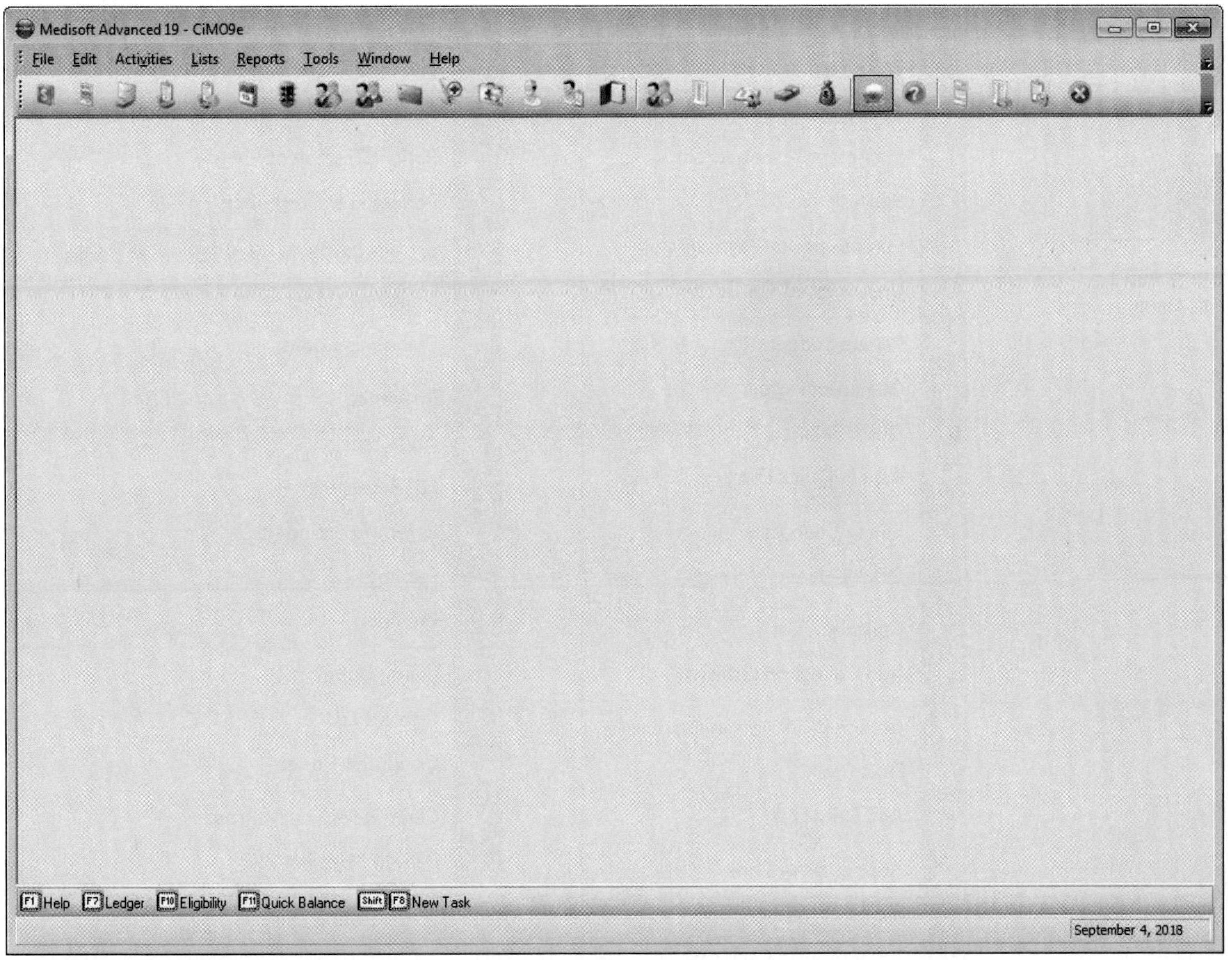

Figure 2-1 Main Medisoft Window

and security options, change the program date, and perform file maintenance activities (see Figure 2-2).

EDIT MENU

The Edit menu contains the basic commands needed to move, change, or delete information (see Figure 2-3). These commands are Cut, Copy, Paste, and Delete.

ACTIVITIES MENU

Most medical office data collected on a day-to-day basis are entered through options on the Activities menu (see Figure 2-4). This menu is used to perform most billing tasks in a medical practice, including:

- Entering financial transactions.
- Creating insurance claims.
- Creating patient statements.
- Entering deposits.
- Viewing unprocessed transactions coming from an electronic health record (EHR).

Figure 2-2 File Menu

Edit	Activities
Cut	
Copy	
Paste	
Delete	

Figure 2-3
Edit Menu

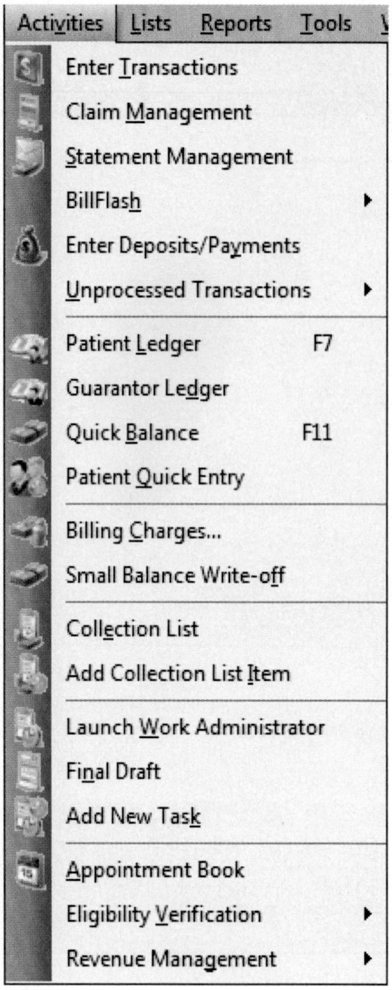

Activities Lists Reports Tools

Enter Transactions
Claim Management
Statement Management
BillFlash ▶
Enter Deposits/Payments
Unprocessed Transactions ▶

Patient Ledger   F7
Guarantor Ledger
Quick Balance   F11
Patient Quick Entry

Billing Charges...
Small Balance Write-off

Collection List
Add Collection List Item

Launch Work Administrator
Final Draft
Add New Task

Appointment Book
Eligibility Verification ▶
Revenue Management ▶

Figure 2-4 Activities Menu

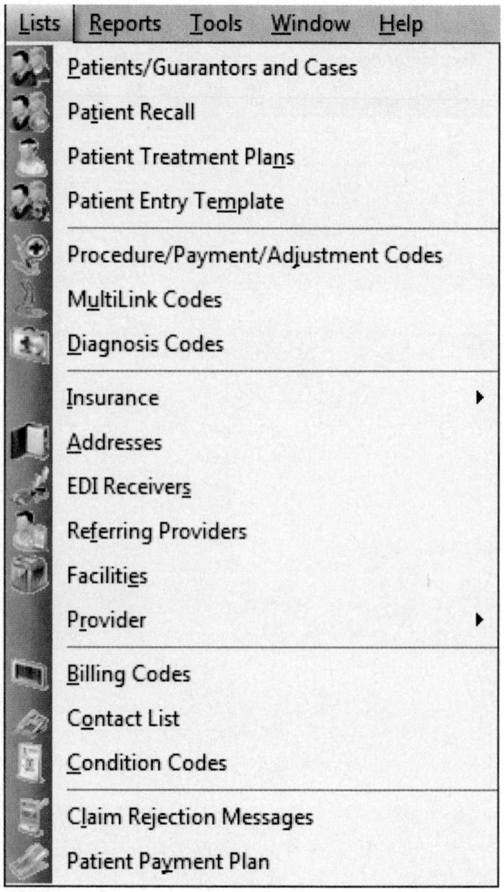

Lists Reports Tools Window Help

Patients/Guarantors and Cases
Patient Recall
Patient Treatment Plans
Patient Entry Template

Procedure/Payment/Adjustment Codes
MultiLink Codes
Diagnosis Codes

Insurance ▶
Addresses
EDI Receivers
Referring Providers
Facilities
Provider ▶

Billing Codes
Contact List
Condition Codes

Claim Rejection Messages
Patient Payment Plan

Figure 2-5 Lists Menu

- Viewing summaries of patient account information.
- Calculating billing charges.
- Writing off small account balances.
- Performing collections activities.
- Opening the appointment scheduler.

The Activities menu also contains options for verifying patient eligibility with insurance carriers (Eligibility Verification) and for launching the Revenue Management functions.

LISTS MENU

Information on new patients, such as name, address, and employer, is entered through the Lists menu (see Figure 2-5). If information needs to be changed on an established patient, it is also updated through this menu. The Lists menu provides access to lists of procedure and diagnosis codes, insurance carriers, electronic data receivers, referring providers, facilities, providers, billing codes,

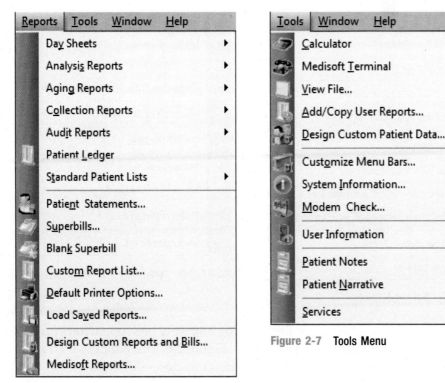

Figure 2-6   Reports Menu

Figure 2-7   Tools Menu

contacts, claim rejection messages, and payment plans. Information on any of these lists may be updated and printed when necessary.

REPORTS MENU

The Reports menu is used to print reports about patients' accounts and other reports about the practice (see Figure 2-6). Medisoft comes with a number of standard report formats, such as day sheets, aging reports, and patient ledgers. There are also several hundred additional reports, which are accessed by selecting the Medisoft Reports option at the bottom of the Reports menu. Practices may create their own report formats using the Design Custom Reports and Bills option.

TOOLS MENU

The Tools menu provides access to a number of utilities that are built into Medisoft, such as a calculator. It is also used to customize various components of the program to meet the needs of the individual practice. Custom collection letters and patient statements can be easily created by using one of the available wizards. The Services option contains commands to set the ICD version and to create ICD-10 mappings. The Tools menu is displayed in Figure 2-7.

WINDOW MENU

Using the Window menu, it is possible to switch back and forth between several open windows. For example, if the Patient List dialog

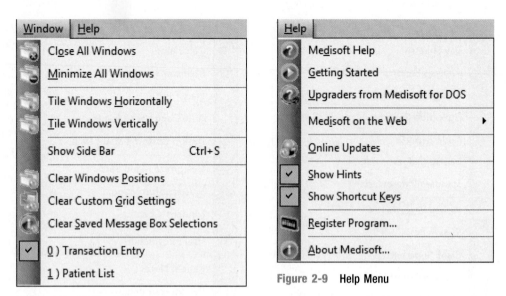

Figure 2-8   Window Menu

Figure 2-9   Help Menu

box and the Transaction Entry dialog box were both open, the Window menu would look like the menu in Figure 2-8. The Window menu also has other selections, such as an option to close all windows.

HELP MENU

The Help menu, shown in Figure 2-9, is used to access Medisoft's built-in help feature. The Help menu also contains an option for identifying the version of the program in use (About Medisoft). For the exercises in this text/workbook to work successfully, you must be using Version 19 of Medisoft (see Figure 2-10).

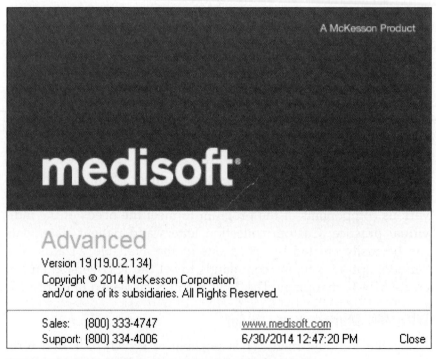

Figure 2-10   Window That Displays the Version of Medisoft in Use

Practice using the Medisoft menus.

1. Start Medisoft.

2. Click the Lists menu on the menu bar.

3. Click Patients/Guarantors and Cases. The Patient List dialog box is displayed.

4. Click the Close button at the bottom of the dialog box.

5. Click the Activities menu.

6. Click Enter Transactions. The Transaction Entry dialog box appears.

7. Click the red "x" button in the upper-right corner of the dialog box.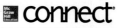

✓ **You have completed Exercise 2-1.**

2.3 THE MEDISOFT TOOLBAR

Located below the menu bar, the toolbar contains twenty-six buttons with icons that represent the most common activities performed in Medisoft (see Figure 2-11 and Table 2-1). These buttons are shortcuts for frequently used menu commands. When you click a button, the corresponding Medisoft dialog box opens. For example, clicking the Claim Management button opens the same dialog box as selecting the Claim Management option on the Activities menu. When you move your cursor over an icon, a description of the icon is displayed. Throughout this text/workbook, the buttons can be used instead of the pull-down menus to perform common tasks.

Practice using buttons on the toolbar. *Note:* **You will need to look at Table 2-1 on pages 56–57 to complete this exercise.**

1. Click the Provider List button. The Provider List dialog box opens.

2. Close the dialog box by clicking the red X in the upper-right corner of the window.

3. Click the Procedure Code List button. The Procedure/Payment/Adjustment List dialog box is displayed.

4. Close the dialog box by clicking the Close button in the lower-right section of the window.

✓ **You have completed Exercise 2-2.**

Figure 2-11 Medisoft Toolbar

TABLE 2-1	Medisoft Toolbar Buttons		
Button	**Button Name**	**Opens**	**Activity**
	Transaction Entry	Transaction Entry dialog box	Enter, edit, or delete transactions
	Claim Management	Claim Management dialog box	Create and transmit insurance claims
	Statement Management	Statement Management dialog box	Create statements
	Collection List	Collection List dialog box	View, add, edit, or delete items on collection list
	Add Collection List Item	Add Collection List Item dialog box	Add items to the collection list
	Appointment Book	Office Hours	Schedule appointments
	View Eligibility Verification Results (F10)	Eligibility Verification Results dialog box	Review results of eligibility verification inquiries
	Patient Quick Entry	Patient Quick Entry dialog box	Use predefined templates to enter new patients
	Patient List	Patient List dialog box	Enter patient information
	Insurance Carriers List	Insurance Carrier List dialog box	Enter insurance carriers
	Procedure Code List	Procedure/Payment/ Adjustment List dialog box	Enter procedure codes
	Diagnosis Code List	Diagnosis List dialog box	Enter diagnosis codes
	Provider List	Provider List dialog box	Enter providers
	Referring Provider List	Referring Provider List dialog box	Enter referring providers

| TABLE 2-1 | *Continued* | | |

	Address List	Address List dialog box	Enter addresses
	Patient Recall Entry	Patient Recall dialog box	Enter Patient Recall data
	Custom Reports List	Open Report dialog box	Open a custom report
	Quick Ledger	Quick Ledger dialog box	View a patient's ledger
	Quick Balance	Quick Balance dialog box	View a patient's balance
	Enter Deposits and Apply Payments	Deposit List dialog box	Enter deposits and payments
	Show/Hide Hints	Show or Hide Hints	Turn the Hints feature on and off
	Medisoft Help	Medisoft Help	Access Medisoft's built-in help feature
	Edit Patient Notes in Final Draft	Final Draft untitled document	Use built-in word processor to create and edit patient notes
	Launch Medisoft Reports	Medisoft Reports window	Provides access to additional reports
	Launch Work Administrator	Assignment List	Assign tasks to practice staff
	Exit Program	Exit Program	Exit the Medisoft program

2.4 ENTERING, EDITING, SAVING, AND DELETING DATA IN MEDISOFT

The process of entering, editing, saving, and deleting data in Medisoft is similar to the way these functions are done in other Windows programs. If you know how to use a word-processing program, for example, the techniques used to manipulate data in Medisoft should be familiar to you.

ENTERING DATA

All data, whether patients' addresses or treatment procedures, are entered into Medisoft through the menus on the menu bar or through the buttons on the toolbar. Selecting an option from the menus or toolbar opens a dialog box. The Tab key is used to move between text boxes within a dialog box. Some information, such as a patient's name, is entered by keying data into a text box. At other times, selections are made from a list of choices already present, such as when making a selection from the drop-down list.

EDITING DATA

If information already entered needs to be changed, the correction is made by following the steps originally used to enter the data. For example, if a patient's phone number has changed, you enter the new number by entering it in the phone number field, right over the old number. Once saved, the newly entered information takes the place of the older data.

EXERCISE 2-3   EDITING DATA

Connect users: go to http://connect.mheducation.com to complete this exercise! Some steps may differ from what is listed here, so be sure to refer to the steps listed in Demo and Practice Modes for guidance.

Edit a procedure code in a charge transaction.

1. Click the Activities menu.

2. Click Enter Transactions.

3. Click the drop-down arrow in the Chart box. The Chart drop-down list is opened (see Figure 2-12).

4. To select James Smith, key the first two letters of his chart number (SMITHJAØ): **SM**. Notice that the system goes to the entry for the first patient whose chart number begins with *SM*, in this case James Smith (see Figure 2-13).

5. Press the Tab key. James Smith's information is displayed (see Figure 2-14). *Note:* if the order of the dates in the Date column on your screen do not match the textbook, click on the shaded triangle to the right of the word Date to re-sort the dates.

6. To edit a transaction, click in the field that needs to be changed. In this case, in the Procedure field, click the entry 92516. Notice that the entry in the field becomes highlighted in blue.

7. Click again in the Procedure field. A pop-up list of procedure codes is displayed.

8. Select a new code from the list by clicking it. Scroll down the pop-up list of codes, and click 99396. Notice that the new code is displayed in the Procedure field, but the entry in the Amount field has not changed. This does not happen until the Tab key is pressed. Press the Tab key now, and watch the entry in the Amount field change (see Figure 2-15).

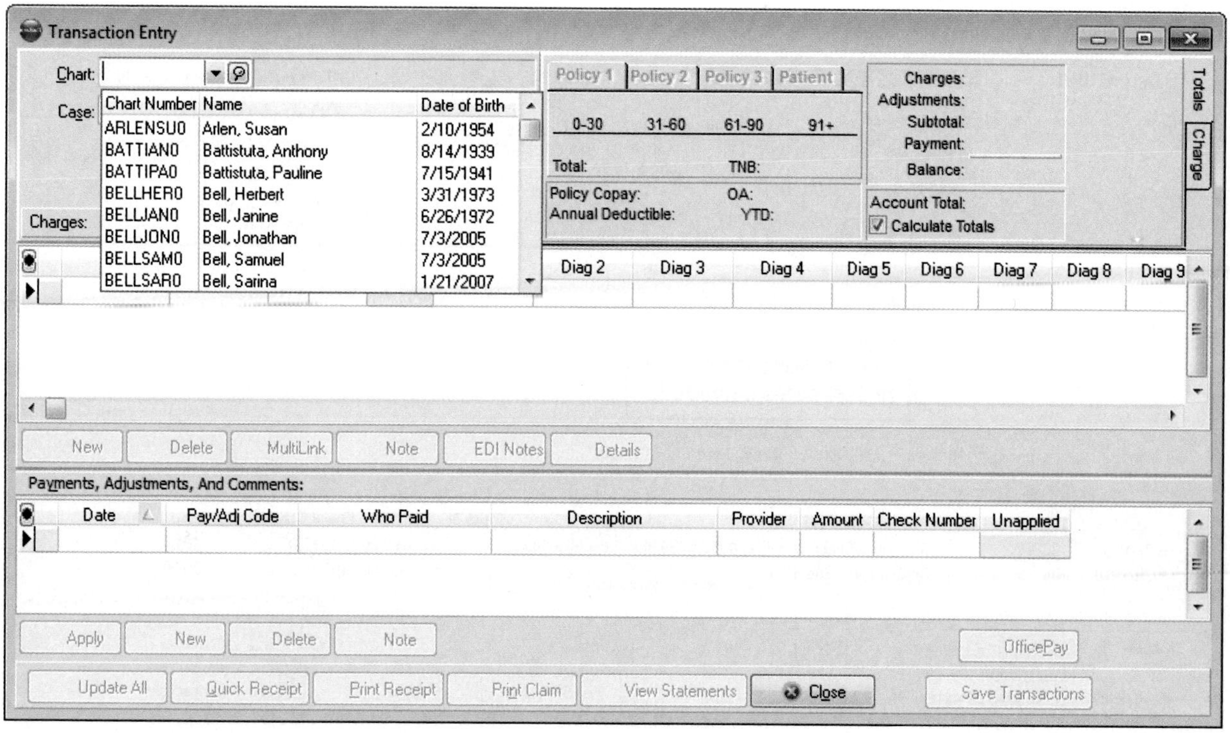

Figure 2-12   Transaction Entry Chart Drop-down List

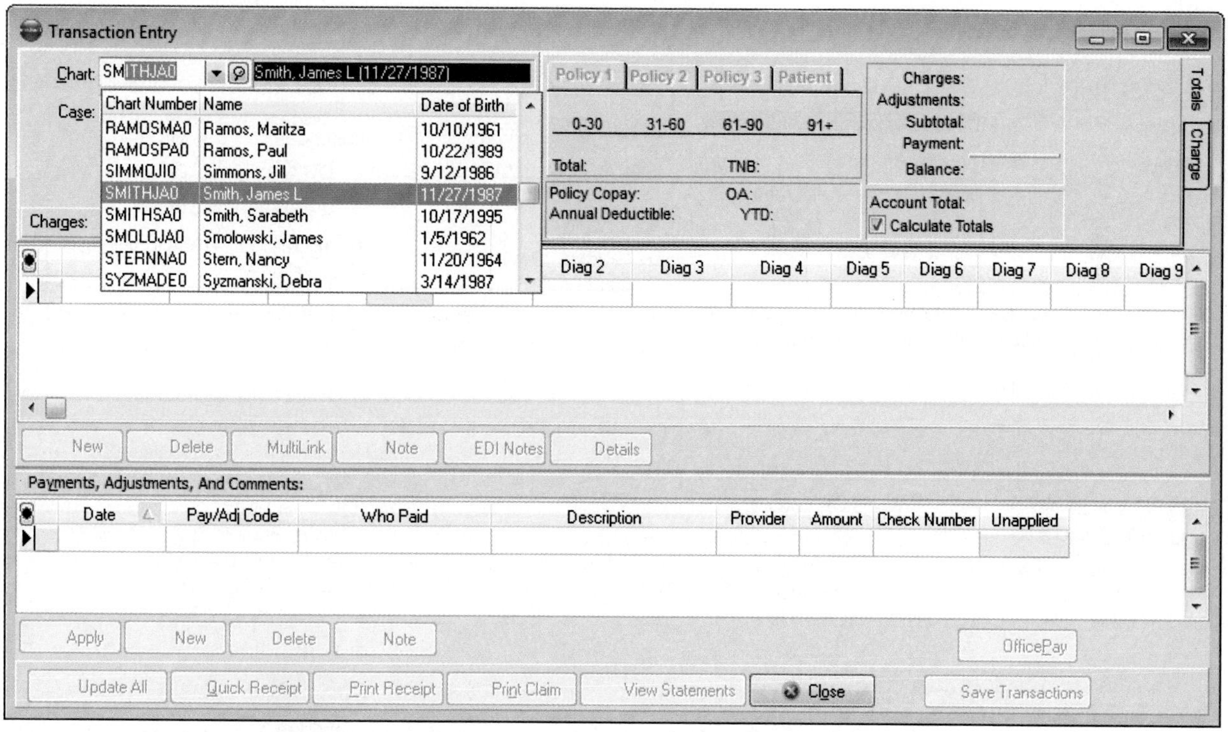

Figure 2-13   Transaction Entry Chart Drop-down List After the Letters *SM* Are Keyed

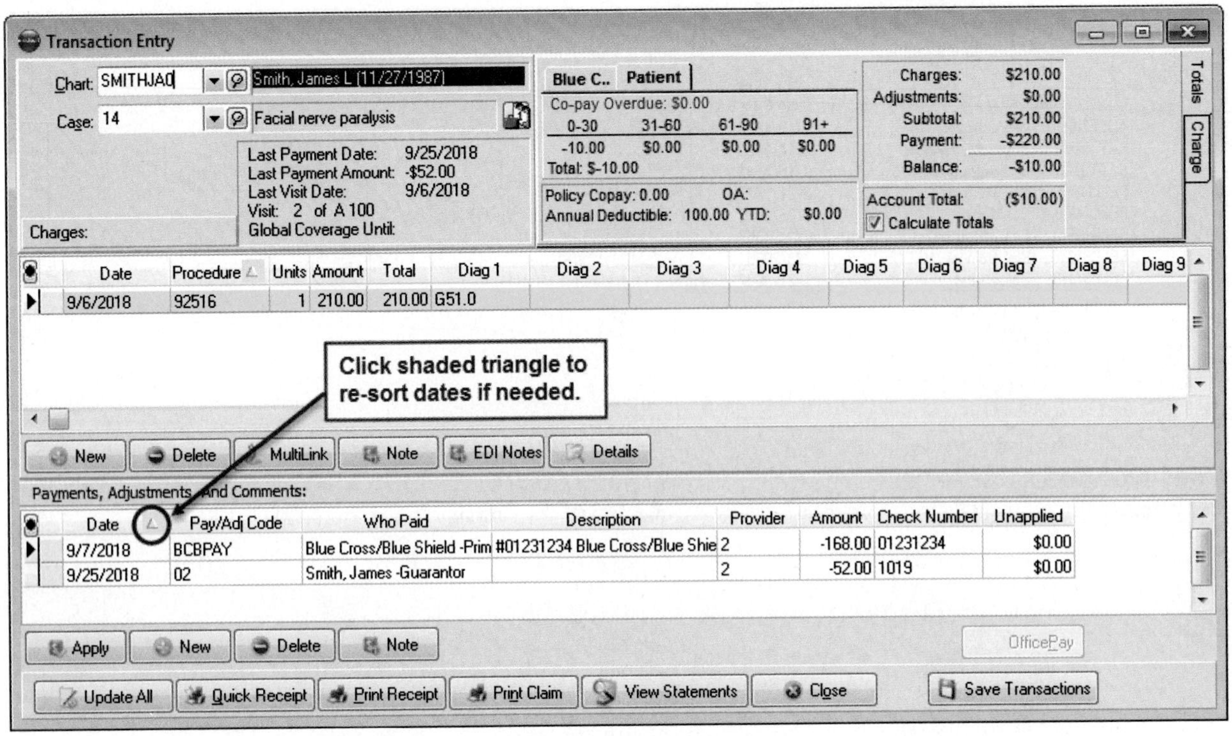

Figure 2-14 Transaction Entry Dialog Box with James Smith's Information Displayed

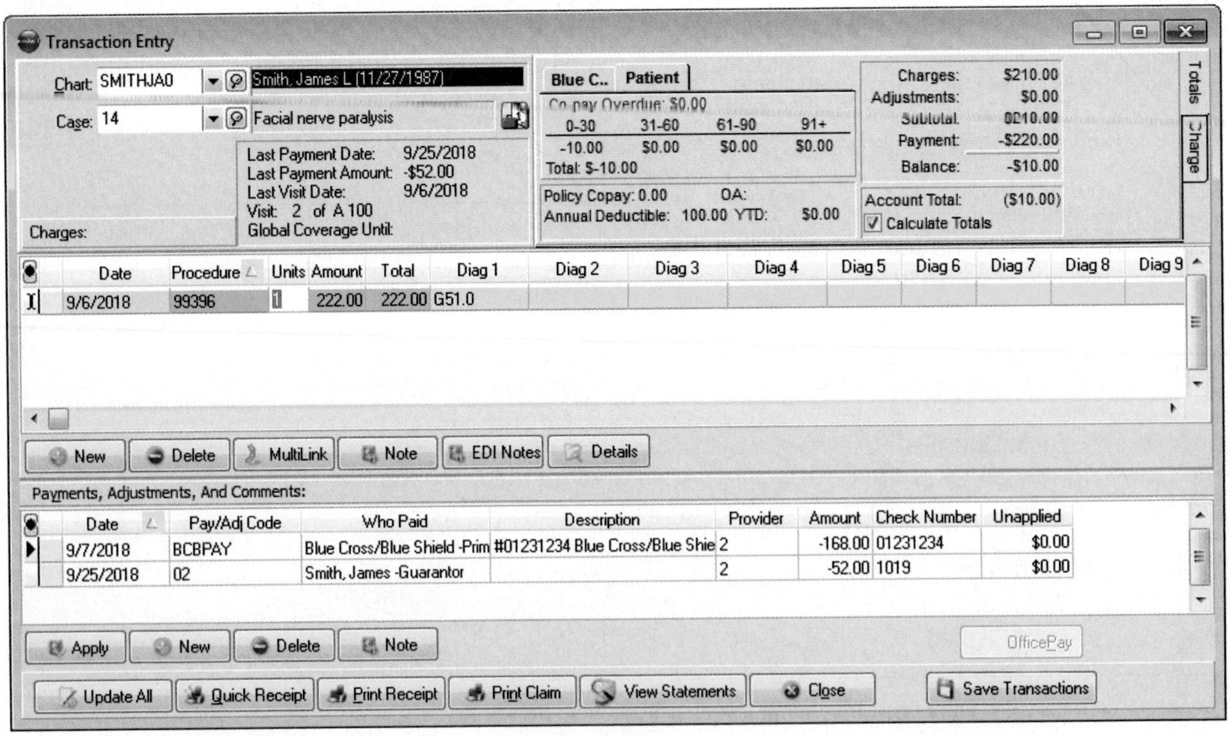

Figure 2-15 Transaction Entry Dialog Box After Code 99396 Is Entered

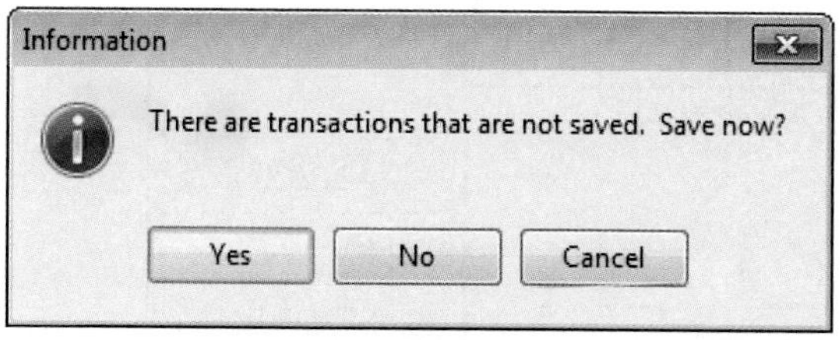

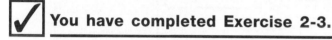

Figure 2-16 Transaction Entry Save Warning Dialog Box

9. Press the Tab key repeatedly, and watch as the cursor moves from box to box.

10. Exit the Transaction Entry dialog box by clicking the Close button or by clicking the close icon in the upper-right corner of the dialog box. An Information box is displayed, asking whether the changes should be saved (see Figure 2-16). In this case, **click the No button**. The changes are not saved, and the Transaction Entry window closes. **ciMC**

✓ **You have completed Exercise 2-3.**

SAVING DATA

Information entered into Medisoft is saved by clicking the Save button that appears in most dialog boxes. In most medical practices, data are saved to the network drive. For the purposes of this text/workbook, your instructor will tell you where to save your data. This may be a hard drive, a directory on a network drive, a flash drive, or some other type of storage device.

DELETING DATA

In some Medisoft dialog boxes, there are buttons for the purpose of deleting data. For example, to delete an insurance carrier, the entry for the carrier is clicked in the Insurance Carrier List dialog box. Then, the Delete button is clicked (see Figure 2-17). Medisoft will ask for a confirmation before deleting the data.

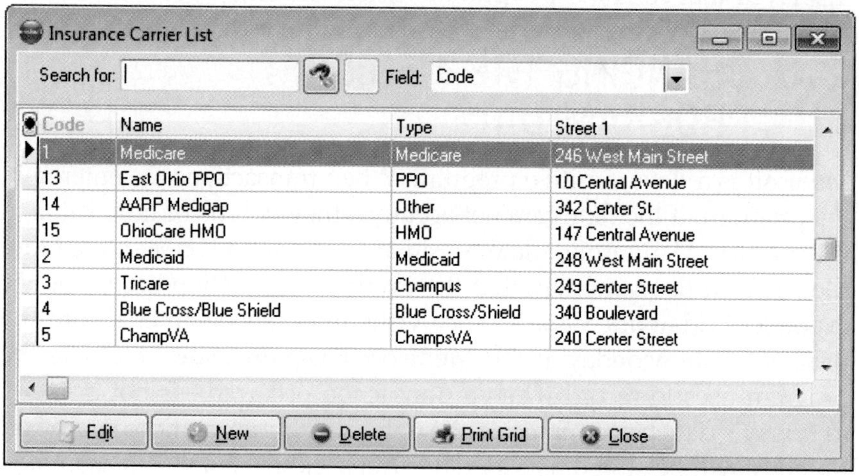

Figure 2-17 Insurance Carrier List Dialog Box with Delete Button Highlighted

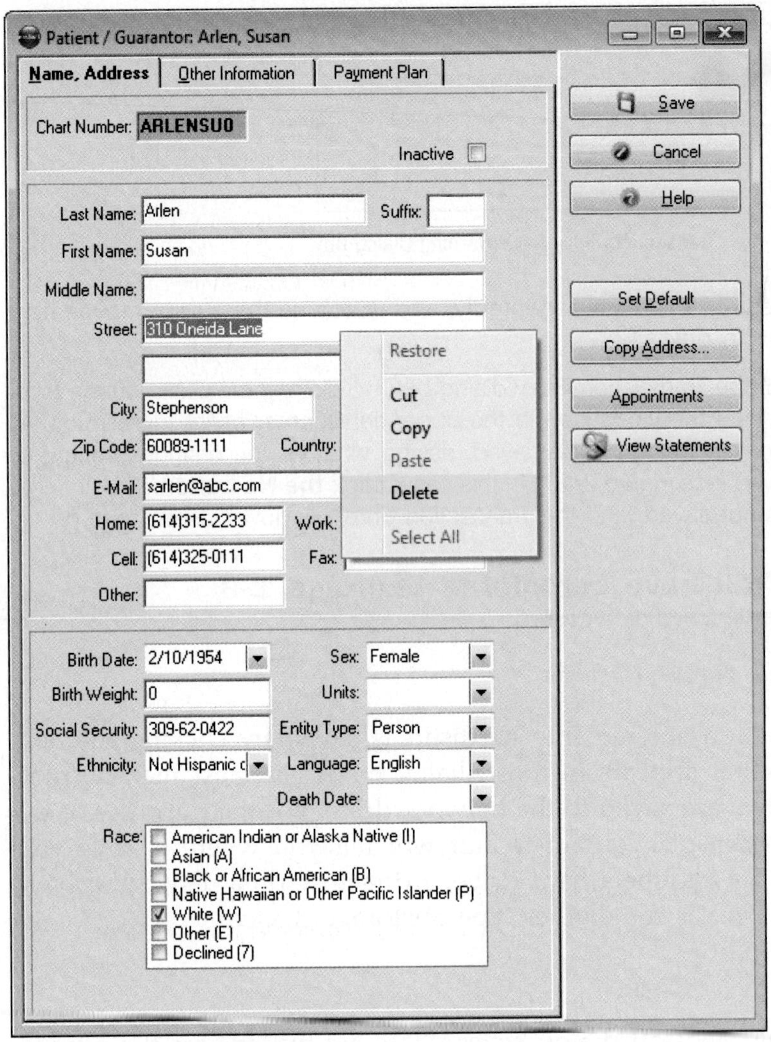

Figure 2-18 Shortcut Menu with Delete Option Available

In other dialog boxes, there is no button for deleting data. In this situation, select the text that is to be deleted, and click either the Delete key on the keyboard or the right mouse button. A shortcut menu is displayed that contains an option to delete the entry (see Figure 2-18).

2.5 CHANGING THE MEDISOFT PROGRAM DATE

Medisoft Program Date date the program uses to record when a transaction occurred.

Medisoft is a date-sensitive program. When transactions are entered in the program, if the dates are not accurate, they will be of little value to the practice. Many times, date-sensitive information is not entered into Medisoft on the same day that the event or transaction occurred. For example, Friday afternoon's office visits may not be entered into the program until Monday. If the **Medisoft Program Date**—the date the program uses to record when a transaction occurred—is not changed to Friday's date before entering the data, all the information entered on Monday will be stored as Monday's transactions. For this reason, it is important to know how to change the Medisoft Program Date.

Figure 2-19a Dialog Box That Appears When a Future Date Is Entered

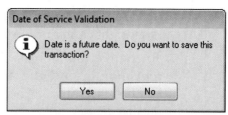

Figure 2-19b Dialog Box That Appears When a Future Date Is Entered While Entering Patient Visit Transactions

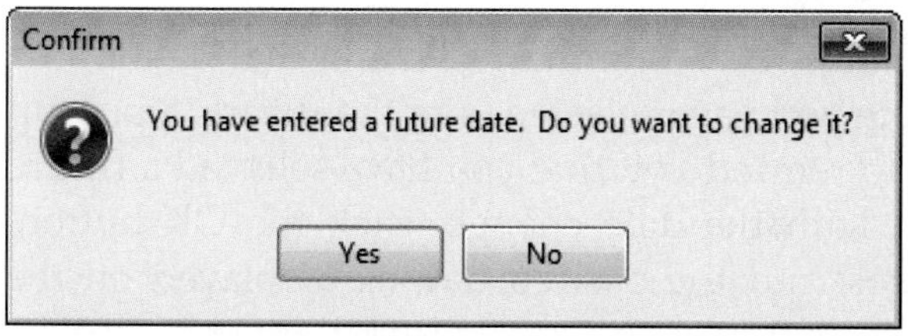

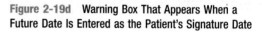

Figure 2-19c Dialog Box That Appears When a Future Date Is Entered While Entering Deposits

Figure 2-19d Warning Box That Appears When a Future Date Is Entered as the Patient's Signature Date

For the exercises in this text/workbook, you will need to change the Medisoft Program Date to the date specified at the beginning of each exercise. Most of the exercises take place in the year 2018. When a date is entered that is in the future (relative to the actual date on which the entry is made), the program displays one of several dialog boxes (see Figures 2-19a, b, c, and d). For example, if the exercise date is September 10, 2019, but the data are actually being entered on February 9, 2016, the program recognizes that a future date has been entered.

Depending on where in the program the date is entered, the dialog box will vary. If a change is made to the pop-up calendar, the dialog box in Figure 2-19a appears as a notification that the date selected is in the future. To keep the future date, click the OK button.

When entering patient office visit transactions, the Date of Service Validation window appears and asks whether the transaction should be saved (see Figure 2-19b). To keep the future date and save the transaction, it is necessary to click the Yes button.

When entering deposits, a Confirm dialog box appears and asks whether the date should be changed (see Figure 2-19c). To keep the future date, the No button must be clicked.

When entering a signature date for a patient, a Warning dialog box states that the date you entered is in the future (see Figure 2-19d). To continue, the OK button is clicked.

The following steps are used to change the Medisoft Program Date in Windows 7 and Windows 8:

1. Click Set Program Date on the File menu. A pop-up calendar is displayed in the lower-right corner of the window (see Figure 2-20).

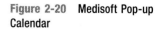

Figure 2-20 Medisoft Pop-up Calendar

	2018		►
Jan	Feb	Mar	Apr
May	Jun	Jul	Aug
Sep	Oct	Nov	Dec

Today: 9/4/2018

Figure 2-21 Calendar Month Window

◄	2010-2019		►
2009	2010	2011	2012
2013	2014	2015	2016
2017	2018	2019	2020

Today: 9/4/2018

Figure 2-22 Calendar Year Window

MMDDCCYY format the way dates must be keyed in Medisoft, in which *MM* stands for the month, *DD* stands for the day, *CC* represents the century, and *YY* stands for the year.

Note: You can also click directly on the date that is displayed in the lower-right corner of the window.

2. To change the month, click the word displayed for the current month, and the abbreviations for the months appear in the calendar window. Click the desired month (see Figure 2-21).

3. To change the year, follow the same procedure. Click the current year, and select the desired year from the years that appear in the window (see Figure 2-22).

4. Select the desired day of the month by clicking that date in the calendar. If the date you have selected is in the future, a pop-up message appears to remind you that you have selected a future date. To continue with the date change, click the OK button. The calendar closes, and the desired date is displayed on the status bar.

In most Medisoft dialog boxes, if a pop-up calendar is not used, dates must be entered manually in the MMDDCCYY format. In the **MMDDCCYY format,** *MM* stands for the month, *DD* stands for the day, *CC* represents the century, and *YY* stands for the year. Each day, month, century, and year entry must contain two digits, and no punctuation can be used. For example, February 1, 2018, would be keyed *02012018*.

> **WARNING!** Dates are very important! If incorrect dates are used when entering data, the information in reports will be inaccurate. Be sure to change the Medisoft Program Date as specified at the beginning of each exercise (If you are using the simulated Medisoft exercises in Connect, you will not need to change the Medisoft Program Date.)

2.6 USING MEDISOFT HELP

Medisoft offers users two different types of help.

HINTS

As the cursor moves over certain fields, hints appear on the status bar at the bottom of the screen. For example, when the cursor is over the New Patient button, a related hint is displayed (see Figure 2-23). The Hint feature can be turned on or off by clicking Show Hints on the Help menu.

BUILT-IN

For more detailed help, Medisoft has an extensive help feature built into the program itself, which is accessed by selecting Medisoft Help on the Help menu (see Figure 2-24).

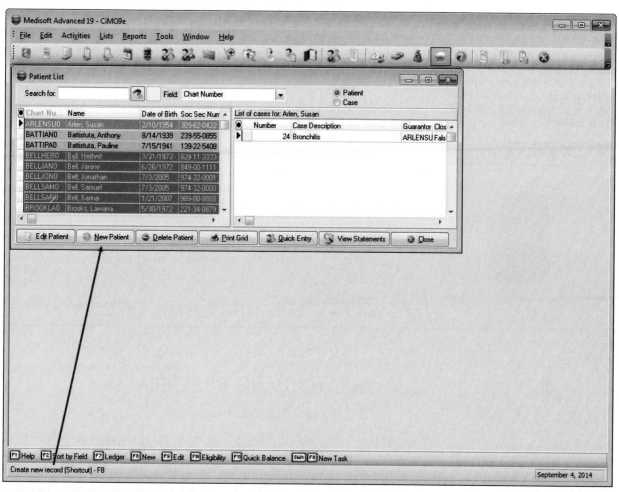

Figure 2-23   Hint Displayed on Status Bar

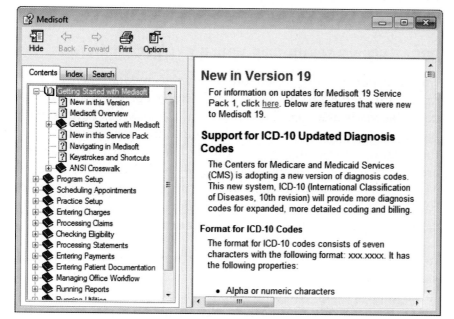

Figure 2-24   Medisoft Built-in Help Feature

Practice using Medisoft's built-in help.

1. Click the Help menu.

2. Click Medisoft Help. Medisoft displays a list of topics for which help is available.

3. In the left column, select the Index tab.

4. Scroll down to locate Diagnosis Entry in the list of terms. Double click Diagnosis Entry. Information on entering diagnosis codes is displayed on the right side of the window. *Note:* You can also locate information by entering the word diagnosis in the blank box below the Index label.

5. Click the red "x" button in the upper-right corner to close the Help window. **CiMC**

✓ **You have completed Exercise 2-4.**

2.7 CREATING AND RESTORING BACKUP FILES

Medisoft is exited by clicking Exit on the File menu or by clicking the Close box. To avoid the inconvenience of exiting and restarting Medisoft many times a day when the computer is needed for a different program, Medisoft can be made temporarily inactive by using the Minimize button, the first of the three small buttons in the upper-right corner of the window. Medisoft can be reactivated at any time by clicking the Medisoft button on the Windows taskbar.

CREATING A BACKUP FILE WHILE EXITING MEDISOFT

backup data a copy of data files made at a specific point in time that can be used to restore data.

Data are periodically saved on removable media, such as flash drives, through a process known as backing up. The extra copy of data files made at a specific point in time is known as **backup data.** Backup data can be used to restore data to the system in the event the data in the system are accidentally lost or destroyed. Backups are performed on a regular schedule, determined by the practice. Many practices back up data at the end of each day. A copy of backup data is usually stored at a location other than the office, in case of a natural or man-made disaster at the office facility.

In a school setting, files are also backed up regularly to store each student's work securely and separately. If you are a student using this book in a school environment, it is important to make a backup copy of your work after each Medisoft session. This ensures that you can restore your work during the next session and be able to use your own data even if another student uses the computer after you or if, for any reason, the data on the school computer are changed or corrupted.

If you are working on your own computer, you do not have to make a backup after each Medisoft session. However, it is still good practice to make a backup on a regular basis, in case something happens to the database. Imagine how you would feel if you almost finished the exercises in this book, and one day you were unable to open the Medisoft database that contains your work! If you did not have a backup for each chapter, you would have to start over with Chapter 3.

In Medisoft, the Backup Data option on the File menu can be used to make a backup copy of the active database at any time. By default, Medisoft also displays a Backup Reminder dialog box every time the program is exited. The Backup Reminder dialog box gives you the opportunity to back up your work every time you exit Medisoft (see Figure 2-25). To perform the backup, click the Back Up Data Now button. A Backup Warning dialog box may appear, indicating that if others are using the same practice data, they should exit Medisoft before the backup is made (see Figure 2-26). To continue

Figure 2-25   Backup Reminder Dialog Box

Figure 2-26   Backup Warning Dialog Box

to exit the program without making a backup, click the Exit Program button in the Backup Reminder dialog box.

By default, Medisoft assigns a name to the backup file, using the current system date. For example, a backup made on March 29, 2018 would be named *mw03-29-2018.mbk*. All Medisoft backup files start with the letter *mw* and end in the extension *.mbk*. The .mbk extension indicates that it is a Medisoft backup file, just as an extension of .docx refers to a Microsoft Word file. This name can be changed by clicking in the Destination File Path and Name field and entering a new name.

Note: Files that contain the .mbk extension cannot be opened by double-clicking; they can only be opened from within the Medisoft program, through a process known as restoring data.

The following exercise provides practice backing up the Medisoft database.

EXERCISE 2-5   BACKING UP

Practice backing up your work on exiting Medisoft.

1. To exit Medisoft, click Exit on the File menu, or click the Exit button on the toolbar.

2. The Backup Reminder dialog box appears, displaying three options: Back Up Data Now, Exit Program, and Cancel. For the purposes of this text, it is recommended that you back up your work each time you exit the program. Your instructor will tell you where to save your backup.

3. Click the Back Up Data Now button. If a Backup Warning dialog box appears, click the OK button.

4. The Medisoft Backup dialog box is displayed (see Figure 2-27). Depending on the last time the dialog box was accessed, the Destination File Path and Name box may already contain an entry. Your instructor will tell you what to enter in this field.

5. Medisoft automatically displays the location of the database files to be backed up in the Source Path box in the lower half of the dialog box.

6. Click the Start Backup button.

7. The program backs up the latest database files and displays an Information dialog box indicating that the backup is complete (see Figure 2-28). Click OK.

8. Close the Medisoft Backup dialog box by clicking the Close button.

9. The Medisoft Backup dialog box disappears, and the Medisoft program closes. **CiMC**

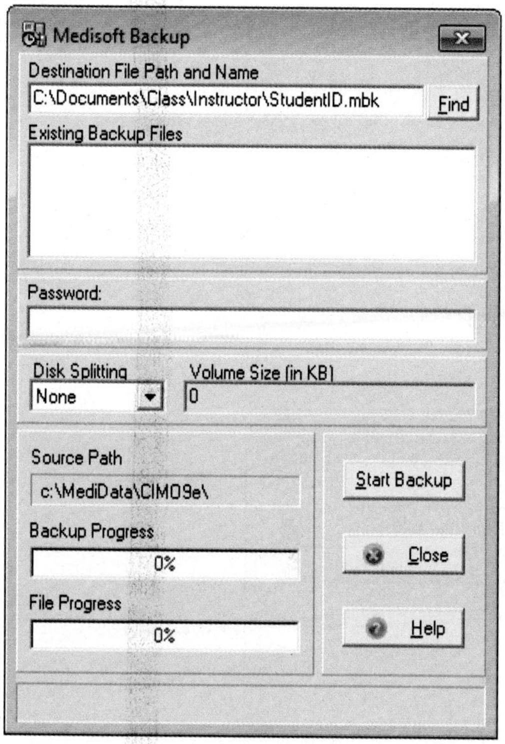

Figure 2-27 Backup Dialog Box

Figure 2-28 Backup Complete Message

✓ **You have completed Exercise 2-5.**

RESTORING THE BACKUP FILE

The process of retrieving data from backup storage devices is referred to as **restoring data.** Whenever a new Medisoft session begins, the following steps can be used to restore the backup file, if required. If you share a computer in an instructional environment, it is recommended that you perform a restore before each new session to be sure you are working with your own data.

restoring data the process of retrieving data from backup storage devices.

RESTORING A BACKUP FILE (CONNECT ONLY) EXERCISE 2-6

WARNING: this exercise can only be completed in Connect, not in the live Medisoft software available on CD.

Practice restoring a backup file.

In this exercise, backups are stored on the C drive, and the Medisoft program files are located on the C drive.

1. Open the File menu, and click Restore Data.

2. When the Warning box in Figure 2-29 appears, click OK.

3. The Restore dialog box appears (see Figure 2-30). To locate the file that is to be restored, click the Find button (located to the right of the Backup File Path and Name field).

4. In the Selection dialog box that appears, locate the folder that contains the file and click once to select the folder. Then click the OK button. The file itself will be selected in the next step.

Connect users: go to http://connect.mheducation.com to complete this exercise! Some steps may differ from what is listed here, so be sure to refer to the steps listed in Demo and Practice Modes for guidance.

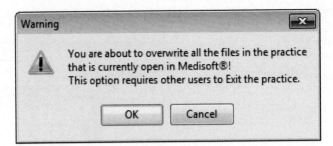

Figure 2-29 Restore Warning Box

Figure 2-30 Restore Dialog Box

5. The backup file(s) located in the folder appear in the list of existing backup files in the Restore dialog box. Click once on the desired backup file.

6. Click the Start Restore button.

7. When the Confirm box appears, click OK.

8. An Information dialog box appears indicating that the restore is complete. Click OK to continue.

9. Click the Close button to close the Restore dialog box.

✓ **You have completed Exercise 2-6.**

2.8 MEDISOFT'S FILE MAINTENANCE UTILITIES

In addition to the backup and restore features, Medisoft provides four features to assist in maintaining data files stored in a system. These four features are found on tabs in the File Maintenance dialog box (see Figure 2-31).

1. Rebuild Indexes
2. Pack Data
3. Purge Data
4. Recalculate Balances

The dialog box is accessed by clicking File Maintenance on the File menu. If the medical office's database is large, Medisoft's utilities may take a long time to finish. For this reason, it is usually a good idea to use the utility functions at the end of the day or when the system will not be needed for a while.

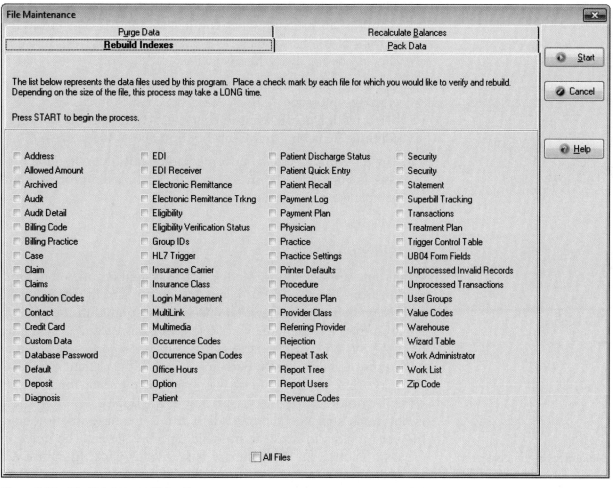

Figure 2-31 File Maintenance Dialog Box

rebuilding indexes a process that checks and verifies data and corrects any internal problems with the data.

REBUILDING INDEXES

Rebuilding indexes is a process that checks and verifies data and corrects any internal data problems. The rebuild does not check or verify the content of the data; it does not change the content of any data files. For example, the system will not check whether John Fitzwilliams paid $50 on his last visit.

To keep files working efficiently, files should be rebuilt about once a month. Files to be rebuilt are selected from the list of files in the Rebuild Indexes tab (refer back to Figure 2-31). If the database is large, rebuilding indexes can take a long time.

To rebuild files in Medisoft in an office, you would complete the following steps:

1. Click File Maintenance on the File menu. The File Maintenance dialog box is displayed with the Rebuild Indexes tab active.
2. Click each check box next to the files that are to be verified and rebuilt. If all files are to be rebuilt, click the All Files box at the bottom of the list of files. This saves the time it would take to click a box for every Medisoft file.
3. Click the Start button. The Confirm dialog box is displayed with the message "All of the checked file processes will be performed. Do you want to continue?" Click the OK button to continue. (Clicking the Cancel button aborts the process.)
4. The rebuild process is performed automatically. When the process is complete, the message "All checked file processes are complete." is displayed.

PACKING DATA

When data are deleted in Medisoft, the system empties the information from the record but keeps the empty slot in the database so it is available when new data need to be entered in the system. For example, if a patient were deleted in the Patient List dialog box, the system would delete all the records pertaining to that patient but would maintain an empty slot in the patient database. The next time a new patient was entered, the data for the new patient would occupy the vacant slot in the database. When there is not much space on the hard disk, it may be desirable to delete the vacant slots to make more disk space available. The deletion of vacant slots from the database is known as **packing data.** Data for packing can be selected from the list of files in the Pack Data tab (see Figure 2-32). (Only transaction files with zero balances

packing data the deletion of vacant slots from the database.

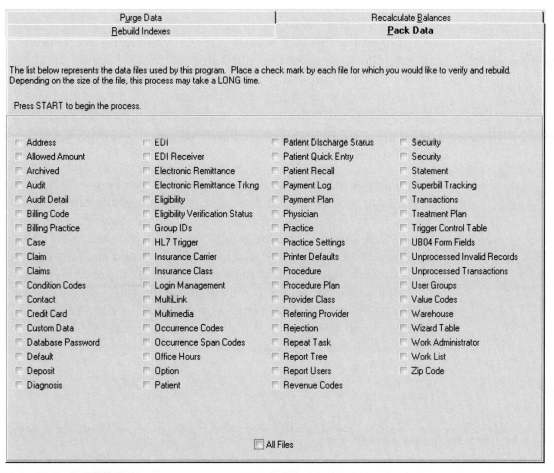

Purge Data		Recalculate Balances	
Rebuild Indexes		**Pack Data**	

The list below represents the data files used by this program. Place a check mark by each file for which you would like to verify and rebuild. Depending on the size of the file, this process may take a LONG time.

Press START to begin the process.

Address	EDI	Patient Discharge Status	Security
Allowed Amount	EDI Receiver	Patient Quick Entry	Security
Archived	Electronic Remittance	Patient Recall	Statement
Audit	Electronic Remittance Trkng	Payment Log	Superbill Tracking
Audit Detail	Eligibility	Payment Plan	Transactions
Billing Code	Eligibility Verification Status	Physician	Treatment Plan
Billing Practice	Group IDs	Practice	Trigger Control Table
Case	HL7 Trigger	Practice Settings	UB04 Form Fields
Claim	Insurance Carrier	Printer Defaults	Unprocessed Invalid Records
Claims	Insurance Class	Procedure	Unprocessed Transactions
Condition Codes	Login Management	Procedure Plan	User Groups
Contact	MultiLink	Provider Class	Value Codes
Credit Card	Multimedia	Referring Provider	Warehouse
Custom Data	Occurrence Codes	Rejection	Wizard Table
Database Password	Occurrence Span Codes	Repeat Task	Work Administrator
Default	Office Hours	Report Tree	Work List
Deposit	Option	Report Users	Zip Code
Diagnosis	Patient	Revenue Codes	

All Files

Figure 2-32   Pack Data Tab

can be deleted.) If the database is large, packing data can take a long time.

To pack files in an office situation, you would complete the following steps:

1. Click File Maintenance on the File menu. The File Maintenance dialog box is displayed with the Rebuild Indexes tab active. Make the Pack Data tab active.

2. Click each check box next to the files that are to be packed.

3. If all files are to be packed, click the All Files box at the bottom of the list of files.

4. Click the Start button. The Confirm dialog box is displayed with the message "All of the checked file processes will be performed. Do you want to continue?" Click the OK button to continue. (Clicking the Cancel button aborts the process.)

5. The pack process is performed automatically. When the process is complete, the message "All checked file processes are complete." is displayed.

PURGING DATA

purging data the process of deleting files of patients who are no longer seen by a provider in a practice.

The process of deleting files of patients who are no longer seen by a provider in a practice is called **purging data.** Purging data frees space on the computer and permits the system to run more efficiently. However, purging should be done with great caution. Once data are purged from the system, they cannot be retrieved, except from a backup file. As a safety precaution, always perform a backup before purging.

The Purge Data tab offers several options (see Figure 2-33). Data can be purged for appointments, claims, statements, recalls, closed cases, and credit card entries. All options except Purge Closed Cases and Credit Card Purge are purged by date. A cutoff date is entered, and Medisoft deletes all data up to that date. For example, if all the data entered prior to December 31, 2010, are to be purged, that date would be entered as the cutoff date. Data entered in cases that have been closed are purged by clicking the check box labeled Purge Closed Cases.

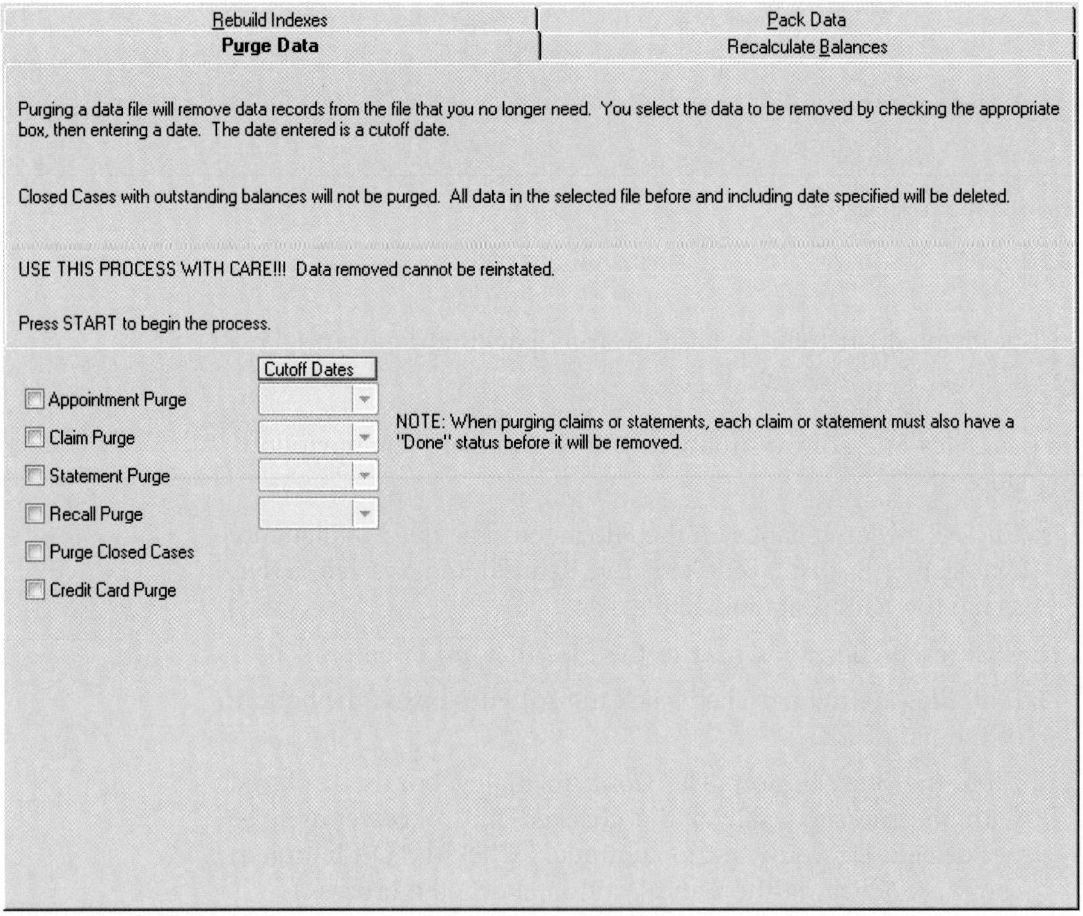

Rebuild Indexes	Pack Data
Purge Data	Recalculate Balances

Purging a data file will remove data records from the file that you no longer need. You select the data to be removed by checking the appropriate box, then entering a date. The date entered is a cutoff date.

Closed Cases with outstanding balances will not be purged. All data in the selected file before and including date specified will be deleted.

USE THIS PROCESS WITH CARE!!! Data removed cannot be reinstated.

Press START to begin the process.

Cutoff Dates

☐ Appointment Purge
☐ Claim Purge
☐ Statement Purge
☐ Recall Purge
☐ Purge Closed Cases
☐ Credit Card Purge

NOTE: When purging claims or statements, each claim or statement must also have a "Done" status before it will be removed.

Figure 2-33 Purge Data Tab

To purge data in an office situation, you would complete the following steps:

1. Click File Maintenance on the File menu. The File Maintenance dialog box is displayed with the Rebuild Indexes tab active. Make the Purge Data tab active.

2. Click each check box next to the files that are to be purged. Enter a cutoff date in the Cutoff Dates box.

3. Click the Start button. The Confirm dialog box is displayed with the message "All of the checked file processes will be performed. Do you want to continue?" Click the OK button to continue. (Clicking the Cancel button aborts the process.)

4. The purge process is performed automatically. When the process is complete, the message "All checked file processes are complete." is displayed.

RECALCULATING PATIENT BALANCES

As transaction entries are changed or deleted, there are times when the balance listed on the screen is not accurate. **Recalculating balances** refers to the process of updating balances to reflect the most recent changes made to the data. This feature is accessed through the Recalculate Balances tab on the File Maintenance dialog box (see Figure 2-34).

recalculating balances the process of updating balances to reflect the most recent changes made to the data.

When balances are recalculated, the system reviews every patient's data and recalculates the balances. The process can be time-consuming. Individual patient balances can be recalculated in the Transaction Entry dialog box by clicking the Account Total column.

To recalculate balances in an office situation, you would complete the following steps:

1. Click File Maintenance on the File menu. The File Maintenance dialog box is displayed with the Rebuild Indexes tab active. Make the Recalculate Balances tab active.

2. Click to place a check mark in the appropriate box(es).

3. Click the Start button. The Confirm dialog box is displayed with the message "All of the checked file processes will be performed. Do you want to continue?" Click the OK button to continue. (Clicking the Cancel button aborts the process.)

4. The recalculate process is performed automatically. When the process is complete, the message "All checked file processes are complete." is displayed.

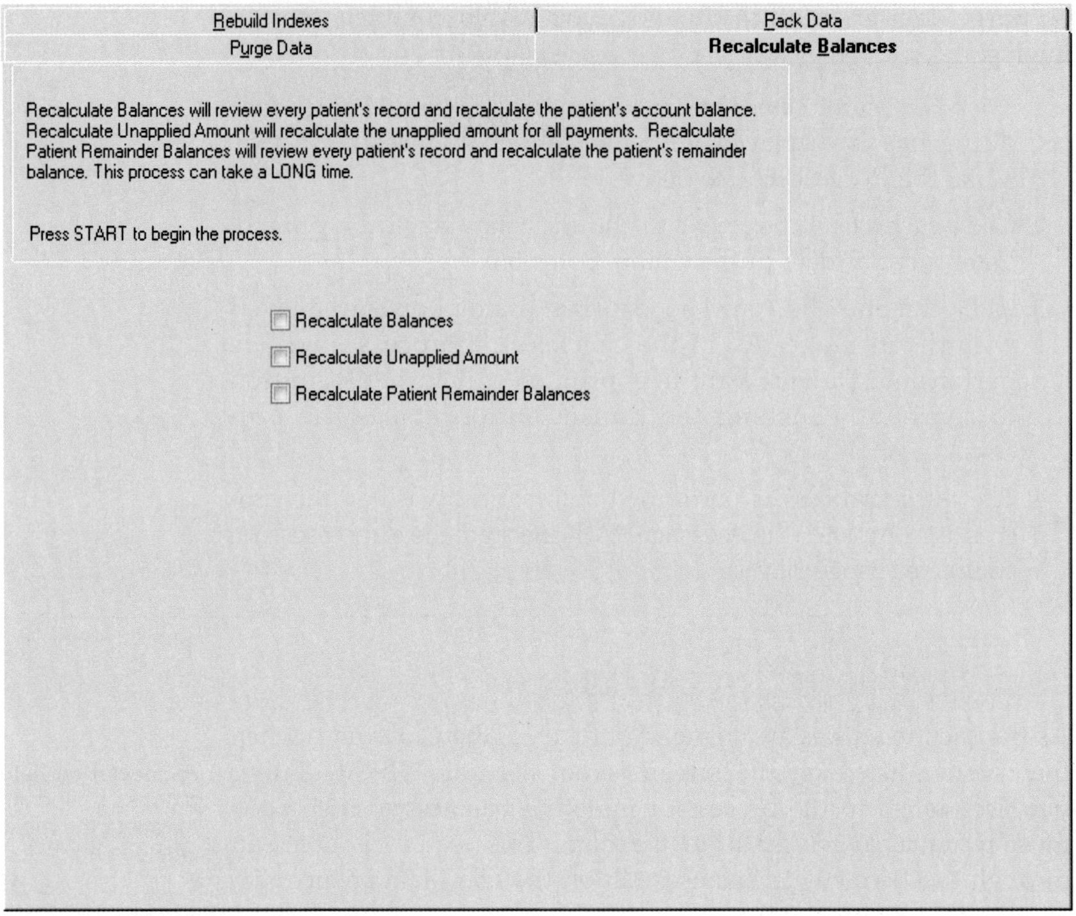

| Rebuild Indexes | | Pack Data |
| Purge Data | | **Recalculate Balances** |

Recalculate Balances will review every patient's record and recalculate the patient's account balance. Recalculate Unapplied Amount will recalculate the unapplied amount for all payments. Recalculate Patient Remainder Balances will review every patient's record and recalculate the patient's remainder balance. This process can take a LONG time.

Press START to begin the process.

☐ Recalculate Balances
☐ Recalculate Unapplied Amount
☐ Recalculate Patient Remainder Balances

Figure 2-34 Recalculate Balances Tab

2.9 USING MEDISOFT SECURITY FEATURES TO ENSURE HIPAA AND HITECH COMPLIANCE

Medisoft offers a number of features to protect the privacy and security of patients' protected health information in accordance with HIPAA and HITECH regulations. Security is set up in Medisoft by first assigning the administrative function to an individual in the practice, usually the office manager. The administrator has unlimited access to the program. The Security Setup option on the File menu is used to set up the administrator. The administrator can assign access rights to each level of security by clicking the Permissions option on the File menu. (*Note*: The Permissions option does not appear in the File menu until the security administrator has been set up in the Security Setup window.) **Access rights** determine which areas of the program a particular user can access, and whether that user can only view data or has rights to enter or edit data.

access rights security option that determines the areas of the program a user can access, and whether the user has rights to enter or edit data.

When the Permissions option is selected on the File menu, the Medisoft Security Permissions dialog box appears (since no security has been set up, this will not appear on your computer). Each function within the program is listed alphabetically in the left side of the dialog box (see Figure 2-35). The right side of the dialog box displays security level assignments. A check mark under a level heading means that anyone with that level of security has the ability to perform that task or has access to that portion of the program.

Medisoft security consists of five levels of program access, with level 1 having the most access rights and level 5 the fewest. Level 1 is for unlimited access and is designed to be used exclusively by the administrator. Levels 2, 3, 4, and 5 are set up to meet the needs of the practice. Generally, the administrator decides what staff roles and tasks belong in what level and assigns users accordingly.

In the Medisoft Security Permissions dialog box illustrated in Figure 2-35, the permissions for the Claim Management features are displayed. Notice that users with access levels 1 through 4 can create claims; only level 5 users cannot create claims. Permission for editing claims is restricted to users in levels 1 through 3, while deleting claims is limited to users in levels 1 and 2.

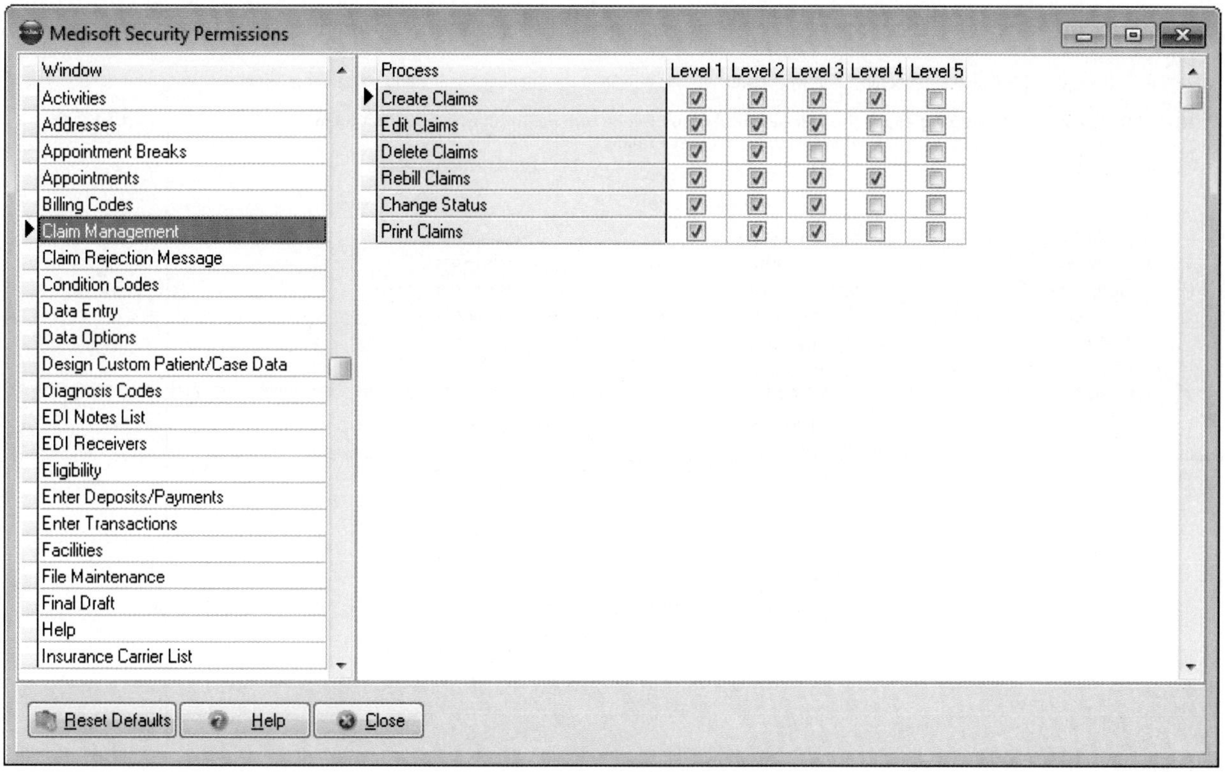

Figure 2-35 Medisoft Security Permissions Dialog Box

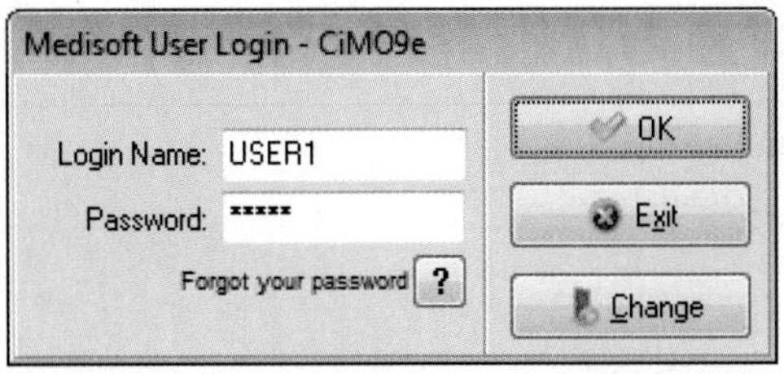

Figure 2-36   Medisoft User Login Dialog Box

USER LOGINS AND AUDIT CONTROLS

Once security has been set up in Medisoft, users are assigned user names and passwords, and they must log in to access the program (see Figure 2-36).

Requiring users to log in limits access to the program to those who have been assigned logins, and also allows tracking the actions of users within the program though an audit report. The audit function can be used to track changes made in the program, as well as who made the changes. Options for the audit report are selected in the Audit tab of the Program Options dialog box, accessed via the File menu (see Figure 2-37). For database tables to be audited, check marks must appear in the boxes in the Update and/or Delete columns. If the Update box is checked, the program tracks changes to the table; if the Delete box is checked, the program tracks deletions of data from the table.

AUTO LOG OFF AND UNAPPROVED CODES

Another tab in the Program Options dialog box allows practice administrators to select options to help protect patient information from unauthorized access. The HIPAA/ICD-10 tab (see Figure 2-38) contains an Auto Log Off option and a Warn on Unapproved Codes

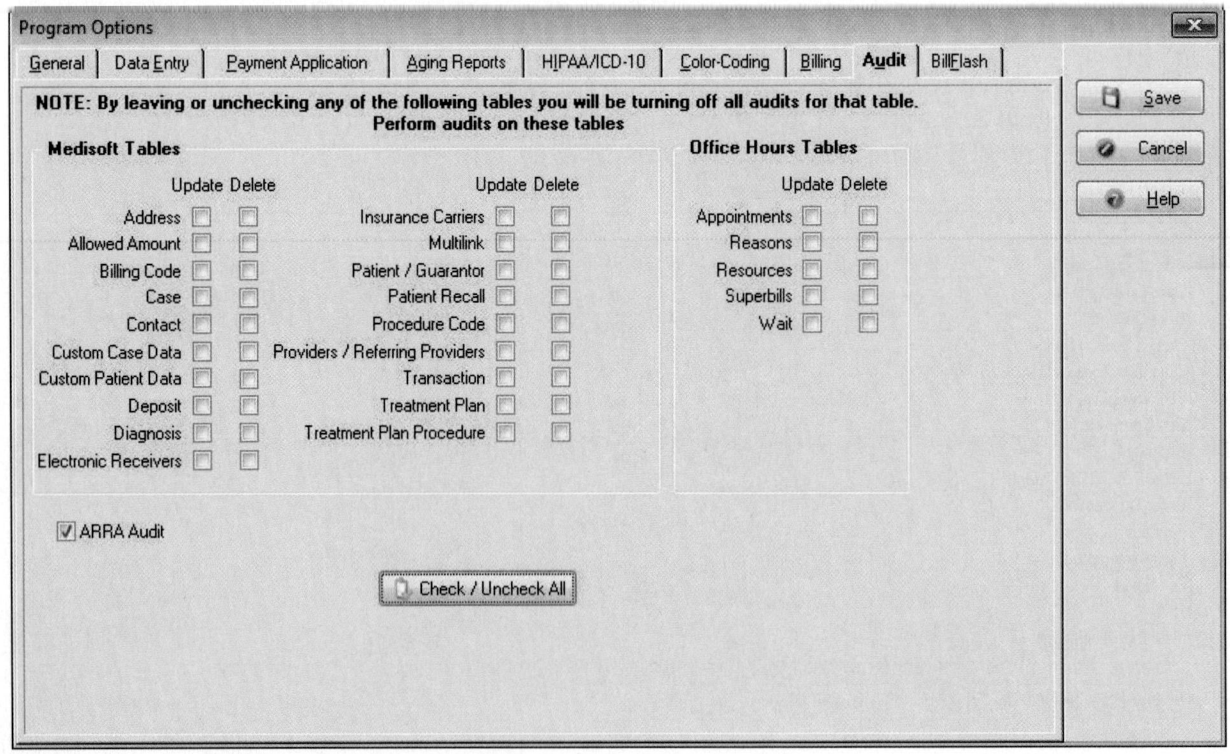

Figure 2-37   Audit Tab of the Program Options Dialog Box

Program Options

| General | Data Entry | Payment Application | Aging Reports | **HIPAA/ICD-10** | Color-Coding | Billing | Audit | BillFlash |

Health Insurance Portability and Accountability Act

☐ Auto Log Off: `15` minutes

☐ Warn on Unapproved Codes

ICD 10 Settings

Medisoft Clinical Preference: Default New Diagnosis Version: `ICD-10 ▾`

[Save]
[Cancel]
[Help]

Figure 2-38 HIPAA Tab of the Program Options Dialog Box

option. The **Auto Log Off** feature is designed to protect data files from unauthorized access by logging a user off after detecting no activity for a specified number of minutes. If a user steps away from his or her desk without first logging off, information in the Medisoft program can be viewed by anyone who uses the computer. This feature automatically logs the user off, preventing access to the program. The Auto Log Off field can be set for up to 59 minutes.

Auto Log Off feature of Medisoft that automatically logs a user out of the program after a period of inactivity.

The Warn on Unapproved Codes box, when checked, is used to trigger a warning box to pop up every time a transaction is saved with a code that has not been marked HIPAA compliant. Codes are marked as compliant by checking the HIPAA Approved box in the Procedure/Payment/Adjustment dialog box for each procedure code, and in the HIPAA Approved box in the Diagnosis dialog box for each diagnosis code.

BE THE DETECTIVE!

If assigned by your instructor, complete the Healthcare IT Video Case in Connect. Put your skills to use learning about the features of Medisoft and enhance your knowledge by exploring the other software used in physician practices.

LEARNING OUTCOMES	CONCEPTS TO REVIEW
2.1 List the six databases Medisoft uses to store information.	– Provider data – Patient data – Insurance carriers – Diagnosis codes – Procedure codes – Transactions
2.2 List the menus in Medisoft.	– File – Edit – Activities – Lists – Reports – Tools – Window – Help
2.3 Explain the function of the Medisoft toolbar.	The toolbar contains buttons that are shortcuts for frequently used menu commands. When you click on a button, the corresponding Medisoft dialog box opens. The buttons can be used instead of the pull-down menus to perform common tasks.
2.4 Explain how to enter, edit, save, and delete data in Medisoft.	– Data are entered by selecting options on the menus or by clicking a button on the toolbar. The Tab key is used to move from text box to text box within a dialog box. Some information is entered by keying data into a text box; at other times, selections are made from a list of choices already present, such as a drop-down list. – Data are edited by entering the correct information directly in the field where the incorrect information exists. – Data are saved by clicking the Save button that is located in most dialog boxes. – Data are deleted in two ways—either by clicking a Delete button (if present), or by right-clicking to display a shortcut menu that contains a Delete option.

LEARNING OUTCOMES	CONCEPTS TO REVIEW
2.5 Describe how to change the Program Date in Medisoft.	Windows 7 or Windows 8 1. Click Set Program Date on the File menu, or click the date displayed in the lower-right corner of the Medisoft window. 2. To change the month, click the word displayed for the current month, and the abbreviations for the months appear in the calendar window. Click the desired month. 3. To change the year, click the current year, and select the desired year from the years that appear in the window. 4. Select the desired day of the month by clicking that date in the calendar.
2.6 Discuss two types of help available in Medisoft.	– Hints appear on the status bar at the bottom of the screen as the cursor moves over certain fields. – Medisoft's extensive built-in help feature is accessed by selecting Medisoft Help on the Help menu.
2.7 Explain how to create and restore backup files in Medisoft.	Creating a Backup File 1. To exit Medisoft and create a backup file, click Exit on the File menu, or click the Exit button on the toolbar. 2. The Backup Reminder dialog box appears. 3. Click the Back Up Data Now button. If a Backup Warning dialog box appears, click the OK button. 4. The Medisoft Backup dialog box is displayed. Your instructor will tell you what to enter in the top field. 5. Click the Start Backup button. 6. The program backs up the latest database files and displays an Information dialog box indicating that the backup is complete. Click OK. 7. Close the Medisoft Backup dialog box by clicking the Close button.

LEARNING OUTCOMES	CONCEPTS TO REVIEW
	Restoring a Backup File
	1. Check the program's title bar at the top of the screen to make sure the CiMO9e database is the active database. (If it is not, use the Open Practice option on the File menu to select it.)
	2. Open the File menu, and click Restore Data.
	3. When the Warning box appears, click OK.
	4. The Restore dialog box appears. In the Backup File Path and Name box at the top of the dialog box, key the location of the backup file, if this name is not already displayed.
	5. Click the Start Restore button.
	6. When the Confirm box appears, click OK.
	7. An Information dialog box appears indicating that the restore is complete. Click OK to continue.
	8. Click the Close button to close the Restore dialog box. The Restore dialog box disappears. You are ready to begin the next session.
2.8 Describe the functions of the file maintenance utilities in Modicoft.	– Rebuilding indexes checks and verifies data and corrects any internal problems with the data. – Packing data deletes vacant slots in the database that remain after data have been deleted from the program. – Purging data deletes all data as of a user-specified date. – Recalculating balances updates balances to reflect the most recent changes made to the data.
2.9 Describe the Medisoft security features used to ensure compliance with HIPAA and HITECH regulations.	– The ability to view and alter data in different areas of the program is restricted by assigning access rights to each user. – Users are assigned logins and passwords to limit access to the program and to track their activities within the program. – The Auto Log Off feature automatically logs a user out of Medisoft after a specified number of minutes pass without any activity, preventing access to the program by unauthorized users. – The Warn on Unapproved Codes feature sends a warning message when a transaction is saved with a code that is not HIPAA approved.

USING TERMINOGY

Match the terms on the left with the definitions on the right.

1. *[LO 2.9]* access rights
2. *[LO 2.9]* Auto Log Off
3. *[LO 2.7]* backup data
4. *[LO 2.1]* database
5. *[LO 2.5]* Medisoft Program Date
6. *[LO 2.5]* MMDDCCYY format
7. *[LO 2.8]* packing data
8. *[LO 2.8]* purging data
9. *[LO 2.8]* rebuilding indexes
10. *[LO 2.8]* recalculating balances
11. *[LO 2.7]* restoring data

a. The process of retrieving data from backup storage devices.

b. A collection of related pieces of information.

c. A feature that automatically logs a user out of the program after a specified number of minutes of inactivity.

d. The process of updating balances to reflect the most recent changes made to the data.

e. The process of deleting files of patients who are no longer seen by a provider in a practice.

f. The way dates must be keyed in Medisoft.

g. An option that determines which areas of the program a user can access, and whether the user can only view data or has rights to enter or edit data.

h. A copy of data files made at a specific point in time that can be used to restore data to the system.

i. The date recorded in Medisoft when a transaction is entered.

j. A process that checks and verifies data and corrects any internal problems with the data.

k. The deletion of vacant slots from the database.

connect Enhance your learning by completing these exercises and more at http://connect.mheducation.com

chapter 2 review

CHECKING YOUR UNDERSTANDING

12. *[LO 2.2]* Describe two ways of issuing a command in Medisoft.

13. *[LO 2.4]* What are two ways data are entered in a box?

14. *[LO 2.6]* What two types of Medisoft help are available?

15. *[LO 2.2]* Which menu provides access to Office Hours, Medisoft's scheduling feature?

16. *[LO 2.5]* What is the format for entering dates in Medisoft?

17. *[LO 2.7]* Describe two ways of exiting Medisoft.

18. *[LO 2.7]* Why is it important to back up data regularly?

19. *[LO 2.8]* Why is extra caution required when purging data?

20. *[LO 2.7]* When is a data restore performed?

21. *[LO 2.9]* Give an example of how Medisoft's Auto Log Off feature protects patient data.

22. *[LO 2.9]* Give two reasons why it is important to assign each user a login ID and password.

23. *[LO 2.1]* List the six Medisoft databases.

24. *[LO 2.3]* What is the purpose of the Medisoft toolbar?

APPLYING YOUR KNOWLEDGE

25. *[LO 2.6]* Use Medisoft's built-in help feature to look up information on the following topics:

   a. How to enter diagnosis codes

   b. How to print procedure code lists from the Medisoft database

26. *[LO 2.7]* You come to work on a Monday morning and find that the office computer is not working. The system manager informs everyone that the computer's hard disk crashed and that all data that were not backed up are lost. What do you do?

27. *[LO 2.5]* Why is it important to know how to change dates in Medisoft? What could happen if dates are entered incorrectly?

28. *[LO 2.7]* Why is it important to know how to back up and restore Medisoft database files?

SCHEDULING

key terms

chart number
Office Hours break
Office Hours calendar
Office Hours patient
  information
provider's daily schedule
provider selection box
recall list

learning outcomes

When you finish this chapter, you will be able to:

3.1 List the four main areas of the Office Hours window.

3.2 Demonstrate how to enter an appointment.

3.3 Demonstrate how to schedule a follow-up appointment.

3.4 Demonstrate how to search for an available time slot.

3.5 Demonstrate how to book an appointment for a new patient.

3.6 Demonstrate how to book repeating appointments.

3.7 Demonstrate how to reschedule and cancel an appointment.

3.8 Demonstrate how to check a patient's insurance eligibility.

3.9 Demonstrate how to check in and check out a patient.

3.10 Demonstrate how to create an overdue balance report for upcoming appointments.

3.11 Demonstrate how to create a recall list.

3.12 Demonstrate how to enter provider breaks in the schedule.

3.13 Demonstrate how to preview and print a provider's schedule.

what you need to know

To use this chapter, you need to know how to:

- Start Medisoft, use menus, and enter and edit text.
- Work with chart numbers and codes.
- Locate patient information.

Appointment scheduling is one of the most important tasks in a medical office. Different medical procedures take different lengths of time, and each appointment must be the right length. On the one hand, a physician wants to be able to go from one appointment to another without unnecessary breaks. On the other hand, a patient should not be kept waiting more than a few minutes for a physician. Managing and juggling the schedule are usually the job of a medical office assistant working at the front desk. Medisoft® provides a special program called Office Hours to handle appointment scheduling.

3.1 THE OFFICE HOURS WINDOW

The Office Hours program has its own window (see Figure 3-1), including its own menu bar and toolbar. The Office Hours menu bar lists the menus available: File, Edit, View, Lists, Reports, Tools, and Help (see Figure 3-2). Under the menu bar is a toolbar with shortcut buttons. The functions of Office Hours are accessed by selecting a choice from one of the menus or by clicking a button on the toolbar.

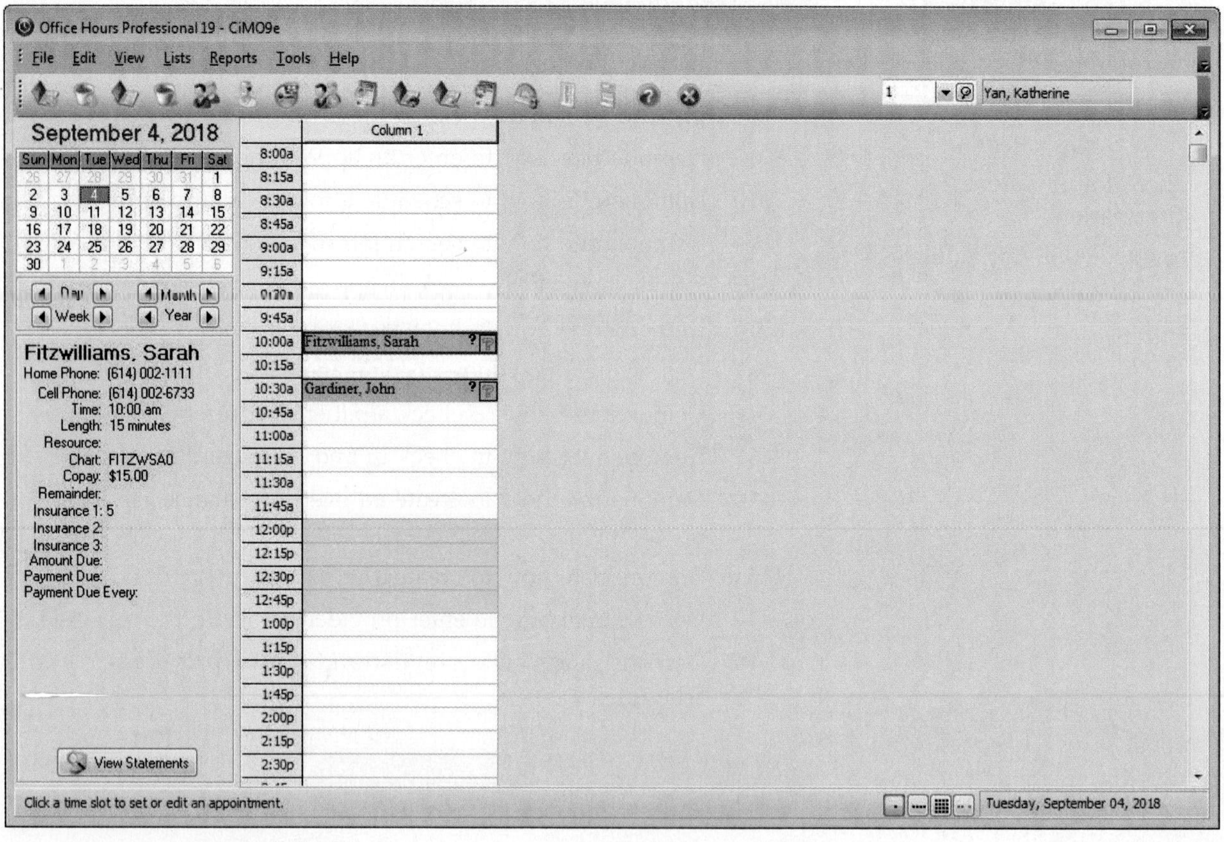

Figure 3-1   The Office Hours Window

Figure 3-2   The Office Hours Menu Bar

Figure 3-3 The Office Hours Toolbar

Located just below the menu bar, the toolbar contains a series of buttons that represent the most common activities performed in Office Hours. These buttons are shortcuts for frequently used menu commands. The toolbar displays seventeen buttons (see Figure 3-3 and Table 3-1).

	TABLE 3-1	Office Hours Toolbar Buttons	
Button	**Button Name**	**Associated Function**	**Activity**
	Appointment Entry	New Appointment Entry dialog box	Enter appointments
	Break Entry	New Break Entry dialog box	Enter breaks
	Appointment List	Appointment List dialog box	Display list of appointments
	Break List	Break List dialog box	Display list of breaks
	Patient List	Patient List dialog box	Display list of patients
	Provider List	Provider List dialog box	Display list of providers
	Resource List	Resource List dialog box	Display list of resources
	Patient Recall List	Patient Recall List dialog box	Add a patient to the Recall List
	Go to a Date	Go to Date dialog box	Change calendar to a different date
	Search for Open Time Slot	Find Open Time dialog box	Locate first available time slot
	Search Again	Find Open Time dialog box	Locate next available time slot
	Go to Today		Return calendar to current date
	Edit Templates	New Template Entry dialog box	Creates or modifies a template for appointments
	Quick Appointment List		Print appointment list
	Edit Patient Notes in Final Draft	Final Draft word processor	Use Final Draft word processor
	Help	Office Hours Help	Display Office Hours Help contents
	Exit	Exit	Exit the Office Hours program

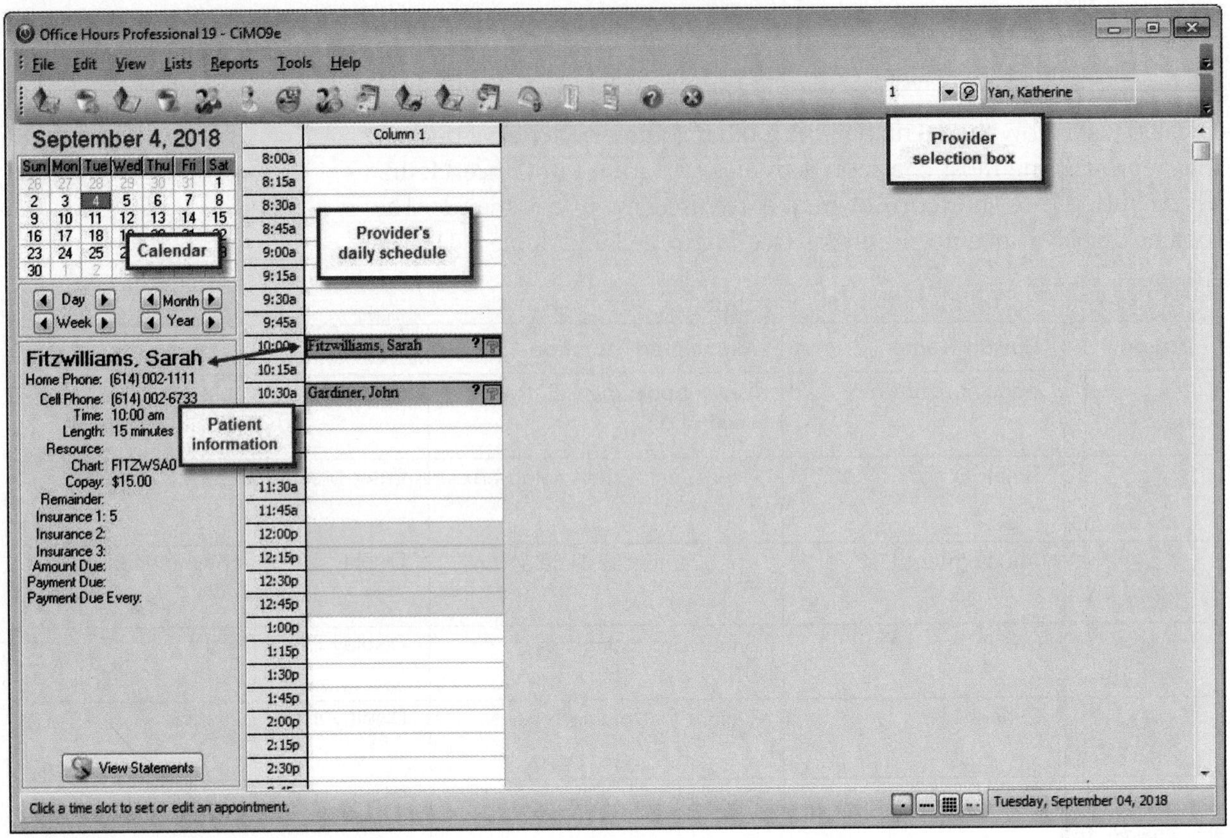

Figure 3-4　The Main Areas of the Office Hours Window

provider selection box a selection box that determines which provider's schedule is displayed in the provider's daily schedule.

provider's daily schedule a listing of time slots for a particular day for a specific provider that corresponds to the date selected in the calendar.

Office Hours calendar an interactive calendar that is used to select or change dates in Office Hours.

Office Hours patient information the area of the Office Hours window that displays information about the patient who is selected in the provider's daily schedule.

Figure 3-5　View Buttons

In addition to the menu bar and toolbar, the Office Hours window contains four main areas (see Figure 3-4). The **provider selection box,** located at the far-right end of the toolbar, is where you select a provider. This selection determines which provider's schedule is displayed in the provider's daily schedule. The **provider's daily schedule,** shown in the right half of the screen, is a listing of time slots for a particular day for a specific provider. The schedule displayed corresponds to the date selected in the calendar, which is located on the left side of the window. The **Office Hours calendar** is used to select or change dates. The right and left arrows that surround Day, Week, Month, and Year are used to move back or ahead on the calendar. When a different date is clicked on the calendar, the calendar switches to the new date. Finally, the area just below the calendar contains **Office Hours patient information** about the patient who is selected in the provider's daily schedule.

In addition to the four main areas of the window, there are four small buttons at the lower right-hand corner of the window, next to the date (see Figure 3-5). These buttons change the view of the provider's daily schedule. From left to right, the buttons are Day View, Week View, Month View, and Multiple Provider/Resource View.

PROGRAM OPTIONS

When Office Hours is installed in a medical practice, it is set up to reflect the needs of that particular practice. Most offices that use Medisoft already have Office Hours set up and running. However, if Medisoft is just being installed, the options to set up the Office Hours program can be found in the Program Options dialog box, which is accessed by clicking Program Options on the Office Hours File menu.

ENTERING AND EXITING OFFICE HOURS

Office Hours can be started from within Medisoft or directly from Windows. To access Office Hours from within Medisoft, Appointment Book is clicked on the Activities menu (see Figure 3-6). Office Hours can also be started by clicking the corresponding shortcut button on the toolbar (see Figure 3-7).

To start Office Hours without entering Medisoft first:

1. Click Start > All Programs.
2. Click Medisoft on the Programs submenu.
3. Click Office Hours Professional on the Medisoft submenu.

The Office Hours program is closed by clicking Exit on the Office Hours File menu or by clicking the Exit button on its toolbar. If Office Hours was started from within Medisoft, exiting will return you to Medisoft. If Office Hours was started directly from Windows, clicking Exit will return you to the Windows desktop.

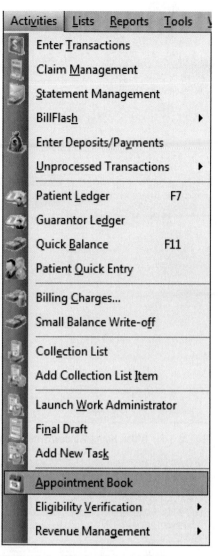

Figure 3-6   The Appointment Book Selection on the Activities Menu

3.2 ENTERING APPOINTMENTS

Entering an appointment begins with selecting the provider for whom the appointment is being scheduled. The current provider is listed in the provider selection box at the upper-right of the screen (see Figure 3-8). Clicking the arrow button displays a drop-down list of providers in the system. To choose a different provider, click the name of the provider on the drop-down list.

Figure 3-7
The Office Hours
Shortcut Button

After the provider is selected, the date of the desired appointment must be chosen. Dates are changed by clicking the Day, Week, Month, and Year right and left arrow buttons located under the calendar (see Figure 3-9). After the provider and date have been selected, patient appointments can be entered.

Appointments are entered by clicking the Appointment Entry shortcut button or by double clicking in a time slot on the schedule.

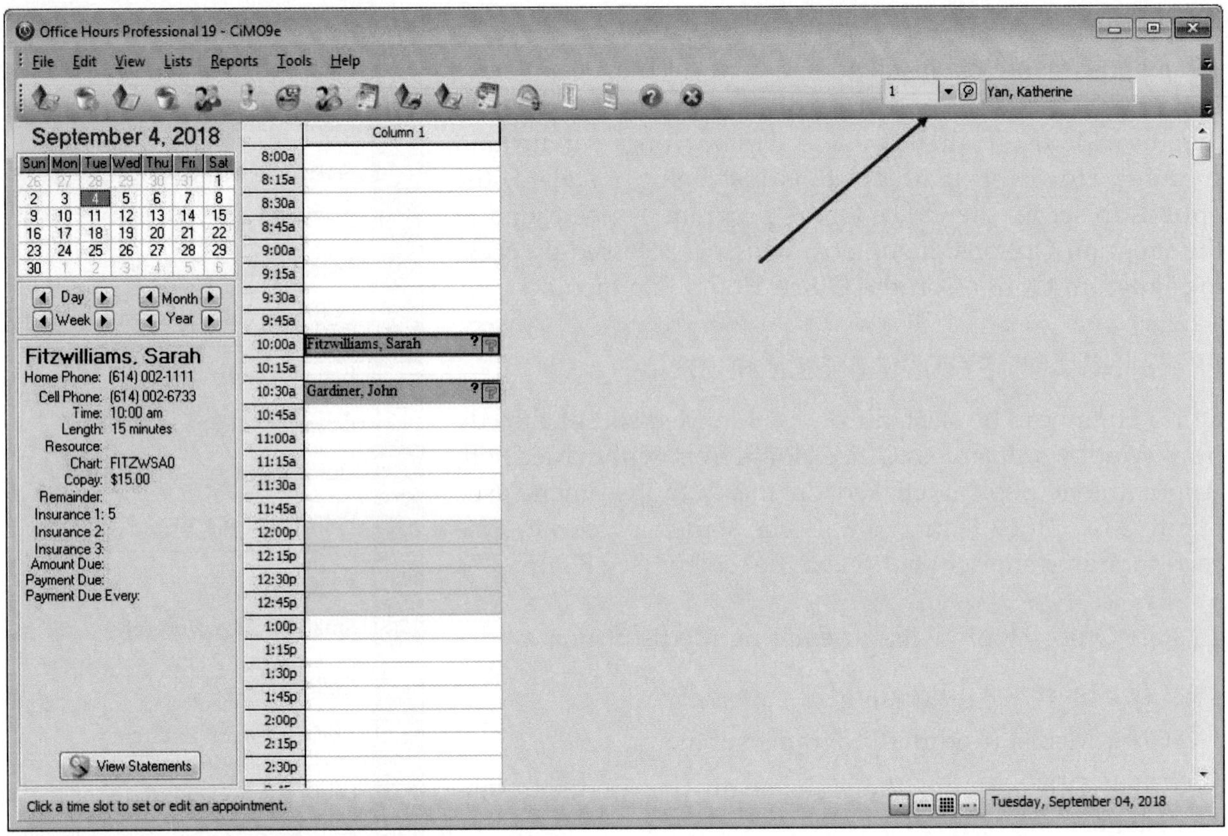

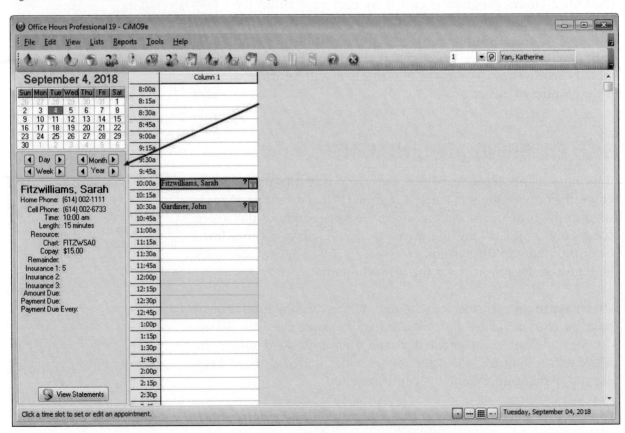

Figure 3-8 Office Hours Window with Provider Box Highlighted

Figure 3-9 Office Hours Window with Day, Week, Month, and Year Arrow Buttons Highlighted

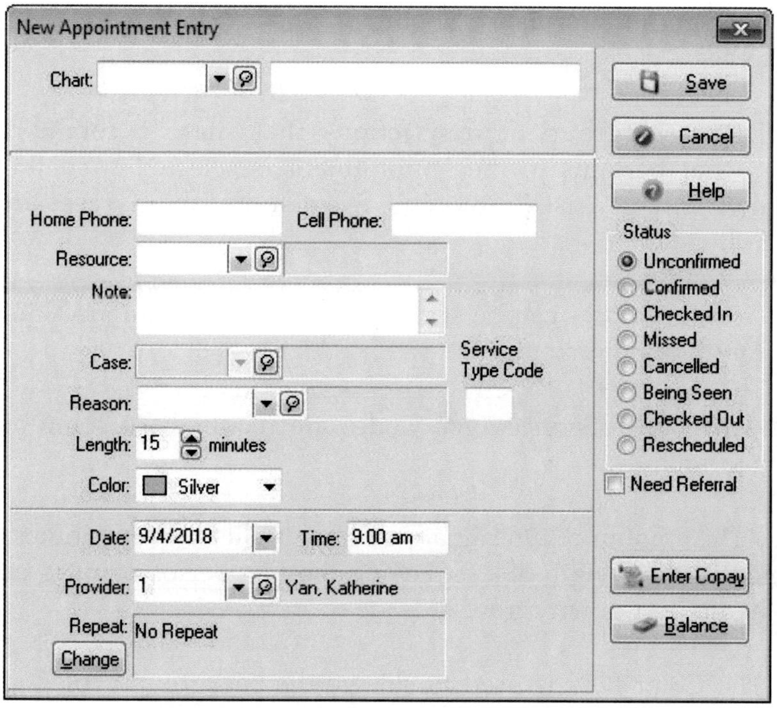

Figure 3-10   New Appointment Entry Dialog Box

When either action is taken, the New Appointment Entry dialog box is displayed (see Figure 3-10).

The New Appointment Entry dialog box contains the following fields:

Chart   The **chart number** is a unique number that identifies a patient. In Medisoft, a chart number links together all the information about a patient that is stored in the different databases, such as name, address, charges, and insurance claims. A patient's chart number is chosen from the Chart drop-down list. To select the desired patient, click on the patient's name in the drop-down list and press Tab. If you are setting up an appointment for a new patient who has not been assigned a chart number, skip the Chart box, and key the patient's name in the blank box to the right of the Chart box using the Lastname, Firstname format.

Home Phone   After a patient's chart is selected, that patient's home phone number is automatically entered in the Home Phone box.

Cell Phone   After a patient's chart is selected, that patient's cell phone number is automatically entered in the Cell Phone box.

Resource   This box is used if the practice assigns codes to resources, such as exam rooms or equipment.

chart number a unique number that identifies a patient.

Note   Any special information about an appointment is entered in the Note box.

Case   The case (group of transactions that share a common element) that pertains to the appointment is selected from the drop-down list of cases. You will learn more about cases in Chapter 5.

Reason   Reason codes can be set up in the program to reflect the reason for an appointment.

Service Type Code   Service Type Codes are required for some of eligibility inquiries.

Length   The amount of time an appointment will take (in minutes) is entered in the Length box by keying the number of minutes or using the up and down arrows.

Color   The Color field is used to change the background color of an appointment on the screen. The default is silver.

Date   The Date box displays the date that is currently displayed on the calendar. If this is not the desired date, it may be changed by keying in a different date or by clicking the arrow button and selecting a date from the pop-up calendar that appears.

Time   The Time box displays the appointment time that is currently selected on the schedule. If this is not the desired time, it may be changed by keying in a different time.

Provider   The provider who will be treating the patient during this appointment is selected from the drop-down list of providers.

Repeat/Change   The Change button is used to enter repeating appointments. Once repeating appointments are scheduled, the Repeat box lists how often the appointments are repeated (daily, weekly, monthly, yearly).

Save, Cancel, and Help   The Save, Cancel, and Help buttons are located at the top right corner of the dialog box.

Status   The Status section of the New Appointment Entry dialog box can be used to keep track of the appointment status. Some practices use a practice management program to track status, while others use an electronic health record program. Right-clicking on an appointment time slot displays a shortcut menu with a list of status options listed (see Figure 3-11).

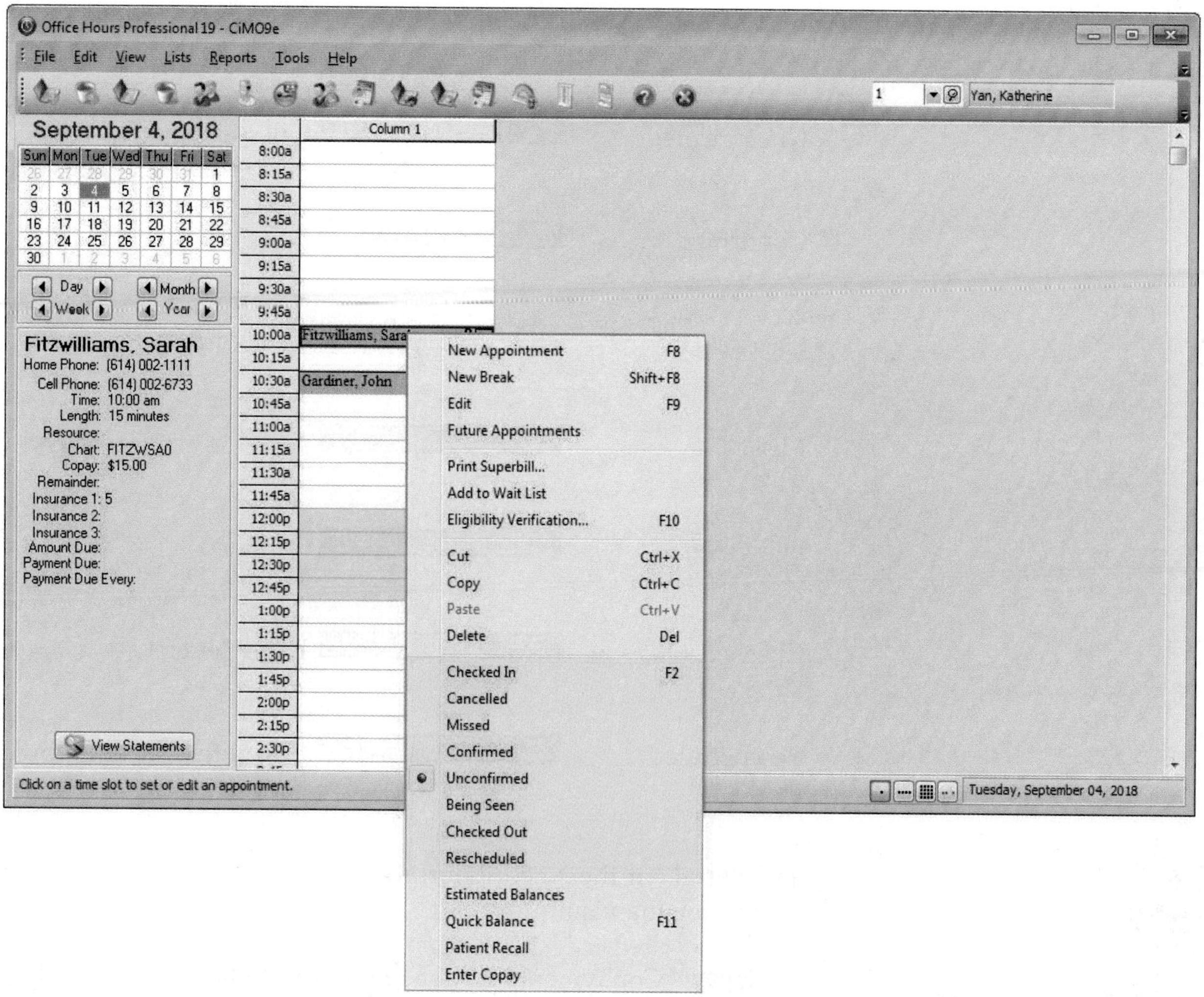

Figure 3-11 Status Options in Shortcut Menu

Selecting a status changes the small icon displayed in upper right corner of the appointment slot (see Figure 3-12).

In the example in Figure 3-12, there is a question mark icon (unconfirmed) visible for Sarah Fitzwilliams's appointment, and a square box icon (confirmed) for John Gardiner's appointment.

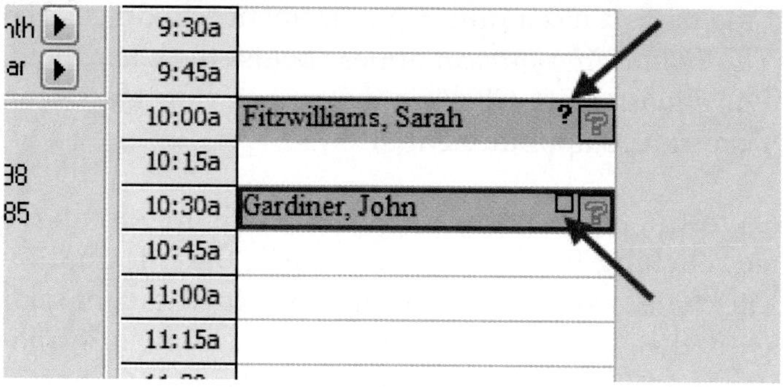

Figure 3-12 Status Icons in Appointment Slot

The icons used to indicate appointment status are as follows:

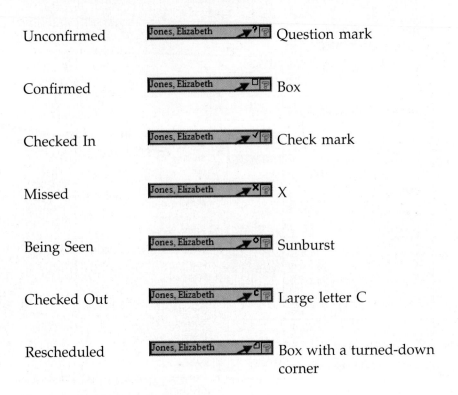

Unconfirmed	Jones, Elizabeth	Question mark
Confirmed	Jones, Elizabeth	Box
Checked In	Jones, Elizabeth	Check mark
Missed	Jones, Elizabeth	X
Being Seen	Jones, Elizabeth	Sunburst
Checked Out	Jones, Elizabeth	Large letter C
Rescheduled	Jones, Elizabeth	Box with a turned-down corner

Need Referral   If the Need Referral is checked, the patient requires a referral for the visit.

Enter Copay   Copayments can be entered in Office Hours, or they can be entered in Medisoft. In the exercises in this text/workbook, copayments will be entered in Medisoft.

Balance   Clicking the Balance button displays a summary of the remainder charges for an account. Remainder charges are amounts remaining after the patient's insurance carrier has paid (or denied) the claim.

Note: When scheduling a new appointment, Office Hours will display an alert if the patient has a future appointment scheduled. The words *Patient Has Future Appointment* appear below the Chart field, with a magnifying glass icon. Clicking the magnifying glass icon shows a list of the future appointment(s).

After the boxes in the New Appointment Entry dialog box have been completed, clicking the Save button enters the information on the schedule. The patient's name appears in the time slot corresponding to the appointment time. In addition, information about the patient's insurance appears in the patient information section in the lower-left corner of the Office Hours window.

ENTERING AN APPOINTMENT, LEILA PATTERSON

EXERCISE 3-1

Enter an appointment for Leila Patterson at 4:30 p.m. on Monday, November 12, 2018. The appointment is thirty minutes in length and is with Dr. John Rudner.

1. Start Medisoft.
2. Start Office Hours by clicking the Appointment Book shortcut button on the toolbar.
3. Select John Rudner from the drop-down list in the Provider field.
4. Change the date on the calendar to Monday, November 12, 2018. Use the arrow keys to change the month and year, and then click the day on the calendar.
5. Locate 4:30 p.m. in the schedule and click once to select it. Figure 3-13 shows the Office Hours window with John Rudner selected as provider, November 12, 2018, on the calendar, and the 4:30 p.m. time slot highlighted. Compare your screen to Figure 3-13.
6. In the schedule, double click the 4:30 p.m. time slot. The New Appointment Entry dialog box is displayed.
7. Select Leila Patterson from the list of names on the drop-down list in the Chart box, and press Tab. The system automatically fills in a number of boxes in the dialog box, such as the patient's name and home and cell phone numbers.

Connect users: go to http://connect.mheducation.com to complete this exercise! Some steps may differ from what is listed here, so be sure to refer to the steps listed in Demo and Practice Modes for guidance.

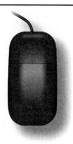

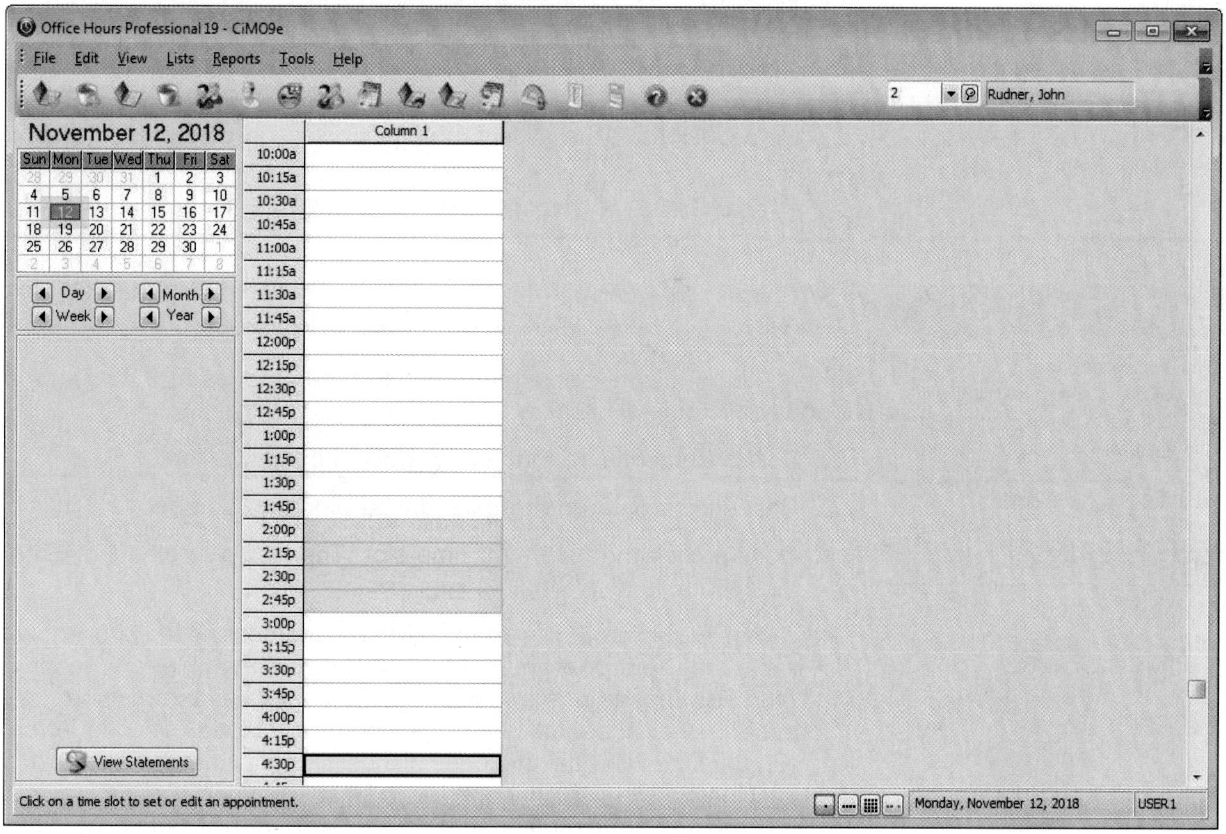

Figure 3-13 Office Hours Window with Selections Highlighted

New Appointment Entry

Chart: PATTELE0 ▼ 🔍 Patterson, Leila

Save

Cancel

Help

Home Phone: (614)666-0099   Cell Phone: (614)666-0014

Resource: ▼ 🔍

Note:

Case: 11 ▼ 🔍 Poison ivy

Reason: ▼ 🔍

Length: 30 ▲▼ minutes

Color: ■ Silver ▼

Service Type Code

Status
◉ Unconfirmed
○ Confirmed
○ Checked In
○ Missed
○ Cancelled
○ Being Seen
○ Checked Out
○ Rescheduled

☐ Need Referral
Copay: $20.00

Date: 11/12/2018 ▼   Time: 4:30 pm

Provider: 2 ▼ 🔍 Rudner, John

Repeat: No Repeat
Change

Enter Copay

Balance

Figure 3-14   Completed New Appointment Entry Dialog Box

8. Notice that the Length box already contains an entry of fifteen minutes. This is the default appointment length in Medisoft. This entry must be changed to thirty minutes. Key **30** in the Length box, or use the up arrow next to the Length box to change the appointment length.

9. Check your entries against Figure 3-14, and then click the Save button. Office Hours saves the appointment and closes the dialog box. Leila Patterson's name is displayed in the 4:30 p.m. time slot on the schedule as well as in the patient information section on the left.   CiMO

✓ **You have completed Exercise 3-1.**

EXERCISE 3-2   **ENTERING AN APPOINTMENT, ELIZABETH JONES**

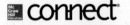

Enter a thirty-minute appointment for Elizabeth Jones at 9:45 a.m. on Monday, October 1, 2018 with Dr. Katherine Yan.

1. Select Katherine Yan in the Provider drop-down list.

2. Change the date on the calendar to Monday, October 1, 2018.

3. Double click the 9:45 a.m. time slot. The New Appointment Entry dialog box is displayed.

4. Select Elizabeth Jones from the list of names on the drop-down list in the Chart box, and press Tab. Notice that the letters Account Alert RB appear in red, indicating that Jones has a remainder balance on her account. When the cursor is placed over the letters RB, the amount of the overdue balance is displayed (see Figure 3-15). Just below the RB notice, the program indicates that the patient has another appointment scheduled. Clicking the magnifying glass icon displays a list of the patient's future appointment(s).

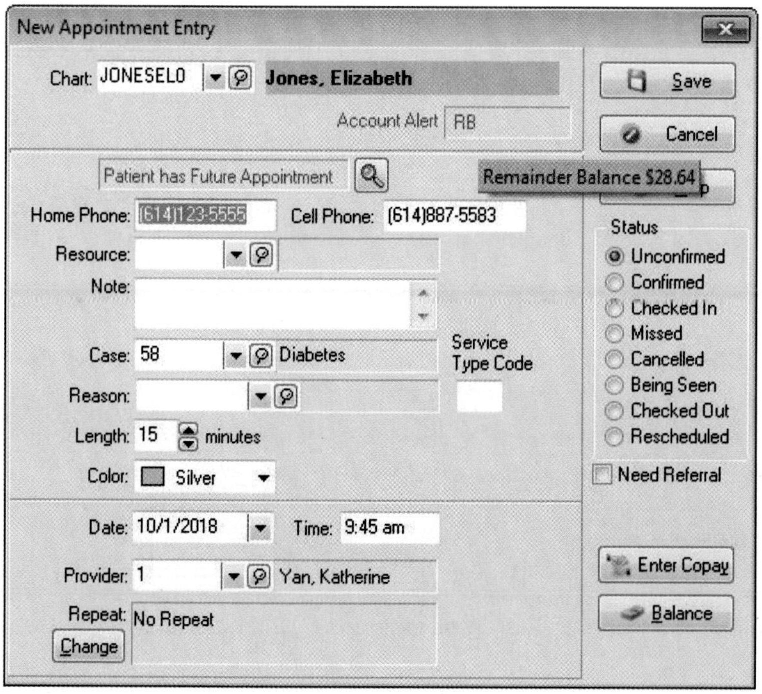

Figure 3-15 New Appointment Entry with Remainder Balance and Future Appointment Alerts

5. Change the value in the Length box to change the appointment length to thirty minutes.

6. Click the Save button. Office Hours saves the appointment and closes the dialog box. Elizabeth Jones' name is displayed in the 9:45 a.m. time slot on the schedule as well as in the patient information section on the left. **CiMO**

✓ **You have completed Exercise 3-2.**

LOOKING UP A PROVIDER AND ENTERING AN APPOINTMENT

EXERCISE 3-3

Enter a fifteen-minute appointment on Monday, October 1, 2018, at 11:00 a.m. for John Fitzwilliams. You do not know his provider, so this information must be looked up before you enter the appointment.

1. Select Patient List on the Lists menu in Office Hours. The Patient List dialog box is displayed.

2. Enter *F* in the Search for box to select John Fitzwilliams (see Figure 3-16).

3. Double click the line that contains John Fitzwilliams's chart number and name, or click the Edit Patient button. The Patient/Guarantor dialog box appears.

4. Click the Other Information tab, and locate the Assigned Provider field to determine the name of John Fitzwilliams's provider.

Connect users: go to http://connect.mheducation.com to complete this exercise! Some steps may differ from what is listed here, so be sure to refer to the steps listed in Demo and Practice Modes for guidance.

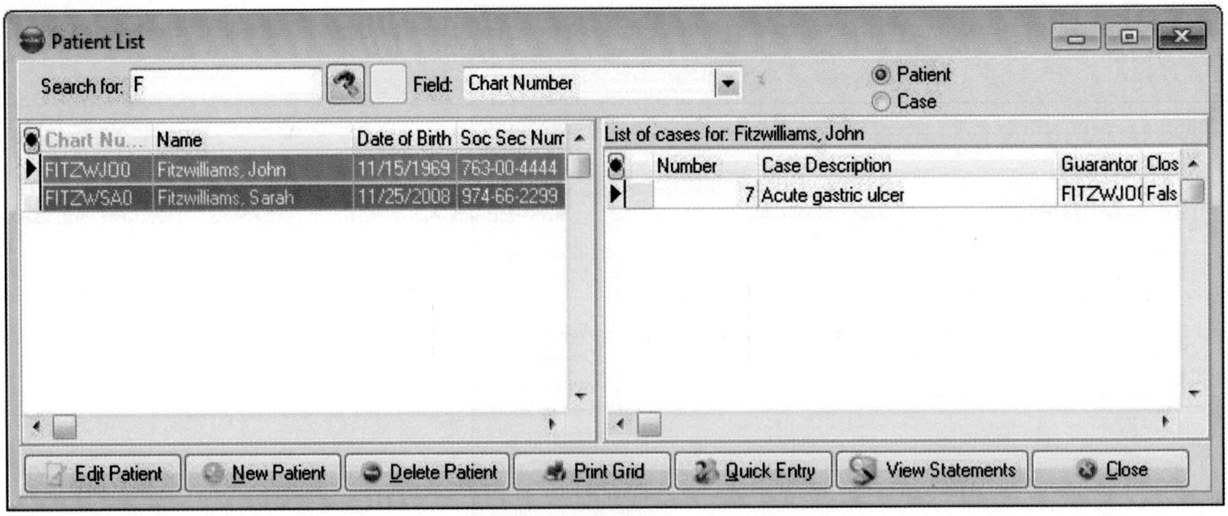

Figure 3-16   Patient List Dialog Box with John Fitzwilliams Selected

5. To close the Patient/Guarantor dialog box, click the Cancel button.

6. Click the Close button to close the Patient List dialog box. You are back to the main Office Hours window.

7. Select John Fitzwilliams's provider in the provider selection box on the toolbar, and enter the appointment. Remember to set the Office Hours calendar to the correct date. **CiMO**

✓ **You have completed Exercise 3-3.**

3.3 BOOKING FOLLOW-UP APPOINTMENTS

Often a patient will need a follow-up appointment at a certain time in the future. For example, suppose a physician would like a patient to return for a checkup in three weeks. The most efficient way to search for a future appointment in Office Hours is to use the Go to a Date shortcut button on the toolbar. (This feature can also be accessed on the Edit menu.)

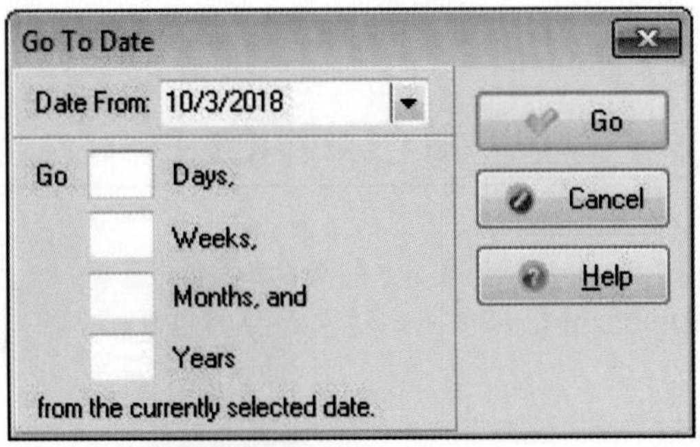

Clicking the Go to a Date shortcut button displays the Go To Date dialog box (see Figure 3-17). Within the dialog box, five boxes offer options for choosing a future date.

Date From   This box indicates the current date in the appointment search.

Go ___ Days   This box is used to locate a date that is a specific number of days in the future. For example, if a patient needs an appointment ten days from the current day, *10* would be entered in this box.

Figure 3-17   Go To Date Dialog Box

Go ___ Weeks This box is used when a patient needs an appointment a specific number of weeks in the future, such as six weeks from the current day.

Go ___ Months This box is used when a patient needs an appointment a specific number of months in the future, such as three months from the current day.

Go ___ Years Similar to the weeks and months options, this box is used when an appointment is needed in one year or several years in the future.

After a future date option has been selected, clicking the Go button closes the dialog box and begins the search. The system locates the future date and displays the calendar schedule for that date.

BOOKING AN APPOINTMENT WITH A FOLLOW-UP   EXERCISE 3-4

Enter a thirty-minute appointment for James Smith on Tuesday, November 13, 2018, at 12:15 p.m., with Dr. John Rudner. Then, schedule a fifteen-minute follow-up appointment for the same time, two weeks later.

Connect users: go to http://connect.mheducation.com to complete this exercise! Some steps may differ from what is listed here, so be sure to refer to the steps listed in Demo and Practice Modes for guidance.

1. Verify that John Rudner is selected in the Provider drop-down list.

2. Change the date on the calendar to Tuesday, November 13, 2018.

3. Double click the 12:15 p.m. time slot. The New Appointment Entry dialog box opens.

4. Select James Smith in the Chart box and press Tab.

5. Change the entry in the Length field to 30.

6. Click the Save button.

7. Click the Go to a Date shortcut button.

8. Key **2** in the Go ___ Weeks box. Click the Go button. The program closes the Go To Date box and displays the appointment schedule for November 27, 2018, at 12:15 p.m.

9. Enter James Smith's follow-up appointment. **ⓒiMⓞ**

✓ **You have completed Exercise 3-4.**

3.4 SEARCHING FOR AVAILABLE TIME SLOTS

Often it is necessary to search for available appointment space on a particular day of the week and at a specific time. For example, a patient needs a thirty-minute appointment and would like it to be during his lunch hour, which is from 12:00 p.m. to 1:00 p.m. He can get away from the office only on Mondays and Fridays. Office

Hours makes it easy to locate an appointment slot that meets these requirements with the Search for Open Time Slot shortcut button.

EXERCISE 3-5	SEARCHING FOR OPEN TIME, RAMOS

Maritza Ramos needs an appointment, but she has very limited times she can come in to the office. Search for the next available appointment slot with Dr. Yan on a Tuesday, 30 minutes in length, between 11:00 a.m. and 2:00 p.m., beginning November 8, 2018.

1. Select Dr. Katherine Yan in the Provider box.

2. Change the calendar to November 8, 2018.

3. On the Edit menu, click Find Open Time, or click the Search for Open Time Slot shortcut button. The Find Open Time dialog box is displayed (see Figure 3-18).

4. Key **30** in the Length box and then press the Tab key.

5. By default, the entry in the Start Time box is 8:00 a.m. The program highlights the default entry in the box. To change the hour from 8 to 11, key **11**. Press the Tab key.

6. Key **2** in the End Time box. Press the Tab key.

7. To search for an appointment on Tuesday, click the Tuesday box in the Day of Week area of the dialog box. The Find Open Time dialog box should look like Figure 3-19.

8. Click the Search button to begin looking for an appointment slot. The Find Open Time dialog box closes and the first available time slot that meets these specifications is located. The time slot is outlined in black on the schedule.

9. Double click the selected time slot.

10. Click Maritza Ramos on the drop-down list in the Chart box.

11. Press the Tab key until the cursor is in the Length box.

12. Key **30** and press the Tab key.

13. Click the Save button.

14. Verify that the appointment has been entered by looking at the schedule. **CiMO**

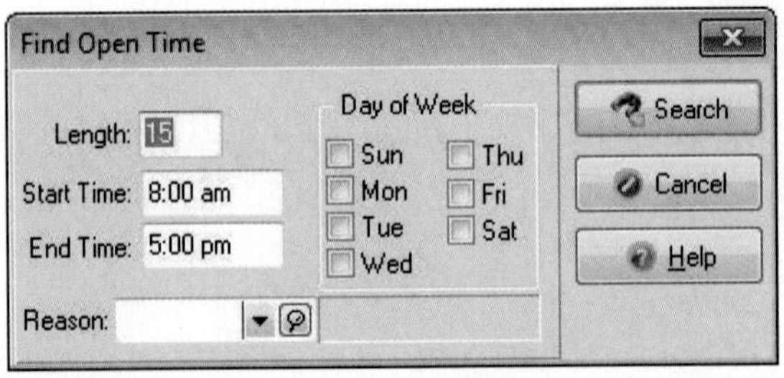

Figure 3-18 Find Open Time Dialog Box

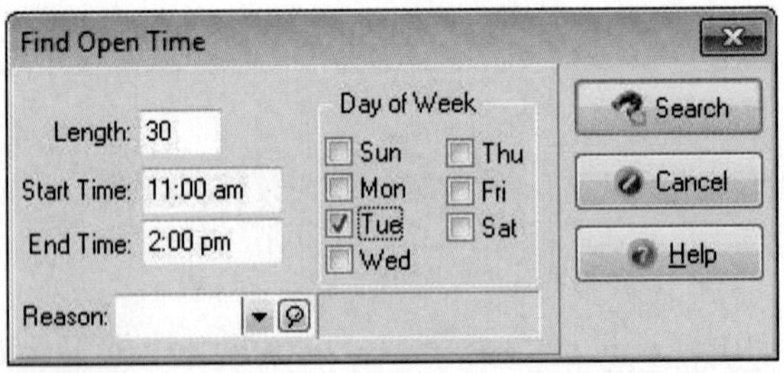

Figure 3-19 Completed Find Open Time Dialog Box

✓ **You have completed Exercise 3-5.**

Schedule Randall Klein for a thirty-minute appointment with Dr. John Rudner sometime after November 12, 2018. Mr. Klein is available only on Mondays between 3:00 p.m. and 5:00 p.m.

1. Select Klein's provider in the Provider box.

2. Confirm that the calendar is still on November 13, 2018.

3. Click Find Open Time on the Edit menu to display the Find Open Time dialog box.

4. Key **30** in the Length box. Press the Tab key to move the cursor to the Start Time box.

5. Key **3** in the Start Time box. Click on "am" to highlight it, and then key **p** to change "am" to "pm." Press Tab to move to the End Time box.

6. Key **5** in the End Time box. Press Tab.

7. In the Day of Week area, select Monday. Click to deselect any other days that are selected.

8. Click the Search button. The first available slot that meets the requirements is outlined on the schedule.

9. Double click in the time slot to open the New Appointment Entry dialog box.

10. Select Randall Klein in the drop-down list in the Chart box. Press tab several times to move the cursor to the Length box.

11. Key **30** in the Length box, and press the Tab key.

12. Click the Save button. The dialog box closes, and Randall Klein's appointment appears on the schedule. **CiMO**

✓ **You have completed Exercise 3-6.**

3.5 ENTERING APPOINTMENTS FOR NEW PATIENTS

When a new patient phones the office for an appointment, the appointment can be scheduled in Office Hours before the patient information is entered in Medisoft. In these instances, it is possible to enter an appointment before a chart number has been assigned to the patient, by entering the patient's name in the field to the right of the Chart field.

Schedule Hiro Tanaka, a new patient, for a thirty-minute appointment with Dr. Katherine Yan on October 1, 2018, at 3:00 p.m.

1. Select Tanaka's provider in the Provider field.

2. Change the calendar to October 1, 2018.

3. Double click the 3:00 p.m. time slot.

4. Click in the blank box to the right of the Chart box, and key **Tanaka, Hiro**. Press the Tab key to move the cursor to the Home Phone box.

5. Key **6145557373** in the Home Phone box, and press Tab to go to the Cell Phone box.

6. Enter **6145550162** in the Cell Phone box. Press Tab repeatedly to go to the Length box.

7. Key **30** in the Length box.

8. Click the Save button. The appointment is displayed on the October 1, 2018, schedule. **CiMC**

✓ **You have completed Exercise 3-7.**

3.6 BOOKING REPEAT APPOINTMENTS

Some patients require appointments on a repeated basis, such as every Thursday for eight weeks. Repeat appointments are also set up in the New Appointment Entry dialog box. The Repeat feature is located at the bottom of the dialog box (see Figure 3-20). When the Change button is clicked, the Repeat Change dialog box is displayed. The Repeat Change dialog box provides a number of choices for setting up repeating appointments (see Figure 3-21).

The left side of the dialog box contains information about the frequency of the appointments. The default is set to None. Other options include Daily, Weekly, Monthly, and Yearly. When an option other than None is selected, the center section of the dialog box changes and displays additional options for setting up the appointments (see Figure 3-22).

In the center section, an option is provided to indicate how often the appointments should be scheduled, such as once every week. Below that there is an option to indicate the day of the week on which the appointments should be scheduled. Finally, there is a box to indicate when the repeating appointments should stop. When all the information has been entered, clicking the OK button closes the Repeat Change dialog box, and the New Appointment Entry dialog box is once again visible. Clicking the Save button enters the repeating appointments on the schedule.

New Appointment Entry

Chart: [　　　▼ 🔎] [　　　　　　　　　]

[💾 Save]

[⊘ Cancel]

[❓ Help]

Home Phone: [　　　]   Cell Phone: [　　　]

Resource: [　▼ 🔎]

Note: [　　　　　]

Case: [　　▼ 🔎]   Service Type Code

Reason: [　　▼ 🔎] [　　]

Length: 15 ⏶⏷ minutes

Color: ■ Silver ▼

Date: 11/12/2018 ▼   Time: 12:00 pm

Provider: 2 [▼ 🔎] Rudner, John

Repeat: No Repeat

[Change]

Status
- ⦿ Unconfirmed
- ○ Confirmed
- ○ Checked In
- ○ Missed
- ○ Cancelled
- ○ Being Seen
- ○ Checked Out
- ○ Rescheduled

☐ Need Referral

[💲 Enter Copay]

[⟿ Balance]

Figure 3-20 New Appointment Entry Dialog Box with Repeat Change Area Highlighted

Repeat Change

Frequency
- ⦿ None
- ○ Daily
- ○ Weekly
- ○ Monthly
- ○ Yearly

Click on the repeat options on the left to set an interval for this repeat.

No Repeat

[✓ OK]
[⊘ Cancel]
[❓ Help]

Figure 3-21 Repeat Change Dialog Box with the Default Settings (None Button Selected)

Repeat Change

Frequency
- ○ None
- ○ Daily
- ⦿ Weekly
- ○ Monthly
- ○ Yearly

Every: 1   Week(s)

On: S M T W T F S
☐ ☑ ☐ ☐ ☐ ☐ ☐

End on: [　　▼]

Every week on Mon

[✓ OK]
[⊘ Cancel]
[❓ Help]

Figure 3-22 Repeat Change Dialog Box When an Option Other Than None Is Selected

---

BOOKING REPEAT APPOINTMENTS   EXERCISE 3-8

Schedule Jo Wong for a fifteen-minute appointment once a week for six weeks with Dr. Katherine Yan. Mr. Wong has requested that the appointments be at the same time every week, preferably in the early morning, beginning on Wednesday, November 14, 2018.

1. Confirm that Wong's provider is selected in the Provider field.

2. Change the schedule to November 14, 2018.

3. Double click in the 8:00 a.m. time slot. The New Appointment Entry dialog box is displayed.

4. Select Jo Wong from the Chart drop-down list. Press the Tab key.

5. Confirm that the entry in the Length box is fifteen minutes.

6. Click the Change button to schedule the repeating appointments.

Connect users: go to http://connect.mheducation.com to complete this exercise! Some steps may differ from what is listed here, so be sure to refer to the steps listed in Demo and Practice Modes for guidance.

[Mc Graw Hill Education] **connect**

7. In the Frequency column, select Weekly.

8. Accept the default entry of 1 in the Every ___ Week(s) field.

9. Accept the default entry of W to accept Wednesday as the day of the week.

10. Enter *12192018* in the End on box.

11. Click the OK button. Notice that "Every week on Wed" is displayed in the Repeat area of the New Appointment Entry dialog box.

12. Click the Save button to enter the appointments. Notice that "Occurs every week on Wed" appears in the lower-left corner of the Office Hours window, below the patient information.

13. Go to December 19, 2018, to verify that Mr. Wong is scheduled for an appointment at 8:00 a.m.

14. Go to December 26, 2018, and confirm that Mr. Wong is not scheduled. This is the seventh week, and his repeating appointments were scheduled for six weeks, so no appointment should appear on December 26, 2018. ⓒiMⓞ

✓ **You have completed Exercise 3-8.**

3.7 RESCHEDULING AND CANCELING APPOINTMENTS

It is often necessary to reschedule a patient's appointment. Changing an appointment is accomplished with the Cut and Paste commands on the Office Hours Edit menu. Similarly, an appointment can be canceled and not rescheduled simply by using the Cut command.

The following steps are used to reschedule an appointment:

1. Locate the appointment that needs to be changed.

2. Click on the time-slot box. A black border surrounds the slot to indicate that it is selected.

3. Click Cut on the Edit menu. The appointment disappears from the schedule.

4. Click the date on the calendar when the appointment is to be rescheduled.

5. Click the desired time-slot box on the schedule. The slot becomes active.

6. Click Paste on the Edit menu. The patient's name appears in the new time-slot box.

The following steps are used to cancel an appointment without rescheduling:

1. Locate the appointment on the schedule.

SHORT CUT

CUTTING AND PASTING

Instead of using the Cut and Paste commands to change or delete an appointment, select the appointment, and press the right mouse button. A shortcut menu appears with several options, including Cut, Copy, and Delete.

2. Click the time-slot box to select the appointment.

3. Click Cut on the Edit menu. The appointment disappears from the schedule.

Change John Gardiner's appointment with Dr. Katherine Yan from Thursday, November 8 at 9:00 a.m. to Friday, November 16 at 9:15 a.m. Change Janine Bell's appointment with Dr. Jessica Rudner from 3:00 p.m. on November 16, 2018 to 4:00 p.m. on the same day.

1. Confirm that Katherine Yan is selected in the Provider drop-down list.

2. Go to Thursday, November 8, 2018, on the calendar.

3. Locate John Gardiner's 9:00 a.m. appointment. Right-click on the appointment and select Cut from the shortcut menu.

4. Go to Friday, November 16, 2018, on the calendar.

5. Right-click in the 9:15 a.m. time slot and select Paste from the shortcut menu.

6. Select Jessica Rudner on the Provider box drop-down list.

7. Locate Janine Bell's 3:00 p.m. appointment on November 16, 2018, on the calendar.

8. Click the 3:00 p.m. time-slot box.

9. Click Cut on the Edit menu. Janine Bell's appointment is removed from the 3:00 p.m. time-slot box. (You may also use the right-mouse-click shortcut.)

10. Click the 4:00 p.m. time-slot box.

11. Click Paste on the Edit menu. Janine Bell's name is displayed in the 4:00 p.m. time-slot box. **cIMC**

✓ **You have completed Exercise 3-9.**

Connect users: go to http://connect.mheducation.com to complete this exercise! Some steps may differ from what is listed here, so be sure to refer to the steps listed in Demo and Practice Modes for guidance.

3.8 VERIFYING INSURANCE ELIGIBILITY AND BENEFITS

Before the patient sees the provider on the day of his or her appointment, the patient's eligibility for insurance benefits must be verified. While the specific information provided by the payer varies, the information generally includes:

- Whether the patient is currently covered by the plan.

- The amount of the copayment, coinsurance, and/or deductible.

- Whether the planned encounter is for a covered service that is medically necessary under the payer's rules.

Previously, to determine a patient's eligibility and benefits, a staff member had to refer to the latest paperwork from the insurance company or phone a representative. Today, most eligibility verification is performed electronically. Electronic transactions are the most efficient because they take only seconds, and can be completed at the practice's convenience. For example, large practices often schedule batches of patient eligibility inquiries to be run overnight. The next morning, the staff reviews the results before patient appointments begin.

Most practice management programs have a feature that enables online inquires to a payer to be sent from within the program. In Medisoft, eligibility can be checked in a number of ways, including:

- By selecting Eligibility Verification on the Activities menu.
- By right-clicking on a Case in the Patient List dialog box.
- By right-clicking on an appointment in Office Hours.

When a patient appointment is visible on the schedule in Office Hours, right-clicking the appointment displays a shortcut menu. Figure 3-23 displays the shortcut menu with Eligibility Verification highlighted.

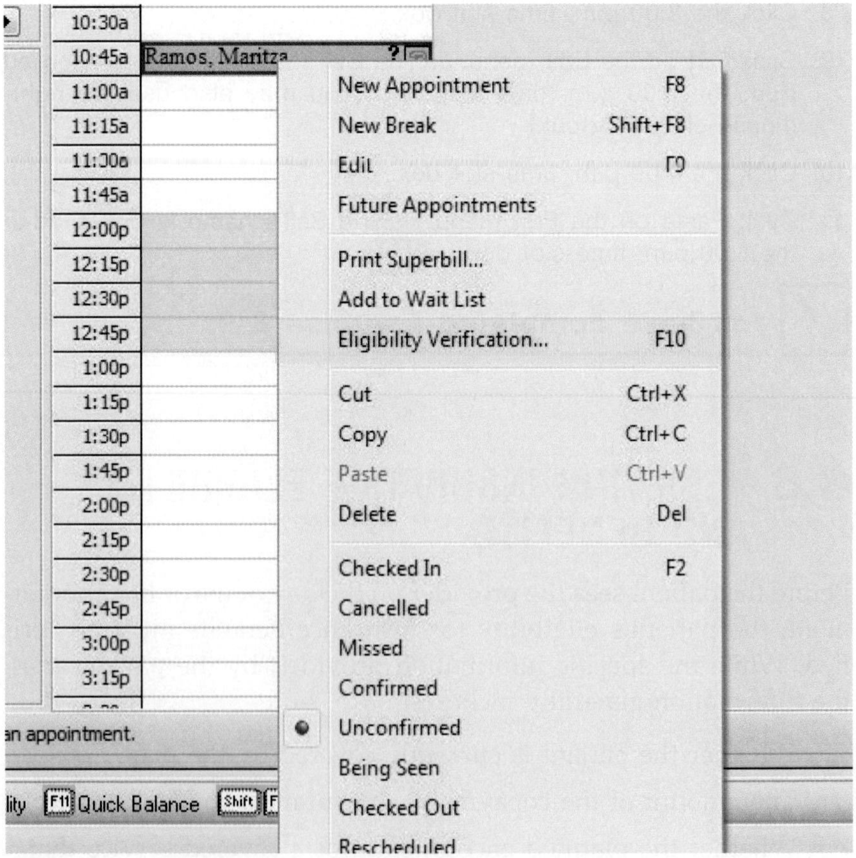

Figure 3-23   Shortcut Menu with Eligibility Verification Highlighted

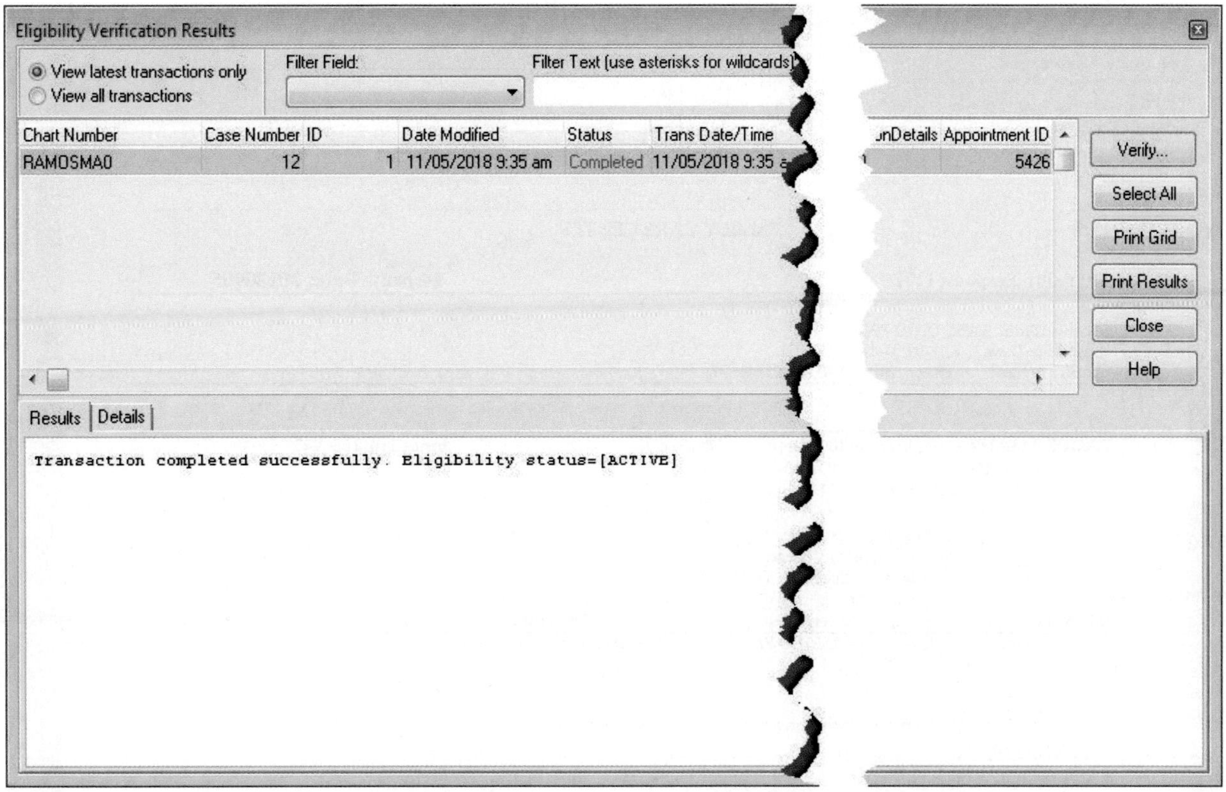

Figure 3-24 Eligibility Verification Results Dialog Box with Verify Button Highlighted

When the option for Eligibility Verification is selected, the Eligibility Verification Results dialog box is displayed (see Figure 3-24).

Clicking the Verify button causes the Real-Time Eligibility Verification dialog box to appear (see Figure 3-25).

This Real-Time Eligibility Verification dialog box lists the patient's name, the provider, the date of service, and the insurance selection (primary, secondary, tertiary). Clicking the Verify button in this dialog box sends the electronic request to the clearinghouse, or payer. The Please Wait dialog box is displayed while the request is processed. When the verification is complete, the Select the Report Format for the Eligibility Response Report dialog box is displayed (see Figure 3-26).

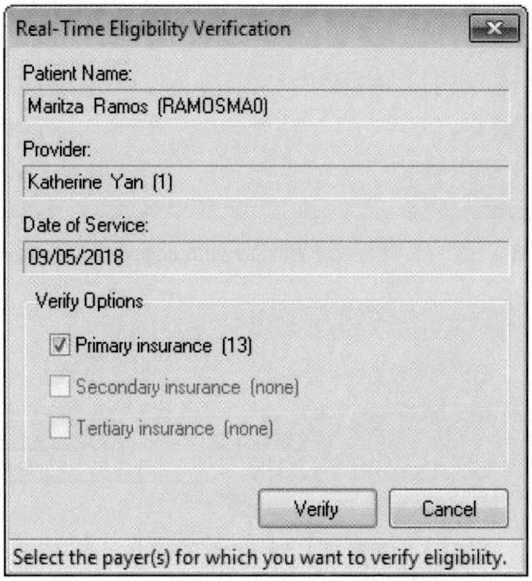

Figure 3-25 Real-Time Eligibility Verification Dialog Box

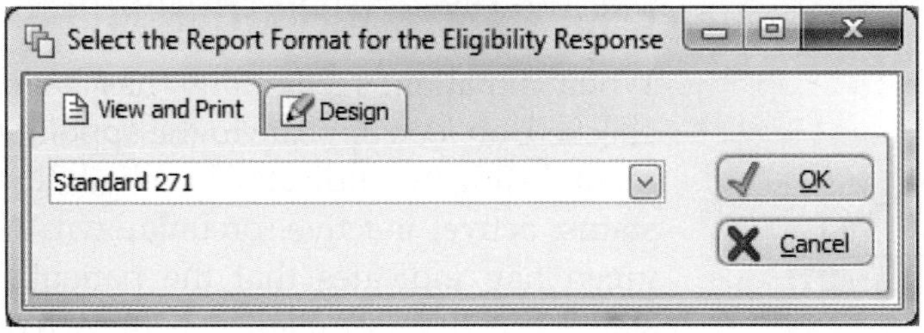

Figure 3-26 Select the Report Format for the Eligibility Response Dialog Box

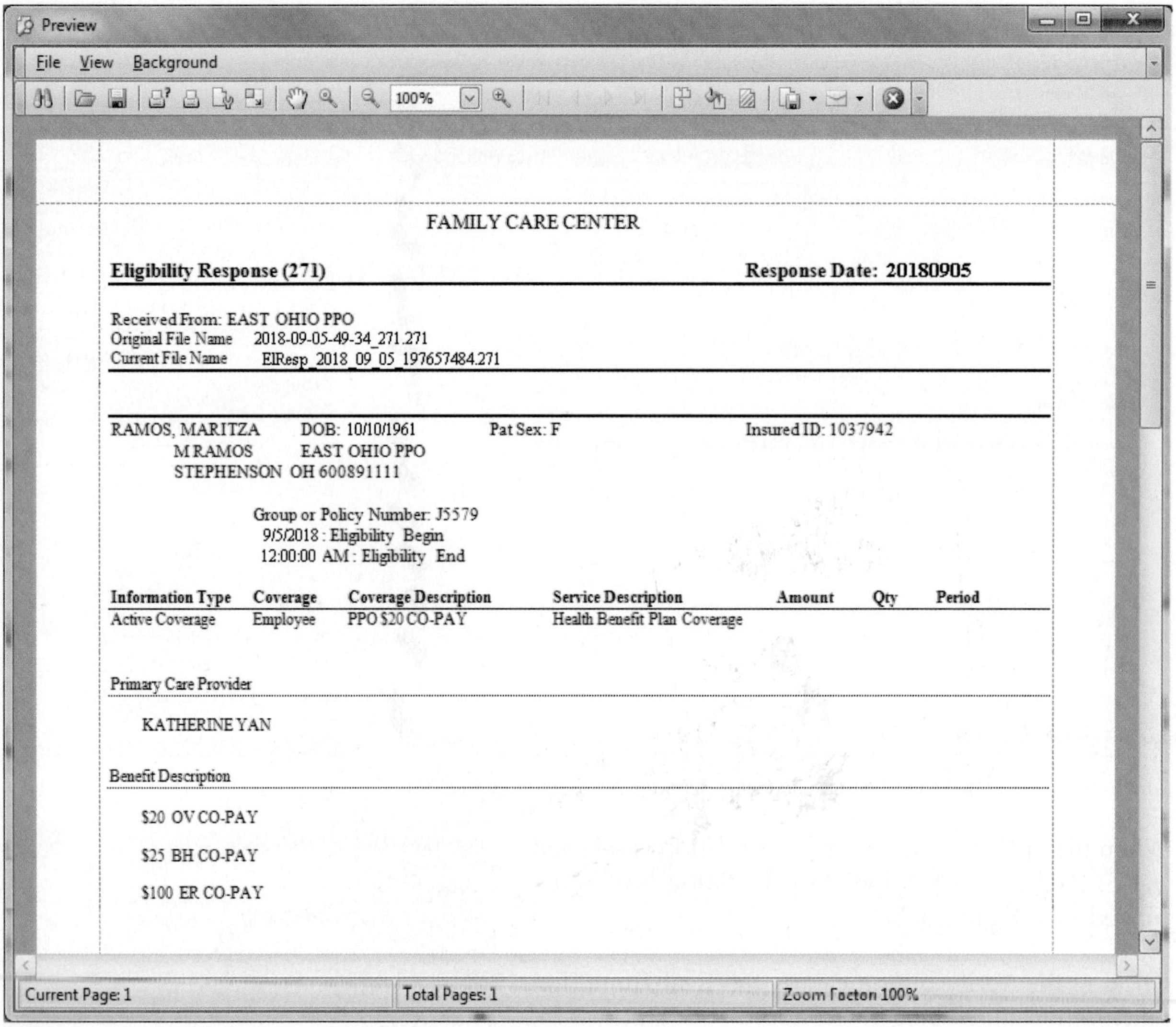

Figure 3-27 Preview Window with Eligibility Response Displayed

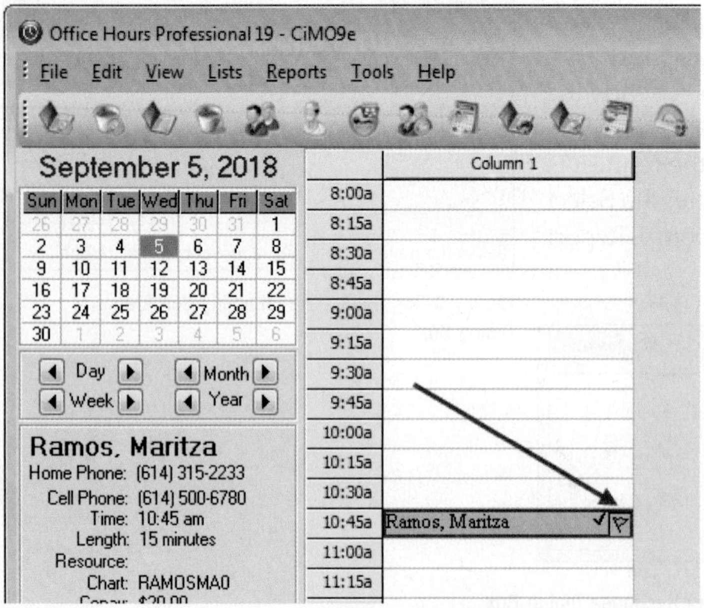

Figure 3-28 Appointment with Green Flag After Eligibility Verified

In the View and Print tab, the Standard 271 eligibility response format is listed. The Design tab provides an option for users who want to customize the view. When the OK button is clicked, the eligibility response report appears in the Preview window (see Figure 3-27.

ELIGIBILITY VERIFICATION ICONS

When a patient's eligibility has been checked, an icon appears in the appointment listing to indicate the eligibility status: active, inactive, or unknown. A green flag indicates that the patient's status is active (see Figure 3-28). A red flag means the patient is inactive. A yellow flag indicates that the patient does not have a successful eligibility verification in the record or that the past results conflict with current results. If the box is blank, no eligibility verification has been attempted.

<table>
<tr><td>VERIFYING A PATIENT'S ELIGIBILITY
(CONNECT ONLY)</td><td>EXERCISE 3-10</td></tr>
</table>

Verify John Fitzwilliams's insurance eligibility for his appointment with Dr. John Rudner on Monday, October 1, 2018.

1. Select John Rudner on the Provider drop-down list.
2. Go to Monday, October 1, 2018, on the calendar.
3. Locate John Fitzwilliams's 11:00 a.m. appointment.
4. Right-click on the appointment to display the shortcut menu and click Eligibility Verification. The Eligibility Verification Results dialog box appears.
5. Notice that Fitzwilliams's appointment is listed in the top section of the dialog box.
6. Click the Verify button. The Real-Time Eligibility Verification dialog box appears.
7. Click the Verify button. The Please Wait box appears while the system processes the request.
8. Once verification is complete, the Select the Report Format for the Eligibility Response Report dialog box is displayed. Accept the default of Standard 271 and click OK.
9. The eligibility response report appears in the Preview window. After viewing the report, close the Preview window by clicking the red circle with the white X in it, which is located on the right-hand side of the toolbar.
10. You are returned to the Eligibility Verification Results dialog box. Click the Close button to close the dialog box. **CiMO**

> ✔ **You have completed Exercise 3-10.**

connect

3.9 CHECKING PATIENTS IN AND OUT

Office Hours can also be used to record the check-in and checkout of patients. Depending on the preferences of the physician practice, patients may be checked in and out in a scheduling program such as Office Hours or in an electronic health record program. In either case, recording this information helps keep track of patients while they are in the office.

In Office Hours, patients are checked in or out by using the status option described earlier in the chapter. For example, to check a patient in:

- Locate the appointment on the Office Hours calendar.
- Click once to select the appointment.
- Right click to view the shortcut menu.
- Click Checked In on the shortcut menu (see Figure 3-29).

	Column 1
8:00a	Jones, Elizabeth
8:15a	
8:30a	
8:45a	
9:00a	
9:15a	
9:30a	
9:45a	
10:00a	
10:15a	
10:30a	
10:45a	
11:00a	
11:15a	
11:30a	
11:45a	
12:00p	
12:15p	
12:30p	
12:45p	
1:00p	
1:15p	
1:30p	
1:45p	

Shortcut menu:

New Appointment	F8
New Break	Shift+F8
Edit	F9
Future Appointments	
Print Superbill...	
Add to Wait List	
Eligibility Verification...	F10
Cut	Ctrl+X
Copy	Ctrl+C
Paste	Ctrl+V
Delete	Del
Checked In	F2
Cancelled	
Missed	
● Confirmed	
Unconfirmed	
Being Seen	
Checked Out	
Rescheduled	

Figure 3-29   Shortcut menu with Checked In highlighted

EXERCISE 3-11   CHECKING IN A PATIENT

It is Monday, October 1, 2018. John Fitzwilliams has arrived in the office for his 11:00 a.m. appointment with Dr. John Rudner. Use Office Hours to change his appointment status to checked in.

1. Select John Rudner on the Provider drop-down list.

2. Go to Monday, October 1, 2018, on the calendar.

3. Locate John Fitzwilliams's 11:00 a.m. appointment. Notice that the current status icon is a question mark, which means it is unconfirmed.

4. Click once to select the appointment, if it is not already selected. (*Note: Once an appointment is selected, it appears with a black border. An unselected appointment has no such border.*)

5. Click the right mouse button. The shortcut menu appears.

6. Click Checked In on the shortcut menu. Notice that the question mark in the status section of his appointment changed to a check mark, to indicate that he has checked in. **ĉiMC**

✓ **You have completed Exercise 3-11.**

3.10 CREATING AN OVERDUE BALANCE REPORT FOR PATIENTS WITH APPOINTMENTS

Medical practices have discovered that it is much easier to collect on overdue accounts when the patient is in the office, rather than by phone or mail. As a result, it is useful to have account balance information available at the front desk when patients check in. In Medisoft, the Appointment List with Remainder Balance report provides this information.

CREATING AN OVERDUE BALANCE REPORT — EXERCISE 3-12

The practice manager would like a list of patients with appointments scheduled in the current month who have overdue balances.

1. Minimize the Office Hours window by clicking the Minimize button.

2. In Medisoft, select Medisoft Reports on the Reports menu.

3. In the left-hand column titled All Folders, double click on the Plus Pack folder. The contents of the Plus Pack folder appear in the pane on the right.

4. Double click on the report titled Appointment List with Remainder Balance (Patient). The Search box appears.

5. Enter **11012018** in the first Date box and **11302018** in the second Date box.

6. Leave the other fields blank and click the OK button.

7. The report is displayed. The first page lists patients scheduled with Dr. Katherine Yan. Additional pages may be viewed by clicking the blue circle with the white arrow, located to the right of the "1," at the upper-left section of the window.

8. Close the Print Preview window. Close the Medisoft Reports window. Click the Office Hours button on the status bar to display it on the screen again. **CIMO**

✓ **You have completed Exercise 3-12.**

Connect users: go to http://connect.mheducation.com to complete this exercise! Some steps may differ from what is listed here, so be sure to refer to the steps listed in Demo and Practice Modes for guidance.

3.11 CREATING A PATIENT RECALL LIST

Medical offices frequently must keep track of patients who need to return for future appointments. Some offices schedule future appointments when the patient is leaving the office. For example, if a patient has just seen a physician and needs to return for a follow-up appointment in six weeks, the appointment is usually made before the patient leaves the office. However, when the appointment is needed farther in the future, such as one year later, it is not always practical to set up the appointment. It is difficult for the patient and the physician to know their schedules a year in

Figure 3-30 Patient Recall List Shortcut Icon

Patient Recall List

Search for: [ ]   Field: Provider, Date Of Recall ▾

Date of R...	Name	Phone	Extension Status	

Edit   **New**   Delete   Print Grid   **Close**

Figure 3-31 Patient Recall List Dialog Box

recall list a list of patients who need to be contacted for future appointments.

advance. For this reason, many offices keep a **recall list**, which is a list of patients who need to be contacted for future appointments. Maintaining an active recall list is an important part of ensuring a consistent cash flow from year-to-year.

In Office Hours, a recall list is created and maintained by clicking the Patient Recall List icon on the toolbar (see Figure 3-30) or by selecting Patient Recall List on the Lists menu. When the Patient Recall List icon is clicked, the Patient Recall List dialog box is displayed (see Figure 3-31). This dialog box organizes the recall information in a column format. To view all the columns, the horizontal scroll bar must be used.

Date of Recall   Lists the date on which the recall is scheduled.

Name   Displays the patient's name.

Phone   Lists the patient's phone number, making it easy to call patients for appointments without having to look up phone numbers in another dialog box.

Extension   Lists the patient's phone extension.

Status   Indicates the patient's recall status: Call, Call Again, Appointment Set, or No Appointment.

Provider   Displays the provider code for the patient's provider.

Message   Displays the entry made in the Message box of the Patient Recall dialog box.

Chart Number   Displays the patient's chart number.

Procedure Code   Lists the procedure code for the procedure for which the patient is being recalled.

The Patient Recall List dialog box contains the following boxes:

Search For   The Search For box is used to locate a specific patient on the recall list. Entering the first few letters or numbers in the Search For box displays the selection that is the closest match to the search criteria.

Field   The choices in the Field box determine the order in which patients are listed in the dialog box. There are three sorting options:

1. Provider, Date of Recall
2. Chart Number, Date of Recall
3. Date of Recall , Provider, Chart Number

The Patient Recall List dialog box also contains these buttons: Edit, New, Delete, Print Grid, and Close.

Edit   Clicking the Edit button displays the Patient Recall dialog box for the patient whose entry is highlighted. The information on the patient can then be edited by making different selections in the boxes.

New   Clicking the New button displays an empty Patient Recall dialog box in which data on a new recall patient can be entered.

Delete   Clicking the Delete button deletes data on the patient whose entry is highlighted from the patient recall list.

Print Grid   Clicking the Print Grid button displays options to print the grid that is used in the Patient Recall dialog box.

Close   The Close button is used to exit the Patient Recall List dialog box.

ADDING A PATIENT TO THE RECALL LIST

Patients are added to the recall list by clicking the New button in the Patient Recall List dialog box. When the New button is clicked, the Patient Recall dialog box is displayed (see Figure 3-32).

The Patient Recall dialog box contains the following boxes:

Recall Date   The date a patient needs to return to see a physician is entered in the Recall Date box.

Provider   A patient's provider is selected from the drop-down list.

Chart   A patient's chart number is selected from the drop-down list, or the first few letters of a patient's chart number are entered in the Chart box.

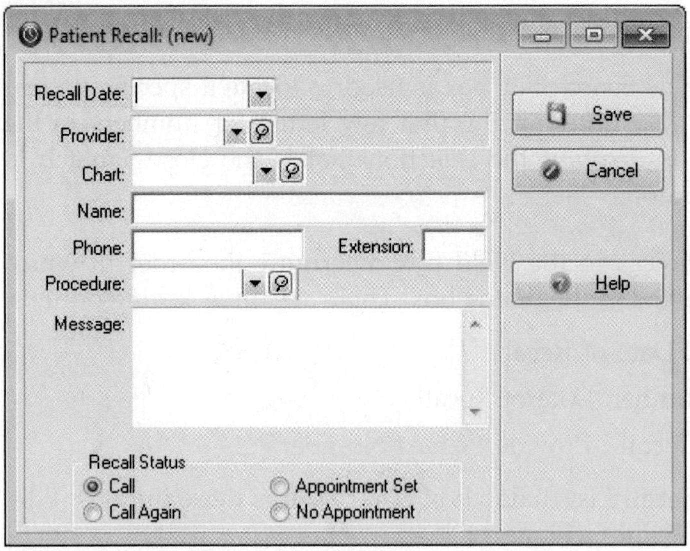

Figure 3-32　Patient Recall (new) Dialog Box

Name, Phone, Extension　After a chart number is entered, the system automatically completes the Name, Phone, and Extension boxes.

Procedure　If the procedure for which a patient is returning is known, it is entered in the Procedure box in one of two ways. The procedure code can be selected from the drop-down list, or the first few numbers can be entered so that the drop-down list will display the entry that most closely matches the entered numbers. This is especially valuable in practices that use hundreds of procedure codes because it eliminates the need to scroll through the codes to locate the desired one.

Message　The Message box is used to record any special notes, reminders, or instructions about a patient and his or her appointment.

Recall Status　The choices in the Recall Status box are used to indicate the action that needs to be taken. They include

- *Call.*　The Call button is used when a patient needs to be telephoned about a future appointment.
- *Call Again.*　The Call Again button is used when a patient has been called once, but contact was not made and an additional call is necessary.
- *Appointment Set.*　The Appointment Set button is used when a patient has an appointment already scheduled.
- *No Appointment.*　The No Appointment button is used when a patient has been contacted for an appointment but has declined for some reason.

After the information has been entered in the dialog box, clicking the Save button saves the data and adds the patient to the recall list. In addition to the Save button, the Patient Recall dialog box contains Cancel, Recall List, and Help buttons. The Cancel button exits the dialog box without saving the data entered. The Recall List button in the Patient Recall dialog box is used to display the Patient Recall List dialog box. The Help button displays Medisoft's online help for the Patient Recall dialog box.

ADDING A PATIENT TO THE RECALL LIST EXERCISE 3-13

Connect users: go to http://connect.mheducation.com to complete this exercise! Some steps may differ from what is listed here, so be sure to refer to the steps listed in Demo and Practice Modes for guidance.

John Fitzwilliams needs to receive a phone call one year from November 12, 2018, to set up an appointment for an annual physical with Dr. John Rudner. Add John Fitzwilliams to the recall list.

1. Click the Patient Recall List shortcut button. The Patient Recall dialog box is displayed.

2. Click the New button. The Patient Recall dialog box is displayed.

3. In the Recall Date box, enter November 12, 2019. Press Tab.

4. Click John Fitzwilliams's provider on the drop-down list in the Provider box. Press Tab.

5. Enter John Fitzwilliams's chart number in the Chart box by keying the first few letters of his last name and pressing Tab. Notice that the system automatically completes the Name and Phone boxes. (The Extension box would also be completed if there were an extension.)

6. Enter the procedure code in the Procedure box by keying **99396** (Preventive est., 40–64 years) and pressing Tab.

7. Verify that the Call radio button in the Recall Status box is selected.

8. Click the Save button to save the entry.

9. Click the Close button to close the Patient Recall List dialog box.

✓ **You have completed Exercise 3-13.**

3.12 CREATING PROVIDER BREAKS

Office Hours provides features for inserting standard breaks in providers' schedules. The **Office Hours break** is a block of time when a physician is unavailable for appointments with patients. Some examples of breaks include Lunch, Meeting, Personal, Emergency, Break, Vacation, Seminar, Holiday, Trip, and Surgery. In Office Hours, breaks can be created one at a time or on a recurring basis for all providers. One-time breaks, such as those for vacations, are set up for individual providers. Other breaks, such as staff meetings, can be entered once for multiple providers.

Office Hours break a block of time when a physician is unavailable for appointments with patients.

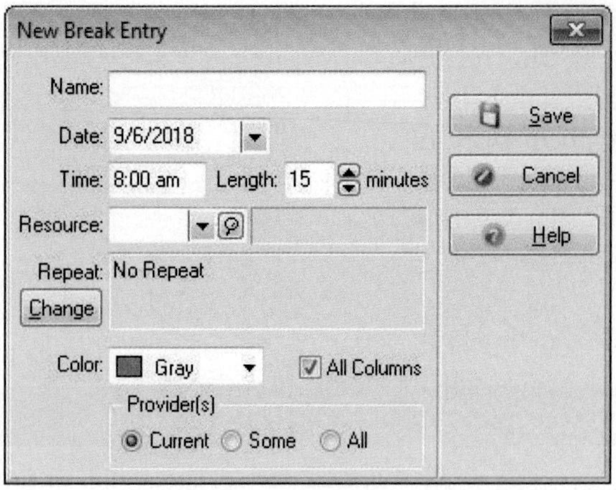

Figure 3-33 New Break Entry Dialog Box

Often breaks need to be inserted into a provider's schedule when he or she is not available for appointments with patients. For example, if a physician will be in surgery on Thursday from 9 a.m. until 12:00 p.m., that time period must be marked as unavailable on his or her schedule.

To set up a break for a current provider (that is, the provider listed in the Office Hours Provider box), click the Break Entry shortcut button. This action causes the New Break Entry dialog box to appear (see Figure 3-33).

The dialog box contains the following options:

Name   The Name field is used to store a name or description of the break.

Date   The Date field displays the current date on the Office Hours calendar. If this is not the correct date for the break entry, a different date can be entered.

Time   The starting time of the break is entered in this box.

Length   This box indicates the length of the break in minutes (from 0 to 720).

Resource   The drop-down list entries in the Resource box display the different types of breaks already set up in Office Hours.

Change   The Change button next to the Repeat box is used to enter breaks that recur at a regular interval.

Color   By selecting a different color from the drop-down list, the color of the break time slot in the schedule can be changed.

All Columns   If the All Columns box is checked, the break will appear across all columns of the schedule (if a practice uses multiple columns in Office Hours).

Provider(s)   The Provider(s) buttons are used to indicate whether a break is to be set for the current provider (the provider selected in the Provider box in Office Hours), some providers, or all providers. If Some is selected, a Provider Selection dialog box will be displayed when the Save button is clicked. The appropriate providers can then be selected.

When all the information has been entered, clicking the Save button closes the dialog box and enters the break(s) in Medisoft.

Dr. Jessica Rudner will be attending a seminar on updates to the Affordable Care Act (ACA) from 10:00 a.m. to 12:00 p.m. on Monday, Tuesday, and Wednesday, December 10–12, 2018. Enter this as a break on her schedule.

1. Select Jessica Rudner in the Provider field.

2. Change the date on the calendar to December 10, 2018.

3. Click once in the 10:00 a.m. time slot (do not double click).

4. Click the Break Entry shortcut button. The New Break Entry dialog box appears.

5. Enter **ACA Update Seminar** in the Name box.

6. Confirm that the date and time are correct.

7. Enter **120** in the Length box to change the length of time to 120 minutes.

8. Select Seminar Break from the drop-down list in the Resource field.

9. Click the Change button (to repeat the break for two additional days). The Repeat Change dialog box is displayed.

10. Click the Daily button in the Frequency column.

11. Accept the default entry of 1 in the Every ____ Day(s) box, since the break occurs every day for a period of three days.

12. Key **12122018** in the End on box.

13. Click the OK button. You are returned to the New Break Entry dialog box.

14. Click the Save button to enter the break in Office Hours. Notice that the time slot from 10:00 a.m. to 12:00 p.m. on December 10, 2018, has been filled in on the calendar.

15. Change the calendar to December 11 and 12, 2018, to verify that the break has been entered correctly. **cIMc**

✔ **You have completed Exercise 3-14.**

Connect users: go to http://connect.mheducation.com to complete this exercise! Some steps may differ from what is listed here, so be sure to refer to the steps listed in Demo and Practice Modes for guidance.

3.13 VIEWING AND PRINTING SCHEDULES

In most medical offices, providers' schedules are printed on a daily basis. To view a list of all appointments for a provider for a given day, the Appointment List option on the Office Hours Reports menu is used. A single provider and date are specified in the Data Selection dialog box for the report. (If the Provider boxes are left blank, schedules are created for all providers.) The schedule created is based on the provider and date specified in the Data Selection dialog box rather than the provider and date selected in the Office Hours window.

The report can be previewed on the screen or sent directly to the printer. If the preview option is selected, the appointment list is

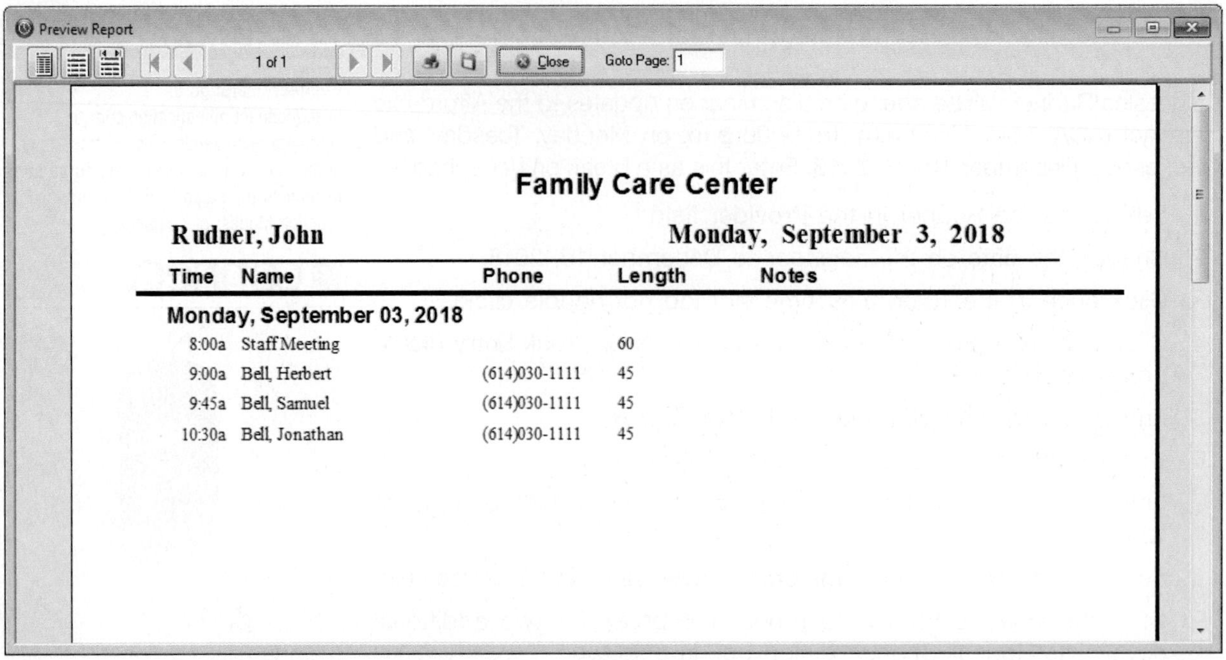

Family Care Center

Rudner, John   **Monday, September 3, 2018**

Time	Name	Phone	Length	Notes
Monday, September 03, 2018				
8:00a	Staff Meeting		60	
9:00a	Bell, Herbert	(614)030-1111	45	
9:45a	Bell, Samuel	(614)030-1111	45	
10:30a	Bell, Jonathan	(614)030-1111	45	

Figure 3-34 Preview Report Window with Appointment List Displayed

displayed in a preview window (see Figure 3-34). Various buttons are used to view the schedule at different sizes, to move from page to page, to print the schedule, and to save the schedule as a file. Clicking the Close button closes the preview window.

The schedule can also be printed without using the Appointment List option on the Office Hours Reports menu by clicking the Print Appointment List shortcut button. If this option is chosen, Office Hours prints the schedule for the date selected in the calendar and for the provider who is listed in the Provider box. To print the schedule for a different date or provider, change the date on the calendar and the entry in the Provider box before printing the schedule.

EXERCISE 3-15   VIEWING A PROVIDER SCHEDULE

Preview Dr. Katherine Yan's schedule for October 1, 2018, using the Appointment List option on the Office Hours Reports menu.

1. Click Appointment List on the Office Hours Reports menu. The Report Setup dialog box appears.

2. Under Print Selection, accept the default entry to preview the report on the screen.

3. Click the Start button. The Data Selection dialog box is displayed.

4. Enter **10012018** in both Dates boxes.

5. Select Katherine Yan in both Providers boxes.

6. Click the OK button. The Preview Report window appears.

7. Click the Close button to close the Preview Report window. **ciMo**

☑ **You have completed Exercise 3-15.**

The Applying Your Skills questions that follow appear in Chapters 3-10. These exercises are NOT OPTIONAL. You must complete these exercises or your results in later chapters will be incorrect!

APPLYING YOUR SKILLS

At the end of each chapter, you will apply what you have learned in an Applying Your Skills exercise. This exercise is similar to the exercises you completed throughout the chapter, with one important difference: step-by-step instructions are not provided. You must rely on what you learned and practiced in the chapter to complete the Applying Your Skills exercise.

1: ENTER AN APPOINTMENT FOR A NEW PATIENT

Book a thirty-minute appointment for a new patient, Lisa Wright, at 2:00 p.m. on October 1, 2018, with Dr. Jessica Rudner. Wright's home phone number is 614-555-7059 and her cell number is 614-505-1397.

APPLYING YOUR SKILLS

2: SEARCH FOR AN OPEN TIME

Herbert Bell needs a sixty-minute appointment with Dr. John Rudner. He would like to come in the week of November 12, 2018, if possible, and then he is only available after 4:00 p.m. Schedule him in the first available time-slot that meets these requirements.

APPLYING YOUR SKILLS

3: PREVIEW A PHYSICIAN'S SCHEDULE

Preview the November 13, 2018 appointment list for Dr. John Rudner.

Remember to create a backup of your work before exiting Medisoft! To help you keep track of your work, name the backup file after the chapter you are working on, for example, StudentID-c3.mbk.

BE THE DETECTIVE!

If assigned by your instructor, complete the Scheduling Problem Video Case in Connect. Put your skills to use identifying mistakes made in Medisoft and enhance your knowledge by determining the impact of those mistakes.

Transferring Appointment Information

The first time Medisoft exchanges information with an electronic health record, all appointments and patient demographics are transferred. After that first transmission, only new or edited appointments and demographics are transmitted. The figure below shows the settings required to exchange appointment information with an electronic health record such as Medisoft Clinical.

Settings

Connection Type	Medisoft Clinical
Source	Medisoft

Shared DB Settings

Server Name (Path)	\\C:\MediData
Database Name	CiMO9e.add
UserID	shareddatauser
Password	••••••••••••

Practice Name	CiMO9e
Target	Medisoft Clinical
Transmit Interval (2-3600 seconds)	30
Protocol	File

[EMR Settings]

☑ Transmit patient demographics
☑ Transmit appointments
☑ Send & receive appointment status updates
☑ Automate provider mappings
☑ Receive billing messages
☐ Transmit demographics to RelayHealth

[OK]   [Delete]   [Cancel]

chapter 3 worksheet

[Note: These questions are designed for students using the live Medisoft CD software, since students may need to refer back to specific screens in the software to answer the questions.]

1. *[LO 3.2]* In Exercise 3-2, what is the meaning of the account alert "RB"?

2. *[LO 3.2]* In Exercise 3-3, who is John Fitzwilliams's provider?

3. *[LO 3.3]* In Exercise 3-4, which dialog box contains the Go ___ Weeks option that is used to schedule a follow-up appointment?

4. *[LO 3.4]* In Exercise 3-5, what is the date and time of Maritza Ramos's appointment?

5. *[LO 3.4]* In Exercise 3-6, what is the date and time of Randall Klein's appointment?

6. *[LO 3.6]* In Exercise 3-8, what are the dates of Jo Wong's appointments?

7. *[LO 3.7]* In Exercise 3-9, Janine Bell's appointment had to be rescheduled. Is anyone scheduled in the time slot following her 4:00 p.m. appointment?

8. *[LO 3.9]* In Exercise 3-11, what appears in the appointment time slot once the patient is checked in?

9. *[LO 3.11]* In Exercise 3-13, what is selected in the Recall Status section of the Patient Recall dialog box?

10. *[LO 3.12]* In Exercise 3-14, what is option is selected in the Frequency column of the Repeat Change dialog box?

11. *[LO 3.13]* In Exercise 3-15, what is listed in the 9:45 a.m. time slot for Dr. Katherine Yan on October 1, 2018?

12. *[LO 3.2]* Today is Friday, August 31, 2018. Dr. Katherine Yan asks you to find out when Sarah Fitzwilliams is coming in for her next appointment. When is the appointment?

13. *[LO 3.4]* Today is November 12, 2018. Samuel Bell would like an appointment with Dr. John Rudner as soon as possible for a thirty-minute appointment between 10:00 a.m. and 12:00 p.m. When is the next available time slot that meets these requirements?

chapter 3 summary

LEARNING OUTCOMES	CONCEPTS TO REVIEW
3.1 List the four main areas of the Office Hours window.	1. Provider selection box 2. Provider's daily schedule 3. Office Hours calendar 4. Office Hours patient information
3.2 Demonstrate how to enter an appointment.	1. Start Office Hours. 2. Select the appropriate provider in the Provider box. 3. Change the date on the calendar to the desired date. 4. Locate the desired time slot in the schedule. 5. Double click in the time slot. 6. Select the patient in the Chart box. 7. Complete the other fields as required, being sure to enter the appointment length in the Length box. 8. When you are finished entering information, click the Save button.
3.3 Demonstrate how to schedule a follow-up appointment.	1. Verify that the correct provider is selected in the Provider box. 2. Click the Go to a Date shortcut button. 3. Confirm the entry in the Date From box. 4. Make an entry in the Go ___ Days, Weeks, Months, or Years boxes. 5. Click the Go button. 6. The calendar changes to the specified date. 7. Double click in the time slot. 8. Select the patient in the Chart box. 9. Complete the other fields as required, being sure to enter the appointment length in the Length box. 10. When you are finished entering information, click the Save button.
3.4 Demonstrate how to search for an available time slot.	1. Verify that the correct provider is selected in the Provider box. 2. Click the Search Open Time Slot button. 3. Make appropriate entries in the Length, Start Time, End Time, and Day of Week boxes. 4. Click the Search button. 5. The calendar displays the first available time slot that matches the specifications. 6. Double click in the time slot. 7. Select the patient in the Chart box. 8. Complete the other fields as required, being sure to enter the appointment length in the Length box. 9. When you are finished entering information, click the Save button.

LEARNING OUTCOMES	CONCEPTS TO REVIEW
3.5 Demonstrate how to book an appointment for a new patient.	1. Verify that the correct provider is selected in the Provider box. 2. Locate the desired date and time for the appointment. 3. Double click in the desired time slot. 4. Click in the blank box to the right of the Chart box, and enter the patient's name (last name, first name). Press the Tab key to move the cursor to the Home Phone box. 5. Enter the patient's home phone. Press Tab to go to the Cell Phone box. 6. Finish entering information in the boxes, as appropriate. 7. Click the Save button.
3.6 Demonstrate how to book repeating appointments.	1. Click the desired provider on the Provider drop-down list. 2. Change the calendar to the appropriate date. 3. Double click in the desired time slot. The New Appointment Entry dialog box is displayed. 4. Select the patient in the Chart box. 5. Finish completing the boxes in the dialog box. 6. Click the Change button to schedule the repeating appointments. The Repeat Change dialog box appears. 7. Make a selection in the Frequency column. 8. Make entries in the additional boxes that appear. (These will vary depending on whether you selected Daily, Weekly, Monthly, or Yearly in the Frequency column.) 9. Click the arrow for the drop-down list in the End on box. A calendar pops up. Set the calendar to the date when the repeating appointment should stop. 10. Click the OK button. 11. Check the calendar to be sure the repeating appointments are correct.
3.7 Demonstrate how to reschedule and cancel an appointment.	1. Locate the appointment that needs to be changed. Make sure the appointment slot is visible on the provider's daily schedule. 2. Click on the existing time-slot box. A black border surrounds the slot to indicate that it is selected. 3. Click Cut on the Edit menu. The appointment disappears from the schedule. If rescheduling the appointment, continue with steps 4-6. 4. Click the date on the calendar when the appointment is to be rescheduled. 5. Click the desired time-slot box on the schedule. The slot becomes active. 6. Click Paste on the Edit menu. The patient's name appears in the new time-slot box.

LEARNING OUTCOMES	CONCEPTS TO REVIEW
3.8 Demonstrate how to verify a patient's insurance eligibility.	1. Locate the patient's appointment. 2. Right-click on the appointment to display the shortcut menu and click Eligibility Verification. The Eligibility Verification Results dialog box appears. 3. Click the Verify button. The Real-Time Eligibility Verification dialog box appears. 4. Click the Verify button. The Please Wait box appears while the system processes the request. 5. Once verification is complete, the Select the Report Format for the Eligibility Response Report dialog box is displayed. Accept the default of Standard 271 and click OK. 6. The eligibility response reports appear in the Preview window. After viewing the report, close the Preview window.
3.9 Demonstrate how to check in and check out a patient.	1. Click the desired provider on the Provider drop-down list. 2. Locate the patient's appointment on the calendar. 3. Click once to select the appointment. 4. Click the right mouse button. 5. Click Checked In on the shortcut menu. 6. To check out a patient, follow steps 1-4 and click Checked Out on the shortcut menu.
3.10 Demonstrate how to create an overdue balance report for upcoming appointments.	1. In Medisoft, select Medisoft Reports on the Reports menu. 2. In the left column titled All Folders, double click on the Plus Pack folder. The contents of the Plus Pack folder appear in the pane on the right. 3. Double click on the report titled Appointment List with Remainder Balance (Patient). The Search box appears. 4. Enter the desired dates in both Date boxes. 5. Complete the other fields if appropriate. 6. Click the OK button. 7. The report is displayed. Notice that the report has more than one page. Each page lists patients for a different provider.
3.11 Demonstrate how to create a recall list.	1. Click the Patient Recall shortcut button. The Patient Recall dialog box is displayed. 2. In the Recall Date box, enter the date the patient needs to have a follow-up appointment. Press Tab. 3. Select the patient's provider from the drop-down list in the Provider box. Press Tab. 4. Select the patient in the Chart box. 5. Enter the procedure code that corresponds to the appointment, if known. 6. Verify that the appropriate radio button is selected in the Recall Status box. 7. Click the Save button to save the entry.

LEARNING OUTCOMES	CONCEPTS TO REVIEW
3.12 Demonstrate how to enter provider breaks in the schedule.	1. Select the provider from the Provider drop-down list. 2. Change the date on the calendar to the date of the break. 3. Click once in the appropriate time slot (do not double click). 4. Click the Break Entry shortcut button. The New Break Entry dialog box appears. 5. Enter a description of the break in the Name box. 6. Confirm that the date and time are correct. 7. Make the appropriate selection in the Length box. 8. Make a selection in the Resource box. 9. If the break is for more than one day, press the Change button. The Repeat Change dialog box is displayed. 10. Complete the Repeat Change box if necessary and click OK. 11. Click the Save button to enter the break in Office Hours. 12. Verify that the break has been entered correctly.
3.13 Demonstrate how to preview and print a provider's schedule.	1. Click Appointment List on the Office Hours Reports menu. The Report Setup dialog box appears. 2. Under Print Selection, accept the default entry to preview the report on the screen before printing. 3. Click the Start button. The Data Selection box is displayed. 4. Enter the desired date in both Dates boxes. 5. Select the appropriate provider in both Providers boxes. 6. Click the OK button. The Preview Report window appears. 7. Click the Print report icon to print the report. 8. Click the Close button to close the Preview Report window.

chapter 3 review

USING TERMINOGY

Define the terms listed.

1. *[LO 3.2]* Chart number
2. *[LO 3.12]* Office Hours break
3. *[LO 3.1]* Office Hours calendar
4. *[LO 3.1]* Office Hours patient information
5. *[LO 3.1]* provider's daily schedule
6. *[LO 3.1]* provider selection box
7. *[LO 3.11]* Recall list

CHECKING YOUR UNDERSTANDING

8. *[LO 3.1]* What are the different ways of starting Office Hours?
9. *[LO 3.2]* If the Office Hours calendar shows October 6, how do you move to November 6?
10. *[LO 3.11]* How is a patient added to the Recall List?
11. *[LO 3.5]* If a patient is new and does not yet have a chart number, what is entered in the New Appointment Entry dialog box (just to the right of the Chart field)?
12. *[LO 3.7]* How is an appointment rescheduled?
13. *[LO 3.9]* How do you check in a patient in Office Hours?
14. *[LO 3.6]* How do you access the dialog box that contains the options for scheduling repeating appointments?
15. *[LO 3.2]* Suppose your office has set up Office Hours so that the default appointment length is fifteen minutes. If you need to make a one-hour appointment for a patient, in what box do you change fifteen to sixty?
16. *[LO 3.8]* You need to check insurance eligibility for a patient who is at the front desk. You locate the appointment in Office Hours. What is the next step?
17. *[LO 3.3]* If a patient is leaving the office and states that he needs to schedule a follow-up visit in one week, what shortcut button would you use?
18. *[LO 3.12]* In the New Break Entry dialog box, what are the three options for selecting providers?
19. *[LO 3.13]* What option on the Office Hours Reports menu is used to print or preview a list of appointments?
20. *[LO 3.4]* Which Office Hours dialog box would you use to locate an available appointment time for a patient who can only come in on Tuesdays and Thursdays after 4:00 p.m.?

APPLYING YOUR KNOWLEDGE

21. *[LO 3.12]* After you entered a personal break for Dr. Katherine Yan for February 24, she tells you that she gave you the wrong date. The break should be February 25. How do you correct the schedule?

22. *[LO 3.2]* A patient calls to request an appointment on a specific day next week. You determine that the appointment is for a routine checkup, not an emergency. What steps should you follow to schedule the appointment?

23. *[LO 3.2]* Why would an office switch from a paper-based system to a computer-based scheduling system? What are some advantages of a computerized scheduling system?

24. *[LO 3.11]* How could the creation of a patient recall list contribute to the financial success of the practice?

25. *[LO 3.10]* Why do medical practices check a patient's balance before the patient comes in for a scheduled appointment?

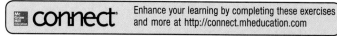

chapter 4

ENTERING PATIENT INFORMATION

Copyright ©2016 McGraw-Hill Education

key terms

established patient
guarantor
new patient

learning outcomes

When you finish this chapter, you will be able to:

4.1 Explain how patient information is organized in Medisoft.

4.2 Discuss how a new patient is added in Medisoft.

4.3 Describe how to search for a patient in Medisoft.

4.4 Describe how patient information is edited in Medisoft.

what you need to know

To use this chapter, you need to know how to:

- Start Medisoft.
- Move around the Medisoft menus.
- Use the Medisoft toolbar.
- Enter and edit data in Medisoft.
- Exit Medisoft.

4.1 HOW PATIENT INFORMATION IS ORGANIZED IN MEDISOFT®

Patient information is accessed through the Patient List dialog box. The Patient List dialog box is displayed when Patients/Guarantors and Cases is clicked on the Lists menu or when the corresponding shortcut button is clicked on the toolbar (see Figure 4-1).

Figure 4-1
Patient List Shortcut Button

The Patient List dialog box (see Figure 4-2) is divided into two primary sections. The left side of the window displays information about patients, and the right side of the window contains information about cases. Cases are covered in Chapter 5.

On the upper-right side of the Patient List dialog box, there are two radio buttons: Patient and Case. When the Patient radio button is clicked, the left side of the window becomes active. Correspondingly, when the Case radio button is clicked, the right side of the window becomes active. The command buttons at the bottom of the dialog box vary, depending on which side of the window is active. When the Patient window is active, the command buttons at the bottom of the screen include Edit Patient, New Patient, Delete Patient, Print Grid, Quick Entry, View Statements, and Close.

The Patient window contains the following fields: Chart Number, Name, Date of Birth, Social Security Number, Patient ID #2, Patient Type, Phone 1, Provider, Last Name, Billing Code, and Patient Indicator. There is not enough room in the Patient window to display all this information, so only a portion is visible at one time. The additional patient information can be viewed by using the scroll bar, maximizing the dialog box, or resizing the Patient area of the dialog box (see Figure 4-3).

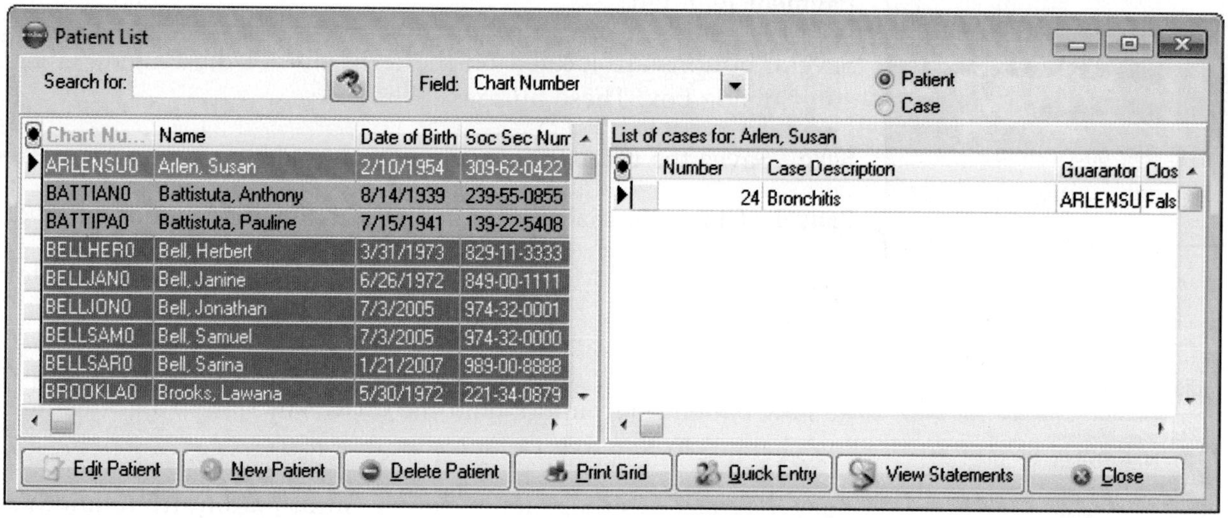

OPENING A PATIENT OR CASE

The quickest way to open a patient or case is to double click on the line associated with a patient or case.

Figure 4-2 Patient List Dialog Box

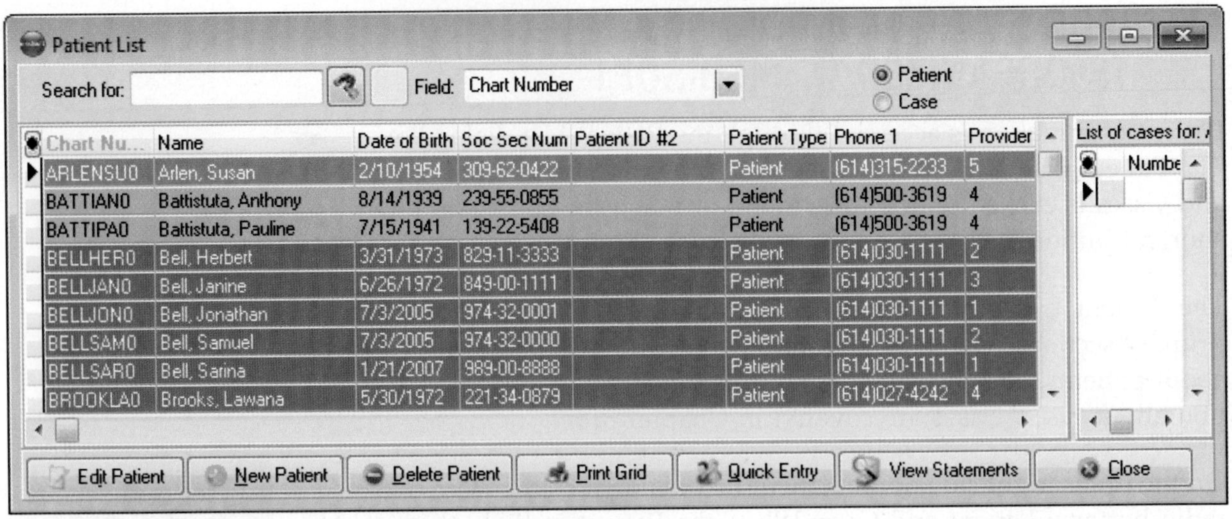

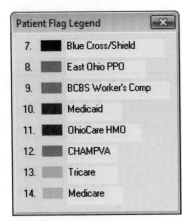

Figure 4-3 Patient Window Expanded to Show Additional Columns

Information in the Patient window is color-coded. In the exercises in this text/workbook, the patient identification color codes shown in Figure 4-4 are assigned to represent the patient's insurance carrier.

4.2 ENTERING NEW PATIENT INFORMATION

A **new patient** is a patient who has not received services from the same provider or a provider of the same specialty or subspecialty within the same practice for a period of three years. An **established patient** is a patient who has been seen by a provider in the practice in the same specialty or subspecialty within three years.

Information on a new patient is entered in Medisoft by clicking the New Patient button at the bottom of the Patient List dialog box (see Figure 4-5). This action opens the Patient/Guarantor dialog box (see Figure 4-6). The Patient/Guarantor dialog box contains three tabs: the Name, Address tab, the Other Information tab, and the Payment Plan tab.

Several buttons are located on the right side of the Patient/Guarantor dialog box. These buttons include:

Save   Saves the information entered in the dialog box.

Cancel   Closes the dialog box and discards any information entered.

Help   Displays the Medisoft help window for Patient/Guarantor Entry.

Set Default   Sets the information in this window as the default for all new patients. (To undo, hold the CTRL key down, and this button changes to Remove Default.)

Copy Address   Copies demographic information from another patient or guarantor entry.

new patient a patient who has not received services from the same provider or a provider of the same specialty or subspecialty within the same practice for a period of three years.

established patient a patient who has been seen by a provider in the practice in the same specialty or subspecialty within three years.

Figure 4-4 Color Legend for Patient List Window

Figure 4-5 New Patient Button

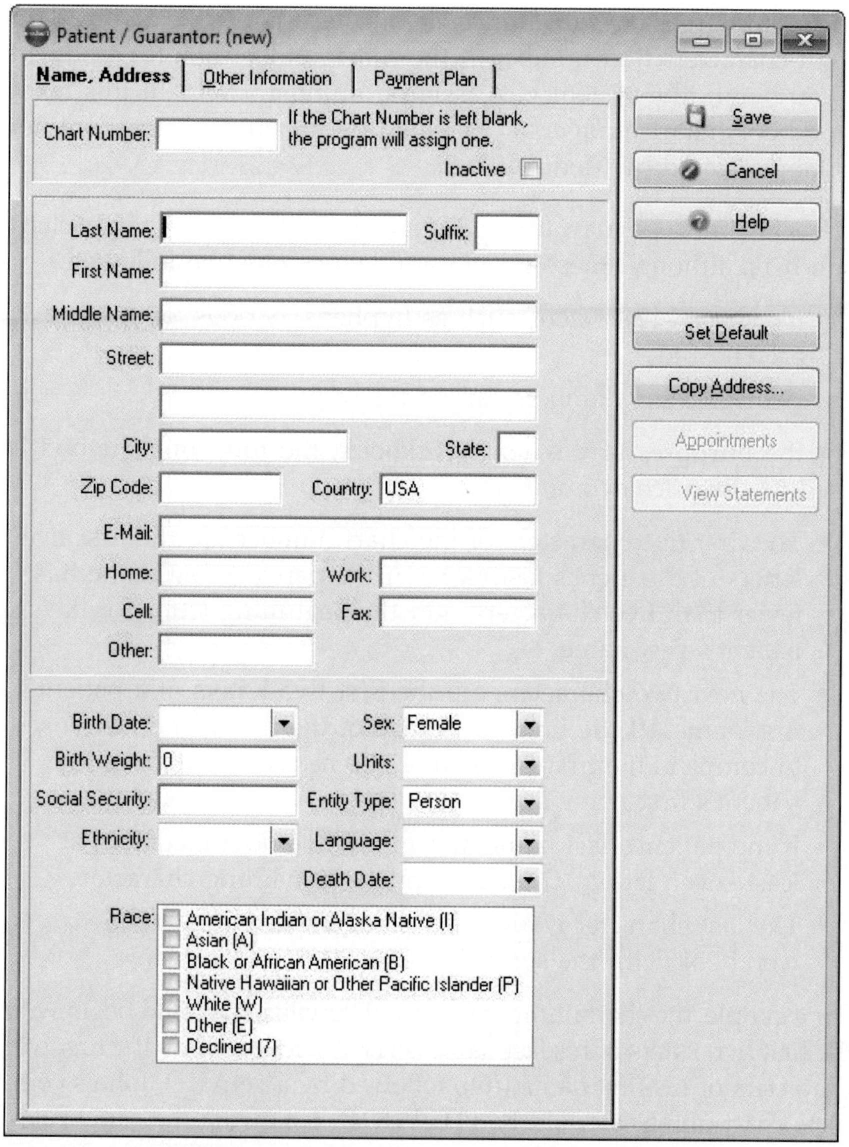

Figure 4-6 Patient/Guarantor Dialog Box with Name, Address Tab Active

Appointments Opens a window with a list of scheduled appointments for the patient. (The Appointments button is grayed and cannot be selected if a patient has no appointments scheduled.)

View Statements This button is used to access the optional BillFlash electronic statement program.

NAME, ADDRESS TAB

The Name, Address tab is where basic patient information is entered (see Figure 4-6).

Chart Number

In Medisoft, a chart number links together all the information about a patient that is stored in the different databases, such as name, address, charges, and insurance claims. Each patient is assigned an eight-character chart number. If the chart number box for a patient is left blank, the system will assign a number. (*Note:* In this text/workbook, chart numbers are created by the student; they are not to be generated by Medisoft.)

Medical practices may use different methods for assigning chart numbers, although these general guidelines must be followed:

- No special characters, such as hyphens, periods, or spaces, are allowed.
- No two chart numbers can be the same.

For the purposes of this text/workbook, the following method is used to assign chart numbers:

- The first five characters of the chart number are the first five letters of a patient's last name. If the patient's last name has fewer than five characters, add the beginning letters of the patient's first name.
- The next two characters are the first two letters of a patient's first name. (If the first two letters of the first name were used to complete the first five letters, the next two letters of the patient's first name are used.)
- If the patient's last name and first name do not contain at least seven letters, use zeros for the remaining characters.
- The last character is always a zero, displayed in this text/workbook with the symbol "Ø."

For example, the chart number for John Fitzwilliams would begin with the first five letters of his last name (FITZW), followed by the first two characters of his first name (JO), followed by a zero (Ø). John's complete chart number would be FITZWJOØ. Following the same rules, his daughter Sarah would have a chart number of FITZWSAØ.

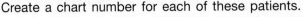

EXERCISE 4-1 CHART NUMBERS

Create a chart number for each of these patients.

Albert Wong

Jessica Sypkowski

John James

☑ **You have completed Exercise 4-1.**

Personal Data

In addition to the chart number, personal information about a patient is entered in the Name, Address tab.

Name, Address, Phone Numbers, E-Mail   Medisoft provides fields for name and address as well as a number of fields for contact methods. There are boxes for e-mail address, home phone, work phone, cell phone, fax, and other. Phone and fax numbers must be entered without parentheses or hyphens.

Birth Date   The patient's birth date is entered in the Birth Date box using the MMDDCCYY format.

Sex   This drop-down list contains choices for the patient's gender: male, female, or unknown.

Birth Weight   If the patient is a newborn, the birth weight is entered in this field.

Units   This field indicates whether the birth weight is listed in pounds or grams.

Social Security   The nine-digit Social Security number is entered without hyphens; Medisoft automatically adds hyphens.

Entity Type   This field is used for the direct transmission of electronic claims to an insurance carrier. The options in this field are person and non-person.

The Affordable Care Act (ACA) requires new standards to more consistently measure a patient's race, ethnicity, sex, and primary language. This data will be used to identify health differences in health status and to direct interventions designed to improve health disparities. This information is usually requested on a practice's patient information form, and completion of this section is always optional.

Ethnicity   This field indicates the patient's ethnicity.

Language   This field lists the patient's primary language—the language that the patient would like to use to communicate with the healthcare provider.

Race   This Race field is used to record the patient's race.

Death Date   If the patient is deceased, enter the death date by clicking in the Death Date field and entering the date, or by selecting the date from the pop-up calendar.

USING COPY ADDRESS

The Copy Address button saves time when entering patients with the same address, such as family members. Clicking on the Copy Address button provides an option to copy demographic information from a patient already in the database.

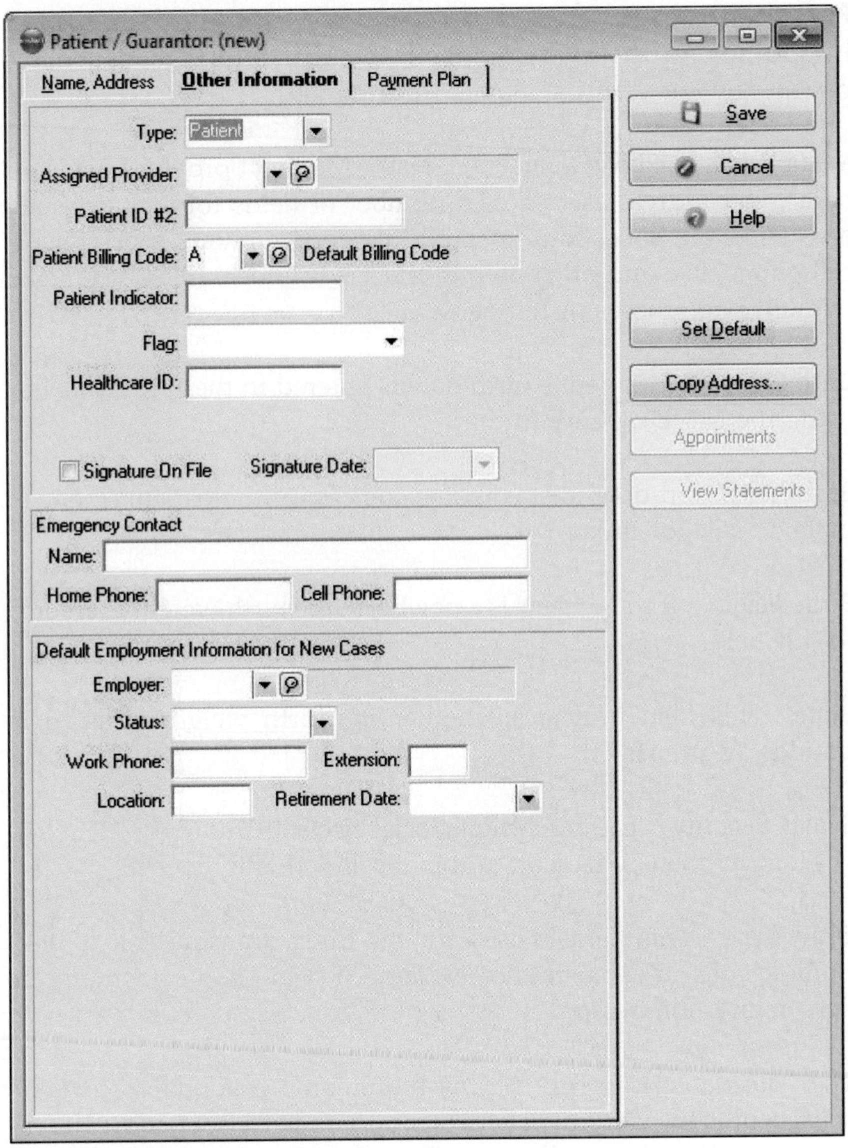

Figure 4-7　Other Information Tab

OTHER INFORMATION TAB

The Other Information tab within the Patient/Guarantor dialog box contains facts about a patient's employment and other miscellaneous information (see Figure 4-7).

Type　The Type drop-down list is used for billing purposes to designate whether an individual is a patient or guarantor. A patient is an individual who is a patient of the practice, whether or not he or she is also the insurance policyholder. The term **guarantor** refers to an individual who may not be a patient of the practice but who is financially responsible for a patient account. For example, if the insurance policy of a parent who is not a patient provides coverage for a child who is a patient, the parent is the guarantor. In this case,

guarantor an individual who may not be a patient of the practice, but who is financially responsible for a patient account.

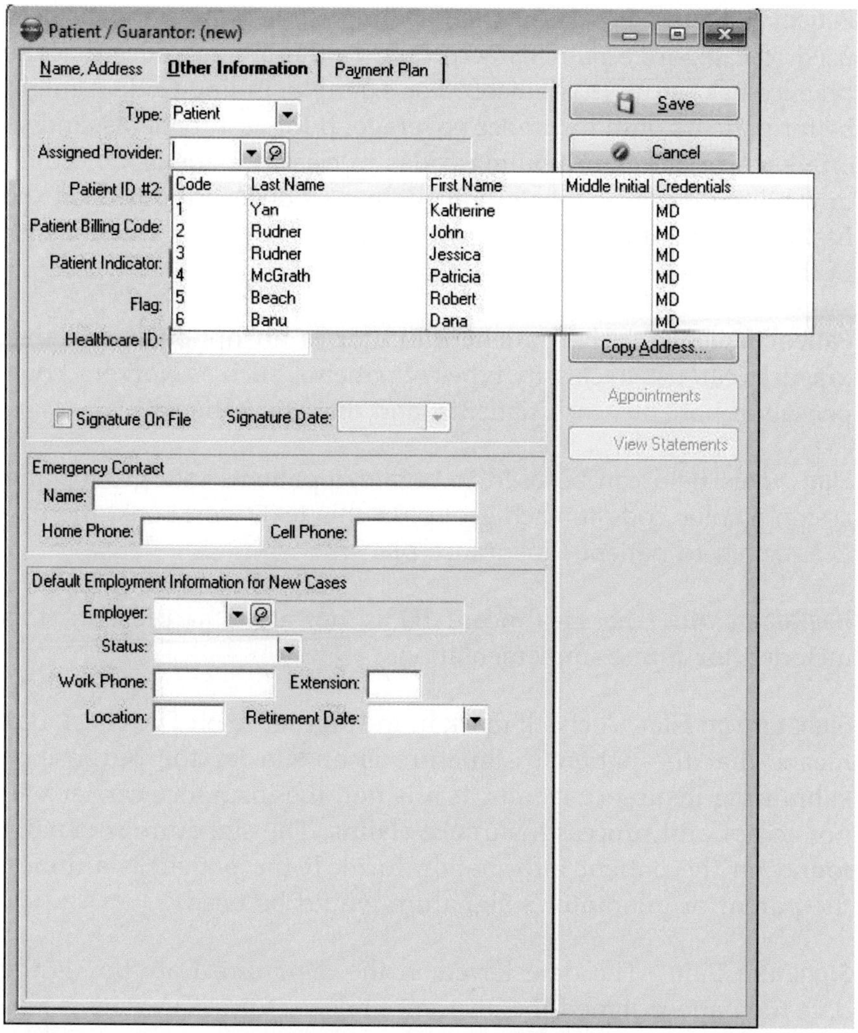

Figure 4-8 Other Information Tab with Assigned Provider Drop-down List Displayed

the guarantor (the parent) is entered in Medisoft first, and then the patient (the child) is entered.

Information about the patient is always entered in Medisoft in the Name/Address tab. When the patient is not the policyholder, information about the guarantor must also be entered in Medisoft for insurance claims to be processed. This information is collected from the patient information or patient update form.

Assigned Provider   The Assigned Provider drop-down list contains codes assigned to the doctors in the practice (see Figure 4-8). The code for the specific doctor providing care to this patient is selected.

Patient ID #2   The Patient ID #2 box is used by some medical practices as a second identification system in addition to chart numbers.

Patient Billing Code   The Patient Billing Code is an optional field used to categorize patients according to the billing codes that the practice has set up in Medisoft. For example, Billing Code A might be for patients with insurance coverage, B for cash patients, and so on. Some practices use billing codes to classify patients according to a billing cycle—patients with Billing Code A are billed on the first of the month, and those with Billing Code B on the fifteenth of the month.

Patient Indicator   The Patient Indicator is an optional field that practices can use to classify types of patients, such as workers' compensation patients, cash patients, and diabetic patients.

Flag   This field can be used to organize patients into groups and assign a color code to each group. In this text/workbook, the flag is assigned to patients' insurance plans.

Healthcare ID   The Healthcare ID is not used at present; it is included for future implementation.

Signature on File   A check mark in the Signature on File check box means that the patient's signature is on file for the purpose of submitting insurance claims. If it is not, the insurance carrier will not accept and process insurance claims. The signature is usually found on the patient information form. If the patient is a minor, the parent or guarantor's signature would be used.

Signature Date   The date keyed in the Signature Date box is the date the patient signed the insurance release form. The date is also found on the patient information form.

Emergency Contact   Information about how to contact someone in case of a patient emergency is entered in these fields.

Employer   The code for the patient's employer is selected from the drop-down list of employers in the database (see Figure 4-9). If the patient's employer is not in the database, this information must be entered before the code can be selected. (This process is described later in the chapter.)

Status   The Status drop-down list displays the following choices for the patient's employment status: Not employed, Full time, Part time, Retired, and Unknown.

Work Phone and Extension   Work phone numbers should be entered without parentheses or hyphens.

Location   Some companies have multiple locations. If the patient supplies information on the specific company location, it is entered in this box.

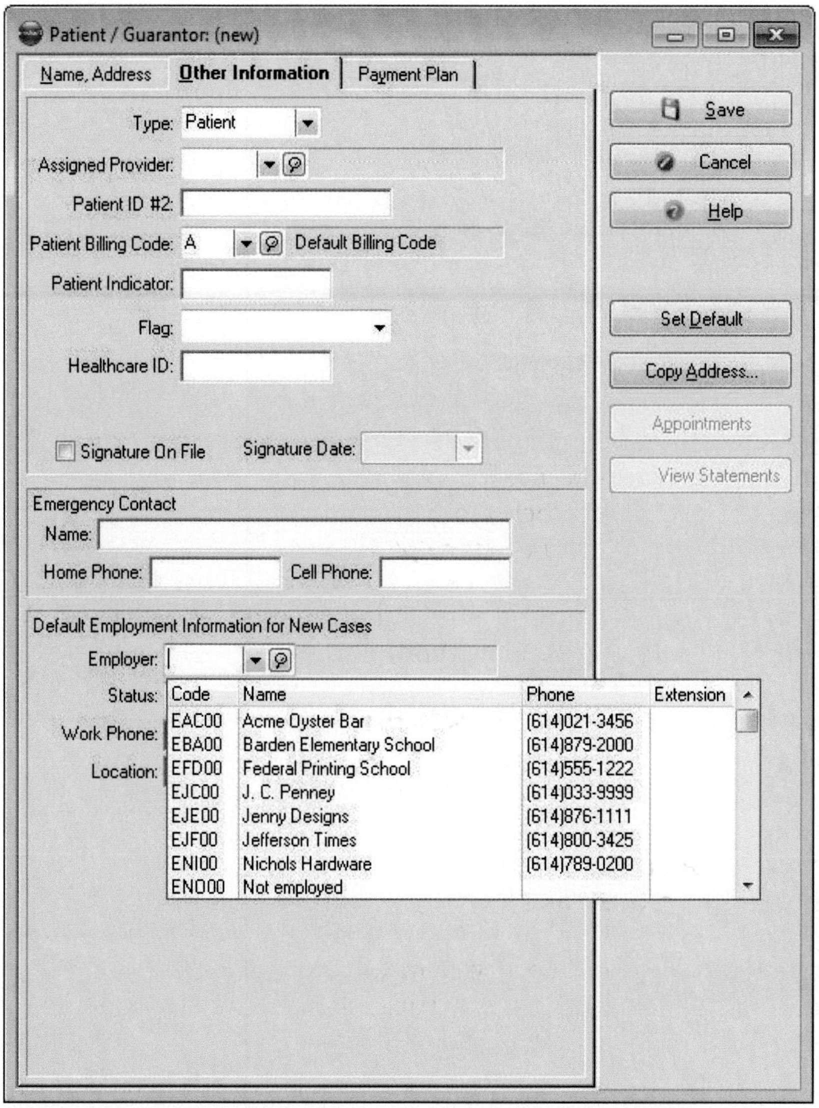

Figure 4-9 Other Information Tab with Employer Drop-down List Displayed

Retirement Date The Retirement Date box is filled in only if the patient is already retired. Retirement dates should be entered in the MMDDCCYY format.

When all of the fields in the Name, Address tab and the Other Information tab have been filled in, entries should be checked for accuracy. If any information needs to be corrected, it can easily be changed. Once the information has been checked and necessary corrections made, it is saved by clicking the Save button.

PAYMENT PLAN TAB

The Payment Plan tab is used when a patient's account is overdue and a payment plan has been created to pay the patient's account (see Figure 4-10).

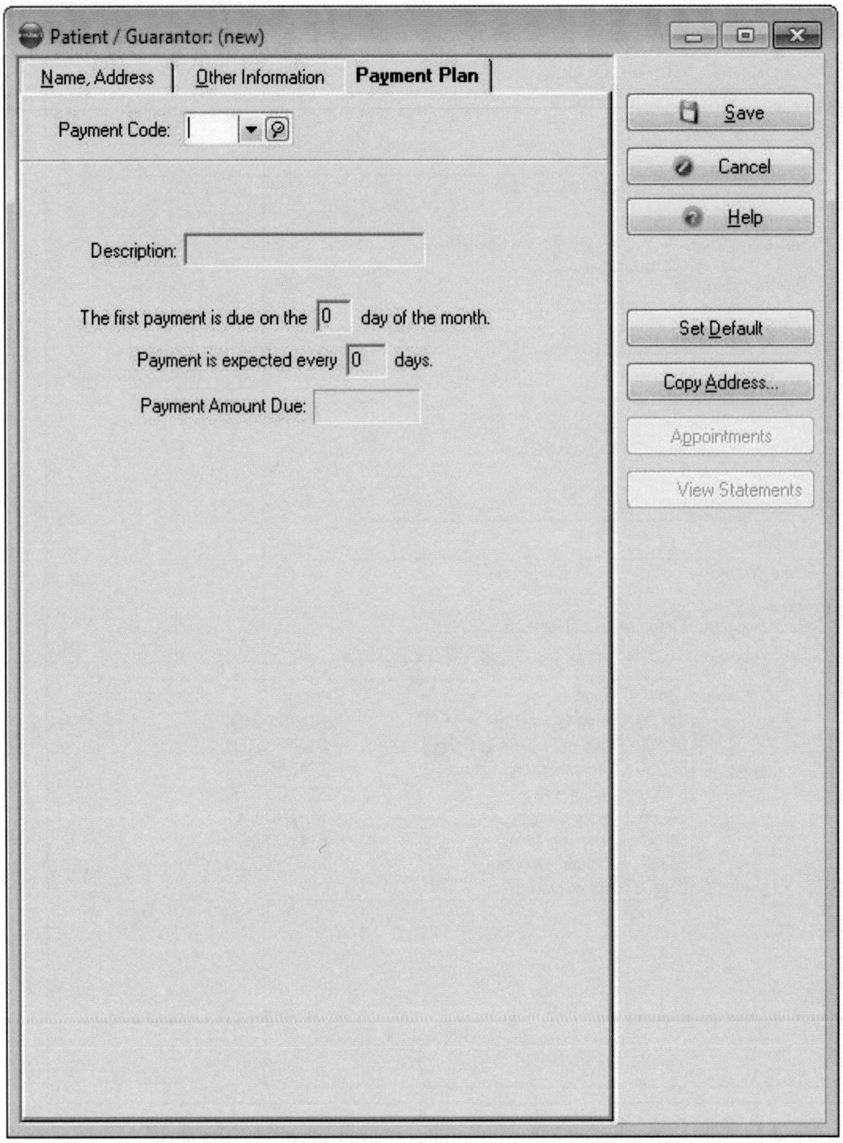

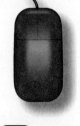

Figure 4-10 **Payment Plan Tab**

EXERCISE 4-2 ADDING A NEW PATIENT

Connect users: go to http://connect.mheducation.com to complete this exercise! Some steps may differ from what is listed here, so be sure to refer to the steps listed in Demo and Practice Modes for guidance.

connect

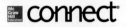

Using Source Document 1 (located in Part 4 of this book), complete the Patient/Guarantor dialog box for Hiro Tanaka, a new patient of Dr. Yan.

1. Start Medisoft by clicking the Start button and selecting All Programs, Medisoft, Medisoft Advanced.
2. On the Lists menu, click Patients/Guarantors and Cases, or click the corresponding shortcut button on the toolbar.
3. Scroll down the list of patients to make sure Hiro Tanaka is not already in the patient database.
4. Click the New Patient button.

5. Create a chart number for this patient. Remember, in this text/workbook, the chart number should be the first five letters of the patient's last name, followed by the first two letters of the patient's first name, followed by a Ø. Click the Chart Number box, and enter the chart number. *Note:* You do not need to enter the chart number in capital letters; the program automatically capitalizes your entry. Press the Tab key twice to advance to the Last Name field.

6. Enter the patient's last name, first name, etc. Fill in the rest of the boxes for which you have data on the Name, Address tab, pressing the Tab key to move from box to box. Check your work against Figure 4-11.

7. Click the Other Information tab. Be sure to select an Assigned Provider (Dr. Yan is Tanaka's assigned provider) so the exercises in this chapter will work.

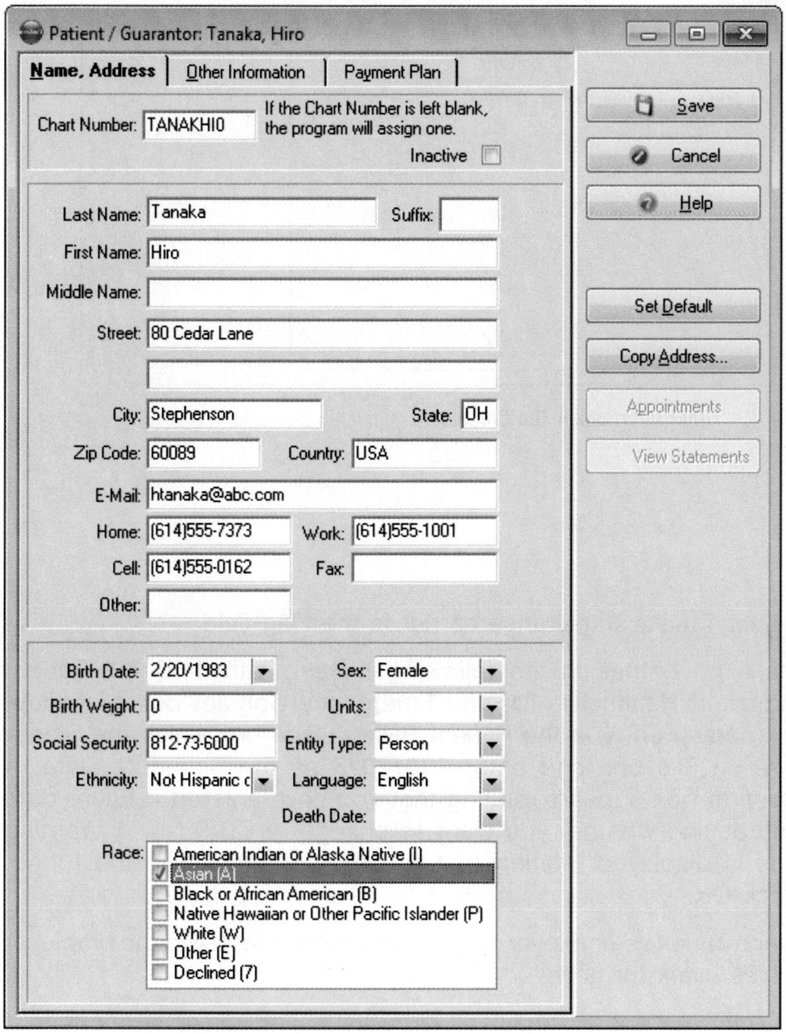

Figure 4-11   Name, Address Tab Completed

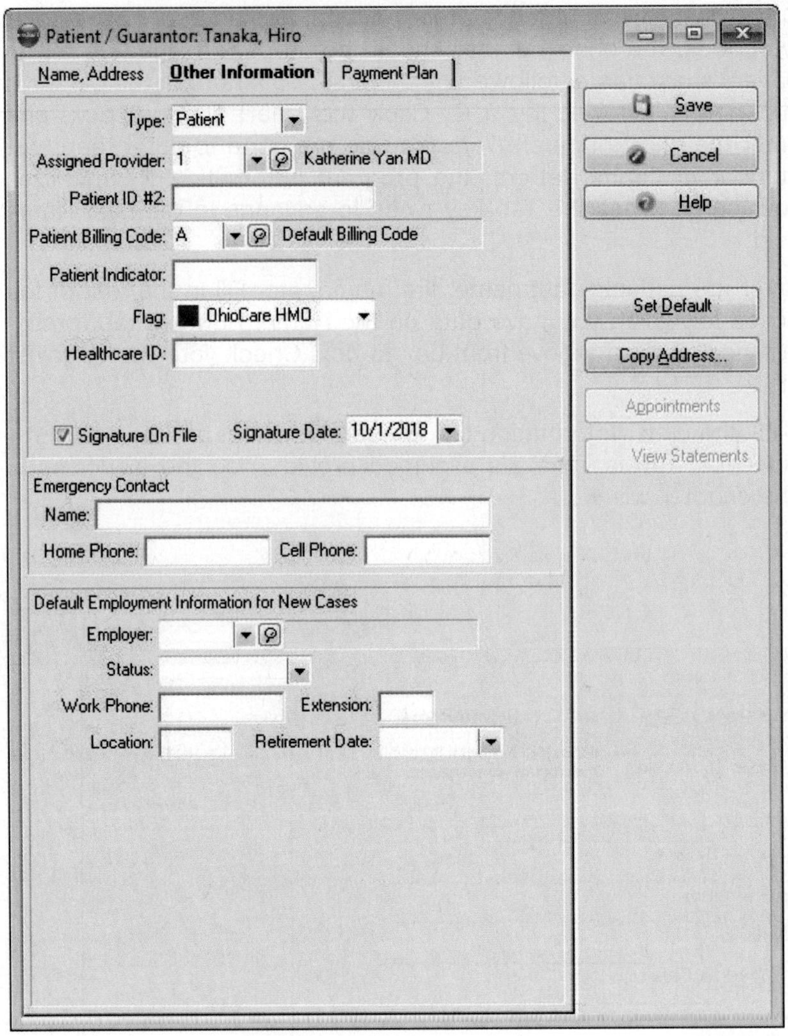

Figure 4-12   Other Information Tab Completed

8. Select Tanaka's insurance carrier in the Flag field.

9. Make no entries in the following boxes: Patient ID #2, Patient Indicator, Healthcare ID, and Emergency Contact boxes. Accept the default entry in the Patient Billing Code box. Click the Signature on File box and enter *10012018* as the Signature Date. A Confirm box appears, stating that you have entered a future date and asking whether you want to change it. Click No. A Warning box is displayed, stating that the date entered is in the future. Click OK.

10. Since Tanaka's employer is not in the database, leave the employer boxes blank for now.

11. Check your entries against Figure 4-12, and make corrections if necessary.

12. Click the Save button to save the data on Tanaka.

13. Verify that Tanaka has been added to the list in the Patient List dialog box.

14. Close the Patient List dialog box.

 You have completed Exercise 4-2.

ADDING AN EMPLOYER TO THE ADDRESS LIST

If the patient's employer does not appear on the Employer drop-down list in the Other Information tab, it must be entered using the Address feature. To enter an address, click Addresses on the Lists menu, which displays the Address List dialog box (see Figure 4-13).

Clicking the New button at the bottom of the Address List dialog box displays the Address dialog box (see Figure 4-14).

The Address dialog box contains the following boxes.

Code   The code for an employer should begin with the letter *E* to indicate that this is an employer. Codes can be a combination of letters and numbers up to a maximum of five characters. If a code is not assigned, the system will assign one.

Name and Address   The employer's name is entered in the Name box. This field allows up to thirty characters. The employer's street, city, state (two characters only), and ZIP code are entered in the boxes provided.

Type   The Type drop-down list displays a list of kinds of addresses: Attorney, Employer, Miscellaneous, and Referral Source. For example, when the address being entered is that of an employer, "Employer" is selected.

Code	Name	Phone	Type	Extension
EAC00	Acme Oyster Bar	(614)021-3456	Employer	
EBA00	Barden Elementary School	(614)879-2000	Employer	
EFD00	Federal Printing School	(614)555-1222	Employer	
EJC00	J. C. Penney	(614)033-9999	Employer	
EJE00	Jenny Designs	(614)876-1111	Employer	
EJF00	Jefferson Times	(614)800-3425	Employer	
ENI00	Nichols Hardware	(614)789-0200	Employer	
ENO00	Not employed		Employer	
ERE00	Retired		Employer	
ESA00	Sara's Dresses	(614)027-2000	Employer	

Figure 4-13   **Address List Dialog Box**

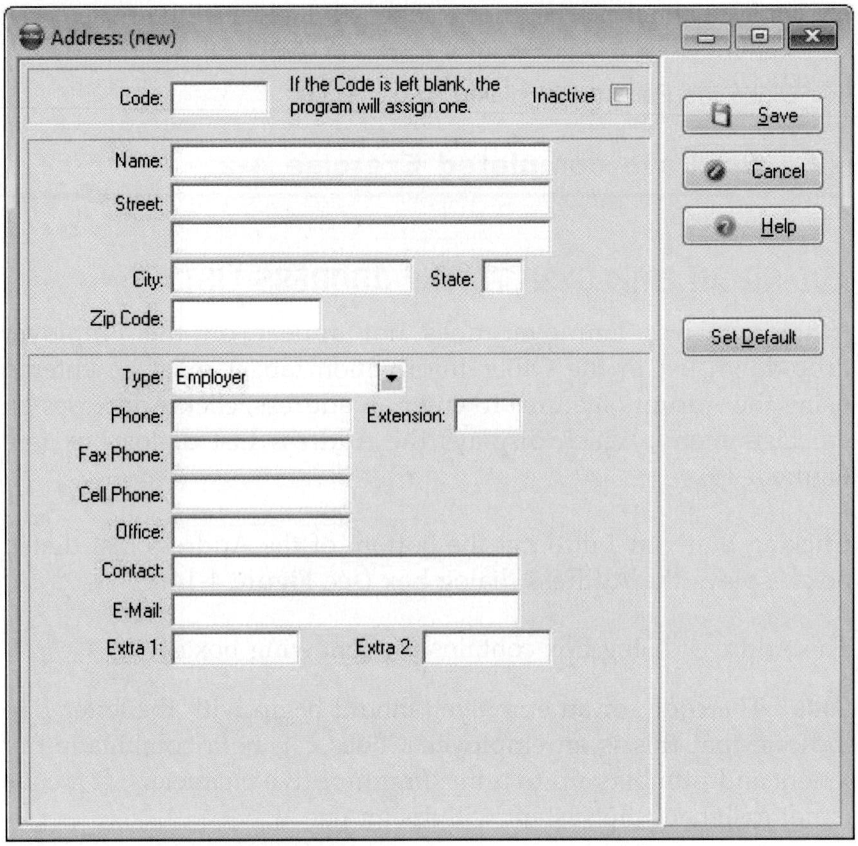

Figure 4-14 Address Dialog Box

SHORT CUT

ENTERING DATA WITH F8

Throughout Medisoft, the F8 function key serves as a shortcut for entering data. For example, clicking once in the Employer box on the Other Information tab and then pressing F8 brings up the Address dialog box, in which a new employer can be entered. The F8 key shortcut enables users to enter data in Medisoft in another part of the program without leaving the current dialog box. Once the F8 key is pressed, the dialog box used to enter new addresses is opened, with the Patient List and Patient/Guarantor dialog boxes still open in the background (see Figure 4-15).

Phone, Extension, Fax Phone, Cell Phone   In the Phone box, the employer's phone number is entered, without parentheses or hyphens. If there is an extension, it is entered in the Extension box. If there is a cell phone, it is entered in the Cell Phone box. The employer's fax number is entered in the Fax Phone box.

Office   This field can be used to note a particular office within an organization.

Contact   The Contact box is used to enter the name of an individual at the place of employment. If there is no contact person, the box is left blank.

E-Mail   This box provides a field for the employer's e-mail address.

Extra 1, Extra 2   The Extra 1 and Extra 2 boxes are available to keep track of additional information that needs to be recorded and stored for future reference.

When all the information on the employer has been entered, it is saved by clicking the Save button.

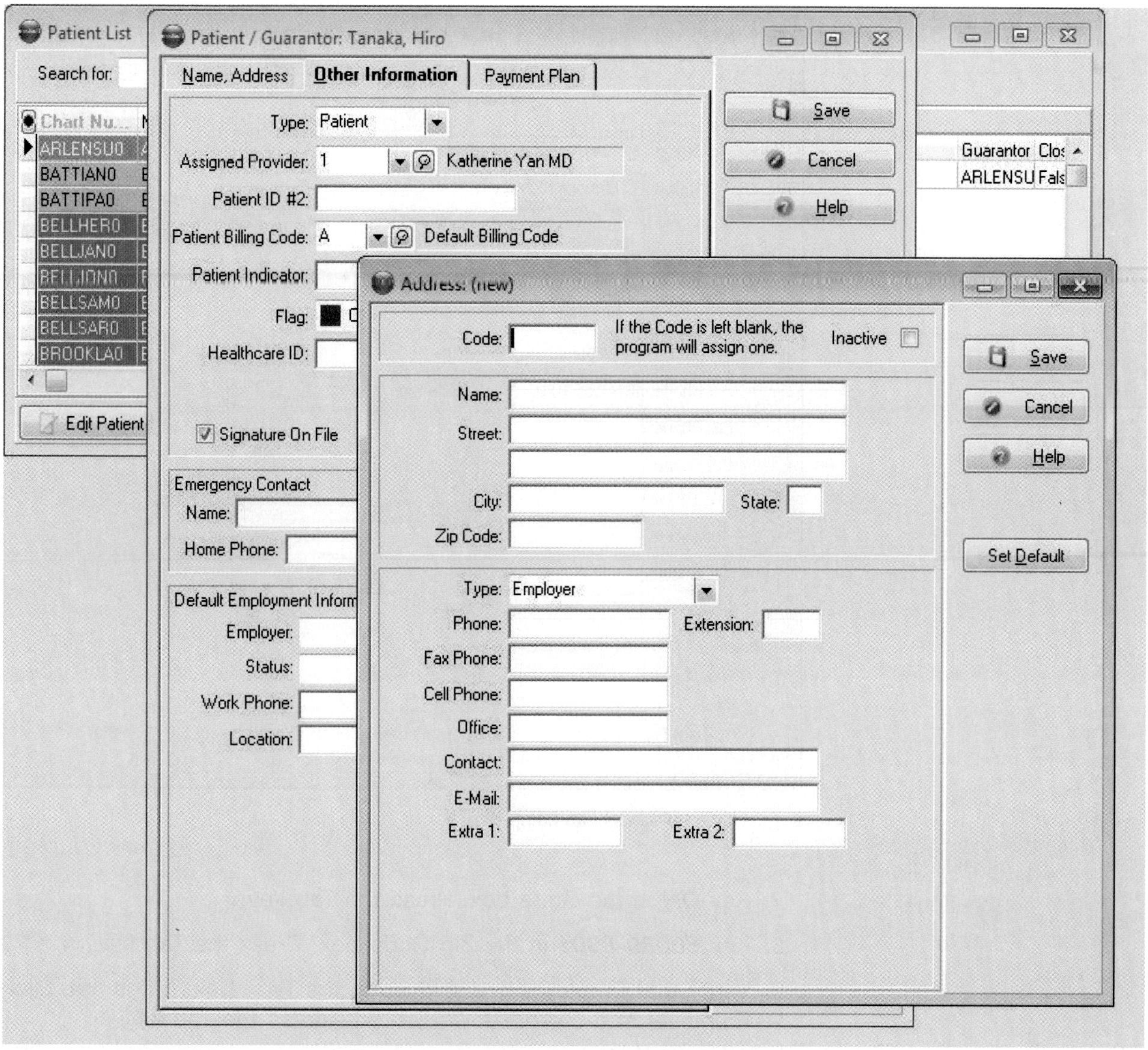

Figure 4-15 Address Dialog Box with Other Dialog Boxes Visible in Background

ADDING AN EMPLOYER EXERCISE 4-3

Practice entering information about an employer.

1. Click Addresses on the Lists menu. The Address List dialog box is displayed.

2. Click the New button at the bottom of the dialog box. The Address dialog box is displayed.

3. In the Code box, key **EMCØØ** for McCray Manufacturing, Inc. (*E* for employer, followed by the first two letters of the employer's name, followed by two zeros). Press the Tab key twice.

4. Key **McCray Manufacturing Inc.** in the Name box. Press the Tab key.

5. In the Street box, key **1311 Kings Highway.** Press the Tab key twice.

6. Key **Stephenson** in the City box. Press the Tab key.

Connect users: go to http://connect.mheducation.com to complete this exercise! Some steps may differ from what is listed here, so be sure to refer to the steps listed in Demo and Practice Modes for guidance.

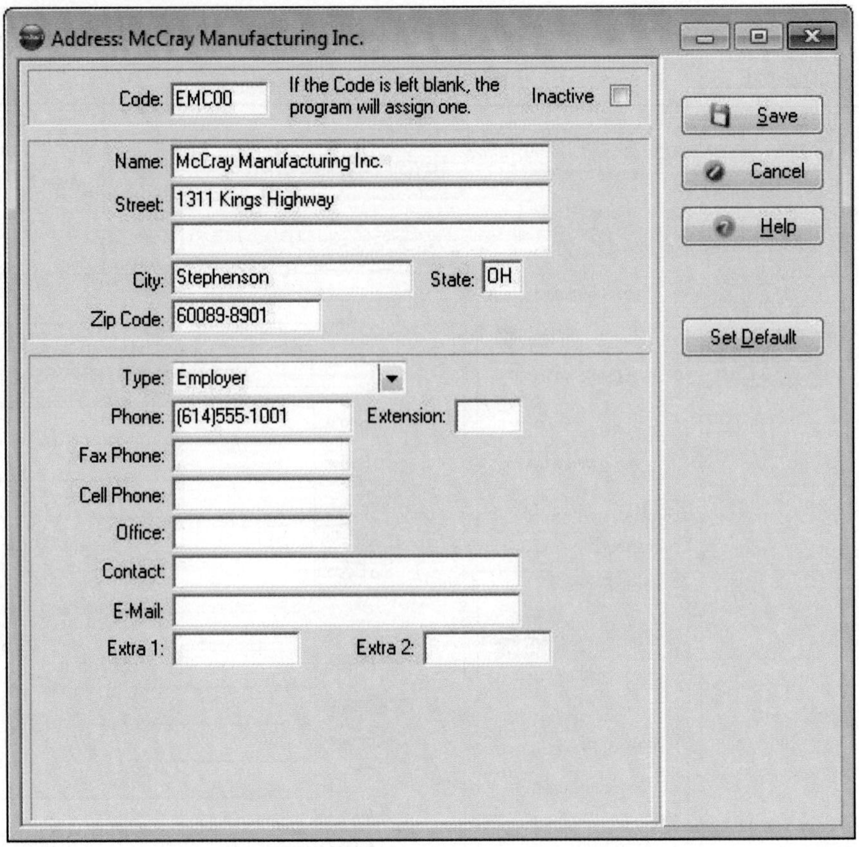

Figure 4-16 Address Tab Completed

7. Key **OH** in the State box. Press the Tab key.

8. Key **60089-8901** in the Zip Code box. Press the Tab key.

9. Verify that Employer is displayed in the Type box. If it is not, click Employer in the drop-down list, and press the Tab key.

10. Key **6145551001** in the Phone box. Press the Tab key.

11. Leave the remaining boxes blank. Check your work against Figure 4-16.

12. Click the Save button to store the information you have entered.

13. Click the Close button to exit the Address List dialog box. **CiMC**

✓ **You have completed Exercise 4-3.**

4.3 SEARCHING FOR PATIENT INFORMATION

A patient who comes to a medical practice for the first time fills out a patient information form. The information on this form needs to be entered into the Medisoft patient/guarantor database before insurance claims can be submitted. However, before information on

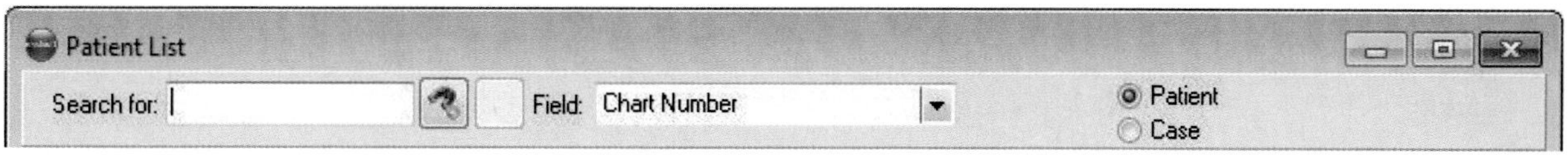

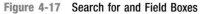

Figure 4-17   Search for and Field Boxes

a patient is entered into the system, it is important to search the database to be certain that the patient does not already exist there.

Medisoft provides two options for conducting searches: Search for and Field boxes, and Locate buttons.

SEARCH FOR AND FIELD OPTION

The Search for and Field boxes at the top of many dialog boxes provide a quick way to search for information in Medisoft (see Figure 4-17).

The Search for box contains the text that is to be searched on. The entry in the Field box controls how the list is sorted. Figure 4-18 displays the Field options in the Patient List dialog box.

When a selection is made in the Field box, the information is re-sorted by the selected criteria. For example, if Social Security Number is selected in the Field box, the entries in the List window are listed in numerical order by Social Security number, from lowest to highest (see Figure 4-19).

The Search for and Field feature is used in the following Medisoft dialog boxes: Patient List, Insurance Carrier List, Procedure/Payment/Adjustment List, Diagnosis Code List, Address List, Provider List, and Referring Provider List. Table 4-1 displays the Field box options for each of these Medisoft dialog boxes.

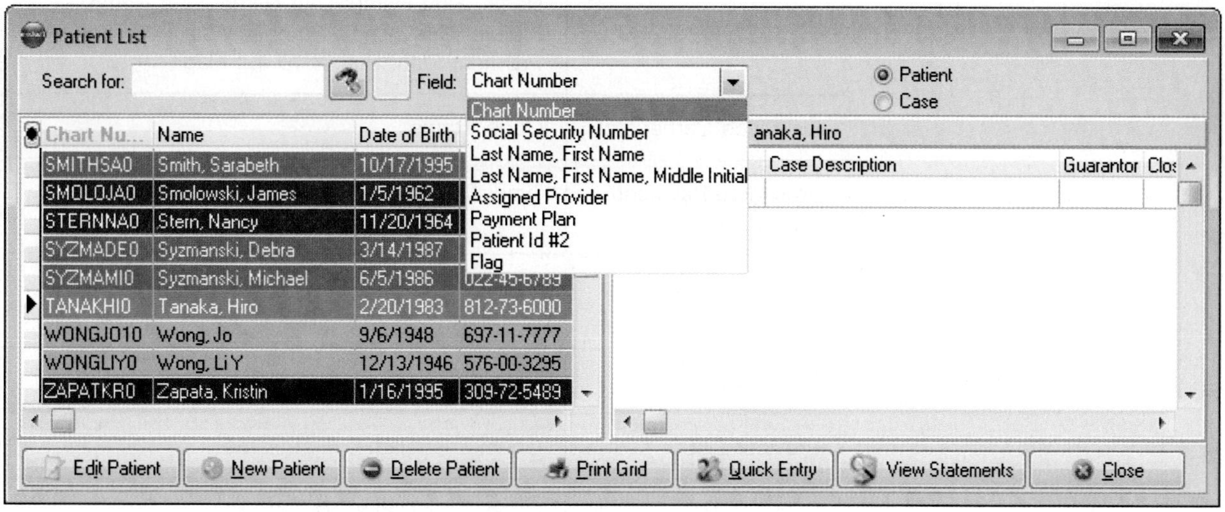

Figure 4-18   Field Options in the Patient List Dialog Box

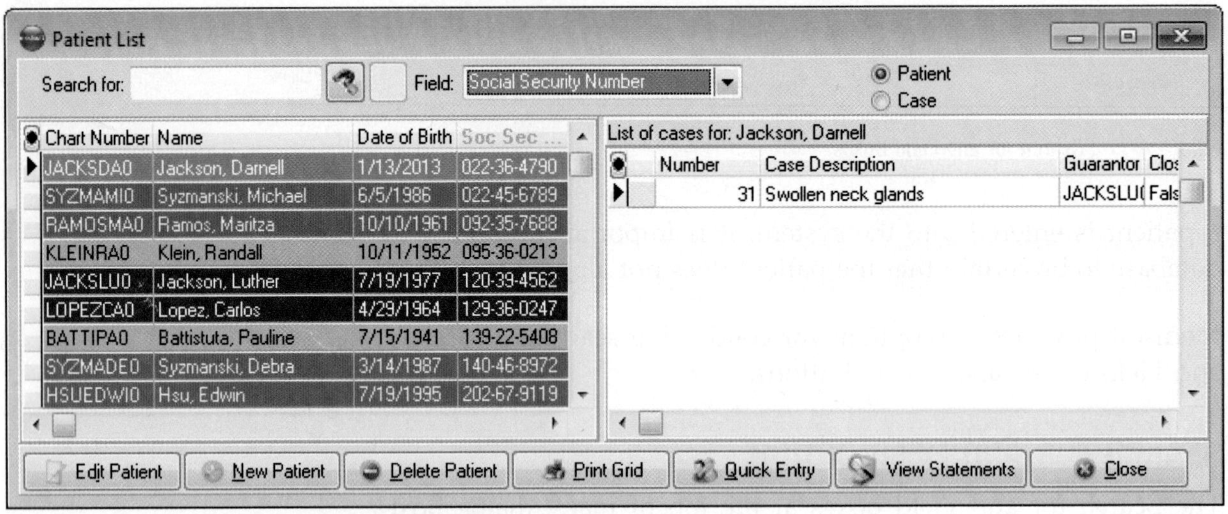

Figure 4-19 List Window Sorted by Social Security Number

After an entry is made in the Field box, the search criteria are entered in the Search field. As each letter or number is entered, the list automatically filters out records that do not match. For example, if the Field box is set to Last Name, First Name in the Patient List dialog box and *S* is entered in the Search field, the program eliminates all data from the list except patients whose last names begin with *S* (see Figure 4-20).

To restore the Patient list to its default setting (all patients listed), delete the entry in the Search for box.

TABLE 4-1	Field Options for Medisoft Searches
List Window	**Field Options**
Patient List	Chart Number; Social Security Number; Last Name, First Name; Last Name, First Name, Middle Initial, Chart Number; Assigned Provider; Payment Plan; Patient ID #2; Flag
Insurance Carrier List	Code, Name
Procedure/Payment/ Adjustment List	Type, Description, Code 1
Diagnosis Code List	Code, Description, ICD-9, ICD-9 Description, ICD-10. ICD-10 Description
Address List	Type, Code, Name
Provider List	Code; Last Name, First Name
Referring Provider List	Code; Last Name, First Name

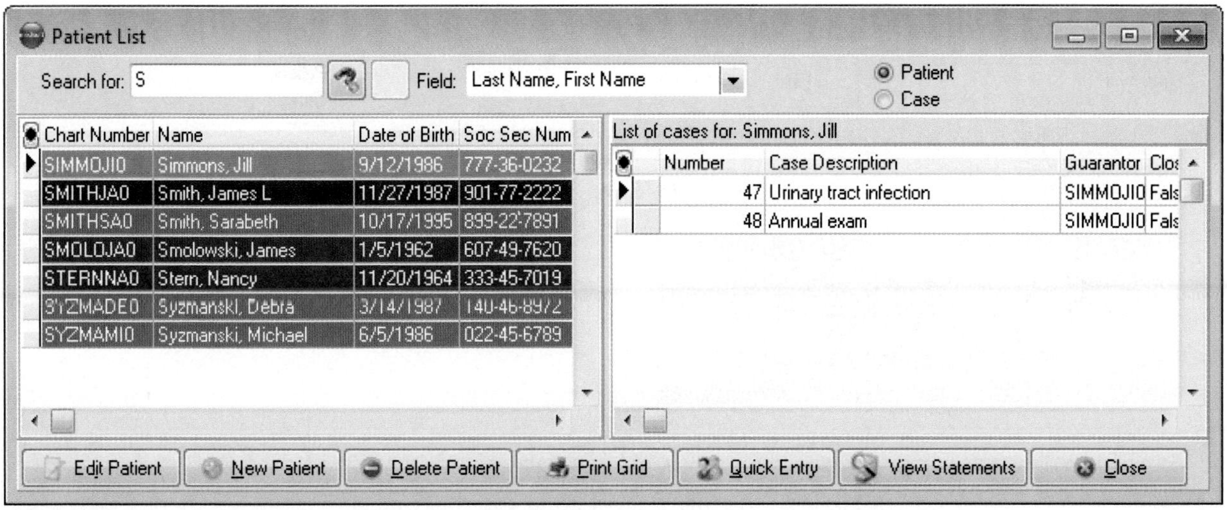

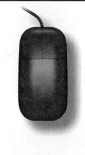

Figure 4-20 **Patient List Dialog Box with Search for Patients Whose Last Names Begin with *S***

SEARCH USING FIELD BOX

EXERCISE 4-4

Connect users: go to http://connect.mheducation.com to complete this exercise! Some steps may differ from what is listed here, so be sure to refer to the steps listed in Demo and Practice Modes for guidance.

Use the Search feature to locate information on James Smolowski.

1. On the Lists menu, click Patients/Guarantors and Cases, or click the corresponding shortcut button. The Patient List dialog box is displayed, and the cursor is blinking in the Search for box. Confirm that the entry in the Field box is Last Name, First Name. If it is not, select Last Name, First Name from the drop-down list.
2. Enter the first letter of the patient's last name. Notice that when you keyed *S*, the list window filtered the data so that only patients whose last names begin with *S* are listed. Now enter the second letter of his last name, ***m***. The list now displays only those patients whose last names begin with the letters *Sm*. Now enter the third letter, ***o***. Smolowski is the only patient whose name begins with the letters *Smo*, so he is the only patient listed.
3. To restore the Patient window so that all patients are listed, delete the letters entered in the Search for box.
4. Click the Close button to exit the Patient List dialog box.

✓ **You have completed Exercise 4-4.**

LOCATE BUTTONS OPTION

Another option for finding information in Medisoft is to use the Locate buttons (see Figure 4-21).

When a Locate button is clicked, a Locate dialog box is displayed. Figure 4-22 shows the Locate Patient dialog box.

Patient List

Search for: [ ] Field: Chart Number ▼   ◉ Patient   ○ Case

Chart Nu...	Name	Date of Birth	Soc Sec Num
ARLENSU0	Arlen, Susan	2/10/1954	309-62-0422
BATTIAN0	Battistuta, Anthony	8/14/1939	239-55-0855
BATTIPA0	Battistuta, Pauline	7/15/1941	139-22-5408
BELLHER0	Bell, Herbert	3/31/1973	829-11-3333
BELLJAN0	Bell, Janine	6/26/1972	849-00-1111
BELLJON0	Bell, Jonathan	7/3/2005	974-32-0001
BELLSAM0	Bell, Samuel	7/3/2005	974-32-0000
BELLSAR0	Bell, Sarina	1/21/2007	989-00-8888
BROOKLA0	Brooks, Lawana	5/30/1972	221-34-0879

List of cases for: Arlen, Susan

Number	Case Description	Guarantor	Clos
24	Bronchitis	ARLENSU	Fals

[Edit Patient] [New Patient] [Delete Patient] [Print Grid] [Quick Entry] [View Statements] [Close]

Figure 4-21 Locate Button Highlighted in Yellow

Locate Patient

Field Value
[ ]

Search Type
☐ Case-sensitive

○ Exact Match
○ Partial Match at Beginning
◉ Partial Match Anywhere

Fields
[Last Name ▼]

[First] [Next] [✗ Cancel]

Figure 4-22 Locate Patient Dialog Box

SHORT CUT

SEARCHING WITH LOCATE WINDOW

To make searching easier, right-click a column heading in a window that contains several columns. From the shortcut menu that appears, select Locate, or press CTRL + L. This opens a Locate window that defaults the Fields selection to the column you selected.

Field Value

The information entered in the Field Value box at the top of the window can be part of a name, birth date, payment date or amount, or assigned provider. Any combination of numbers and letters can be used.

Search Type

Case-Sensitive Use to make the search sensitive to uppercase or lowercase letters.

Exact Match Use when an entry in the Field Value box is exactly as entered in the program.

Partial Match at Beginning Use when unsure of the correct spelling or entry at the end of the word.

Partial Match Anywhere Use when unsure of the correct spelling or entry.

Fields

The Fields box provides a drop-down list from which to choose the field that contains the information that is being matched. For example, if searching for a patient by last name, select the Last Name field. The available fields are determined by the type of information you are working with. For example, if you are looking for a particular chart number, you have nineteen fields from which to choose as the basis of your search. Searching for cases gives access to up to ninety-one fields.

Once the criteria are selected, clicking the First button starts a search for the first match to the criteria. If a match is found, the Locate window is closed, and the search result is highlighted in the Search window. If a match is not found, a message is displayed.

Practice searching for and editing information on Hiro Tanaka.

Connect users: go to http://connect.mheducation.com to complete this exercise! Some steps may differ from what is listed here, so be sure to refer to the steps listed in Demo and Practice Modes for guidance.

1. Open the Patient List dialog box.

2. Click the Locate button to the right of the Search for field. The Locate Patient dialog box appears.

3. Enter **TANAKA** in the Field Value box.

4. The Case-sensitive field should not be checked.

5. The Partial Match Anywhere button should be selected.

6. The Field drop-down list should be set to Last Name.

7. Click the First button. In the left side of the Patient List dialog box, the selection triangle should be pointing at Tanaka, Hiro (see Figure 4-23).

8. Keep this Patient List window open, since you will use it to edit Hiro Tanaka's information in Exercise 4-6. **CIMO**

Chart Nu...	Name	Date of Birth	Soc Sec Num
SMITHSA0	Smith, Sarabeth	10/17/1995	899-22-7891
SMOLOJA0	Smolowski, James	1/5/1962	607-49-7620
STERNNA0	Stern, Nancy	11/20/1964	333-45-7019
SYZMADE0	Syzmanski, Debra	3/14/1987	140-46-8972
SYZMAMI0	Syzmanski, Michael	6/5/1986	022-45-6789
TANAKHI0	Tanaka, Hiro	2/20/1983	812-73-6000
WONGJO10	Wong, Jo	9/6/1948	697-11-7777
WONGLIY0	Wong, Li Y	12/13/1946	576-00-3295
ZAPATKR0	Zapata, Kristin	1/16/1995	309-72-5489

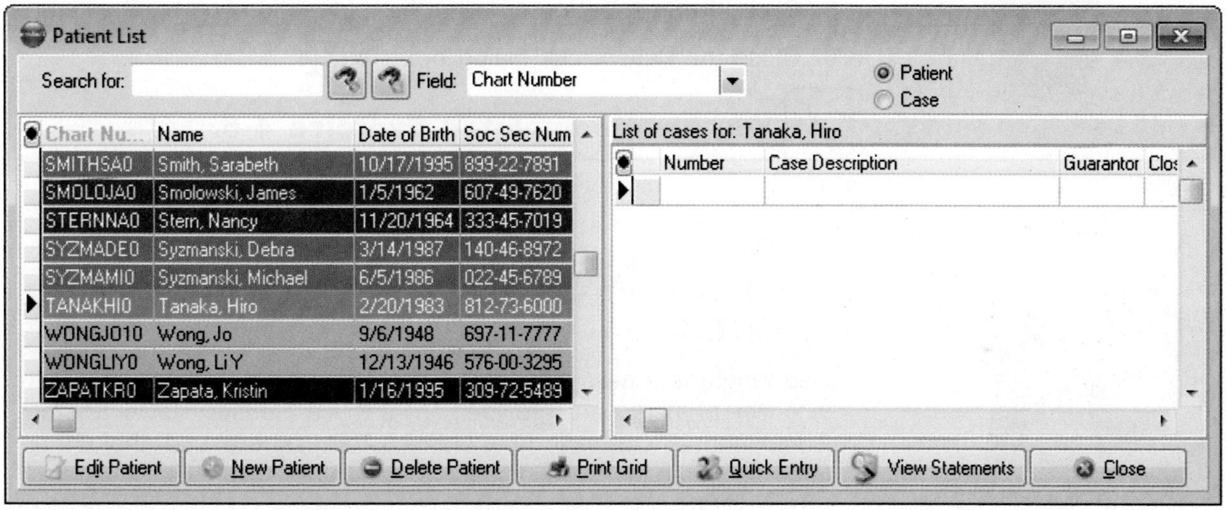

Figure 4-23 Selection Triangle Pointing to Hiro Tanaka

✓ **You have completed Exercise 4-5.**

4.4 EDITING PATIENT INFORMATION

From time to time, patients notify the practice that they have moved, changed jobs or insurance carriers, and so on. When this happens, information needs to be updated in Medisoft's patient/guarantor database.

The process of changing information about a patient is similar to that of entering information for a new patient. The Patients/Guarantors and Cases command is selected from the Lists menu. A search is usually performed to locate the chart number of the patient whose record needs to be updated. Clicking the Edit button displays the Patient/Guarantor dialog box, where changes can be made. Clicking the Save button stores the changes.

| EXERCISE 4-6 | EDITING PATIENT INFORMATION |

Practice editing information on Hiro Tanaka.

1. With the Patient List window still open to Hiro Tanaka, click the Edit Patient button.

2. Click the Other Information tab.

3. Click the down arrow button in the Employer box. Click McCray Manufacturing Inc. on the drop-down list. Notice that the program automatically enters the phone number in the Work Phone box.

4. Select Full time from the Status drop-down list.

5. Click the Save button to store the information you have entered.

6. Close the Patient List dialog box. CiMC

✓ **You have completed Exercise 4-6.**

APPLYING YOUR SKILLS
4: ENTERING A NEW PATIENT

Lisa Wright is a new patient who has just arrived for her office visit with her primary care provider, Dr. Jessica Rudner. Using Source Document 2, complete the Name, Address tab and the Other Information tab in the Patient/Guarantor dialog box. (*Note:* Not all text boxes will have entries.)

Remember to create a backup of your work before exiting Medisoft! To help you keep track of your work, name the backup file after the chapter you are working on, for example, StudentID-c4.mbk.

Transferring Patient Information

Some practice management programs and electronic health record programs are able to exchange patient information. This saves time and reduces errors, since patient information is entered in one program and then transferred to the other, eliminating the need to enter the information twice.

Patient information in Medisoft, such as that displayed in the illustration below, is transferred to an electronic health record program.

The next illustration shows a log of patient information that has been received by Medisoft from an electronic health record program.

```
20180903_10:20:09:90114FLSTDReceived messageStringMSH | ^~\&|Medisoft|Family Care
Center|Medisoft|Family Care Center|2018090301510+0000^S|NO SECURITY|ADT^A04|20|D\2.5.1|||| EVN|A04|
2018090301510+0000^S||01|PID|1|ARLENSU0|ARLENSU0|ARLENSU0|Arlen^Susan|309620422|F|W|310 Oneida
Lane^^Stephenson^OH^60089|(614)315-2233^(614)325-0111^^sarlen@abc.com|(614)202-0000
|English|F|ARLENSU0|309-62-0422||||||||||||||5|Robert Beach MD|||East Ohio PPO||||20180101
||||||||||||EBA00^||||||||Barden Elementary School|||Full time|||^^||||||(614)202-0000
|||AAAA|||||||||||U||||||||))))IN1|3||||||||||||||||||||AAAA|||||||||||||
```

BE THE DETECTIVE!

If assigned by your instructor, complete the Chart Number Video Case in Connect. Put your skills to use identifying mistakes made in Medisoft and enhance your knowledge by determining the impact of those mistakes.

[Note: These questions are designed for students using the live Medisoft CD software, since students may need to refer back to specific screens in the software to answer the questions.]

1. *[LO 4.2]* What is entered in the Chart Number field for Hiro Tanaka (Name, Address tab)?

2. *[LO 4.3]* Which patient is found as a result of the search in Exercise 4-4?

3. *[LO 4.3]* Which patient is found as a result of the search in Exercise 4-5?

4. *[LO 4.4]* What is the entry in the Employer field for Hiro Tanaka (Other Information tab)?

5. *[LO 4.2]* What is the entry in the Signature Date box for Hiro Tanaka (Other Information tab)?

6. *[LO 4.2]* What is entered in the Chart Number field for Lisa Wright (Name, Address tab)?

7. *[LO 4.2]* What is entered in the Flag field for Lisa Wright (Other Information tab)?

8. *[LO 4.2]* What is entered in the Work Phone field for Hiro Tanaka (Other Information tab)?

9. *[LO 4.2]* What is entered in the Status field for Lisa Wright (Other Information tab)?

10. *[LO 4.2]* What is entered in the Birth Date field for Lisa Wright (Name, Address tab)?

11. *[LO 4.3]* How many patients in the database have the last name of Smith?

12. *[LO 4.3]* What is the name of the patient who is found when you search for the letters JO?

13. *[LO 4.2, 4.3]* What is Li Y. Wong's chart number?

LEARNING OUTCOMES	CONCEPTS TO REVIEW
4.1 Explain how patient information is organized in Medisoft.	Patient information is accessed through the Patient List dialog box. This box is displayed when the Patients/Guarantors and Cases option is clicked on the Lists menu or when the shortcut button is clicked on the toolbar. The Patient List dialog box has two primary sections: – Patient The left side of the window displays information about patients. – Cases The right side of the window contains information about cases.
4.2 Discuss how a new patient is added in Medisoft.	1. Click Patients/Guarantors and Cases on the Lists menu. 2. Click the New Patient button. 3. Complete the Name, Address and Other Information tabs. 4. Click the Save button.
4.3 Describe how to search for a patient in Medisoft.	There are two ways of searching for a patient in Medisoft. 1. In the Patient List dialog box, enter a search term in the Search for box and make a corresponding selection in the Field box. 2. In the Patient List dialog box, click the Locate button. In the Locate Patient box that appears, enter a search term or number in the Field Value field, and make appropriate selections in the remaining fields. When finished making selections, click the First button to display the first record that matches the search.
4.4 Describe how patient information is edited in Medisoft.	Information about a patient is edited in the same way it is entered. To edit patient information, select Patients/Guarantors and Cases on the Lists menu. A search is usually performed to locate the chart number of the patient whose record needs to be updated. Clicking the Edit button displays the Patient/Guarantor dialog box, where changes can be made. Clicking the Save button stores the changes.

USING TERMINOLOGY

Define the terms listed.

1. *[LO 4.2]* established patient
2. *[LO 4.2]* guarantor
3. *[LO 4.2]* new patient

CHECKING YOUR UNDERSTANDING

4. *[LO 4.3]* To search for Paul Ramos, can you key either "Paul" or "Ramos"? Explain.
5. *[LO 4.2]* Create a chart number for a patient named William Burroughs.
6. *[LO 4.2]* Sam Wu has no insurance of his own but is covered by his wife's insurance policy. How would you indicate this in the Patient/Guarantor dialog box?
7. *[LO 4.4]* A patient's phone number has changed. How would you replace the existing phone number in Medisoft?
8. *[LO 4.2]* How would you enter the Social Security number 123-45-6789?

APPLYING YOUR KNOWLEDGE

9. *[LO 4.2, 4.3]* Jane Taylor-Burke comes to the office. She thinks she saw Dr. Yan a few years ago for a flu shot, but she is not sure. You need to decide whether to enter Ms. Taylor-Burke as a new patient in the Medisoft database. What should you do?
10. *[LO 4.1]* Why does each patient need to be assigned a chart number?
11. *[LO 4.1]* Why are guarantors entered in Medisoft when they are not patients of the practice?

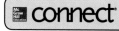 Enhance your learning by completing these exercises and more at http://connect.mheducation.com

chapter 5

WORKING WITH CASES

key terms

capitated plan

case

crossover claim

primary insurance carrier

progress notes

referring provider

sponsor

learning outcomes

When you finish this chapter, you will be able to:

5.1 Describe when it is necessary to create a new case in Medisoft.

5.2 List the eleven tabs in the Case dialog box.

5.3 Review the information contained in the Personal tab and the Account tab.

5.4 Discuss the information recorded in the Policy 1, 2, 3, and Medicaid and Tricare tabs in Medisoft.

5.5 Describe the information contained in the Diagnosis tab and the Condition tab in Medisoft.

5.6 Review the purpose of the Miscellaneous, Comment, and EDI tabs in Medisoft.

5.7 Describe how to edit information in a case.

what you need to know

To use this chapter you need to know how to:

- Use the Medisoft Search feature.
- Enter patient information in Medisoft.
- Locate and change information about an established patient.

5.1 UNDERSTANDING CASES

Each time a physician treats a patient, a record is made of the encounter. The information in the record is used to document the patient's medical condition, and also to bill for services. In Medisoft®, this information is entered and stored in a **case**, which is a grouping of transactions that share a common element. These transactions represent the services and treatments that the physician provided to the patient during the visit. To receive payment, the office must transmit these transactions to the patient's insurance carrier in the form of an insurance claim. In Chapter 6, you will discover how to add transactions to cases.

case a grouping of transactions that share a common element.

WHEN TO SET UP A NEW CASE

Most often, transactions are grouped into cases based on the medical condition for which a patient seeks treatment. For example, if a patient has a chronic condition such as diabetes, charges for all visits related to diabetes are stored in one case. If the same patient also has hypertension, all visits for treatment of hypertension are stored in another case. Patients with chronic conditions often have many transactions in a single case.

On the other hand, a patient may require more than one case per office visit if treatment is provided for two or more unrelated conditions. For example, a patient who visits the physician complaining of migraine headaches may also ask for an influenza vaccination. Since the two conditions are unrelated, two cases would need to be created: one for the migraine headaches and one for the vaccination. In contrast, a patient who is treated for shortness of breath and chest pain during exertion would require one case if the physician determines that the two complaints are related to the same diagnosis.

In these examples just described, it is the patient's medical condition that determines whether more than one case is needed, since each different medical condition requires its own case. There are other instances when a separate case must be created, such as a change in insurance. When a patient changes insurance plans, a new case is set up, even if the same condition is being treated. This makes it easier to submit insurance claims to the appropriate carrier. Transactions that took place while the previous policy was in effect must be submitted under that policy. Transactions that occur after the change in policies must be submitted to the new carrier. By opening a new case, transactions for the two insurance carriers can be kept separate. The information needed to submit claims to the previous carrier is still intact, while information for claims under the new policy is current.

Similarly, when a patient is injured at work and is treated under workers' compensation insurance, a new case must be created so that the claims are billed to the workers' compensation plan, not to the patient's personal policy.

CASE EXAMPLES

The following scenarios provide examples of when new cases are—and are not—required.

Example 1

Among Dr. Yan's patients today is Josephine Tremblay, a Medicare patient. Josephine has a number of chronic health conditions, including diabetes, arthritis, hypertension, and asthma. She has four cases already set up in Medisoft, one for each of her chronic conditions. Today she is seeing Dr. Yan because she is experiencing lower back pain. From this information alone, we cannot determine whether to create a new case since the back pain may be due to one of her existing conditions. When the billing assistant reviews the electronic encounter form, she sees that Dr. Yan has diagnosed Mrs. Tremblay with lower back pain due to arthritis. Since arthritis is one of Mrs. Tremblay's existing cases, no new case is needed.

Example 2

Dr. Jessica Rudner has just finished examining Kimberly DeJong. Ms. DeJong is a twenty-five-year-old woman who has an existing case for rosacea, a chronic skin condition. Today, Ms. DeJong received an antimalarial prescription in preparation for her travel to India. Since this visit is not related to her existing case for rosacea, a new case will be created.

Example 3

Jose Gonzales has been a patient of Dr. John Rudner for three months. During that time, he was diagnosed with hypertension and started on medication. He has come in today for a follow-up visit, to see how well the medication is working. The front desk staff asks him if any information has changed since his last visit, and he indicates that he changed jobs and has a new health plan. Even though he is being treated for the same condition (hypertension), claims for today's visit must be sent to the new insurance carrier. To ensure that today's charges are submitted to the new carrier, a new case must be created.

Example 4

David Weber is the seven-year-old son of Marcia and Ronald Weber, who are divorced. David has not been seen by Dr. Yan except for routine immunizations each year before school starts. David has been covered by his father's insurance plan since the divorce. David's father recently lost his job, and David is now covered by his mother's health plan. Today, David's father has brought him in for his annual immunizations. A new case must be created, even though David has an existing case for annual immunizations, because he is covered by a different insurance plan. If a new case were not created, the charges would be submitted to the insurance plan listed in the existing case, and the claim would be rejected.

5.2 NAVIGATING CASES IN MEDISOFT

In Chapter 4, you learned that certain patient information is stored in the Patient/Guarantor dialog box. The data stored in the Patient/Guarantor dialog box are primarily demographic, including a patient's name, address, date of birth, Social Security number, employer, and so on.

The information about a patient's medical conditions and treatments—including the diagnosis, procedures, provider, and insurance plan—is stored in the Case dialog box. The same Patient List dialog box that you worked with in Chapter 4 is used to access the Case dialog box. It is accessed by choosing Patients/Guarantors and Cases from the Lists menu.

CASE COMMAND BUTTONS

When the Case radio button in the Patient List dialog box is clicked, the following command buttons appear at the bottom of the Patient List dialog box: Edit Case, New Case, Delete Case, Copy Case, Print Grid, View Statements, and Close (see Figure 5-1).

Edit Case   The Edit Case button is used to add, delete, or change information in an existing case. When the Edit Case button is clicked, the Case dialog box is displayed. Case information to be updated is contained in eleven different tabs. For example, if a patient gets married, information needs to be updated in the Personal tab. The only item in the Case dialog box that cannot be changed is the case number. All other boxes are edited by moving the cursor to the box and making the change, whether this involves rekeying, selecting and deselecting check boxes, or clicking a different option on a drop-down list.

New Case   The New Case button creates a new case.

Delete Case   The Delete Case button deletes a case from the system if the case has no open transactions. Open transactions are charges

SHORT CUT

OPENING CASES FOR EDITING

Cases can also be opened for editing by double-clicking on the case number/description in the Case window within the Patient List dialog box.

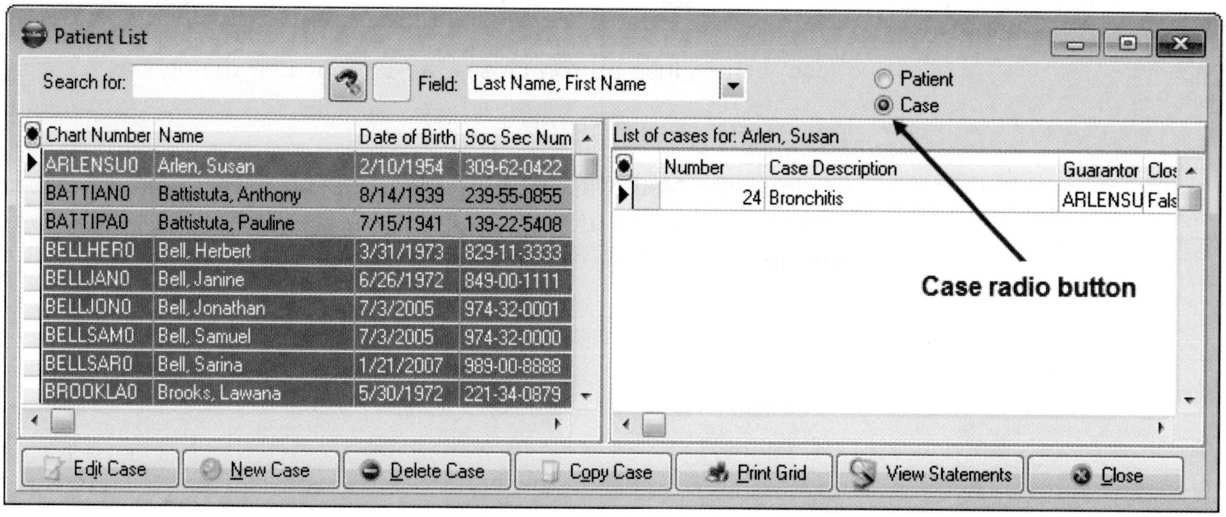

Figure 5-1   Patient List Dialog Box with Case Radio Button Selected

that have not been fully paid by the insurance carrier or the policy-holder. The Delete Case button should be used with caution; once deleted, information cannot be retrieved. Cases should be deleted only when it is definite that the patient's records will never be needed again. Medical offices usually have policies about when a patient's records are deleted, such as five years after the patient's last visit to the practice. In most instances, it is more appropriate to close a case than to delete it. Cases are closed by clicking the Case Closed box in the Personal tab of the Case dialog box.

Cases are deleted in the Patient List dialog box. With the Case radio button clicked, the specific case to be deleted is selected by clicking the line that displays the case number and description. The case is then deleted by clicking the Delete Case button at the bottom of the dialog box. The system will ask, "Are you sure you want to delete this case?" Clicking the Yes button deletes the case from the system.

Copy Case   The Copy Case button copies all the information from an existing case into a new case. This feature is useful when creating a new case for a patient who already has a case in the system. Copy Case makes it unnecessary to reenter the information in all eleven tabs; instead, the information in the existing case is copied into a new case. Then the information that needs to be changed can be edited to reflect the new case. The fields that almost always require editing are the case description, the referring provider, and the patient's diagnosis. Sometimes those may be the only changes; other times data must be changed in all the tabs of the Case folder. For this reason, when copying a case it is important to check each tab to make sure the copied information is accurate for the new case. The information that remains the same from the previous case can be left as is.

Print Grid   The Print Grid button is used to select or deselect columns of information for printing purposes.

View Statements   The View Statements button is used in practices that use the BillFlash option for electronic statements.

Close   The Close button closes the Patient List dialog box.

THE CASE DIALOG BOX

Clicking the New Case button brings up the Case dialog box (see Figure 5-2). Information about a patient is entered in eleven different tabs in the Case dialog box:

1. Personal
2. Account
3. Diagnosis
4. Policy 1
5. Policy 2
6. Policy 3

SHORT CUT

USING COPY CASE

When creating a new case for an established patient, it is faster to use the Copy Case button than to create a new case using the New Case button.

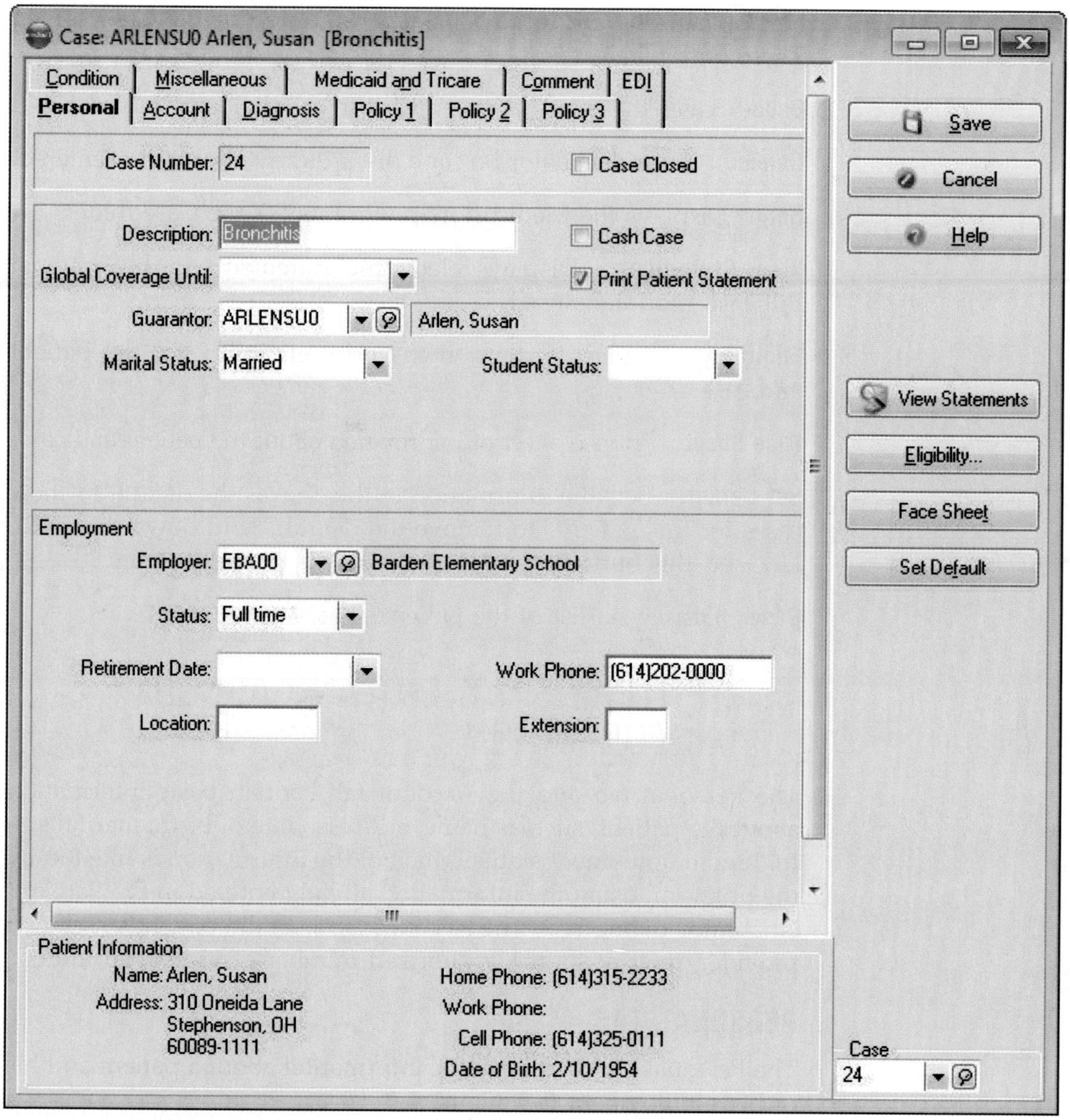

Figure 5-2 Case Dialog Box

7. Condition

8. Miscellaneous

9. Medicaid and Tricare

10. Comment

11. EDI

The information required to complete the eleven tabs comes from documents found in a patient's medical record, or chart. The patient information form supplies basic information, such as name and address, as well as information about insurance coverage, allergies, whether the condition is related to an accident, and the referral source. The **progress notes** contain the physician's notes about a patient's condition and diagnosis. The encounter form is a list of services performed and the charges for them.

progress notes a physician's notes about a patient's condition and diagnosis.

Several buttons are located on the right side of the Case folder. These buttons are:

Save   Saves the information entered in the dialog box.

Cancel   Closes the dialog box and discards any information entered.

Help   Displays the Medisoft help window for the Case folder.

View Statements   Displays electronic statements if the optional BillFlash module is used.

Eligibility   Displays an option to verify eligibility for the patient and case.

Face Sheet   Prints a sheet of information about the patient and case.

Set Default   Sets the information in the case as the default for new cases for this patient. To remove the default, hold down the CTRL key, and this button changes to a Remove Default button.

Case   Displays a list of the patient's cases.

5.3 ENTERING PATIENT AND ACCOUNT INFORMATION

The Personal tab and the Account tab contain basic information about the patient, such as name, address, date of birth, marital status, and employment status. Much of the information is filled in by the program, using the information already entered in the Patient/Guarantor dialog box. The Account tab lists the patient's assigned provider, referral source, authorized number of visits, and more.

PERSONAL TAB

The Personal tab contains basic information about a patient and his or her employment (see Figure 5-3).

Case Number   The case number is a sequential number assigned by Medisoft. To avoid confusion, case numbers are unique; no two patients ever have the same case number.

Case Closed   A case is marked as closed by placing a check mark in the Case Closed box. At times it is appropriate to close a case. Closing a case indicates that no more data will be entered into the case. When is it appropriate to close a case? Policies vary from practice to practice, but generally cases are closed when a patient changes insurance carriers, has recovered completely from a condition (such as the flu), or is no longer a patient at the practice. *Note:* The Case Closed box does not appear until a case is created and saved.

Description   Information entered in the Description box indicates a patient's complaint, or reason for seeing a physician. For example, if a patient comes to see a physician for an annual physical examination,

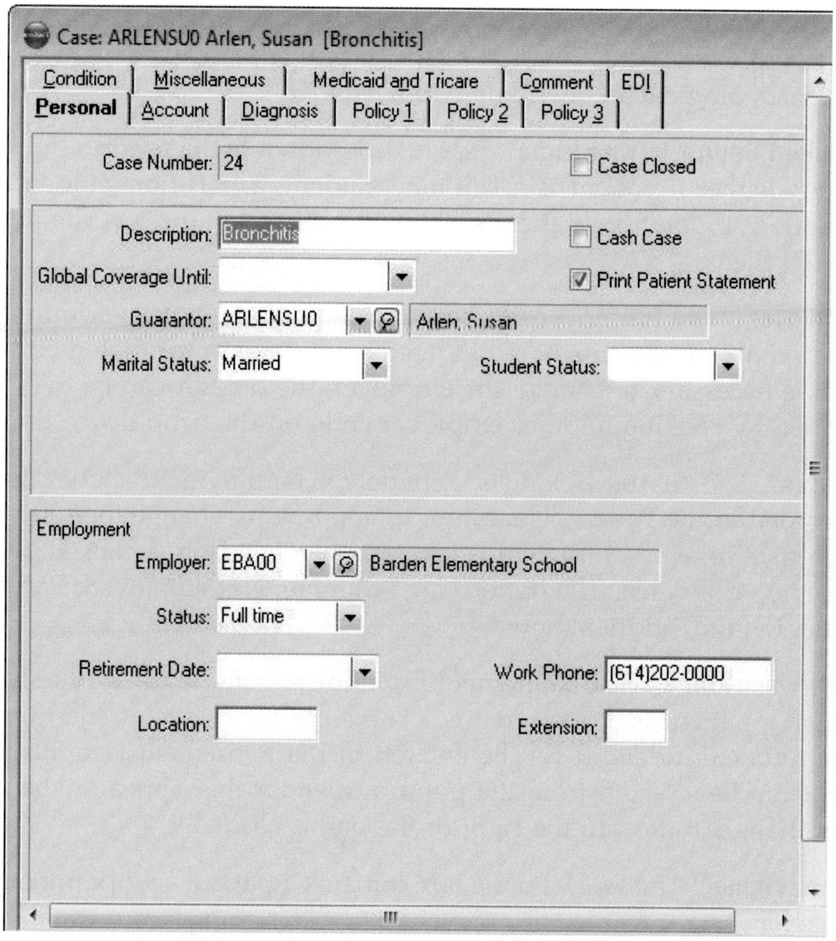

Case: ARLENSU0 Arlen, Susan [Bronchitis]

| Condition | Miscellaneous | Medicaid and Tricare | Comment | EDI |

Personal | Account | Diagnosis | Policy 1 | Policy 2 | Policy 3 |

Case Number: 24

☐ Case Closed

Description: Bronchitis

☐ Cash Case

Global Coverage Until: [   ] ▼

☑ Print Patient Statement

Guarantor: ARLENSU0 ▼ ⊘ Arlen, Susan

Marital Status: Married ▼   Student Status: [   ] ▼

Employment

Employer: EBA00 ▼ ⊘ Barden Elementary School

Status: Full time ▼

Retirement Date: [   ] ▼   Work Phone: (614)202-0000

Location: [   ]   Extension: [   ]

Figure 5-3   Personal Tab

the Description box would read "annual physical." Other examples of entries are sore throat, stomach pains, dog bite, and accident at work. A patient's complaint can be found in his or her chart.

Cash Case   If the Cash Case box is checked, the patient is paying cash and has no insurance coverage.

Global Coverage Until   Certain services are paid for under what are known as "global fees." These fees include reimbursement for services performed at different times by the same provider (or group) when performed in conjunction with one medical procedure or episode of care. For example, preoperative, intraoperative, and postoperative services are included in the single payment for a global surgical procedure. The entry in this field indicates the date on which charges are no longer considered part of the global fee.

Print Patient Statement   If this box is checked, a statement for the patient is automatically printed when statements for the practice are printed.

Guarantor   The Guarantor box lists the name of the person responsible for paying the bill. The drop-down list contains the chart numbers and names of all potential guarantors in the database.

Marital Status   The drop-down list provides the following choices to indicate a patient's marital status: Divorced, Legally separated, Married, Single, Unknown, or Widowed.

Student Status   The Student Status drop-down list is used to indicate whether a patient is a full-time student, a part-time student, or a non-student. If a patient's status is not known, the box should be left blank.

Employer   The Employer box contains the default employer information that has been entered in the Patient/Guarantor dialog box. If it is necessary to change the employer, the default can be overridden by clicking another employer code on the drop-down list.

Status   The Status box lists a patient's employment status as recorded in the Patient/Guarantor dialog box. To change the selection that appears in the Status box, another selection is clicked on the drop-down list. The options are Full-time, Not employed, Part-time, Retired, and Unknown.

Retirement Date   The Retirement Date box should be filled in only when a patient is already retired. There are two ways of entering the retirement date. It can be entered in the Retirement Date box, or it can be selected from the pop-up calendar that appears when the triangle button to the right of the box is clicked.

Work Phone   The Work Phone box contains a patient's work phone number.

Location   If a patient has supplied a specific work location, such as "Fifth Avenue Branch," it is entered in the Location box.

Extension   The Extension box lists a patient's work phone extension.

EXERCISE 5-1	ENTERING DATA IN THE PERSONAL TAB

Create a new case for patient Hiro Tanaka and enter information in the Personal tab. The information needed to complete this exercise is found on Source Document 1. (*Note:* All Source Documents are located in the back of the book.)

Date: October 1, 2018

1. Start Medisoft and restore the data from your last work session.

2. Change the Medisoft Program Date to the date listed above, October 1, 2018.

3. On the Lists menu, click Patients/Guarantors and Cases. The Patient List dialog box is displayed.

4. Search for Hiro Tanaka by keying *T* in the Search for box. The arrow should point to the entry line for Hiro Tanaka.

5. Click the Case radio button to activate the case portion of the Patient List dialog box.

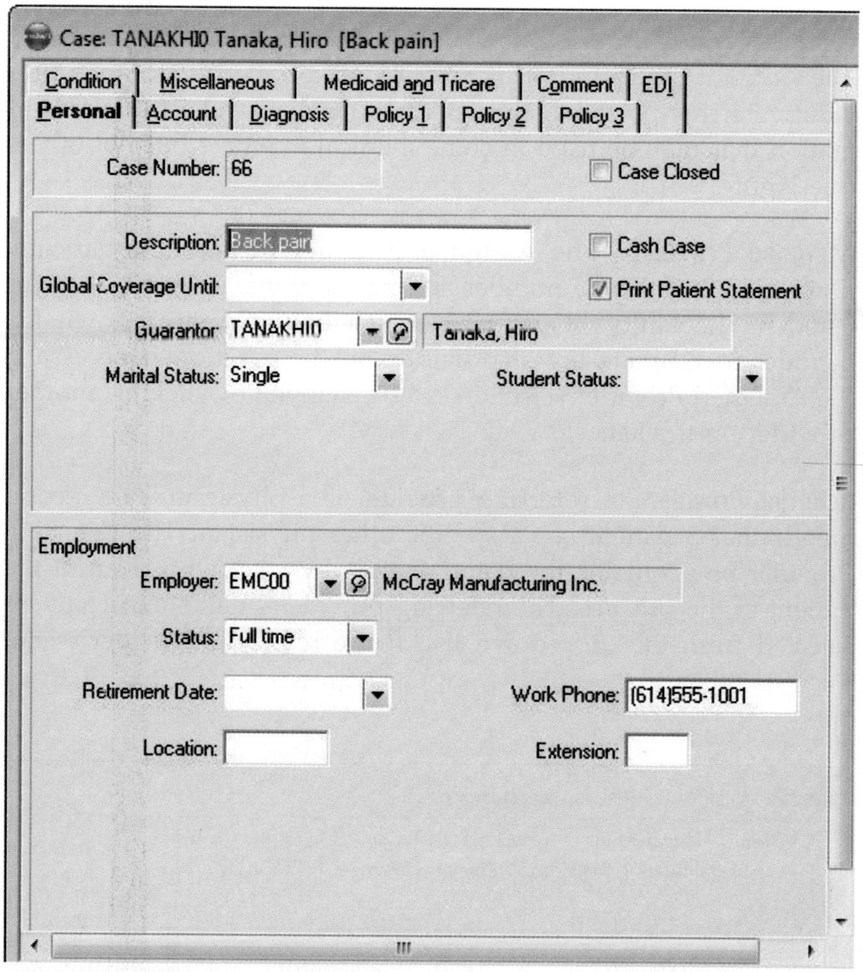

Figure 5-4   Personal Tab, Hiro Tanaka

6. Click the New Case button. The dialog box labeled Case: TANAKHIØ Tanaka, Hiro (new) is displayed. The Personal tab is the current active tab. Notice that some information is already filled in.

7. Enter Tanaka's reason for seeing the doctor in the Description box.

8. Choose the correct entry for Tanaka's marital status from the drop-down list in the Marital Status box. The Student Status box can be left blank.

9. Notice that the information on Tanaka's employment is already filled in. The system copies the information entered in the Patient/Guarantor dialog box to the Case folder for you.

10. Use the completed Personal tab in Figure 5-4 to check your entries for accuracy. (*Note:* The case number is entered by the program; do not be concerned if your screen shows a different case number.)

11. Click the Save button to save the case information you just entered. The Patient List dialog box redisplays. Notice that the case you just created is listed in the right side of the dialog box in the area labeled List of cases for: Tanaka, Hiro.

12. Do not close the Patient List dialog box. **ciMC**

☑ **You have completed Exercise 5-1.**

ACCOUNT TAB

The Account tab includes information on a patient's assigned provider, referring provider, and referral source, as well as other information that may be used in some medical practices but not others (see Figure 5-5).

Assigned Provider The Assigned Provider box is automatically filled in with the code number and name of the assigned provider listed in the Patient/Guarantor dialog box. The drop-down list includes a complete list of providers in the practice. If necessary, the Assigned Provider selection can be changed by clicking another provider on the list.

referring provider a physician who recommends that a patient see a specific other physician.

Referring Provider A **referring provider** is a physician who recommends that a patient see a specific other physician. The Referring Provider box contains the name of the physician who referred the patient to the practice. The referring provider's name and code are selected from the drop-down list. If the referring provider is not

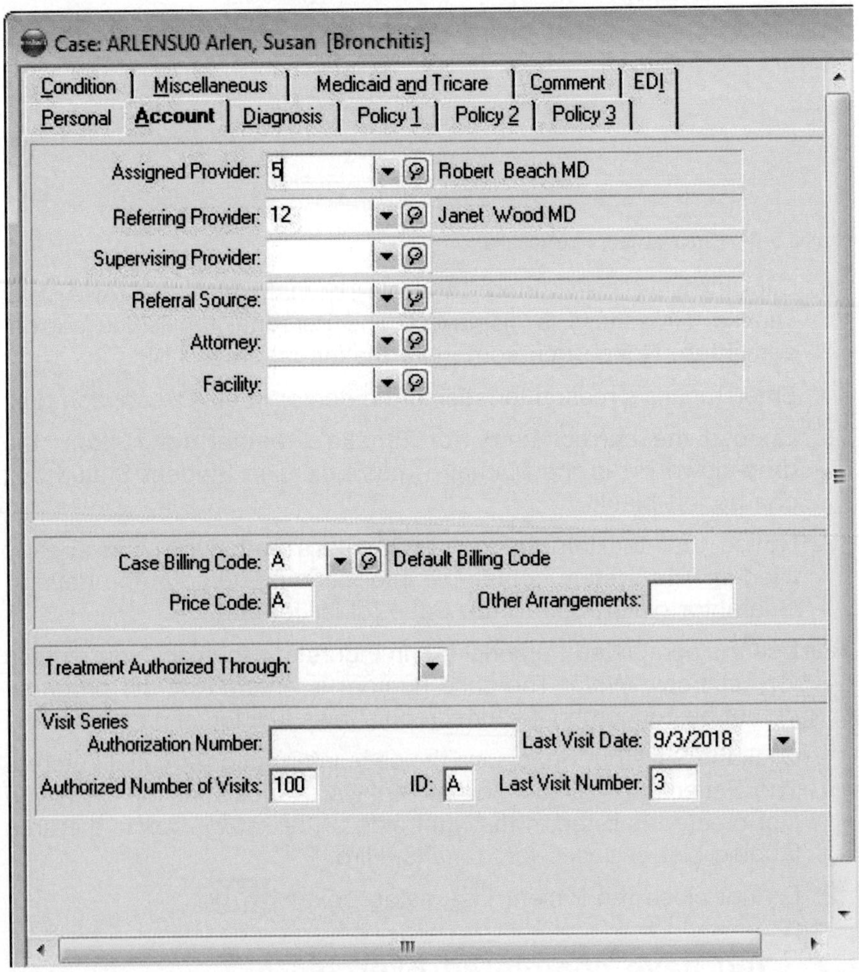

Figure 5-5 Account Tab

listed on the drop-down list, he or she will need to be added to the Referring Provider list, which is found on the Lists menu. It is not necessary to close the Case dialog box to add a referring provider to the database. To add a new referring provider, click Referring Providers on the Lists menu As an alternative, click in the Referring Provider field and either click F8 or click the right mouse button. The Referring Provider List dialog box opens in front of the other dialog boxes displayed on the screen, and a new provider can be entered.

Supervising Provider   When the provider rendering services is being supervised by a physician, the supervising physician's information is included on the claim.

Referral Source   If known, the source of a patient's referral is selected from the drop-down list of choices.

Attorney   The Attorney box is used for accident cases. If a patient has an attorney, the name of the attorney should be selected from the drop-down list. If the attorney is not listed, he or she will need to be added to the system by clicking Addresses on the Lists menu and entering information about the attorney.

Facility   The Facility box lists the place where a patient is receiving treatment. A facility is selected from the drop-down list. When necessary, facilities can be added to the database by clicking Facilities on the Lists menu and entering the necessary information.

Case Billing Code   The Case Billing Code box is a one- or two-character box used by some practices to classify and sort patients by insurance carrier, diagnosis, billing cycle, or other kinds of information.

Price Code   The Price Code box determines which set of fees is used when entering transactions for this case. The Price Code fees are entered and stored in the Amounts tab of the Procedure/ Payment/Adjustment List dialog box, accessed through the Lists menu.

Other Arrangements   If a special arrangement is made for billing, it is indicated in the Other Arrangements box.

Treatment Authorized Through   A date can be entered in this box if the insurance carrier has authorized treatment only through a certain date.

Visit Series   Information in the Visit Series section of the Account tab is used primarily by psychotherapy practices and chiropractors.

Complete the Account tab for Hiro Tanaka. The information needed to complete this exercise is found on Source Document 1.

Date: October 1, 2018

1. Confirm that Hiro Tanaka is still listed in the Patient List dialog box and that the Case radio button is selected.

2. Click the Edit Case button to add information to Tanaka's case file. The Case dialog box is displayed, with the Personal tab active.

3. Make the Account tab active. The word *Account* should now be displayed in boldface type, and the boxes on the Account tab should be visible.

4. Notice that the Assigned Provider box is already filled in with the name of Tanaka's assigned provider, Katherine Yan. The system copies this information from data stored in the Patient/Guarantor dialog box.

5. Click the name of Tanaka's referring provider on the Referring Provider drop-down list. Press Tab.

6. Accept the default entry of "A" in the Price Code box.

7. Check your work for accuracy.

8. Save the changes. The Patient List dialog box is redisplayed.

9. Do not close the Patient List dialog box. **CiMO**

☑ **You have completed Exercise 5-2.**

5.4 ENTERING INSURANCE INFORMATION

primary insurance carrier the first carrier to whom claims are submitted.

The **primary insurance carrier** is the first carrier to whom claims are submitted. There may also be a secondary carrier (Policy 2 tab) or a tertiary carrier (Policy 3 tab). The Medicaid and Tricare tab is used to enter specific information for Medicaid and TRICARE claims.

POLICY 1 TAB

The Policy 1 tab is where information about a patient's primary insurance carrier and coverage is recorded (see Figure 5-6).

Insurance 1   The Insurance 1 box lists the code number and name of the insurance carrier. The drop-down list shows the carriers already in the system. If the carrier is not listed, it must be added to the database. It is not necessary to close the Case dialog box to add an insurance carrier to the database. When Insurance is clicked on the Lists menu, and Carriers is clicked on the submenu, the Insurance Carrier List dialog box is displayed in front of the other dialog boxes on the screen.

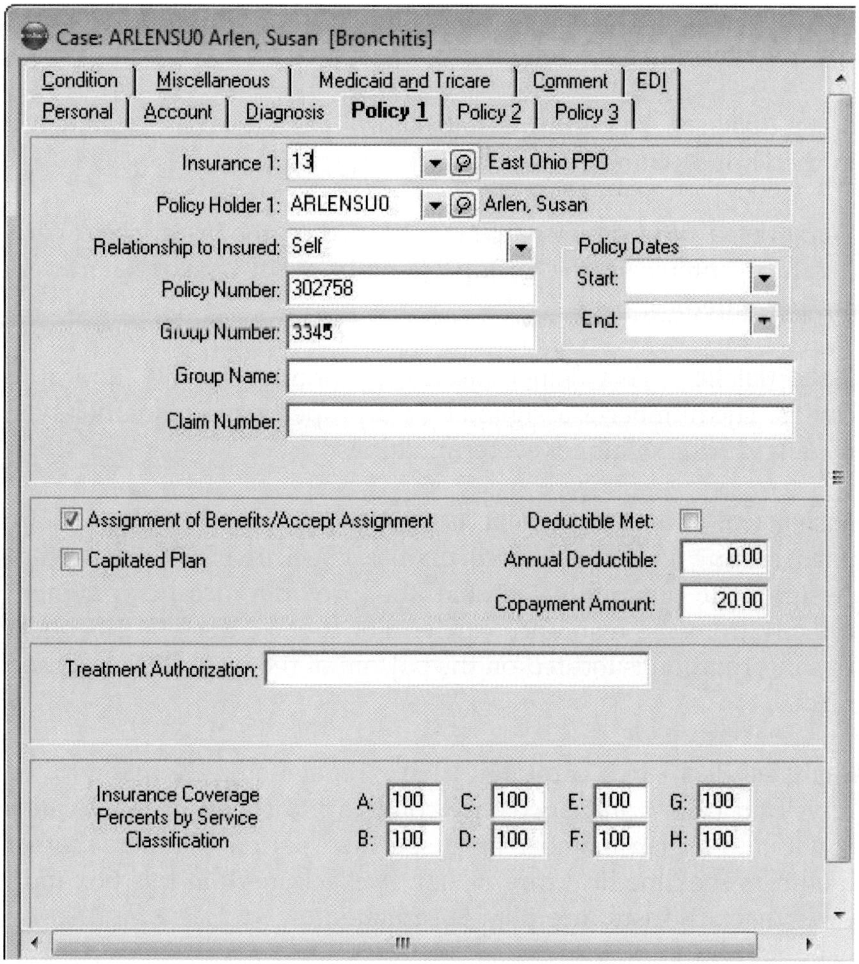

Case: ARLENSU0 Arlen, Susan [Bronchitis]

Condition | Miscellaneous | Medicaid and Tricare | Comment | EDI
Personal | Account | Diagnosis | **Policy 1** | Policy 2 | Policy 3

Insurance 1: 13 ▼ 🔍 East Ohio PPO

Policy Holder 1: ARLENSU0 ▼ 🔍 Arlen, Susan

Relationship to Insured: Self ▼

Policy Dates

Policy Number: 302758   Start: ▼

Group Number: 3345   End: ▼

Group Name:

Claim Number:

☑ Assignment of Benefits/Accept Assignment   Deductible Met: ☐

☐ Capitated Plan   Annual Deductible: 0.00

Copayment Amount: 20.00

Treatment Authorization:

Insurance Coverage Percents by Service Classification

A: 100   C: 100   E: 100   G: 100
B: 100   D: 100   F: 100   H: 100

Figure 5-6   Policy 1 Tab

Policy Holder 1   The Policy Holder 1 box lists the person who is the insured under a particular policy. For example, if the patient is a child covered under his or her parent's insurance plan, the parent's chart number would be entered in this box. The insured's chart number is selected from the choices on the drop-down list. (If the insured is not a patient of the practice, he or she must be entered as a guarantor in Medisoft, and a chart number must be established.)

Relationship to Insured   This box describes a patient's relationship to the individual listed in the Policy Holder 1 box.

Policy Number   A patient's policy number is entered in the Policy Number box.

Policy Dates—Start/End   The date a patient's insurance policy went into effect is entered in the Policy Dates—Start box. If the date is not known, the date the patient first came to the practice for treatment can be entered. If the policy has ended, for example, because the carrier changed or the coverage expired, the date on which coverage terminated is entered in the Policy Dates—End box.

Group Number   The group number for a patient's policy is entered in the Group Number box.

Group Name   If a group name is provided by the insurance carrier, it can be entered in the Group Name box. Up to sixty characters are permitted.

Claim Number   This field is used on property, casualty, and auto claims. The number is assigned by the property and casualty payer, usually during eligibility determinations.

Assignment of Benefits/Accept Assignment   For physicians who are participating in an insurance plan, a check mark in the Accept Assignment box indicates that the provider accepts payment directly from the insurance carrier. For the exercises in this book, this information is located on the bottom of the patient information form.

Capitated Plan   In a **capitated plan**, prepayments are made to the physician from a managed care company to cover the physician's services to a plan member for a specified period of time, whether members seek medical care or not. A check mark in this box indicates that this insurance plan is capitated.

Deductible Met   This box is checked if the patient has met the deductible for the current year.

Annual Deductible   The dollar amount of the insured's insurance plan deductible is entered in this box.

Copayment Amount   The dollar amount of a patient's copayment per visit is entered in the Copayment Amount box.

Treatment Authorization   This field is used to record the treatment authorization code from an insurance company for UB-04 claims. The UB-04 is the standard uniform bill (UB) that is used for institutional healthcare providers such as hospitals.

Insurance Coverage Percents by Service Classification   The percentage of fees that an insurance carrier covers is entered in the Insurance Coverage Percents by Service Classification box. Some insurance plans pay different percentages of charges based on the type of service provided. For example, if a plan pays 80 percent of necessary medical procedures, box A would contain 80. If the plan covered 100 percent of lab work, box B would contain 100, and so on.

Complete the Policy 1 tab for Hiro Tanaka. The information needed to complete this exercise is found on Source Document 1.

Date: October 1, 2018

1. Confirm that the Low back pain case for Hiro Tanaka is still open.

2. Click the Policy 1 tab to make it active.

3. Select Tanaka's primary insurance carrier from the drop-down list in the Insurance 1 box. Press Tab.

4. The program completes the Policy Holder 1 field with the name of the patient. Since Tanaka is the policyholder, accept this entry.

5. Notice that the Relationship to Insured box already has "Self" entered. Since this is correct, do not make any changes.

6. Enter Tanaka's insurance policy number in the Policy Number box. Press Tab.

7. Enter Tanaka's group number in the Group Number box. Press Tab.

8. In the Policy Dates—Start box, key **01012018** (January 1, 2018) as the start date of the policy. Press Tab. The program displays a Confirm message stating that the date entered is in the future and asking whether you want to change it. Click No.

9. Dr. Yan accepts assignment for this carrier, so click the Assignment of Benefits/Accept Assignment box.

10. The insurance plan is capitated, so check the Capitated Plan box.

11. Key **20** in the Copayment Amount box if it does not already appear. Press Tab.

12. Key **100** in each of the Insurance Coverage Percents by Service Classification boxes.

13. Check your work for accuracy.

14. Save the changes.

15. Do not close the Patient List dialog box. **CiMO**

☑ **You have completed Exercise 5-3.**

Connect users: go to http://connect.mheducation.com to complete this exercise! Some steps may differ from what is listed here, so be sure to refer to the steps listed in Demo and Practice Modes for guidance.

POLICY 2 TAB

Claims are usually not submitted to a secondary carrier until the primary carrier has paid. The secondary carrier must have access to the remittance advice of the primary carrier to see what has already been paid on the claim. Delayed secondary billing may be set up so a claim is not created for the secondary carrier until a response has been received from the primary carrier.

The boxes in the Policy 2 tab are the same as those in the Policy 1 tab, with a few exceptions. The Copayment Amount, Capitated Plan, Annual Deductible, and Deductible Met boxes are only in the

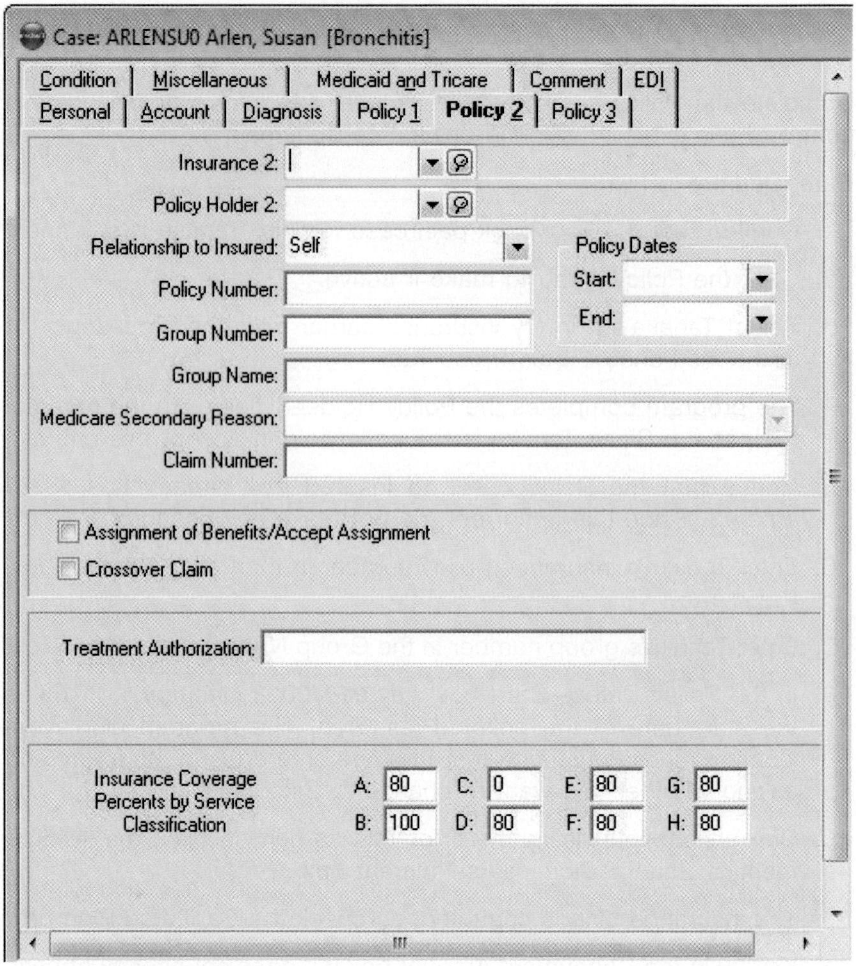

Figure 5-7   Policy 2 Tab

Policy 1 tab. Only the Policy 2 tab has a Crossover Claim box and a Medicare Secondary Reason field (see Figure 5-7). **Crossover claims** are claims that are processed by Medicare and then transferred to Medicaid, or to a payer that provides supplemental insurance benefits to Medicare beneficiaries. Medicare secondary reasons are required when another payer or insurer pays on a patient's claim prior to Medicare.

crossover claims claims that are processed by Medicare and then transferred to Medicaid, or to a payer that provides supplemental insurance benefits to Medicare beneficiaries.

Medicare Secondary Reason   When Medicare is the secondary payer, the reason must be indicated in this field.

Crossover Claim   A check mark in this box indicates that the claim is processed by one payer such as Medicare and then automatically sent to the secondary payer.

POLICY 3 TAB

The Policy 3 tab does not contain the Copayment Amount, Capitated Plan, Annual Deductible, Deductible Met, Medicare Secondary Reason, or Crossover Claim boxes. Otherwise, the boxes are the same as those in the Policy 1 and Policy 2 tabs (see Figure 5-8).

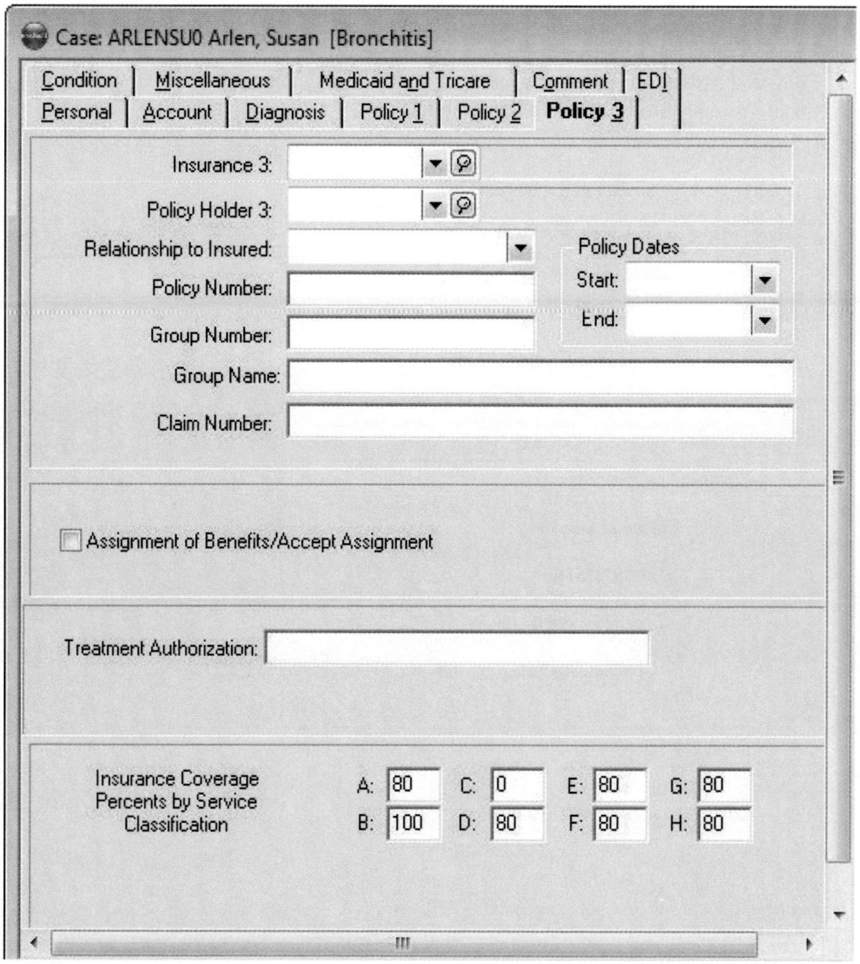

Case: ARLENSU0 Arlen, Susan [Bronchitis]

Condition | Miscellaneous | Medicaid and Tricare | Comment | EDI
Personal | Account | Diagnosis | Policy 1 | Policy 2 | **Policy 3**

Insurance 3:

Policy Holder 3:

Relationship to Insured:

Policy Number:

Group Number:

Group Name:

Claim Number:

Policy Dates

Start:

End:

☐ Assignment of Benefits/Accept Assignment

Treatment Authorization:

Insurance Coverage
Percents by Service
Classification

A: 80   C: 0   E: 80   G: 80
B: 100   D: 80   F: 80   H: 80

Figure 5-8   Policy 3 Tab

MEDICAID AND TRICARE TAB

For patients covered by Medicaid or TRICARE, the Medicaid and Tricare tab is used to enter additional information about the government programs (see Figure 5-9).

Medicaid

EPSDT   *EPSDT* stands for Early and Periodic Screening, Diagnosis, and Treatment. This is a Medicaid program for patients under the age of twenty-one that provides comprehensive healthcare services. The program includes periodic health screening, vision, dental, and hearing services. A check mark in the EPSDT box indicates that a patient's visit is part of the EPSDT program.

Family Planning   A check mark in the Family Planning box specifies that a patient's condition is related to Medicaid family planning services.

Resubmission Number   For claims being resubmitted to Medicaid, the resubmission number is entered in this box.

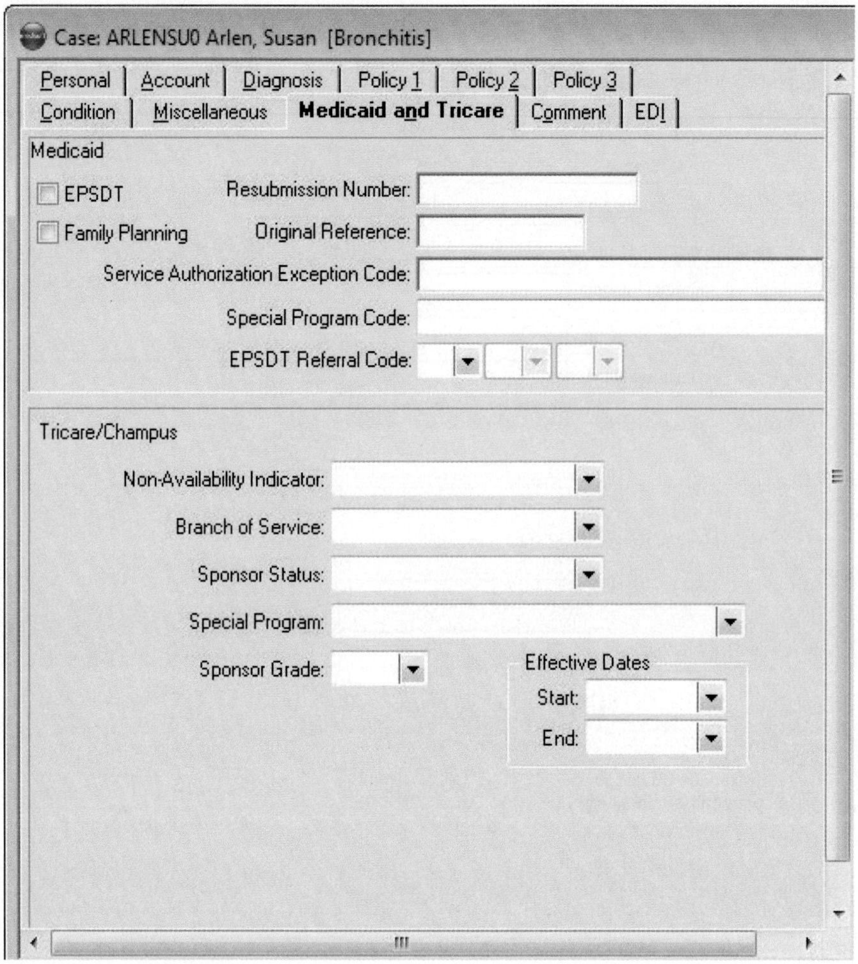

Figure 5-9   Medicaid and Tricare Tab

Original Reference   For claims being resubmitted to Medicaid, the original reference number is recorded in the Original Reference box.

Service Authorization Exception Code   This code is required on some Medicaid claims. If a service authorization code was not obtained before seeing the patient, enter one of the following codes:

1. Immediate/Urgent Care
2. Services Rendered in a Retroactive Period
3. Emergency Care
4. Client as Temporary Medicaid
5. Request from County for Second Opinion to Recipient Can Work
6. Request for Override Pending
7. Special Handling

Special Program Code   The Special Program Code is used for Medicaid claims. The choices in the drop-down list include:

Disability (05)

Physically Handicapped Children's Program (02)

Second Opinion or Surgery (09)

Special Federal Funding (03)

EPSDT Referral Code   If appropriate, an Early and Periodic Screening Diagnosis and Treatment referral code is selected from the drop-down list:

AV (Patient Refused Referral)

NU (Patient Not Referred)

S2 (Under Treatment)

ST (New Services Requested)

TRICARE/TRICARE for Life

TRICARE is the government insurance program that serves spouses and children of active-duty service members, military retirees and their families, some former spouses, and survivors of deceased military members. TRICARE for Life provides military healthcare coverage to TRICARE beneficiaries 65 years of age or older, as a secondary plan to Medicare.

Non-Availability Indicator   The Non-Availability Indicator box specifies whether a non-availability (NA) statement is required. The choices on the drop-down list are NA statement not needed, NA statement obtained, and Other carrier paid at least 75%.

Branch of Service   The Branch of Service box indicates the particular branch of service: Army, Air Force, Marines, Navy, Coast Guard, Public Health Service, NOAA, and CHAMPVA.

Sponsor Status   The **sponsor** is the active-duty service member. The sponsor's family members are covered by the TRICARE insurance plan. The drop-down list in the Sponsor Status box provides choices to indicate the sponsor's status in the service, such as Active, Civilian, and National Guard.

sponsor in TRICARE, the active-duty service member.

Special Program   The Special Program drop-down list contains codes for special TRICARE programs.

Sponsor Grade   The two-character sponsor grade is entered in the Sponsor Grade box.

Effective Dates—Start/End   The start date of the TRICARE policy is entered in the Effective Dates—Start box. If there is an end date, it is entered in the Effective Dates—End box. Specific dates can be entered, or a selection can be made from the pop-up calendar.

5.5 ENTERING HEALTH INFORMATION

Information about a patient's health is recorded in the Diagnosis and Condition tabs in Medisoft.

DIAGNOSIS TAB

The Diagnosis tab contains a patient's diagnosis, information about allergies, and electronic claims (EDI) notes (see Figure 5-10).

Principal Diagnosis and Default Diagnosis 2 Through 12 A patient's diagnosis is selected from the drop-down list of diagnoses. If a patient has more than one diagnosis for the same condition, the primary diagnosis is entered in the Principal Diagnosis field. Additional diagnoses are entered in the Default Diagnosis 2 through 12 fields.

In Medisoft, diagnosis codes are updated and new codes are entered by selecting Diagnosis Codes on the Lists menu. Similarly, procedure codes are entered and updated by selecting Procedure/Payment/Adjustment Codes on the Lists menu.

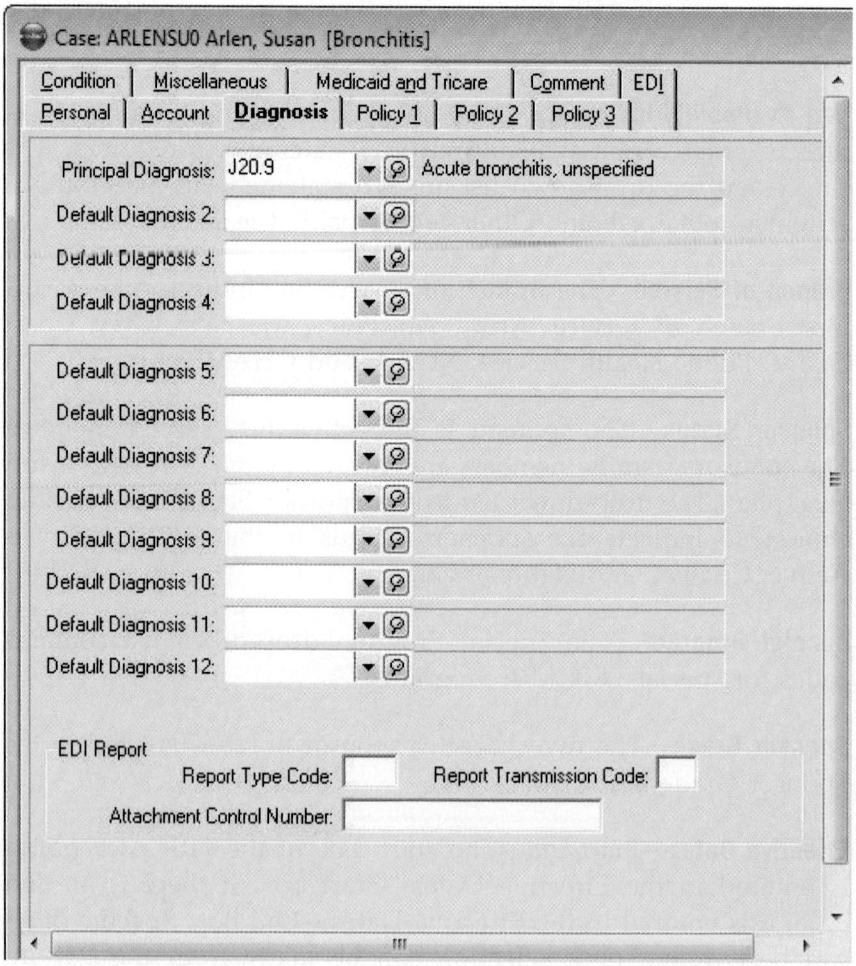

Case: ARLENSU0 Arlen, Susan [Bronchitis]
Condition
Miscellaneous
Medicaid and Tricare
Comment
EDI
Personal
Account
Diagnosis
Policy 1
Policy 2
Policy 3
Principal Diagnosis:
J20.9
Acute bronchitis, unspecified
Default Diagnosis 2:
Default Diagnosis 3:
Default Diagnosis 4:
Default Diagnosis 5:
Default Diagnosis 6:
Default Diagnosis 7:
Default Diagnosis 8:
Default Diagnosis 9:
Default Diagnosis 10:
Default Diagnosis 11:
Default Diagnosis 12:
EDI Report
Report Type Code:
Report Transmission Code:
Attachment Control Number:

Figure 5-10 Diagnosis Tab

EDI Report

The EDI Report section of the Diagnosis tab contains fields for entering information about electronic claim attachments.

Report Type Code The Report Type Code is a two-character code that indicates the title or contents of a document, report, or supporting item sent with electronic claims. For example, DG is the code for a diagnostic report. Other codes include:

77 Support data for verification. REFERRAL: use this code to indicate a completed referral form

AS Admission summary

B2 Prescription

B3 Physician order

B4 Referral form

CT Certification

DA Dental models

DG Diagnostic report

DS Discharge summary

EB Explanation of benefits (coordination of benefits or Medicare secondary payer)

MT Models

NN Nursing notes

OB Operative note

OZ Support data for claim

PN Physician therapy notes

PO Prosthetics or orthotic certification

PZ Physical therapy certification

RB Radiology films

RR Radiology reports

RT Report of tests and analysis report

Report Transmission Code This box is used to record the report transmission code, a two-character code that indicates the means by which the report will be transmitted to the payer (for example, via mail, e-mail, or fax). Possible codes include:

AA Available on request at provider site. This means that the paperwork is not being sent with the claim at this time. Instead, it is available to the payer (or appropriate entity) at its request.

BM By mail.

EL Electronically only. Used to indicate that the attachment is being transmitted in a separate X12 functional group.

EM By e-mail.

FX By fax.

Attachment Control Number This box contains the attachment's reference number (up to seven digits, assigned by the practice). This number is required if the transmission code is anything other than AA.

EXERCISE 5-4   ENTERING DATA IN THE DIAGNOSIS TAB

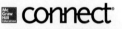

Complete the Diagnosis tab for Hiro Tanaka. The information needed to complete this exercise is found on Source Documents 1 and 3.

Date: October 1, 2018

1. Edit the case for Hiro Tanaka.

2. Make the Diagnosis tab active.

3. From the list of choices in the drop-down list, select Tanaka's diagnosis.

4. Check your work for accuracy.

5. Save the changes. The Patient List dialog box is redisplayed.

6. Do not close the Patient List dialog box.

✓ **You have completed Exercise 5-4.**

CONDITION TAB

The Condition tab stores data about a patient's illness, accident, disability, and hospitalization (see Figure 5-11). This information is used by insurance carriers to process claims.

Injury/Illness/LMP Date The date of a patient's injury, illness, or last menstrual period (LMP) is entered in the Injury/Illness/LMP Date box. (For an illness, the date when the symptoms first appeared is entered.)

Illness Indicator The Illness Indicator box specifies whether a patient's condition is an illness, a last menstrual period in the case of a pregnancy, or an injury.

Initial Treatment Date The date of the patient's first visit to the physician for this condition is entered in the Initial Treatment Date box. The actual date can be entered, or the pop-up calendar can be activated and dates selected.

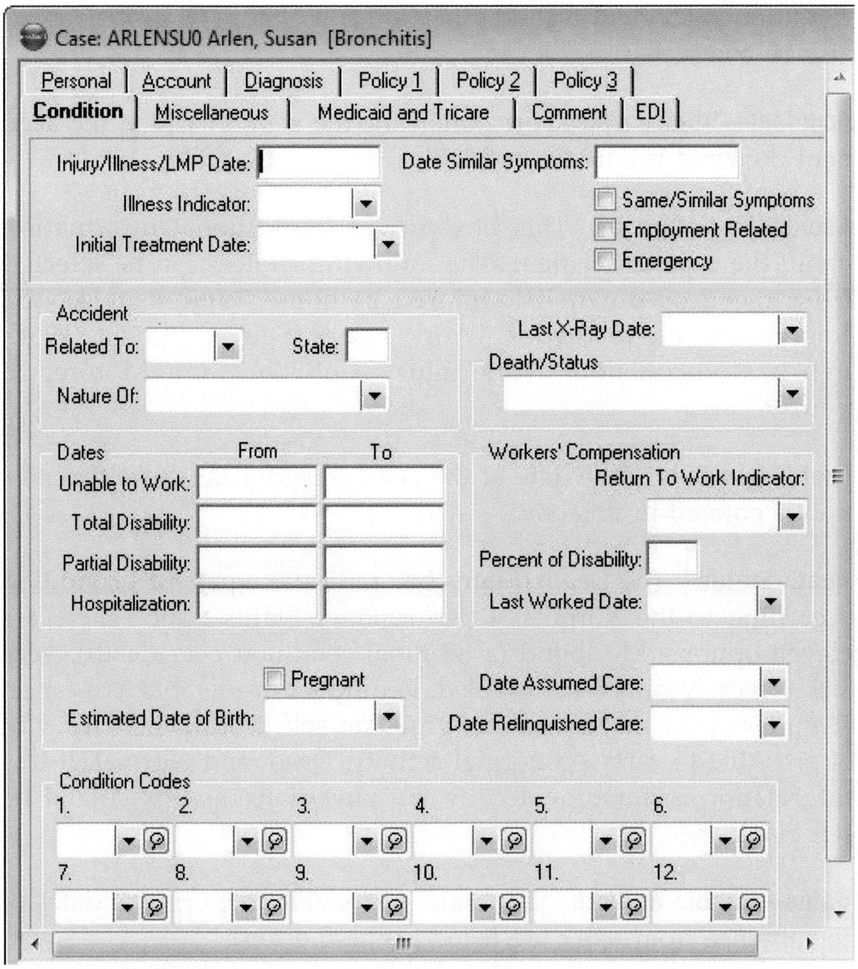

Figure 5-11   Condition Tab

Date Similar Symptoms   If a patient has had similar symptoms in the past, enter the date of those symptoms in the Date Similar Symptoms box.

Same/Similar Symptoms   A check mark in the Same/Similar Symptoms box indicates that a patient has had the same or similar symptoms in the past.

Employment Related   If the Employment Related box is checked, it means that the illness or accident is in some way related to a patient's employment.

Emergency   If a patient sees the provider on an emergency visit, a check mark is entered in the Emergency box.

Accident—Related To   The Accident—Related To box indicates whether a patient's condition is related to an accident. The drop-down list offers three choices: Auto, if an automobile accident is involved; No, if it is not accident-related; and Yes, if it is accident-related but not related to an auto accident. If a patient's condition is accident-related, the State and Nature Of boxes should also be completed.

Accident—State   The abbreviation for the state in which the accident occurred is entered in this box.

Accident—Nature Of   This box provides additional information about the type of accident. The following choices can be selected from the drop-down list: Injured at home, Injured at school, Injured during recreation, Work injury/Self employed, Work injury/Non-collision, Work injury/Collision, and Motorcycle injury.

Last X-Ray Date   The date of the last X-rays for the current condition is entered in this box.

Death/Status   The Death/Status box indicates a patient's condition according to the Karnofsky Performance Status Scale. There are eleven options: Moribund (a terminal condition near death), Very sick, Severely disabled, Disabled, Requires considerable assistance, Requires occasional assistance, Cares for self, Normal activity with effort, Able to carry on normal activity, Dead, and Normal. If this information is not provided by the physician, the box should be left blank.

Dates—Unable to Work   If a patient is unable to work, the dates of the absence from work are listed in these boxes.

Dates—Total Disability   If a patient is totally disabled, the dates of the total disability are entered in these boxes.

Dates—Partial Disability   If a patient is partially disabled, the dates of the partial disability are listed in these boxes.

Dates—Hospitalization   If a patient is hospitalized, the dates of the hospitalization are entered in these boxes.

Workers' Compensation—Return To Work Indicator   If a patient has been out of work on workers' compensation, the patient's return to work status is selected from the drop-down list of choices: Limited, Normal, or Conditional. If the status is Conditional or Limited, the Percent of Disability box should also be completed.

Workers' Compensation—Percent of Disability   This box indicates a patient's percentage of disability upon returning to work.

Workers' Compensation—Last Worked Date   The last day the patient worked is listed in this box.

Pregnant   This box is checked if a woman is pregnant.

Estimated Date of Birth   If the patient is pregnant, enter the date the baby is due.

Date Assumed Care   This field is used when providers share postoperative care. Enter the date the provider assumed care for this patient.

Date Relinquished Care   This field is used when providers share postoperative care. Enter the date the provider relinquished care of the patient.

Condition Codes   Condition codes identify conditions or other factors that may affect the processing of claims. Condition codes are used primarily for UB-04 (institutional) claims.

ENTERING DATA IN THE CONDITION TAB   EXERCISE 5-5

Complete the Condition tab for Hiro Tanaka. The information needed to complete this exercise is found on Source Documents 1, 3, and 4.

Date: October 3, 2018

1. Edit the case for Hiro Tanaka.

2. Make the Condition tab active.

3. Enter the date of the injury in the Injury/Illness/LMP Date box.

4. Select Injury in the Illness Indicator box.

5. In the Initial Treatment Date box, enter the date Tanaka first saw Dr. Yan for this condition, which is 10/1/2018. Press Tab. The program displays a Confirm message stating that the date entered is in the future and asking whether you want to change it. Click No.

6. Since this visit resulted from a non-work-related accident, leave the Date Similar Symptoms box, the Same/Similar Symptoms box, and the Employment Related box blank.

7. Choose Yes in the Accident—Related To box, to indicate that the fall was an accident.

8. Since the accident did not involve an automobile, leave the Accident—State box blank.

9. Tanaka was injured while cleaning leaves out of the gutters on her house. Complete the Accident—Nature Of box regarding the type of accident with Injured at home.

10. Leave the remaining fields blank.

11. Check your work for accuracy.

12. Save the changes.

13. Do not close the Patient List dialog box.

✓ **You have completed Exercise 5-5.**

Connect users: go to http://connect.mheducation.com to complete this exercise! Some steps may differ from what is listed here, so be sure to refer to the steps listed in Demo and Practice Modes for guidance.

5.6 ENTERING OTHER INFORMATION

MISCELLANEOUS TAB

The Miscellaneous tab records a variety of miscellaneous information about the patient and his or her treatment (see Figure 5-12).

Outside Lab Work   If the Outside Lab Work box is checked, the lab work was performed by a lab other than the physician's office. If the lab bills the provider rather than the patient, then the provider bills the patient for the lab work even though it was performed by an outside lab.

Lab Charges   The charges for lab work, whether performed inside or outside the practice, are entered in the Lab Charges box.

Local Use A and B   These boxes may be used by some medical practices to record information specific to the local office.

Indicator   If an indicator code is used to categorize patients or services, it is entered in the Indicator box. For example, patients might

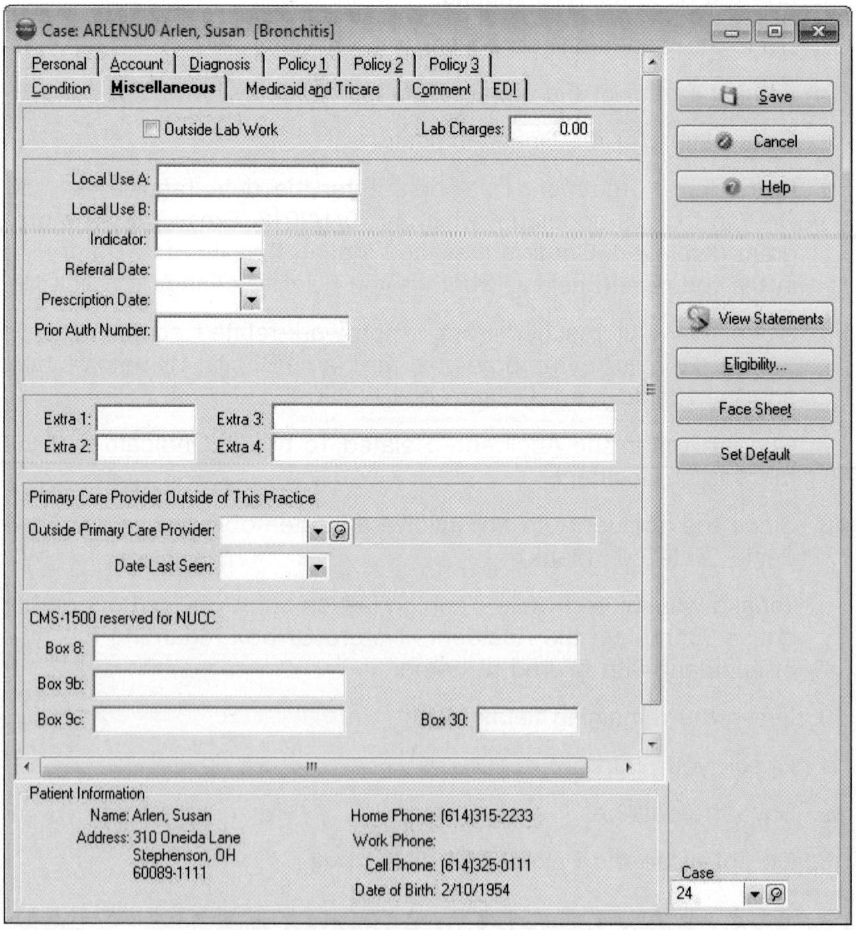

Figure 5-12   Miscellaneous Tab

be categorized according to the primary diagnosis. Services might be divided into such categories as lab work, consultations, and hospital visits.

Referral Date   If the patient was referred to the provider, enter the date of the referral.

Prescription Date   This field is required for hearing and vision claims.

Prior Auth Number   Before some services are performed, prior authorization must be obtained from the appropriate insurance carrier. If an insurance carrier has issued an authorization number for treatment that has not yet occurred, the number is entered in the Prior Auth Number box.

Extra 1, 2, 3, and 4   The Extra 1, 2, 3, and 4 boxes are used for different purposes depending on the medical practice.

Outside Primary Care Provider   If a patient is covered by a managed care plan and the patient's primary care provider is outside the medical practice, the name of the provider is selected from the drop-down list in this box.

Date Last Seen   The Date Last Seen box lists the date a patient was last seen by the outside primary care provider.

CMS-1500 Reserved for NUCC   If necessary, these fields can be used for populating the boxes on the 02/12 CMS-1500 claim form.

COMMENT TAB

The Comment tab is used to enter allergies and notes, EDI notes, contract information, and case notes (see Figure 5-13).

Notes entered in the Comment box will print on statements if statements are formatted to include case comments.

Allergies and Notes   If a patient has allergies or other special conditions that need to be recorded, they are entered in the Allergies and Notes box. The information entered in this field is for internal staff use; it is not used in any claim files.

Note Reference Code   A description of the EDI notes can be selected from the drop-down list:

ADD = Additional Information

CER = Certification Narrative

DCP = Goals, Rehabilitation Potential, or Discharge Plans

DGN = Diagnosis Description

TPO = Third Party Organization Notes

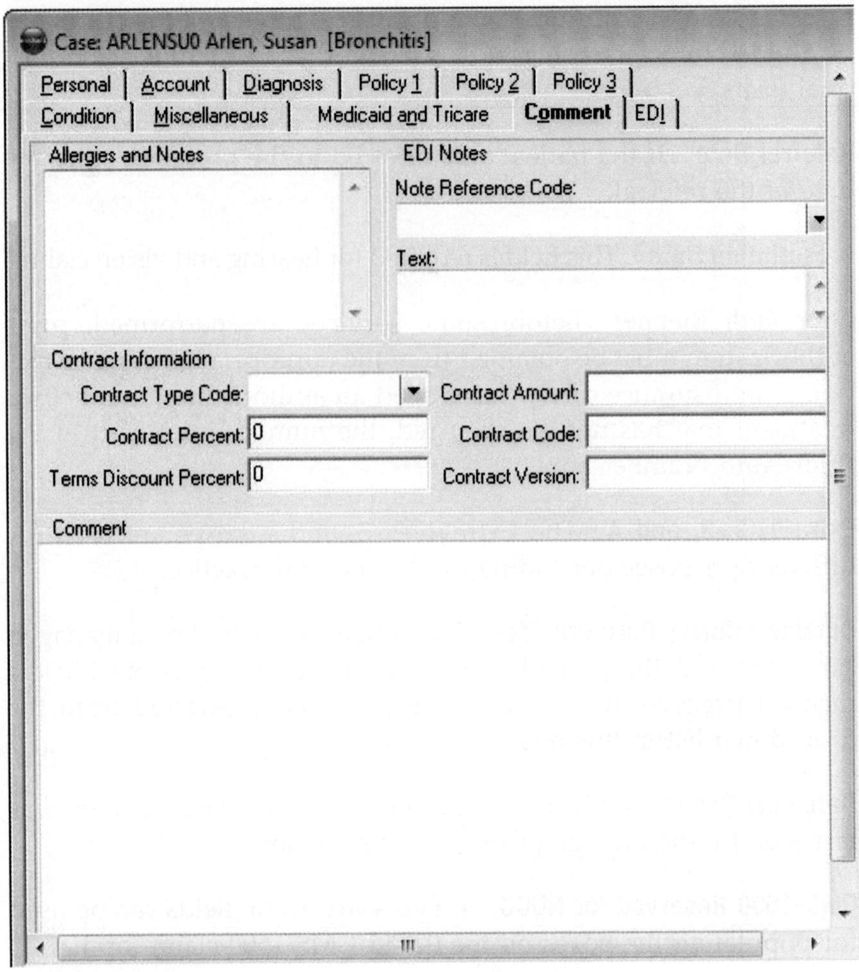

Figure 5-13   Comment Tab

Text   If a patient's electronic claims require special handling, notes about the procedure, such as an explanation about the charges for supplies, are entered in this box.

Contract Type Code   Primarily used when the payer's contract arrangement with the provider is other than fee-for-service. Options on the drop-down list include:

01 = Diagnosis Related Group (DRG)

02 = Per Diem

03 = Variable Per Diem

04 = Flat

05 = Capitated

06 = Percent

09 = Other

Contract Amount   If the provider is required by contract to supply this information on the claim, the amount of the contract agreement is entered in this field.

Contract Percent   If the provider is required by contract to supply this information on the claim, enter the percentage of the contract agreement.

Contract Code   If the provider is required by contract to supply this information on the claim, enter the contract code. Up to fifty characters may be entered.

Terms Discount Percent   If the provider is required by contract to supply this information on the claim, enter the discount percent that is part of the agreement.

Contract Version   If the provider is required by contract to supply this information on the claim, enter the contract version. Up to thirty characters may be entered.

ENTERING DATA IN THE COMMENT TAB   EXERCISE 5-6

Record Hiro Tanaka's allergy in the Comment tab. The information needed to complete this exercise is found on Source Document 1.

Date: October 1, 2018

1. Edit the case for Hiro Tanaka.
2. Make the Comment tab active.
3. Enter the allergy in the Allergies and Notes box.
4. Leave the remaining fields blank.
5. Check your work for accuracy.
6. Save the changes.
7. Do not close the Patient List dialog box.

✓ **You have completed Exercise 5-6.**

Connect users: go to http://connect.mheducation.com to complete this exercise! Some steps may differ from what is listed here, so be sure to refer to the steps listed in Demo and Practice Modes for guidance.

EDI TAB

The EDI tab is used to enter information for electronic claims specific to this case (see Figure 5-14). Only fields that are relevant for the particular case need to be completed.

Care Plan Oversight #   If a physician is billing for home health and hospice care plan oversight (CPO), enter the care plan oversight number.

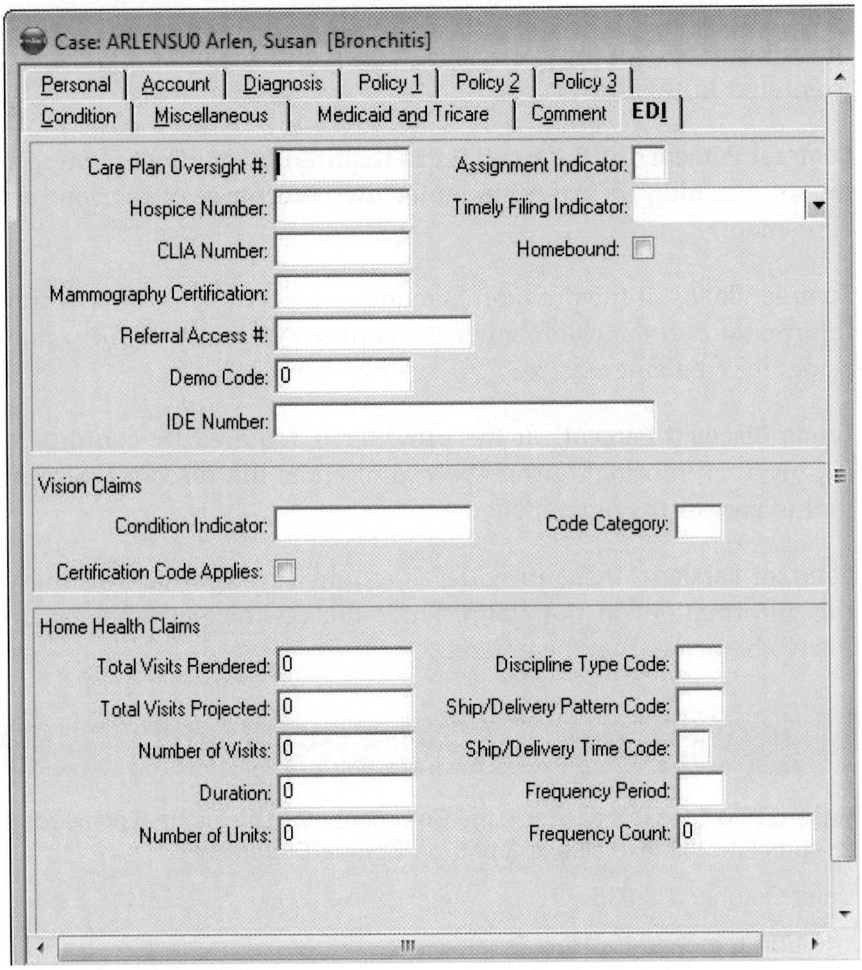

Figure 5-14   EDI Tab

Hospice Number   If a physician is billing for hospice care, enter the hospice number.

CLIA Number   When laboratory claims are billed electronically, the Clinical Laboratory Improvement Act (CLIA) number must be included in the claim. This number is assigned to labs and required on all laboratory claims billed to Medicare.

Mammography Certification   This box lists the provider's or facility's mammography certification number.

Referral Access #   The referring physician's Medicaid referral access number for the patient is entered in this field.

Demo Code   This field is used when filing claims for this patient under demonstration projects.

IDE Number   The IDE number is required when there is an investigational device exemption on the claim. This is usually for vision claims but can also be assigned for other types of claims.

Assignment Indicator   The entry in this field is the assignment indicator for this case. Valid codes are:

A Assigned

B Assignment accepted on clinical lab services only

C Not assigned

P Patient refuses to assign benefits

Timely Filing Indicator   If a response to a request for information from an insurance carrier was delayed, the reason for the delay is selected from the drop-down list of entries:

Administration delay in the prior approval process (10)

Authorization delays (3)

Delay in certifying provider (4)

Delay in delivery of custom-made appliances (6)

Delay in eligibility determination (8)

Delay in supplying billing forms (5)

Litigation (2)

Natural disaster (15)

Original claim rejected or denied (9)

Other (11)

Proof of eligibility unknown or unavailable (1)

Third-party processing delay (7)

Homebound   If the patient is under homebound care, this box should be checked.

Vision Claims

If a provider submits vision claims, entries are made in these fields.

Condition Indicator   The code indicator is entered in this field.

Code Category   The code category for the vision device is entered in this field.

Certification Code Applies   This box is checked if a certification code is applicable.

Home Health Claims

If a provider submits home health claims, these fields are filled in.

Total Visits Rendered   This field indicates the total number of visits.

Total Visits Projected　This field lists the total number of visits projected.

Number of Visits　The total number of visits is entered in this field.

Duration　The duration of the home health visits is recorded in this field.

Number of Units　This field contains the number of units for the home visits.

Discipline Type Code　The provider's discipline type code is entered.

Ship/Delivery Pattern Code　Enter the pattern code for the home visits.

Ship/Delivery Time Code　This field records the time code for the home visits.

Frequency Period　The frequency period for the home visits is listed.

Frequency Count　The frequency count for the home visits is entered.

5.7 EDITING CASE INFORMATION

Information in an existing case is modified by selecting the case to be edited and clicking the Edit Case button at the bottom of the Patient List dialog box. (The Case radio button must be clicked for the Edit Case button to be displayed.) Alternatively, a case can be opened for editing by double-clicking directly on the case line in the right half of the dialog box.

EXERCISE 5-7　　**EDITING A CASE**

Connect users: go to http://connect.mheducation.com to complete this exercise! Some steps may differ from what is listed here, so be sure to refer to the steps listed in Demo and Practice Modes for guidance.

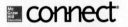

John Fitzwilliams, an established patient, has just divorced. Edit the information in his Case dialog box to reflect this change.

Date: October 1, 2018

1. Click in the Search for field in the Patient List dialog box and press Backspace to delete the existing entry.

2. Enter **F** in the Search for field. All patients who have last names beginning with the letter *F* are displayed.

3. Since John Fitzwilliams is selected (the selection arrow is pointing to his record), click the Edit Case button. Verify that Acute Gastric Ulcer is listed in the Description field.

. 4. In the Personal tab, change the entry in the Marital Status box from Married to Divorced.

5. Click the Save button. **CiMC**

✓ **You have completed Exercise 5-7.**

James Smith has come in for his appointment with Dr. John Rudner to receive an influenza immunization. Using the Copy Case button, create a new case for Mr. Smith.

Date: October 1, 2018

Connect users: go to http://connect.mheducation.com to complete this exercise! Some steps may differ from what is listed here, so be sure to refer to the steps listed in Demo and Practice Modes for guidance.

1. Enter **S** in the Search for field in the Patient List dialog box. All patients who have last names beginning with the letter S are displayed. Click on the line that contains his entry to select him.

2. In the Case section of the dialog box, click on the listing for the Facial Nerve Paralysis case. *Note:* Do not double-click or you will open the case.

3. Click the Copy Case button.

4. In the Personal tab, press the Delete key to remove the existing information. Then enter *Influenza Immunization*.

5. Click on the Diagnosis tab.

6. Change the entry in the Primary Diagnosis field to Z23, Immunization.

7. Click the Save button. **CiMO**

✓ **You have completed Exercise 5-8.**

APPLYING YOUR SKILLS

5: CREATING A CASE FOR A NEW PATIENT

October 1, 2018

Lisa Wright is a new patient who has just arrived for her office visit with Dr. Jessica Rudner. Dr. Rudner accepts assignment from Blue Cross/Blue Shield. Using Source Document 2, complete the Personal, Account, and Policy 1 tabs in the Case dialog box. In the Policy 1 tab, enter **100** in all the Insurance Coverage by Service Classification boxes. (*Note:* Not all tabs and text boxes will have entries.)

Remember to create a backup of your work before exiting Medisoft! To help you keep track of your work, name the backup file after the chapter you are working on; for example, StudentID-c5.mbk.

Creating Cases for Imported Transactions

Transactions received from an electronic health record will not always be related to an existing case in Medisoft. As illustrated below, the Unprocessed Transactions Edit dialog box contains a blank Case field and a message, "Case number does not exist. (Error)".

To process the transaction, a new case must be created. This can be done from the Unprocessed Transactions Edit dialog box simply by pressing the F8 shortcut key, which opens a new Case dialog box in Medisoft.

BE THE DETECTIVE!

If assigned by your instructor, complete the Case Error Video Case in Connect. Put your skills to use identifying mistakes made in Medisoft and enhance your knowledge by determining the impact of those mistakes.

chapter 5 worksheet

[Note: These questions are designed for students using the live Medisoft CD software, since students may need to refer back to specific screens in the software to answer the questions.]

1. *[LO 5.3]* What is the entry in the Referring Provider box for Hiro Tanaka (Account tab)?

2. *[LO 5.6]* What is the entry in the Allergies and Notes box for Hiro Tanaka (Comment tab)?

3. *[LO 5.3]* What is the code for John Fitzwilliams's employer (Personal tab)?

4. *[LO 5.5]* What is listed in the Principal Diagnosis field for Hiro Tanaka (Diagnosis tab)?

5. *[LO 5.4]* Is Hiro Tanaka's insurance plan capitated (Policy 1 tab)?

6. *[LO 5.4]* What is the entry in the Copayment Amount box for Hiro Tanaka (Policy 1 tab)?

7. *[LO 5.4]* What code is entered in the Insurance 1 box for Hiro Tanaka (Policy 1 tab)?

8. *[LO 5.3]* What is entered in the Description box for Lisa Wright (Personal tab)?

9. *[LO 5.3]* What is the entry in the Price Code box for Lisa Wright (Account tab)?

10. *[LO 5.4]* Has Lisa Wright met her deductible for the year (Policy 1 tab)?

11. *[LO 5.4]* Using the information contained in the Case dialog box, list Randall Klein's primary and secondary insurance carriers.

12. *[LO 5.3]* Who is the guarantor for Janine Bell's account?

chapter 5 summary

LEARNING OUTCOMES	CONCEPTS TO REVIEW
5.1 Describe when it is necessary to create a new case in Medisoft.	Cases are organized around a common element. Most often this element is the patient's medical condition. A new case must be created when the patient is treated for a different medical condition. A new case also must be created when the patient changes insurance plans or when treatment is covered by another policy, such as in the case of workers' compensation injuries.
5.2 List the eleven tabs in the Case dialog box.	1. Personal 2. Account 3. Diagnosis 4. Policy 1 5. Policy 2 6. Policy 3 7. Condition 8. Miscellaneous 9. Medicaid and Tricare 10. Comment 11. EDI
5.3 Review the information contained in the Personal tab and the Account tab.	The Personal tab contains basic information about a patient, including: – A description of the case. – Name of guarantor. – Marital and student status. – Employment information. The Account tab tracks basic information about the patient's account, including providers, referral source, attorney, and facility. It also includes accounting codes and visit authorization information.
5.4 Discuss the information recorded in the Policy 1, 2, 3, and Medicaid and Tricare tabs in Medisoft.	The Policy 1, 2, and 3 tabs contain information about the patient's insurance coverage, including: – Insurance carrier – Policy holder – Relationship to insured – Policy and group number – Policy start and end dates There is also information about the assignment of benefits, deductible, and copayment, as well as other insurance-related information. The Medicaid and Tricare tab is used to enter information specific to those claims.

LEARNING OUTCOMES	CONCEPTS TO REVIEW
5.5 Describe the information contained in the Diagnosis tab and the Condition tab in Medisoft.	– The Diagnosis tab contains the patient's principal diagnosis and up to 11 additional diagnoses. There are also fields for entering information specific to electronic claims. – The Condition tab contains information about the general status or condition of the patient. There are many fields for recording data about the dates of an illness or injury. It also includes workers' compensation information.
5.6 Review the purpose of the Miscellaneous, Comment, and EDI tabs in Medisoft.	– The Miscellaneous tab is used to enter information that may be required to submit a claim, including outside lab work and lab charges, a prior authorization number, or the name of an outside primary care provider. – The Comment tab is used to enter allergies, EDI notes, contract information, and notes that can be printed on patient statements. – The EDI tab contains numerous fields in which carrier-specific information for electronic claims is entered.
5.7 Describe how to edit information in a case.	Information in an existing case is edited in the same way it is entered; changes are made directly in the field that contains the information that requires editing.

chapter 5 review

USING TERMINOGY

Match the terms on the left with the definitions on the right.

1. *[LO 5.4]* capitated plan
2. *[LO 5.1]* case
3. *[LO 5.4]* crossover claims
4. *[LO 5.4]* primary insurance carrier
5. *[LO 5.2]* progress notes
6. *[LO 5.3]* referring provider
7. *[LO 5.4]* sponsor

a. Physician's notes about a patient's condition and diagnosis.

b. A physician who recommends that a patient make an appointment with a particular doctor.

c. An insurance plan in which payments are made to primary care providers whether patients visit the office or not.

d. Claims that are processed by Medicare and then transferred to Medicaid, or to a payer that provides supplemental insurance benefits to Medicare beneficiaries.

e. The insurance company that receives claims before they are submitted to any other payer.

f. A grouping of transactions organized around a common element.

g. The active-duty service member on the TRICARE government insurance program.

CHECKING YOUR UNDERSTANDING

8. *[LO 5.4]* Sarina Bell has no insurance of her own but is covered by her father's insurance policy. How would this be indicated in the Policy 1 tab for Sarina Bell?

9. *[LO 5.1]* Is it necessary to set up a new case when a patient changes insurance carriers? Why?

10. *[LO 5.5]* In the Case dialog box, where would you enter information about a work-related accident?

11. *[LO 5.5]* Where is information needed to complete the Diagnosis tab usually found?

12. *[LO 5.1]* A patient has been seeing the doctor regularly for treatment of diabetes. She was hospitalized yesterday, and the doctor saw her in the hospital for treatment of her diabetes. Do you need to set up a new case for the hospitalization?

connect Enhance your learning by completing these exercises and more at http://connect.mheducation.com

Copyright ©2016 McGraw-Hill Education

13. *[LO 5.2]* If the Copy Case command is used to create a new case for a patient, what fields almost always must be changed?

14. *[LO 5.3]* Which tab contains the name of the assigned and referring providers?

15. *[LO 5.6]* Where is allergy information recorded in the Case folder?

16. *[LO 5.7]* Describe the procedure for editing information in a case.

APPLYING YOUR KNOWLEDGE

17. *[LO 5.3]* While you are entering case information for a new patient, you realize that the patient's referring provider is not one of the choices in the Referring Provider box in the Account tab. What should you do?

18. *[LO 5.4]* An established patient has changed insurance carriers from Blue Cross and Blue Shield to OhioCare HMO. What specific boxes need to be changed in the Case dialog box?

19. *[LO 5.1]* Why are patient transactions grouped into cases? What could happen if transactions were not organized by case?

Enhance your learning by completing these exercises and more at http://connect.mheducation.com

chapter 6

ENTERING CHARGE TRANSACTIONS AND PATIENT PAYMENTS

When you finish this chapter, you will be able to:

6.1 Describe the three types of transactions recorded in Medisoft.

6.2 Discuss how to select a patient and case in Transaction Entry.

6.3 Demonstrate how to enter charge transactions in Medisoft.

6.4 Demonstrate how to enter payments made at the time of an office visit.

6.5 Demonstrate how to print a walkout receipt.

6.6 Demonstrate how to process a refund for a patient.

6.7 Demonstrate how to post a nonsufficient funds (NSF) check.

what you need to know

To use this chapter, you need to know how to:

- Start Medisoft, use menus, and enter and edit text.
- Enter patient information in Medisoft.
- Work with chart and case numbers.

key terms

adjustments	MultiLink codes	payments
charges	NSF check	walkout receipt

6.1 UNDERSTANDING CHARGES, PAYMENTS, AND ADJUSTMENTS

Three types of transactions are recorded in Medisoft®: charges, payments, and adjustments. **Charges** are the amounts a provider bills for the services performed. **Payments** are monies received from patients and insurance carriers. **Adjustments** are changes to patients' accounts. Examples of adjustments include returned checks, refunding of overpayments, and differences between the amount billed and the amount allowed per contract. This chapter covers charge transactions and patient payments and adjustments. Chapter 8 covers insurance payment and adjustment transactions.

charges amounts a provider bills for the services performed.

payments monies received from patients and insurance carriers.

adjustments changes to patients' accounts that alter the amounts charged or paid.

The primary document needed to enter charge transactions in Medisoft is a patient's encounter form. Typically, the physician indicates the appropriate procedure and diagnosis codes on the encounter form during or just after the patient visit. Charges and payments listed on an encounter form are later entered in the Transaction Entry dialog box in Medisoft by an insurance billing specialist. If the office uses an electronic health record program that exchanges data with Medisoft, the charges may not require manual posting. After charge transactions are entered, they are checked for accuracy. If all the information is correct, the transaction data are saved and a walkout receipt is printed for the patient. If it is incorrect, the data are edited and then saved.

In Medisoft, transactions are entered in the Transaction Entry dialog box, which is accessed by selecting Enter Transactions on the Activities menu. The Transaction Entry dialog box consists of three main sections, each consuming about a third of the window (see Figure 6-1):

1. Patient/Account Information: The top third contains information about the patient, the insurance coverage, and the patient's account.

2. Charge Transactions: The middle section is where charge transactions are entered.

3. Payment/Adjustment Transactions: The bottom third is where patient payments and different types of adjustments are entered and applied.

6.2 SELECTING A PATIENT AND CASE

The Patient/Account Information section comprises the top third of the Transaction Entry dialog box (see Figure 6-2). It contains two critical pieces of information: chart number and case number. Boxes for entering these numbers are found at the top left of the dialog box.

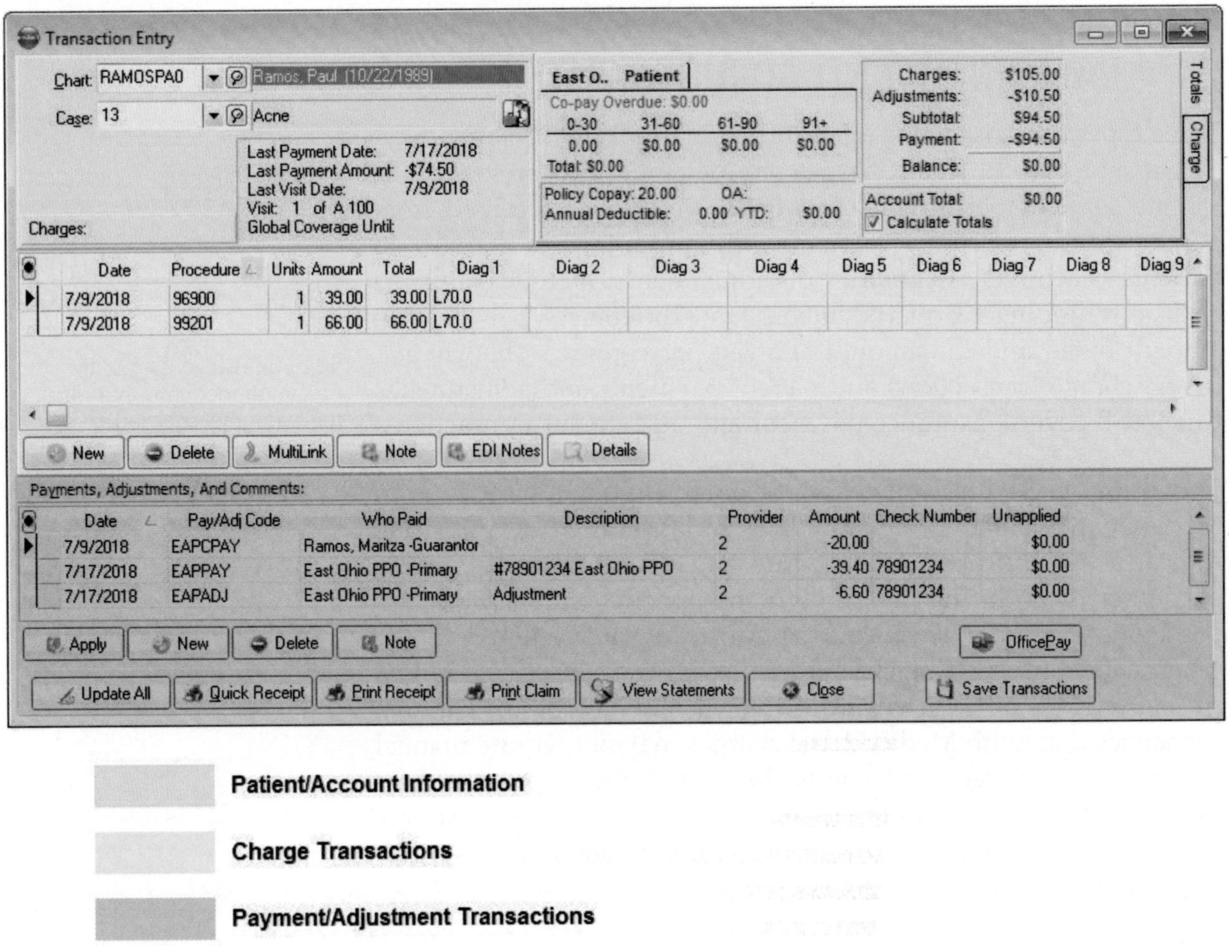

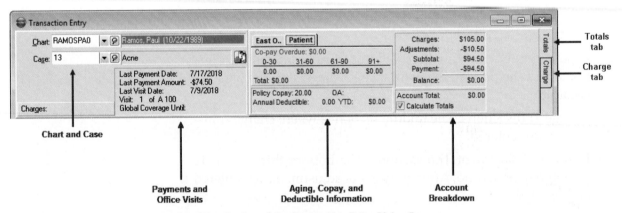

Figure 6-1 Transaction Entry Dialog Box with Three Sections Highlighted

Figure 6-2 The Patient/Account Information Section of the Transaction Entry Dialog Box

CHART

The Chart drop-down list includes all patients in the practice. In large practices, the list of chart numbers could be very long, so it is important to know how to search for a chart number. One way

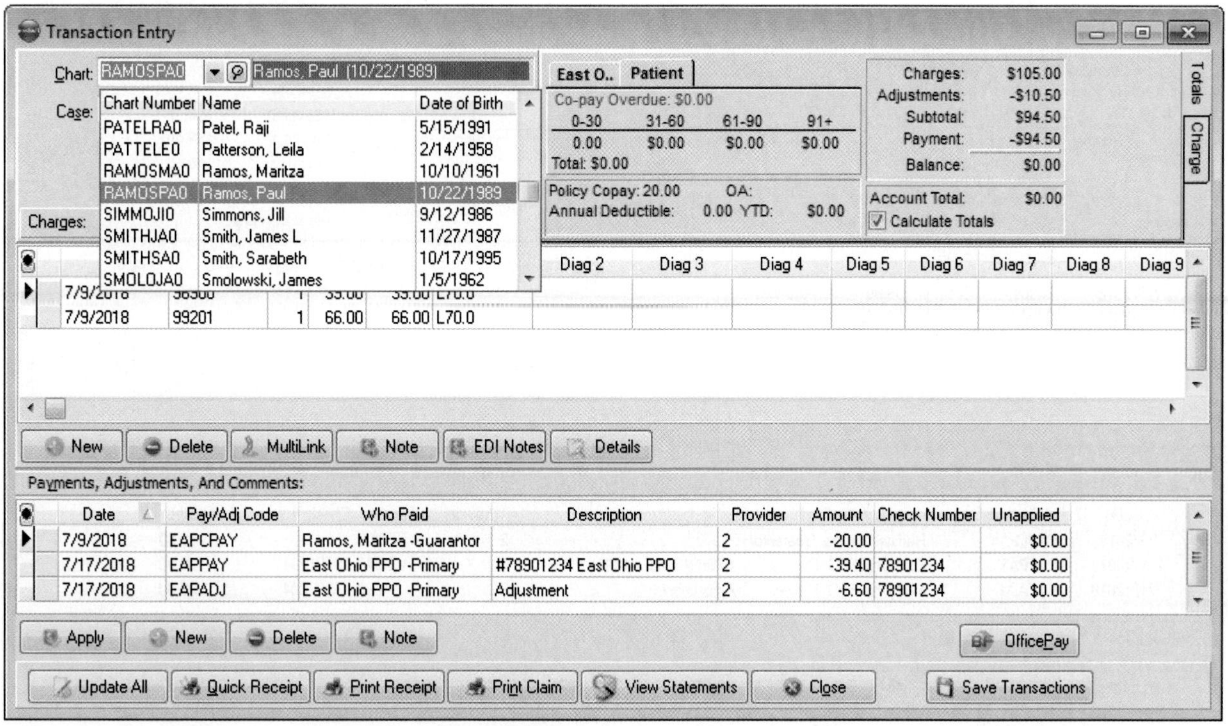

Figure 6-3 Chart Drop-down List after *RAMOSP* Is Keyed

to locate a chart number is to key the first several letters of a patient's last name. As the letters are keyed, the first chart number in the list that matches is highlighted. In the example in Figure 6-3, the letters *RAMOSP* were keyed. The program highlights the first patient with a chart number beginning with those letters—in this case, Paul Ramos. If this is the correct patient, pressing Tab selects the patient and closes the drop-down list. If a different patient is desired, the up and down arrow keys are used to move up or down in the list.

CASE

Once the patient's chart number has been located, the case that relates to the current charges or payments must be selected. Recall from what you learned in Chapter 5 that transactions are linked to a case. The drop-down list in the Case box displays case numbers and descriptions for the patient (see Figure 6-4). By default, the transactions for the most recent case are displayed. Transactions for other cases can be displayed by changing the selection in the Case box. Only one case can be opened at a time.

ADDITIONAL INFORMATION

The remaining areas in the Patient/Account Information section of the Transaction Entry dialog box contain information that is entered automatically by the program and cannot be edited. The dates and

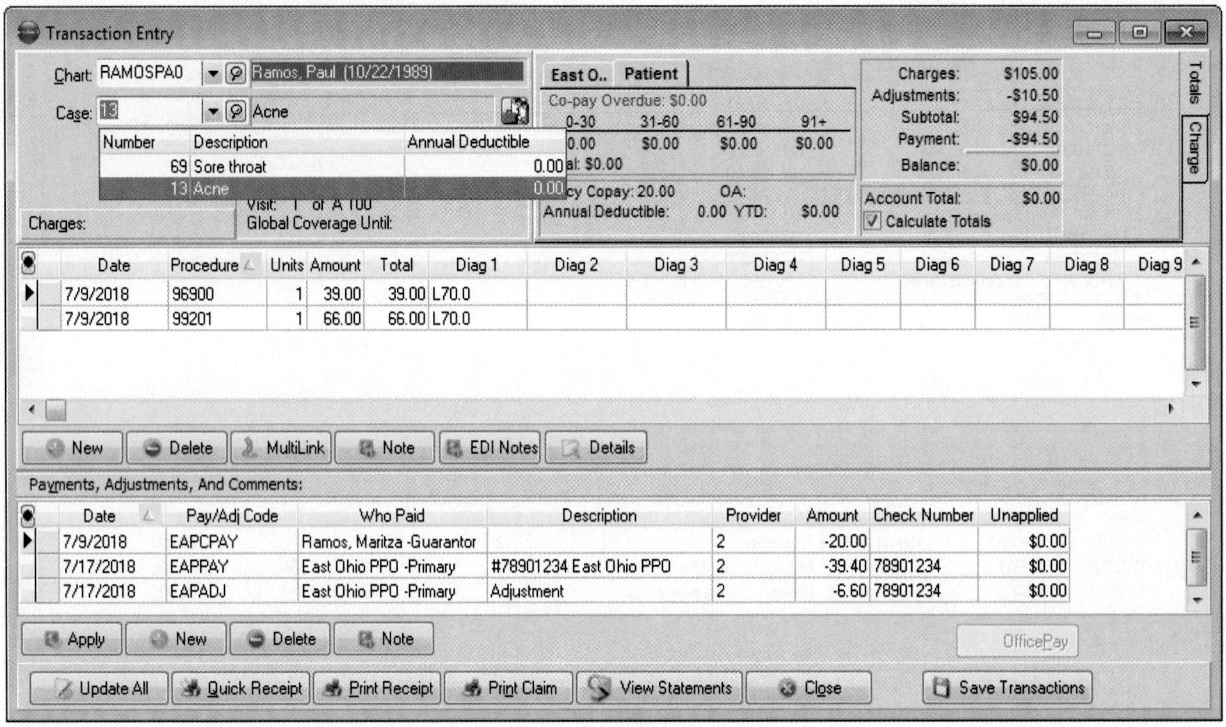

Figure 6-4 Case Drop-down List for the Patient Listed in the Chart Box

figures are automatically updated after a new transaction is entered and saved.

The Aging, Copay, and Deductible section (see Figure 6-2) displays account aging information for the patient and the insurance carrier(s). By default, the Patient tab is displayed. The Patient tab contains the following information:

- Whether a copayment is overdue.
- The outstanding balance for 0–30, 31–60, 61–90, and 91+ days, and the total amount outstanding.
- The amount of the copayment per the patient's health plan.
- The amount of the annual deductible and the amount paid toward the deductible year-to-date.

The Insurance tab, which is not visible until you click on the tab title (the name of the patient's insurance carrier), contains similar information, except it displays aging information for the carrier.

6.3 ENTERING CHARGE TRANSACTIONS

Charges for procedures performed by a provider are entered in the Charges section in the middle of the Transaction Entry dialog box (see Figure 6-5). The process of entering a charge transaction in

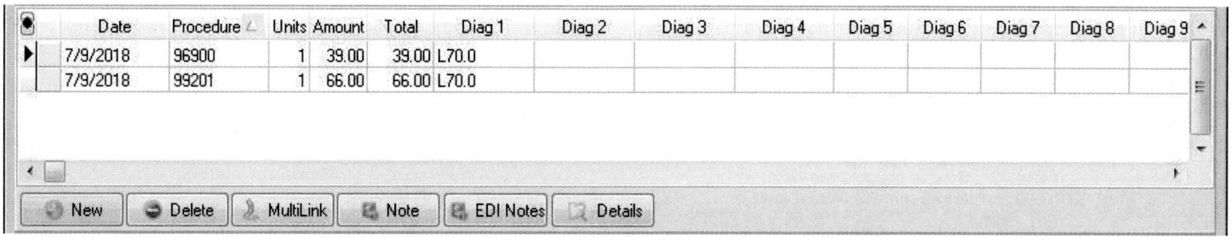

	Date	Procedure △	Units	Amount	Total	Diag 1	Diag 2	Diag 3	Diag 4	Diag 5	Diag 6	Diag 7	Diag 8	Diag 9
▶	7/9/2018	96900	1	39.00	39.00	L70.0								
	7/9/2018	99201	1	66.00	66.00	L70.0								

New   Delete   MultiLink   Note   EDI Notes   Details

Figure 6-5 Charges Area in the Transaction Entry Dialog Box, with the New Button Highlighted

Medisoft begins with clicking the New button, located just below the list of individual charges.

Date When the New button is clicked, the program automatically enters the current date (the date that the Medisoft Program Date is set to) in the Date box (see Figure 6-6). If this is not the date on which the procedures were performed, it must be changed to reflect the actual date of the procedures. To change the default date for these boxes, any of these methods can be used:

- The Set Program Date command on the File menu can be clicked.
- The Date button in the lower-right corner of the screen can be clicked. (This must be done before the New button is clicked in the Transaction Entry dialog box.)
- The information that is already in the Date box can be keyed over with the desired date.

Procedure After the date is entered, the next information required is the code for the procedure performed by the provider. The procedure code is selected from a drop-down list of CPT® codes already in the database. Again, it is more efficient to locate a code by entering the full code number or the first several digits than to scroll through the entire list of codes. In the example in Figure 6-7, the numbers *8, 0,* and *0* were entered, and the first CPT code that matches is highlighted. To select the code, press Tab. If a different code is desired, use the up and down arrow keys on the keyboard to move up or down in the list.

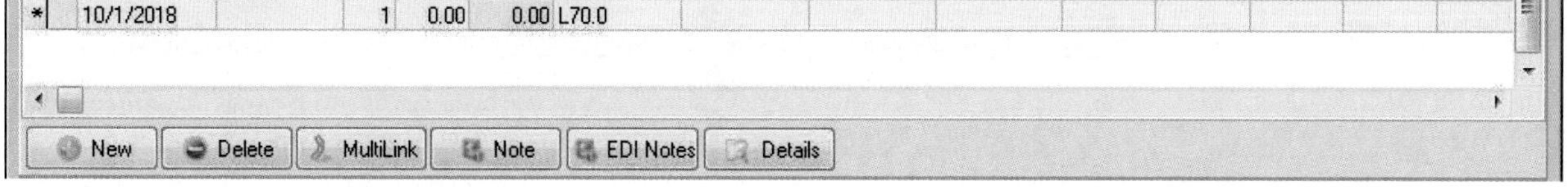

	Date	Procedure △	Units	Amount	Total	Diag 1	Diag 2	Diag 3	Diag 4	Diag 5	Diag 6	Diag 7	Diag 8	Diag 9
	7/9/2018	99201	1	66.00	66.00	L70.0								
	7/9/2018	96900	1	39.00	39.00	L70.0								
*	10/1/2018		1	0.00	0.00	L70.0								

New   Delete   MultiLink   Note   EDI Notes   Details

Figure 6-6 Date Displayed in the Date Column After the New Button Is Clicked (New entry highlighted in yellow)

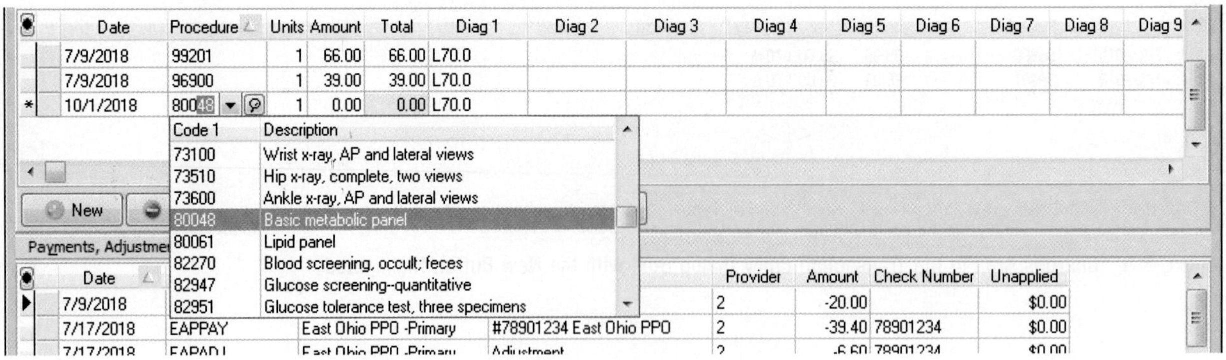

Date	Procedure	Units	Amount	Total	Diag 1	Diag 2	Diag 3	Diag 4	Diag 5	Diag 6	Diag 7	Diag 8	Diag 9
7/9/2018	99201	1	66.00	66.00	L70.0								
7/9/2018	96900	1	39.00	39.00	L70.0								
10/1/2018	80048	1	0.00	0.00	L70.0								

Code 1	Description
73100	Wrist x-ray, AP and lateral views
73510	Hip x-ray, complete, two views
73600	Ankle x-ray, AP and lateral views
80048	Basic metabolic panel
80061	Lipid panel
82270	Blood screening, occult; feces
82947	Glucose screening--quantitative
82951	Glucose tolerance test, three specimens

New

Payments, Adjustme

Date				Provider	Amount	Check Number	Unapplied
7/9/2018				2	-20.00		$0.00
7/17/2018	EAPPAY	East Ohio PPO -Primary	#78901234 East Ohio PPO	2	-39.40	78901234	$0.00
7/17/2018	EAPADJ	East Ohio PPO -Primary	Adjustment	2	-6.60	78901234	$0.00

Figure 6-7 Procedure Drop-down List After the Numbers *8*, *0*, and *0* Are Entered

Only one procedure code can be selected for each transaction. If multiple procedures were performed for a patient, each must be entered as a separate transaction (unless a MultiLink code, which is discussed later in the chapter, is used).

If a CPT code for a procedure is not listed, it can be added to the database by pressing the F8 key or by clicking Procedure/Payment/Adjustment Codes on the Lists menu. This may be done without exiting the Transaction Entry dialog box.

After the code is selected and the Tab key is pressed, the program automatically enters data in the other columns (see Figure 6-8). These entries are described in the paragraphs that follow. If additional information must be added, use the Tab key to move to the box in the appropriate column.

Units The Units box indicates the quantity of the procedure. Normally, the number of units is one. In some cases, however, it may be more than one.

Amount The Amount box lists the charge amount for a procedure. The amount is entered automatically by the system based on the CPT code and insurance carrier. Each CPT code stored in the system has a charge amount associated with it. The charge amount can be edited if necessary. These amounts are determined by the fee schedule(s) for a particular office.

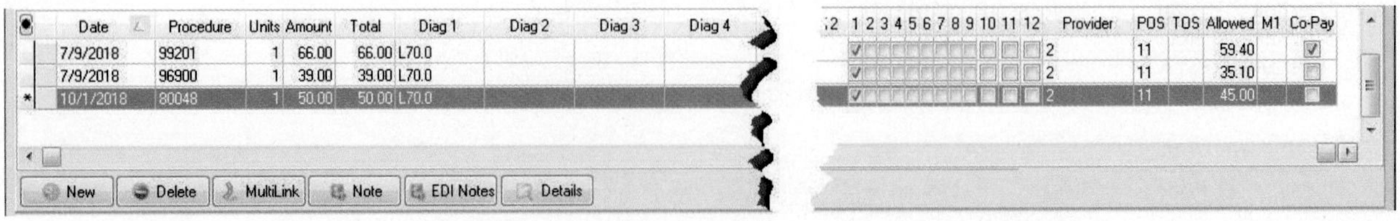

Date	Procedure	Units	Amount	Total	Diag 1	Diag 2	Diag 3	Diag 4
7/9/2018	99201	1	66.00	66.00	L70.0			
7/9/2018	96900	1	39.00	39.00	L70.0			
10/1/2018	80048	1	50.00	50.00	L70.0			

2 1 2 3 4 5 6 7 8 9 10 11 12	Provider	POS	TOS	Allowed	M1	Co-Pay
✓	2	11		59.40		✓
✓	2	11		35.10		
✓	2	11		45.00		

New   Delete   MultiLink   Note   EDI Notes   Details

Figure 6-8 Charges Section of the Transaction Entry Dialog Box After a Procedure Code Is Selected

Total To the right of the Amount box is the Total box. This field displays the total charges for the procedures performed. The amount is calculated by the system; the number in the Units box is multiplied by the number in the Amount box. For example, suppose a patient had three X-rays done at a charge of $45.00 per X-ray. The Units box would read "3" and the Amount box would read "$45.00." The Total box would read "$135.00," which is 3 × $45.00.

Diagnosis The Diag 1 through Diag 12 boxes correspond to the information in the Diagnosis tab of the Case folder. If a patient has several different diagnoses, the diagnosis that is most relevant to the procedure is used.

1 through 12 The 1 through 12 boxes to the right of the Diag 1 through 12 boxes indicate which diagnoses should be used for this charge. A check mark appears in each Diagnosis box for which a diagnosis was entered in the Diag 1 through 12 boxes. Diagnoses can be checked or unchecked as needed.

Provider The Provider box lists the code number of a patient's assigned provider. If a patient sees a different provider for a visit, the Provider box can be changed to list that provider instead.

POS The POS, or place of service, box indicates where services were performed. The standard numerical codes used are:

11   Provider's office

21   Inpatient hospital

22   Outpatient hospital

23   Hospital emergency room

When Medisoft is set up for use in a practice, an option is provided to set a default POS code. In addition, POS codes can be assigned to specific procedure codes when they are set up in the Procedure/Payment/Adjustment Codes List. For purposes of this book, the default code has been set to 11 for provider's office.

TOS *TOS* stands for "type of service." Medical offices may set up a list of codes to indicate the type of service performed. For example, 1 may indicate an examination, 2 a lab test, and so on. The TOS code is specified in the Procedure/Payment/Adjustment entry for each CPT code.

Allowed This is the amount allowed by the payer for this procedure. This value comes from the Allowed Amounts tab of the Procedure/Payment/Adjustment dialog box.

M1 The M1 box is for a CPT code modifier. The grid in the Transaction Entry dialog box can be changed to allow entry of up to four modifiers per line.

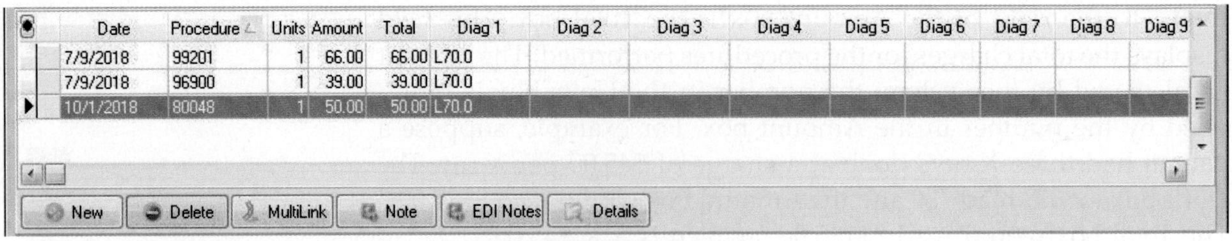

	Date	Procedure	Units	Amount	Total	Diag 1	Diag 2	Diag 3	Diag 4	Diag 5	Diag 6	Diag 7	Diag 8	Diag 9
	7/9/2018	99201	1	66.00	66.00	L70.0								
	7/9/2018	96900	1	39.00	39.00	L70.0								
▶	10/1/2018	80048	1	50.00	50.00	L70.0								

New | Delete | MultiLink | Note | EDI Notes | Details

Figure 6-9 Transaction Selected for Deletion Indicated by Triangle at Left

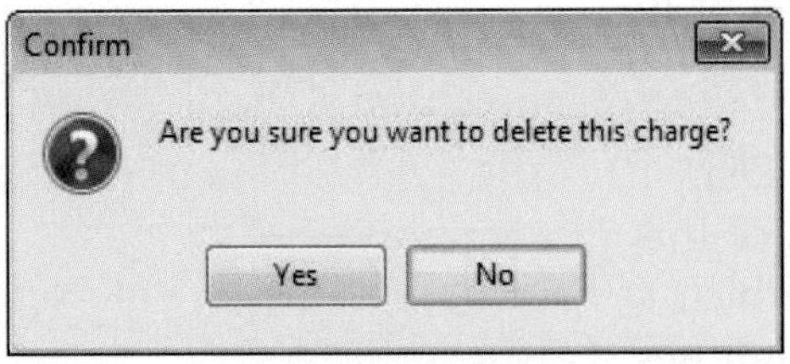

Confirm

Are you sure you want to delete this charge?

Yes   No

Figure 6-10 Confirm Dialog Box Displayed After Clicking the Delete Button

Co-Pay A check mark in this box indicates that the code entered in the Procedure column requires a copayment.

BUTTONS IN THE CHARGES AREA OF THE TRANSACTION ENTRY DIALOG BOX

Six buttons are provided at the bottom of the Charges area: New, Delete, MultiLink, Note, EDI Notes, and Details. The New button, used to create a new charge entry, has already been discussed.

Delete Button To delete a charge transaction, it is necessary to select the particular charge that is to be deleted. This is accomplished by clicking in any of the boxes associated with that transaction (Date, Procedure, Units, Amount, and so on). Clicking in a box selects the transaction, indicated by the black triangle at the far left box on the line (see Figure 6-9).

Once the desired transaction is selected, it is ready for deletion. Clicking the Delete button causes a confirmation message to be displayed (see Figure 6-10). To continue with the deletion, click the Yes button. To cancel the deletion, click the No button.

● All transactions can be deleted from within the Transaction Entry dialog box. Caution should be exercised when using the Delete feature. Deleted data cannot be recovered!

MultiLink codes groups of procedure code entries that relate to a single activity.

MultiLink Medisoft provides a feature that saves time when entering multiple CPT codes that are related to the same activity. **MultiLink codes** are groups of procedure code entries that relate to a single activity. For example, a MultiLink code could be created for the procedures related to diagnosing a strep throat: 99211 OF— Established patient, minimal; 87430 Strep test; and 85025 Complete CBC w/auto diff. WBC.

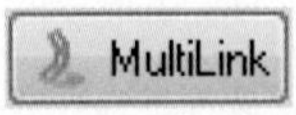

MultiLink

Figure 6-11 MultiLink Button

When the MultiLink button is clicked, the code STREPM is selected from a drop-down list of MultiLink codes already in the database (see

Figures 6-11 and 6-12). All three procedure codes associated with diagnosing a strep throat are entered automatically by the system, eliminating the need to enter each CPT code separately. The MultiLink feature saves time by reducing the number of procedure code entries, and it also reduces omission errors. When procedure codes are entered as a MultiLink, it is impossible to forget to enter a procedure, since all the codes that are in the Multi-Link group are entered automatically.

Clicking the MultiLink button (see Figure 6-11) in the Transaction Entry dialog box displays the MultiLink dialog box (see Figure 6-12). After a MultiLink code is selected from the MultiLink drop-down list, the Create Transactions button is clicked.

The codes and charges for each procedure are automatically added to the list of transactions at the bottom of the Transaction Entry dialog box (see Figure 6-13).

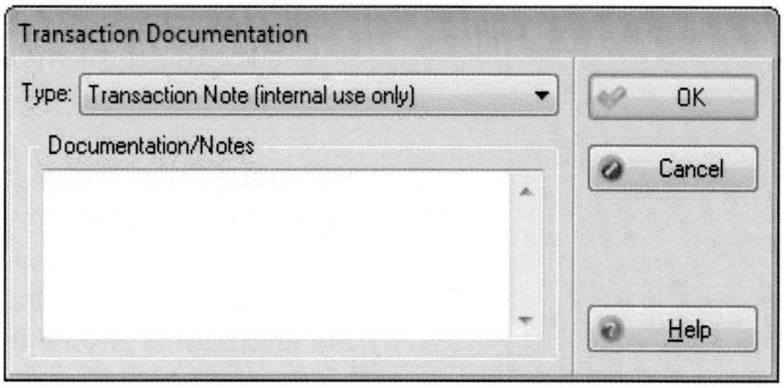

Note The Note button is used to enter additional information about a particular procedure. When the Note button is clicked, the Transaction Documentation dialog box is displayed (see Figure 6-14).

In the Type field, Medisoft provides a list of types of documentation in the drop-down list (see Figure 6-15). Some of the information entered here is transmitted with an insurance claim when claims are transmitted electronically.

EDI Notes Click this button to add notes of the following types: Line Note (NTE), Test Results (MEA), Contract Information (CN1), and Line Supplemental Information (PWK).

Details When clicked, the Details button displays a dialog box that is used to enter drug/prescription information for a charge.

Figure 6-12 MultiLink Code Drop-down List

Figure 6-13 Charge Transactions Created with STREPM MultiLink Code

Figure 6-14 Transaction Documentation Dialog Box, Where Notes About a Transaction Are Entered

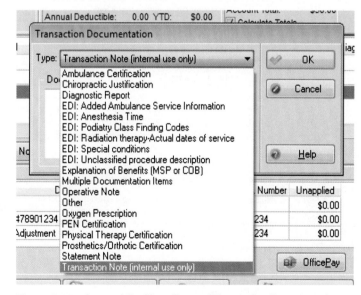

Figure 6-15 Some of the Many Types of Transaction Documentation Available in Medisoft

COLOR CODING IN TRANSACTION ENTRY

Transactions in Medisoft are color-coded, making it easy to determine the status of a charge or payment. No color can be assigned to more than one transaction type at the same time. Color codes are set up using the Program Options selection on the File menu.

In the medical practice used in this text/workbook, the codes have already been determined. Three color codes are applied to the status of a charge:

1. No payment (gray)
2. Partially paid charge (aqua)
3. Overpaid charge (yellow)

Charges that have been paid in full are not colored and appear white.

To display a list of color codes used in the Transaction Entry dialog box, click the right mouse button in the white area below the list of transactions, and a shortcut menu is displayed (see Figure 6-16).

When the Show Color Legend option is selected, the Color-Coding Legend box appears on the screen (see Figure 6-17). The box lists the meaning of the color codes used in Transaction Entry—three for charges and three for payments. The color codes used to indicate the status of a payment are discussed later in the chapter.

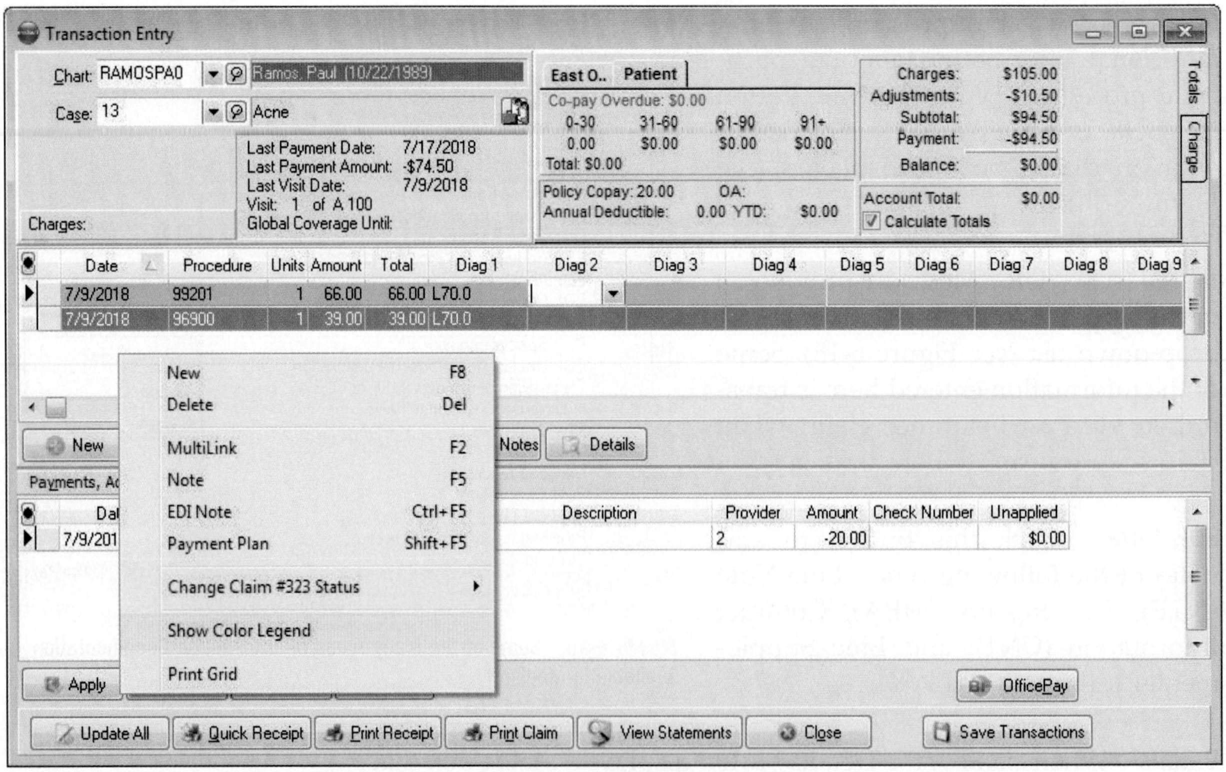

Figure 6-16   Shortcut Menu with Show Color Legend Option Highlighted

In Figure 6-16, the change entry for 99201 on 7/9/2018 is shaded aqua to indicate that it has been partially paid. The other charge, 96900, is shaded gray, indicating that no payment has been made for this charge.

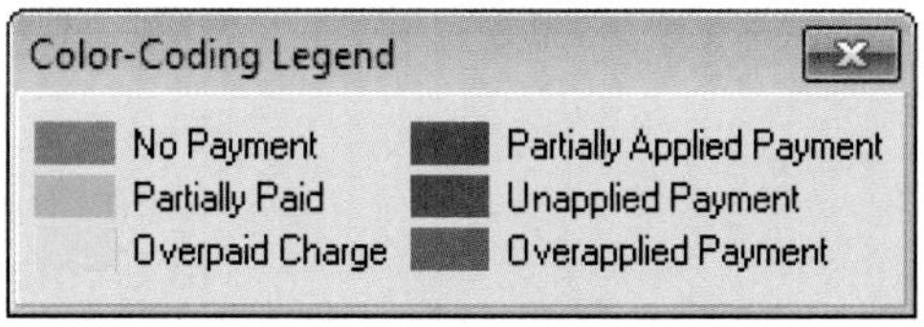

Figure 6-17   Color-Coding Legend Box

SAVING CHARGES

When all the charge information has been entered and checked for accuracy, the transactions must be saved. Transactions are saved by clicking the Save Transactions button, which is located at the bottom of the Transaction Entry dialog box (see Figure 6-18).

Transactions can also be saved by clicking the Update All button located in the same row of buttons. When Update All is clicked, the transactions are saved and the program checks all fields for missing or invalid information and displays various messages, such as a warning that the date entered is in the future.

The other buttons located in this row, Quick Receipt and Print Receipt, are used to print a *walkout receipt* for a patient (covered later in this chapter). The Print Claim button is used to print a paper claim. The View Statements button opens the optional add-on BillFlash Settings dialog box. The Close button simply closes the Transaction Entry dialog box.

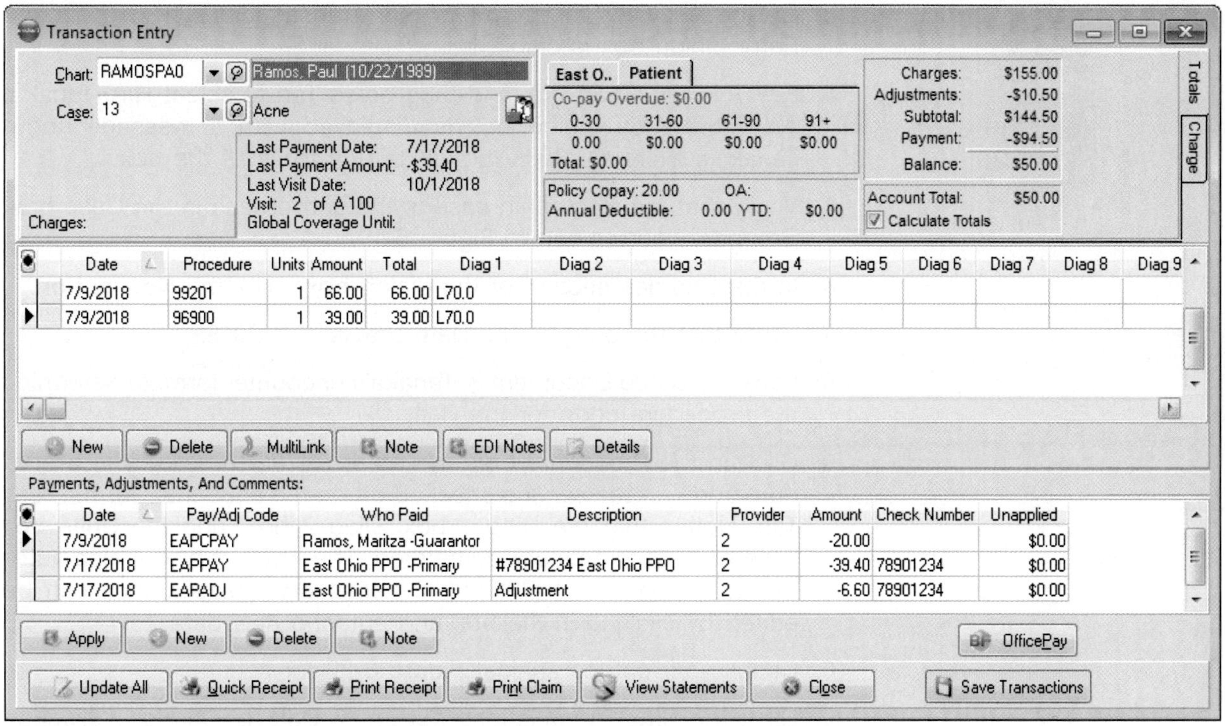

Figure 6-18   Transaction Entry Dialog Box with Save Transactions Button Highlighted

EDITING TRANSACTIONS

The most efficient way to edit a transaction is to click in the field that needs to be changed and enter the correct information. For example, to change the procedure code, click in the Procedure box and either key a new code or select a new code from the drop-down list. After changes are made, the data must be saved. To view the updated amounts in the Patient/Account Information area, click the Update All button near the bottom of the Transaction Entry dialog box.

Depending on the type of edit, the program may display several message boxes. For example, if an attempt is made to change the Payment Type or Who Paid fields, a message is displayed to confirm the change. If someone tries to change a diagnosis code that is already included in a claim, the program asks whether to remove the transaction from the existing claim and create a new claim, or to replace the original diagnosis code in the transaction.

EXERCISE 6-1	ENTERING A CHARGE FOR HIRO TANAKA

Using Source Document 3, enter a charge transaction for Hiro Tanaka's accident case.

Date: October 1, 2018

1. Start Medisoft and restore the data from your last work session.

2. Change the Medisoft Program Date to October 1, 2018, if it is not already set to that date.

3. On the Activities menu, click Enter Transactions. The Transaction Entry dialog box is displayed.

4. Key **T** in the Chart box and then press Tab to select Hiro Tanaka. An Information dialog box is displayed with a message about Tanaka's allergies. Click the OK button to close the box.

5. Verify that the Back pain case is the active case in the Case box. Compare your screen to Figure 6-19.

6. In the Charges section of the dialog box, click the New button.

7. Verify that the entry in the Date box is 10/1/2018.

8. Look at Source Document 3, Tanaka's encounter form, to determine the procedure code for the visit.

9. Click in the Procedure box and enter **99202** to select the procedure code for the service checked off on the encounter form. Press Tab. Notice that the Diag 1 box, Diag 2 box, and the Units box have been automatically completed. The Amount box is also automatically completed ($88.00). If necessary, these entries can be edited by clicking in the box and entering new data.

10. Check your entries against Figure 6-20 for accuracy.

11. Click the Save Transactions button. A Date of Service Validation message appears. Click Yes to save the transaction.

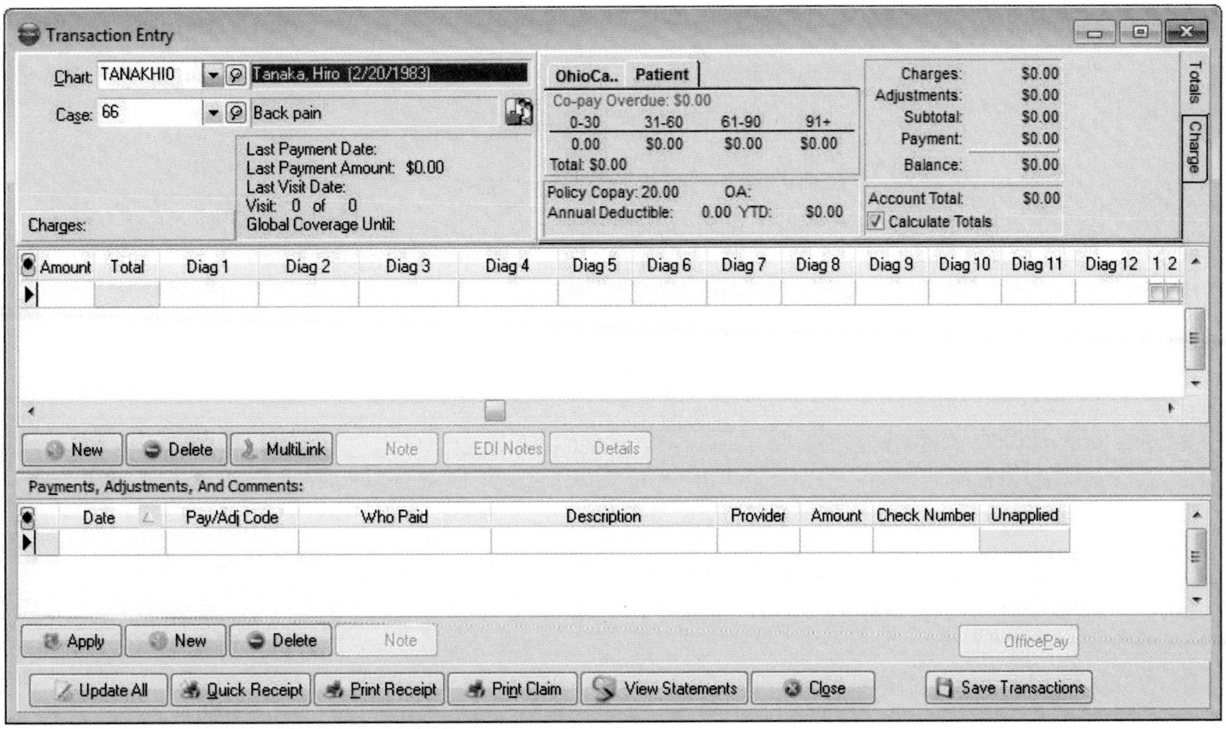

Figure 6-19   Transaction Entry Dialog Box with Hiro Tanaka Selected

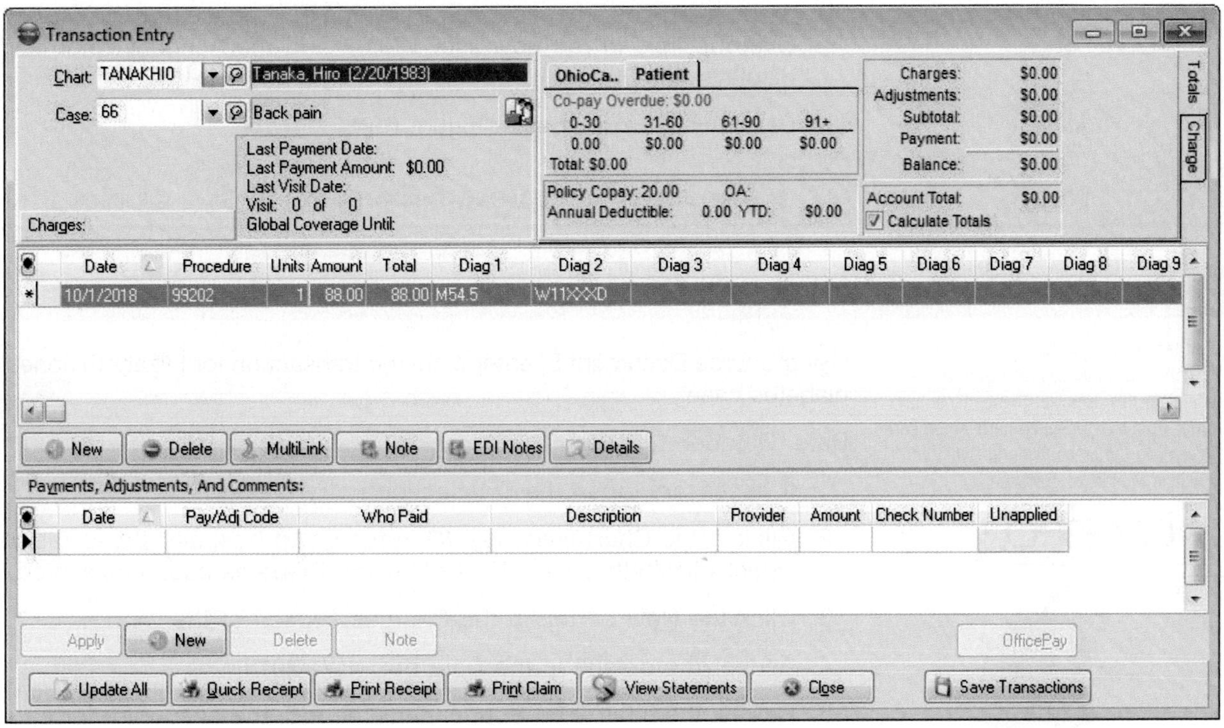

Figure 6-20   Transaction Entry Dialog Box with Charge Entered

| Transaction Entry | | | | | | | | | | | | | | |

Chart: TANAKHI0   Tanaka, Hiro (2/20/1983)

Case: 66   Back pain

Last Payment Date:
Last Payment Amount: $0.00
Last Visit Date: 10/1/2018
Visit: 1 of A100
Global Coverage Until:

Charges:

OhioCa..	Patient

Co-pay Overdue: $20.00

0-30	31-60	61-90	91+
0.00	$0.00	$0.00	$0.00

Total: $0.00

Policy Copay: 20.00   OA:
Annual Deductible: 0.00 YTD: $0.00

Charges:	$88.00
Adjustments:	$0.00
Subtotal:	$88.00
Payment:	$0.00
Balance:	$88.00

Account Total: $88.00
☑ Calculate Totals

Totals / Charge

	Date	Procedure	Units	Amount	Total	Diag 1	Diag 2	Diag 3	Diag 4	Diag 5	Diag 6	Diag 7	Diag 8	Diag 9
▶	10/1/2018	99202	1	88.00	88.00	M54.5	W11XXXD							

[New] [Delete] [MultiLink] [Note] [EDI Notes] [Details]

Payments, Adjustments, And Comments:

	Date	Pay/Adj Code	Who Paid	Description	Provider	Amount	Check Number	Unapplied
▶								

[Apply] [New] [Delete] [Note]   [OfficePay]

[Update All] [Quick Receipt] [Print Receipt] [Print Claim] [View Statements] [Close] [Save Transactions]

Figure 6-21   Transaction Entry Dialog Box with Transaction Saved

12. A message appears that a $20.00 copayment is due. This will be entered later in the chapter, in the section on copayments. Click the OK button.

13. At the top of the Transaction Entry dialog box, notice that the Co-pay Overdue field in red now lists $20.00 and the Account Total field displays $88.00.

14. Check your work against Figure 6-21. CiMC

 You have completed Exercise 6-1.

EXERCISE 6-2   ENTERING A CHARGE FOR ELIZABETH JONES

Using Source Document 5, enter a charge transaction for Elizabeth Jones' diabetes case.

Date: October 1, 2018

1. If necessary, open the Transaction Entry dialog box.

2. Click in the Chart field; key **JO** in the Chart box; and press Tab to select Elizabeth Jones. Verify that the Diabetes case is selected.

3. Click the New button in the Charges section of the window.

4. Accept the default in the Date box (10/1/2018).

5. Review the charge on Source Document 5, the encounter form for her visit.

6. Key **99213** in the Procedure box to select the procedure code for the services checked off on the encounter form. Press Tab.

7. Accept the entry of "1" in the Units field.

8. Accept the charge for the procedure that is displayed in the Amount box ($72.00).

9. Review the entries in the other boxes.

10. Click the Save Transactions button. When the Date of Service Validation box appears, click Yes.

✔ **You have completed Exercise 6-2.**

6.4 ENTERING PAYMENTS MADE AT THE TIME OF AN OFFICE VISIT

Payments are entered in two different areas of the Medisoft program: the Transaction Entry dialog box and the Deposit List dialog box, which will be discussed in Chapter 8. Practices have different preferences for how payments are entered, depending on their billing procedures. In this text/workbook, you will be introduced to both methods of payment entry.

Patient payments made at the time of an office visit are entered in the Transaction Entry dialog box. Payments that are received electronically or by mail, such as insurance payments and mailed patient payments, are entered in the Deposit List dialog box. The Deposit List feature is very efficient for entering large insurance payments that must be split up and applied to a number of different patients.

The first step when entering a patient payment is to select a patient's chart number and case number in the Transaction Entry dialog box. After the chart and case numbers have been selected, a payment transaction can be entered. Payments are entered in the Payments, Adjustments, And Comments section of the Transaction Entry dialog box (see Figure 6-22).

The process of creating a payment transaction begins with clicking the New button. When the New button is clicked, the program automatically enters the current date (the date to which the Medisoft program date is set) in the Date box (see Figure 6-23).

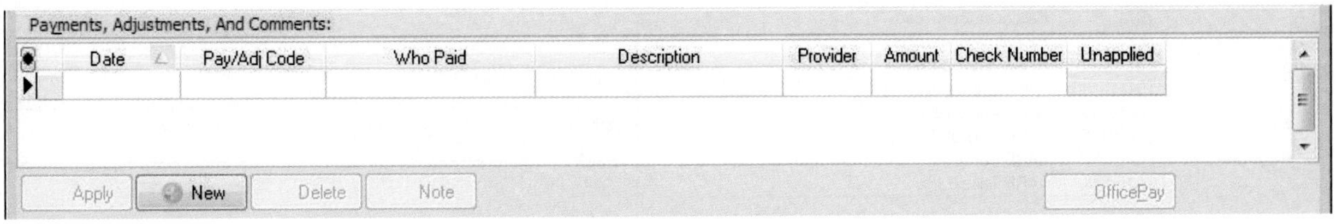

Date	Pay/Adj Code	Who Paid	Description	Provider	Amount	Check Number	Unapplied

Apply | New | Delete | Note | OfficePay

Figure 6-22 Payments, Adjustments, and Comments Area of the Transaction Entry Dialog Box

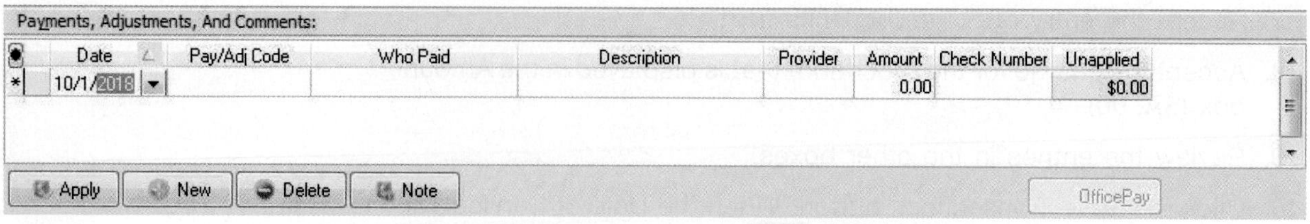

Figure 6-23 Payments, Adjustments, And Comments Area After Clicking the New Button

If this is not the date on which the payment was received, the date must be changed to reflect this date. To change the default date for these boxes, any of these methods can be used:

- The Set Program Date command on the File menu can be clicked.
- The Date button in the lower-right corner of the screen can be clicked. (This must be done before the New button is clicked in the Transaction Entry dialog box.)
- The date that is already in the Date box can be keyed over.

Pay/Adj Code Once the correct date is entered, pressing the Tab key moves the cursor to the Payment/Adjustment Code box. The code for a payment is selected from the drop-down list of payment codes already entered in the system (see Figure 6-24).

If a payment code is not listed, it can be added to the database by pressing the F8 key or by clicking Procedure/Payment/Adjustment Codes on the Lists menu. This may be done without exiting the Transaction Entry dialog box.

Who Paid After the code is selected and the Tab key is pressed, the program automatically completes the Who Paid box based on information stored in the database (see Figure 6-25). The Who Paid field displays a drop-down list of guarantors and carriers that are assigned in the patient case folder.

Description The Description field can be used to enter other information about the payment, if desired.

Provider The Provider column lists the code number of the provider.

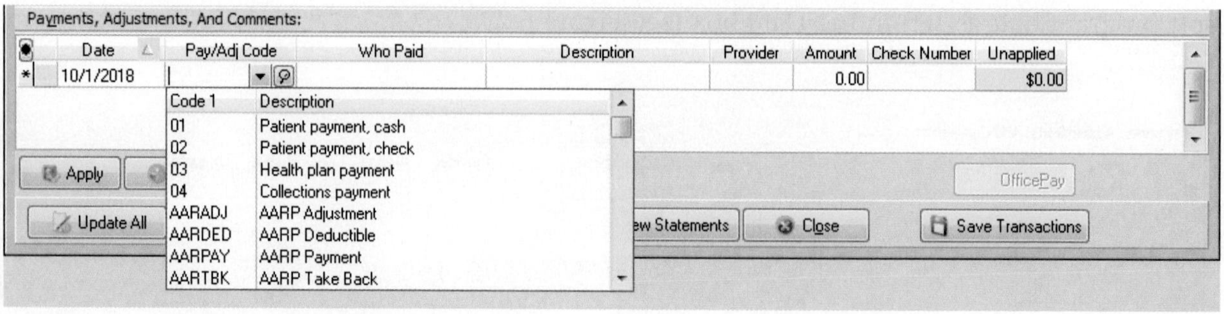

Figure 6-24 Payment/Adjustment Code Drop-down List

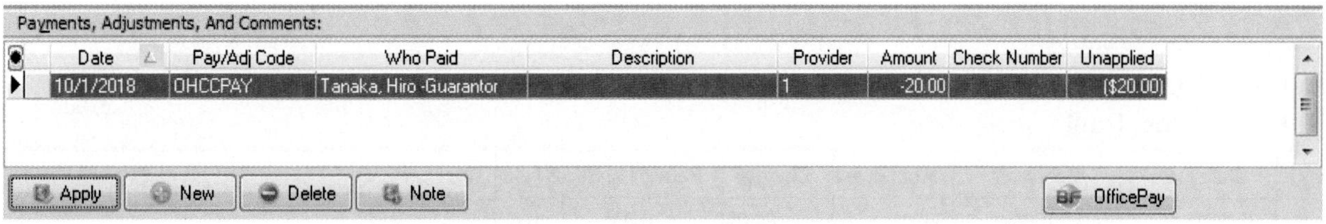

Figure 6-25   Payments, Adjustments, And Comments Area After Payment/Adjustment Code Is Entered

Amount   The Amount field contains the amount of payment received. If the payment is a copayment from a patient, this box is completed automatically when a payment/adjustment code is selected. Again, the program uses information stored in the database.

Check Number   The Check Number field is used to record the number of the check used for payment.

Unapplied   The dollar value in the Unapplied box is the amount that has not yet been applied to a charge transaction.

APPLYING PAYMENTS TO CHARGES

Payments are color-coded to indicate payment status (see Figure 6-26). Three color codes are applied to the status of a payment:

1. Partially applied payment (blue)
2. Unapplied payment (red)
3. Overapplied payment (pink)

Payments that have been fully applied are not colored and appear white.

Once all the necessary information is entered, it is time to apply the payment to specific charges. This is accomplished by clicking the Apply button, which causes the Apply Payment to Charges dialog box to be displayed. The Apply Payment to Charges dialog box lists information about all unpaid charges for a patient, including the date of the procedure, the document number, the procedure code, the charge, the balance, and the total amount paid (see Figure 6-27).

In the upper-right corner of the dialog box, the amount of payment that has not yet been applied to charges is listed in the Unapplied box.

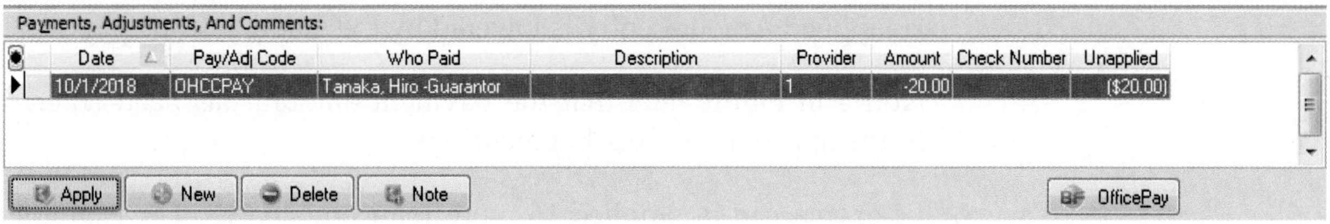

Figure 6-26   Payments, Adjustments, And Comments Area with a Color-Coded Unapplied Payment and Apply Button Highlighted

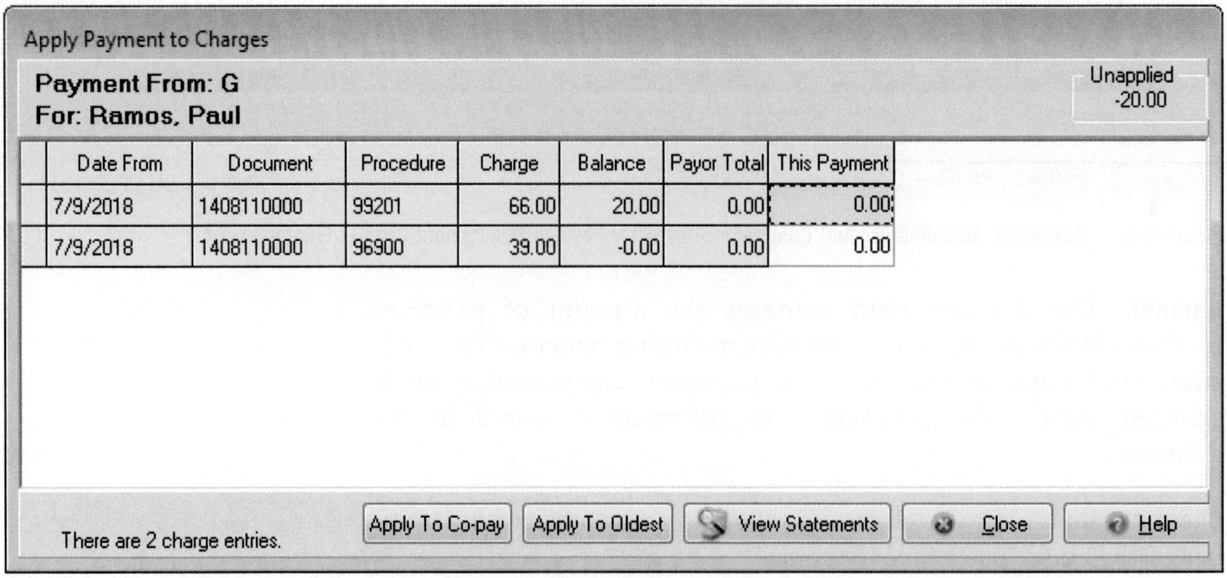

Figure 6-27 Apply Payment to Charges Dialog Box with This Payment Box Highlighted

The first step in applying a payment is to determine the charge(s) to which the payment should be applied. Payments may be applied to charges that require a copayment, charges that are the oldest, or any other charges.

If the payment is a copayment, then the Apply To Co-pay button is clicked. When the Apply To Co-pay button is clicked, the program automatically applies the payment to the charge on that date that requires a copayment. Information about whether a procedure code requires a copayment is located in the General tab of the Procedure/Payment/Adjustment dialog box for that code. In the exercises in this text/workbook, copayments are required for Evaluation and Management Codes—procedure codes that cover physicians' services performed to determine the optimum course for patient care.

If the payment should be applied to the oldest charge, then the Apply To Oldest button is clicked. When the Apply To Oldest button is used, the program automatically applies the payment to the oldest charge.

Payments may also be manually applied by clicking in the box in the This Payment column on the line that contains the charge. To select a box, click in it; a dotted rectangle appears around the outside of the box. Enter the amount of the payment (without a decimal point), and press the Enter key. The payment is applied, and the Unapplied Amount entry is lowered by the amount of the payment.

Notice in Figure 6-28 that the payment amount has been entered in the appropriate This Payment box.

Payments can be applied to more than one charge. For example, suppose that the payment is $200.00 and three charges have not

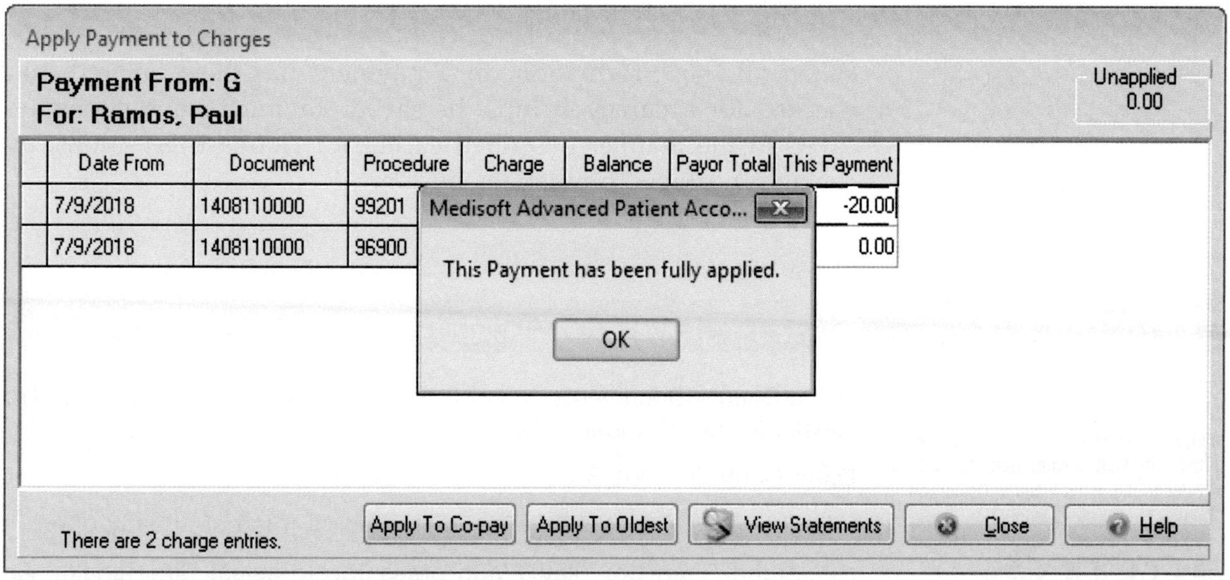

Figure 6-28   Apply Payment to Charges Dialog Box with Payment Entered

been paid. The $200.00 payment can be applied to one, two, or all three of the charges.

Once the box is closed, the payment appears in the Payments, Adjustments, And Comments area of the Transaction Entry dialog box (see Figure 6-29).

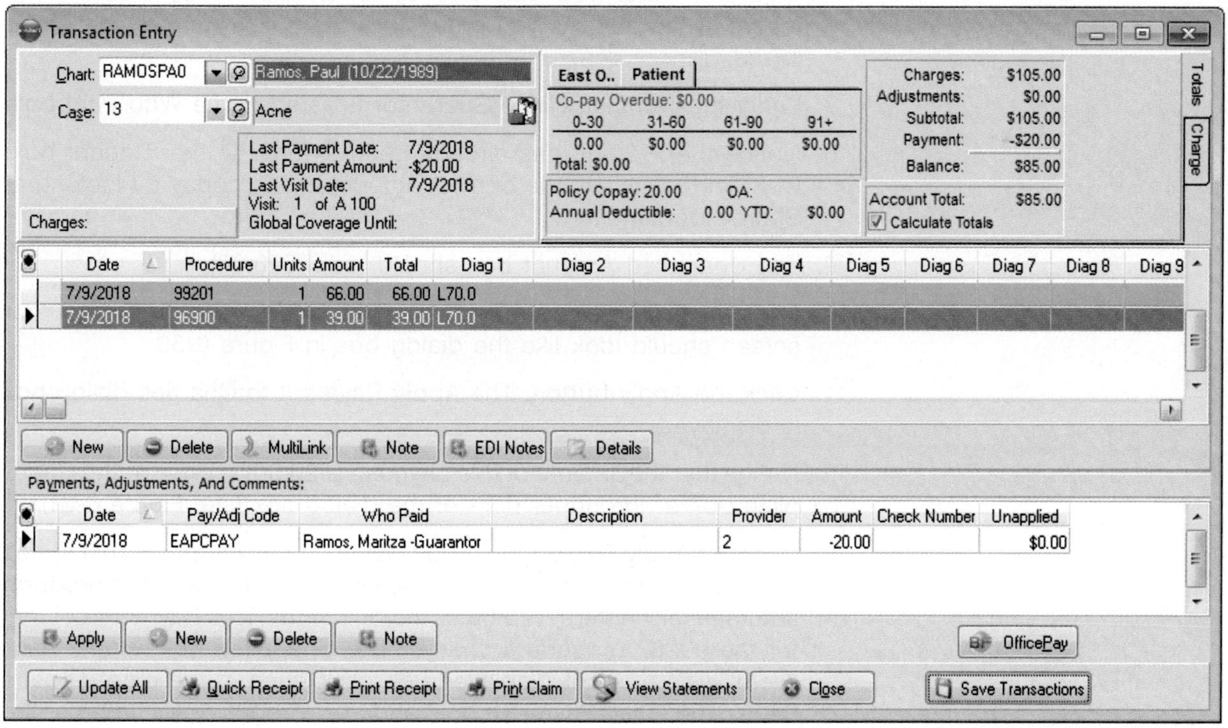

Figure 6-29   Payments, Adjustments, And Comments Area with Payment Listed and Charges Color-Coded as Partially Paid (Aqua) and No Payment (Gray)

SAVING PAYMENT INFORMATION

When all the information on a payment has been entered and checked for accuracy, it must be saved. Payment transactions are saved in the manner described earlier for charge transactions, by clicking the Save Transactions button.

EXERCISE 6-3	ENTERING A COPAYMENT

Connect users: go to http://connect.mheducation.com to complete this exercise! Some steps may differ from what is listed here, so be sure to refer to the steps listed in Demo and Practice Modes for guidance.

Using Source Documents 1 and 3, enter the copayment made by Hiro Tanaka for her October 1, 2018, office visit.

Date: October 1, 2018

1. Open the Transaction Entry dialog box if it is not already open.

2. In the Chart box, key **T** and press Tab to select Hiro Tanaka. An Information box is displayed with information about Tanaka's allergies. Click the OK button.

3. Verify that Back pain is the active case in the Case box.

4. Click the New button in the Payments, Adjustments, And Comments section of the dialog box.

5. Accept the default entry of 10/1/2018 in the Date box.

6. Click in the Pay/Adj Code box. From the drop-down list, select OHCCPAY (the code for OhioCare HMO copayment) and press Tab. Notice that some of the boxes have been completed by the program. *Note:* You can also select OHCCPAY by entering the letters in the box. As you press Tab, the boxes will be highlighted in red.

7. Verify that Tanaka, Hiro—Guarantor is listed in the Who Paid box.

8. Notice that −20.00 has already been entered in the Amount box. Confirm that this is the correct amount of the copay by looking at Source Document 1.

9. The Unapplied Amount box should read ($20.00).

10. Click in the Check Number box, enter **123**, and press Tab. Your screen should look like the dialog box in Figure 6-30.

11. Click the Apply button. The Apply Payment to Charges dialog box is displayed.

12. Notice that the amount of this payment (−20.00) is listed in the Unapplied box at the upper right of the dialog box (see Figure 6-31).

13. Click the Apply To Co-pay button. When the box appears that states "This payment has been fully applied," click OK. The program automatically enters −20.00 in the box in the This Payment column for the 99202 procedure charge. The Unapplied box is now zero. (*Note:* If zero is not displayed yet, click once in the empty space below the This Payment box and the program will update the Unapplied box.) See Figure 6-32.

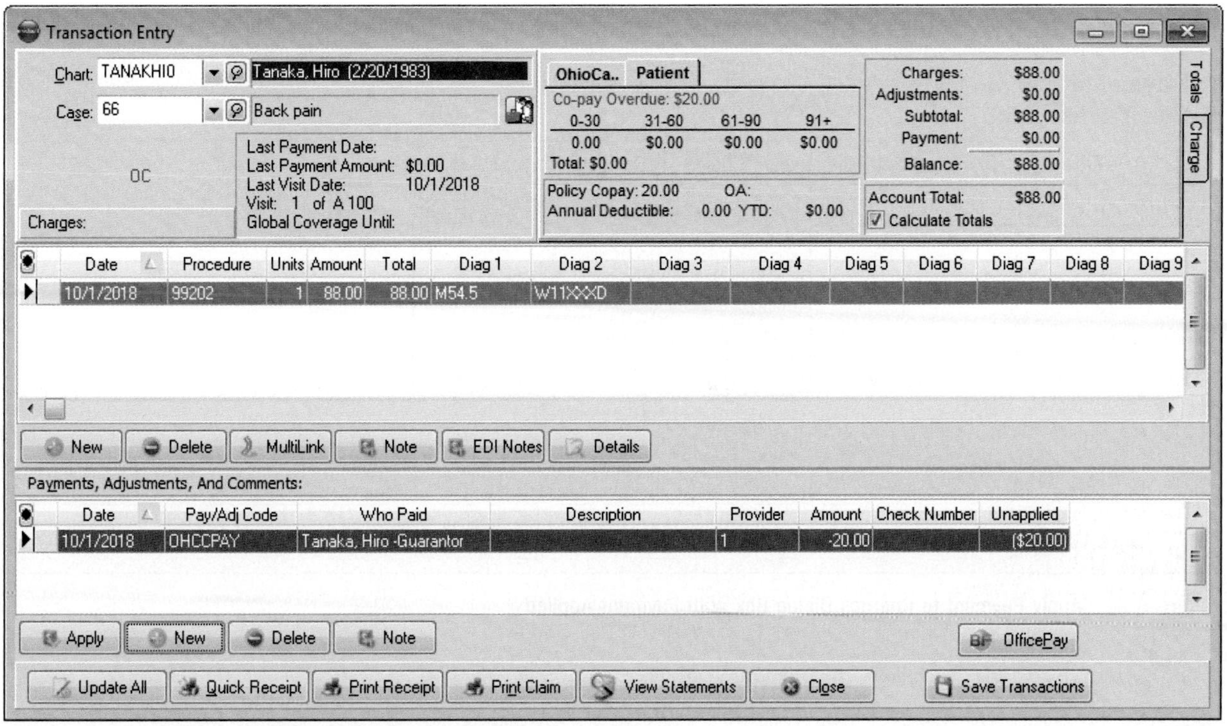

Figure 6-30　Transaction Entry Dialog Box with Copayment Entered

14. Click the Close button.

15. Click the Save Transactions button. When the date warning box appears, click Yes. If an Information box appears with a reminder about the copay, click OK.

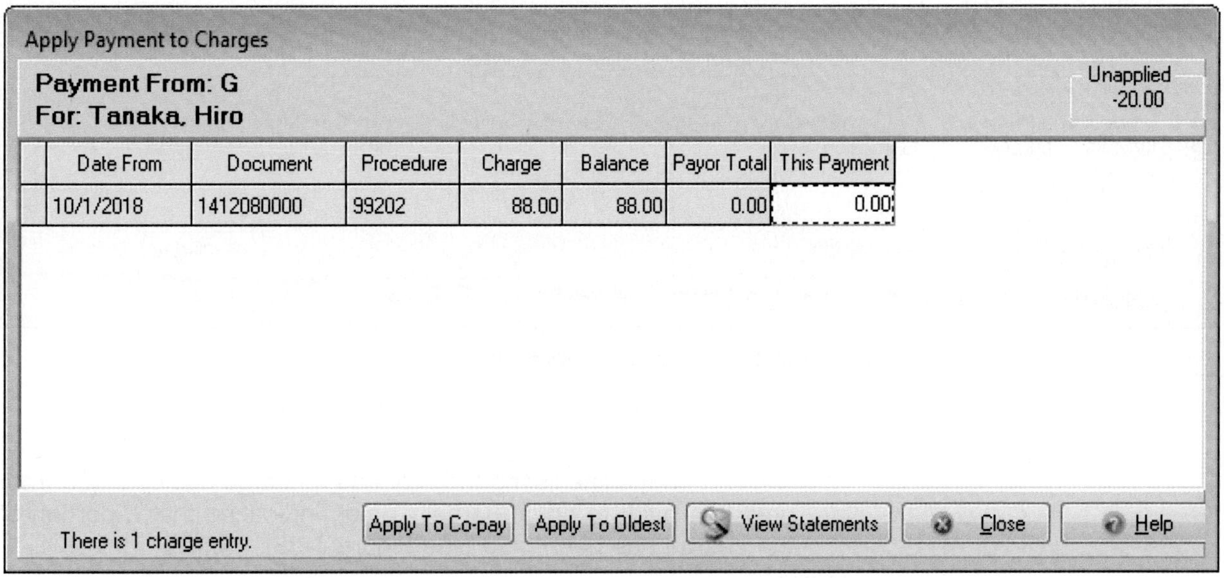

Figure 6-31　Apply Payment to Charges Dialog Box with Payment Unapplied

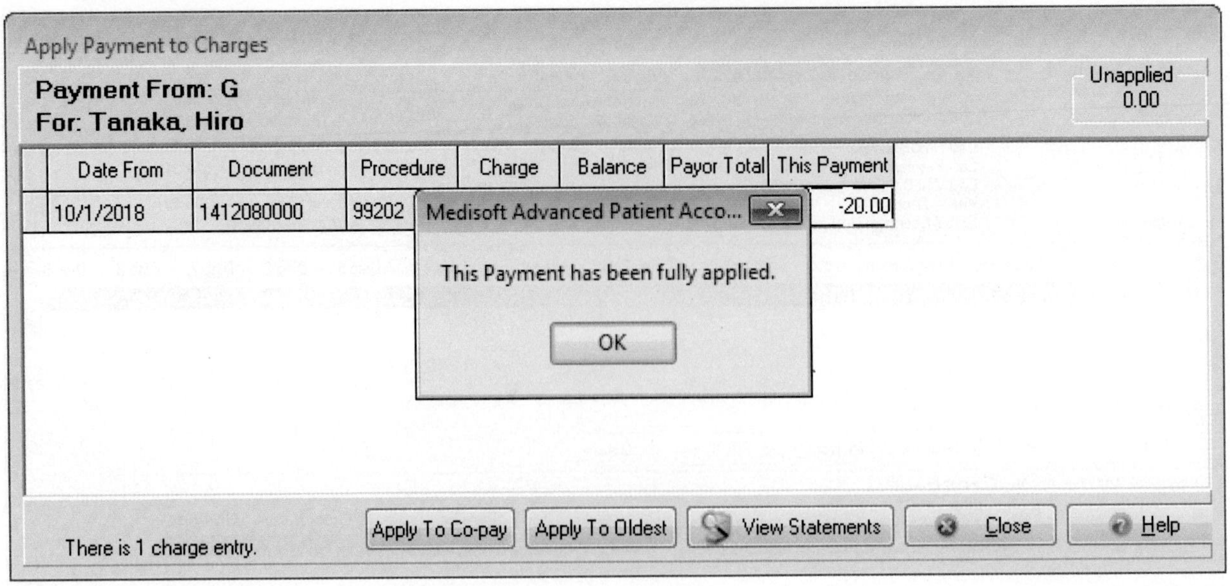

Apply Payment to Charges

Payment From: G
For: Tanaka, Hiro

Unapplied
0.00

Date From	Document	Procedure	Charge	Balance	Payor Total	This Payment
10/1/2018	1412080000	99202				-20.00

Medisoft Advanced Patient Acco... ✕

This Payment has been fully applied.

[OK]

There is 1 charge entry.

[Apply To Co-pay] [Apply To Oldest] [🔍 View Statements] [⊗ Close] [❓ Help]

Figure 6-32 Apply Payment to Charges Dialog Box with Payment Applied

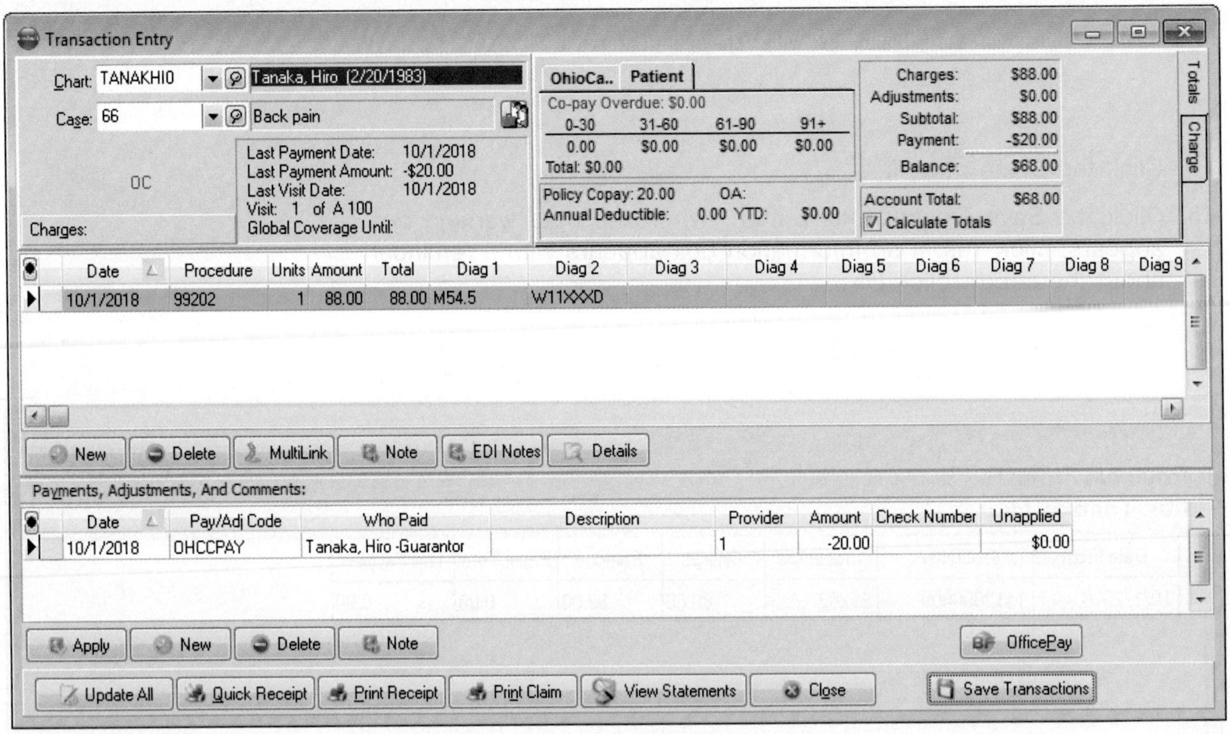

Transaction Entry

Chart: TANAKHI0 ▾ 🔍 Tanaka, Hiro (2/20/1983)

Case: 66 ▾ 🔍 Back pain

OC

Charges:

Last Payment Date: 10/1/2018
Last Payment Amount: -$20.00
Last Visit Date: 10/1/2018
Visit: 1 of A 100
Global Coverage Until:

OhioCa.. | Patient

Co-pay Overdue: $0.00

0-30	31-60	61-90	91+
0.00	$0.00	$0.00	$0.00

Total: $0.00

Policy Copay: 20.00   OA:
Annual Deductible: 0.00 YTD: $0.00

Charges:	$88.00
Adjustments:	$0.00
Subtotal:	$88.00
Payment:	-$20.00
Balance:	$68.00

Account Total: $68.00
☑ Calculate Totals

Totals | Charge

	Date	Procedure	Units	Amount	Total	Diag 1	Diag 2	Diag 3	Diag 4	Diag 5	Diag 6	Diag 7	Diag 8	Diag 9
▶	10/1/2018	99202	1	88.00	88.00	M54.5	W11XXXD							

[◉ New] [⊖ Delete] [🔗 MultiLink] [📋 Note] [📋 EDI Notes] [🔲 Details]

Payments, Adjustments, And Comments:

	Date	Pay/Adj Code	Who Paid	Description	Provider	Amount	Check Number	Unapplied
▶	10/1/2018	OHCCPAY	Tanaka, Hiro -Guarantor		1	-20.00		$0.00

[📋 Apply] [◉ New] [⊖ Delete] [📋 Note]   [🔳 OfficePay]

[📝 Update All] [🧾 Quick Receipt] [🖨 Print Receipt] [🖨 Print Claim] [🔍 View Statements] [⊗ Close] [💾 Save Transactions]

Figure 6-33 Transaction Entry Dialog Box with Copayment Entry Applied and Saved

16. Notice that the line listing the procedure charge has changed from gray (not paid) to aqua (partially paid), indicating that a portion of the charge has been paid (see Figure 6-33). **ᏟᎥᎷᏟ**

✓ **You have completed Exercise 6-3.**

Using Source Document 6, enter the procedure charges and copayment for John Fitzwilliams's acute gastric ulcer case.

Date: October 1, 2018

1. Open the Transaction Entry dialog box, if it is not already open. Click in the Chart box and key **F**. Notice that the chart number for John Fitzwilliams is highlighted on the drop-down list. Press the Tab key. Verify that Acute gastric ulcer is the active case in the Case box.

2. Notice that there are already charges and payments listed for this case, since this is an existing medical condition for which the patient has been treated in the past.

3. Click the New button in the Charges section of the dialog box.

4. Accept the default in the Date box (10/1/2018).

5. Select the procedure code for the services checked off on the encounter form. There is more than one procedure. Enter the first procedure code (99212). Press Tab.

6. Accept the default entries in the other boxes.

7. Check your entries for accuracy.

Now enter the second procedure code marked on the encounter form by following these steps.

8. Click the New button.

9. Accept the default in the Date box.

10. Select the procedure code for the second service checked off on the encounter form (82270). Press Tab.

11. Accept the default entries in the other boxes.

12. Check your entries for accuracy.

13. Click the Save Transactions button. Click Yes when the Date of Service Validation box appears. If an Information box appears with a reminder about the copay, click OK.

Now enter the copayment listed on the encounter form by completing the remaining steps.

14. Click the New button in the Payments, Adjustments, And Comments section of the dialog box.

15. Accept the default entry of 10/1/2018 in the Date box.

16. On the Pay/Adj Code drop-down list, click CHVCPAY (CHAMPVA Copayment), and press Tab. Notice that all the remaining boxes except Check Number and Description are once again filled in. Verify that the entries are correct.

17. Enter **456** in the Check Number box and press Tab.

18. Click the Apply button. The Apply Payment to Charges dialog box is displayed.

19. Notice that the amount of this payment (−15.00) is listed in the Unapplied box at the upper right of the dialog box.

Connect users: go to http://connect.mheducation.com to complete this exercise! Some steps may differ from what is listed here, so be sure to refer to the steps listed in Demo and Practice Modes for guidance.

20. Click the Apply To Co-pay button. When the box appears that states "This payment has been fully applied," click OK.

21. Click the Close button.

22. Click the Save Transactions button. When the date warning box appears, click the Yes button. If an Information box appears with a reminder about the copay, click OK.

23. Notice that the amount listed in the Unapplied Amount column is now zero. Also notice that the line listing the 99212 charge on 10/1/2018 is now aqua rather than gray, indicating that the charge has been partially paid.

24. Notice also that the program moves the most recent transaction in the Payments, Adjustments, And Comments section (the transaction dated 10/1/2018) up to the first row after it is applied. Clicking once on a Date column heading in the Transaction Entry dialog box reorders the transaction dates chronologically from newest to oldest. Clicking again reorders them in the reverse way, from oldest to newest. The order of the dates can be toggled back and forth, depending on your preference. **CiMO**

✓ **You have completed Exercise 6-4.**

6.5 PRINTING WALKOUT RECEIPTS

After a patient payment has been entered in the Transaction Entry dialog box, a walkout receipt is printed and given to the patient before he or she leaves the office. A **walkout receipt**, also known as a walkout statement, is a receipt given to the patient after a payment is made that lists the procedures, diagnosis, charges, and payment. If there is a balance due, the receipt serves as a reminder to the patient of the amount owed.

walkout receipt a receipt given to the patient after a payment is made that lists the procedures, diagnosis, charges, and payment.

In the Transaction Entry dialog box, walkout receipts are created via the Print Receipt or Quick Receipt button (see Figure 6-34). The Quick Receipt option remembers the user's preferred report format and eliminates several steps in the creation of a receipt. (*Note:* A Print Claim button also appears in the Transaction Entry dialog box; claim management is discussed in detail in Chapter 7.)

When the Print Receipt button is clicked, the Open Report window appears with the first report highlighted, Walkout Receipt (All Transactions), as shown in Figure 6-35.

	Date	Pay/Adj Code	Who Paid	Description	Provider	Amount	Check Number	Unapplied	
▶	7/9/2018	EAPCPAY	Ramos, Maritza -Guarantor		2	-20.00		$0.00	

Payments, Adjustments, And Comments:

[Apply] [New] [Delete] [Note]   [OfficePay]

[Update All] [Quick Receipt] [Print Receipt] [Print Claim] [View Statements] [Close] [Save Transactions]

Figure 6-34 Quick Receipt and Print Receipt Buttons Highlighted in Yellow

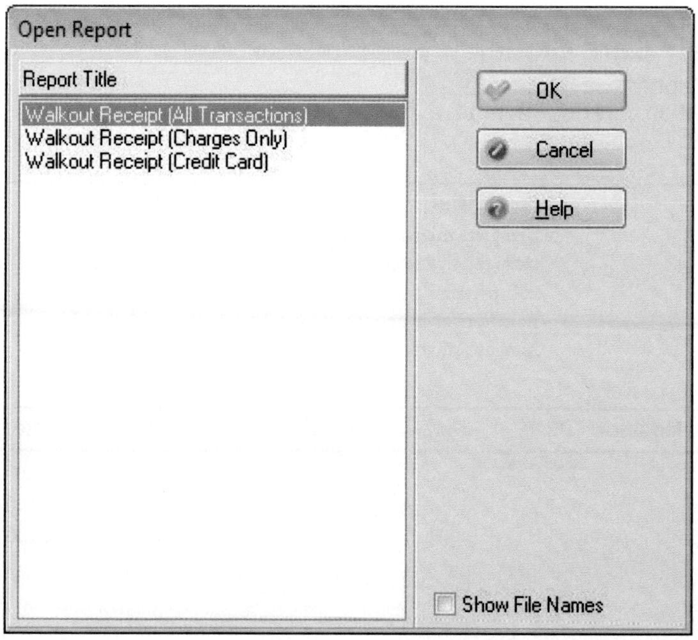

Figure 6-35   Open Report Window with Walkout Receipt (All Transactions) Selected

After clicking the OK button in the Open Report window, the Print Report Where? dialog box is displayed, and three options are provided (see Figure 6-36):

1. Preview the report on the screen

2. Print the report on the printer

3. Export the report to a file

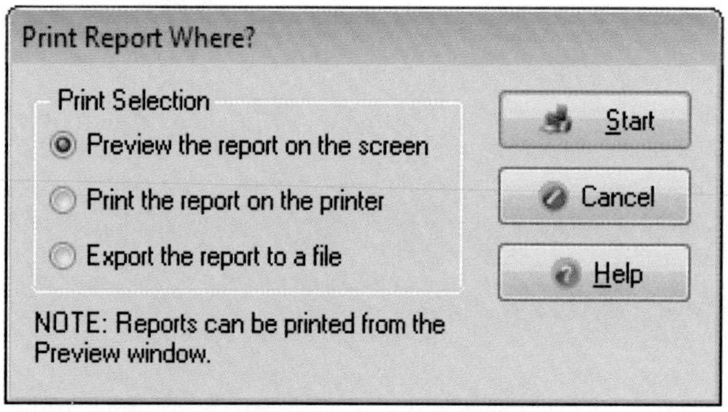

Once a printing choice is made, clicking the Start button causes the Data Selection Questions window to open (see Figure 6-37). This is where the data for the receipt are selected.

Figure 6-36   Print Report Where? Dialog Box

Finally, when the OK button is clicked, the report is sent to its destination (on screen, to the printer, or to a file; see Figure 6-38).

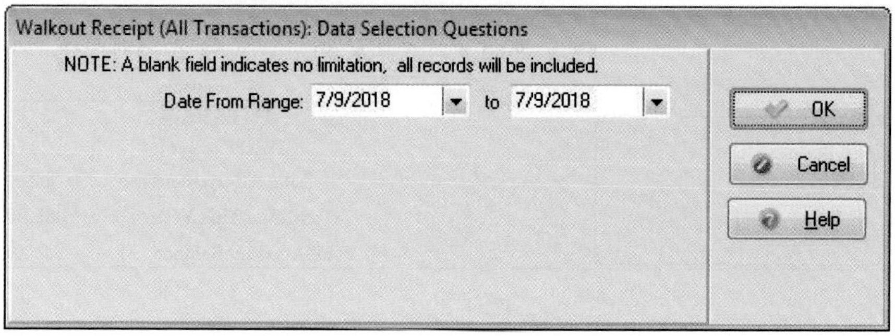

Figure 6-37   Data Selection Questions Window

Family Care Center

285 Stephenson Boulevard
Stephenson, OH 60089-1111
(614)555-0000

Page: 1   7/9/2018

Patient:	Paul Ramos	**Instructions:**
	39 Locust Avenue	Complete the patient information portion of your insurance
	Stephenson, OH 60089-1111	claim form. Attach this bill, signed and dated, and all other
		bills pertaining to the claim. If you have a deductible policy,
Chart #:	RAMOSPA0	hold your claim forms until you have met your deductible.
Case #:	13	Mail directly to your insurance carrier.

Date	Description	Procedure	Modifier	Dx 1	Dx 2	Dx 3	Dx 4	Units	Charge
7/9/2018	OF--new patient, minimal	99201		L70.0				1	66.00
7/9/2018	Ultraviolet light treatment	96900		L70.0				1	39.00
7/9/2018	East Ohio PPO Copayment	EAPCPAY						1	-20.00

Provider Information			Total Charges:	$ 105.00
Provider Name:	John Rudner MD		Total Payments:	-$ 20.00
License:	84701		Total Adjustments:	$ 0.00
Insurance PIN:			**Total Due This Visit:**	**$ 85.00**
SSN or EIN:	504-39-0020		Total Account Balance:	$ 85.00

Figure 6-38   Sample Walkout Receipt

222   cIMO   **PART 2** MEDISOFT ADVANCED TRAINING

CREATING A WALKOUT RECEIPT · EXERCISE 6-5

Create a walkout receipt for John Fitzwilliams.

Date: October 1, 2018

1. With the Transaction Entry dialog box open to John Fitzwilliams's acute gastric ulcer case, click the Print Receipt button. The Open Report dialog box opens with Walkout Receipts (All Transactions) selected.

2. Click the OK button. The Print Report Where? dialog box is displayed.

3. In the Print Report Where? dialog box, accept the default selection to preview the report on the screen. Click the Start button. The Walkout Receipt (All Transactions): Data Selection Questions dialog box appears.

4. Confirm that 10/01/2018 is displayed in both Date From Range fields.

5. Click OK. The Preview Report window opens, displaying the walkout receipt.

6. Review the charge and payment entries listed in the top half of the receipt.

7. Scroll down and review the total charges, payments, and adjustments listed in the lower-right area of the receipt.

8. Click the Close button to exit the Preview Report window. **CiMC**

✓ **You have completed Exercise 6-5.**

Connect users: go to http://connect.mheducation.com to complete this exercise! Some steps may differ from what is listed here, so be sure to refer to the steps listed in Demo and Practice Modes for guidance.

6.6 PROCESSING A PATIENT REFUND

Sometimes it is necessary to make an adjustment to a patient account. This can happen for a number of reasons. Some practices ask patients to make an estimated payment at the time of the office visit. This amount is an estimate of the amount the patient will owe after the expected payment is received from the insurance company. When the actual payment is received from the insurance carrier, it may be greater or less than the estimated amount. If it is greater than estimated, the practice must issue the patient a refund of the overpayment.

Adjustments to patient accounts are entered in the same manner as payments are recorded, in the lower third of the Transaction Entry dialog box. Clicking the New button begins the process of entering an adjustment. When the New button is clicked, the program automatically enters the current date (the date to which the Medisoft program date is set) in the Date box. The other fields include the following:

Pay/Adj Code This code indicates the type of adjustment transaction, such as PTREFUND (patient refund).

Who Paid In the case of a refund, the chart number of the patient who is receiving the refund is entered.

Description The reason for the refund, such as "patient payment more than expected," is entered.

Provider The Provider column lists the code number of the provider.

Amount The amount of the refund is shown.

Check Number The number of the check used for the refund is entered.

Unapplied The dollar value in the Unapplied box is the amount that has not yet been applied to a transaction.

If the patient's account has a positive balance because the patient overpaid, the patient's charge in the Transaction Entry dialog box is color-coded yellow (see Figure 6-39). This indicates the patient is due a refund for that procedure, and an adjustment needs to be made.

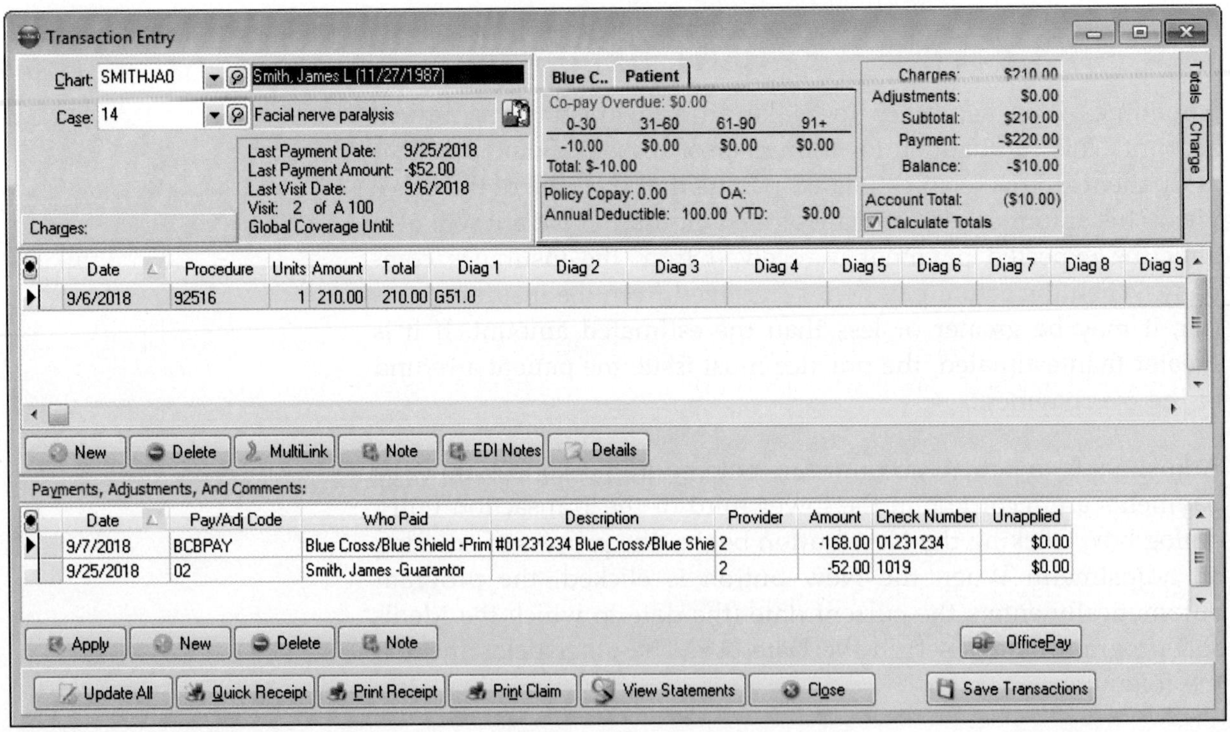

Figure 6-39 Transaction Entry Dialog Box with the Overpaid Charge Highlighted in Yellow

Process a refund for a patient who has overpaid on his account.

Date: October 1, 2018

1. Open the Transaction Entry dialog box, if it is not already open.

2. In the Chart box, key **SM** and press Tab to select James L. Smith.

3. Select Facial nerve paralysis in the Case box.

4. Notice that the entry in the Charges section of the window is highlighted in yellow, indicating that this is an overpaid charge. According to the patient's insurance plan, the plan pays 80 percent of charges and the patient pays 20 percent. In this case, 20 percent of the charges ($210.00) would be $42.00. However, the patient paid $52 and is therefore due a refund of $10.00.

5. Click the New button in the Payments, Adjustments, And Comments section of the dialog box.

6. Accept the default entry of 10/1/2018 in the Date box.

7. Click in the Pay/Adj Code box. Select PTREFUND (the code for a patient refund) from the drop-down list and press Tab.

8. Select Smith, James—Guarantor in the Who Paid box.

9. Enter **Overpaid—refund** in the Description box and press Tab twice to get to the Amount box.

10. Enter **10** in the Amount box and press Tab. Notice that the amount is listed as a positive amount.

11. The Unapplied Amount box should read $10.00.

12. Enter **456** in the Check Number box and press Tab. Check your work against Figure 6-40.

13. Click the Apply button. The Apply Adjustment to Charges dialog box is displayed.

14. Notice that the amount of this refund ($10.00) is listed in the Unapplied box at the upper right of the dialog box.

15. Click in the white box in the This Adjust. column. Enter **10** and press Enter. Your screen should look like Figure 6-41.

16. Click the Close button.

17. Click the Save Transactions button. When a Date of Service Validation box appears, click Yes.

18. Notice that the line listing the procedure charge has changed from yellow (overpaid) to white (fully paid), indicating that the expected amount has been paid (see Figure 6-42). **CiMO**

Connect users: go to http://connect.mheducation.com to complete this exercise! Some steps may differ from what is listed here, so be sure to refer to the steps listed in Demo and Practice Modes for guidance.

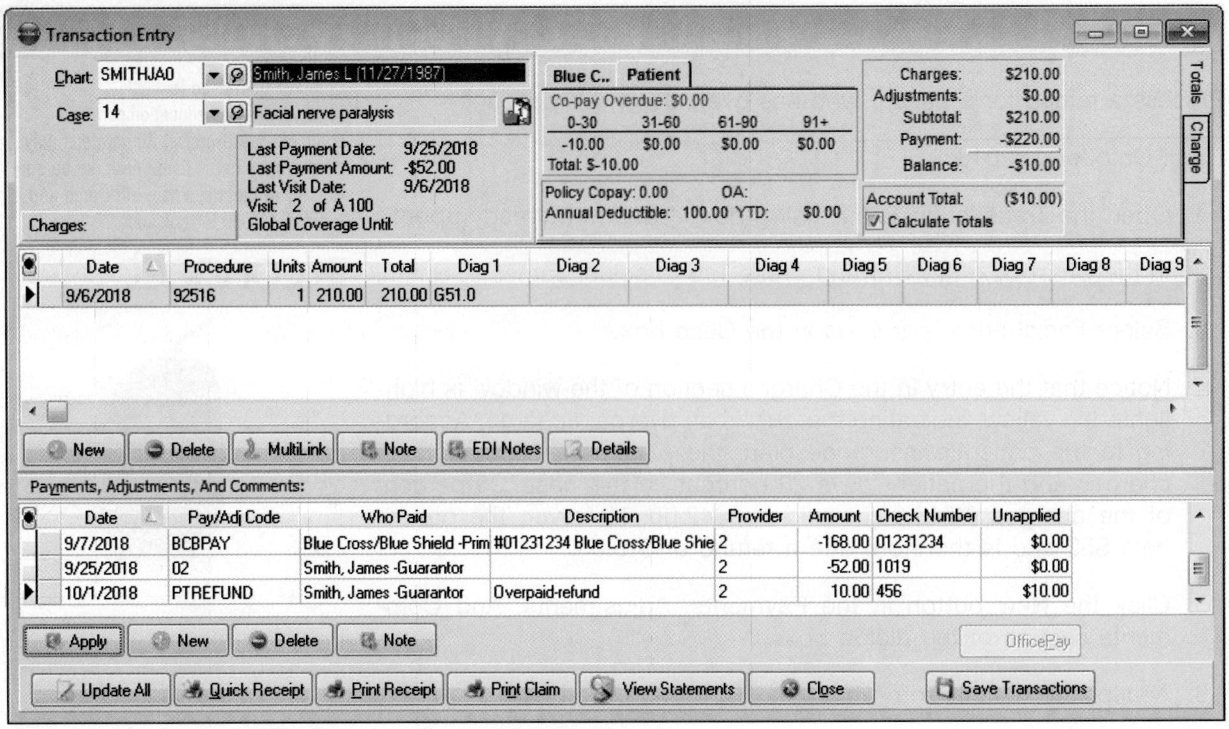

Figure 6-40   Transaction Entry Dialog Box with Unapplied Patient Refund Adjustment

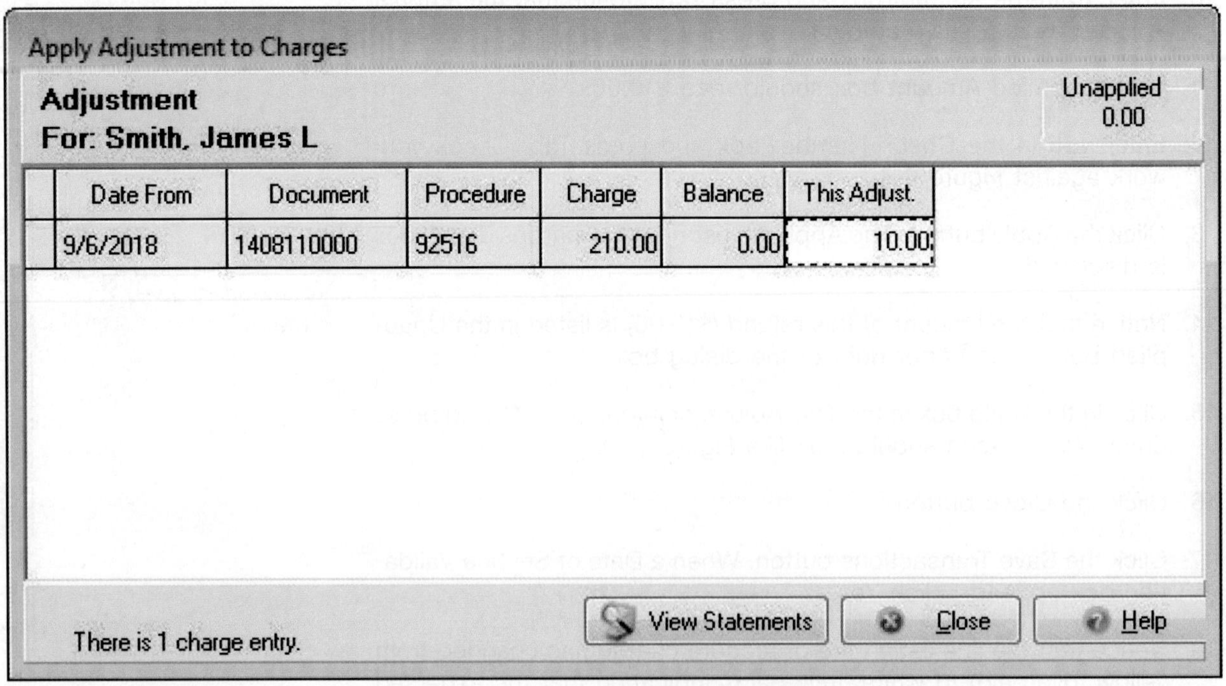

Figure 6-41   Apply Adjustment to Charges Dialog Box with $10.00 Refund Adjustment Applied

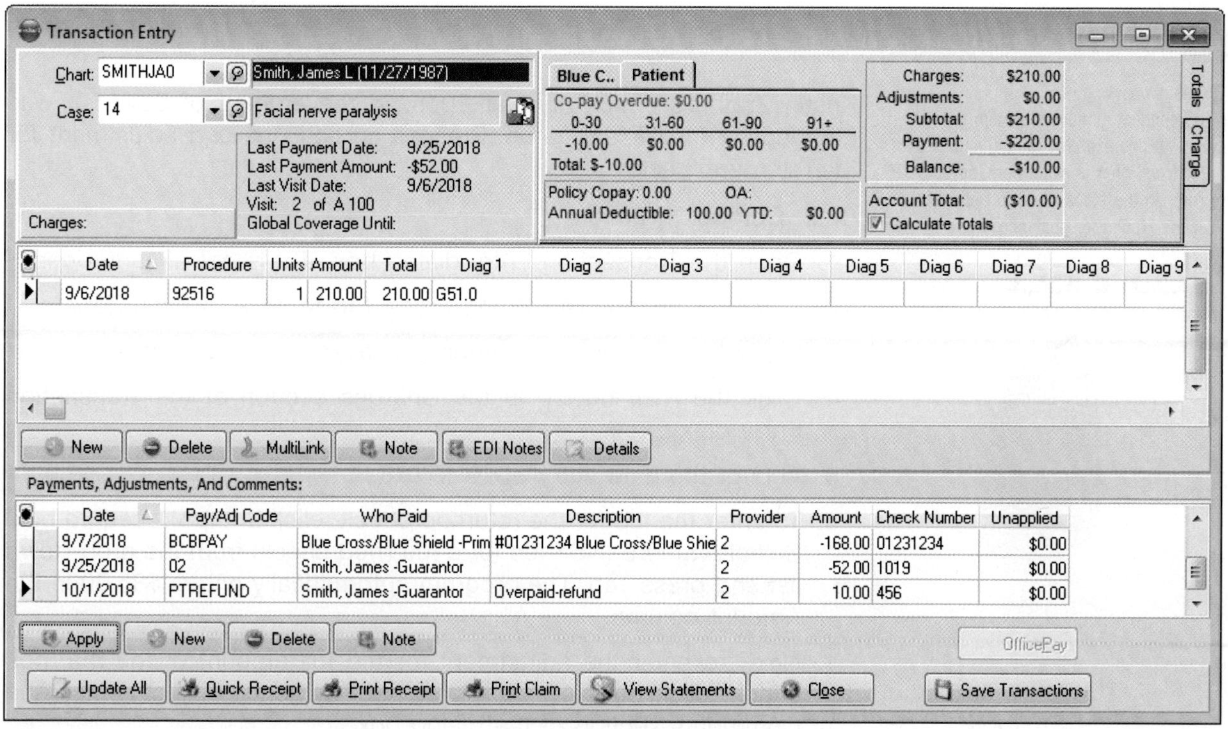

Figure 6-42 Transaction Entry Dialog Box No Longer Showing Overpayment

✓ **You have completed Exercise 6-6.**

6.7 PROCESSING A NONSUFFICIENT FUNDS (NSF) CHECK

When a patient makes a payment by check and does not have adequate funds in his or her checking account to cover the check, it is not honored by the bank. These checks are referred to as **NSF checks**, for "nonsufficient funds." They are also commonly called "bounced" and "returned" checks. A bank also may not honor a check if the account has been closed. When a practice receives an NSF notice from a bank, an adjustment is made in the patient's account, since the patient now owes the practice the amount of the returned check. In addition, most practices charge a fee for a returned check. The maximum amount of the fee is governed by state laws.

NSF check a check that is not honored by a bank because the account it was written on does not have sufficient funds to cover it.

In Medisoft, the fee for the returned check is entered in the Charges section of the Transaction Entry dialog box and the adjustment is entered in the Payments, Adjustments, And Comments section.

Kristin Zapata's check number 1078, in the amount of $247.50, was returned for insufficient funds. Process an NSF fee and adjustment for the returned check.

Date: October 1, 2018

1. Open the Transaction Entry dialog box, if it is not already open.

2. In the Chart box, key **Z** and press Tab to select Kristin Zapata.

3. Verify that Preventive Exam is displayed in the Case box.

4. Click the New button in the Charges section of the Transaction Entry dialog box.

5. Accept the date entry of 10/1/2018.

6. To enter the fee for the returned check, click in the Procedure box. Select NSFFEE (NSF fee for a returned check) from the drop-down list and press Tab. The program automatically enters $35.00 in the Amount column.

7. Next, to enter the adjustment for the full amount of the returned check, click the New button in the Payments, Adjustments, And Comments section of the dialog box.

8. Accept the default entry of 10/1/2018 in the Date box.

9. Click in the Pay/Adj Code box. Select NSF (the code for a returned check) from the drop-down list and press Tab twice (no information is entered in the Who Paid box).

10. Enter **Returned Check** in the Description box and press Tab twice to go to the Amount box.

11. Enter **$247.50** in the Amount box and press Tab. Notice that the amount is listed as a positive amount.

12. Press Tab and enter the check number in the Check Number field.

13. Click the Apply button. The Apply Adjustment to Charges dialog box is displayed.

14. Notice that the amount of the adjustment ($247.50) is listed in the Unapplied box at the upper right of the dialog box.

15. Click in the white box in the This Adjust. column for the $247.50 charge on 8/27/2018. Enter **247.50** and press Enter.

16. Click the Close button.

17. In the Charges section of the dialog box, notice that the line for the charge that was white (fully paid) is now gray (no payment received). The line for the $35.00 fee (NSFFEE) is also gray, since it has not been paid.

18. Click the Save Transactions button. When the date warning box appears, click Yes.

    Note: To see the NSF adjustment you just entered, you may need to scroll down in the Payments, Adjustments, And Comments section of the dialog box. **CiMO**

✓ **You have completed Exercise 6-7.**

APPLYING YOUR SKILLS

6: ADD A DIAGNOSIS AND ENTER PROCEDURE CHARGES

October 1, 2018

Lisa Wright has just been seen by Dr. Jessica Rudner. Using Source Document 7, enter the diagnosis in the Case folder, and then enter the procedure charges in the Transaction Entry dialog box. Be sure to enter the charge in the second column of the encounter form.

Remember to create a backup of your work before exiting Medisoft! To help you keep track of your work, name the backup file after the chapter you are working on; for example, StudentID-c6.mbk.

ELECTRONIC HEALTH RECORD EXCHANGE

Electronic Workflow

Charge transactions imported from an electronic health record (EHR) are processed differently than transactions entered from paper encounter forms. The imported charges are held as unprocessed transactions until they are reviewed and posted by a member of the billing staff.

In Medisoft, the Unprocessed Charges dialog box displays transactions transmitted from the EHR program that have yet to be posted in Medisoft. This dialog box provides detailed information about the visit, including the procedure codes, the diagnosis codes, and the standard fees for the procedures. The dialog box provides editing capability should changes need to be made before posting.

ID	Post	Transaction Status	Chart_Number	Case	Provider	Date_From	Diagnosis_Code_1	Diagnosis_Code_2	Diagnosis_Code_3	Diagnosis
696c9	☐	✓	FITZJWOO	-1	2	3/7/2019	I10			

☑ Align Dx Codes during Posting · Refresh · Edit · Help · Post · Close

Once the charges have been reviewed, they are ready to be posted to the patient's account. This is accomplished by clicking the Post button in the Unprocessed Charges dialog box (highlighted in yellow in the figure). Once the button is clicked, the charge(s) automatically appear in the Transaction Entry dialog box, just as they would if they had been entered manually.

BE THE DETECTIVE!

If assigned by your instructor, complete the Transaction Error Video Case in Connect. Put your skills to use identifying mistakes made in Medisoft and enhance your knowledge by determining the impact of those mistakes.

[Note: These questions are designed for students using the live Medisoft CD software, since students may need to refer back to specific screens in the software to answer the questions.]

1. *[LO 6.5]* What are the total charges listed on John Fitzwilliams's walkout receipt?

2. *[LO 6.4]* What is entered in the Pay/Adj Code box for Hiro Tanaka's copayment on 10/1/2018 (Transaction Entry dialog box)?

3. *[LO 6.4]* What is listed as the annual deductible for John Fitzwilliams (Transaction Entry dialog box)?

4. *[LO 6.3]* What is listed in the Allowed Amount box for procedure 99212 on 10/1/2018 for John Fitzwilliams (Transaction Entry dialog box)?

5. *[LO 6.3]* What is entered in the Total box for procedure 99213 on 10/1/2018 for Elizabeth Jones (Transaction Entry dialog box)?

6. *[LO 6.3]* What is entered in the Diag 1 box for procedure 99202 on 10/1/2018 for Hiro Tanaka (Transaction Entry dialog box)?

7. *[LO 6.3]* What is entered in the Provider box for procedure 99202 on 10/1/2018 for Hiro Tanaka (Transaction Entry dialog box)?

8. *[LO 6.7]* What is the amount of the returned check fee for Kristin Zapata on 10/1/2018 (Transaction Entry dialog box)?

9. *[LO 6.3]* What is entered in the Amount box for procedure 99203 on 10/1/2018 for Lisa Wright (Transaction Entry dialog box)?

10. *[LO 6.3]* What two procedure codes are listed for Lisa Wright on 10/1/2018 (Transaction Entry dialog box)?

11. *[LO 6.3, 6.4]* What are the procedure codes and charges for Randall Klein for September 4, 2018?

12. *[LO 6.3]* What is the amount of the procedure charge entered on September 7, 2018, for patient Jo Wong?

13. *[LO 6.3]* What is the total amount that John Fitzwilliams paid in copayments in September 2018? (*Hint*: Include his daughter Sarah in the calculation.)

LEARNING OUTCOMES	CONCEPTS TO REVIEW
6.1 Describe the three types of transactions recorded in Medisoft.	1. Charges are the amounts a provider bills for the services performed. 2. Payments are monies received from patients and insurance carriers. 3. Adjustments are changes to patients' accounts.
6.2 Discuss how to select a patient and case in Transaction Entry.	To select a patient, click the Chart drop-down list. Enter the first few letters of the patient's last name, and when you find the patient's entry, click to select it. To select a case for the patient, click the Case drop-down list and click on the desired case.
6.3 Demonstrate how to enter charge transactions in Medisoft.	1. Select the patient and case in the Transaction Entry dialog box. 2. In the Charges section of the dialog box, click the New button. 3. Accept or change the date listed. 4. Click the Procedure drop-down list and find the correct code. Click the code to enter it. You may also key in the code manually. Press the Tab key to get to the end of the line. 5. Review the information you entered. 6. Click the Save Transactions button. (If a Date of Service Validation box opens because the date is in the future, click Yes to continue saving.)

6.4 Demonstrate how to enter payments made at the time of an office visit.	1. Select the patient and case in the Transaction Entry dialog box.
	2. In the Payments, Adjustments, And Comments section of the dialog box, click the New button.
	3. Accept or change the date listed.
	4. Click the Pay/Adj Code drop-down list and find the correct code. Click the code to enter it. Press the Tab key.
	5. Click in the Who Paid column and select the appropriate entry. Press the Tab key.
	6. Entering information in the Description field is optional.
	7. To record a check number, press Tab to get to the Check Number field.
	8. Review the information you entered.
	9. Click the Apply button. The Apply Payment to Charges window appears.
	  – If the payment is a copayment, click the Apply To Co-pay button. Click OK in response to the message that the payment has been fully applied. Then click the Close button.
	  – If the payment is not a copayment, click in the box in the This Payment column next to the appropriate charge. Enter the amount of the payment and press Enter. Then click the Close button.
	10. Click the Save Transactions button. (If a Date of Service Validation box opens because the date is in the future, click Yes to continue saving.)

LEARNING OUTCOMES	CONCEPTS TO REVIEW
6.5 Demonstrate how to print a walkout receipt.	1. Select the patient and case in the Transaction Entry dialog box. 2. Click the Print Receipt or Quick Receipt button in the Transaction Entry dialog box. 3. In the Open Report window, confirm that the Walkout Receipt (All Transactions) option is selected, and then click OK. 4. In the Print Report Where? dialog box, select an option to preview the report, print the report, or save the report as a file, and then click Start. 5. In the Walkout Receipt (All Transactions) box, confirm that the correct dates are selected in both Date From Range boxes and click OK. 6. The receipt is created and appears on the screen (if a preview), is sent to a printer, or is saved to a file.
6.6 Demonstrate how to process a refund for a patient.	1. Select the patient and the appropriate case in the Transaction Entry dialog box. 2. In the Payments, Adjustments, And Comments section of the dialog box, click the New button. 3. Accept or change the date listed. 4. Click the Pay/Adj Code drop-down list and select the PTREFUND code. Press the Tab key. 5. Click in the Who Paid column and select the patient. Press the Tab key. 6. Enter *Overpaid—refund* in the Description field. Press Tab twice. 7. Enter the amount of the refund and press Tab. 8. Review the information you entered. 9. Click the Apply button. The Apply Adjustment to Charges dialog box appears. 10. Click in the white box in the This Adjust. column next to the overpaid charge. Enter the amount of the refund and press Enter. Then click the Close button. 11. Click the Save Transactions button. (If a Date of Service Validation box opens because the date is in the future, click Yes to continue saving.)

LEARNING OUTCOMES	CONCEPTS TO REVIEW
6.7 Demonstrate how to post a nonsufficient funds (NSF) check.	Begin by entering the NSF fee for the returned check. 1. Select the patient and case in the Transaction Entry dialog box. 2. In the Charges section of the dialog box, click the New button. 3. Accept or change the date listed. 4. Click the Procedure drop-down list and select the NSFFEE code. Click the code to enter it. Press the Tab key. Confirm that the correct amount is listed in the Amount field. 5. Review the information you entered. Now enter the returned check as an adjustment to the account. 6. In the Payments, Adjustments, And Comments section of the dialog box, click the New button. 7. Accept or change the date listed. 8. Click the Pay/Adj Code drop-down list and select the NSF code. Leave the Who Paid field blank. Press the Tab key. 9. Enter ***Returned Check*** in the Description box. Press Tab twice. 10. Enter the amount of the returned check in the Amount field and press Tab. 11. Review the information you entered. 12. Click the Apply button. The Apply Adjustment to Charges window appears. 13. Click in the white box in the This Adjust. column next to the entry for the check. Enter the amount of the returned check and press Enter. Then click the Close button. 14. Click the Save Transactions button. (If a Date of Service Validation box opens because the date is in the future, click Yes to continue saving.)

USING TERMINOGY

Match the terms on the left with the definitions on the right.

1. *[LO 6.1]* adjustments
2. *[LO 6.1]* charges
3. *[LO 6.3]* MultiLink codes
4. *[LO 6.7]* NSF check
5. *[LO 6.1]* payments
6. *[LO 6.5]* walkout receipt

a. Changes to patients' accounts that alter the amount charged or paid.

b. The amounts billed by a provider for particular services.

c. A payment not honored by a bank because the account it was written on does not have sufficient funds to cover the check.

d. A receipt given to the patient after a payment is made that lists the procedures, diagnosis, charges, and payment.

e. Monies paid to a medical practice by patients and insurance carriers.

f. Groups of procedure code entries that are related to a single activity.

CHECKING YOUR UNDERSTANDING

7. *[LO 6.1]* Give an example of each of the three types of transactions recorded in Medisoft.
8. *[LO 6.2]* In a large medical practice, what is one method of locating a patient in the Chart field?
9. *[LO 6.3]* What are the two key pieces of information you must have before entering a procedure charge?
10. *[LO 6.3]* List two advantages of using MultiLink codes.
11. *[LO 6.5]* When is it appropriate to print a walkout receipt?
12. *[LO 6.4]* What is the color code for an unapplied payment?
13. *[LO 6.6]* What does it mean if a patient's charge transaction is color-coded yellow?
14. *[LO 6.7]* In Medisoft, what area of the Transaction Entry dialog box is used to enter a fee for an NSF or bounced check?

Enhance your learning by completing these exercises and more at http://connect.mheducation.com

APPLYING YOUR KNOWLEDGE

15. *[LO 6.3]* After you have entered a charge for procedure code 99393, you realize it should have been 99394. What should you do?

16. *[LO 6.3]* The receptionist working at the front desk phones to tell you that Maritza Ramos has just seen the physician and would like to know—before she leaves the office—what the charges were for her September 8, 2018, office visit. You are in the middle of entering charges from an encounter form for another patient. What should you do first? What is your reasoning?

17. *[LO 6.4]* After you have entered a patient copayment for $20.00, you realize it should have been $30.00. What should you do?

18. *[LO 6.1]* What is the purpose of entering charges in Medisoft? What would happen to a medical practice that did not record charges?

19. *[LO 6.2]* Why is it important to make sure the correct case is selected before entering transactions?

20. *[LO 6.4]* Why is it necessary to enter patient payments in Medisoft? Would it be sufficient to give the patient a receipt instead of entering the payment in Medisoft?

21. *[LO 6.6]* Describe a situation in which an office would need to issue a refund to a patient.

CREATING CLAIMS

key terms

capitation

clean claims

CMS-1500

coinsurance

copayment

deductible

filter

health maintenance
   organization (HMO)

high-deductible health
   plan with savings option
   (HDHP/SO)

indemnity plan

managed care

medical necessity

navigator buttons

payer

point-of-service (POS)
   plan

policyholder

preferred provider
   organization (PPO)

premiums

X12 837 Health Care
   Claim (837P)

learning outcomes

When you finish this chapter, you will be able to:

7.1 Describe the five most common types of health
insurance plans.

7.2 Describe the role of claims in the billing cycle.

7.3 Discuss the information contained in the Claim
Management dialog box.

7.4 Demonstrate how to create claims in Medisoft.

7.5 Describe how to locate a claim that has already been
submitted.

7.6 Discuss how claims are edited in Medisoft.

7.7 Explain how to change the status of a claim.

7.8 List the steps required to submit electronic claims in
Medisoft.

7.9 Describe how to add attachments to electronic claims.

what you need to know

To use this chapter, you need to know how to:

- Start Medisoft, use menus, and enter and edit text.
- Work with chart numbers and codes.

7.1 THE BASICS OF MEDICAL INSURANCE

policyholder a person or entity who buys an insurance plan; the insured.

Medical insurance represents an agreement between a person or entity, known as the **policyholder,** and a health plan. A health plan is any plan, program, or organization that provides health benefits; it may be an insurance company, also called a carrier, a government program, or a managed care organization (MCO). Payments made to the health plan by the policyholder for insurance coverage are called **premiums.** In exchange for the payments, the health plan agrees to pay for the insured's medical services according to the terms of the insurance policy or agreement.

premiums the periodic amount of money the insured pays to a health plan for insurance coverage.

There are many sources of medical insurance in the United States. Most insured people are covered by group policies, often through their employers. Some people have individual plans. Insurance coverage may be supplied by a private company, such as CIGNA, or by a government plan. CMS—Centers for Medicare and Medicaid Services—runs the Medicare and Medicaid programs. These are the most common government plans:

- **Medicare** Medicare is a federal health plan that covers persons aged sixty-five and over, people with disabilities and with end-stage renal disease (ESRD), and dependent widows.

- **Medicaid** People with low incomes who cannot afford medical care are covered by Medicaid, which is cosponsored by the federal and state governments. Qualifications and benefits vary by state.

- **TRICARE** TRICARE is a government program that covers medical expenses for dependents of active-duty members of the uniformed services and for retired military personnel. Formerly known as CHAMPUS, it also covers dependents of military personnel who were killed while on active duty.

- **CHAMPVA** The Civilian Health and Medical Program of the Veterans Administration is for veterans with permanent service-related disabilities and their dependents. It also covers surviving spouses and dependent children of veterans who died from service-related disabilities.

- **Workers' compensation** People with job-related illnesses or injuries are covered under workers' compensation insurance. Workers' compensation benefits vary according to state law.

payer private or government organization that insures or pays for healthcare on behalf of beneficiaries.

Whether it is a private company or a government program, the health plan is called a **payer.** The term *third-party payer* is also used, because the primary relationship is between the provider and the patient, and the health plan is the third party.

TYPES OF HEALTH PLANS

Most insured patients have medical coverage under a managed care plan. **Managed care** is a type of health insurance in which organizations control both the financing and the delivery of healthcare to policyholders. The managed care organization establishes contracts with physicians and other healthcare providers that control fees. A much smaller number of patients are covered by an **indemnity plan,** also known as a *fee-for-service plan.* Under an indemnity plan, healthcare providers receive a fee for each service such as an office visit, test, or procedure. The type of health plan affects the payments that patients must make for medical services, so it is important for medical office administrative staff to understand the plans' key features.

managed care a type of insurance in which the carrier is responsible for both the financing and the delivery of healthcare.

indemnity plan also known as a fee-for-service plan; a health plan that reimburses the policyholder for a percentage of covered medical expenses.

Indemnity Plans

Indemnity plans used to be the norm. As Figure 7-1 shows, up until 1996, indemnity plans were the most common type of employer-sponsored health plan in the United States. Today, less than 1 percent of patients who receive insurance through their employer are covered by an indemnity plan. Under an indemnity plan, policyholders are repaid for the costs of healthcare. Usually, a **deductible**—an amount due before benefits begin—must be paid. Then, the health plan pays a percentage of charges—usually 70 or 80 percent. The portion of charges that an insured person must pay is known as **coinsurance.**

deductible amount due before benefits begin.

coinsurance percentage of charges that an insured person must pay for healthcare services after payment of the deductible amount.

Preferred Provider Organizations

Today, the most common type of health plan is a **preferred provider organization (PPO)** (see Figure 7-1). A PPO is a network of providers under contract to perform services for plan members at discounted fees. In most cases, an individual does not need prior approval to see a provider in the network. Usually, members may choose to receive care from other doctors or providers outside the network, but they pay a higher cost. These plans usually include a copayment or coinsurance. A **copayment** is a fixed fee, such as $25—made to the provider at the time of an office visit.

preferred provider organization (PPO) managed care network of healthcare providers who agree to perform services for plan members at discounted fees.

copayment a fixed fee paid by the patient at the time of an office visit.

Health Maintenance Organizations

An individual covered by a **health maintenance organization (HMO)** is assigned a primary care physician (PCP) and must use the HMO's network of providers except in an emergency. If they seek services from a provider who is not in the health plan, the plan does not pay for the care. In most HMOs, a patient pays a copayment.

health maintenance organization (HMO) a managed healthcare system in which providers agree to offer healthcare to the organization's members for fixed payments.

Some providers who contract with an HMO are paid fixed rates at regular intervals, such as monthly, to provide necessary contracted

Year	Traditional Indemnity	HMO	PPO	POS	HDHP/SO
1988	73%	16%	11%		
1993	46%	21%	26%	7%	
1996	27%	31%	28%	14%	
1999	10%	28%	39%	24%	
2000	8%	29%	42%	21%	
2001	7%	24%	46%	23%	
2002	4%	27%	52%	18%	
2003	5%	24%	54%	17%	
2004	5%	25%	55%	15%	
2005	3%	21%	61%	15%	
2006	3%	20%	60%	13%	4%
2007	3%	21%	57%	13%	5%
2008	2%	20%	58%	12%	8%
2009	1%	20%	60%	10%	8%
2010	1%	19%	58%	8%	13%
2011	1%	17%	55%	10%	17%
2012	1%	16%	56%	9%	19%
2013	<1%	14%	57%	9%	20%
2014	<1%	13%	58%	8%	20%

Traditional Indemnity: Patients are billed and repaid for all or part of each service performed, subject to deductibles.

HMO: Patients pay a fixed premium for coverage and must use doctors, hospitals, and suppliers approved by the HMO.

PPO: Patients may use any doctors or hospitals, but they are charged less if they use those on an approved list.

POS: Patients meet most of their medical needs using doctors and hospitals on an approved list but may go outside the network if they are willing to pay extra.

HDHP/SO: Patients pay for medical costs out of a health savings account, and once the deductible is met, become eligible for reimbursement under the insurance plan.

Figure 7-1   Enrollment in Employer-Sponsored Health Plans by Type, 1988 to 2014

(NOTE: Information was not obtained for POS plans in 1988. A portion of the change in plan type enrollment for 2005 is likely attributable to incorporating more recent Census Bureau estimates of the number of state and local government workers and removing federal workers from the weights. See the Survey Design and Methods section from the 2005 Kaiser/HRET Survey of Employer-Sponsored Health Benefits for additional information.

SOURCE: Kaiser/HRET Survey of Employer-Sponsored Health Benefits, 1999–2014; KPMG Survey of Employer-Sponsored Health Benefits, 1993, 1996; The Health Insurance Association of America (HIAA), 1988)

capitation payment to a provider that covers each plan member's healthcare services for a certain period of time.

point-of-service (POS) plan a plan, combining features of an HMO and a PPO, in which members may choose from providers in a primary or secondary network.

high-deductible health plan with savings option (HDHP/SO) a type of insurance plan in which a high-deductible plan is combined with a pretax savings account to cover out-of-pocket medical expenses.

services to patients who are plan members. This fixed payment is referred to as **capitation**. In other HMO plans, negotiated per-service fees are paid. These fees are less than the regular rate for a service that the provider normally charges.

Point-of-Service (POS) Plans

A **point-of-service (POS) plan** combines features of an HMO and a PPO. Members may choose from providers in a primary or secondary network. The primary network is HMO-like, and the secondary network is often a PPO network. Like HMOs, POS plans charge annual premiums and copayments for office visits.

High-Deductible Health Plan

In recent years, employers have turned to a new type of health plan in an effort to control costs. A **high-deductible plan with a savings option (HDHP/SO)** is a type of insurance in which a high-deductible plan is combined with a pretax savings account to cover out-of-pocket medical expenses. These plans, also known as *consumer-driven health plans*, typically include two elements. The first is an insurance plan with a high deductible (such as $2,500), for which the policyholder pays a lower premium than for a plan with a lower deductible.

The second element is a designated health savings account (HSA) that is used to pay medical bills before the deductible has been met. The savings account, similar to an individual retirement account (IRA), lets people set aside untaxed wages to cover their out-of-pocket medical expenses. Some employers contribute to employees' accounts as a benefit. If money is left in the account at the end of a plan year, it rolls over to help cover the next year's health expenses.

As Figure 7-1 illustrates, HDHP/SOs are gaining a greater share of the health insurance market, rising from 4 percent in 2006 to 20 percent in 2014.

7.2 THE ROLE OF CLAIMS IN THE BILLING CYCLE

Health insurance claims communicate information about a patient's diagnosis, procedures, and charges to a payer. The insurance claim is the most important document for correct reimbursement. Whether physicians are paid by health plans for treating patients depends in part on the diagnosis and procedure codes assigned to the office visit. The medical office staff member who does the coding must have specialized knowledge. In some medical practices, the physicians assign the codes; in others, a *medical coder* or a medical insurance specialist handles this task.

MEDICAL NECESSITY

Before the practice submits the encounter information to an insurance plan for payment, the codes must be reviewed for compliance. In the area of coding, compliance requires checking that the codes are up-to-date and follow the official guidelines of the American Hospital Association and the American Medical Association (AMA). Also, the diagnosis and the medical services that are documented in the patient's medical record should be logically connected, so that the **medical necessity** of the charges is clear to the health plan. The AMA has defined medical necessity as "services or products that a prudent physician would provide to a patient for the purpose

medical necessity treatment provided by a physician to a patient for the purpose of preventing, diagnosing, or treating an illness, injury, or its symptoms in a manner that is appropriate and is provided in accordance with generally accepted standards of medical practice.

of preventing, diagnosing, or treating an illness, injury, or its symptoms in a manner that is:

1. In accordance with generally accepted standards of medical practice.

2. Clinically appropriate in terms of type, frequency, extent, site, and duration.

3. Not primarily for the convenience of the patient, physician, or other healthcare provider."

If medical necessity is not met, the physician will not receive payment from the health plan.

CLEAN CLAIMS

A physician practice depends on the billing specialist to submit **clean claims**—claims with all the correct information necessary for payer processing. An error on a claim may cause the claim to be delayed or denied. Rejected claims can cost the practice twice as much as clean claims and can result in reduced cash flow. Claims that are not paid in full also have a negative effect on the practice's bottom line.

CMS-1500 AND X12 837 HEALTH CARE CLAIM

Today, almost all claims are sent electronically. The HIPAA standard transaction for electronic claims is the HIPAA **X12 837 Health Care Claim or Equivalent Encounter Information (837P).** The paper format is known as the **CMS-1500** claim form. Both types of insurance claims are prepared in the practice management program.

The National Uniform Claim Committee (NUCC), led by the American Medical Association, determines the content of both the 837P and the CMS-1500. The CMS-1500 claim has 33 numbered boxes representing about 150 discrete data elements, while the 837P has a maximum of 244 segments representing about 1,054 elements. However, many of these data elements are conditional and apply to particular specialties only. The CMS-1500 is pictured in Figure 7-2.

The built-in help feature in Medisoft® contains a "clickable" CMS-1500 form. When you click in a box on the form, a pop-up window describes the location of the data in Medisoft. Exercise 7-1 provides an opportunity to explore this form. The information in Table 7-1 lists the data elements on the CMS-1500 and the corresponding location of those data in Medisoft. This is a summary of the information provided in the clickable CMS-1500 form.

HEALTH INSURANCE CLAIM FORM

APPROVED BY NATIONAL UNIFORM CLAIM COMMITTEE (NUCC) 02/12

☐☐ PICA   PICA ☐☐

1. ☐ MEDICARE (Medicare#)	☐ MEDICAID (Medicaid#)	☐ TRICARE (ID#/DoD#)	☐ CHAMPVA (Member ID#)	☐ GROUP HEALTH PLAN (ID#)	☐ FECA BLK LUNG (ID#)	☐ OTHER (ID#)

1a. INSURED'S I.D. NUMBER (For Program in Item 1)

2. PATIENT'S NAME (Last Name, First Name, Middle Initial)

3. PATIENT'S BIRTH DATE MM ⎮ DD ⎮ YY   SEX   M ☐   F ☐

4. INSURED'S NAME (Last Name, First Name, Middle Initial)

5. PATIENT'S ADDRESS (No., Street)

6. PATIENT RELATIONSHIP TO INSURED   Self ☐   Spouse ☐   Child ☐   Other ☐

7. INSURED'S ADDRESS (No., Street)

CITY   STATE

8. RESERVED FOR NUCC USE

CITY   STATE

ZIP CODE   TELEPHONE (Include Area Code) ( )

ZIP CODE   TELEPHONE (Include Area Code) ( )

9. OTHER INSURED'S NAME (Last Name, First Name, Middle Initial)

10. IS PATIENT'S CONDITION RELATED TO:

11. INSURED'S POLICY GROUP OR FECA NUMBER

a. OTHER INSURED'S POLICY OR GROUP NUMBER

a. EMPLOYMENT? (Current or Previous)   ☐ YES ☐ NO

a. INSURED'S DATE OF BIRTH MM ⎮ DD ⎮ YY   SEX   M ☐   F ☐

b. RESERVED FOR NUCC USE

b. AUTO ACCIDENT?   PLACE (State)   ☐ YES ☐ NO

b. OTHER CLAIM ID (Designated by NUCC)

c. RESERVED FOR NUCC USE

c. OTHER ACCIDENT?   ☐ YES ☐ NO

c. INSURANCE PLAN NAME OR PROGRAM NAME

d. INSURANCE PLAN NAME OR PROGRAM NAME

10d. CLAIM CODES (Designated by NUCC)

d. IS THERE ANOTHER HEALTH BENEFIT PLAN?   ☐ YES ☐ NO   **If yes**, complete items 9, 9a, and 9d.

READ BACK OF FORM BEFORE COMPLETING & SIGNING THIS FORM.

12. PATIENT'S OR AUTHORIZED PERSON'S SIGNATURE I authorize the release of any medical or other information necessary to process this claim. I also request payment of government benefits either to myself or to the party who accepts assignment below.

SIGNED _____ DATE _____

13. INSURED'S OR AUTHORIZED PERSON'S SIGNATURE I authorize payment of medical benefits to the undersigned physician or supplier for services described below.

SIGNED _____

14. DATE OF CURRENT ILLNESS, INJURY, or PREGNANCY (LMP) MM ⎮ DD ⎮ YY   QUAL.

15. OTHER DATE QUAL. ⎮ MM ⎮ DD ⎮ YY

16. DATES PATIENT UNABLE TO WORK IN CURRENT OCCUPATION FROM MM ⎮ DD ⎮ YY   TO MM ⎮ DD ⎮ YY

17. NAME OF REFERRING PROVIDER OR OTHER SOURCE   17a.   17b. NPI

18. HOSPITALIZATION DATES RELATED TO CURRENT SERVICES FROM MM ⎮ DD ⎮ YY   TO MM ⎮ DD ⎮ YY

19. ADDITIONAL CLAIM INFORMATION (Designated by NUCC)

20. OUTSIDE LAB?   ☐ YES ☐ NO $ CHARGES

21. DIAGNOSIS OR NATURE OF ILLNESS OR INJURY Relate A-L to service line below (24E)   ICD Ind. ⎮

A. |_____   B. |_____   C. |_____   D. |_____
E. |_____   F. |_____   G. |_____   H. |_____
I. |_____   J. |_____   K. |_____   L. |_____

22. RESUBMISSION CODE   ORIGINAL REF. NO.

23. PRIOR AUTHORIZATION NUMBER

24. A. DATE(S) OF SERVICE From MM DD YY	To MM DD YY	B. PLACE OF SERVICE	C. EMG	D. PROCEDURES, SERVICES, OR SUPPLIES (Explain Unusual Circumstances) CPT/HCPCS ⎮ MODIFIER	E. DIAGNOSIS POINTER	F. $ CHARGES	G. DAYS OR UNITS	H. EPSDT Family Plan	I. ID. QUAL.	J. RENDERING PROVIDER ID. #
1										NPI
2										NPI
3										NPI
4										NPI
5										NPI
6										NPI

25. FEDERAL TAX I.D. NUMBER   SSN ☐ EIN ☐

26. PATIENT'S ACCOUNT NO.

27. ACCEPT ASSIGNMENT? (For govt. claims, see back)   ☐ YES ☐ NO

28. TOTAL CHARGE $

29. AMOUNT PAID $

30. Rsvd for NUCC Use

31. SIGNATURE OF PHYSICIAN OR SUPPLIER INCLUDING DEGREES OR CREDENTIALS (I certify that the statements on the reverse apply to this bill and are made a part thereof.)

SIGNED _____ DATE _____

32. SERVICE FACILITY LOCATION INFORMATION   a. NPI   b.

33. BILLING PROVIDER INFO & PH # ( )   a. NPI   b.

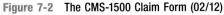

Figure 7-2   The CMS-1500 Claim Form (02/12)

Box	CMS-1500 Field Name	Data Source in Medisoft	Dialog Box/Tab/Field Name in Medisoft
Top 1	Insurance Name/Address	Insurance	**Insurance Carrier**, Address, *Name, etc.*
Top 2	Primary, Secondary, Tertiary	Insurance	Determined by claim form selected
1	Insurance Type	Insurance	**Insurance Carrier**, EDI/Eligibility, *Type*
1a	Insured's ID No.	Case	**Case**, Policy 1, 2, 3, *Policy No.*
2	Patient's Name	Patient	**Patient/Guarantor**, Name, Address, *Last Name, First Name, Middle Initial*
3	Patient Birth Date, Sex	Patient	**Patient/Guarantor**, Name, Address, *Birth Date, Sex*
4	Insured's Name	Case	**Case**, Policy 1, 2, 3, *Policy Holder 1, 2, 3*
5	Patient's Address	Patient	**Patient/Guarantor**, Name, Address, *Street, City, State, Zip*
6	Patient Relation to Insured	Case	**Case**, Policy 1, 2, 3, *Relationship to Insured*
7	Insured's Address	Patient	**Patient/Guarantor**, Name, Address, *Street, City, State, Zip*
8	Reserved for NUCC Use	Case	**Case**, Miscellaneous, *CMS-1500 Reserved for NUCC, Box 8*
9	Other Insured's Name	Case	**Case**, Policy 1, 2, 3, *Policy Holder 1, 2, 3*
9a	Other Insured's Policy/ Group No.	Case	**Case**, Policy 1, 2, 3, *Policy Number, Group Number*
9b	Reserved for NUCC Use	Case	**Case**, Miscellaneous, *CMS-1500 Reserved for NUCC, Box 9b*
9c	Reserved for NUCC Use	Case	**Case**, Miscellaneous, *CMS-1500 Reserved for NUCC, Box 9c*
9d	Insurance Plan Name, Program	Insurance	**Insurance Carrier**, Address, *Plan Name*; if empty, prints carrier name
10a	Condition Related to Employment	Case	**Case**, Condition, *Employment Related* check box
10b	Condition Related to Auto Accident	Case	**Case**, Condition, *Accident, Related To*
10o	Condition Related to Other Accident	Case	**Case**, Condition, *Accident, Related To*
10d	Claim Codes	Case	**Case**, Diagnosis, *Condition Codes 1-12*
11	Insured's Policy Group/ FECA#	Case	**Case**, Policy 1, *Policy Number, Group Number*
11a	Insured's Date of Birth, Sex	Patient	**Patient/Guarantor**, Name, Address, *Birth Date, Sex*
11b	Other Claim ID	Case	**Case**, Policy 1, *Claim Number*
11c	Insurance Plan Name/ Program	Insurance	**Insurance Carrier**, Address, *Plan Name*; if empty, prints carrier name
11d	Another Health Benefit Plan?	Case	**Case,** Policy 2, 3
12	Patient Signature or Authorized Signature	Patient	**Patient/Guarantor**, Other Information, *Signature on File*; **Insurance Carrier**, Options and Codes, *Patient Signature on File*
13	Insured's Signature or Authorized Signature	Patient	**Patient/Guarantor**, Other Information, *Signature on File*; **Insurance Carrier**, Options and Codes, *Insured Signature on File*
14	Date Current Ill/Inj/LMP	Case	**Case**, Condition, *Injury/Illness/LMP Date* and *Illness Indicator*
15	Other Date	Case	**Case**, Condition, *Date Similar Symptoms*
16	Dates Unable to Work	Case	**Case**, Condition, *Dates—Unable to Work*
17	Referring Provider	Case or Insurance Carrier	**Case**, Account, *Referring Provider, Supervising Provider* or **Insurance Carrier**, EDI/Eligibility, *Send Ordering Provider in Loop 2420E*

TABLE 7-1 (*continued*)

Box	CMS-1500 Field Name	Data Source in Medisoft	Dialog Box/Tab/Field Name in Medisoft
17a	Referring Provider, Other Identifier, Qualifier	Referring Provider	***Referring Provider***, Referring Provider IDs, *NPI*
17b	Referring Provider NPI	Referring Provider	***Referring Provider***, Referring Provider IDs, *NPI*
18	Hospitalization Dates	Case	***Case***, Condition, *Dates—Hospitalization*
19	Additional Claim Information		If there is a Taxonomy Code in the Provider ID grid for the provider in Box 24j, Medisoft will use that information first for Box 19. The qualifier ZZ followed by the taxonomy value will print. If there is a value in the Legacy Identifier 2 field for that provider, the Legacy Identifier 2 qualifier and value will print. If the Payer type is Worker's Comp, three blank spaces and the Transaction Entry EDI notes for PWK, in addition to the IDs listed above, will print. If none of these conditions are met, Medisoft will print the value in the Local Use B field on the Case – Miscellaneous tab.
20	Outside Lab? $ Charges	Case	***Case***, Miscellaneous, *Outside Lab Work*
21	Diagnosis	Transaction Entry	***Transaction Entry***, Charges, *Diag 1-12*
22	Medicaid Resubmission	Case	***Case***, Medicaid and Tricare, *Resubmission No., Original Reference*
23	Prior Authorization #	Case	***Case***, Miscellaneous, *Prior Authorization Number*
24a	Dates of Service	Transaction	***Transaction Entry***, Date From, Date To
24b	Place of Service	Transaction	***Transaction Entry***, Place of Service
24c	EMG		***Payer Specific Code***
24d	Procedures, Services, or Supplies	Transaction	***Transaction Entry***, Procedure, M1, M2, M3, M4
24e	Diagnosis Pointer	Transaction	***Transaction Entry***, *Diag 1, Diag 2, Diag 3, Diag 4*
24f	$ Charges	Transaction	***Transaction Entry***, *Amount*
24g	Days or Units	Transaction	***Transaction Entry***, *Units*
24h	EPSDT	Case	***Case***, Medicaid and Tricare, *EPSDT*
24i	Rendering Provider, Other ID, Qualifier	Provider	***Provider***, Provider IDs
24j	Rendering Provider ID#	Provider	***Provider***, Provider IDs
25	Federal Tax ID	Practice	***Provider***, Provider IDs, *Tax ID/SSN*
26	Patient's Account No.	Patient	***Patient/Guarantor***, Name, Address, *Chart No.*
27	Accept Assignment?	Case	***Case***, Policy 1, 2, 3, *Assignment of Benefits/ Accept Assignment*
28	Total Charge	Transaction	Calculated field
29	Amount Paid	Transaction	***Transaction Entry***, *Payment*
30	Rsvd for NUCC Use		No longer in use
31	Physician's Signature	Provider	***Provider***, Address, *Signature on File*; ***Insurance Carrier***, Address, *Signature on File*
32	Facility Address	Practice	***Facility***, Address
32a	Facility NPI	Address	***Facility***, Facility IDs, *NPI*
33	Billing Provider Information	Provider	***Provider***, Address, *First Name, Middle Initial, Last Name, Street, City, State, Zip*
33a	Billing Provider NPI	Provider	***Provider:*** Provider IDs, *NPI*

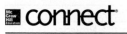

Connect users: go to http://connect.mheducation.com to complete this exercise! Some steps may differ from what is listed here, so be sure to refer to the steps listed in Demo and Practice Modes for guidance.

Explore the clickable CMS-1500 form that is provided in Medisoft's built-in help feature.

1. Start Medisoft and restore the data from your last work session.

2. Click Medisoft Help on the Help menu. The Help window appears.

3. Click on the Search tab to select it (see Figure 7-3).

4. In the field labeled *Type in the keyword to find*, enter **clickable.**

5. Click the List Topics button. Compare your screen to Figure 7-4.

6. Click on the clickable CMS-1500 form 02/12 Version.

7. Click the Display button. The Clickable CMS-1500 Form 02/12 Version appears in the right-hand pane of the window.

8. Maximize the window by clicking the Maximize button, which is the middle of the three buttons located at the top right corner of the window. The claim form fills the screen.

9. Click in the different boxes of the form. Notice that when you click in a box, a pop-up window appears, containing information about the location of the data that corresponds to that field in Medisoft. Figure 7-5 displays the pop-up window for Box 1 on the form.

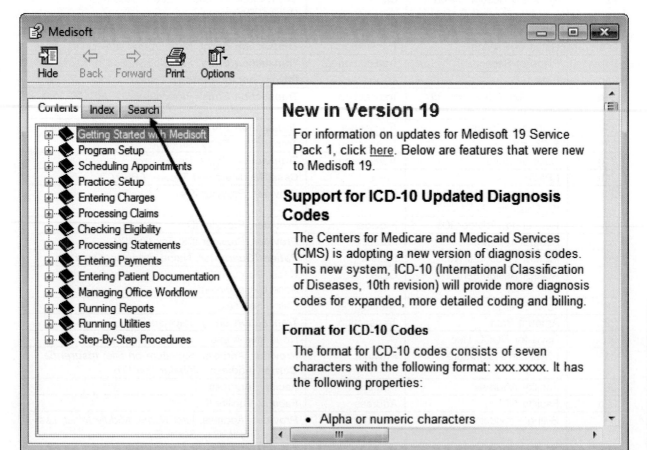

Figure 7-3   Medisoft Help Window with Search tab Selected

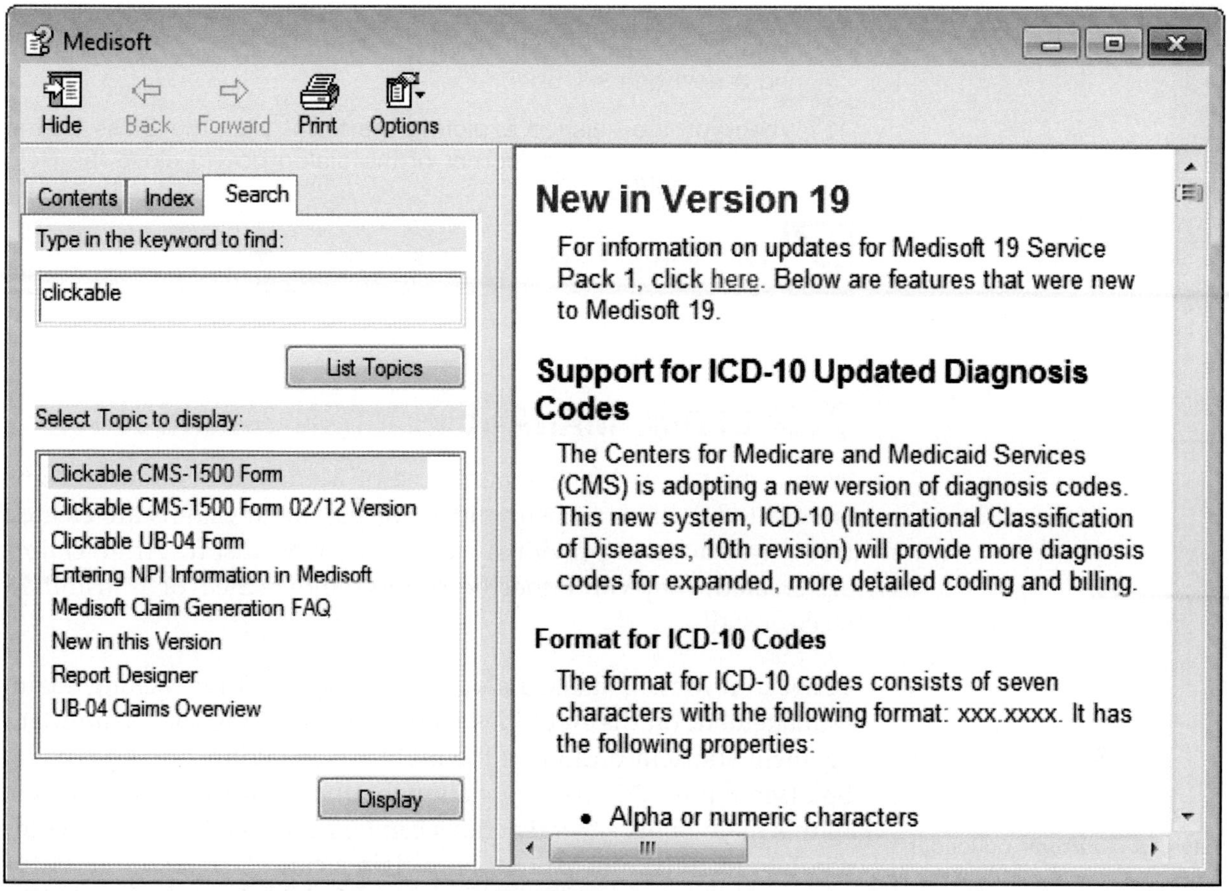

Medisoft

Hide | Back | Forward | Print | Options

Contents | Index | **Search**

Type in the keyword to find:

clickable

[List Topics]

Select Topic to display:

Clickable CMS-1500 Form
Clickable CMS-1500 Form 02/12 Version
Clickable UB-04 Form
Entering NPI Information in Medisoft
Medisoft Claim Generation FAQ
New in this Version
Report Designer
UB-04 Claims Overview

[Display]

New in Version 19

For information on updates for Medisoft 19 Service Pack 1, click here. Below are features that were new to Medisoft 19.

Support for ICD-10 Updated Diagnosis Codes

The Centers for Medicare and Medicaid Services (CMS) is adopting a new version of diagnosis codes. This new system, ICD-10 (International Classification of Diseases, 10th revision) will provide more diagnosis codes for expanded, more detailed coding and billing.

Format for ICD-10 Codes

The format for ICD-10 codes consists of seven characters with the following format: xxx.xxxx. It has the following properties:

- Alpha or numeric characters

Figure 7-4   Medisoft Help Window after Clicking List Topics Button

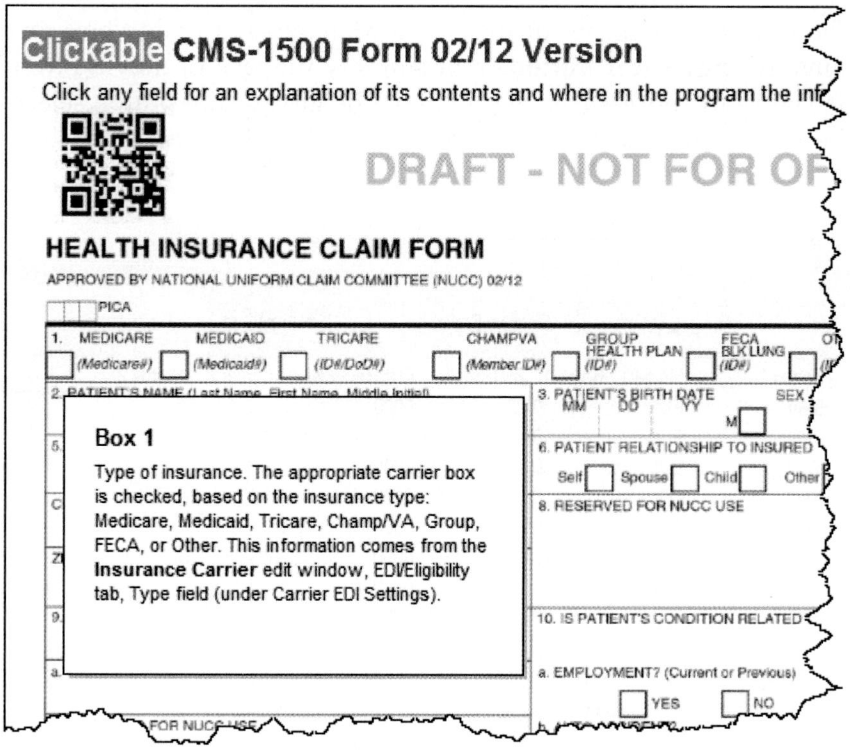

Clickable CMS-1500 Form 02/12 Version

Click any field for an explanation of its contents and where in the program the inf

DRAFT - NOT FOR OF

HEALTH INSURANCE CLAIM FORM

APPROVED BY NATIONAL UNIFORM CLAIM COMMITTEE (NUCC) 02/12

PICA

1. MEDICARE   MEDICAID   TRICARE   CHAMPVA   GROUP HEALTH PLAN   FECA BLK LUNG   O

(Medicare#)   (Medicaid#)   (ID#/DoD#)   (Member ID#)   (ID#)   (ID#)   (I

2. PATIENT'S NAME (Last Name, First Name, Middle Initial)   3. PATIENT'S BIRTH DATE   SEX
MM | DD | YY   M

Box 1

Type of insurance. The appropriate carrier box is checked, based on the insurance type: Medicare, Medicaid, Tricare, Champ/VA, Group, FECA, or Other. This information comes from the **Insurance Carrier** edit window, EDI/Eligibility tab, Type field (under Carrier EDI Settings).

6. PATIENT RELATIONSHIP TO INSURED

Self   Spouse   Child   Other

8. RESERVED FOR NUCC USE

10. IS PATIENT'S CONDITION RELATED

a. EMPLOYMENT? (Current or Previous)
YES   NO

FOR NUCC USE

Figure 7-5   Clickable CMS-1500 Form After Clicking in Box 1

10. When you are finished reading the information in a pop-up window, click on another box on the form. The current pop-up will close and a new one will open.

11. When you are finished exploring the form, click the Close button (the X) in the top right corner of the dialog box to close the Help window. **ciMc**

✓ **You have completed Exercise 7-1.**

7.3 CLAIM MANAGEMENT IN MEDISOFT

Within the Claim Management area of Medisoft, insurance claims are created, edited, and submitted for payment. Claims are created from transactions previously entered in Medisoft. After claims are created, they can either be printed and mailed or transmitted electronically.

The Claim Management dialog box is displayed by clicking Claim Management on the Activities menu or by clicking the Claim Management shortcut button on the toolbar (see Figure 7-6). The dialog box (see Figure 7-7) lists all claims that have already been created. In this dialog box, several actions can be performed: existing claims can be reviewed and edited, new claims can be created, the status of existing claims can be changed, and claims can be printed or submitted electronically.

navigator buttons buttons that simplify the task of moving from one entry to another.

Figure 7-6
Claim Management
Shortcut Button

The upper-right corner of the Claim Management dialog box contains five **navigator buttons** that simplify the task of moving from one entry to another (see Figure 7-8). The First Claim button selects the first claim in the list and makes it active. The Previous Claim

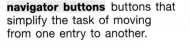

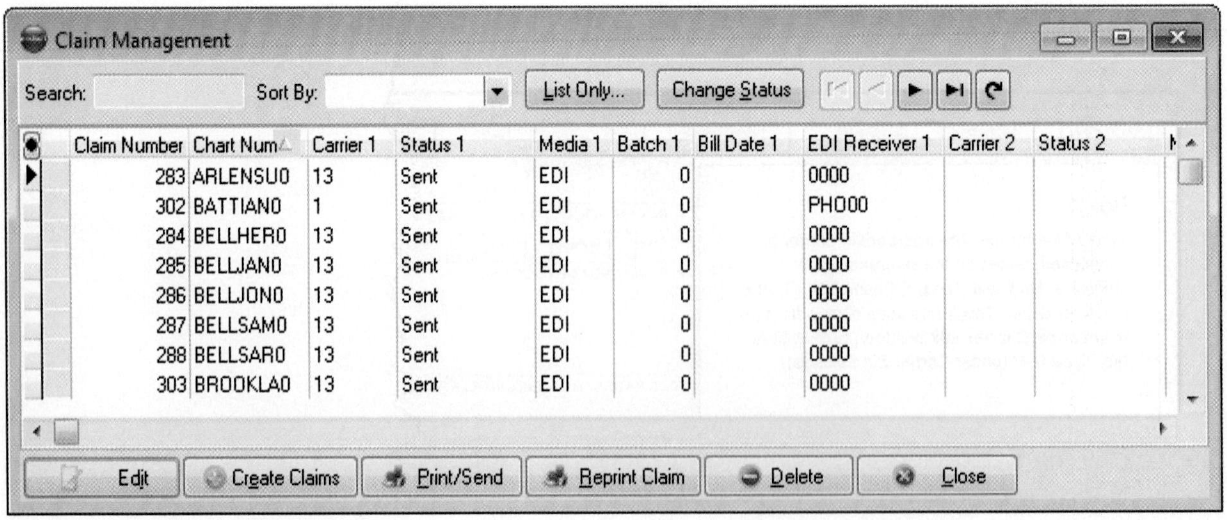

	Claim Number	Chart Num△	Carrier 1	Status 1	Media 1	Batch 1	Bill Date 1	EDI Receiver 1	Carrier 2	Status 2	
	283	ARLENSU0	13	Sent	EDI	0		0000			
	302	BATTIAN0	1	Sent	EDI	0		PHO00			
	284	BELLHER0	13	Sent	EDI	0		0000			
	285	BELLJAN0	13	Sent	EDI	0		0000			
	286	BELLJON0	13	Sent	EDI	0		0000			
	287	BELLSAM0	13	Sent	EDI	0		0000			
	288	BELLSAR0	13	Sent	EDI	0		0000			
	303	BROOKLA0	13	Sent	EDI	0		0000			

Figure 7-7   Claim Management Dialog Box

button reactivates the claim that was most recently active. The Next Claim button makes the next claim in the list active. The Last Claim button makes the last claim in the list active. The Refresh Data button is used to restore data when necessary.

Figure 7-8 Navigator Buttons

The bottom of the Claim Management dialog box contains a number of buttons that are used for various functions (see Figure 7-7).

Edit Opens a claim for editing.

Create Claims Opens the Create Claims dialog box.

Print/Send Begins the process of sending electronic claims or printing paper claims.

Reprint Claim Reprints a claim that has already been printed.

Delete Deletes the selected claim and releases the transactions bound to the claim.

Close Closes the Claim Management dialog box.

7.4 CREATING CLAIMS

Claims are created in the Create Claims dialog box. The Create Claims dialog box (see Figure 7-9) is accessed by clicking the Create Claims button in the Claim Management dialog box. This dialog box provides several filters to customize the creation of claims. A **filter** is a condition that data must meet to be selected. For example, claims can be created for services performed between the first and the fifteenth of the month.

filter a condition that data must meet to be selected.

In this case, the filter is the condition that services must have been performed between the first and fifteenth of the month. Transactions that meet this criterion are included in the selection; transactions that do not fall within the date range are not included. Filters can be used to create claims for a specific patient, for a specific insurance carrier, and for transactions that exceed a certain dollar amount, among others. The following filters can be applied within the Create Claims dialog box.

Transaction Dates The Transaction Dates boxes are used to specify the starting and ending dates for which claims will be

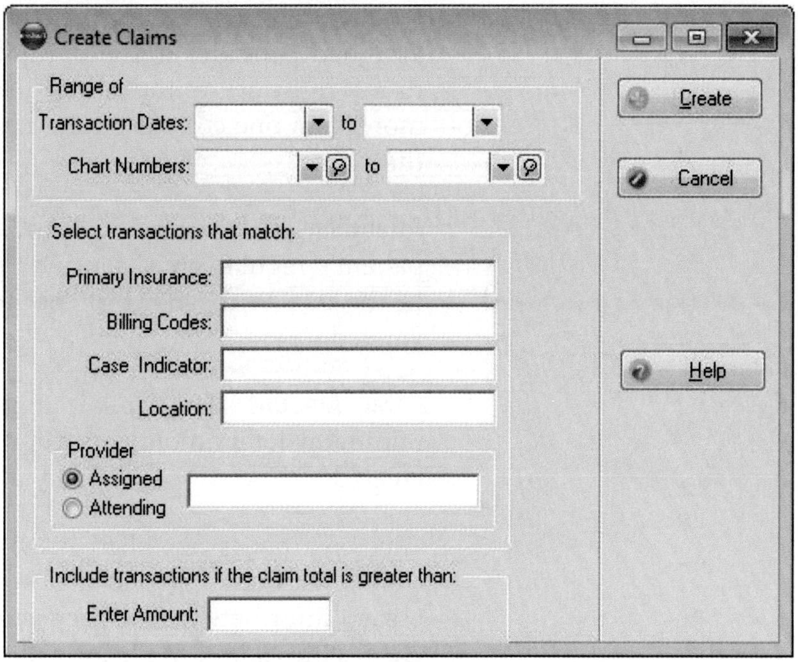

Figure 7-9 Create Claims Dialog Box

created. If the boxes are left blank, transactions for all dates will be included.

Chart Numbers   In the Chart Numbers boxes, the starting and ending chart numbers for which claims will be created are entered. If the boxes are left blank, all chart numbers will be included.

Primary Insurance   The carrier code for the insurance company is entered in the Primary Insurance box. If claims are being sent to a clearinghouse, more than one insurance carrier code can be entered. When more than one code is entered, commas must be placed between the codes. If claims are being sent directly to the carrier, only that carrier's code is entered.

Billing Codes   The billing code is entered in the Billing Codes box. If more than one code is entered, commas must be placed between the codes. (The Billing Code is an optional code that can be used to group patients.)

Case Indicator   If case indicators are used to classify patients (such as by type of illness for workers' compensation cases), the case indicator can be listed in the Case Indicator box. If more than one indicator is entered, commas must be placed between them.

Location   Sometimes a sort is needed by location, such as all procedures done at a hospital. The location code is entered in the Location box. If more than one code is entered, commas must be placed between the codes.

Assigned   The radio buttons in the Provider box indicate whether the provider is the assigned or attending provider. The assigned provider is the patient's regular physician. In the box to the right of the radio button, the provider code is entered. If more than one code is entered, commas must be placed between the codes.

Attending   The attending provider is someone other than the patient's regular physician who provides treatment to the patient. In the box to the right of the radio button, the provider code is entered.

Enter Amount   The dollar amount entered in this box is the minimum total amount required for a case before a claim can be created.

Any box that is not filled in will default to include all data, and claims with any entry in that box will be included. When all necessary information has been entered, clicking the Create button creates the claims. Medisoft will create a file of matching claims but will include only those that have not yet been billed.

Note: When creating claims, Medisoft uses the Windows System Date—the date you are actually completing the exercise—for some fields, such as the Claim Created date. If you see dates that are current rather than the year 2018 or 2019, these are not the result of anything you did, and will not be counted as errors.

Create insurance claims for patients.

Date: November 2, 2018

1. Set the Medisoft Program Date to November 2, 2018.

2. On the Activities menu, click Claim Management. The Claim Management dialog box is displayed.

3. Click the Create Claims button.

4. Enter **09012018** in the first Transaction Dates box and **11022018** in the second. When the program asks you whether you want to change the date (because it is in the future), click the No button.

5. Leave the remaining boxes in the Create Claims dialog box blank. Your screen should look like Figure 7-10.

6. Click the Create button.

7. Click on the column heading Status 1 to sort claims by status. This will make it easier to see the claims just created, which have a status of Ready to Send.

Connect users: go to http://connect.mheducation.com to complete this exercise! Some steps may differ from what is listed here, so be sure to refer to the steps listed in Demo and Practice Modes for guidance.

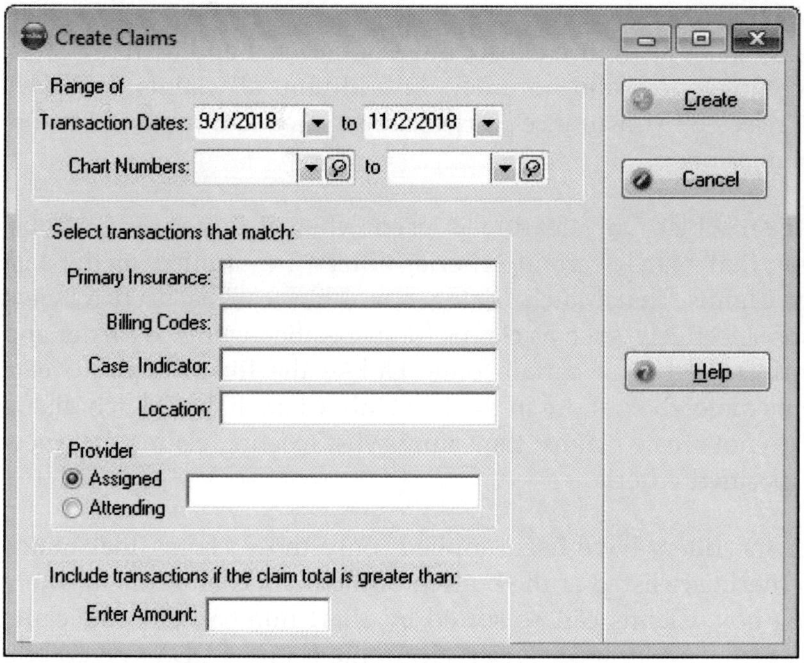

Figure 7-10 Create Claims Dialog Box with Dates Entered

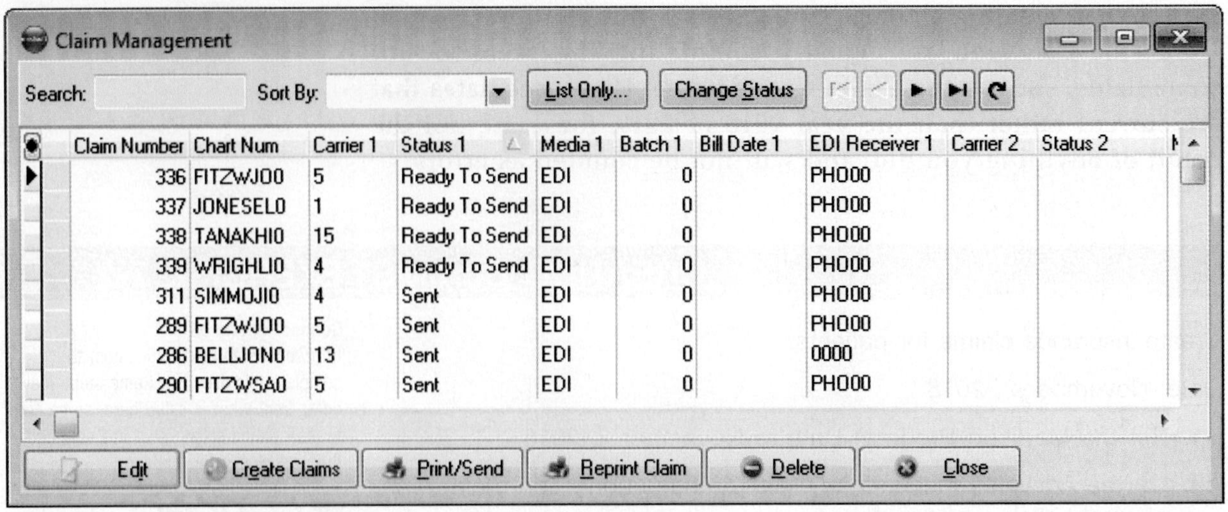

Figure 7-11   Claim Management Dialog Box with New Claims Displayed

Claim Management window contents:

	Claim Number	Chart Num	Carrier 1	Status 1	Media 1	Batch 1	Bill Date 1	EDI Receiver 1	Carrier 2	Status 2
▶	336	FITZWJO0	5	Ready To Send	EDI	0		PHO00		
	337	JONESEL0	1	Ready To Send	EDI	0		PHO00		
	338	TANAKHI0	15	Ready To Send	EDI	0		PHO00		
	339	WRIGHLI0	4	Ready To Send	EDI	0		PHO00		
	311	SIMMOJI0	4	Sent	EDI	0		PHO00		
	289	FITZWJO0	5	Sent	EDI	0		PHO00		
	286	BELLJON0	13	Sent	EDI	0		0000		
	290	FITZWSA0	5	Sent	EDI	0		PHO00		

Toolbar: Search: _____ Sort By: _____ | List Only... | Change Status |
Buttons: Edit | Create Claims | Print/Send | Reprint Claim | Delete | Close

8. Confirm that you have created the claims with a Ready to Send status that are visible in Figure 7-11.

9. Before you close the dialog box, note your answers to questions 1 and 2 on the Chapter 7 Worksheet on page 268.

10. Click the Close button. **CiMO**

✓ **You have completed Exercise 7-2.**

7.5 LOCATING CLAIMS

At times it is necessary to select and view specific claims that have already been created. For example, any claims prepared for submission to an insurance carrier must be selected and then reviewed for completeness and accuracy. In addition, all claims that have been rejected by insurance carriers are selected and reviewed before resubmission.

Medisoft's List Only feature is used when it is necessary to list claims that match certain criteria. Filters are applied in the List Only Claims That Match dialog box. They can be used to view claims selectively, such as claims for a specific insurance carrier and claims created on a certain date. Unlike the filters in the Create Claims dialog box, those in the List Only Claims That Match dialog box do not create claims; they simply list existing claims that meet the specified criteria.

Once the filters have been applied, only those claims that match the criteria are listed at the bottom of the main Claim Management dialog box. Claims can be sorted by chart number, date the claim was created, insurance carrier, electronic claim (EDI) receiver, billing method, billing date, batch number, and claim status. Not all the boxes need to be filled in, only the ones that will be used to select the desired claims.

The List Only feature is activated by clicking the List Only. . . button in the Claim Management dialog box (see Figure 7-12). Clicking the button causes the List Only Claims That Match dialog box to be displayed (see Figure 7-13).

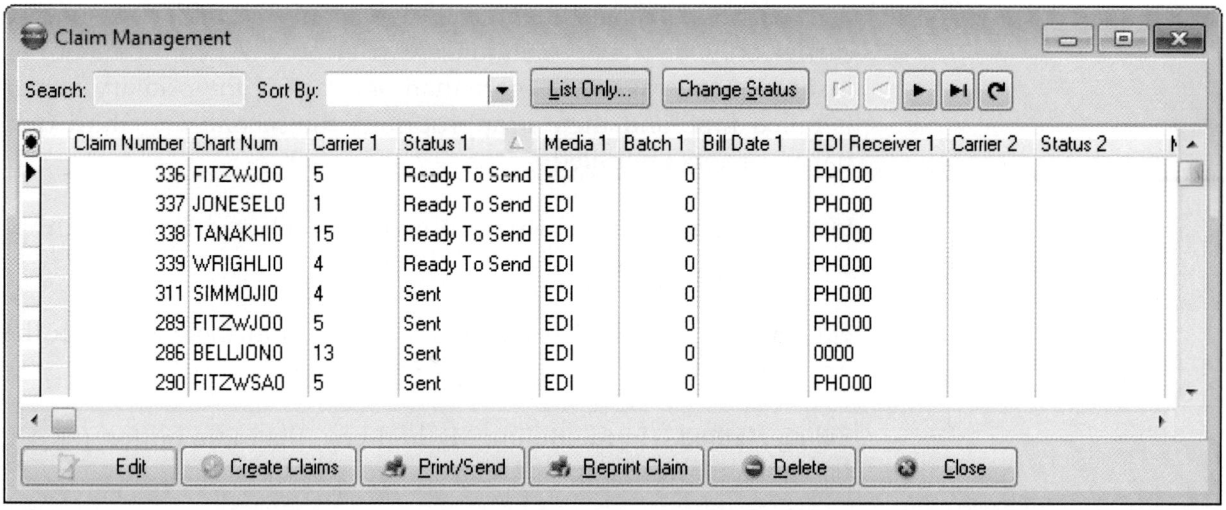

Figure 7-12   Claim Management Dialog Box with List Only. . . Button Highlighted in Yellow

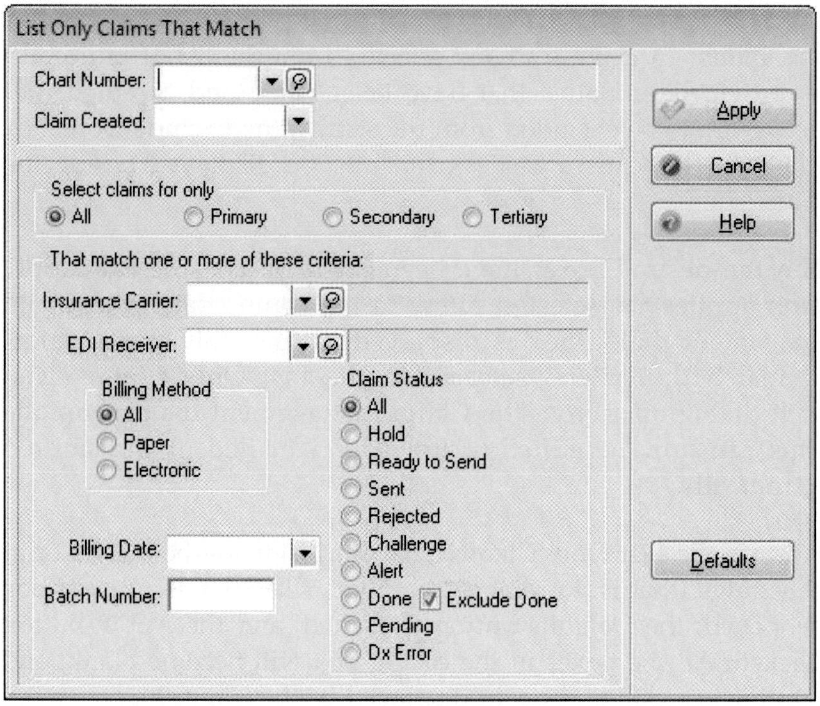

Figure 7-13   List Only Claims That Match Dialog Box

The following filters are available in the List Only Claims That Match dialog box.

Chart Number   A patient's chart number is selected from the drop-down list of patients' chart numbers.

Claim Created   The date that a claim was created is entered in MMDDCCYY format.

Select Claims for Only   A radio button is clicked for either all insurance carriers, primary insurance carrier only, secondary insurance carrier only, or tertiary insurance carrier only. When a patient has insurance coverage with more than one carrier, the primary carrier is billed first, and then, if appropriate, the second and third (tertiary) carriers are billed.

Insurance Carrier   An insurance carrier is selected from the drop-down list of choices.

EDI Receiver   An EDI receiver is selected from the choices on the drop-down list.

Billing Method   In the Billing Method box, the radio button for All, Paper, or Electronic is clicked.

Billing Date   The date of billing is entered in the Billing Date box.

Batch Number   A batch number is entered in the Batch Number box.

Claim Status   A claim status is selected from the list of radio buttons provided. If claims that have been billed and accepted (not rejected) are to be excluded from the search, the Exclude Done box is clicked. This causes a check mark to be displayed beside the option.

When the desired boxes have been filled in, clicking the Apply button applies the selected filters to the claims data. The Claim Management dialog box is displayed, listing only those claims that match the criteria selected in the List Only Claims That Match dialog box. From the Claim Management dialog box, the claims can now be edited, printed, and mailed or transmitted electronically.

To restore the List Only Claims That Match dialog box to its original settings (that is, to remove the filters selected), the dialog box is reopened; the Defaults button is clicked; and the Apply button is clicked. All the boxes in the dialog box will become blank, and the full list of claims is again displayed in the Claim Management dialog box.

Find all insurance claims for Medicare that have a status of Sent.

Date: November 2, 2018

Connect users: go to http://connect.mheducation.com to complete this exercise! Some steps may differ from what is listed here, so be sure to refer to the steps listed in Demo and Practice Modes for guidance.

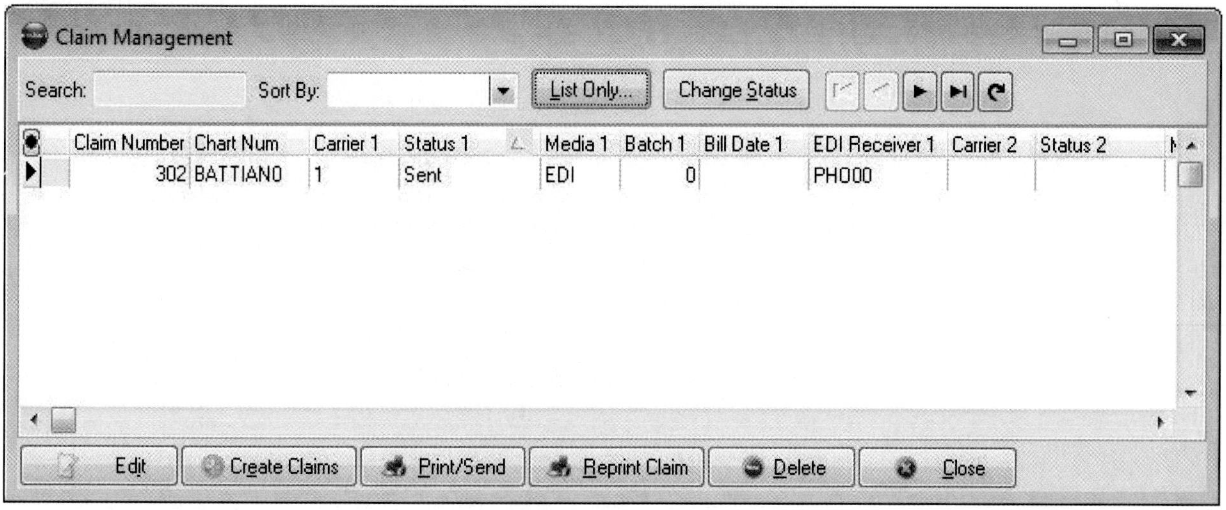

1. If necessary, open the Claim Management dialog box by selecting it on the Activities menu. The Claim Management dialog box is displayed.

2. Click the List Only. . . button. The List Only Claims That Match dialog box is displayed.

3. Leave the Chart Number and Claim Created fields blank.

4. In the Select Claims for Only section, make sure All is selected.

5. Select 1-Medicare from the drop-down list in the Insurance Carrier field.

6. Leave the EDI Receiver field blank.

7. Select Electronic as the Billing Method.

8. Leave the Billing Date and Batch Number fields blank.

9. Select Sent as the Claim Status.

10. Click the Apply button.

11. Your screen should look like the window in Figure 7-14.

12. To restore the full list of claims in the Claim Management box, click the List Only. . . button, and then click the Defaults button.

13. Click the Apply button. **CiMO**

	Claim Number	Chart Num	Carrier 1	Status 1	Media 1	Batch 1	Bill Date 1	EDI Receiver 1	Carrier 2	Status 2
▶	302	BATTIANO	1	Sent	EDI	0		PHO00		

Figure 7-14 Claim Management Dialog Box with Selected Claim Displayed

✓ **You have completed Exercise 7-3.**

7.6 EDITING CLAIMS

Medisoft's Claim Edit feature allows claims to be reviewed and edited before they are submitted to insurance carriers for payment. The more problems that can be spotted and solved before claims are sent to insurance carriers, the sooner the practice will receive payment.

When a claim is active in the Claim Management dialog box, it can be edited by clicking the Edit button or by double clicking the claim itself. The Claim dialog box is displayed (see Figure 7-15). The top section of the Claim dialog box lists the claim number, the date the claim was created, the chart number, the patient's name, and the case number. This information cannot be edited, although the information in the six tabs can be edited.

CARRIER 1 TAB

The Carrier 1 tab displays information about claims being submitted to a patient's primary insurance carrier. The following boxes are listed in the Carrier 1 tab:

Claim Status   The Claim Status box indicates the status of a particular claim: Hold, Ready to Send, Sent, Rejected, Challenge, Alert, Done, Pending, and Dx Error. The radio button that reflects a claim's status should be clicked.

Billing Method   The Billing Method box displays two choices: Paper and Electronic. The radio button that describes the billing method should be clicked.

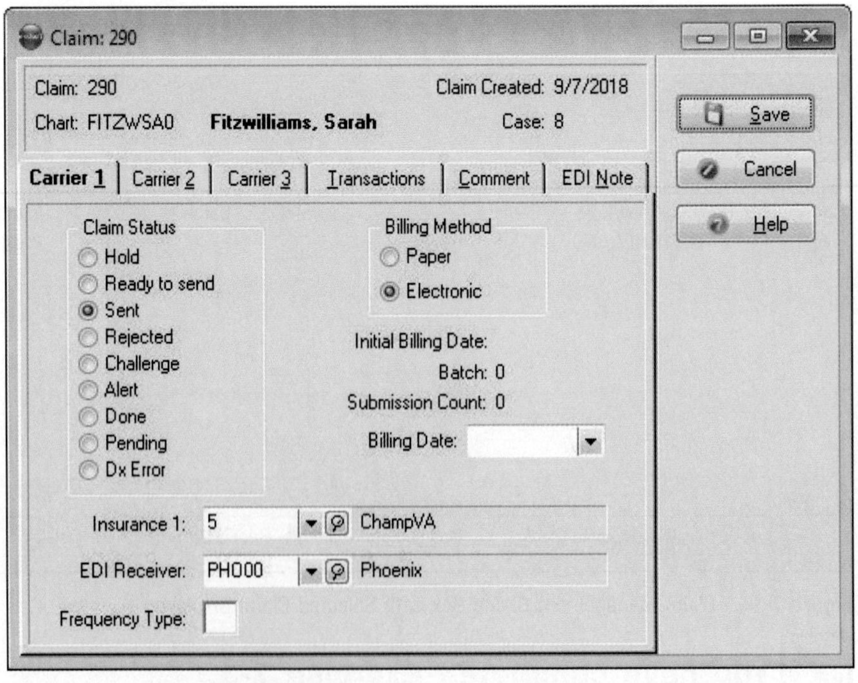

Figure 7-15   Claim Dialog Box

Initial Billing Date   If the claim was sent more than once, this box automatically displays the initial billing date.

Batch   If the claim has been assigned to a batch, the batch number is displayed.

Submission Count   The Submission Count area lists the number of claims submitted.

Billing Date   The Billing Date box lists the most recent date the bill was sent (if the claim was submitted more than once).

Insurance 1   The Insurance 1 box lists a patient's primary insurance carrier.

EDI Receiver   The EDI receiver is selected from the drop-down list.

Frequency Type   This field is used with some insurance carriers when sending claims electronically. Allowed entries in this field are:

   1-Original (admission through discharge claim)

   6-Corrected (adjustment of prior claim)

   7-Replacement (replacement of prior claim)

   8-Void (voiding/cancellation of prior claim)

CARRIER 2 AND CARRIER 3 TABS

The Carrier 2 and Carrier 3 tabs display information about claims being submitted to a patient's secondary (Carrier 2) and tertiary (Carrier 3) insurance carriers. The boxes in these tabs are the same as the boxes in the Carrier 1 tab, with the exception of the Claim Status box and the Frequency Type box. In the Carrier 2 and Carrier 3 tabs, there is no Pending radio button in the Claim Status box, and there is no Frequency Type box. Otherwise the three tabs are the same.

TRANSACTIONS TAB

The Transactions tab lists information about the transactions included in a claim. The scroll bars can be used to view all the information in the Transactions tab (see Figure 7-16).

Diagnosis   The diagnosis for the listed transactions is displayed.

Date From   The Date From box lists the date on which service was provided.

Document   The Document box lists the document number of a transaction.

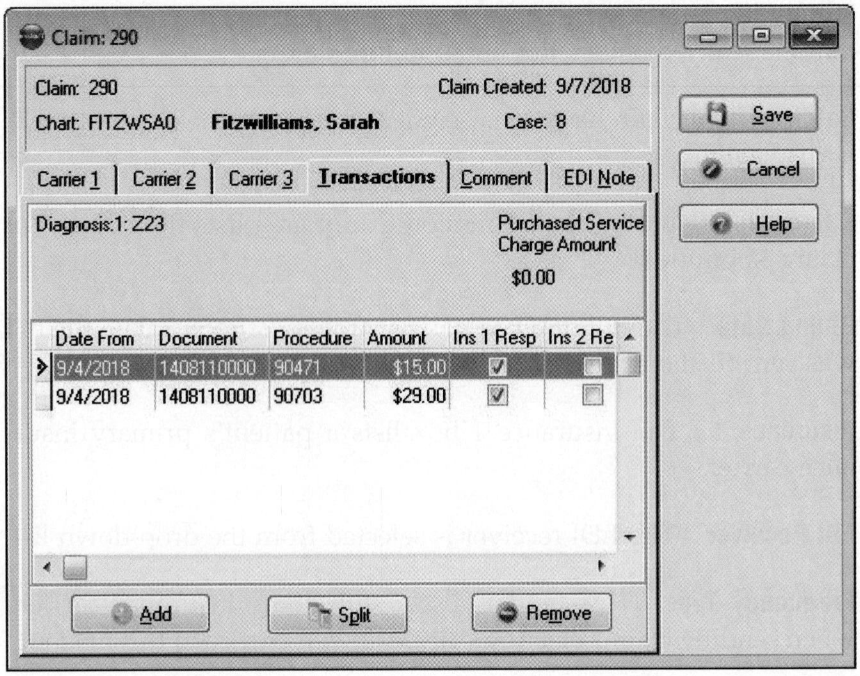

Figure 7-16 Transactions Tab

Procedure The Procedure box displays the procedure code for a performed procedure.

Amount In the Amount box, the dollar cost of a service is displayed.

Ins 1 Resp If this box is checked, the primary insurance carrier is responsible for the claim.

Ins 2 Resp If this box is checked, the secondary insurance carrier is responsible for the claim.

Ins 3 Resp If this box is checked, the tertiary insurance carrier is responsible for the claim.

The Transactions tab also contains three buttons at the bottom of the dialog box:

Add The Add button is used to add a transaction to an existing claim.

Split The Split button removes a single transaction from an existing claim and places it on a new claim.

Remove The Remove button deletes a transaction from the claim database.

COMMENT TAB

The Comment tab provides a place to include any specific notes or comments about the claim (see Figure 7-17). The comments are for internal use and are not transmitted or printed.

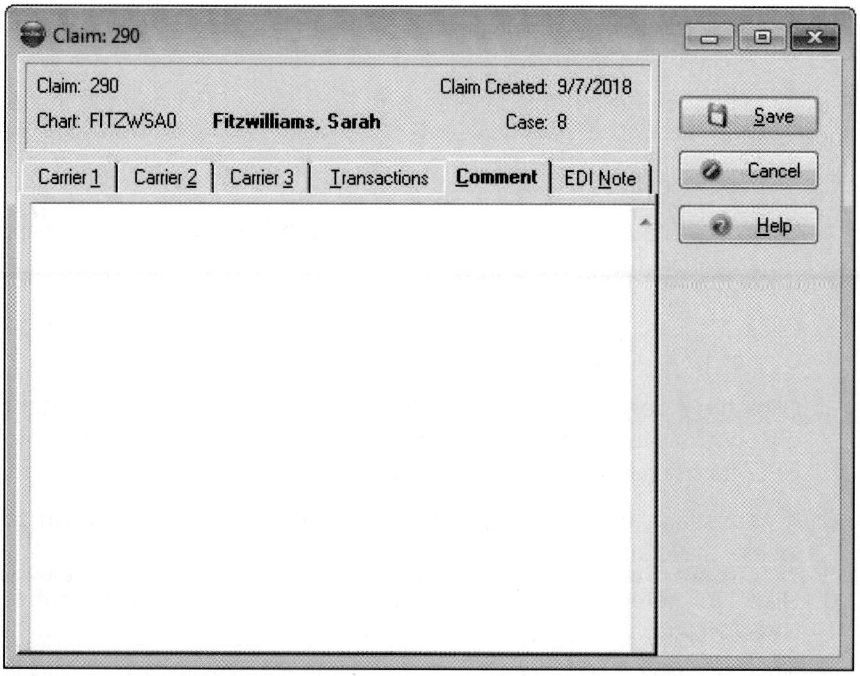

![Figure 7-17 Comment Tab — Claim: 290 window showing the Comment tab selected. Header reads: Claim: 290, Chart: FITZWSA0, Fitzwilliams, Sarah, Claim Created: 9/7/2018, Case: 8. Tabs: Carrier 1, Carrier 2, Carrier 3, Transactions, Comment, EDI Note. Buttons: Save, Cancel, Help.]

Figure 7-17   Comment Tab

EDI NOTE TAB

The EDI Note tab displays the electronic claim and contract information from the Comment tab of the Case folder (see Figure 7-18). The information may be changed before the claim is sent by editing the fields here or in the Case folder.

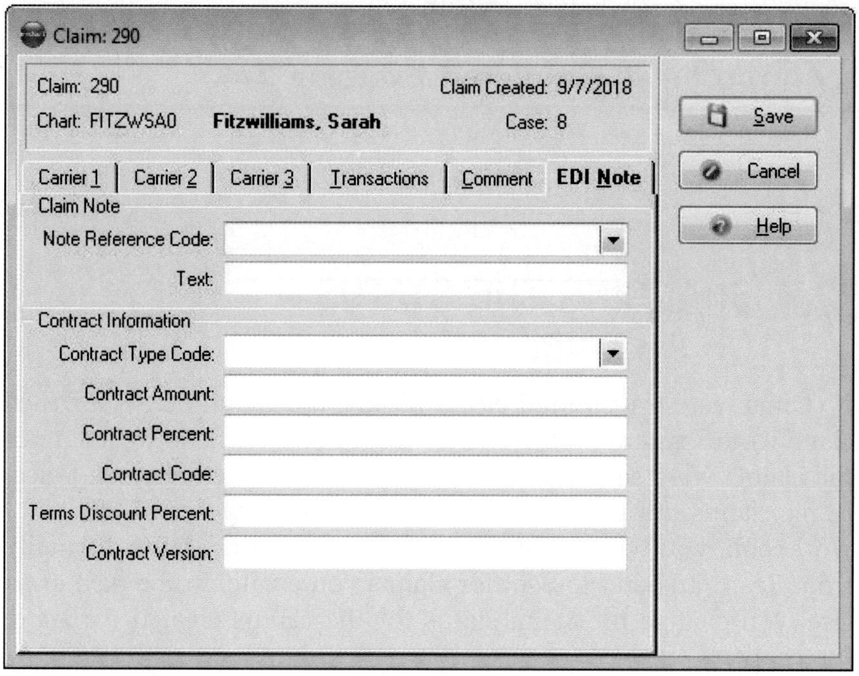

![Figure 7-18 EDI Note — Claim: 290 window showing the EDI Note tab selected. Header reads: Claim: 290, Chart: FITZWSA0, Fitzwilliams, Sarah, Claim Created: 9/7/2018, Case: 8. Tabs: Carrier 1, Carrier 2, Carrier 3, Transactions, Comment, EDI Note. Claim Note section with Note Reference Code and Text fields. Contract Information section with Contract Type Code, Contract Amount, Contract Percent, Contract Code, Terms Discount Percent, Contract Version fields. Buttons: Save, Cancel, Help.]

Figure 7-18   EDI Note

Review insurance claims for patients with East Ohio PPO as their insurance carrier.

Date: November 2, 2018

1. Open the Claim Management dialog box, if it is not already open.

2. Click the List Only. . . button.

3. Click 13 East Ohio PPO on the drop-down list in the Insurance Carrier box.

4. Click the Apply button. You are returned to the Claim Management dialog box. Notice that only claims for patients who have East Ohio PPO as their insurance carrier are listed.

5. If necessary, click the Scroll Bar several times to scroll down to locate the claim for Lawana Brooks.

6. Click to select the claim for Lawana Brooks (chart number BROOKLAØ).

7. Click the Edit button to review the claim. The Claim dialog box is displayed.

8. Review the information in the Carrier 1 tab.

9. Review the information in the Transactions tab.

10. Click the Cancel button to exit the Claim dialog box without saving any changes. (The Cancel button does not cancel the claim; it just cancels any changes that may have been made.)

11. To restore the full list of claims in the Claim Management box, click the List Only. . . button, and then click the Defaults button.

12. Click the Apply button.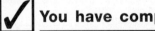

✓ **You have completed Exercise 7-4.**

7.7 CHANGING THE STATUS OF A CLAIM

If claims were transmitted electronically, the Claim Status for each claim would automatically change from Ready to Send to Sent once the claims were sent. Since it is not possible to actually send electronic claims during these exercises, for the purposes of this text/workbook, you will be asked to change the claim status manually from Ready to Send to Sent for claims you create. In the next exercise, you change the claim status for the claims created earlier in the chapter.

CHANGING CLAIM STATUS EXERCISE 7-5

Change the Claim Status for the claims created on November 2, 2018, from Ready to Send to Sent.

Date: November 2, 2018

1. In the Claim Management dialog box, click the Change Status button. The Change Claim Status/Billing Method dialog box appears.
2. Click Batch, and accept the default entry of 0.
3. Select Ready to Send in the Status From column.
4. Select Sent in the Status To column. Check your screen against Figure 7-19.
5. Click the OK button. The dialog box closes, and the Claim Management dialog box reappears with the Claim Status column displaying Sent for the new claims.
6. Before you close the dialog box, note your answer to question 4 on the Chapter 7 Worksheet on page 268.
7. Close the Claim Management dialog box. CiMO

Connect users: go to http://connect.mheducation.com to complete this exercise! Some steps may differ from what is listed here, so be sure to refer to the steps listed in Demo and Practice Modes for guidance.

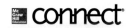

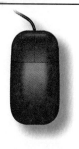

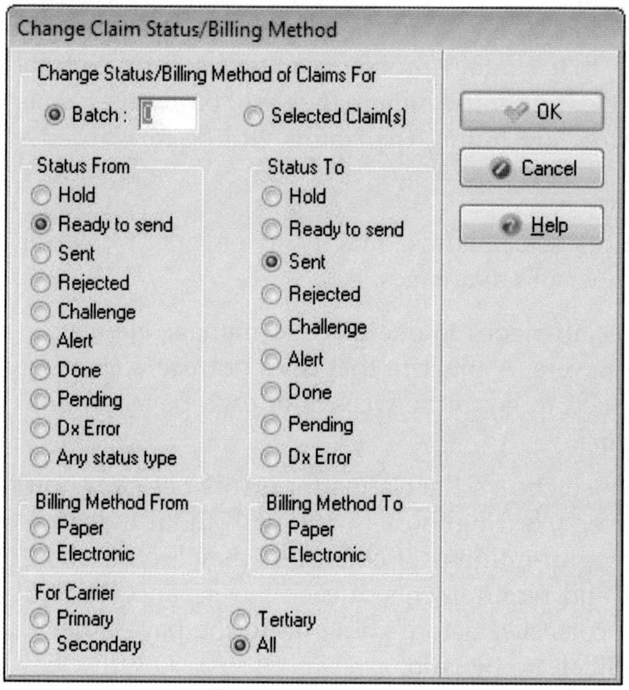

Figure 7-19 Selections in Change Claim Status/Billing Method Dialog Box

You have completed Exercise 7-5.

7.8 ELECTRONIC CLAIMS WORKFLOW

When claims are created in a practice management program such as Medisoft, an electronic claim file is created. The electronic file contains the information required by the payer to process the claim. Before the claim file reaches the payer, it will go through a series of reviews designed to find any problems that could prevent the claim from being paid. While some practice management programs perform preliminary claim reviews that identify problems, most of the checking is done by a clearinghouse.

A clearinghouse acts as a middleman between the practice and the payer. When a clearinghouse receives a claim, it performs a series of reviews known as edits, checking to see that all necessary information is included in the claim file. It checks for missing data and obvious errors, such as procedures performed on a date earlier than the patient's insurance coverage was in effect. After the edit is complete, a report is sent from the clearinghouse to the practice. This report lists problems that need to be corrected before the claim can be sent to the health plan.

Claims that are clean—problem-free—are sent on to the payer. Once the payer receives the claims and performs its own first round of edits, it sends a report to the clearinghouse indicating which claims have been accepted for adjudication. The clearinghouse sends this information on to the practice in the form of a report. Any claims that contain problems must be corrected and resubmitted to the clearinghouse, where they will be checked again for errors. If no errors are found, the claims will be forwarded to the payer.

While some practices send claims directly to payers, a clearinghouse offers a number of advantages:

- The billing specialist goes to one place to manage claims from multiple payers. A practice that does not use a clearinghouse would need to go to the website of each payer, login, and check claims.

- The clearinghouse checks the claims for errors before sending it on to the payer. Clearinghouses work with thousands of payers and transmit millions of claims, so they are familiar with the rules and requirements of each payer. Since errors are found and corrected before going on to the payer, the claim is more likely to be paid.

- The clearinghouse sends reports to the practice on a regular basis (daily, if not more often), so the practice is always aware of where each claim is in the processing cycle. Most clearinghouses also send special alerts when a claim contains an error.

PERFORM AN ELECTRONIC CLAIM EDIT CHECK (CONNECT ONLY) — EXERCISE 7-6

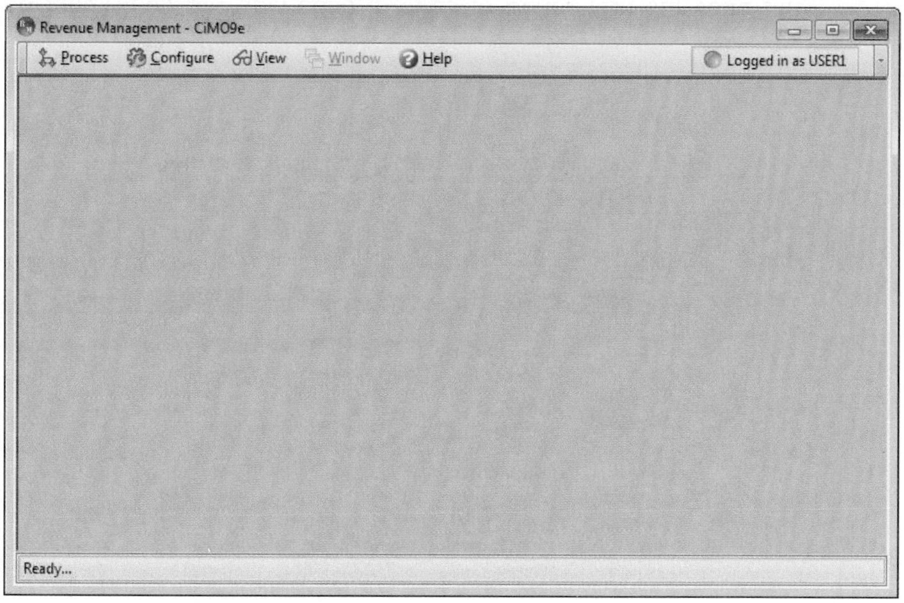

Connect users: go to http://connect.mheducation.com to complete this exercise! Some steps may differ from what is listed here, so be sure to refer to the steps listed in Demo and Practice Modes for guidance.

connect

Prepare a batch of electronic claims for transmission to a clearinghouse and review the claim edit report.

Date: July 10, 2018

1. Select Revenue Management > Revenue Management . . . on the Activities menu. The Revenue Management main window opens (see Figure 7-20).
2. Select Claims on the Process menu (see Figure 7-21).
3. Select an EDI receiver. In this case, the receiver is Phoenix, listed here by the code PHO00. A list of claims ready to be sent is displayed. Notice that the entries in the Edit Status column are all "Not Checked" (see Figure 7-22).
4. To perform an edit check on the claims, click Check Claims and PHO00, the EDI receiver (see Figure 7-23). The claims are checked against a number of edits.
5. When the edit check is finished, the Edit Status column displays the status of each claim—indicated by a green, yellow, or red flag (see Figure 7-24). A green flag indicates that the claim passed the edits and is ready to send. A yellow flag indicates

Figure 7-20 The Revenue Management Window

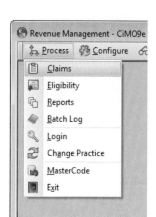

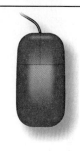

Figure 7-21 Process Menu with Claims Option Highlighted

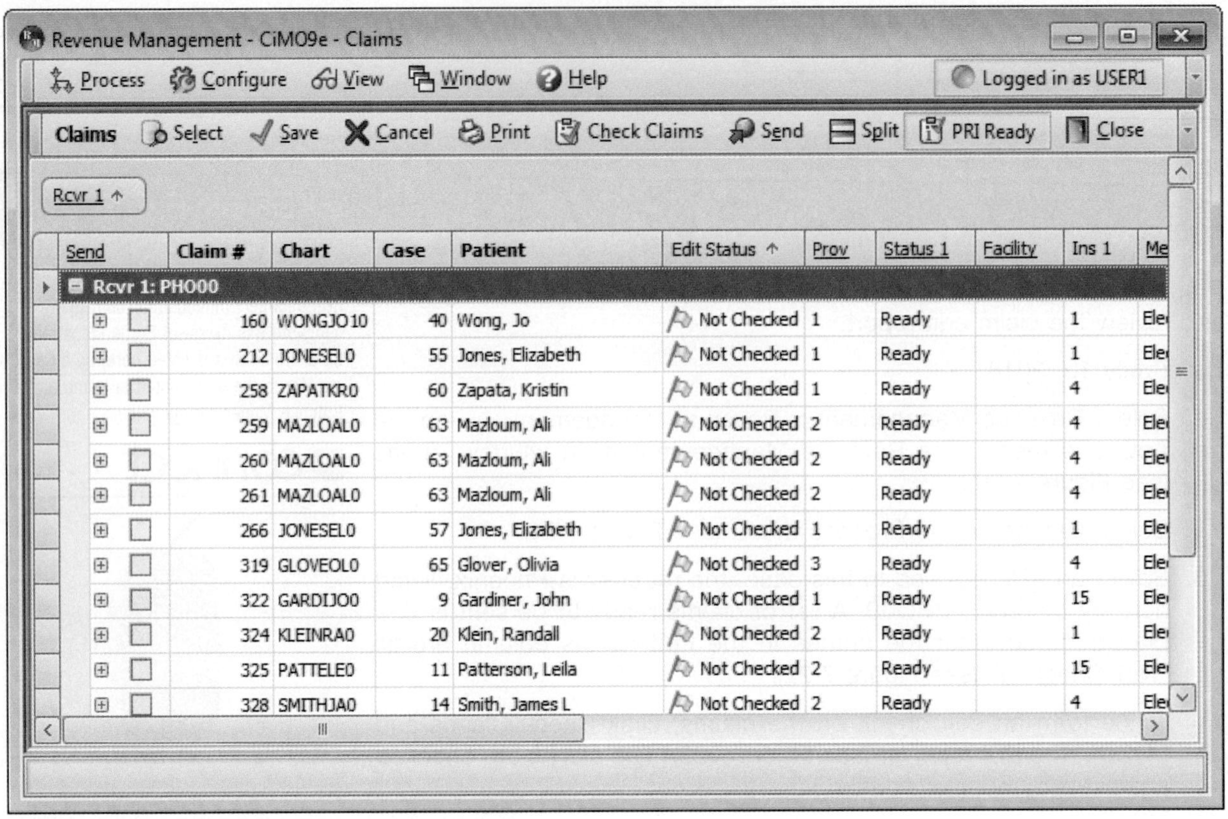

Figure 7-22 List of Claims Ready to be Sent, by EDI Receiver

Figure 7-23 Check Claims Menu with RELAY Selected

that there are issues with the claim—not serious enough to prevent it from being sent, but increasing the possibility that it will be rejected by the payer. A red flag indicates that the claim did not pass the first round of edits. Claims with red flags must be

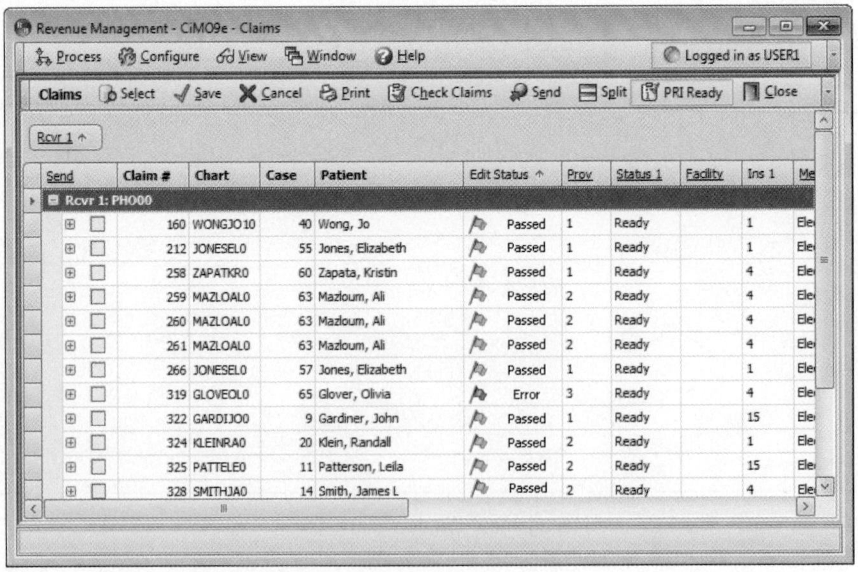

Figure 7-24 List of Claims after Edits Performed

corrected before they can be sent. You can view and correct the errors now, or print an error report and fix the claims at a later time.

6. To print a list of claims with errors, select Edits on the Print menu (see Figure 7-25).

7. The Claim Edits Report appears in the Preview window (see Figure 7-26). This report lists the error message associated with the claim. **CIMO**

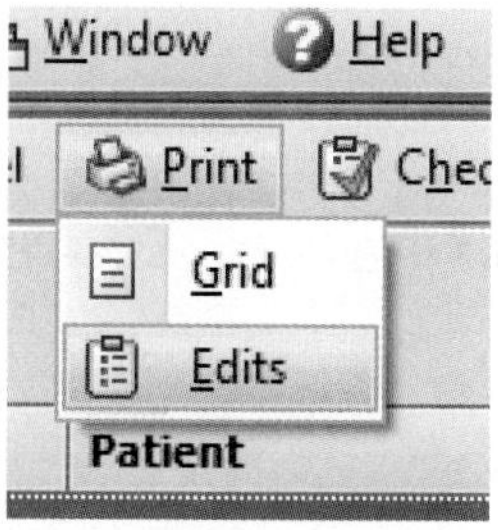

Figure 7-25 Print Menu with Edits Selected

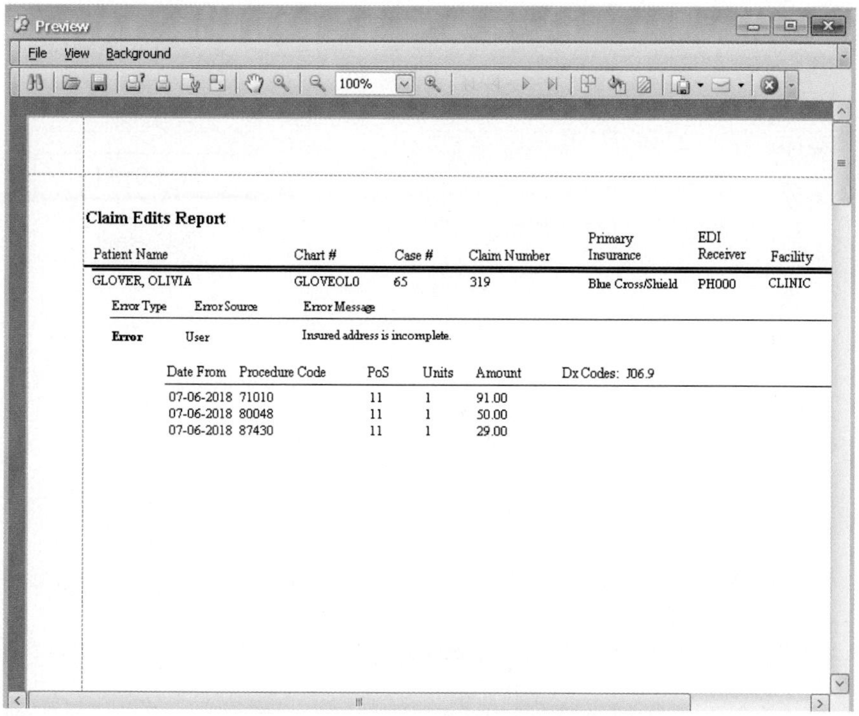

Claim Edits Report

Patient Name	Chart #	Case #	Claim Number	Primary Insurance	EDI Receiver	Facility
GLOVER, OLIVIA	GLOVEOL0	65	319	Blue Cross/Shield	PH000	CLINIC

Error Type	Error Source	Error Message
Error	User	Insured address is incomplete.

Date From	Procedure Code	PoS	Units	Amount	Dx Codes: J06.9
07-06-2018	71010	11	1	91.00	
07-06-2018	80048	11	1	50.00	
07-06-2018	87430	11	1	29.00	

Figure 7-26 Preview Window with Claim Edits Report Displayed

✓ **You have completed Exercise 7-6.**

7.9 SENDING ELECTRONIC CLAIM ATTACHMENTS

When a claim is sent electronically, an attachment that needs to accompany the claim, such as radiology films, must be attached to the claim. In Medisoft, the EDI Report area in the Diagnosis tab of the Case folder is used to indicate to the payer when an attachment will accompany the claim and how the attachment will be transmitted (see Figure 7-27).

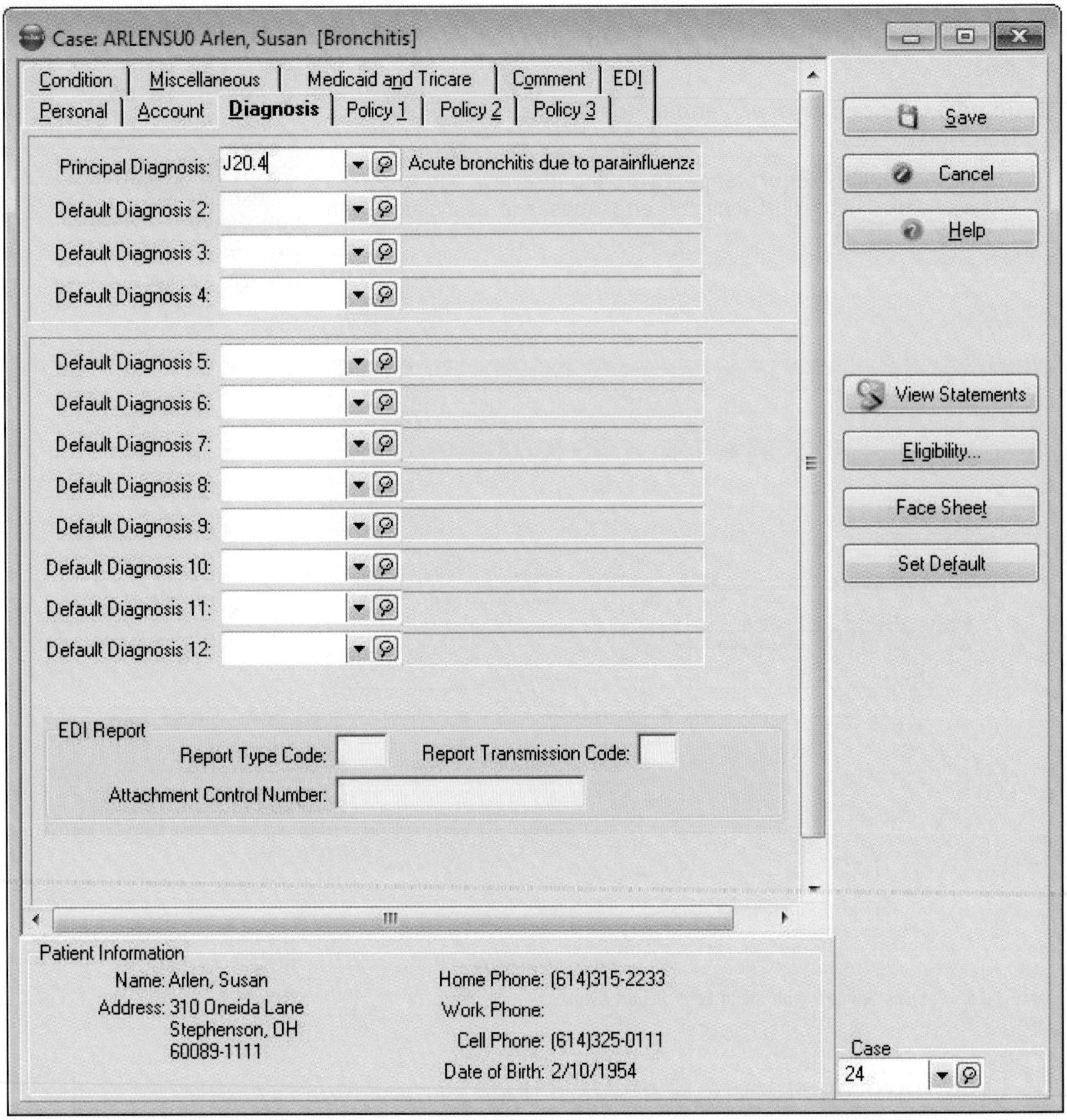

Figure 7-27 Diagnosis Tab with EDI Report Fields Highlighted

If additional information that does not require an attachment is required by the patient's insurance carrier, notes can be entered by clicking the EDI Notes button in the Transaction Entry dialog box (see Figure 7-28).

Figure 7-28 Transaction Entry Dialog Box with EDI Notes Button Highlighted

APPLYING YOUR SKILLS

7: REVIEWING CLAIMS

November 2, 2018
Using the List Only . . . feature, locate all claims for the insurance
carrier BCBS. (*Note:* Do not include claims with a status of Done.)

*Remember to create a backup of your work before exiting Medisoft!
To help you keep track of your work, name the backup file after the
chapter you are working on, for example, StudentID-c7.mbk.*

BE THE DETECTIVE!

If assigned by your instructor, complete the Rejected Claim Video
Case in Connect. Put your skills to use identifying mistakes made in
Medisoft and enhance your knowledge by determining the impact of
those mistakes.

chapter 7 worksheet

[Note: These questions are designed for students using the live Medisoft CD software, since students may need to refer back to specific screens in the software to answer the questions.]

1. *[LO 7.4]* List the names of patients for whom claims were created in Exercise 7-2.

2. *[LO 7.7]* After completing Exercise 7-2, what was listed in the Status 1 column for the claims created?

3. *[LO 7.6]* What transactions are listed on Lawana Brooks's insurance claim?

4. *[LO 7.7]* After completing Exercise 7-5, what is listed in the Status 1 column for the claims for John Fitzwilliams and Elizabeth Jones?

5. *[LO 7.6]* What transactions are listed on Lisa Wright's insurance claim?

6. *[LO 7.5]* Which patients have claims listed in the Claim Management dialog box for Blue Cross/Blue Shield with a status of Sent?

7. *[LO 7.9]* What transactions are included on the claim for Sheila Giles?

Copyright ©2016 McGraw-Hill Education

LEARNING OUTCOMES	CONCEPTS TO REVIEW
7.1 Describe the five most common types of health insurance plans.	– Preferred provider organization (PPO) A type of managed care plan in which providers contract with the organization to provide services to patients at a discounted fee. – Health maintenance organization (HMO) A type of managed care plan in which providers are paid a predetermined amount at regular intervals to cover services they provide to patients. – Point-of-service (POS) plan A plan that combines features of an HMO and a PPO, in which members choose from providers in a primary or secondary network. – Indemnity plan A health plan in which policyholders are repaid for the cost of healthcare after meeting a deductible. – High-deductible health plan with savings option (HDHP/SO) A type of managed care plan with a high deductible, in which a policyholder uses a pretax savings account to cover medical expenses up to the deductible.
7.2 Describe the role of claims in the billing cycle.	Once the services a patient has received from a provider have been entered into the practice management program, the next step is to create insurance claims. The insurance claim is the most important document for correct reimbursement. Claims communicate information about a patient's diagnosis and procedures and the charges to a payer.
7.3 Discuss the information contained in the Claim Management dialog box.	The Claim Management dialog box contains a list of all claims created, and buttons used for editing claims, creating claims, printing/sending claims, reprinting claims, and deleting claims.
7.4 Demonstrate how to create claims in Medisoft.	1. On the Activities menu, click Claim Management. The Claim Management dialog box is displayed. 2. Click the Create Claims button. 3. Enter dates in the Transaction Dates boxes, or leave the boxes blank to create claims for any date. When the program asks whether you want to change the date (because it is in the future), click the No button. 4. Enter the appropriate value(s) in the other fields as needed; remember that if a field is left blank, claims with any value in that field will be created. 5. When you have made your selections, click the Create button. The Create Claims box closes, and the new claims are listed in the Claim Management dialog box.

LEARNING OUTCOMES	CONCEPTS TO REVIEW
7.5 Describe how to locate a claim that has already been submitted.	The List Only feature is used to locate a claim. 1. Click the List Only . . . button in the Claim Management dialog box. 2. In the List Only Claims That Match dialog box, complete the fields to filter claim selection by the options listed. 3. When you have made your selections, click Apply. The List Only Claims That Match dialog box closes, and the selected claim(s) are listed in the Claim Management dialog box.
7.6 Discuss how claims are edited in Medisoft.	In the Claim Management dialog box, click the claim once to select it. With the claim selected, click the Edit button. Locate the information that requires editing in the tabs in the Claim dialog box. To save the changes, click the Save button.
7.7 Explain how to change the status of a claim.	In the Claim Management dialog box, click the claim once to select it. With the claim selected, click the Change Status button. The Change Claim Status/Billing Method dialog box is displayed. Click the appropriate fields in the Status, Billing Method, and For Carrier sections of the dialog box. Click the OK button to change the status.
7.8 List the steps required to submit oloctronic claims in Medisoft.	1. Select Revenue Management > Revenue Management . . . on the Activities menu. 2. The Revenue Management main window opens. 3. Select Claims on the Process menu. 4. Select an EDI receiver. A list of claims ready to be sent is displayed. 5. Click Check Claims and select the EDI receiver. 6. Review claims that did not pass the edit. Correct the errors now or print an error report and fix the claims at a later time. 7. To continue with the ready-to-send claims, select Send, select Claims, and select the EDI receiver. Medisoft creates a claims file and displays a preview report. 8. The preview report checks the claims for ANSI errors. If any errors are found, the claims must be edited before they can be transmitted. Clicking the Remove Claims button removes the selected claim from the claims file. 9. Click the Send button to send the claims files. The file is transmitted to the payer and the claim status is updated in Medisoft.
7.9 Describe how to add attachments to electronic claims.	Information regarding claim attachments is entered in the EDI report section of the Diagnosis tab (within the Case folder). Fields include: – Report Type Code – Report Transmission Code – Attachment Control Number

Copyright ©2016 McGraw-Hill Education

USING TERMINOLOGY

Match the terms on the left with the definitions on the right.

1. *[LO 7.1]* capitation
2. *[LO 7.2]* clean claims
3. *[LO 7.2]* CMS-1500
4. *[LO 7.1]* coinsurance
5. *[LO 7.1]* copayment
6. *[LO 7.1]* deductible
7. *[LO 7.1]* health maintenance organization (HMO)
8. *[LO 7.1]* high-deductible health plan with savings option (HDHP/SO)
9. *[LO 7.1]* indemnity plan
10. *[LO 7.1]* managed care
11. *[LO 7.2]* medical necessity
12. *[LO 7.1]* payer
13. *[LO 7.1]* point-of-service (POS) plan
14. *[LO 7.1]* preferred provider organization (PPO)

15. *[LO 7.2]* X12 837 Health Care Claim or Equivalent Encounter Information (837P)

a. Private or government organization that insures or pays for healthcare.

b. A type of managed care insurance in which a high-deductible plan is combined with a pretax savings account to cover out-of-pocket medical expenses.

c. Percentage of charges that an insured person must pay for healthcare services after payment of the deductible amount.

d. A network of healthcare providers who agree to provide services to plan members at a discounted fee.

e. The electronic format of the claim used by physician offices to bill for services.

f. A plan, combining features of an HMO and a PPO, in which members may choose from providers in a primary or secondary network.

g. A small fee paid by the patient at the time of an office visit.

h. A fixed amount that is paid to a provider to provide medically necessary services to patients.

i. A type of insurance in which the carrier is responsible for the financing and delivery of healthcare.

j. An insurance plan in which policyholders are reimbursed a percentage of healthcare costs.

 Enhance your learning by completing these exercises and more at http://connect.mheducation.com

k. The amount a policyholder must spend on medical services before benefits begin.

l. The mandated paper insurance claim form.

m. A type of managed care system in which providers are paid fixed rates at regular Intervals.

n. Healthcare claims with all the correct information necessary for payer processing.

o. Healthcare services that are reasonable, necessary, and/or appropriate, based on evidence-based clinical standards of care.

CHECKING YOUR UNDERSTANDING

16. *[LO 7.5]* A claim needs to be submitted for John Fitzwilliams. How would you select only those claims pertaining to John Fitzwilliams?

17. *[LO 7.6]* If an error is found on a claim, how is it corrected?

18. *[LO 7.2]* What is meant by a "clean claim"?

19. *[LO 7.2]* What is HIPAA X12 837?

20. *[LO 7.5]* What is the List Only feature in the Claim Management dialog box used for?

21. *[LO 7.9]* In Medisoft, where is information about electronic claim attachments entered?

APPLYING YOUR KNOWLEDGE

22. *[LO 7.4]* You are asked to create a claim for Samuel Bell. After entering his chart number in the Create Claims dialog box, you receive the message "No new claims were created." Why were no claims created for Samuel Bell?

23. *[LO 7.4]* How would you create claims for one specific insurance carrier?

24. *[LO 7.8]* You are not sure whether an electronic claim for a particular patient was transmitted. How would you find out?

25. *[LO 7.9]* A new billing specialist in the office tells you it is less costly to submit electronic claims directly to insurance carriers without using a clearinghouse. Why do you think offices use clearinghouses? What are the benefits?

26. *[LO 7.2]* If claims were not created and transmitted, what would the consequence be?

27. *[LO 7.2]* Why is it important that claims be submitted soon after the patient's visit?

28. *[LO 7.2]* Why is it important that claims be submitted with complete and correct information?

connect Enhance your learning by completing these exercises and more at http://connect.mheducation.com

POSTING PAYMENTS AND CREATING PATIENT STATEMENTS

learning outcomes

When you finish this chapter, you will be able to:

8.1 Describe how an adjustment is calculated if the payer pays less than the provider's usual fee.

8.2 List the five steps for processing a remittance advice.

8.3 Demonstrate how to enter insurance payments.

8.4 Demonstrate how to apply insurance payments to charges.

8.5 Demonstrate how to enter and apply a patient payment received by mail.

8.6 Demonstrate how to enter capitation payments.

8.7 Demonstrate how to create patient statements.

8.8 Explain how statements are edited.

8.9 Demonstrate how to preview and print patient statements.

what you need to know

To use this chapter, you need to know how to:

- Start Medisoft, use menus, and enter and edit text.
- Edit information in an existing case.
- Work with chart and case numbers.
- Select patients and cases for transaction entry.

key terms

autoposting

capitation payments

cycle billing

electronic funds transfer (EFT)

fee schedule

once-a-month billing

patient statement

payment schedule

remainder statements

standard statements

8.1 THIRD-PARTY REIMBURSEMENT OVERVIEW

fee schedule a document that specifies the amount the provider bills for provided services.

payment schedule a document that specifies the amount the payer agrees to reimburse the provider for a service.

The amount a physician is reimbursed for a service depends on the patient's insurance benefits and the provider's agreement with the third-party payer. Providers establish a list of standard fees, known as a **fee schedule**, for procedures and services—this is the amount the provider bills the payer. Payers also develop a list of standard fees, but their **payment schedule** is based on a rate established in a contract with the provider. Most of the time, the amount the provider bills and the rate specified in the contract with the payer differ. The difference between the amount billed (the fee schedule) and the amount paid per contract (the payment schedule) is an adjustment that is entered in the billing area of the practice management program.

The following examples illustrate how reimbursement is calculated for an indemnity plan, a managed care plan, and a Medicare plan.

INDEMNITY PLAN EXAMPLE

In an indemnity plan, insurers often reimburse 80 percent of "reasonable charges," and the patient pays the remaining 20 percent.

Provider's usual fee	$100.00
Allowed charge	100.00
Insurance payment	80.00
Patient coinsurance	20.00

In this example, the amount allowed by the payer is the same as the provider's charge. The payer reimburses at 80 percent and the patient is responsible for the remaining 20 percent. The provider is paid for the entire billed amount; no adjustment is necessary.

MANAGED CARE EXAMPLE

Providers enter into contracts with managed care companies in which they agree to accept reduced fees for services. A managed care plan may require the patient to pay a fixed copayment.

Provider's usual fee	$100.00
Allowed charge	90.00
Patient copayment	20.00
Insurance payment	70.00
Adjustment	10.00

In this example, the provider charges $100.00. However, the provider's contract with the payer requires the provider to accept

90 percent of the usual and customary charge as full payment. This amount is known as the approved amount. The provider must enter an adjustment to write off the $10.00 difference between the amount charged and the amount approved per the contract. The patient pays a fixed copayment of $20.00, which is subtracted from the approved charge.

MEDICARE PARTICIPATING EXAMPLE

Medicare uses its own payment schedule, known as the Medicare Physician Fee Schedule (MPFS), which is updated annually. Providers who agree to participate in Medicare must accept the fee listed in the MPFS as payment in full. Medicare is responsible for paying 80 percent of this amount and the patient is responsible for the other 20 percent (after a deductible has been met).

Provider's usual fee	$100.00
Medicare allowed charge	64.00
Medicare pays 80 percent	51.20
Patient pays 20 percent	12.80
Adjustment	36.00

In this example, the provider charges $100.00. The maximum allowed amount in the Medicare Physician Fee Schedule is $64.00. The difference between $100.00 and $64.00 must be written off by the provider. Medicare pays 80 percent of the allowed amount and the patient is billed for the remaining 20 percent, or $12.80.

Note: Providers who do not participate in the Medicare program may accept assignment on a claim-by-claim basis, but they are paid 5 percent less than providers who participate. Providers who do not participate and who do not accept assignment of a claim are subject to Medicare's limiting charge. This rule limits the amount a provider can charge to 115 percent of the fee listed in the Medicare nonparticipating fee schedule.

The chart displayed in Figure 8-1 contains the fee schedules for the providers and payers used in the exercises in this text/workbook. The information on the chart includes the following:

CPT Code The procedure code for the service provided.

Provider's Usual Fee The usual amount the provider bills for the service.

Managed Care Allowed The discounted fee specified by contract.

Medicare Allowed The maximum fee a participating provider can collect for the service.

CPT Code	Provider's Usual Fee	Managed Care Allowed	Medicare Allowed
12011	$202.00	$181.80	$148.70
29125	$99.00	$89.10	$61.21
29540	$121.50	$109.35	$40.50
50390	$551.00	$495.90	$101.47
71010	$91.00	$81.90	$26.77
71020	$112.00	$100.80	$34.71
71030	$153.00	$137.70	$45.25
73070	$102.00	$91 80	$27.06
73090	$99.00	$89.10	$27.44
73100	$93.00	$83.70	$26.37
73510	$124.00	$111.60	$32.56
73600	$96.00	$86.40	$26.37
80048	$50.00	$45.00	$11.20
80050	$80.00	$72.00	$20.50
80061	$90.00	$81.00	$18.72
82270	$19.00	$17.10	$4.54
82947	$25.00	$22.50	$5.48
82951	$63.00	$56.70	$16.12
83718	$43.00	$38.70	$11.44
84478	$29.00	$26.10	$8.04
85007	$21.00	$18.90	$4.81
85018	$13.00	$11.70	$3.31
85025	$13.60	$12.24	$10.79
85651	$24.00	$21.60	$4.96
86580	$25.00	$22.50	$6.86
87076	$75.00	$67.50	$11.29
87077	$60.00	$54.00	$11.29
87086	$51.00	$45.90	$11.28
87430	$29.00	$26.10	$16.01
87880	$24.00	$21.60	$16.01
90471	$15.00	$13.50	$17.82

CPT Code	Provider's Usual Fee	Managed Care Allowed	Medicare Allowed
90656	$25.00	$22.50	$14.00
90662	$50.00	$45.00	$33.30
90703	$29.00	$26.10	$14.30
92516	$210.00	$189.00	$59.32
93000	$84.00	$75.60	$25.72
93015	$401.00	$360.90	$103.31
96372	$40.00	$36.00	$18.74
96900	$39.00	$35.10	$16.42
99201	$66.00	$59.40	$35.58
99202	$88.00	$79.20	$63.28
99203	$120.00	$108.00	$94.28
99204	$178.00	$160.20	$133.56
99205	$229.00	$206.10	$169.28
99211	$36.00	$32.40	$20.68
99212	$54.00	$48.60	$37.36
99213	$72.00	$64.80	$51.03
99214	$105.00	$94.50	$80.15
99215	$163.00	$146.70	$116.96
99381	$210.00	$189.00	$100.27
99382	$218.00	$196.20	$108.13
99383	$224.00	$201.60	$106.00
99384	$262.50	$236.25	$115.30
99385	$247.50	$222.75	$115.30
99386	$267.00	$240.30	$135.69
99387	$298.50	$268.65	$147.13
99391	$165.00	$148.50	$76.39
99392	$184.50	$166.05	$85.69
99393	$192.00	$172.80	$84.63
99394	$222.00	$199.80	$93.56
99395	$204.00	$183.60	$94.63
99396	$222.00	$199.80	$104.64
99397	$236.00	$212.40	$115.37

Figure 8-1 Fee Schedule/Payment Schedule for Payers in Contract with the Family Care Center

8.2 REMITTANCE ADVICE (RA) PROCESSING

Once a claim has been received and accepted, it is processed and the appropriate payment is determined. The payer then generates a remittance advice (RA) and sends it to the provider. A remittance advice lists the transactions included on the claims and the amount paid; if appropriate, it provides an explanation of why certain charges were not paid in full or were denied entirely. It contains payments for multiple claims for a number of different patients. A sample RA appears in Figure 8-2.

The RA may be sent in electronic format, called an electronic remittance advice (ERA), or in paper format. Although similar information is contained on an ERA and a paper RA, the ERA may offer additional data. The ERA that is mandated for use by HIPAA is called the ASC X12 835 Remittance Advice Transaction, or simply the 835.

Steps for Processing a Remittance Advice

1. Compare the RA to the original insurance claim. Make sure that all procedures listed on the claim are represented on the RA and that the CPT codes have not changed.
2. Review the payment amount against the expected amount.

```
(1) ABC, Corp
    ADDRESS 1                                                    MEDICARE
    ADDRESS 2                                                    REMITTANCE
    CITY, STATE ZIP                                              NOTICE
    (999) 111-2222

    PROVIDER NAME                    PROVIDER #: 1234567890
    ADDRESS 1                        PAGE #: 1 OF 10
    ADDRESS 2                        DATE: 06/05/15
    CITY, STATE ZIP                  CHECK/EFT #: 12345678901234567890
                                     REMITTANCE # 12345678901234567890 (NOT A REQUIRED FIELD)
........................................................................................................
********************************************************************************************************
                                                                                           *
                 WELCOME TO THE MEDICARE PART B STANDARD PAPER REMITTANCE                   *
                                                                                           *
                                                                                           *
********************************************************************************************************
```

(2) PERF PROV SERV DATE POS NOS PROC MODS BILLED ALLOWED DEDUCT COINS GRP/ RC AMT PROV PD

```
NAME: BUNYAN, PAUL  HIC 123456789    ACNT 1234567890234567890  ICN 123456789012345   ASG Y   MOA
123456ABC    0225 022515  11   1     99213        66.00    49.83   0.34   9.97  CO-42  16.17  $39.52

PT RESP 10.31                    CLAIM TOTALS  66.00    49.83   0.34   9.97         16.17  $39.52 NET
```
___
```
NAME: FISCHER, BENNY  HIC 999999999   ACNT FISC6123133-01      ICN 0202199306850     ASG Y   MOA MA01 MA07
123456ABC    0117 011715  11   1     99213        66.00    49.83   0.00   9.97  PR-96  16.17  $39.86

PT RESP  9.97                    CLAIM TOTALS  66.00    49.83   0.00   9.97         16.17

CLAIM INFORMATION FORWARDED TO:          MEDICAID                                          $39.86 NET
```
___
```
NAME: HURT, I.M.       HIC 999999999   ACNT HURT5-329           ICN 0202199326870     ASG Y   MOA MA01
123456ABC    0117 011715  11   1     90659        25.00    3.32    0.00   0.00  CO-42  21.68  $3.32
123456ABC    0117 011715  11   1     G0008        10.00    4.46    0.00   0.00  CO-42   5.54  $4.46
                                                                                  27.22  $7.78 NET
PT RESP 0.00
```
___
```
NAME: FINE, R.U.       HIC 9999999999  ACNT FINE7-002           ICN 0202199000150     ASG Y   N257 MA130
123456ABC    0526 052615  11   1     73560  LT   79.00    0.00    0.00   0.00  CO-16  79.00
REM: N257
PT RESP 0.00                     CLAIM TOTALS  79.00    0.00    0.00   0.00         79.00   0.00
```

(3) TOTALS: # OF   BILLED   ALLOWED   DEDUCT   COINS   TOTAL   PROV PD   PROV   CHECK
             CLAIMS   AMT   AMT   AMT   AMT   AMT   RC-AMT   AMT   ADJ AMT   AMT
               4   167.00   107.44   0.34   19.94   59.56   87.16   0.00 $87.16

(4) PROVIDER ADJ DETAILS: PLB REASON CODE   FCN   HIC   AMOUNT
___

(5) GLOSSARY: Group, Reason, MOA, Remark and Offset Codes
    CO-42   Contractual Obligation. Amount for which the provider is financially liable. The patient may not be billed for this amount.
                 Claim/service denied/reduced because this procedure/service is not paid separately. Charges exceed our fee schedule or
                 maximum allowable amount.
    M80   We cannot pay for this when performed during the same session as another approved procedure for this beneficiary
    MA07   The claim information has also been forwarded to Medicaid for review.

    1 Carrier and Provider Identification
    2 Claim and Detail Information
    3 Total Summary
    4 Provider Adjustment Details
    5 Glossary

Figure 8-2   Example of a Payer's Remittance Advice
```
```

3. Identify the reasons for denials or payment reductions; resubmit claim or appeal if necessary.

4. Post payment information for individual claims to the appropriate patient accounts.

5. Bill the patient's secondary healthcare plan (if appropriate).

Providers who receive electronic remittance advices have the option of using an automated process called **autoposting** to record the information in the program. In autoposting, the electronic data in the remittance advice are automatically posted to patient accounts in the PMP. While this approach saves the time that would be required to manually enter the information, the information still must be reviewed by a person to identify any payments that are not as expected.

autoposting the automatic posting of data in the remittance advice to a practice management program.

CLAIM ADJUSTMENTS AND DENIALS

In most cases, insurance carriers do not fully pay the amount billed by the provider. The provider bills according to the provider's fee schedule. The amount charged is adjusted by the payer, based on the rate specified in the provider's contract, the policyholder's benefit coverage, and any payment expected from the patient. When the RA is reviewed, the billing specialist checks to see that the amount paid is the expected amount. If a payment is not as expected, the specialist must determine the reason for the discrepancy.

Charges may be denied by insurance carriers for a number of reasons. For example, a procedure may not be covered by the patient's plan, or a procedure or diagnosis may be coded incorrectly. If the reimbursement on an RA is lower than the amount expected, it is important to determine the reason and to take action to collect the correct amount. The problem could have originated in the provider's office, or it could have occurred during processing by the payer. When an error has been made in the provider's office, the billing staff member must correct the error in the billing software and resubmit the claim to the payer. If the error occurs during processing by the third-party payer, an appeal process may be started. Table 8-1 lists common errors that result in reduced or denied payments.

PROCESSING PAYMENTS

In the past, paper remittance advice forms were accompanied by a check, which was deposited in the practice's bank account. Today, most practices receive payment in the form of an electronic funds transfer (EFT). **Electronic funds transfer** is the electronic movement of money from one bank account to another. In this case, the payer transfers funds directly to the practice's bank account,

electronic funds transfer (EFT) the electronic movement of money from one bank account to another.

TABLE 8-1	Common Claim Errors
Remittance Advice Result	**Possible Reasons**
Reimbursement is made at a reduced rate.	• Clerical error was made. • Precertification or preapproval guidelines were not followed.
Reimbursement is denied.	• Clerical error was made. • Precertification or preapproval guidelines were not followed. • Insufficient documentation was provided to establish medical necessity. • All information required by payer was not included. • The wrong payer was billed.
Payment is not received.	• Claim is missing or lost in the system.
Multiple procedures were not paid.	• Payer either missed the additional procedures or grouped them with the primary procedure.

eliminating the steps necessary to create, deliver, and deposit a paper check.

8.3 ENTERING INSURANCE PAYMENTS IN MEDISOFT

In contrast to patient payments that are made at the time of an office visit, which are entered in the Transaction Entry dialog box, insurance payments in Medisoft are entered in the Deposit List dialog box (see Figure 8-3). The Deposit List dialog box is opened by selecting Enter Deposits/Payments on the Activities menu or by clicking the Enter Deposits and Apply Payments shortcut button. The Deposit/Payments area of the program is very efficient for entering large insurance payments that must be split up and applied to a number of different patients.

THE DEPOSIT LIST DIALOG BOX

The Deposit List dialog box contains the following information:

Deposit Date The program displays the current date (the Medisoft Program Date). The date can be changed by keying over the default date.

Show All Deposits If this box is checked, all payments are displayed, regardless of the date entered.

Show Unapplied Only If the Show Unapplied Only box is checked, only payments that have not been fully applied to charge transactions are displayed. If the box is not checked, all payments—both applied and unapplied—are listed.

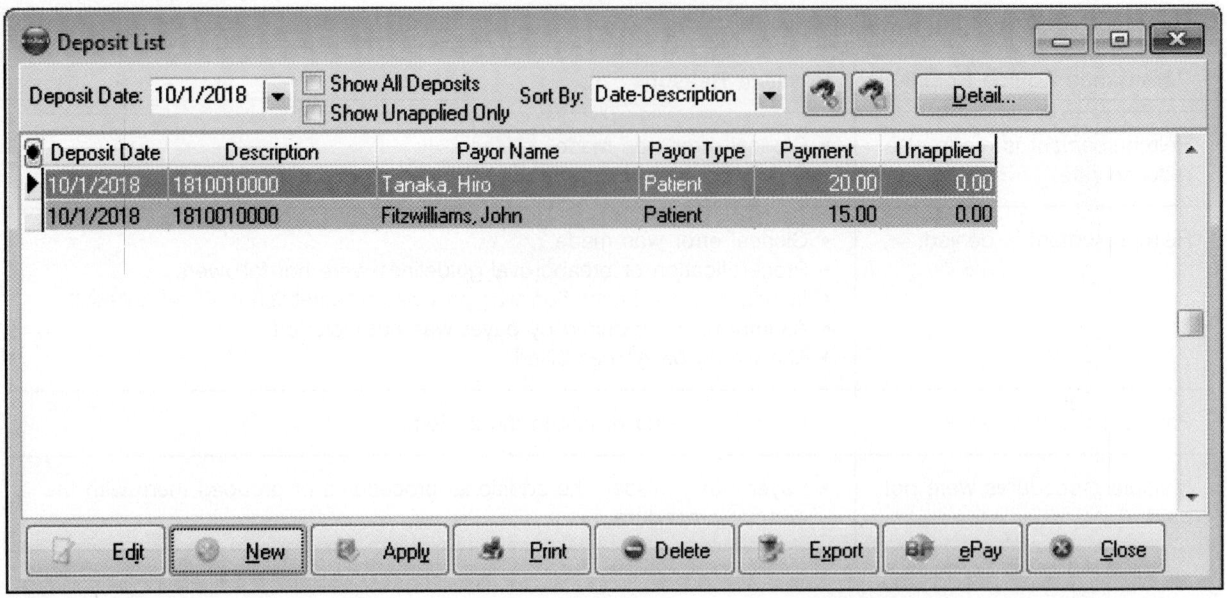

Figure 8-3 Deposit List Dialog Box

Sort By The Sort By drop-down list offers several choices for how payment information is listed. The default is sorting payments by date and description. Payments can also be sorted by other data fields (see Figure 8-4).

Locate Buttons The Locate and Locate Next buttons, indicated by the two magnifying glass icons, are used to search for a deposit.

Detail To view a specific deposit in more detail, highlight the deposit and click the Detail button. A dialog box opens with more information about the selected deposit (see Figure 8-5).

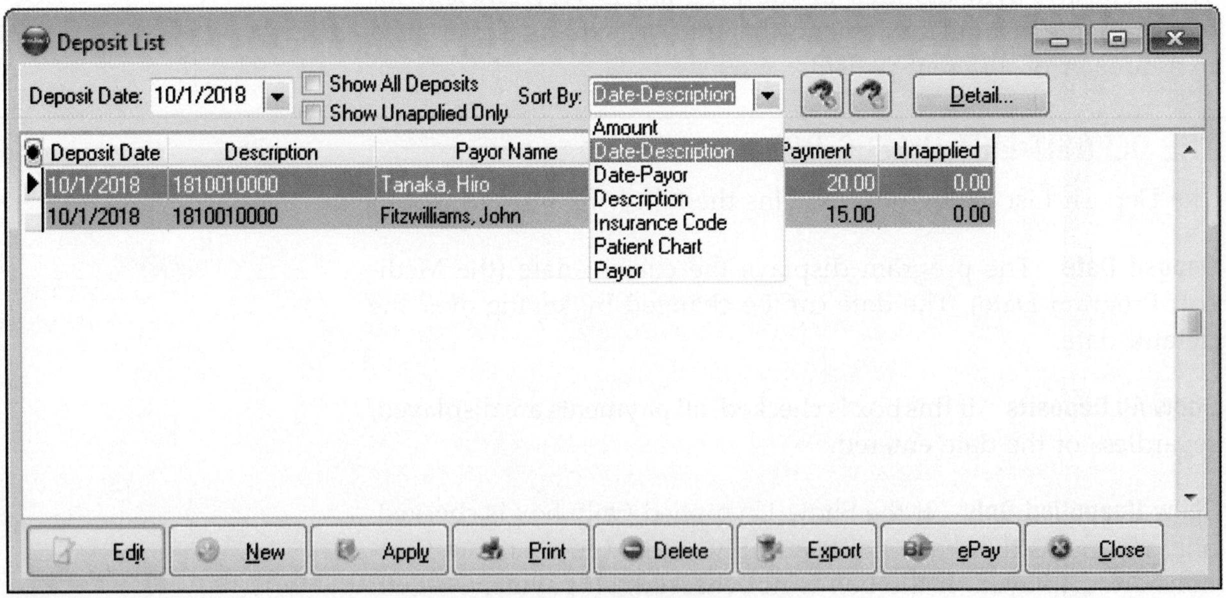

Figure 8-4 Deposit List Dialog Box with Sort By Drop-down List Displayed

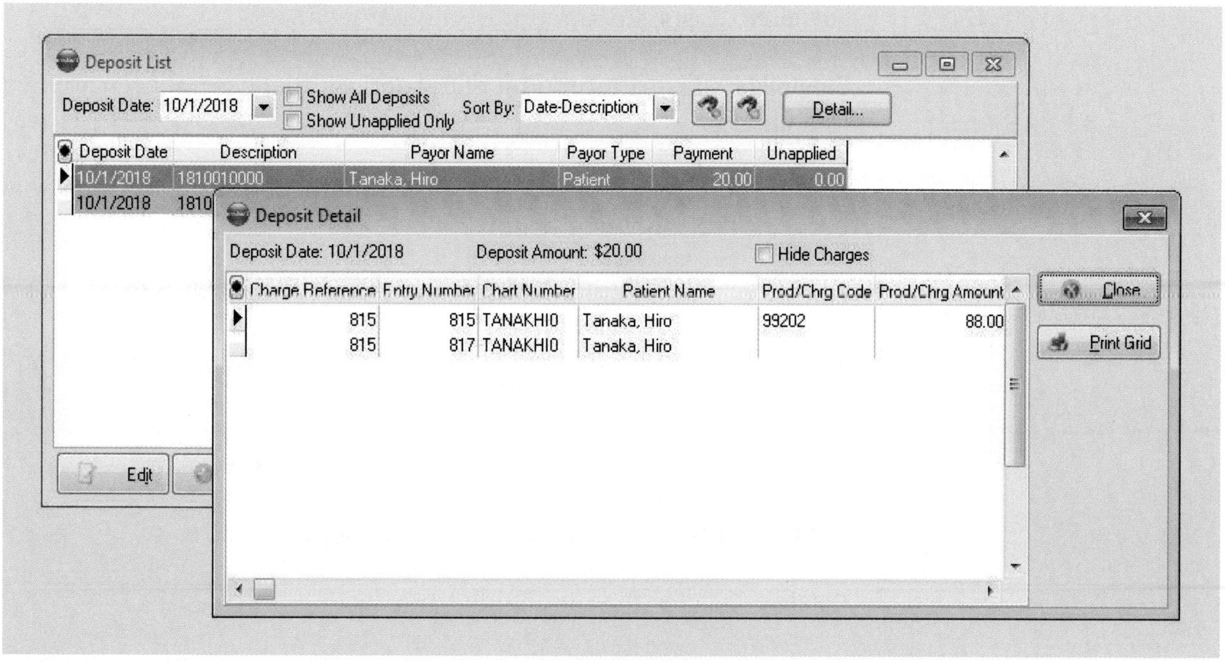

Figure 8-5 Deposit Detail Dialog Box with Deposit List Dialog Box in Background

In the middle section of the Deposit List dialog box, information is listed for each deposit and payment, including the following:

Deposit Date   Lists the date of the deposit or payment.

Description   Displays whatever was entered in the Description or Check Number box in the Deposit dialog box. The Deposit dialog box is where new payments and deposits are recorded (see Figure 8-6). It is accessed by clicking the New button in the Deposit List dialog box.

Payor Name   Lists the name of the insurance carrier or individual who made the payment.

Payor Type   A classification column that lists whether the payment is an insurance payment, a patient payment, or a capitation payment. **Capitation payments** are made to physicians on a regular basis (such as monthly) for providing services to patients in a managed care insurance plan. In traditional insurance plans, physicians are paid based on the specific procedures they perform and the number of times the procedures are performed. Under a capitated plan, a flat fee is paid to the physician no matter how many times a patient receives treatment, up to the maximum number of treatments allowed per year. For example, a primary care physician with fifty patients may receive a payment of $2,500 per month for those patients, regardless of whether the physician has seen them during that month.

capitation payments payments made to physicians on a regular basis for providing services to patients in a managed care plan.

Payment   Lists the amount of the payment.

Unapplied   Lists the amount of the deposit that has not been applied to a charge.

At the bottom of the Deposit List dialog box are buttons that perform the following actions:

Edit   Opens the highlighted payment or deposit for editing.

New   Opens the Deposit dialog box, where new payments and deposits are recorded.

Apply   Applies payments to specific charge transactions.

Print   Sends a command to print the deposit list.

Delete   Deletes the highlighted transaction.

Export   Exports the data in either Quicken or QuickBooks program formats.

ePay   Applies to practices that use the optional BillFlash add-on module.

Close   Exits the Deposit List dialog box.

THE DEPOSIT DIALOG BOX

When the New button is clicked in the Deposit List dialog box, the Deposit dialog box appears (see Figure 8-6).

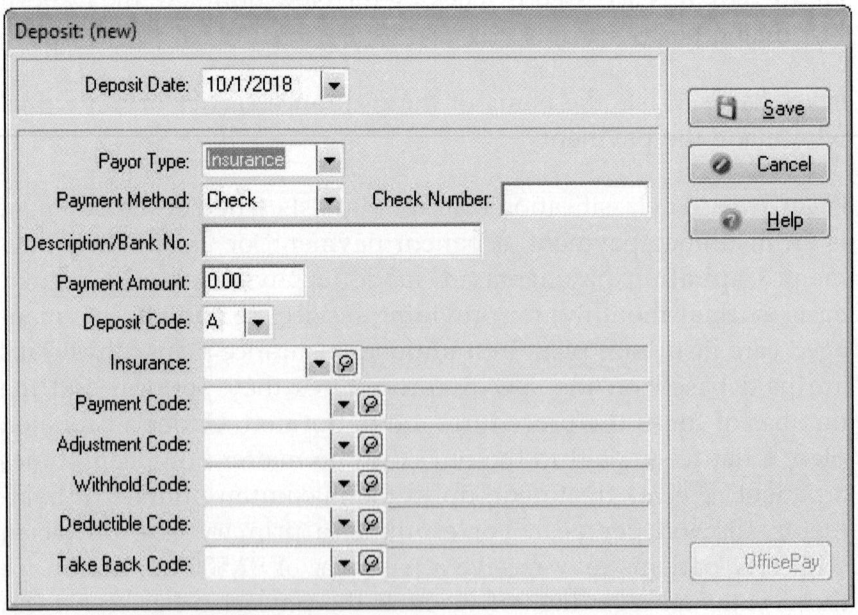

Figure 8-6   Deposit Dialog Box

PART 2 MEDISOFT ADVANCED TRAINING

The Deposit dialog box contains the following fields:

Deposit Date   The program's current date is displayed by default and must be changed if it is not the date of the deposit.

Payor Type   The drop-down options in this box indicate whether the payer is an insurance carrier, a capitation plan, or a patient (see Figure 8-7). Some of the boxes at the bottom of the Deposit dialog box change based on the selection in this box. If Insurance is selected, the dialog box is as illustrated in Figure 8-6. If Capitation is selected, all the boxes below Insurance disappear. If Patient is chosen, the boxes listed below Deposit Code become Chart Number, Payment Code, Adjustment Code, and Copayment Code.

Payment Method   This box lists whether the payment is check, cash, credit card, or electronic.

Check Number   If payment is made by check, the number of the check is entered in this box.

Description/Bank No.   This box can be used to enter a description of the payment, if desired.

Payment Amount   The total amount of the payment is entered in this box.

Deposit Code   This field can be used by practices to sort deposits according to user-defined categories.

Insurance   The insurance carrier that is making the payment is selected.

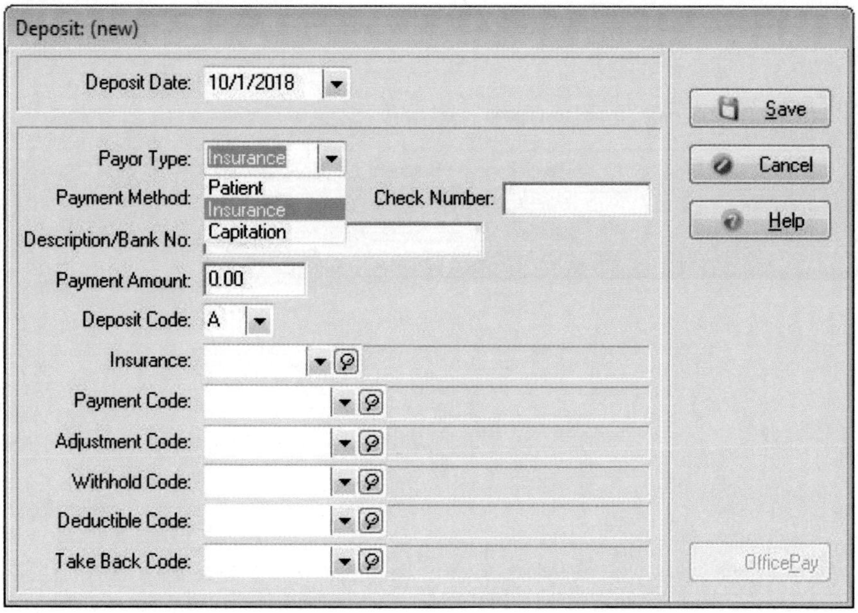

Figure 8-7   Payor Type Options in the Deposit Dialog Box

Payment Code, Adjustment Code, Withhold Code, Deductible Code, and Take Back Code The appropriate codes for the insurance carrier are selected.

Once all the information has been entered and checked for accuracy, the deposit is saved by clicking the Save button (see Figure 8-8). When the deposit entry is saved, the Deposit dialog box closes and the Deposit List dialog box reappears, with the new deposit listed (see Figure 8-9).

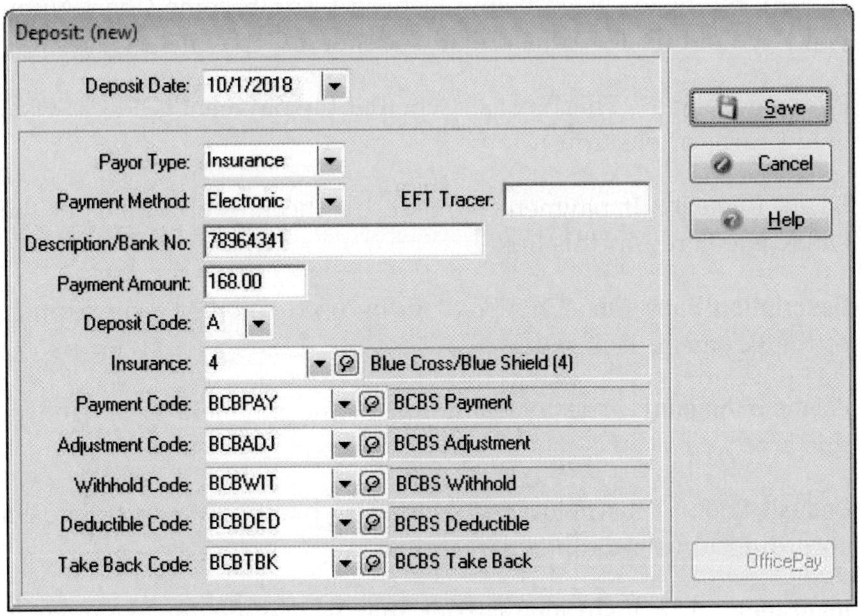

Figure 8-8 Deposit Dialog Box with Information Entered

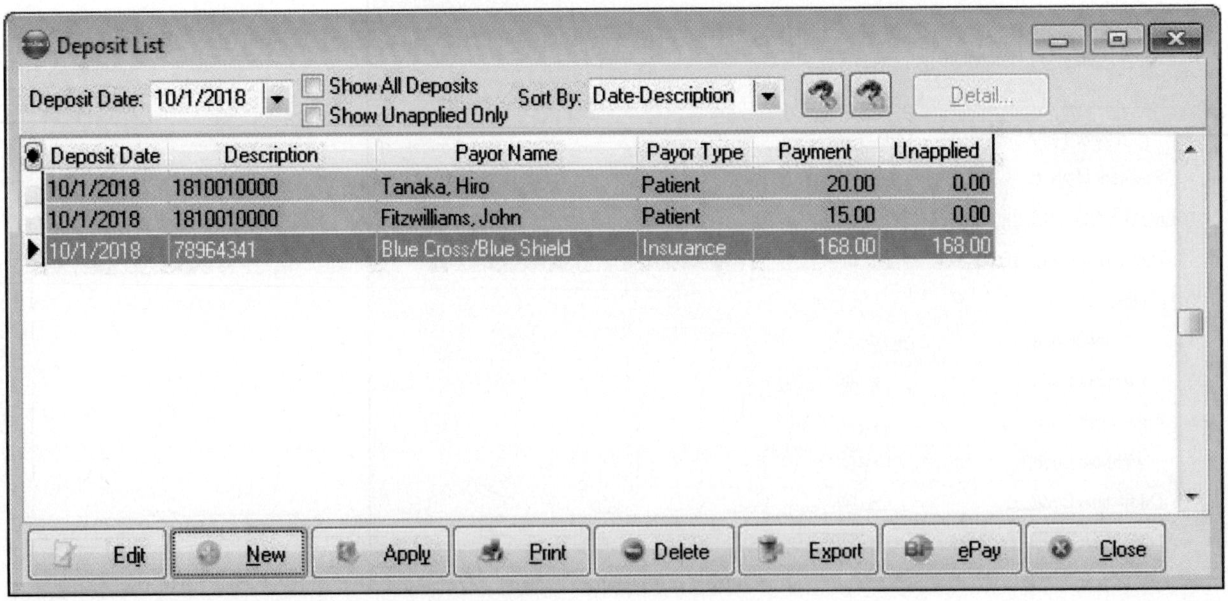

Figure 8-9 Deposit List Dialog Box with Deposit Entered

Using Source Document 8, enter the payment received from John Fitzwilliams's insurance carrier for services provided on September 4, 2018. Note that John is guarantor for his daughter Sarah, so her charges and payments are included on the remittance advice.

Connect users: go to http://connect.mheducation.com to complete this exercise! Some steps may differ from what is listed here, so be sure to refer to the steps listed in Demo and Practice Modes for guidance.

Date: October 1, 2018

1. Start Medisoft and restore the data from your last work session.

2. Change the Medisoft Program Date to October 1, 2018.

3. Enter Deposits/Payments on the Activities menu. The Deposit List dialog box is displayed.

4. Verify that 10/1/2018 is displayed in the Deposit Date box and that the two check boxes—Show All Deposits and Show Unapplied Only—are not checked. If they are checked, click in the box to remove the check mark.

5. Change the entry in the Sort By box to Date-Payor. Click No in response to the message about changing the date. Compare your screen to Figure 8-10.

6. Click the New button. The Deposit dialog box is displayed. Verify that the Deposit Date is 10/1/2018.

7. Since this is a payment from an insurance carrier, confirm that Insurance is selected in the Payor Type box. If it is not, change the selection in the Payor Type box to Insurance.

8. Accept the default entry (Check) in the Payment Method box.

9. Enter **214778924** in the Check Number box and press Tab twice. (The Description/Bank No. field can be left blank.)

10. Enter the amount of the payment (**28.02**) in the Payment Amount box. Press Tab.

11. Accept the default entry (A) in the Deposit Code box. Press Tab.

Deposit Date	Description	Payor Name	Payor Type	Payment	Unapplied
10/1/2018	1810010000	Fitzwilliams, John	Patient	15.00	0.00
10/1/2018	1810010000	Tanaka, Hiro	Patient	20.00	0.00

Deposit Date: 10/1/2018 — Show All Deposits — Show Unapplied Only — Sort By: Date-Payor — Detail...

Edit   New   Apply   Print   Delete   Export   ePay   Close

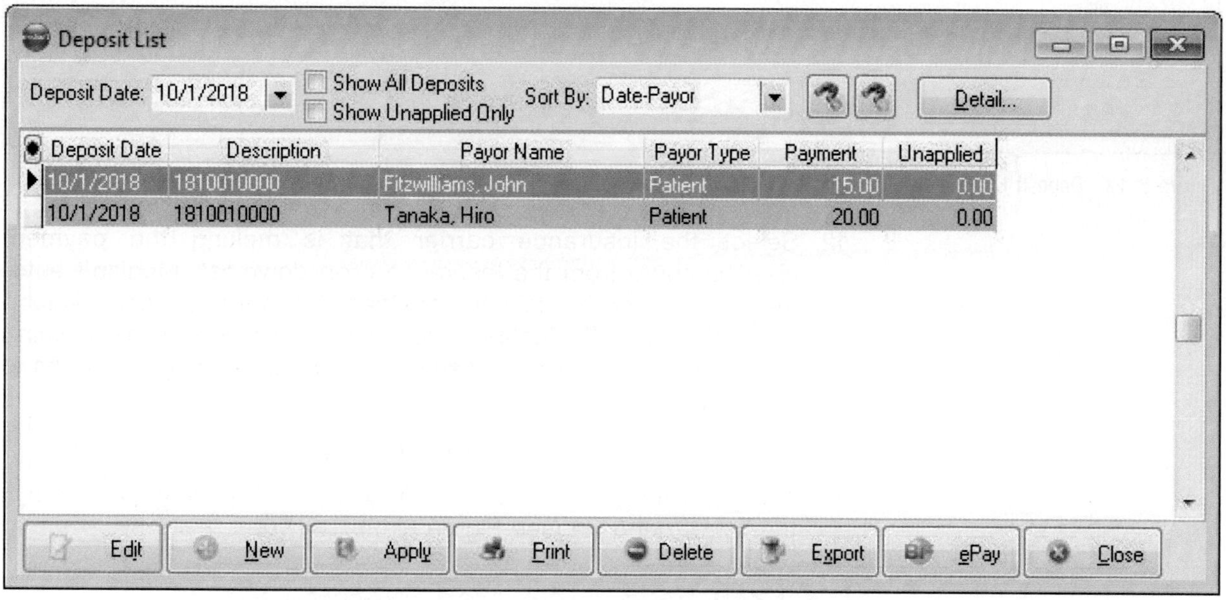

Figure 8-10   Deposit List with 10/1/2018 in Deposit Date Field and Date-Payor Selected in the Sort By Field

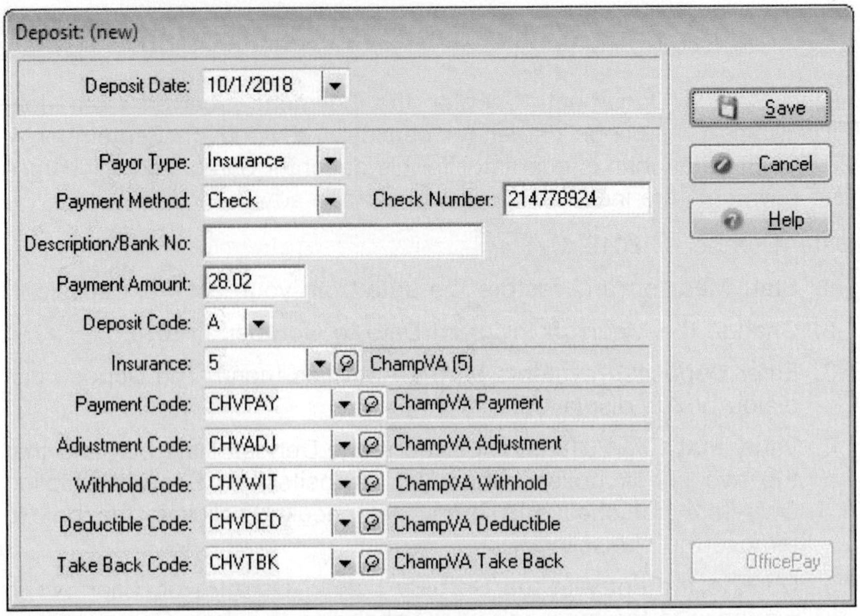

Deposit: (new)

Deposit Date: 10/1/2018 ▼

Payor Type: Insurance ▼
Payment Method: Check ▼   Check Number: 214778924
Description/Bank No:
Payment Amount: 28.02
Deposit Code: A ▼
Insurance: 5 ▼ 🔍 ChampVA (5)
Payment Code: CHVPAY ▼ 🔍 ChampVA Payment
Adjustment Code: CHVADJ ▼ 🔍 ChampVA Adjustment
Withhold Code: CHVWIT ▼ 🔍 ChampVA Withhold
Deductible Code: CHVDED ▼ 🔍 ChampVA Deductible
Take Back Code: CHVTBK ▼ 🔍 ChampVA Take Back

[Save] [Cancel] [Help] [OfficePay]

Figure 8-11   Completed Deposit Dialog Box

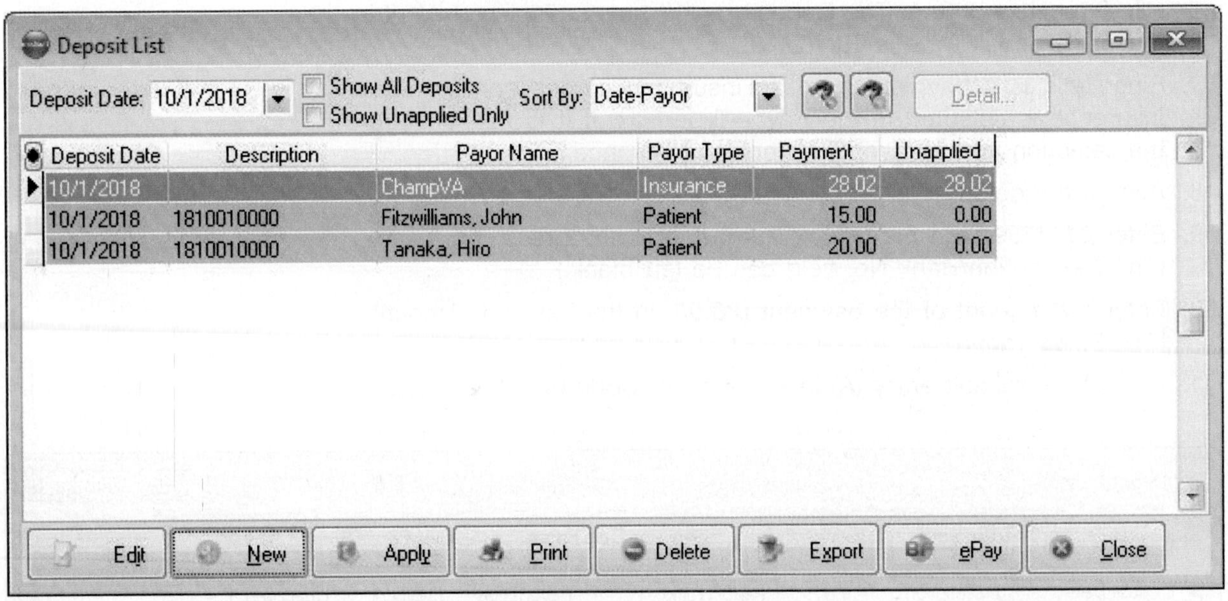

Deposit List

Deposit Date: 10/1/2018 ▼   ☐ Show All Deposits   ☐ Show Unapplied Only   Sort By: Date-Payor ▼   [Detail...]

Deposit Date	Description	Payor Name	Payor Type	Payment	Unapplied
10/1/2018		ChampVA	Insurance	28.02	28.02
10/1/2018	1810010000	Fitzwilliams, John	Patient	15.00	0.00
10/1/2018	1810010000	Tanaka, Hiro	Patient	20.00	0.00

[Edit] [New] [Apply] [Print] [Delete] [Export] [ePay] [Close]

Figure 8-12   Deposit List Dialog Box with New Deposit Entered

12. Select the insurance carrier that is making the payment (5—ChampVA) from the Insurance drop-down list. Medisoft automatically enters the defaults for ChampVA in the Payment, Adjustment, Withhold, Deductible, and Take Back Code boxes. Confirm that your screen looks the same as Figure 8-11 before going on to the next step.

13. Click the Save button to save the entry.

14. The Deposit List box reappears. The insurance payment appears in the list of deposits (see Figure 8-12). 🔷iMC

✓ **You have completed Exercise 8-1.**

8.4 APPLYING INSURANCE PAYMENTS TO CHARGES

After a deposit has been entered, the next step is to apply the payment to the applicable transactions for each patient listed on the RA using the Apply Payment/Adjustments to Charges dialog box. To apply a deposit, the payment is highlighted in the Deposit List dialog box and the Apply button is clicked. The Apply Payment/Adjustments to Charges dialog box opens (see Figure 8-13).

The top section of the dialog box contains information about the payer, the patient, and the amount of the payment that is unapplied.

The upper-left corner of the dialog box displays the payer's name in bold type, and it is also listed in the Ins 1 field. In Figure 8-13, the payer is Blue Cross and Blue Shield. The patient who has a transaction listed on the remittance advice is selected from the drop-down list in the For box.

The upper-right area of the dialog box lists the amount of the deposit that has not yet been applied (Unapplied Amount).

Note: If a patient is selected who does not have coverage with the insurance carrier that is making the deposit, a Select Payor window opens (see Figure 8-14) with the message that the payer does not match any case for the patient. Clicking the Cancel button closes the dialog box.

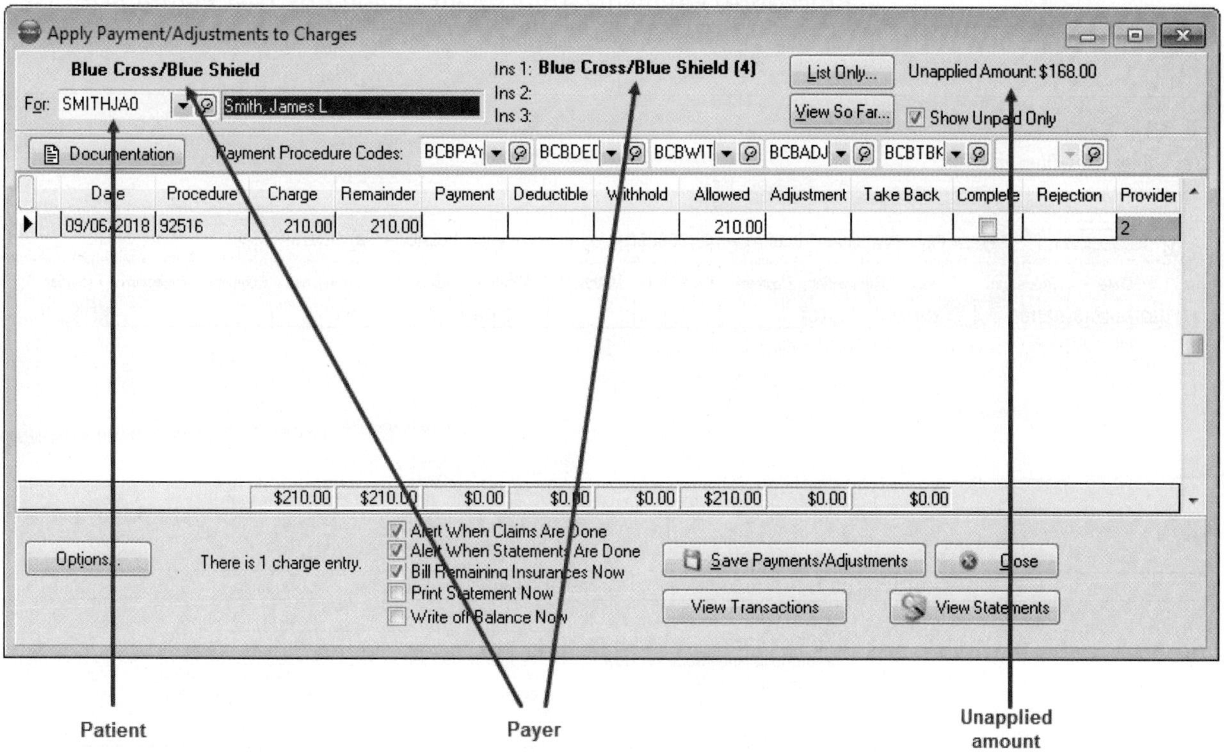

Figure 8-13 Apply Payment/Adjustments to Charges Dialog Box

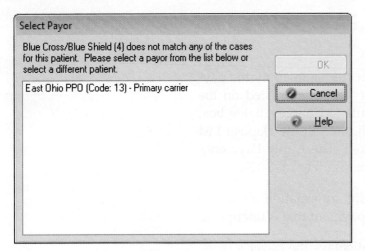

Select Payor

Blue Cross/Blue Shield (4) does not match any of the cases for this patient. Please select a payor from the list below or select a different patient.

East Ohio PPO (Code: 13) - Primary carrier

OK
Cancel
Help

Figure 8-14 Select Payor Dialog Box

The middle section of the Apply Payment/ Adjustments to Charges dialog box is where payments are entered and applied (see Figure 8-15).

Date, Procedure, Charge, Remainder These fields show the date of service, procedure code, charge amount, and amount remaining for each transaction, as already entered in the database. This information cannot be edited in the dialog box.

Payment The amount of the payment for this procedure is entered. The program automatically makes this a negative sum, so it is not necessary to enter a minus sign.

Deductible If applicable, enter the amount of the deductible listed on the RA.

Withhold Some insurance companies may withhold money for multiple charges and then pay out all at once. If applicable, enter the withholding amount in this field.

Allowed This is the amount allowed by the payer for this procedure. These values are located in the Allowed Amounts tab of the Procedure/Payment/Adjustment dialog box (see Figure 8-16).

Apply Payment/Adjustments to Charges

Blue Cross/Blue Shield   Ins 1: **Blue Cross/Blue Shield (4)**   List Only...   Unapplied Amount: $168.00

For: SMITHJA0   Smith, James L   Ins 2:   Ins 3:   View So Far...   ☑ Show Unpaid Only

Documentation   Payment Procedure Codes: BCBPAY ▾ 🔎 BCBDEC ▾ 🔎 BCBWIT ▾ 🔎 BCBADJ ▾ 🔎 BCBTBK ▾ 🔎 ▾ 🔎

Date	Procedure	Charge	Remainder	Payment	Deductible	Withhold	Allowed	Adjustment	Take Back	Complete	Rejection	Provider
09/06/2018	92516	210.00	210.00				210.00			☐		2

| | | $210.00 | $210.00 | $0.00 | $0.00 | $0.00 | $210.00 | $0.00 | $0.00 | | | |

Options...   There is 1 charge entry.

☑ Alert When Claims Are Done
☑ Alert When Statements Are Done
☑ Bill Remaining Insurances Now
☐ Print Statement Now
☐ Write off Balance Now

Save Payments/Adjustments   Close
View Transactions   View Statements

Figure 8-15 Apply Payment/Adjustments to Charges Dialog Box with Payment Entry Area Highlighted Yellow

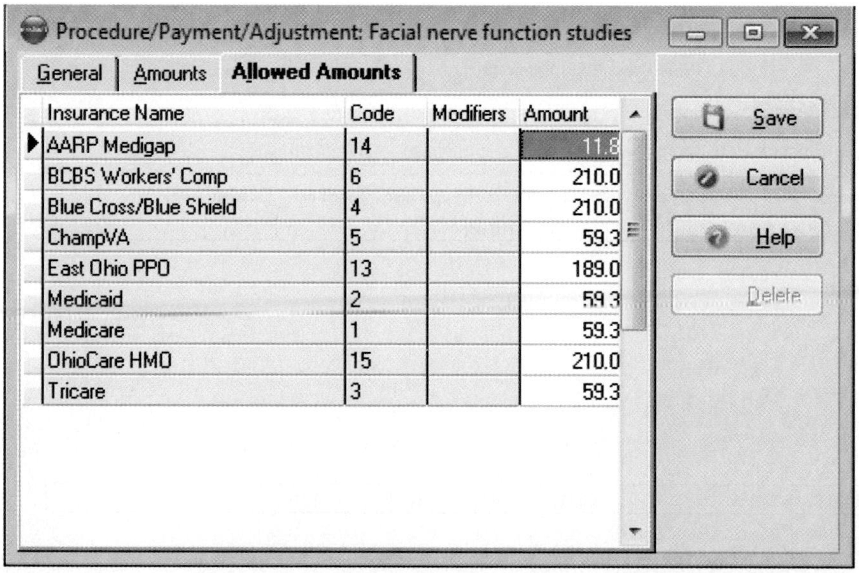

Figure 8-16 Allowed Amounts Tab in the Procedure/Payment/Adjustment Dialog Box

Adjustment The amount entered here is the charge amount minus whatever is entered in the Allowed field. This amount is calculated by the program.

Take Back This field contains only positive adjustment amounts. It is provided for situations in which the insurance company overpays on one charge and then indicates that the overpayment should be applied as a payment for another transaction. Most times, the take back should be applied to the same charge that had the overpayment.

Complete The program places a check in this box to indicate that the payer's responsibility is complete for this transaction.

Rejection If desired, a rejection message from the RA can be entered.

Provider This field lists the provider assigned to the transaction.

Figure 8-17 shows an Apply Payment/Adjustments to Charges dialog box with a payment entered.

The lower third of the Apply Payment/Adjustments to Charges dialog box contains several options that affect claims and statements (see Figure 8-18).

Options The Options . . . button is used to change the default settings for patient payment application codes.

Alert When Claims Are Done This field determines whether a message appears as notification that a claim is done for a payer.

Alert When Statements Are Done This field determines whether a message appears as notification that a statement is done for a patient.

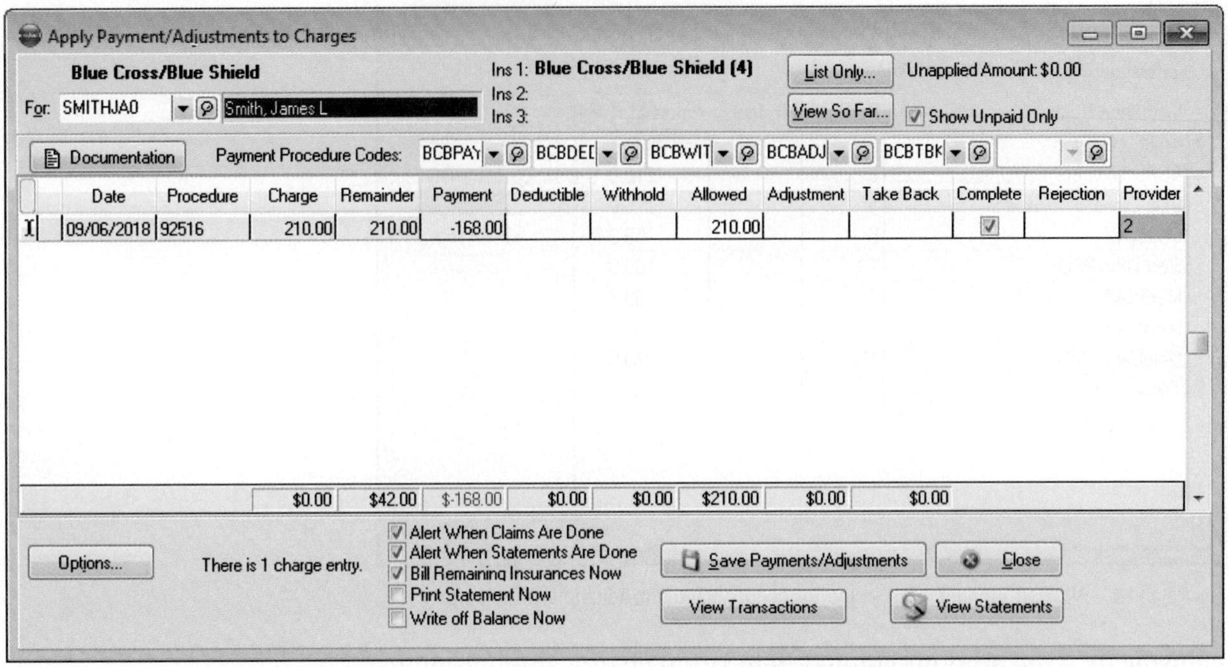

Figure 8-17 Apply Payment/Adjustments to Charges Dialog Box with Insurance Payment Entered and Highlighted

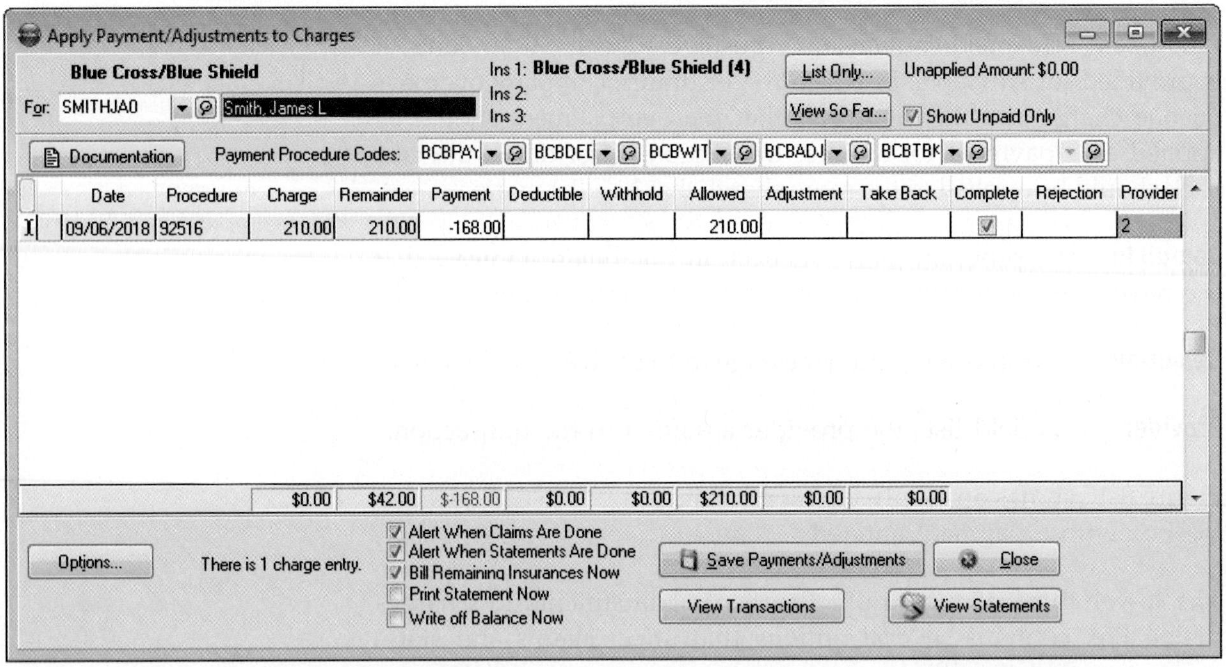

Figure 8-18 Apply Payment/Adjustments to Charges Dialog Box with Save Payments/Adjustments Button Highlighted

Bill Remaining Insurances Now If this box is checked, claims for any secondary or tertiary payer associated with the claim are created when the current insurance payment is saved.

Print Statement Now If a check mark appears in this box, the program creates a patient statement when the current insurance payment is saved.

Write Off Balance Now   This field allows patient remainder balances to be written off from within this window.

Save Payments/Adjustments   Clicking this button saves the payment currently being applied. Once the payment is saved, another patient can be selected in the For field, or the dialog box can be closed.

View Transactions   Clicking this button opens the Transaction Entry dialog box so that the selected patient's transactions can be viewed.

View Statements   Practices that use the optional BillFlash module to create electronic statements may view statements by clicking this button.

APPLYING PAYMENTS TO CHARGES: CHAMPVA EXERCISE 8-2

Using Source Document 8, apply the payment received from John Fitz-williams's insurance carrier for services provided on September 4, 2018.

Date: October 1, 2018

1. Open the Deposit List dialog box, if it is not still open from Exercise 8-1.

2. With the ChampVA payment entry highlighted, click the Apply button. Click No in response to the message about changing the date. The Apply Payment/Adjustments to Charges dialog box appears. In the lower portion of the dialog box, make sure the first three check boxes are checked and the last two (Print Statement Now and Write off Balance Now) are unchecked.

3. Key **F** in the For box and press Tab to select John Fitzwilliams, since a portion of this payment is for his account. All the charge entries for John Fitzwilliams that have not been paid in full are listed. Notice that the amount listed in the Unapplied box in the upper-right corner shows the full deposit amount, since nothing has been applied yet.

4. Refer to Source Document 8 to determine the first payment amount, which is for the 99211 procedure completed on 09/04/2018. Notice that the cursor is blinking in the Payment box for this charge. Enter **5.68** in the Payment box and press Tab.

5. Medisoft automatically places a minus sign before the amount. Notice that once the payment is applied, the Complete box to the right of the dialog box is checked. This indicates that the transaction is complete for this payer. Also notice that the Unapplied amount has been reduced by $5.68. Press Tab to move through each column until you reach the end of the first row so that the program can update the amounts. When you tab past the end of row 1, notice that the amount in the Remainder column changes to 0.00 and the amount in the Adjustment column now displays −15.32.

6. Now enter the payment for the 84478 procedure charge. Enter **8.04** in the Payment box. Press Tab to move through each column until you reach the end of the first row so that the program can update the amounts. When you tab past the end of the row, the amount in the Remainder column changes to 0.00 and the amount in the

Connect users: go to http://connect.mheducation.com to complete this exercise! Some steps may differ from what is listed here, so be sure to refer to the steps listed in Demo and Practice Modes for guidance.

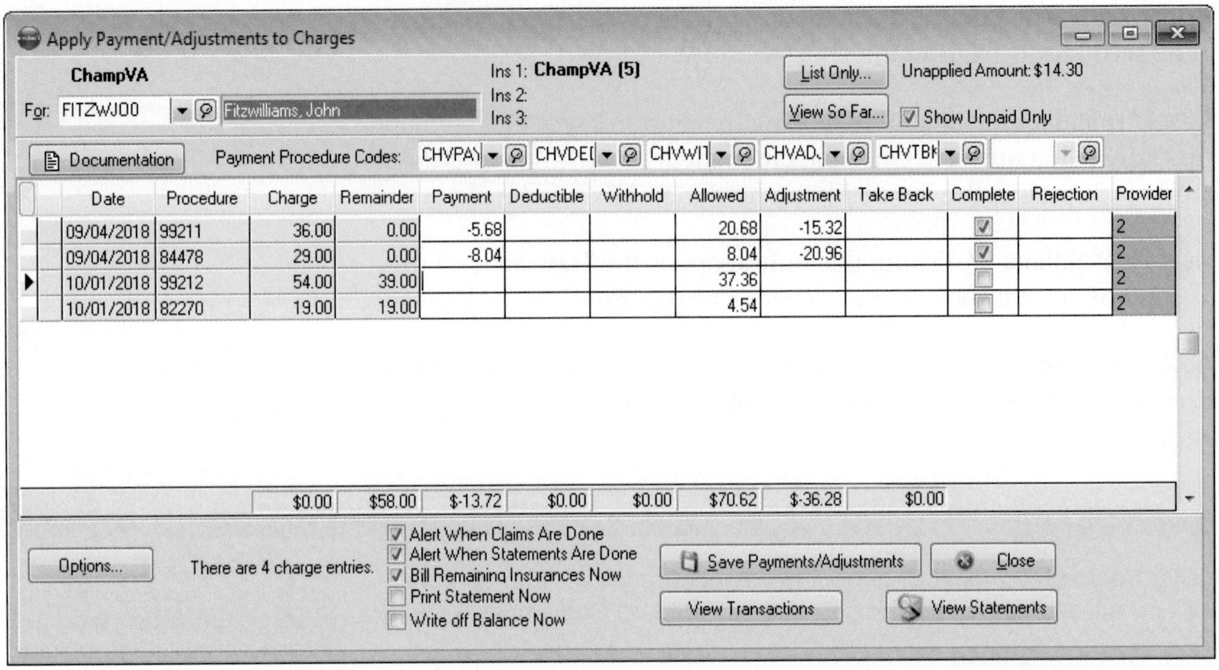

Figure 8-19 Apply Payment/Adjustments to Charges Dialog Box with Two Payments Entered for John Fitzwilliams

Adjustment column now displays −20.96. Check your work against Figure 8-19.

7. Click the Save Payments/Adjustments button to save your entry. When you click this button, an Information dialog box displays the message that the claim has been marked "done" for the primary insurance. Click OK. The dialog box is cleared of the current transaction and is ready for a new transaction.

8. Now enter a payment for Sarah Fitzwilliams. Key **F** in the For box and then locate her name in the drop-down list. Click on her chart number to display her data. Notice on the RA and in the Apply Payment/Adjustments to Charges dialog box that her $15.00 copayment was applied to the charge for procedure 90471, so that the procedure now has a 0.00 remainder balance. A zero payment from the insurance plan must be entered in the Payment column. Do this now and press Tab until the cursor is in the Payment column for the second charge. Now enter the payment for procedure 90703 and again press Tab to the end of the line. Compare your screen to Figure 8-20.

9. Click the Save Payments/Adjustments button. When the Information box appears stating that the claim has been marked done, click OK.

10. Click the Close button to exit the Apply Payment/Adjustments to Charges dialog box. The Deposit List box reappears. Notice that the unapplied amount for the ChampVA deposit is now 0.00.

11. Without closing the Deposit List dialog box, open the Transaction Entry dialog box, select John Fitzwilliams, and scroll through the list of payments and adjustments at the bottom of the screen. In addition to the patient's copayment, there are two payments with corresponding adjustments, dated 10/1/2018. Payments entered in the Deposit List dialog box also appear in the Transaction Entry dialog box. In the Totals tab area of the dialog box, notice that

Apply Payment/Adjustments to Charges

ChampVA   Ins 1: **ChampVA (5)**   [List Only...]   Unapplied Amount: $0.00

For: FITZWSA0 ▼ 🔍 Fitzwilliams, Sarah   Ins 2:   Ins 3:   [View So Far...]   ☑ Show Unpaid Only

[📄 Documentation]   Payment Procedure Codes: CHVPAY ▼🔍 CHVDEI ▼🔍 CHVWI ▼🔍 CHVAD ▼🔍 CHVTBI ▼🔍   ▼🔍

	Date	Procedure	Charge	Remainder	Payment	Deductible	Withhold	Allowed	Adjustment	Take Back	Complete	Rejection	Provider
	09/04/2018	90471	15.00	0.00				15.00			☐		1
▶	09/04/2018	90703	29.00	0.00	-14.30			14.30	-14.70		☑		1

| | | $0.00 | $0.00 | $-14.30 | $0.00 | $0.00 | $29.30 | $-14.70 | $0.00 | | | |

[Options...]   There are 2 charge entries.
☑ Alert When Claims Are Done
☑ Alert When Statements Are Done
☑ Bill Remaining Insurances Now
☐ Print Statement Now
☐ Write off Balance Now

[💾 Save Payments/Adjustments]   [⊗ Close]

[View Transactions]   [View Statements]

Figure 8-20   Apply Payment/Adjustments to Charges Dialog Box with One Payment Entered for Sarah Fitzwilliams

there is still a balance of $58.00 due on Fitzwilliams's account, for his office visit on 10/1/2018.

12. Now select Sarah Fitzwilliams. The payment and corresponding adjustment from ChampVA appear in the Payments, Adjustments, And Comments section, and the Account Total balance in the Totals tab area is now 0.00.

13. Close the Transaction Entry dialog box.

☑ **You have completed Exercise 8-2.**

ENTERING A DEPOSIT AND APPLYING PAYMENTS: EAST OHIO PPO   EXERCISE 8-3

The medical office has just received an ERA from East Ohio PPO (see Source Document 9). The total amount of the electronic funds transfer (EFT) is $450.60. This amount includes payments for a number of patients. Enter the insurance carrier payment and apply it to the appropriate patients. (*Note:* Source Document 9 consists of two pages.)

Date: October 1, 2018

1. Verify that the entry in the Deposit Date box in the Deposit List dialog box is 10/1/2018.

2. Click the New button. (If a message about changing the date appears, click No and press the New button again.) The Deposit dialog box is displayed.

3. Select Insurance in the Payor Type box.

Connect users: go to http://connect.mheducation.com to complete this exercise! Some steps may differ from what is listed here, so be sure to refer to the steps listed in Demo and Practice Modes for guidance.

connect

4. Select Electronic in the Payment Method box, since this payment was sent electronically to the practice's bank account. Notice the Check Number box becomes an EFT Tracer box. Press Tab twice.

5. Enter the ERA ID number, **00146972**, in the Description/Bank No. box.

6. Enter **450.60** in the Payment Amount box and press Tab.

7. Accept the default entry in the Deposit Code box.

8. Select 13—East Ohio PPO in the Insurance box. Medisoft automatically completes the Payment, Adjustment, Withhold, Deductible, and Take Back Code boxes.

9. Click the Save button.

10. The payment entry appears in the Deposit List dialog box.

11. Now apply the payment to the specific transaction charges.

12. With the East Ohio PPO line highlighted, click the Apply button. The Apply Payment/Adjustments to Charges dialog box is displayed.

13. Key **A** in the For box and press Tab to select Susan Arlen.

14. Locate the charge on the ERA for procedure code 99212 on 09/3/2018. Key the amount of the payment, **28.60**, in the Payment box and press Tab. Notice that Medisoft automatically checks the Complete box, since Susan Arlen has only one insurance carrier (there is no payment forthcoming from any other carrier, so the charge is complete). Tab through to the end of the line to have Medisoft update the adjustment amount and the new remainder amount.

15. Click the Save Payments/Adjustments button and then click the OK button when the Information box appears, reporting that the claim has been marked "done." The data for Susan Arlen that were visible in the Apply Payment/Adjustments to Charges dialog box are cleared and the dialog box is ready for the next payment or adjustment. Notice also that the amount listed in the Unapplied column for East Ohio PPO has been reduced by the amount of the Arlen payment.

16. Now enter the payment for the next patient listed on the ERA, Herbert Bell.

17. Key **BE** in the For box and press Tab to select Herbert Bell.

18. Enter the payment of **12.40** in the Payment box for the 99211 charge on 09/3/2018. Tab to the end of the line.

19. Click the Save Payments/Adjustments button and then click the OK button.

20. Key **BELLSAM** in the For box and press Tab to select Samuel Bell.

21. Enter the payment of **28.60** in the Payment box for the 99212 charge on 09/3/2018. Tab to the end of the line.

22. Click the Save Payments/Adjustments button and then click the OK button.

23. Continue to apply the insurance payments for Janine Bell, Jonathan Bell, and Sarina Bell using the information on Source Document 9.

Click the Save Payments/Adjustments button after you complete the payment entries for each patient. When you have applied all the payments, the amount in the Unapplied box for the East Ohio PPO payment should be 0.00.

24. Close the Apply Payment/Adjustments to Charges dialog box.

> ✓ **You have completed Exercise 8-3.**

ENTERING A DEPOSIT AND APPLYING PAYMENTS: BLUE CROSS AND BLUE SHIELD — EXERCISE 8-4

The medical office has just received an ERA from Blue Cross and Blue Shield (see Source Document 10). The total amount of the remittance is $214.40. This amount includes payments for a number of patients. Enter the insurance carrier payment for each patient. You will need to enter a zero payment on a charge for Sheila Giles, as one of her procedures was denied.

Connect users: go to http://connect.mheducation.com to complete this exercise! Some steps may differ from what is listed here, so be sure to refer to the steps listed in Demo and Practice Modes for guidance.

Date: November 1, 2018

1. In the Deposit List dialog box, change the date in the Deposit Date box to 11/1/2018 and press the Tab key. A Confirm box is displayed, stating that the date entered is in the future and asking if you want to change it. Click the No button to keep the new date.

2. Click the New button.

3. Select Insurance in the Payor Type box. Press Tab.

4. Change the entry in the Payment Method box to Electronic.

5. Enter the ERA ID number, **001234**, in the Description/Bank No. box.

6. Enter **214.40** in the Payment Amount box. Press Tab.

7. Accept the default entry in the Deposit Code box. Press Tab.

8. Select 4—Blue Cross/Blue Shield in the Insurance box. Medisoft automatically completes the Payment, Adjustment, Withhold, Deductible, and Take Back Code boxes.

9. Click the Save button.

10. The payment entry appears in the Deposit List dialog box.

11. Now apply the payment to the specific transaction charges.

12. With the Blue Cross/Blue Shield line highlighted, click the Apply button. The Apply Payment/Adjustments to Charges dialog box is displayed.

13. Key **GI** in the For box to select Sheila Giles and then press Tab.

14. Three charges are listed. Locate the charge for procedure code 99213 on 10/26/2018. Key the amount of the payment, **57.60**, in the Payment box and press Tab. Medisoft automatically checks the Complete box, since Sheila Giles has only one insurance carrier (no payment is forthcoming from any other carrier, so the charge is complete). Continue pressing the Tab key until the amount listed in the Remainder column changes to $14.40.

15. Now enter the payment for the next procedure listed on the ERA—71010. (*Note:* The order of procedures is different on the ERA than it is in the Apply Payment/Adjustments to Charges window. Be sure to apply the payment to the correct procedure.) Remember to click the Tab key until the amount in the Remainder column changes.

16. Look again at Source Document 10. Notice that the amount paid for the final procedure, 87430, is $0.00. Read the note listed to determine why the charge was not paid. This denial of payment must be entered in Medisoft so that the practice billing staff will be aware that Sheila Giles is responsible for the entire amount of that charge, $29.00.

17. Click in the Payment box for the charge for procedure 87430. Enter **0** and press Tab. Notice that the amount listed in the Remainder column is the full amount of the charge, $29.00. The charge has also been marked as complete, since the insurance carrier is not responsible for the remainder amount.

18. Click the Save Payments/Adjustments button. An Information box is displayed, indicating that the claim has been marked "done" for the primary insurance. Click the OK button.

19. Close the Apply Payment/Adjustments to Charges dialog box; then, without closing the Deposit List dialog box, open the Transaction Entry dialog box.

20. Locate Sheila Giles's upper respiratory infection case. In the Charges area, notice that two of the charges appear in an aqua color, which indicates that they have been partially paid. The charge that was denied by the insurance carrier—87430—is still in gray, indicating that no payment has been made.

21. Now look at the Account Total in the Totals tab area in the Transaction Entry dialog box. Sheila Giles is listed as being responsible for paying $61.60, which breaks down as follows:

Code	Charge Amount	Patient Responsible for
99213	$72.00	$14.40 (20% of charge)
71010	$91.00	$18.20 (20% of charge)
87430	$29.00	$29.00 (100% of charge)
Totals	**$192.00**	**$61.60**

22. Close the Transaction Entry dialog box.

23. Back in the Deposit List dialog box, make sure the Blue Cross/Blue Shield line is still highlighted and click the Apply button. You are returned to the Apply Payment/Adjustments to Charges dialog box with the Unapplied Amount for the Blue Cross/Blue Shield payment displayed as $84.00. Enter the payments for the second patient listed on Source Document 10, Jill Simmons.

24. Key **S** in the For box and press Tab to select Jill Simmons.

25. Enter the payment of **43.20** in the Payment box for the 99212 charge on 10/26/2018. Tab to the end of the row.

26. Enter the other payment for Jill Simmons. Then notice that the amount listed in the Unapplied area is now 0.00, indicating that the entire payment has been entered.

27. Click the Save Payments/Adjustments button and then click OK.

28. Close the Apply Payment/Adjustments to Charges dialog box.

29. The Deposit List dialog box reappears and the amount in the Unapplied column is now zero. **¢iM¢**

✓ **You have completed Exercise 8-4.**

8.5 PROCESSING A PATIENT PAYMENT RECEIVED BY MAIL

While payments that patients make while in the office are entered in the Transaction Entry dialog box, payments from patients that are received by mail are entered in Medisoft using the Deposit List dialog box. Creating a deposit from the Deposit List dialog box provides the medical biller with options not available in Transaction Entry, such as the ability to see transactions from more than one case on the same screen. The steps followed to enter a patient payment using the Deposit List option are very similar to the steps used to enter an insurance payment: first the deposit is entered and then the payment is applied to the individual charges in the patient's account.

ENTERING A PATIENT PAYMENT RECEIVED BY MAIL	EXERCISE 8-5

The medical office has just received a check from Elizabeth Jones in the amount of $28.64. The check number is 3109. Enter the deposit and apply the payment to the outstanding charges.

Date: November 13, 2018

Connect users: go to http://connect.mheducation.com to complete this exercise! Some steps may differ from what is listed here, so be sure to refer to the steps listed in Demo and Practice Modes for guidance.

1. In the Deposit List dialog box, change the date in the Deposit Date box to 11/13/2018 and press the Tab key. A Confirm box is displayed, stating that the date entered is in the future. Click the No button to keep the new date.

2. Click the New button.

3. Select Patient in the Payor Type box. Press Tab.

4. Accept the default entry of Check in the Payment Method field.

5. Enter the check number, **3109**, in the Check Number field. Press Tab twice.

6. Enter **28.64** in the Payment Amount box. Press Tab.

7. Accept the default entry in the Deposit Code box. Press Tab.

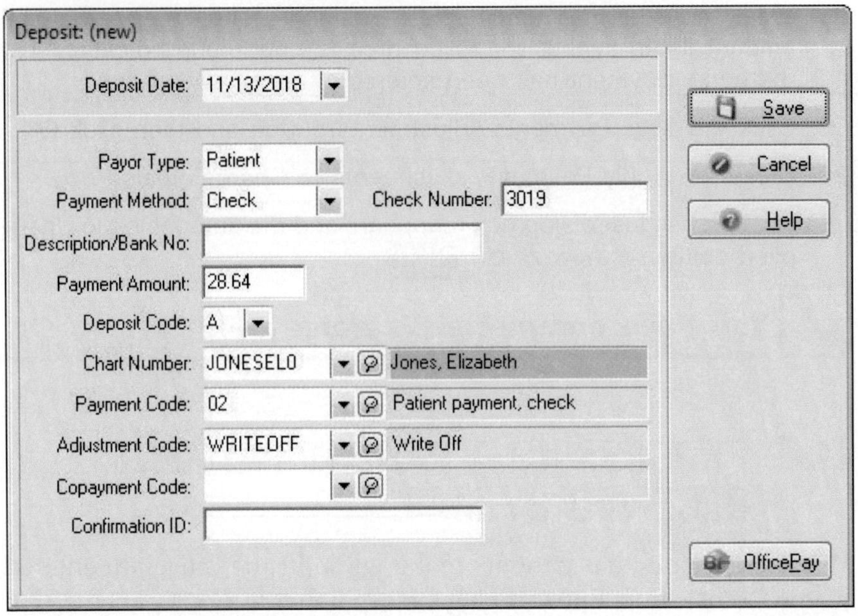

Figure 8-21 Deposit Dialog Box for Patient Payment

8. Select Jones's chart number in the Chart Number field. Medisoft automatically completes the Payment Code and Adjustment Code boxes.

9. Check your work against Figure 8-21.

10. Click the Save button.

11. The payment entry appears in the Deposit List dialog box.

12. With the deposit for Jones highlighted, click the Apply button. The Apply Payment/Adjustments to Charges dialog box is displayed (see Figure 8-22).

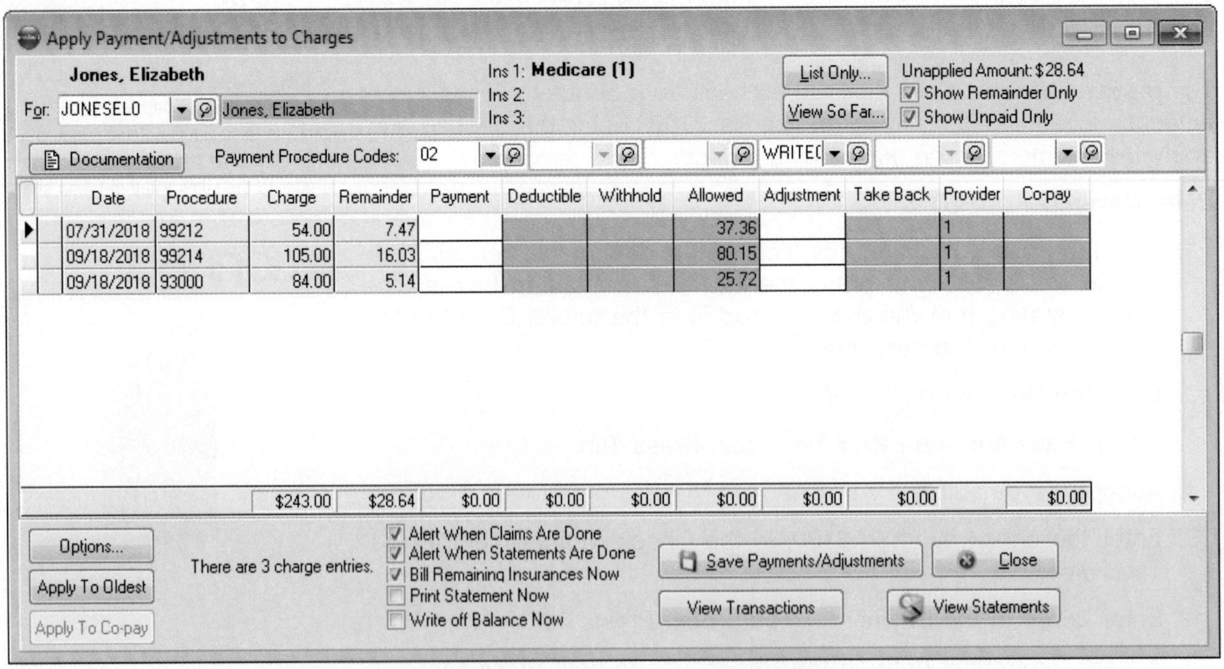

Figure 8-22 Apply Payment/Adjustments to Charges Dialog Box for a Patient Payment

13. Notice that two different office visits are listed—one on July 31, 2018, and one on September 18, 2018. The amount listed in the Remainder column for each procedure is the amount the patient owes for that service. Enter an amount equal to the amount in the Remainder column (**7.47**) for the first procedure, 99212. Press Tab twice. The cursor moves to the Payment field on the line with the second procedure.

14. Enter a payment amount equal to the amount in the Remainder column for procedure 99214. Press Tab twice.

15. Enter a payment amount equal to the amount in the Remainder column for procedure 93000. Press Tab once. Notice that the Unapplied Amount listed in the top-right corner of the dialog box is now $0.00.

16. Click the Save Payments/Adjustments button.

17. An Information box appears confirming that the statement has been marked done. Click OK.

18. Click the Close button. The Apply Payment/Adjustments to Charges dialog box closes. Jones's deposit still appears in the Deposit List dialog box, but now the Unapplied Amount is 0.00. **cIMO**

✓ **You have completed Exercise 8-5.**

8.6 ENTERING CAPITATION PAYMENTS

Capitation payments are entered in the Deposit List dialog box. To indicate a capitation payment, Capitation is selected from the Payor Type drop-down list in the Deposit window (see Figure 8-23).

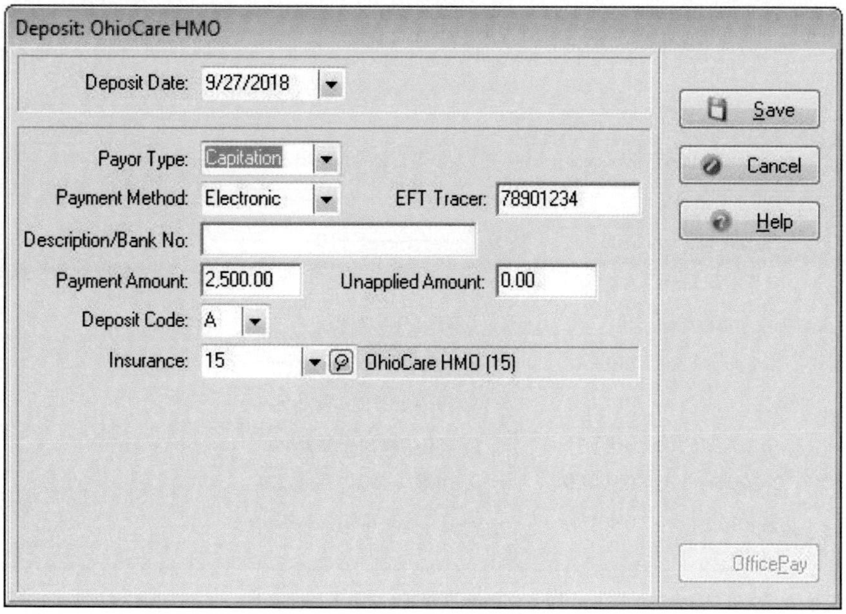

Figure 8-23 Deposit Dialog Box for a Capitation Payment

When a capitation payment is entered in Medisoft, the payment is not applied to the charges of individual patients. Under capitated plans, the insurance carrier pays the practice a set fee to cover all the insured patients who elect to use the practice. This designated payment is made regardless of whether any of the patients visit the practice, or how often they visit. However, the charges in each patient's account who have used the practice during the month covered by the capitation payment still must be adjusted to a zero balance to indicate that the insurance company has met its obligation (through the capitation payment) and that the patient has also done so (by paying a copayment at the time of the office visit).

In order to adjust the patient accounts of those covered by the capitated plan, a second deposit is entered as an insurance payment with a zero amount (see Figure 8-24).

Once the zero amount deposit is saved, the deposit appears in the Deposit List window (see Figure 8-25). The Payment column lists "EOB Only," since there is no payment associated with the zero amount deposit.

The next step is to locate patients who have claims during the month covered by the capitation payment. This is accomplished using the List Only . . . button in the Claim Management dialog box (see Figure 8-26).

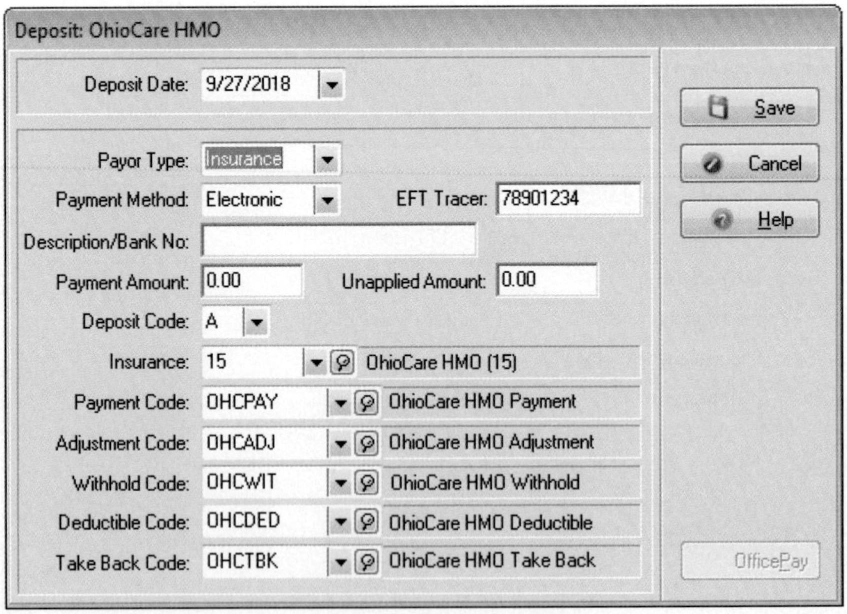

Deposit: OhioCare HMO

Deposit Date:	9/27/2018
Payor Type:	Insurance
Payment Method:	Electronic EFT Tracer: 78901234
Description/Bank No:	
Payment Amount:	0.00 Unapplied Amount: 0.00
Deposit Code:	A
Insurance:	15 OhioCare HMO (15)
Payment Code:	OHCPAY OhioCare HMO Payment
Adjustment Code:	OHCADJ OhioCare HMO Adjustment
Withhold Code:	OHCWIT OhioCare HMO Withhold
Deductible Code:	OHCDED OhioCare HMO Deductible
Take Back Code:	OHCTBK OhioCare HMO Take Back

Save   Cancel   Help   OfficePay

Figure 8-24   Deposit Dialog Box with a Zero Payment Amount

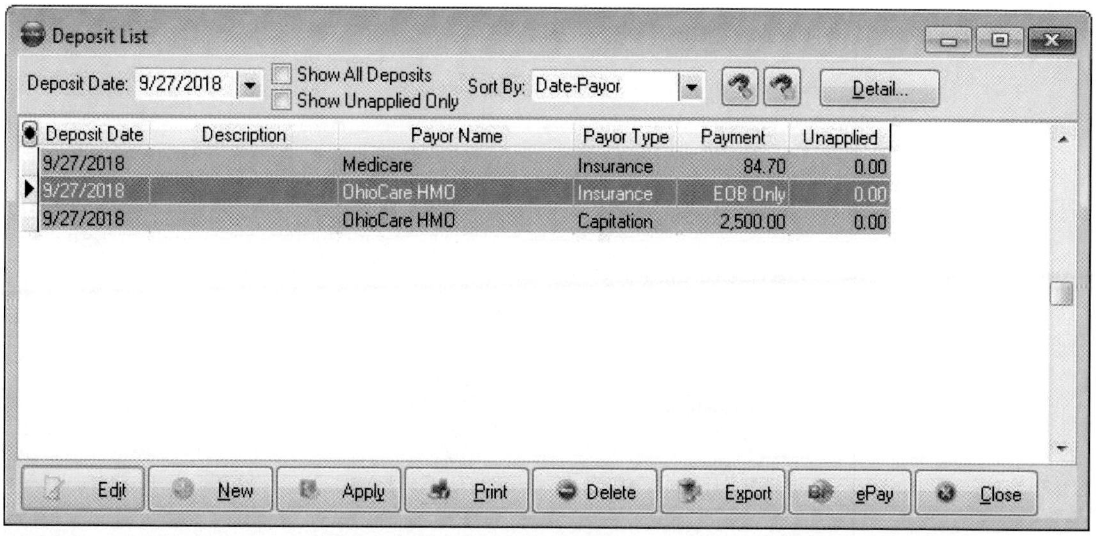

Figure 8-25 Deposit List Dialog Box with a Capitation Payment and a Zero Insurance Payment Entered

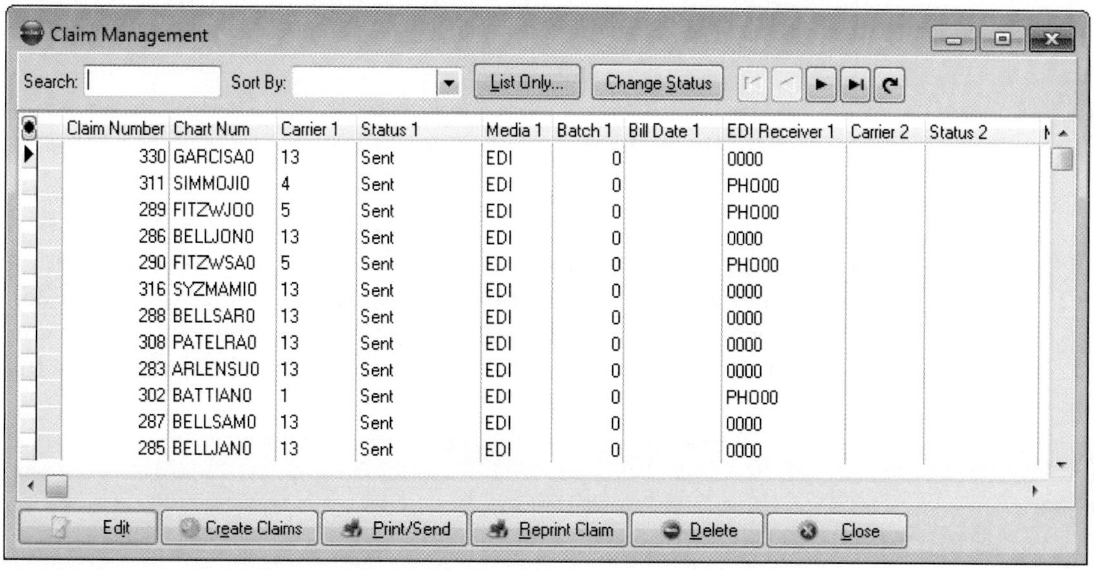

Figure 8-26 Claim Management Dialog Box with List Only . . . Button Highlighted

When the List Only . . . button is clicked, the List Only Claims That Match dialog box appears. The List Only Claims That Match dialog box (see Figure 8-27) provides an option for searching for claims by insurance carrier. Using this option, patients with active capitated claims from a given carrier can be identified.

Once patients have been identified, the Claim Management dialog box is closed and the Deposit List dialog box is opened. The identified patient accounts must be adjusted to a zero balance in the Apply Payment/Adjustments to Charges dialog box.

To apply the zero payment amount to these patient accounts, select the line for the deposit and click the Apply button. In the Apply

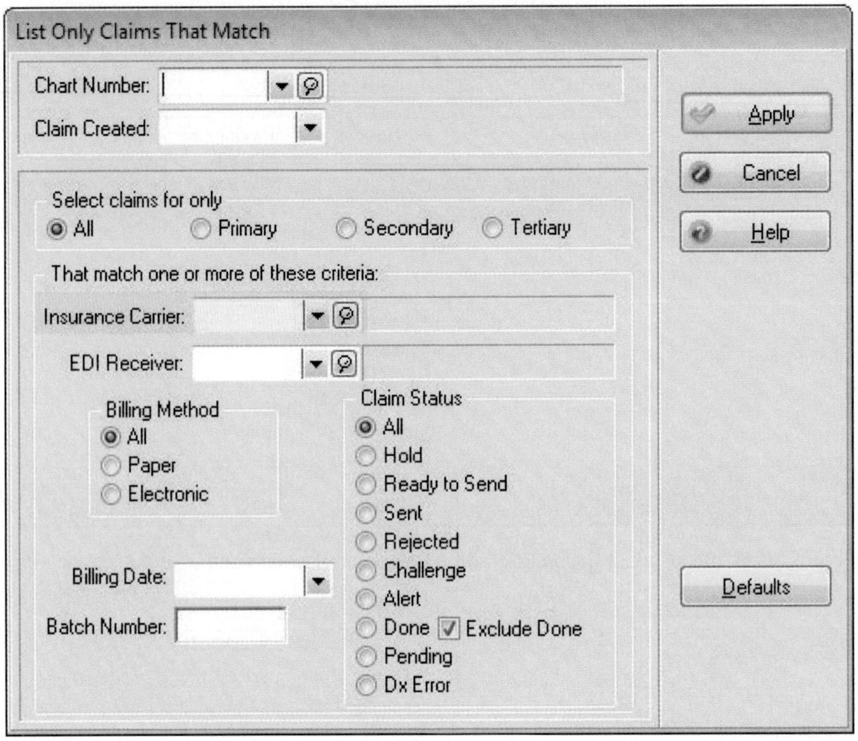

Figure 8-27 List Only Claims That Match Dialog Box with Insurance Carrier Field Highlighted

Payment/Adjustments to Charges dialog box, select the chart number of each patient covered by the zero payment and enter an adjustment equal to the outstanding balance (see Figure 8-28). In the example in Figure 8-28, the amount in the Remainder column is $34.00. This is the amount that must be entered in the

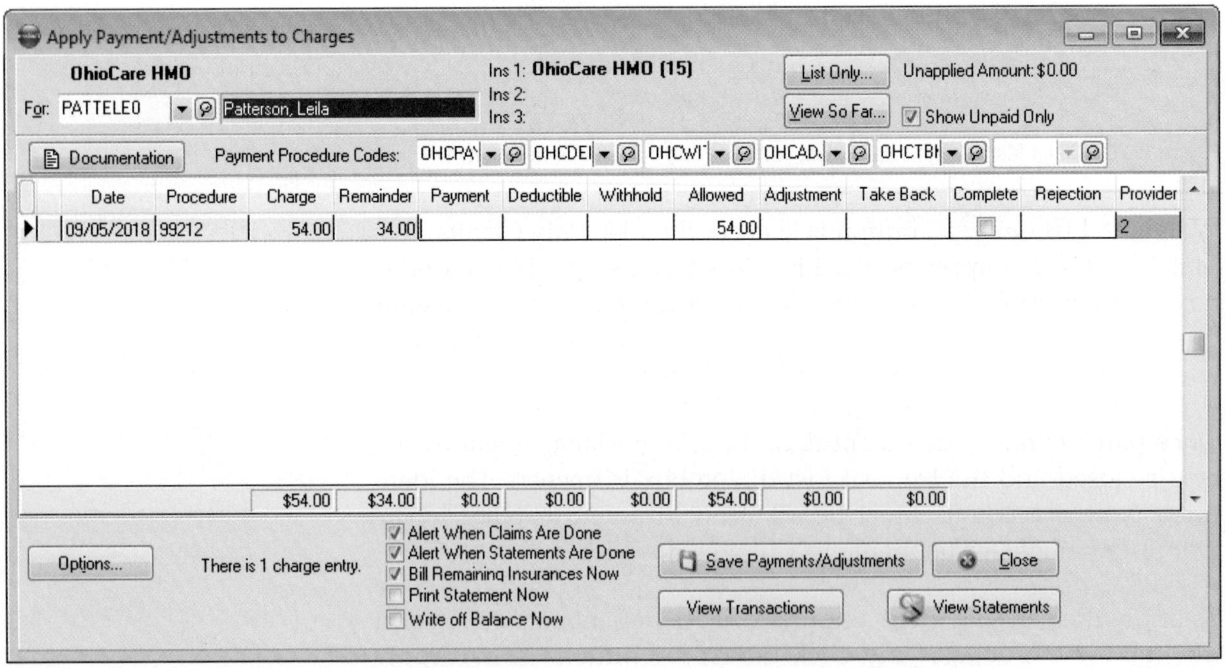

Figure 8-28 Apply Payment/Adjustments to Charges Dialog Box with Capitated Patient Account Displayed

Apply Payment/Adjustments to Charges

OhioCare HMO					Ins 1: **OhioCare HMO (15)**			List Only...	Unapplied Amount: $0.00			
For: PATTELE0 ▼ 🔎 Patterson, Leila					Ins 2:			View So Far...	☑ Show Unpaid Only			
					Ins 3:							

📄 Documentation   Payment Procedure Codes: OHCPA▼ 🔎 OHCDEI ▼ 🔎 OHCWI ▼ 🔎 OHCAD. ▼ 🔎 OHCTBI ▼ 🔎   ▼ 🔎

	Date	Procedure	Charge	Remainder	Payment	Deductible	Withhold	Allowed	Adjustment	Take Back	Complete	Rejection	Provider
▶	09/05/2018	99212	54.00	0.00				54.00	-34.00		☐		2

			$0.00	$0.00	$0.00	$0.00	$0.00	$54.00	$-34.00	$0.00		

Options...   There is 1 charge entry.

☑ Alert When Claims Are Done
☑ Alert When Statements Are Done
☑ Bill Remaining Insurances Now
☐ Print Statement Now
☐ Write off Balance Now

💾 Save Payments/Adjustments   ⊘ Close
View Transactions   🔍 View Statements

Figure 8-29 Apply Payment/Adjustments to Charges Dialog Box After the Patient Account Has Been Adjusted to a Zero Balance

Adjustment column to take the account to a zero balance. Figure 8-29 shows the dialog box after the $34.00 adjustment has been applied. Notice that the amount in the Remainder column is now zero. This procedure must be followed for each patient who has transactions during the time period covered by the capitation payment.

ENTERING A CAPITATION PAYMENT   EXERCISE 8-6

Using Source Document 11, enter a capitation payment from OhioCare HMO for the month of October 2018. The total amount of the electronic funds transfer is $2,500.00.

Date: November 1, 2018

1. In the Deposit List dialog box, change the date in the Deposit Date box to 11/1/2018.

2. Click the New button. (If a Confirm box appears with a message about entering a future date, click No and then click the New button again.) The Deposit dialog box appears.

3. In the Payor Type box, select Capitation. Press Tab.

4. Select Electronic in the Payment Method box. Press Tab twice.

5. Key **001006003** in the Description/Bank No. box. This is the ID number that is listed on the ERA. Press Tab.

6. Key **2500** in the Payment Amount box and press Tab.

7. Accept the default entry of A in the Deposit Code box. Press Tab.

8. Click 15—OhioCare HMO in the Insurance drop-down list.

Connect users: go to http://connect.mheducation.com to complete this exercise! Some steps may differ from what is listed here, so be sure to refer to the steps listed in Demo and Practice Modes for guidance.

connect®

9. Click the Save button.

10. The Deposit List window reappears, displaying the payment just entered. As mentioned, unlike other insurance payments, capitation payments are not applied to individual charges. However, amounts do need to be adjusted in the patient accounts. The next two exercises provide practice. First, a zero amount payment is entered in the Deposit List dialog box. Then the zero amount payment is used to adjust the active accounts for capitated patients to a zero balance.

✓ **You have completed Exercise 8-6.**

EXERCISE 8-7 ENTERING A ZERO AMOUNT PAYMENT

Enter a zero payment amount deposit for OhioCare HMO.

Date: November 1, 2018

1. In the Deposit List dialog box, click the New button. The Deposit dialog box appears.

2. In the Payor Type box, select Insurance. Press Tab.

3. Select Electronic in the Payment Method box.

4. Verify that 0.00 is the amount displayed in the Payment Amount box.

5. Accept the default entry of A in the Deposit Code box.

6. Click 15—OhioCare HMO in the Insurance drop-down list.

7. Click the Save button. The Deposit List dialog box reappears with the zero amount payment displayed.

✓ **You have completed Exercise 8-7.**

EXERCISE 8-8 ADJUSTING A CAPITATED ACCOUNT

Using the List Only Claims That Match option in Claim Management, locate the OhioCare HMO patients who visited the practice in October 2018, as these are the patients with active capitated accounts. Then, in the Apply Payment/Adjustments to Charges dialog box, enter any adjustments needed to zero out their accounts.

Date: November 1, 2018

1. Without closing the Deposit List dialog box, open the Claim Management dialog box by selecting Claim Management on the Activities menu.

2. Click the List Only . . . button.

3. In the List Only Claims That Match dialog box, select 15—OhioCare HMO in the Insurance Carrier drop-down list. In the Claim Status options, make sure the All button is selected and the Exclude Done check box is checked to exclude claims that have already been paid (see Figure 8-30).

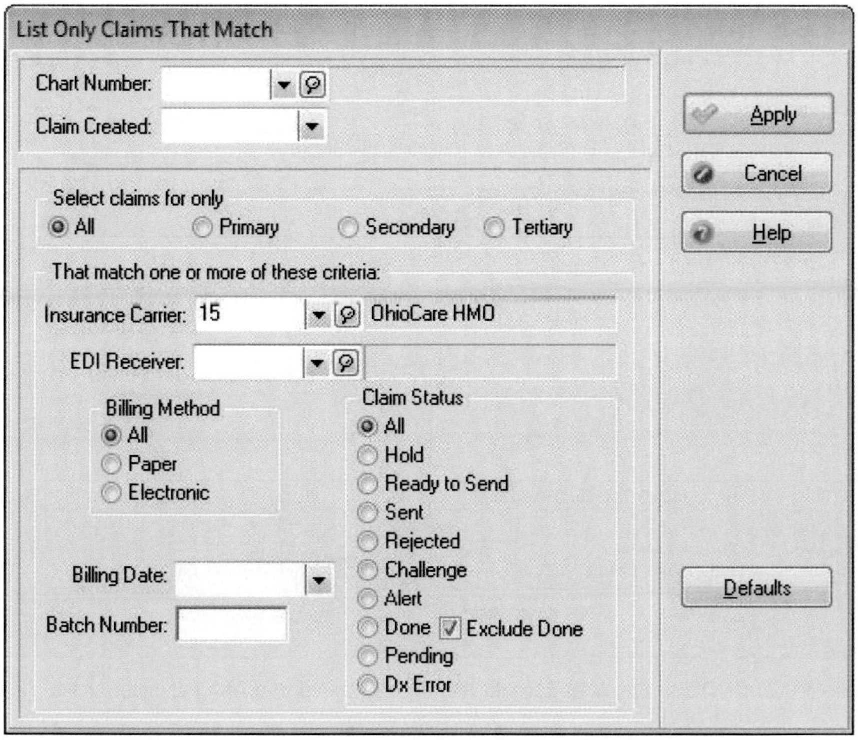

Figure 8-30 List Only Claims That Match Dialog Box with 15—OhioCare HMO Selected

4. Click the Apply button. The Claim Management window appears with the capitated claim listed. In this case, there is only one capitated claim. Check your screen against Figure 8-31.

5. Use the Edit button and click the Transactions tab to view the details of the claim, verifying that any transactions listed took place in October 2018. Make a note of the patient's name and close the Claim dialog box and the Claim Management dialog box.

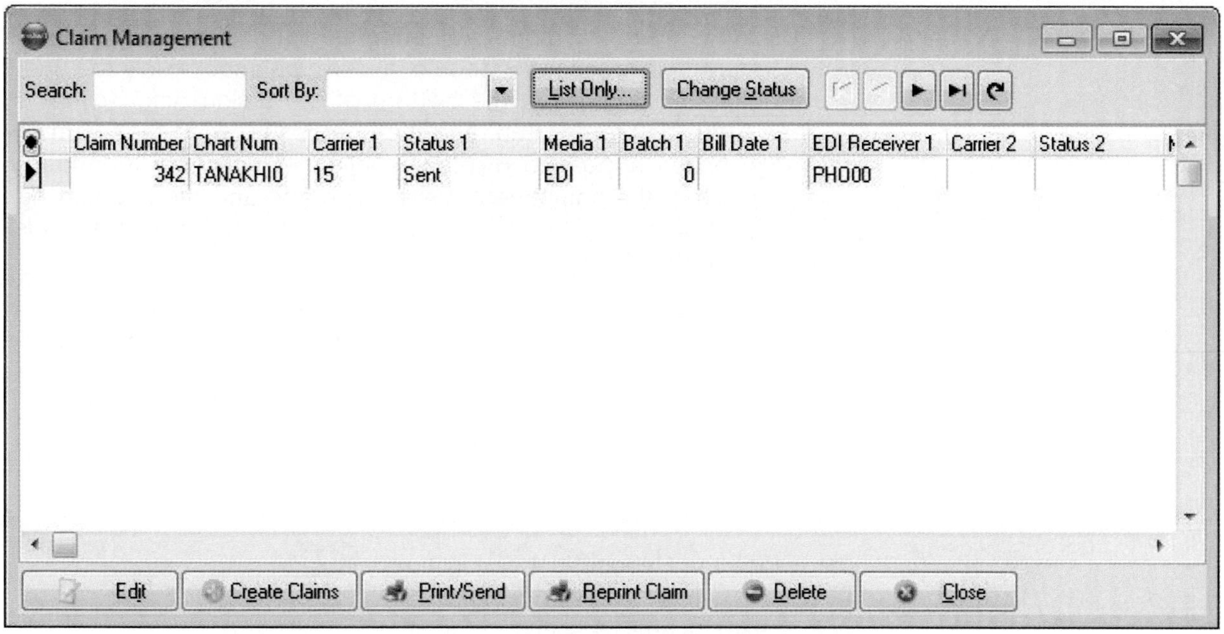

Figure 8-31 Claim Management Dialog Box with OhioCare HMO Patient Listed

Apply Payment/Adjustments to Charges

OhioCare HMO				Ins 1: **OhioCare HMO (15)**			List Only...	Unapplied Amount: $0.00		

For: TANAKHIO ▾ 🔎 Tanaka, Hiro   Ins 2:   Ins 3:   View So Far...   ☑ Show Unpaid Only

📄 Documentation   Payment Procedure Codes: OHCPA' ▾ 🔎 OHCDEl ▾ 🔎 OHCW1' ▾ 🔎 OHCAD, ▾ 🔎 OHCTBI ▾ 🔎   ▾ 🔎

	Date	Procedure	Charge	Remainder	Payment	Deductible	Withhold	Allowed	Adjustment	Take Back	Complete	Rejection	Provider
▶	10/01/2018	99202	88.00	0.00				88.00	-68.00		☐		1

			$0.00	$0.00	$0.00	$0.00	$0.00	$88.00	$-68.00	$0.00			

Options...   There is 1 charge entry.

☑ Alert When Claims Are Done
☑ Alert When Statements Are Done
☑ Bill Remaining Insurances Now
☐ Print Statement Now
☐ Write off Balance Now

💾 Save Payments/Adjustments   ⊗ Close

View Transactions   View Statements

Figure 8-32   Apply Payment/Adjustments to Charges Dialog Box After Account Has Been Adjusted to a Zero Balance, Tanaka

6. You are returned to the Deposit List dialog box. Select the OhioCare HMO deposit that has EOB Only listed in the Payment column and click the Apply button.

7. Select the capitated patient in the For field and press Tab.

8. Notice there is only one procedure on the claim. To enter the correct amount for the adjustment, identify the amount in the Remainder column and enter an equal amount in the Adjustment column. *Note:* Be sure to enter the amount in the Adjustment column and not the Payment column. Press Tab repeatedly, until the remainder amount changes to zero. Your screen should look like Figure 8-32.

9. Click the Save Payments/Adjustments button. To verify that the account has been adjusted to a zero balance, click the View Transactions button at the bottom of the dialog box. Key **TA** in the Chart box, press Tab, and then press OK when the two message boxes appear to display Tanaka's transaction information. Notice that the adjustment has been made and the account has a zero balance. When finished viewing the data, close the Transaction Entry dialog box.

10. You are back in the Apply Payment/Adjustments to Charges dialog box. If there were other OhioCare HMO patients with capitated claims in October, you would use the For field to display their information and repeat the process for each patient's account, entering an adjustment for each transaction line that had a remainder amount.

11. Close the Apply Payment/Adjustments to Charges dialog box.

12. Close the Deposit List dialog box.

✅ **You have completed Exercise 8-8.**

8.7 CREATING STATEMENTS

A **patient statement** lists the amount of money a patient owes, organized by the amount of time the money has been owed, the procedures performed, and the dates the procedures were performed. Patient statements are created after an insurance claim has been filed and a remittance advice has been received. A patient statement is sent to collect the balance on an account that is the patient's responsibility. This may include coinsurance charges and charges for procedures that were not covered by the insurance company.

Statements are created using the Statement Management feature, which is listed on the Activities menu. Just as Claim Management provides a range of options for billing insurance carriers, Statement Management offers multiple choices for billing patients.

STATEMENT MANAGEMENT DIALOG BOX

The Statement Management dialog box is displayed by clicking Statement Management on the Activities menu or by clicking the Statement Management shortcut button on the toolbar (see Figure 8-33). The dialog box lists all statements that have already been created (see Figure 8-34). In this dialog box, several actions can be performed: existing statements can be reviewed and edited, new statements can be created, the status of existing statements can be changed, and statements can be printed.

Stmt # The Stmt # column lists the statement number, which is generated by the program in sequential order.

Guarantor In the Statement Management dialog box, guarantors rather than patients are listed because statements are created only for those financially responsible for accounts. For example, if a

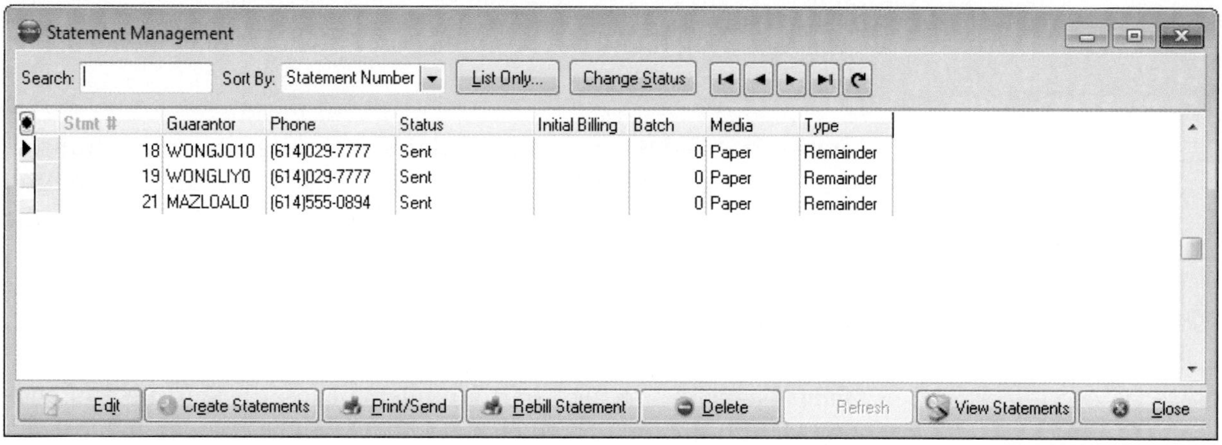

patient statement a list of the amount of money a patient owes, the procedures performed, and the dates the procedures were performed.

Figure 8-33 Statement Management Shortcut Button

Figure 8-34 Statement Management Dialog Box

patient's father is the guarantor, a statement is created for the patient's father, not for the patient. In the Statement Management dialog box, the statement is listed under the father's chart number. If the man is also guarantor on his wife's account, his chart number will appear twice in the Statement Management window. When statements are printed, however, all transactions for the guarantor's child and wife are billed on one statement.

Phone   The Phone column lists guarantors' phone numbers.

Status   The status assigned by Medisoft to each statement depends on whether the statement has been billed and whether the account has a zero balance:

- **Ready to Send.** Transactions that have not been billed.
- **Sent.** Transactions that have been billed but not fully paid.
- **Done.** Transactions that have been billed and fully paid.

Initial Billing   The date the statement was initially sent appears in the Initial Billing column. If a statement has been sent more than once, the most recent date is shown in the Billing Date field located in the General tab of the Statement dialog box, which is used for editing statements.

Batch   The batch number assigned by Medisoft is displayed.

Media   The format for the statement, either paper or electronic, is designated.

Type   The type of statement, either Standard or Remainder, is listed.

CREATE STATEMENTS DIALOG BOX

The Create Statements dialog box is where information is entered that determines which statements are generated (see Figure 8-35).

The following filters can be applied in the Create Statements dialog box:

Transaction Dates   A range of dates is entered to select transactions that occur within those dates. The dates can be entered directly by keying in the boxes, or they can be selected from the calendar that appears when the drop-down arrow is clicked. To create statements for all available transactions, leave both date boxes blank.

Chart Numbers   In the Chart Numbers boxes, the starting and ending chart numbers for which statements will be created are entered. If the boxes are left blank, all chart numbers will be included.

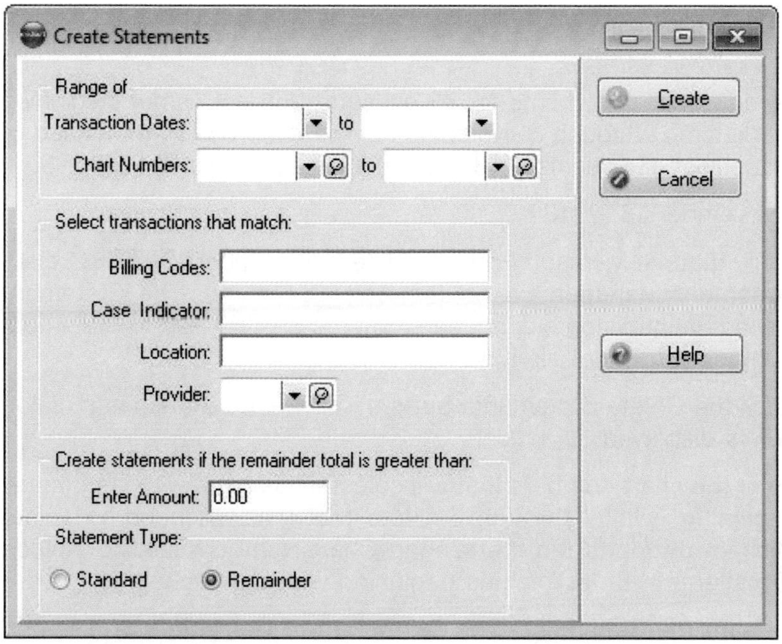

Figure 8-35   Create Statements Dialog Box

Select Transactions That Match   The options in this portion of the dialog box provide filters for creating statements for billing codes, case indicators, locations, and provider. In all instances except provider, commas must be placed between entries if more than one code is entered.

Create Statements If the Remainder Total Is Greater Than . . . Enter Amount   The dollar amount entered in this box is the minimum outstanding balance required for a statement to be created. For example, if 5.00 is entered in this box, the program will not create statements for accounts with balances below $5.00. If this field is left blank, statements will be created for all accounts, regardless of the balances.

Statement Type   Standard statements show all available charges regardless of whether the insurance has paid on the transactions. Remainder statements list only those charges that are not paid in full after all insurance carrier payments have been received. Once a statement type is selected, the setting remains in effect until the other type of statement is selected.

After all selections are complete in the Create Statements dialog box, clicking the Create button instructs the program to generate statements. (*Note:* If you click the Create button and no statements can be created, the following message appears: "No new statements were created." Click OK to close the dialog box that contains the message.)

standard statements
statements that show all charges regardless of whether the insurance has paid on the transactions.

remainder statements
statements that list only those charges that are not paid in full after all insurance carrier payments have been received.

EXERCISE 8-9 CREATING STATEMENTS

Connect users: go to http://connect.mheducation.com to complete this exercise! Some steps may differ from what is listed here, so be sure to refer to the steps listed in Demo and Practice Modes for guidance.

connect

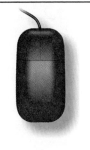

Create remainder statements for all patients with last names beginning with the letters *H* through *S*. *Note:* Be sure to enter *SYZMAM* instead of just *S* to select all patients whose last names begin with the letter *S*.

Date: November 13, 2018

1. Verify that the Medisoft Program Date is November 13, 2018. Select Statement Management on the Activities menu. The Statement Management dialog box appears. Set the Sort By field to Statement Number, if it is not already selected.
2. Click the Create Statements button. The Create Statements dialog box is displayed.
3. Enter the chart numbers that will select all patients with last names beginning with *H* through *S*. Note that you will need to select Michael Syzmanski in the second Chart Numbers field to include all patients with last names beginning with the letter *S*.
4. Be sure the Statement Type field is set to Remainder. If it is not, click the Remainder button. Check your work against Figure 8-36 and then click the Create button to generate statements.
5. A message appears stating the number of statements that have been created (see Figure 8-37). Click the OK button.
6. You are returned to the Statement Management dialog box. Change the entry in the Sort By field to Statement Number, if it is not already listed. Any new statements that were created are added to the list of statements in the Statement Management dialog box, with a Ready to Send status (see Figure 8-38). CiMO

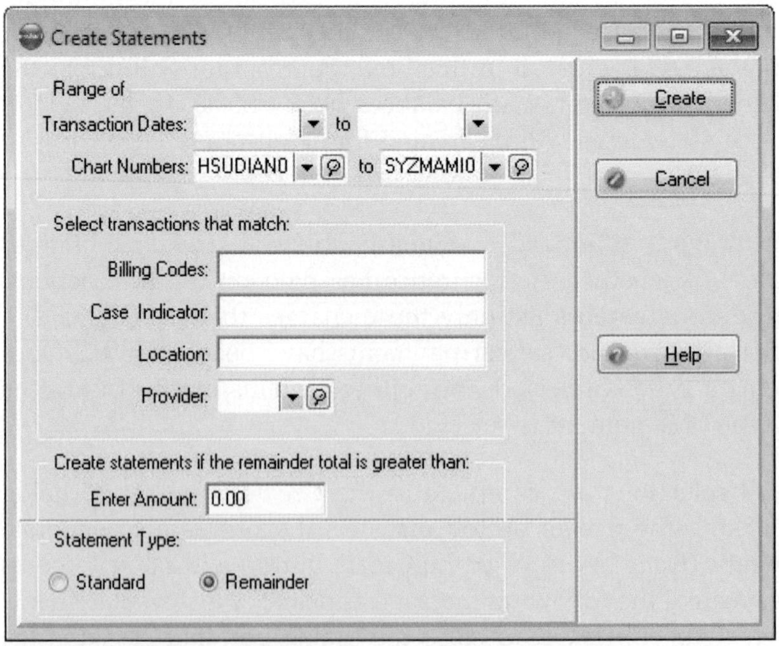

Figure 8-36 Create Statements Dialog Box with Selections Made

Figure 8-37 Information Box Indicating the Number of Statements Created

Stmt #	Guarantor	Phone	Status	Initial Billing	Batch	Media	Type
18	WONGJO10	(614)029-7777	Sent		0	Paper	Remainder
19	WONGLIYO	(614)029-7777	Sent		0	Paper	Remainder
21	MAZLOAL0	(614)555-0894	Sent		0	Paper	Remainder
22	SIMMOJI0	(614)011-6767	Ready To Send		0		Remainder

Figure 8-38 Statement Management Dialog Box with New Statement Created for Jill Simmons

✓ You have completed Exercise 8-9.

8.8 EDITING STATEMENTS

The Edit button in the Statement Management dialog box brings up the Statement dialog box, which is used to perform edits on account statements (see Figure 8-39). The three tabs in the Statement dialog box contain important information about the statement.

GENERAL TAB

The following information is located in the General tab:

Status These buttons indicate the current status of the statement.

Billing Method The statement can be either paper or electronic.

Type The Type field indicates whether the statement is standard or remainder.

Initial Billing Date The Initial Billing Date is the date the statement was first created.

Batch The batch number assigned to the statement appears.

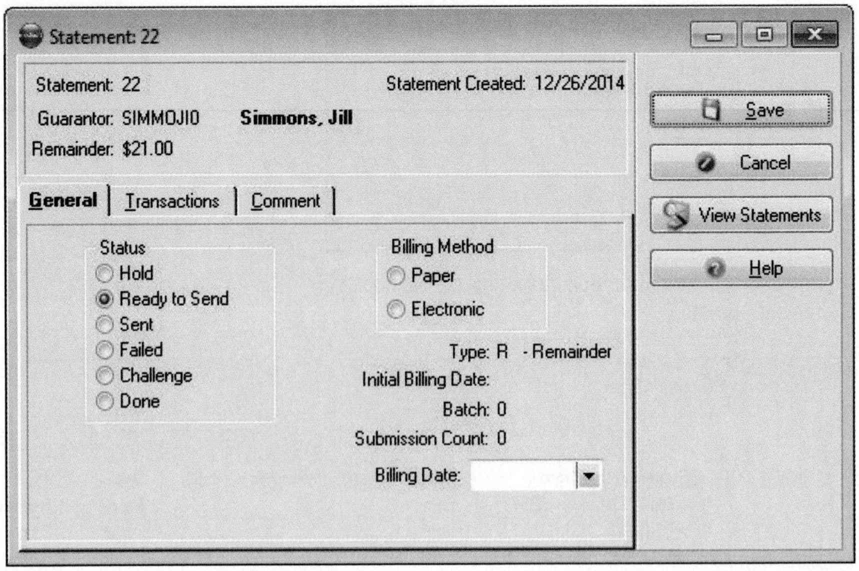

Figure 8-39   The Statement Dialog Box

Submission Count   This entry shows how many times a statement has been sent or printed.

Billing Date   The most current billing date is displayed.

TRANSACTIONS TAB

The Transactions tab lists the transactions placed on the statement (see Figure 8-40). The buttons at the bottom of the tab are used to split transactions, or remove transactions from the statement.

COMMENT TAB

The Comment tab provides a place to include notes about the statement (see Figure 8-41).

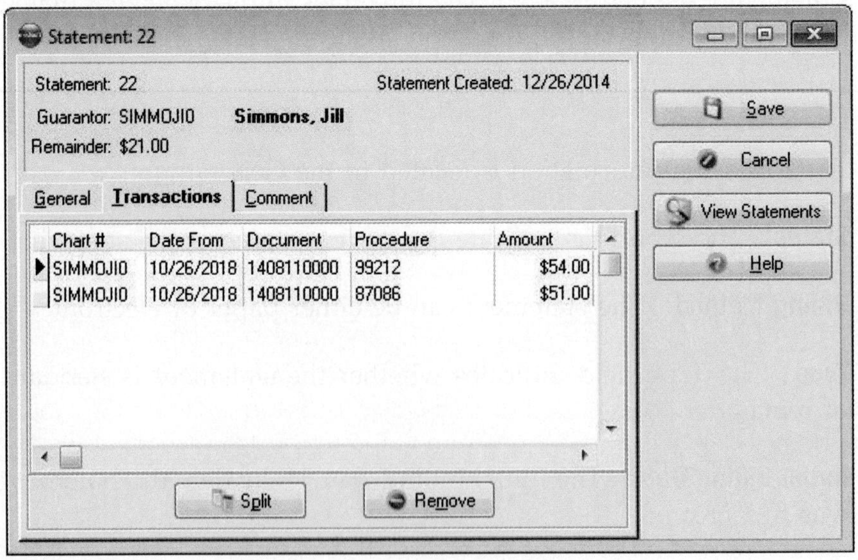

Figure 8-40   Transactions Tab

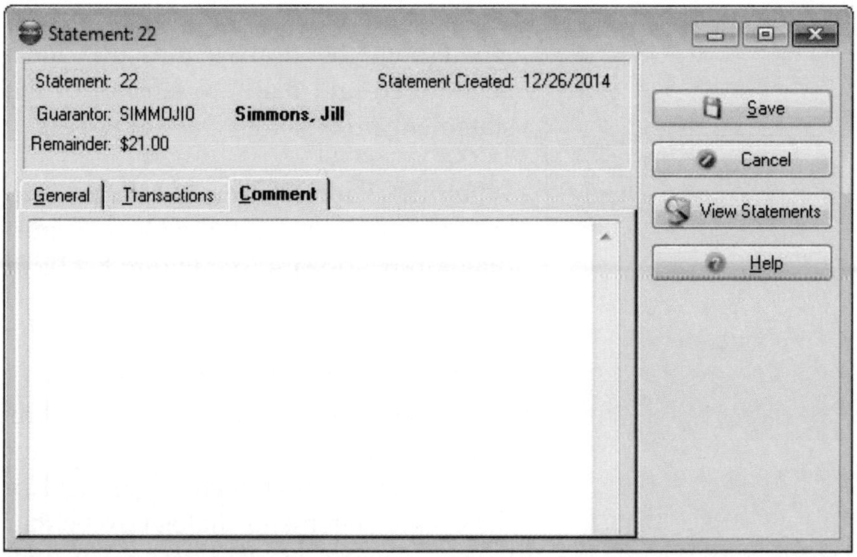

Statement: 22

Statement: 22   Statement Created: 12/26/2014
Guarantor: SIMMOJI0   **Simmons, Jill**
Remainder: $21.00

General | Transactions | **Comment**

Save

Cancel

View Statements

Help

Figure 8-41   Comment Tab

REVIEWING A STATEMENT — EXERCISE 8-10

Review the statement created in Exercise 8-8.

Date: November 13, 2018

1. If it is not already highlighted, click on the statement created for Jill Simmons in Exercise 8-9 to highlight it.

2. Click the Edit button.

3. Review the information in the General tab.

4. Click on the Transactions tab to see the transactions that are on the statement.

5. Click the Cancel button to close the Statement dialog box. **CiMO**

✓ **You have completed Exercise 8-10.**

8.9 PRINTING STATEMENTS

Once statements have been created, the next step is to send them to a printer or to transmit them electronically. When the Print/Send button is clicked, the Print/Send Statements dialog box is displayed (see Figure 8-42). This dialog box lists options for choosing the type of statement that will be created—Paper or Electronic. Paper statements are printed and mailed by the practice. Electronic statements are sent electronically to a processing center, which prints and mails them.

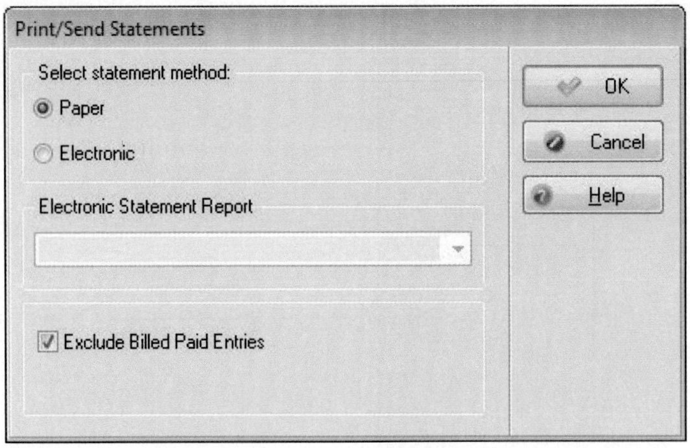

Figure 8-42   Print/Send Statements Dialog Box

The Exclude Billed Paid Entries box designates whether transactions that have been billed and paid are left out of the statement processing.

When the Paper button is selected and the OK button clicked, the Open Report dialog box appears (see Figure 8-43).

SELECTING A FORMAT

The report selected in this dialog box must match the type of statement selected in the Statement Type field of the Create Statements dialog box—either Standard or Remainder. If Remainder was checked, statements will print only if one of the Remainder Statement report formats is selected in the Open Report window:

1. Remainder Statement (0, 30, 60, 90)

2. Remainder Statement (All Payments)

3. Remainder Statement (All Pmts/Deduct)

4. Remainder Statement (Combined Payments)

Likewise, for Standard statements to print, one of the other patient statement report formats on the list must be chosen, such as Patient Statement (All Payments).

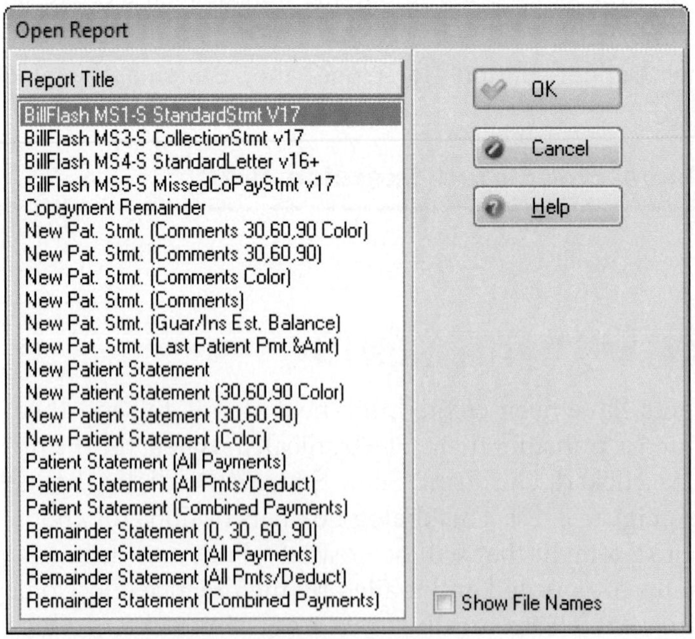

Figure 8-43   Open Report Dialog Box

After selecting the report format, click the OK button to display the Print Report Where? dialog box, which asks whether to preview the report on screen, send the report directly to the printer, or export the report to a file format (see Figure 8-44).

Once the Start button is clicked, the Data Selection Questions dialog box appears (see Figure 8-45).

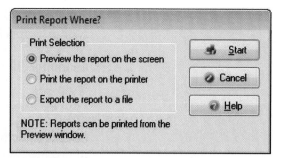

Figure 8-44   Print Report Where? Dialog Box

SELECTING THE FILTERS AND PRINTING THE STATEMENTS

The fields in the Data Selection Questions dialog box are used to filter statement selections. For example, to print statements for a certain group of patients, entries are made in the Chart Number Range field. In **once-a-month billing**, all statements are printed and mailed at once. Many practices use cycle billing instead. In a **cycle billing** system, patients are divided into groups and statement printing and mailing is staggered throughout the month. For example, statements for guarantors whose last names begin with the letters A to G are mailed on the first of the month, those with last names that begin with H to S are mailed on the eighth of the month, and so on.

In addition to the Chart Number Range filter, other available filters include:

Date From Range   Statements within a range of dates.

Insurance Carrier #1 Range   Statements for a range of insurance carriers.

once-a-month billing a type of billing in which statements are mailed to all patients at the same time each month.

cycle billing a type of billing in which statement printing and mailing are staggered throughout the month.

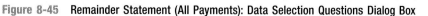

Figure 8-45   Remainder Statement (All Payments): Data Selection Questions Dialog Box

Statement Total Range Statements for guarantors with a balance within a specified range.

Guarantor Billing Code Range Statements for a range of guarantors assigned billing codes (from the Other Information tab in the Patient/Guarantor dialog box).

Patient Indicator Match Statements for patients assigned a particular patient indicator (from the Other Information tab in the Patient/Guarantor dialog box).

Txn Sort Order Transactions can be listed on the statement by Date of Service (Date From), Document Number, or Entry Number.

Statement Number Range Statements for a range of statement numbers (assigned by Medisoft).

Batch Number Match Statements in a particular batch (assigned by Medisoft).

Statements Older Than (Days) Statements that are older than a specified number of days.

In Collections Match Statements for accounts that are in collections.

If no changes are made to the default entries in the Data Selection Questions dialog box, all statements that have a status of Ready to Send or Sent are included in the batch. To avoid printing statements with a Sent status, and to only print those with a Ready to Send status, a zero is entered in the Batch Number Match field. All statements that are Ready to Send have a batch number of zero. Figure 8-46 displays a sample remainder statement.

EXERCISE 8-11	PRINTING STATEMENTS

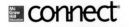

Print remainder statements for all patients with last names beginning with the letter *H* and ending with the letter *S*. *Note:* Be sure to enter *SYZMAM* instead of just *S* to select all patients whose last names begin with the letter *S*.

Note: If you do not have access to a printer, manually change the statement status to Sent using the method you used to change claim status in Chapter 7.

Date: November 13, 2018

1. Click the Print/Send button in the Statement Management dialog box. The Print/Send Statements dialog box is displayed.

2. Select Paper as the statement method. Verify that the Exclude Billed Paid Entries box is checked. Click the OK button.

3. In the Open Report dialog box that appears, select Remainder Statement (All Payments). Click the OK button.

Family Care Center
285 Stephenson Boulevard
Stephenson, OH 60089-1111
(614)555-0000

Statement Date	Chart Number	Page
11/13/2018	SIMMOJI0	1

Jill Simmons
30 Arbor Way
Stephenson, OH 60089-1111

Make Checks Payable To:
Family Care Center
285 Stephenson Boulevard
Stephenson, OH 60089-1111
(614)555-0000

Date of Last Payment: 11/1/2018	Amount: -84.00		Previous Balance:	0.00

Patient: Jill Simmons   Chart Number: SIMMOJI0   Case: Urinary tract infection

Dates	Procedure	Charge	Paid by Primary		Paid By Guarantor	Adjustments	Remainder
10/26/18	99212	54.00	-43.20			0.00	10.80
10/26/18	87086	51.00	-40.80			0.00	10.20

Amount Due
21.00

Figure 8-46   Sample Remainder Statement

4. In the Print Report Where? dialog box, choose the option to preview the report on screen. Click the Start button. The Data Selection Questions dialog box is displayed.

5. In the Chart Number Range boxes, enter the chart numbers that will select all patients with last names beginning with *H* through *S*. In the Batch Number Match field, key *0* so that only statements with a Ready to Send status will be printed. Click the OK button.

6. Scroll down through the statement displayed in the Preview Report window. Click the Print button. After printing, close the Preview window.

7. Notice that Jill Simmons's statement now has a status of Sent. Close the Statement Management dialog box. **CiMC**

✓ **You have completed Exercise 8-11.**

APPLYING YOUR SKILLS
8: ENTER INSURANCE PAYMENTS

October 26, 2018
Using Source Document 12, enter the payment information from the remittance advice and apply payments to the patient's account.

APPLYING YOUR SKILLS
9: CREATE STATEMENTS

November 13, 2018
Create remainder statements for all patients with last names beginning with *T* through the end of the alphabet. Print the statements just created.

Remember to create a backup of your work before exiting Medisoft! To help you keep track of your work, name the backup file after the chapter you are working on; for example, StudentID-c8.mbk.

BE THE DETECTIVE!

If assigned by your instructor, complete the Payment Posting Video Case in Connect. Put your skills to use identifying mistakes made in Medisoft and enhance your knowledge by determining the impact of those mistakes.

chapter 8 worksheet

[Note: These questions are designed for students using the live Medisoft CD software, since students may need to refer back to specific screens in the software to answer the questions.]

1. *[LO 8.4]* What is the amount the insurance carrier paid for procedure 99211 for John Fitzwilliams on 9/4/2018?

2. *[LO 8.4]* What is the amount the insurance carrier paid for procedure 99211 for Herbert Bell on 9/3/2018?

3. *[LO 8.4]* What is the amount the insurance carrier paid for procedure 90471 for Sarah Fitzwilliams on 9/4/2018?

4. *[LO 8.4]* What is listed as the Last Payment Amount on Herbert Bell's account after the East Ohio PPO payments were entered on 10/1/2018 (Transaction Entry dialog box)?

5. *[LO 8.4]* What is the remaining balance on Sheila Giles's account after the Blue Cross and Blue Shield payments were entered on 11/1/2018?

6. *[LO 8.4]* What is listed as the Last Payment Amount on John Fitzwilliams's account after the ChampVA payments were entered on 10/1/2018 (Transaction Entry dialog box)?

7. *[LO 8.4]* What is listed as the Last Payment Amount on Sheila Giles's account after the Blue Cross and Blue Shield payments were entered on 11/1/2018 (Transaction Entry dialog box)?

8. *[LO 8.7]* A statement was created for which patient(s) in Exercise 8-9?

9. *[LO 8.4]* What is the amount of the Blue Cross and Blue Shield payment for procedure 71020 for Lisa Wright on 10/1/2018 (Transaction Entry dialog box)?

10. *[LO 8.8]* What is listed as the amount due on Lisa Wright's statement created in Applying Your Skills 9?

11. *[LO 8.3]* What is the total amount of the deposits entered on October 26, 2018? (*Hint:* Include payments from patients and insurance carriers.)

12. *[LO 8.7, 8.8, 8.9]* What charges are listed on the November 13 statement for Kristin Zapata?

CiMO
chapter 8 summary

LEARNING OUTCOMES	CONCEPTS TO REVIEW
8.1 Describe how an adjustment is calculated if the payer pays less than the provider's usual fee.	If the provider enters into a contract with the payer and agrees to accept reduced fees, the difference between what the provider bills and the contracted discount is recorded as an adjustment.
8.2 List the five steps for processing a remittance advice.	1. Compare the RA to the original insurance claim to be sure that all procedures listed on the claim are represented on the RA and that the CPT codes have not changed. 2. Review the payment amount against the expected amount. 3. Identify the reasons for denials or payment reductions; resubmit claim or appeal if necessary. 4. Post payment information for individual claims to the appropriate patient accounts. 5. Bill the patient's secondary healthcare plan if appropriate.
8.3 Demonstrate how to enter insurance payments.	1. Click Enter Deposits/Payments on the Activities menu. The Deposit List dialog box is displayed. 2. Confirm that the correct date is displayed in the Deposit Date box. 3. Click the New button. The Deposit dialog box is displayed. 4. Verify that the desired date is in the Deposit Date field. 5. Select Insurance in the Payor Type box. 6. Select the appropriate entry in the Payment Method box. 7. Complete the Check Number box if entering a check or the EFT Tracer box if entering an electronic payment. 8. Enter the ERA ID number or other number as appropriate in the Description/Bank No. field. 9. Enter the amount of the payment in the Payment Amount box. 10. Accept the default entry (A) in the Deposit Code box. 11. Select the insurance carrier from the Insurance drop-down list. The program automatically completes the remaining fields. 12. Click the Save button to save the entry.

LEARNING OUTCOMES	CONCEPTS TO REVIEW
8.4 Demonstrate how to apply insurance payments to charges.	1. Click Enter Deposits/Payments on the Activities menu. The Deposit List dialog box is displayed. 2. Confirm that the correct date is displayed in the Deposit Date box. 3. In the list of deposits, click once on the payment that will be applied. The Apply Payment/Adjustments to Charges dialog box appears. 4. In the For box, select the first patient listed on the remittance advice. 5. Locate the first charge, enter the payment in the Payment column, and press Tab to the end of the first row. Follow the same steps for each procedure charge for that patient. 6. Click the Save Payments/Adjustments button. An Information dialog box displays the message that the claim has been marked "done" for the primary insurance. Click OK. If there are additional patients for whom the payment should be applied, repeat the procedure for each patient. 7. When all payments have been applied, click the Close button.
8.5 Demonstrate how to enter and apply a patient payment received by mail.	1. Click Enter Deposits/Payments on the Activities menu. The Deposit List dialog box is displayed. 2. Confirm that the correct date is displayed in the Deposit Date box. 3. Click the New button. The Deposit dialog box is displayed. 4. Verify that the desired date is in the Deposit Date field. 5. Select Patient in the Payor Type box. 6. Select the appropriate entry in the Payment Method box. 7. Complete the Check Number box. 8. Enter the amount of the payment in the Payment Amount box. 9. Accept the default entry (A) in the Deposit Code box. 10. Select the patient from the Chart Number drop-down list. The program automatically completes some or all of the remaining fields. 11. Click the Save button to save the entry. 12. In the Deposit List dialog box, click once on the line that contains the patient's payment. The Apply Payment/Adjustments to Charges dialog box appears. 13. Locate the first charge that is listed with an amount in the Remainder column and enter a payment equal to that amount in the Payment column. If the patient has more than one procedure with a remainder balance, follow the same steps for each procedure charge for that patient. 14. Click the Save Payments/Adjustments button. An Information dialog box displays the message that the statement has been marked "done." Click OK. 15. Click the Close button.

LEARNING OUTCOMES	CONCEPTS TO REVIEW
8.6 Demonstrate how to enter capitation payments.	1. Click Enter Deposits/Payments on the Activities menu. The Deposit List dialog box is displayed. 2. Confirm that the correct date is displayed in the Deposit Date box. 3. Click the New button. The Deposit dialog box is displayed. 4. Verify that the desired date is displayed in the Deposit Date box. 5. Select Capitation in the Payor Type box. 6. Select the appropriate entry in the Payment Method box. 7. Complete the Check Number box if entering a check or the EFT Tracer box if entering an electronic payment. 8. Enter the ERA ID number or other number as appropriate in the Description/Bank No. field. 9. Enter the amount of the payment in the Payment Amount box. 10. Accept the default entry (A) in the Deposit Code box. 11. Select the insurance carrier from the Insurance drop-down list. 12. Click the Save button to save the entry and close the Deposit dialog box. 13. Use the List Only option in the Claim Management dialog box to identify patients insured by the capitated plan who have claims for the period covered by the capitation payment. 14. In the Deposit List dialog box, click the New button. The Deposit List dialog box appears. 15. In the Payor Type field, select Insurance. 16. Select Electronic in the Payment Method field. 17. Verify that 0.00 is the amount displayed in the Payment Amount field. 18. Select the appropriate entry in the Deposit Code field. 19. Select the insurance carrier in the Insurance Carrier drop-down list. 20. Click the Save button. The Deposit List dialog box reappears with the zero amount payment displayed. 21. Select the capitated deposit that has EOB Only listed in the Payment column and click the Apply button. 22. In the For field, select the first capitated patient that was identified in Step 13 and press Tab. 23. Locate the amount listed in the Remainder column and enter an equal amount in the Adjustment column. Press Tab repeatedly, until the remainder amount changes to zero. 24. Continue this procedure for all patients identified in Step 13. When finished, click the Save Payments/Adjustments button.

LEARNING OUTCOMES	CONCEPTS TO REVIEW
8.7 Demonstrate how to create patient statements.	1. Select Statement Management on the Activities menu. The Statement Management dialog box appears. 2. Click the Create Statements button. The Create Statements dialog box is displayed. 3. Enter the appropriate dates in the Transaction Dates fields. 4. Enter the chart numbers of the appropriate patients, or leave these fields blank to select all patients. 5. Set the Statement Type field to Standard or Remainder. 6. Click the Create button to generate statements. A message appears stating the number of statements that have been created. Click the OK button.
8.8 Explain how statements are edited.	1. Select Statement Management on the Activities menu. 2. Click once on the statement to be edited. 3. Click the Edit button. 4. Review the information in the three tabs of the Statement dialog box and make changes as necessary. 5. Click the Save button to save your changes.
8.9 Demonstrate how to preview and print patient statements.	1. Click the Print/Send button in the Statement Management dialog box. The Print/Send Statements dialog box is displayed. 2. Select the statement method (paper or electronic). Click the OK button. 3. In the Open Report dialog box that appears, select Remainder Statement (All Payments). Click the OK button. 4. If previewing statements, accept the default (Preview the report on the screen) in the Print Report Where? dialog box and choose the option to print the reports on the printer. Click the Start button. If printing the statements without previewing, select Print the report to the printer in the Print Report Where? dialog box. In either case, the Data Selection Questions dialog box is displayed. 5. In the Chart Number Range boxes, enter the chart numbers that will select the appropriate patients. 6. Make other selections in the Data Selection Questions dialog box, if appropriate. When finished, click the OK button. 7. The statements are sent to the printer. 8. Close the Statement Management dialog box.

USING TERMINOGY

Match the terms on the left with the definitions on the right.

1. *[LO 8.2]* autoposting
2. *[LO 8.3]* capitation payments
3. *[LO 8.9]* cycle billing
4. *[LO 8.2]* electronic funds transfer (EFT)
5. *[LO 8.1]* fee schedule
6. *[LO 8.9]* once-a-month billing
7. *[LO 8.7]* patient statement
8. *[LO 8.1]* payment schedule
9. *[LO 8.7]* remainder statements
10. *[LO 8.7]* standard statements

a. A list of the amount of money a patient owes, organized by the amount of time the money has been owed, the procedures performed, and the dates the procedures were performed.

b. A type of billing in which patients are divided into groups and statement printing and mailing are staggered throughout the month.

c. A document that specifies the amount the provider bills for provided services.

d. The automatic posting of data in the remittance advice to a practice management program.

e. Statement that shows all charges regardless of whether the insurance has paid on the transactions.

f. Payments made to physicians on a regular basis (such as monthly) for providing services to patients in a managed care insurance plan.

g. The electronic movement of monies from one bank account to another.

h. A document that specifies the amount the payer agrees to pay the provider for a service, based on a contracted rate of reimbursement.

i. A type of billing in which statements are mailed to all patients at the same time each month.

j. Statements that list only those charges that are not paid in full after all insurance carrier payments have been received.

Copyright ©2016 McGraw-Hill Education

CHECKING YOUR UNDERSTANDING

11. *[LO 8.3]* Why is it easier to enter large insurance payments in the Deposit List dialog box than in the Transaction Entry dialog box?

12. *[LO 8.4]* When all payments on a remittance advice have been successfully entered and applied to charges, what should appear in the Unapplied box in the upper-right corner of the Deposit List dialog box?

13. *[LO 8.6]* Why do charges need to be adjusted for patients who are covered under a capitated insurance plan?

14. *[LO 8.7]* If a practice did not want to create statements for patients with an account balance of less than $5.00, how would this be done?

15. *[LO 8.1]* A patient is covered by an indemnity plan and is responsible for 30 percent coinsurance. The charge for a recent office visit was $120. What is the amount owed by the patient, assuming the claim is paid?

16. *[LO 8.2]* What is the first step to be completed when processing a remittance advice?

17. *[LO 8.7]* The process of creating patient statements begins with selecting Statement Management on the _____ menu.

18. *[LO 8.8]* If you wanted to know which transactions were listed on a statement that was already created, what would you do?

19. *[LO 8.9]* If you wanted to print statements for all patients with a particular insurance carrier, which fields would you need to complete in the Data Selection Questions dialog box to select the carrier?

20. *[LO 8.6]* What is listed in the Payment column of the Deposit List dialog box when a zero amount deposit has been entered for a capitation payment?

APPLYING YOUR KNOWLEDGE

21. *[LO 8.3, 8.4]* Randall Klein calls. He would like to know whether Medicare has paid any of the charges for his September office visit. How would you look up this information in Medisoft?

22. *[LO 8.7]* Why do many practices send out remainder statements rather than standard statements?

23. *[LO 8.1]* Why is it important to understand the differences among different types of health plans?

24. *[LO 8.6]* What would happen if a capitated patient account was not adjusted to a zero balance?

25. *[LO 8.2]* What is the purpose of reviewing a remittance advice before entering payments and adjustments?

26. *[LO 8.2]* If payments and adjustments listed on a remittance advice were not posted and applied to patients' accounts, what would the consequence be?

27. *[LO 8.7]* If statements were not created and mailed to patients, what would the consequence be?

chapter 9

CREATING REPORTS

learning outcomes

When you finish this chapter, you will be able to:

9.1 List the three types of reports available in Medisoft.

9.2 Explain why accounts receivable reports are critical to a practice's financial success.

9.3 Distinguish between patient, procedure, and payment day sheets.

9.4 Demonstrate how to create a practice analysis report.

9.5 Demonstrate how to create a patient ledger report.

9.6 Demonstrate how to create a standard patient list report.

9.7 Describe how to use Medisoft Reports to create a report.

9.8 Demonstrate how to create a patient aging report.

9.9 Explain how to access Medisoft's built-in custom reports.

9.10 Demonstrate how to open a report for editing in Medisoft's Report Designer.

what you need to know

To use this chapter, you need to know how to:

- Start Medisoft, use menus, and enter and edit text.
- Work with chart numbers and codes.

9.1 CREATING REPORTS IN MEDISOFT

Medisoft® offers several options for creating reports, all of which can be accessed via the Reports menu (see Figure 9-1). These options include:

- Standard reports
- Medisoft Reports . . .
- Design Custom Reports and Bills . . .

Standard reports include many of the basic reports used by a medical office, such as day sheets, practice analysis reports, and patient ledgers. Medisoft Reports, an option on the Reports menu, includes over a hundred reports not included in the standard reports. Finally, custom reports are created and modified using the Medisoft Report Designer program. In this chapter, you will learn about some of the reports used throughout the billing process and you will gain experience creating all three types of reports.

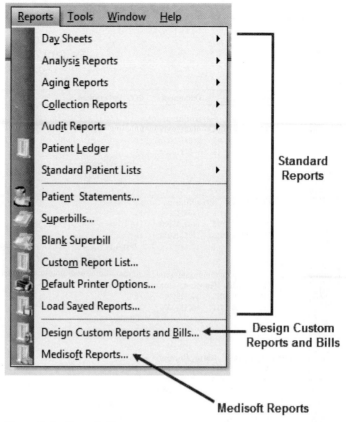

Figure 9-1   Reports Menu

SELECTING PRINT OPTIONS

In Medisoft, the process of creating a report begins with selecting a report from the Reports menu. When a report is selected, a dialog box appears with options to preview the report on the screen, send it to a printer, or export it to a file (see Figure 9-2).

If the preview option is selected, the report will be displayed in a Print Preview window. This window, common to all reports, provides options for viewing or printing a report (see Figure 9-3). The

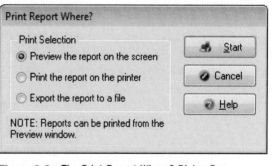

Figure 9-2   The Print Report Where? Dialog Box

buttons on the Print Preview toolbar control how a report is displayed on the screen and how to move from page to page within a report (see Figure 9-4).

Print   The Print button is used to print the report or to save the report as a file, such as a PDF.

Search Data   The Search Data button performs a case-sensitive text search in the report displayed in the preview window.

Window Display   The next three buttons are used to change the display of the report, which makes locating specific information in

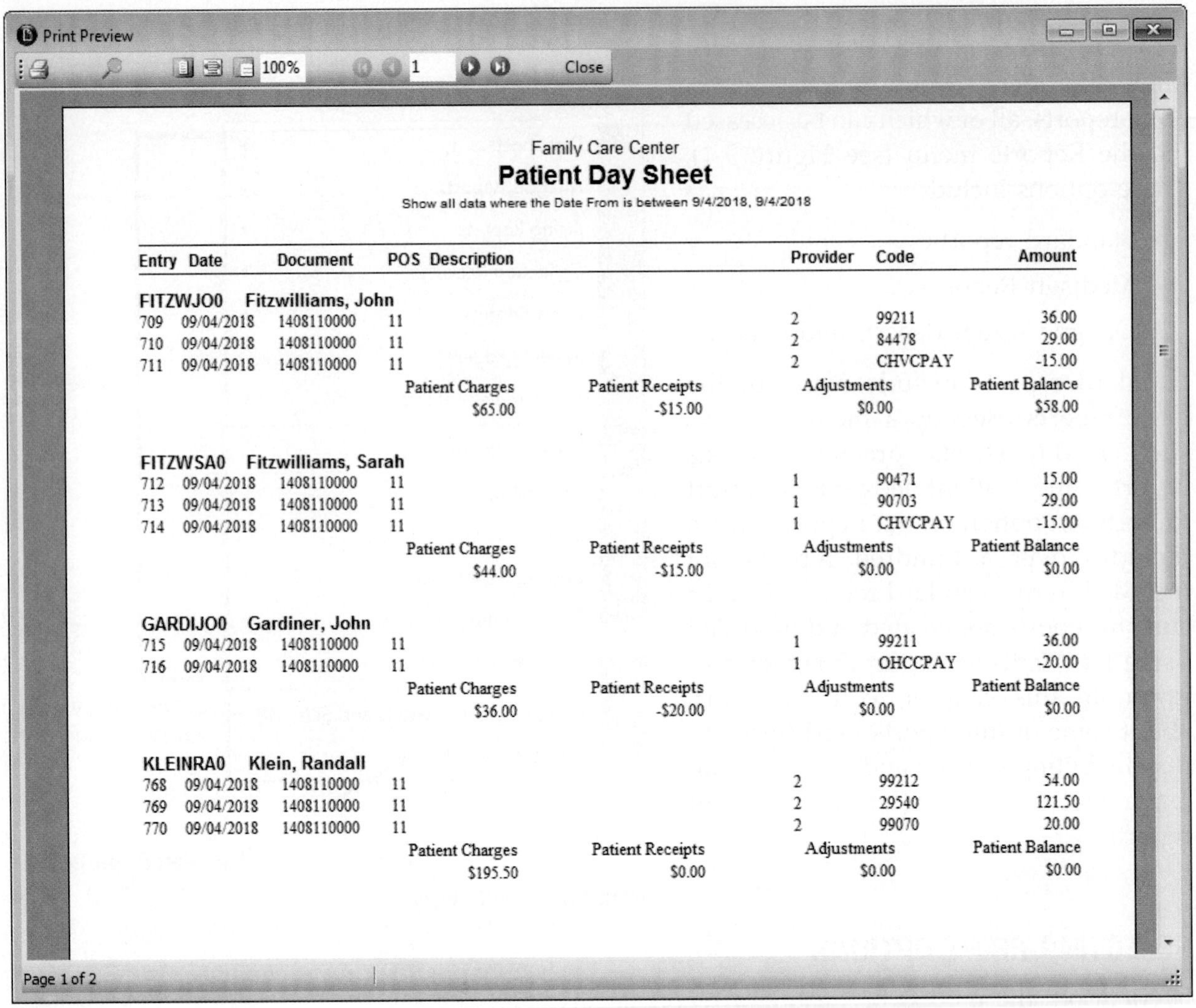

Print Preview

100% 1 Close

Family Care Center

Patient Day Sheet

Show all data where the Date From is between 9/4/2018, 9/4/2018

Entry	Date	Document	POS	Description	Provider	Code	Amount
FITZWJO0	**Fitzwilliams, John**						
709	09/04/2018	1408110000	11		2	99211	36.00
710	09/04/2018	1408110000	11		2	84478	29.00
711	09/04/2018	1408110000	11		2	CHVCPAY	-15.00
		Patient Charges		Patient Receipts	Adjustments		Patient Balance
		$65.00		-$15.00	$0.00		$58.00
FITZWSA0	**Fitzwilliams, Sarah**						
712	09/04/2018	1408110000	11		1	90471	15.00
713	09/04/2018	1408110000	11		1	90703	29.00
714	09/04/2018	1408110000	11		1	CHVCPAY	-15.00
		Patient Charges		Patient Receipts	Adjustments		Patient Balance
		$44.00		-$15.00	$0.00		$0.00
GARDIJO0	**Gardiner, John**						
715	09/04/2018	1408110000	11		1	99211	36.00
716	09/04/2018	1408110000	11		1	OHCCPAY	-20.00
		Patient Charges		Patient Receipts	Adjustments		Patient Balance
		$36.00		-$20.00	$0.00		$0.00
KLEINRA0	**Klein, Randall**						
768	09/04/2018	1408110000	11		2	99212	54.00
769	09/04/2018	1408110000	11		2	29540	121.50
770	09/04/2018	1408110000	11		2	99070	20.00
		Patient Charges		Patient Receipts	Adjustments		Patient Balance
		$195.50		$0.00	$0.00		$0.00

Page 1 of 2

Figure 9-3 Print Preview Window

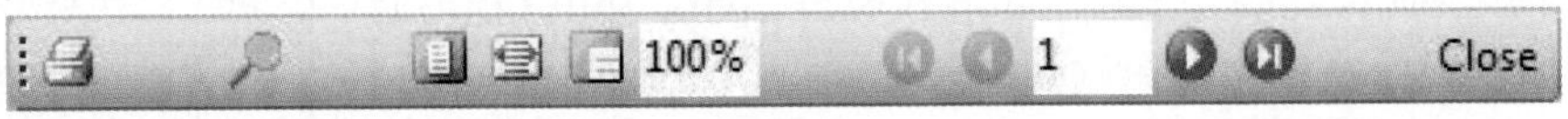

Figure 9-4 Buttons on Print Preview Toolbar

it easier. From left to right, the choices are whole page, page width, and percentage. A percentage can be entered in place of 100 percent for zooming in or out of the report.

Navigate Four triangle buttons, two on the left and two on the right, are used to move through pages of a multipage report. The First Page button, farthest on the left, moves to the beginning of a report. The Prior Page button moves to the page that precedes the one currently displayed. The bar between the two sets of triangle buttons indicates the number of the current page. To the right of the bar are the other two triangle buttons. The Next Page button moves to the page following the current one. The Last Page button moves to the end of a report. If a button is dimmed, it means that there are no more pages in the direction indicated by the triangle. If a button is bright blue, there is an additional page or pages in the report.

Close   This command is used to close the Print Preview window.

SELECTING DATA FOR A REPORT

Once a selection is made in the Print Report Where? dialog box and the Start button is clicked, the Search dialog box is displayed. This dialog box is used to select the range of data that will be included in the report (see Figure 9-5). While the exact contents of the Search box vary from report to report, the way selections are made does not change. Once you learn how to use the Search dialog box, you can create any report.

The Search dialog box contains a number of fields called selection boxes. Some reports have one selection box in a Search box, while others, such as the Patient Day Sheet Search box in Figures 9-5 and 9-6, have many. The selection boxes determine what data are included in the report.

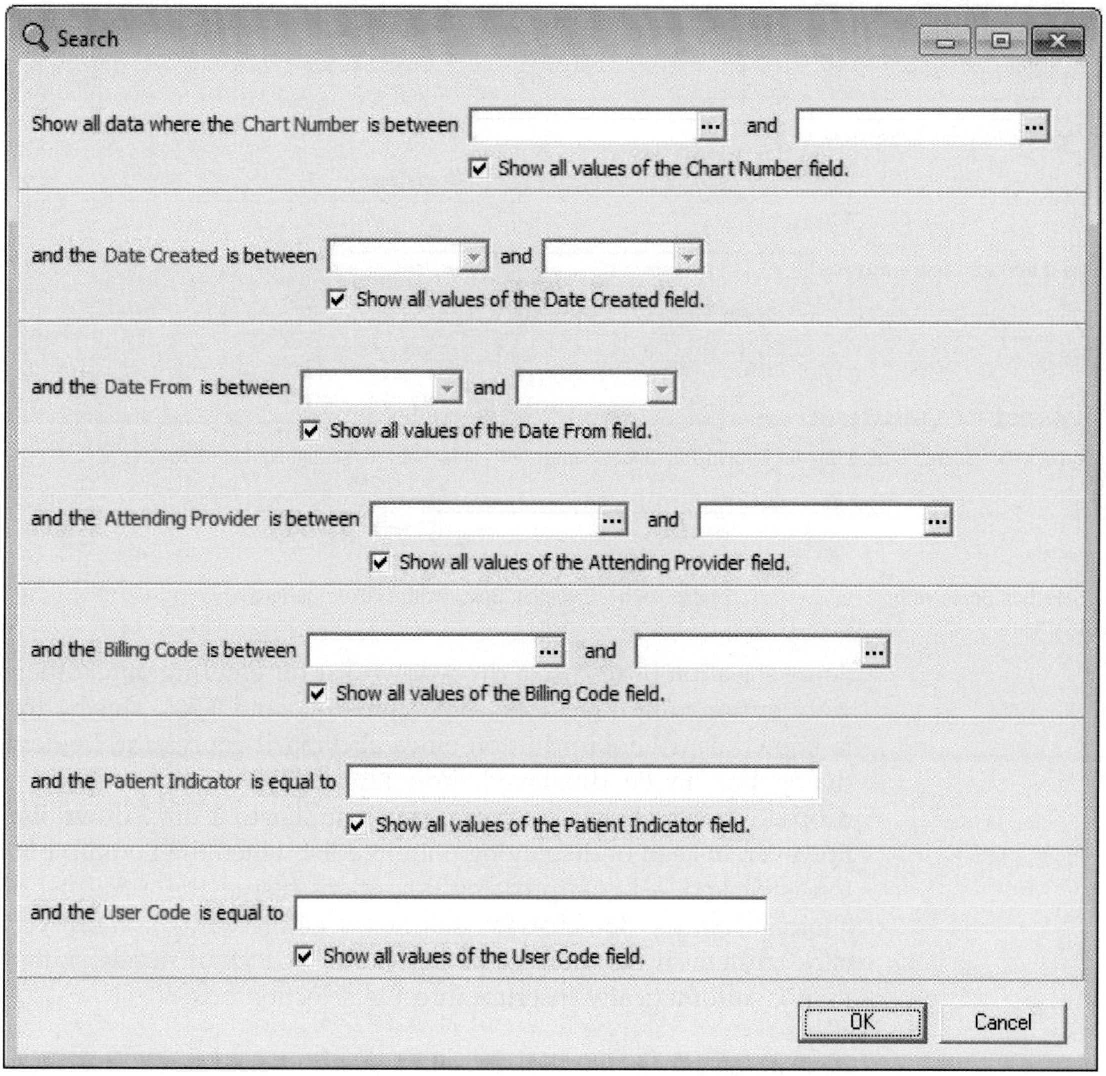

Figure 9-5   Search Dialog Box for Patient Day Sheet Report

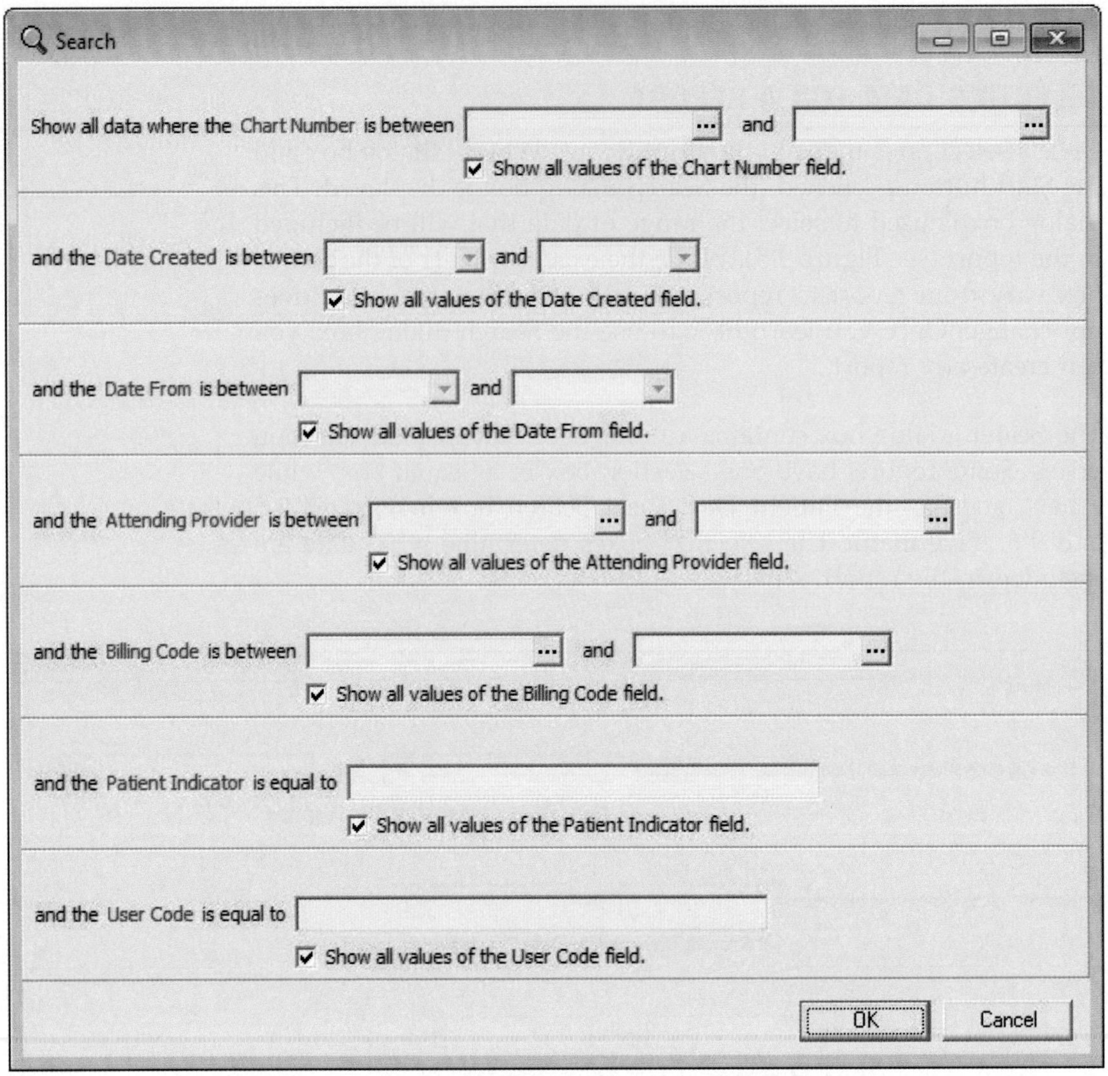

Figure 9-6 Search Dialog Box for Patient Day Sheet Report with Selection Boxes Highlighted in Yellow

Figure 9-7a Selection Boxes with Drop-down List Buttons

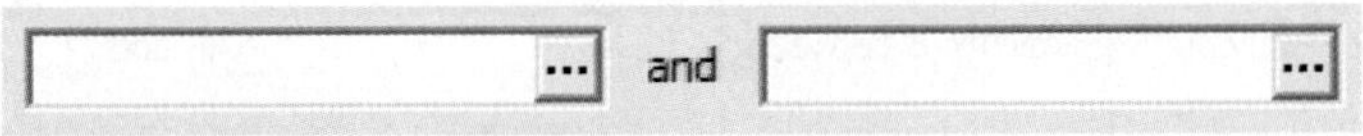

Figure 9-7b Selection Boxes with Lookup Buttons

Some selection boxes use a drop-down list for entering data; others use a button with three dots (see Figures 9-7a and 9-7b). This button is known as a Lookup button since clicking it causes the Lookup dialog box to be displayed. You already know how to use a drop-down list. The Lookup button is similar to a drop-down list; however, instead of displaying a limited list, when the Lookup button is clicked, a Lookup dialog box opens displaying a full list of choices from the database for that field (see Figure 9-8). When you click an item in the dialog box (for example, a chart number), that item is automatically inserted into the selection box.

Beneath each selection box or set of boxes in the Search box, there is an option labeled Show all values of the _____ field. If you are

Lookup											
Search Characters											
Chart Number	Last Name	First Name	Middle Initial	Street 1		Social Security Number	Signature on File	Patient Type	Patient ID #2	Sex	Date of Birth	Ass
ARLENSU0	Arlen	Susan		310 Oneida Lane		309-62-0422	True	Patient		Female	2/10/1954	5
BATTIAN0	Battistuta	Anthony		22 Mountain Blvd.		239-55-0855	True	Patient		Male	8/14/1939	4
BATTIPA0	Battistuta	Pauline		22 Mountain Blvd.		139-22-5408	True	Patient		Female	7/15/1941	4
BELLHER0	Bell	Herbert		727 Willow Lane		829-11-3333	True	Patient		Male	3/31/1973	2
BELLJAN0	Bell	Janine		727 Willow Lane		849-00-1111	True	Patient		Female	6/26/1972	3
BELLJON0	Bell	Jonathan		727 Willow Lane		974-32-0001	True	Patient		Male	7/3/2005	1
BELLSAM0	Bell	Samuel		727 Willow Lane		974-32-0000	True	Patient		Male	7/3/2005	2
BELLSAR0	Bell	Sarina		727 Willow Lane		989-00-8888	True	Patient		Female	1/21/2007	1
BROOKLA0	Brooks	Lawana		1774 Grand Street		221-34-0879	True	Patient		Female	5/30/1972	4
FITZWJO0	Fitzwilliams	John		1627 Forest Avenue		763-00-4444	True	Patient		Male	11/15/1969	2

Search By

Chart Number

✓ OK   ✗ Cancel

Figure 9-8 The Lookup Dialog Box That Is Displayed When the Lookup Button in the Chart Number Selection Box Is Clicked

printing a report and want all values for the field included (for example, all patients), you will need to make sure this box is checked. If instead you want only some of the values included (for example, only patients with last names beginning with the letter *H*), you will need to make entries in the selection boxes. Clicking one of the selection boxes automatically removes the check mark from the Show all values box.

In the Patient Day Sheet Search box pictured in Figures 9-5 and 9-6, selections can be made to include some or all of the following data:

Chart Number (Show all data where the Chart Number is between) In the two Chart Number boxes, a range of chart numbers for patients is entered. If a report on just one patient is needed, that patient's chart number is entered in both boxes. If a report on all patients is needed, a check mark must remain in the Show all values of the Chart Number field box.

Date Created (and the Date Created is between) The Date Created entries refer to the actual dates the information was entered in the computer. The date created may or may not be the same as the date a transaction took place. For example, suppose transactions from Friday, September 28, are entered in Medisoft on Monday morning, October 1. In this example, the Date Created value is the date the transaction was entered—October 1. The transaction date is the date on which the patient was in the office—September 28.

By default, Medisoft enters the Windows System Date in both Date Created boxes. The Windows System Date is today's date—the day you are sitting at your computer working on the exercises in this chapter. *Note:* **Always check to be sure the box labeled** *Show all values of the Date Created* **has a checkmark. Do not enter actual dates in these fields.** If you do not show all values, because the exercises take place in the future (2018), the program will not find all the data it needs to create the report, and no report will be created.

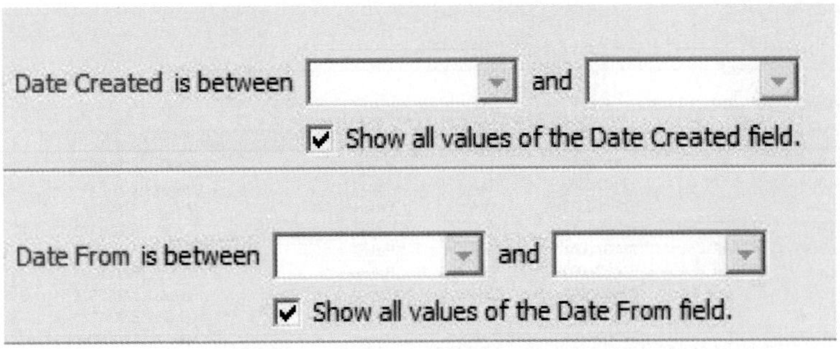

Figure 9-9   Down Arrows (Highlighted in Yellow) Used to Display the Pop-up Calendar

Date From (and the Date From is between)   The Date From entries refer to the actual dates of the transactions. If the day sheet report is for September 3, 2018, then 09032018 is entered in both fields. *At the beginning of each exercise, the Date From fields must be changed to the date listed before step 1 of the exercise.*

Note: There are two ways of changing dates in the Search dialog box. You can use the keyboard to enter the numbers. You do not need to enter the slashes; as long as you enter 8 digits for the dates, Medisoft will automatically insert the slashes. For example, January 1, 2018, would be keyed as 01012018. The other way of entering dates

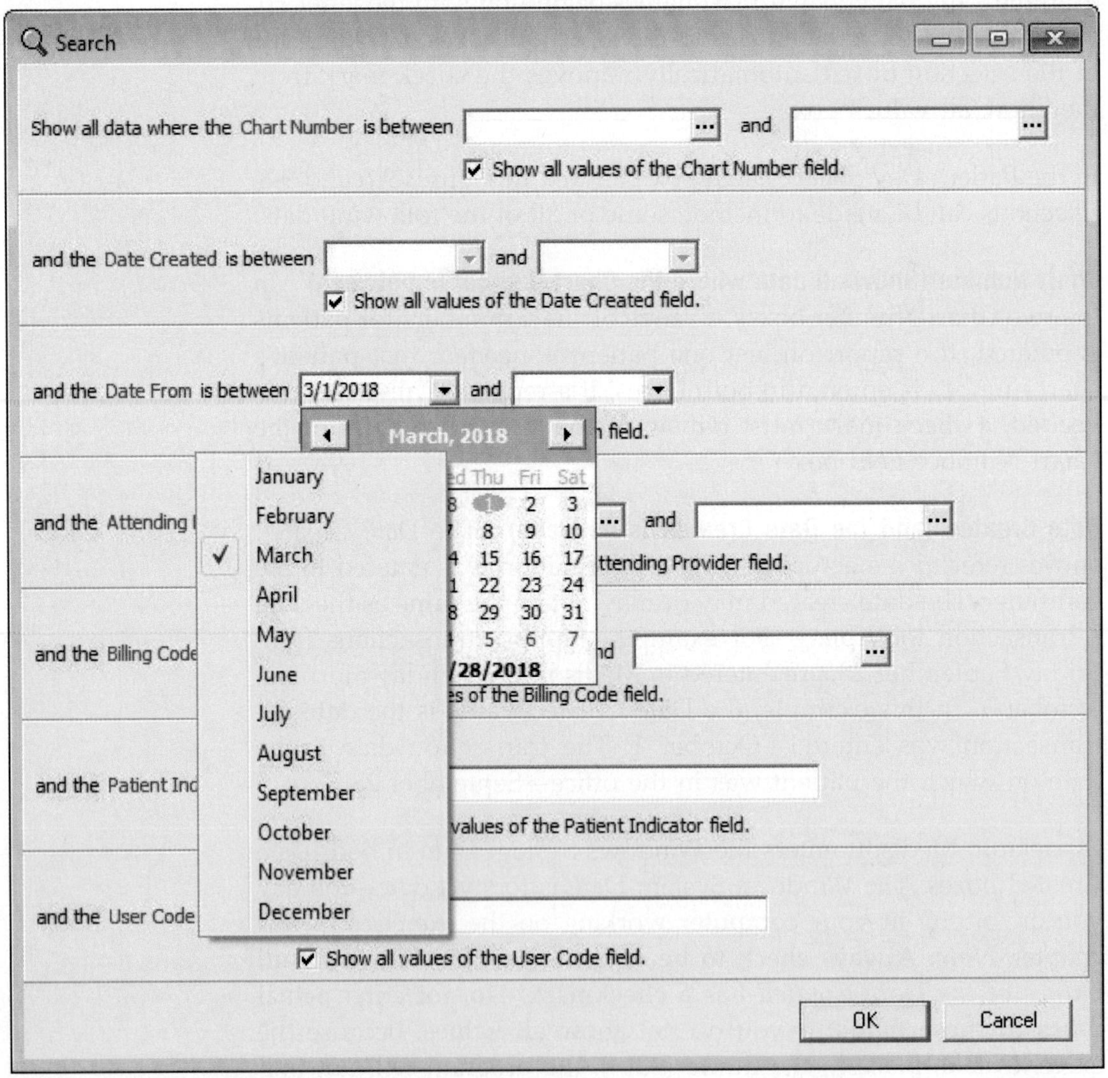

Figure 9-10   List of Months in the Pop-up Calendar

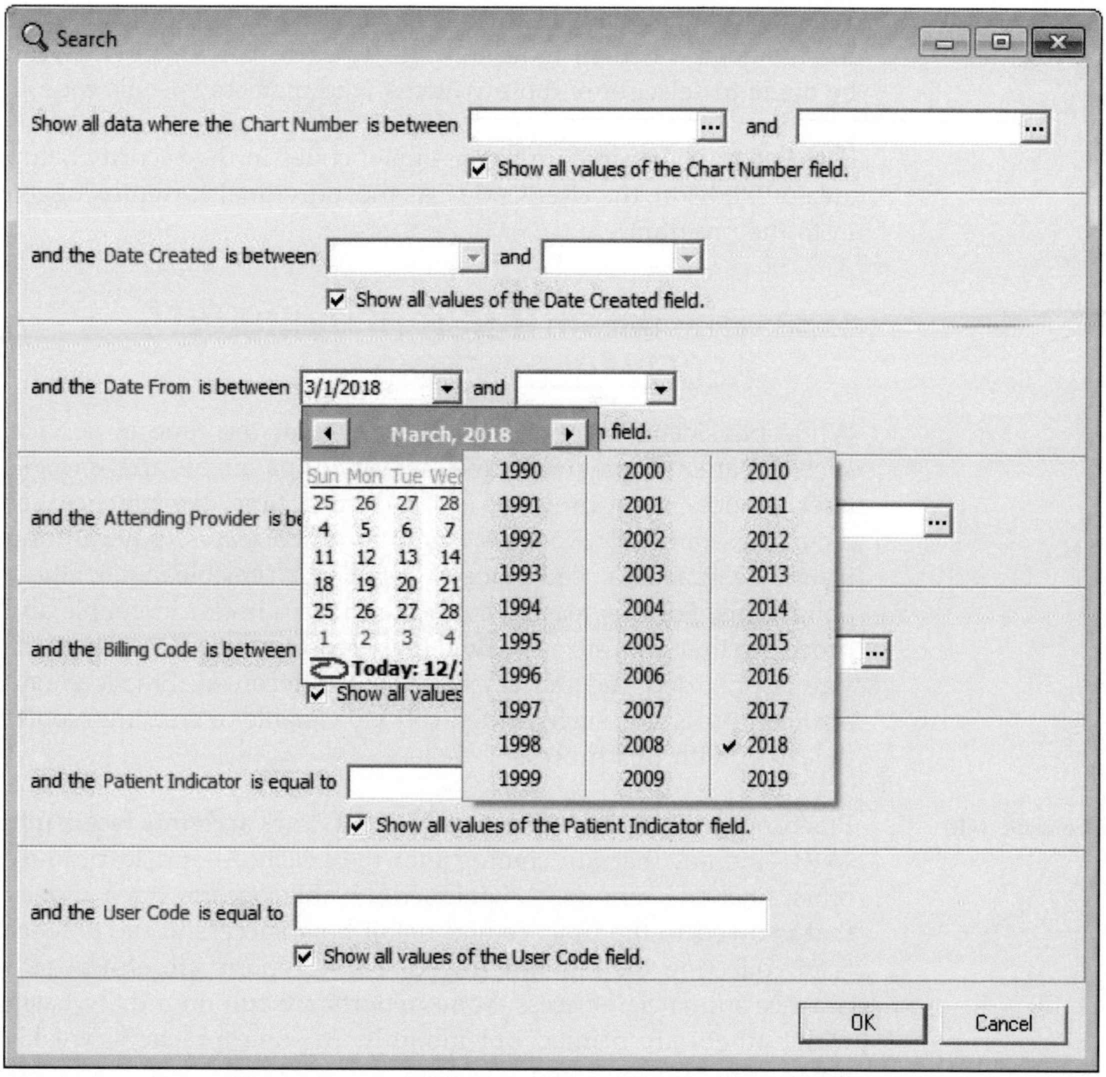

Figure 9-11 List of Years in the Pop-up Calendar

is to use the pop-up calendar. The pop-up calendar is displayed when you click the down arrows at the right side of the box that contains the date (see Figure 9-9). Once this calendar is visible, clicking the month in the blue banner at the top of the calendar displays a list of the months (see Figure 9-10). Clicking any month in the list changes the calendar to that month. Clicking the year in the blue banner displays a list of years. Clicking any year in the list changes the calendar to that year (see Figure 9-11). The day is changed by clicking the desired day in the calendar below the blue banner.

Attending Provider (and the Attending Provider is between)   A range of codes for the attending providers is entered in the Attending Provider fields.

Billing Code (and the Billing Code is between)   If the practice uses Medisoft's Billing Code feature, codes can be entered in this box to select only those patients with the designated billing codes.

Patient Indicator (and the Patient Indicator is equal to)   If the practice has assigned a Patient Indicator code to each patient, an entry can be made to select only those patients who match a specific code.

User Code   If the practice has assigned codes in the Security Setup area of Medisoft, the User Code lists the individual currently logged in to the program.

9.2 THE IMPORTANCE OF ACCOUNTS RECEIVABLE REPORTS

While physicians receive some payments at the time of service, such as patient copayments, the majority of payments arrive weeks after services were provided. At the same time, the practice has recurring standard expenses, such as office leases, payroll, and insurance. Practices need a steady cash flow to be able to meet these obligations. For this reason, medical practices invest in people and processes that minimize the time that elapses between the date service is provided and the date payment is received. Practice management programs such as Medisoft are capable of creating reports that help with this process.

accounts receivable (AR) monies that are coming into the practice.

Practice management programs are used to track **accounts receivable (AR)**—monies that are coming into the practice—and to produce other financial reports. Accounts receivable reports track money that is owed to the practice and detail how successful the practice is in collecting the amounts owed. These reports are critical to a practice's financial success. Some reports are run on a daily basis, while others are printed out monthly. In some practices, weekly reports are also reviewed.

DAILY REPORTS

day sheet a report that provides information on practice activities for a twenty-four-hour period.

A **day sheet** is a standard report that provides information on practice activities for a twenty-four-hour period, including the number of patients, number of procedures, and total charges, payments, and adjustments.

Day sheets can be used to reconcile daily bank deposit slips with the payments entered in the practice management program. To reconcile a day, the amount received in the form of checks and cash is compared to the amount listed in the payment section of the day sheet. To close out the day, the amounts must agree. For example, if a deposit of $320.00 consists of $300.00 in patient checks and $20.00 in cash, the amounts listed on the day sheet report should be $300.00 for check payments and $20.00 for cash payments.

Day sheets can also be used to confirm that all patients seen in the office on a given day also have charges. This can be accomplished by assembling the front desk sign-in sheet and an appointment list (printed from the scheduling program) and then comparing these to the day sheet. Each patient on the sign-in sheet and on the appointment list should have a corresponding charge entry on the day sheet.

MONTHLY REPORTS

Practices rely on a number of monthly financial reports to determine the financial health of the practice. For example, practices review productivity reports, usually on a monthly basis. These reports detail the productivity of the practice, broken down by provider. The report lists the total charges billed, the amount that was collected, and the amount that was adjusted. The totals can be compared to previous months or the same month one year earlier. A regular review of these reports ensures that any sudden increase or decrease in income or productivity can be spotted and addressed before it becomes a serious problem.

Other monthly reports that can be helpful in managing accounts receivable include:

- Outstanding copayments.
- Appointments without charges.
- Unbilled charges (not placed on an insurance claim or billed to the patient).

Aging Reports

Aging reports are of particular importance to medical billing specialists. An **aging report** lists the amount of money owed to the practice, organized by the amount of time the money has been owed. Medical practices use aging reports to determine which accounts require follow-up to collect past-due balances. An aging report groups accounts into what are called *aging buckets*: 0–30 days old, 31–60, 61–90, and over 120 days.

aging report a report that lists the amount of money owed to the practice, organized by the amount of time the money has been owed.

In an ideal world, all accounts would fall into the 0–30 bucket. In reality, many accounts are more than thirty days old. Practices do not like to see large dollar amounts in the older buckets since the older the account, the harder it is to collect the money. Insurance companies have deadlines for filing claims. If patients intend to pay what is owed, they usually do so within thirty days of receiving a bill.

Patient Aging Reports   Prompt collection of patient payments has become more important as patients assume a greater share of the costs for their healthcare. Patient copayments and coinsurance are becoming a more substantial source of practice revenue.

A **patient aging report** lists a patient's balance by age, date, and amount of the last payment. Significant patient balances may indicate a problem with billing processes. Are patient statements

patient aging report a report that lists a patient's balance by age, date, and amount of the last payment.

being mailed regularly? Are accounts being moved to collections when appropriate? These and other questions must be asked to determine the cause of the large overdue balances.

Patient accounts that are more than 90 or 120 days outstanding may be turned over to an internal collections group or to an outside collection agency. Account follow-up and collections are the focus of Chapter 10.

Insurance Aging Reports Aging reports are created for payers as well as patients. An **insurance aging report** details how long it takes for claims to be paid. It provides a breakdown of the claims submitted to insurance carriers, sorted by payer. As with patient aging reports, the amounts owed are sorted into buckets of 0–30 days old, 31–60, 61–90, and over 120 days.

insurance aging report a report that lists how long a payer has taken to respond to insurance claims.

The report is used to identify problem payers, or to uncover problems in the claims creation and submission process. Generally, payer accounts should be in the 0–30 bucket or 31–60 bucket, since clean claims are usually processed within thirty days. Accounts past sixty days should be researched to determine the reason for the payment delay. Is the payer slow in paying, or is there a problem with the claim? If a payer is routinely responding to claims ten days later than the claim turnaround time specified in the contract, the situation should be addressed with the payer representative. On the other hand, are claims submitted in a timely manner? Is claim status monitored on a daily basis? Are rejected claims reviewed, corrected, and resubmitted on a regular basis?

9.3 CREATING DAY SHEETS

In Medisoft, there are three types of day sheet reports: patient day sheets, procedure day sheets, and payment day sheets. Options to view or print the three types of day sheets are located on the Reports menu, within the Day Sheets submenu (see Figure 9-12).

PATIENT DAY SHEET

patient day sheet a summary of patient activity on a given day.

At the end of the day, a medical practice often prints a **patient day sheet**, which is a summary of the patient activity on that day (see Figures 9-13a and 9-13b). Medisoft's version of this report lists the procedures for a particular day, grouped by patient, in alphabetical order by chart number. It includes:

- Procedures performed for a particular patient or group of patients.
- Charges, receipts, adjustments, and balances for a particular patient or group of patients.
- A summary of a practice's charges, payments, and adjustments.

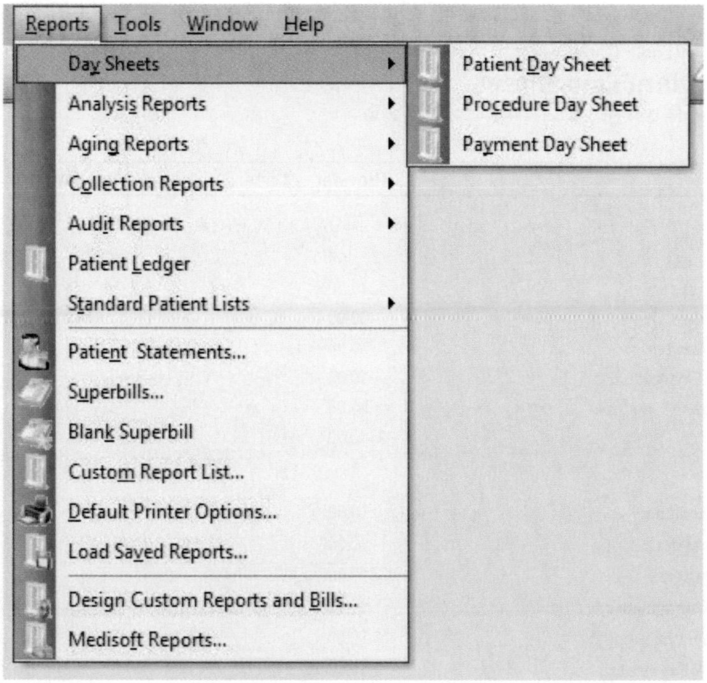

Reports	Tools	Window	Help

Day Sheets ▶ | Patient Day Sheet
Analysis Reports ▶ | Procedure Day Sheet
Aging Reports ▶ | Payment Day Sheet
Collection Reports ▶
Audit Reports ▶
Patient Ledger
Standard Patient Lists ▶

Patient Statements...
Superbills...
Blank Superbill
Custom Report List...
Default Printer Options...
Load Saved Reports...

Design Custom Reports and Bills...
Medisoft Reports...

Figure 9-12 Reports Menu with Day Sheets Submenu Displayed

Family Care Center
Patient Day Sheet
Show all data where the Date From is between 9/4/2018, 9/4/2018

Entry	Date	Document	POS	Description	Provider	Code	Amount
FITZWJO0	**Fitzwilliams, John**						
709	09/04/2018	1408110000	11		2	99211	36.00
710	09/04/2018	1408110000	11		2	84478	29.00
711	09/04/2018	1408110000	11		2	CHVCPAY	-15.00

	Patient Charges	Patient Receipts	Adjustments	Patient Balance
	$65.00	-$15.00	$0.00	$58.00

Entry	Date	Document	POS	Description	Provider	Code	Amount
FITZWSA0	**Fitzwilliams, Sarah**						
712	09/04/2018	1408110000	11		1	90471	15.00
713	09/04/2018	1408110000	11		1	90703	29.00
714	09/04/2018	1408110000	11		1	CHVCPAY	-15.00

	Patient Charges	Patient Receipts	Adjustments	Patient Balance
	$44.00	-$15.00	$0.00	$0.00

Entry	Date	Document	POS	Description	Provider	Code	Amount
GARDIJO0	**Gardiner, John**						
715	09/04/2018	1408110000	11		1	99211	36.00
716	09/04/2018	1408110000	11		1	OHCCPAY	-20.00

	Patient Charges	Patient Receipts	Adjustments	Patient Balance
	$36.00	-$20.00	$0.00	$0.00

Entry	Date	Document	POS	Description	Provider	Code	Amount
KLEINRA0	**Klein, Randall**						
768	09/04/2018	1408110000	11		2	99212	54.00
769	09/04/2018	1408110000	11		2	29540	121.50
770	09/04/2018	1408110000	11		2	99070	20.00

	Patient Charges	Patient Receipts	Adjustments	Patient Balance
	$195.50	$0.00	$0.00	$0.00

Figure 9-13a Page 1 of a Patient Day Sheet Report

Family Care Center

Patient Day Sheet

Show all data where the Date From is between 9/4/2018, 9/4/2018

Entry	Date	Document	POS	Description	Provider	Code	Amount

Total # Patients	4
Total # Procedures	8
Total Procedure Charges	$340.50
Total Product Charges	$0.00
Total Inside Lab Charges	$0.00
Total Outside Lab Charges	$0.00
Total Billing Charges	$0.00
Total Charges	$340.50
Total Insurance Payments	$0.00 *
Total Cash Copayments	$0.00
Total Check Copayments	-$50.00
Total Credit Card Copayments	$0.00
Total Patient Cash Payments	$0.00
Total Patient Check Payments	$0.00
Total Credit Card Payments	$0.00
Total Receipts	-$50.00
Total Credit Adjustments	$0.00
Total Debit Adjustments	$0.00
Total Insurance Debit Adjustments	$0.00
Total Insurance Credit Adjustments	$0.00
Total Insurance Withholds	$0.00
Total Adjustments	$0.00
Net Effect on Accounts Receivable	$290.50

*Total Insurance Payments include Insurance Takeback Adjustments of $0.00

Figure 9-13b Page 2 of a Patient Day Sheet Report

EXERCISE 9-1 PRINTING A PATIENT DAY SHEET

Connect users: go to http://connect.mheducation.com to complete this exercise! Some steps may differ from what is listed here, so be sure to refer to the steps listed in Demo and Practice Modes for guidance.

connect

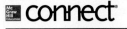

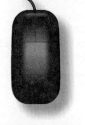

Print a patient day sheet report for October 1, 2018.

Date: October 1, 2018

Note: It is not necessary to change the Medisoft Program Date before each exercise in this chapter as Medisoft uses the Windows System Date as the default date when creating reports. You will, however, need to enter the date(s) listed at the beginning of each exercise in the Date From date range boxes as you create each report.

1. Start Medisoft and restore the data from your last work session.
2. On the Reports menu, click Day Sheets and then Patient Day Sheet. The Print Report Where? dialog box appears.
3. Accept the default selection to preview the report on screen. Click the Start button. The Search dialog box is displayed.

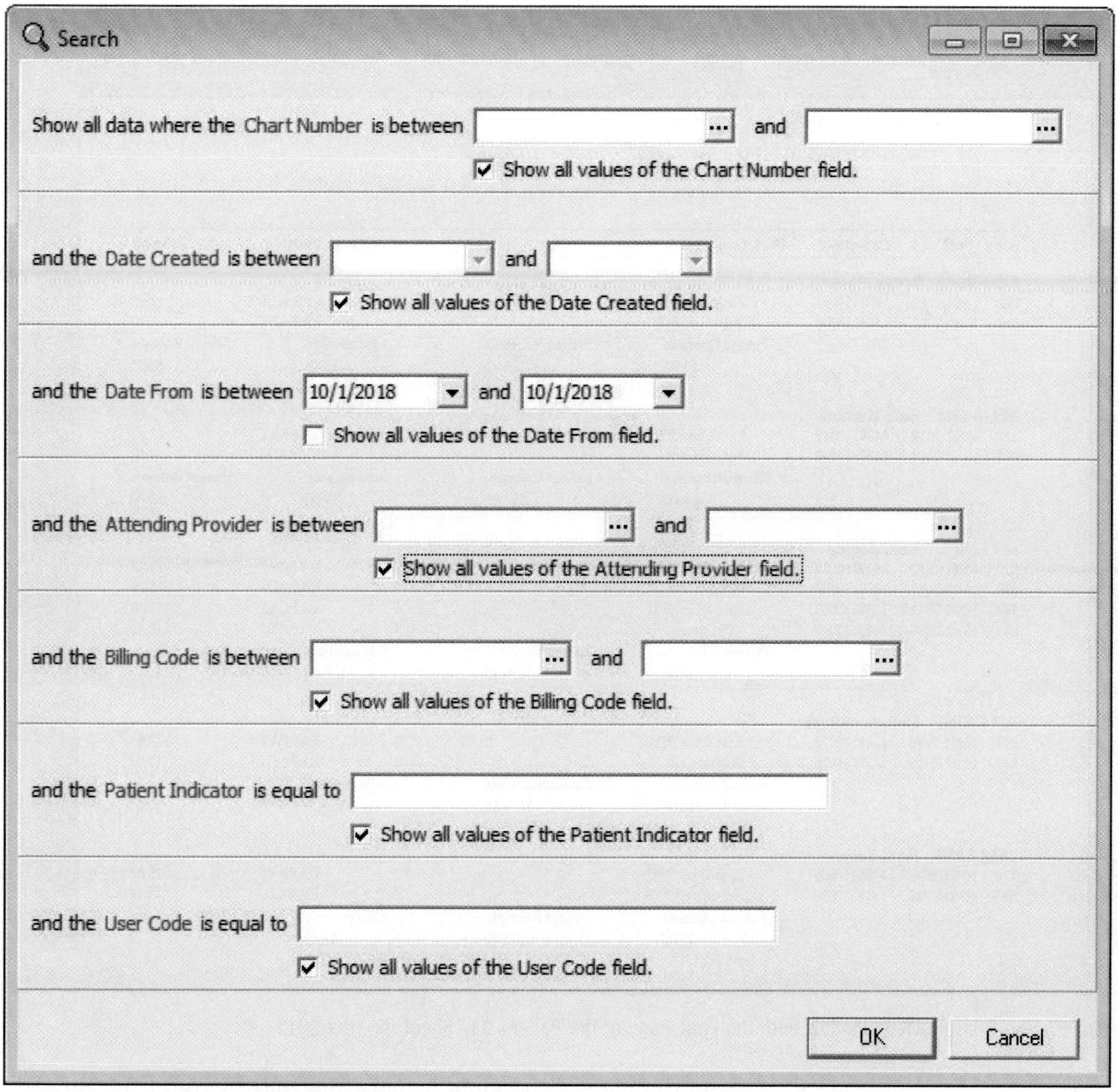

Search

Show all data where the Chart Number is between [ ] ··· and [ ] ···

☑ Show all values of the Chart Number field.

and the Date Created is between [▾] and [▾]

☑ Show all values of the Date Created field.

and the Date From is between [10/1/2018 ▾] and [10/1/2018 ▾]

☐ Show all values of the Date From field.

and the Attending Provider is between [ ] ··· and [ ] ···

☑ Show all values of the Attending Provider field.

and the Billing Code is between [ ] ··· and [ ] ···

☑ Show all values of the Billing Code field.

and the Patient Indicator is equal to [ ]

☑ Show all values of the Patient Indicator field.

and the User Code is equal to [ ]

☑ Show all values of the User Code field.

[OK] [Cancel]

Figure 9-14   Search Dialog Box with Entries

4. Leave the Chart Number fields blank.

5. Leave the Date Created fields blank.

6. Click in the first Date From box and then enter *10012018* in both Date From boxes, or use the pop-up calendar to change the date to October 1, 2018. Leave all other fields in the Search box blank. This will select data for all patients and attending providers for October 1, 2018. Your screen should look like the dialog box in Figure 9-14.

7. Click the OK button. The patient day sheet report is displayed in the Print Preview window (see Figure 9-15).

8. If necessary, use the scroll bar to view additional entries on the first page of the report.

9. Notice at the top of the Print Preview window that the triangle next to the number 1 is bright blue. This indicates that there are more than one page in the report. Click the triangle just to the right of 1 to advance to the second page of the report.

Family Care Center

Patient Day Sheet

Show all data where the Date From is between 10/1/2018, 10/1/2018

Entry	Date	Document	POS	Description		Provider	Code	Amount
ARLENSU0	**Arlen, Susan**							
832	10/01/2018	1408110000		East Ohio PPO		5	EAPPAY	-28.60
833	10/01/2018	1408110000		Adjustment		5	EAPADJ	-5.40
				Patient Charges	Patient Receipts	Adjustments		Patient Balance
				$0.00	-$28.60	-$5.40		$0.00
BELLHER0	**Bell, Herbert**							
834	10/01/2018	1408110000		East Ohio PPO		2	EAPPAY	-12.40
835	10/01/2018	1408110000		Adjustment		2	EAPADJ	-3.60
				Patient Charges	Patient Receipts	Adjustments		Patient Balance
				$0.00	-$12.40	-$3.60		$0.00
BELLJAN0	**Bell, Janine**							
838	10/01/2018	1408110000		East Ohio PPO		3	EAPPAY	-44.80
839	10/01/2018	1408110000		Adjustment		3	EAPADJ	-7.20
840	10/01/2018	1408110000		East Ohio PPO		3	EAPPAY	-111.60
841	10/01/2018	1408110000		Adjustment		3	EAPADJ	-12.40
				Patient Charges	Patient Receipts	Adjustments		Patient Balance
				$0.00	-$156.40	-$19.60		$0.00
BELLJON0	**Bell, Jonathan**							
842	10/01/2018	1408110000		East Ohio PPO		1	EAPPAY	-179.80
843	10/01/2018	1408110000		Adjustment		1	EAPADJ	-22.20
				Patient Charges	Patient Receipts	Adjustments		Patient Balance
				$0.00	-$179.80	-$22.20		$0.00
BELLSAM0	**Bell, Samuel**							
836	10/01/2018	1408110000		East Ohio PPO		2	EAPPAY	-28.60
837	10/01/2018	1408110000		Adjustment		2	EAPADJ	-5.40
				Patient Charges	Patient Receipts	Adjustments		Patient Balance
				$0.00	-$28.60	-$5.40		$0.00

Page 1 of 3

Figure 9-15 The Print Preview Window with the First Page of the Patient Day Sheet for 10/1/2018

10. Follow the same procedure to view the third page of the report.

11. Click the Print button and then click the OK button to print the report.

12. Click the red Close box at the top right of the window to exit the Print Preview window. **CiMO**

✓ **You have completed Exercise 9-1.**

PROCEDURE DAY SHEET

procedure day sheet a report that lists all the procedures performed on a particular day, in numerical order.

A **procedure day sheet** lists all procedures performed on a particular day and gives the dates, patients, document numbers, places of service, debits, and credits relating to them (see Figure 9-16). Procedures are listed in numerical order.

Procedure day sheets are printed by clicking Day Sheets and then Procedure Day Sheet on the Reports menu. The same Search dialog

Family Care Center

Procedure Day Sheet

Show all data where the Date From is between 9/4/2018, 9/4/2018

Entry	Date	Chart	Name	Document	POS	Debits	Credits
29540							
769	9/4/2018	KLEINRA0	Klein, Randall	1408110000	11	121.50	
		Total of 29540			Quantity: 1	$121.50	$0.00
84478							
710	9/4/2018	FITZWJO0	Fitzwilliams, John	1408110000	11	29.00	
		Total of 84478			Quantity: 1	$29.00	$0.00
90471							
712	9/4/2018	FITZWSA0	Fitzwilliams, Sarah	1408110000	11	15.00	
		Total of 90471			Quantity: 1	$15.00	$0.00
90703							
713	9/4/2018	FITZWSA0	Fitzwilliams, Sarah	1408110000	11	29.00	
		Total of 90703			Quantity: 1	$29.00	$0.00
99070							
770	9/4/2018	KLEINRA0	Klein, Randall	1408110000	11	20.00	
		Total of 99070			Quantity: 1	$20.00	$0.00
99211							
709	9/4/2018	FITZWJO0	Fitzwilliams, John	1408110000	11	36.00	
715	9/4/2018	GARDIJO0	Gardiner, John	1408110000	11	36.00	
		Total of 99211			Quantity: 2	$72.00	$0.00
99212							
768	9/4/2018	KLEINRA0	Klein, Randall	1408110000	11	54.00	
		Total of 99212			Quantity: 1	$54.00	$0.00
CHVCPAY							
711	9/4/2018	FITZWJO0	Fitzwilliams, John	1408110000	11		-15.00
714	9/4/2018	FITZWSA0	Fitzwilliams, Sarah	1408110000	11		-15.00
		Total of CHVCPAY			Quantity: 2	$0.00	-$30.00
OHCCPAY							
716	9/4/2018	GARDIJO0	Gardiner, John	1408110000	11		-20.00
		Total of OHCCPAY			Quantity: 1	$0.00	-$20.00
					Total of Codes:	$340.50	-$50.00
					Balance:	$290.50	

Figure 9-16 Procedure Day Sheet

box used for a patient day sheet is displayed, except that a range of procedure codes rather than patients can be selected. A procedure day sheet will be generated only for data that meet the selection criteria. If any box is left blank, all values are included in the report. The report can be previewed on the screen, printed, or exported to a file.

PAYMENT DAY SHEET

A **payment day sheet** lists all payments received on a particular day, organized by provider (see Figure 9-17). It is printed by clicking

payment day sheet a report that lists all payments received on a particular day, organized by provider.

Family Care Center

Payment Day Sheet

Show all data where the Date From is between 9/4/2018, 9/4/2018

Entry	Date	Document	Description	Chart	Code	Amount
1	**Yan, Katherine**					
714	9/4/2018	1408110000		FITZWSA0	CHVCPAY	-15.00
716	9/4/2018	1408110000		GARDIJO0	OHCCPAY	-20.00
			Count: 2		**Provider Total**	-$35.00
2	**Rudner, John**					
711	9/4/2018	1408110000		FITZWJO0	CHVCPAY	-15.00
			Count: 1		**Provider Total**	-$15.00

Report Totals

Total # Payments 3

Total Payments -50.00

Figure 9-17   Payment Day Sheet

Day Sheets and then Payment Day Sheet on the Reports menu. The same Search dialog box is displayed, but with fewer data fields.

A payment day sheet will be generated only for data that meet the selection criteria. If any box is left blank, all values for that box are included in the report. Again, the report can be previewed on the screen, printed, or exported to a file.

9.4 CREATING ANALYSIS REPORTS

Medisoft includes a number of standard reports that provide information about practice productivity, referral sources, unapplied payments, insurance eligibility, and electronic claims. These reports are known as analysis reports. The Analysis Reports submenu is shown in Figure 9-18. The following paragraphs provide a description of each report. (*Note:* Not all reports can be created in student exercises because data have not been sent to actual insurance carriers and patients.)

BILLING/PAYMENT STATUS REPORT

The billing/payment status report lists the status of all transactions that have responsible insurance carriers, showing who has paid and who has not been billed (see Figures 9-19a and 9-19b). The report is in a column format sorted

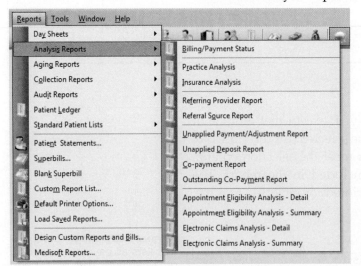

Figure 9-18   The Analysis Reports Submenu

first by chart number and then by case. Every chart number listed shows a patient balance and any unapplied payments or unapplied adjustments. Information in this report can be used by practices to determine whether billing charges can be applied to a patient account.

Family Care Center
Billing/Payment Status Report
Show all data where the Patient Reference Balance is between 0.01,999999999999.99
Show all data where the Date From is between 10/1/2018, 10/31/2018

Date	Document	Procedure	Amount	Policy 1	Policy 2	Policy 3	Guarantor	Adjustments	Balance
BATTIAN0	Anthony Battistuta	(614)500-3619							
Case 25	1: Medicare				(215)599-0000				
	2:								
	3:								
10/25/2018	1009280000	82947	25.00	Not Billed	0.00*	0.00*	Not Billed	0.00	25.00
10/25/2018	1009280000	99212	54.00	Not Billed	0.00*	0.00*	Not Billed	0.00	54.00
							SubTotal:		79.00
						Unapplied Payments and Adjustments:			0.00
							Case Balance:		79.00
						Patient Reference Balance:			79.00
BROOKLA0	Lawana Brooks	(614)027-4242							
Case 27	1: East Ohio PPO				(419)444-1505				
	2:								
	3:								
10/26/2018	1408110000	73600	96.00	Not Billed	0.00*	0.00*	Not Billed	0.00	96.00
10/26/2018	1408110000	99212	54.00	Not Billed	0.00*	0.00*	-20.00	0.00	34.00
							SubTotal:		130.00
						Unapplied Payments and Adjustments:			0.00
							Case Balance:		130.00
						Patient Reference Balance:			130.00
FITZWJO0	John Fitzwilliams	(614)002-1111							
Case 7	1: ChampVA				(614)024-7000				
	2:								
	3:								
10/1/2018	1810010000	82270	19.00	Not Billed	0.00*	0.00*	Not Billed	0.00	19.00
10/1/2018	1810010000	99212	54.00	Not Billed	0.00*	0.00*	-15.00	0.00	39.00
							SubTotal:		58.00
						Unapplied Payments and Adjustments:			-50.00
							Case Balance:		8.00
						Patient Reference Balance:			58.00
GARCISA0	Santiago Garcia	(614)769-4262							
Case 64	1: East Ohio PPO				(419)444-1505				
	2:								
	3:								
10/2/2018	1412050000	90656	25.00	Not Billed	0.00*	0.00*	-5.00	0.00	20.00
							SubTotal:		20.00
						Unapplied Payments and Adjustments:			0.00
							Case Balance:		20.00
						Patient Reference Balance:			20.00

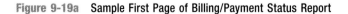
Figure 9-19a Sample First Page of Billing/Payment Status Report

Family Care Center
Billing/Payment Status Report
Show all data where the Patient Reference Balance is between 0.01,999999999999.99
Show all data where the Date From is between 10/1/2018, 10/31/2018

Date	Document	Procedure	Amount	Policy 1	Policy 2	Policy 3	Guarantor	Adjustments	Balance
WRIGHLI0	**Lisa**	**Wright (614)555-7059**							
Case 68	1:	Blue Cross/Blue Shield		(614)024-9000					
	2:								
	3:								
10/1/2018	1810010000	71020	112.00	-89.60*	0.00*	0.00*	12/26/2014	0.00	22.40
10/1/2018	1810010000	99203	120.00	-96.00*	0.00*	0.00*	12/26/2014	0.00	24.00
								SubTotal:	46.40
						Unapplied Payments and Adjustments:			0.00
								Case Balance:	46.40
							Patient Reference Balance:		46.40
ZAPATKR0	**Kristin**	**Zapata (614)033-0044**							
Case 60	1:	Blue Cross/Blue Shield		(614)024-9000					
	2:								
	3:								
10/1/2018	1810010000	NSFFEE	35.00	0.00*	0.00*	0.00*	12/26/2014	0.00	35.00
								SubTotal:	35.00
						Unapplied Payments and Adjustments:			247.50
								Case Balance:	282.50
							Patient Reference Balance:		282.50
								Report Balance:	$1,904.08

Figure 9-19b Sample Last Page of Billing/Payment Status Report

PRACTICE ANALYSIS REPORT

practice analysis report a report that analyzes the revenue of a practice for a specified period of time.

Medisoft's **practice analysis report** analyzes the revenue of a practice for a specified period of time, usually a month or a year (see Figures 9-20a and 9-20b). The report can be used to generate medical practice financial statements. It also can be used for profit analysis. The summary at the end of the report breaks down the information into total charges, total payments and copayments, and total adjustments.

EXERCISE 9-2

SAVING A PRACTICE ANALYSIS REPORT AS A PDF FILE

Connect users: go to http://connect.mheducation.com to complete this exercise! Some steps may differ from what is listed here, so be sure to refer to the steps listed in Demo and Practice Modes for guidance.

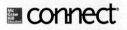

Print a practice analysis report for October 2018. **Remember to enter the exercise dates in the *Date From* fields.**

Date: October 1–31, 2018

1. On the Reports menu, click Analysis Reports and then Practice Analysis. The Print Report Where? dialog box appears.

2. Accept the default option to preview the report and click the Start button. The Search dialog box is displayed.

3. Leave the Code 1 fields blank.

4. Enter **10012018** in the first Date From box and **10312018** in the second. This will select data for the month of October 2018.

5. Click the OK button. The Print Preview window opens, displaying the report.

6. Click the Print icon in the Print Preview toolbar. The Print dialog box is displayed.

7. Click the Print to File box.

8. Select PDF File from the drop-down list in the Type field.

9. Click the Lookup button located to the right of the Where field. The Save As dialog box opens.

10. Select a location for the file in the Save in field.

11. Enter a name in the File name field.

12. Click the Save button. You are returned to the Print dialog box.

13. Click the OK button to save the report as a PDF file.

14. Click the Close button to close the Print Preview window. **ciMc**

✓ **You have completed Exercise 9-2.**

Family Care Center
Practice Analysis
Show all data where the Date From is between 9/1/2018, 9/30/2018

Code	Description	Amount	Units	Average	Cost	Net
02	Patient payment, check	-299.50	2	-149.75	0.00	-299.50
29540	Strapping, ankle	121.50	1	121.50	0.00	121.50
50390	Aspiration of renal cyst by needle	551.00	1	551.00	0.00	551.00
73510	Hip x-ray, complete, two views	124.00	1	124.00	0.00	124.00
84478	Triglycerides test	29.00	1	29.00	0.00	29.00
90471	Immunization administration	15.00	1	15.00	0.00	15.00
90703	Tetanus injection	29.00	1	29.00	0.00	29.00
92516	Facial nerve function studies	210.00	1	210.00	0.00	210.00
93000	Electrocardiogram--ECG with interpre	84.00	1	84.00	0.00	84.00
99070	Supplies and materials provided	20.00	1	20.00	0.00	20.00
99201	OF--new patient, minimal	66.00	1	66.00	0.00	66.00
99211	OF--established patient, minimal	144.00	4	36.00	0.00	144.00
99212	OF--established patient, low	324.00	6	54.00	0.00	324.00
99213	OF--established patient, detailed	216.00	3	72.00	0.00	216.00
99214	OF--established patient, moderate	105.00	1	105.00	0.00	105.00
99394	Preventive est., 12-17 years	222.00	1	222.00	0.00	222.00
AARPAY	AARP Payment	-19.57	3	-6.52	0.00	-19.57
BCBDED	BCBS Deductible	0.00	1	0.00	0.00	0.00
BCBPAY	BCBS Payment	-168.00	2	-84.00	0.00	-168.00
CHVCPAY	ChampVA Copayment	-30.00	2	-15.00	0.00	-30.00
EAPADJ	East Ohio PPO Adjustment	-12.60	2	-6.30	0.00	-12.60
EAPCPAY	East Ohio PPO Copayment	-160.00	8	-20.00	0.00	-160.00
EAPPAY	East Ohio PPO Payment	-73.40	2	-36.70	0.00	-73.40
MCDADJ	Medicaid Adjustment	-479.95	2	-239.97	0.00	-479.95
MCDCPAY	Medicaid Copayment	-10.00	1	-10.00	0.00	-10.00
MCDPAY	Medicaid Payment	-127.05	2	-63.52	0.00	-127.05
MEDADJ	Medicare Adjustment	-212.73	6	-35.46	0.00	-212.73
MEDPAY	Medicare Payment	-209.42	7	-29.92	0.00	-209.42
OHCADJ	OhioCare HMO Adjustment	-50.00	2	-25.00	0.00	-50.00
OHCCPAY	OhioCare HMO Copayment	-40.00	2	-20.00	0.00	-40.00

Figure 9-20a Page 1 of a Sample Practice Analysis Report

Family Care Center
Practice Analysis
Show all data where the Date From is between 9/1/2018, 9/30/2018

Code	Description		Amount	Units	Average	Cost	Net
		Total Procedure Charges					$2,260.50
		Total Global Surgical Procedures					$0.00
		Total Product Charges					$0.00
		Total Inside Lab Charges					$0.00
		Total Outside Lab Charges					$0.00
		Total Billing Charges					$0.00
		Total Insurance Payments					-$597.44
		Total Cash Copayments					$0.00
		Total Check Copayments					-$240.00
		Total Credit Card Copayments					$0.00
		Total Patient Cash Payments					$0.00
		Total Patient Check Payments					-$299.50
		Total Credit Card Payments					$0.00
		Total Debit Adjustments					$0.00
		Total Credit Adjustments					$0.00
		Total Insurance Debit Adjustments					$0.00
		Total Insurance Credit Adjustments					-$755.28
		Total Insurance Withholds					$0.00
		Net Effect on Accounts Receivable					$368.28

Practice Totals

Total # Procedures		63
Total Charges		$5,033.50
Total Payments		-$2,398.28
Total Adjustments		-$731.14
Accounts Receivable		$1,904.08

Figure 9-20b   Page 2 of a Sample Practice Analysis Report

INSURANCE ANALYSIS REPORT

The insurance analysis report tracks charges, insurance payments received during a specified period, and copayments applied to accounts that include those procedures. It is usually printed at the end of the month. The amount listed as the outstanding balance displays the total charges, subtracting the full amount of the charge if the insurance payment was made.

REFERRING PROVIDER REPORT

The referring provider report enables a practice to determine the origins of revenue derived from providers who have referred patients to the practice. The report lists the percentage of total income that was generated by referring providers.

REFERRAL SOURCE REPORT

The referral source report tracks the source of referrals that are not from other medical offices or providers, such as referrals from established patients.

UNAPPLIED PAYMENT/ADJUSTMENT REPORT

The unapplied payment/adjustment report lists payments or adjustments that have not been fully applied. Information about the payment or adjustment includes the case, document number, posting date, code, code description, transaction amount, and unapplied amount.

UNAPPLIED DEPOSIT REPORT

The unapplied deposit report lists deposits that have unapplied amounts. The report includes the date, code, payer name, payer type, deposit amount, and unapplied amount.

CO-PAYMENT REPORT

This report lists patients who have copayment transactions. It shows the amount paid, how much was applied, and how much, if any, was left unapplied.

OUTSTANDING CO-PAYMENT REPORT

This report shows patients who have outstanding copayment transactions. The report shows the copayment amount expected, the actual amount paid, and the amount due.

APPOINTMENT ELIGIBILITY ANALYSIS—DETAIL AND SUMMARY

These two reports display the eligibility of patients for insurance coverage. The reports list the appointment date and time, the name, the provider name, the reason code, and the status of insurance eligibility. The report also indicates the number of appointments that were checked for eligibility. These reports are used to document eligibility verification for Meaningful Use requirements.

ELECTRONIC CLAIMS ANALYSIS—DETAIL AND SUMMARY

The electronic claims analysis reports display the billing date, insurance carrier, claim number, patient chart and name, status of the claim, and whether it is to be filed electronically or by paper. The reports also show a summary of the claims, with total not billed, total electronic and paper, and the percentage filed electronically. These reports are used to document electronic claim submission for Meaningful Use requirements.

patient ledger a report that lists the financial activity in each patient's account.

A **patient ledger** lists the transaction details of a patient's account, including charges, payments, and adjustments (see Figures 9-21a and 9-21b). The information it provides is especially useful when there is a question about a patient's account.

Family Care Center
Patient Account Ledger
As of October 31, 2018
Show all data where the Date From is between 1/1/1980, 10/31/2018

Entry	Date	POS	Description	Procedure	Document	Provider	Amount
ARLENSU0	**Susan Arlen**			(614)315-2233			
	Last Payment: -28.60		On: 10/1/2018				
695	09/03/2018	11		99212	1408110000	5	54.00
696	09/03/2018	11		EAPCPAY	1408110000	5	-20.00
832	10/01/2018		East Ohio PPO	EAPPAY	1408110000	5	-28.60
833	10/01/2018		Adjustment	EAPADJ	1408110000	5	-5.40
						Patient Total:	0.00
BATTIAN0	**Anthony Battistuta**			(614)500-3619			
	Last Payment: 0.00		On:				
425	10/25/2018	11		99212	1009280000	4	54.00
426	10/25/2018	11		82947	1009280000	4	25.00
						Patient Total:	79.00
BELLHER0	**Herbert Bell**			(614)030-1111			
	Last Payment: -12.40		On: 10/1/2018				
694	09/03/2018	11		EAPCPAY	1408110000	2	-20.00
693	09/03/2018	11		99211	1408110000	2	36.00
834	10/01/2018		East Ohio PPO	EAPPAY	1408110000	2	-12.40
835	10/01/2018		Adjustment	EAPADJ	1408110000	2	-3.60
						Patient Total:	0.00
BELLJAN0	**Janine Bell**			(614)030-1111			
	Last Payment: -156.40		On: 10/1/2018				
697	09/03/2018	11		99213	1408110000	3	72.00
698	09/03/2018	11		73510	1408110000	3	124.00
699	09/03/2018	11		EAPCPAY	1408110000	3	-20.00
838	10/01/2018		East Ohio PPO	EAPPAY	1408110000	3	-44.80
839	10/01/2018		Adjustment	EAPADJ	1408110000	3	-7.20
840	10/01/2018		East Ohio PPO	EAPPAY	1408110000	3	-111.60
841	10/01/2018		Adjustment	EAPADJ	1408110000	3	-12.40
						Patient Total:	0.00
BELLJON0	**Jonathan Bell**			(614)030-1111			
	Last Payment: -179.80		On: 10/1/2018				
700	09/03/2018	11		99394	1408110000	1	222.00
701	09/03/2018	11		EAPCPAY	1408110000	1	-20.00
842	10/01/2018		East Ohio PPO	EAPPAY	1408110000	1	-179.80
843	10/01/2018		Adjustment	EAPADJ	1408110000	1	-22.20
						Patient Total:	0.00
BELLSAM0	**Samuel Bell**			(614)030-1111			
	Last Payment: -28.60		On: 10/1/2018				
702	09/03/2018	11		99212	1408110000	2	54.00
703	09/03/2018	11		EAPCPAY	1408110000	2	-20.00
836	10/01/2018		East Ohio PPO	EAPPAY	1408110000	2	-28.60
837	10/01/2018		Adjustment	EAPADJ	1408110000	2	-5.40
						Patient Total:	0.00

Figure 9-21a First Page of Patient Account Ledger Report

Family Care Center
Patient Account Ledger
As of October 31, 2018

Show all data where the Date From is between 1/1/1980, 10/31/2018

Entry	Date	POS	Description	Procedure	Document	Provider	Amount
ZAPATKR0	**Kristin Zapata**			(614)033-0044			
	Last Payment: -247.50		On: 9/19/2018				
580	08/27/2018	11		99385	0803270000	1	247.50
766	09/08/2018		#23451234 Blue Cross/Blue Shie	BCBPAY	0803270000	1	0.00
767	09/08/2018		Carrier 1 Deductible -$247.50	BCBDED	0803270000	1	0.00
791	09/19/2018	11		02	1408110000	1	-247.50
822	10/01/2018	11		NSFFEE	1810010000	1	35.00
823	10/01/2018	11	Returned Check	NSF	1810010000	1	247.50
						Patient Total:	282.50
						Ledger Total:	$2,215.12

Figure 9-21b Last Page of Patient Account Ledger Report

The patient account ledger report is created by clicking Patient Ledger on the Reports menu. The Print Report Where? dialog box is displayed. After the preview, print, or export selection is made, the Search dialog box is displayed, as it is with the other reports. It provides options to select by chart numbers, patient reference balances, dates, attending providers, billing codes, and patient indicators. A patient account ledger is generated only for data that meet the selection criteria.

PRINTING A PATIENT ACCOUNT LEDGER   EXERCISE 9-3

Print a patient account ledger for October 2018 for patients whose last names begin with the letters *R* through *Z*.

Date: October 1–October 31, 2018

1. On the Reports menu, click Patient Ledger. The Print Report Where? dialog box is displayed.

2. Select the choice to send the report to the printer and then click Start. The Search box is displayed.

3. In the selection area for Chart Number, rather than select all values of the Chart Number field, you will use the Lookup button to select a range of chart numbers. Click in the Show all values of the Chart Number field box to remove the check mark. Then click the Lookup button that is located to the right of the first Chart Number selection box (see Figure 9-22). A portion of the Lookup dialog box for the Chart Number fields is pictured in Figure 9-23.

Connect users: go to http://connect.mheducation.com to complete this exercise! Some steps may differ from what is listed here, so be sure to refer to the steps listed in Demo and Practice Modes for guidance.

Search
Show all data where the Chart Number is between
and
Show all values of the Chart Number field.

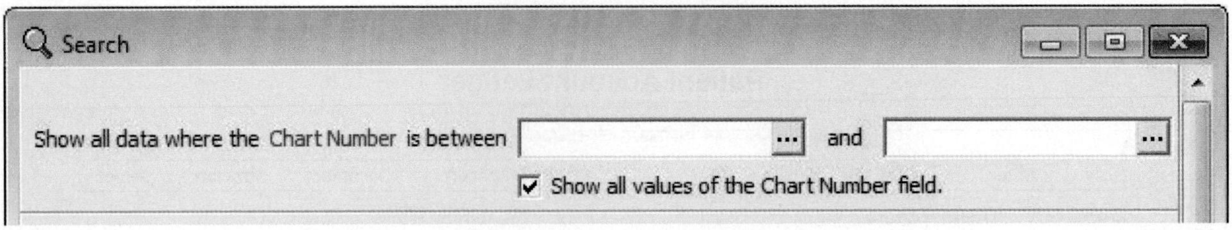

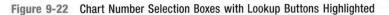

Figure 9-22 Chart Number Selection Boxes with Lookup Buttons Highlighted

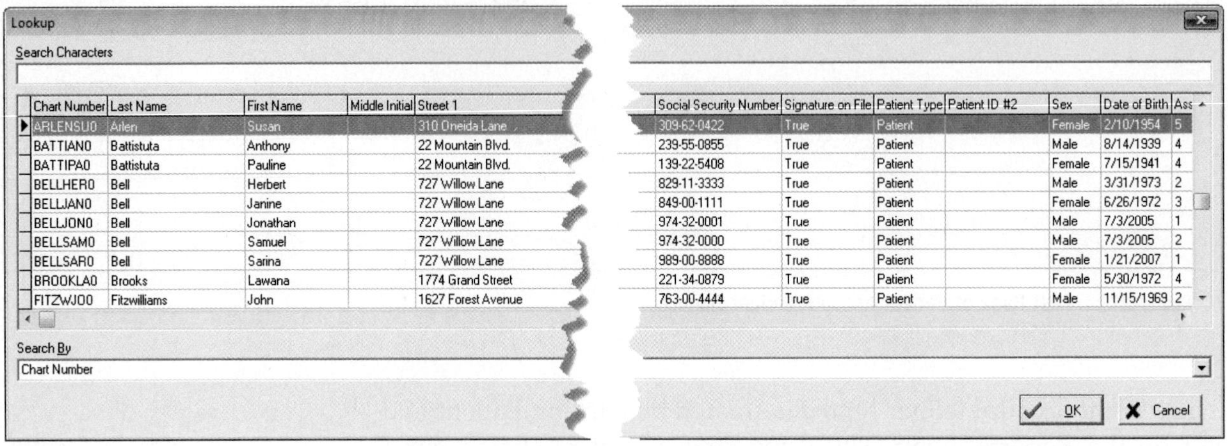

Lookup
Search Characters
Chart Number | Last Name | First Name | Middle Initial | Street 1
Social Security Number | Signature on File | Patient Type | Patient ID #2 | Sex | Date of Birth
ARLENSU0 Arlen Susan 310 Oneida Lane 309-62-0422 True Patient Female 2/10/1954 5
BATTIAN0 Battistuta Anthony 22 Mountain Blvd. 239-55-0855 True Patient Male 8/14/1939 4
BATTIPA0 Battistuta Pauline 22 Mountain Blvd. 139-22-5408 True Patient Female 7/15/1941 4
BELLHER0 Bell Herbert 727 Willow Lane 829-11-3333 True Patient Male 3/31/1973 2
BELLJAN0 Bell Janine 727 Willow Lane 849-00-1111 True Patient Female 6/26/1972 3
BELLJON0 Bell Jonathan 727 Willow Lane 974-32-0001 True Patient Male 7/3/2005 1
BELLSAM0 Bell Samuel 727 Willow Lane 974-32-0000 True Patient Male 7/3/2005 2
BELLSAR0 Bell Sarina 727 Willow Lane 989-00-8888 True Patient Female 1/21/2007 1
BROOKLA0 Brooks Lawana 1774 Grand Street 221-34-0879 True Patient Female 5/30/1972 4
FITZWJO0 Fitzwilliams John 1627 Forest Avenue 763-00-4444 True Patient Male 11/15/1969 2
Search By
Chart Number
OK
Cancel

Figure 9-23 Lookup Dialog Box for Chart Number Selection Boxes

4. In the Search Characters field in the Lookup dialog box, key ***R***. Notice that the program moves to RAMOSMA0, the first chart number that begins with the letter *R*. Click the OK button at the lower-right corner of the dialog box to accept the chart number selection. The Lookup box disappears and you are returned to the Search dialog box. Notice that the chart number for the patient you selected in the Lookup box is now in the first Chart Number selection field.
5. Click the Lookup button in the second Chart Number selection field. The Lookup box appears. Key ***Z*** in the Search Characters box. The chart for Kristin Zapata is selected. Click the OK button to accept the selection.
6. Now you need to enter the dates. Click the first Date From field and enter ***10012018***.
7. Click the second Date From field and enter ***10312018***. Your Search box should look like Figure 9-24.
8. Click the OK button.
9. The Print dialog box for your printer appears. Click OK.
10. The report is sent to the printer. CiMO

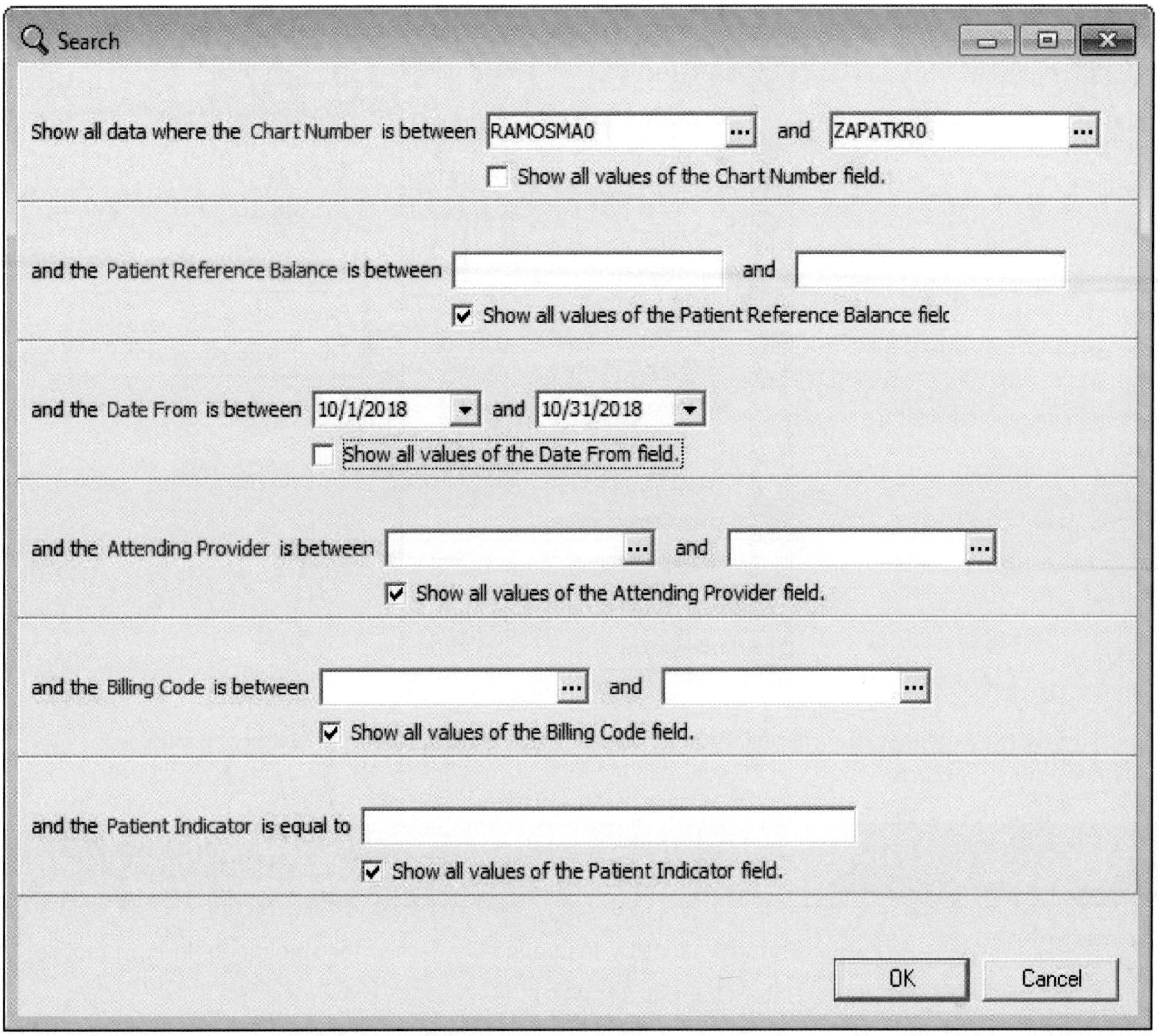

Figure 9-24   Search Dialog Box with Chart Number and Date From Selection Boxes Complete

✓ **You have completed Exercise 9-3.**

9.6 CREATING STANDARD PATIENT LIST REPORTS

Medisoft includes several convenient reports for identifying patients by diagnosis or insurance carrier. These reports are accessed via the Standard Patient Lists submenu on the Reports menu (see Figure 9-25).

The Patient by Diagnosis report lists diagnosis code, chart number, patient name, age, attending provider, facility, and date of last visit. The Patient by Insurance Carrier report lists patients sorted by provider or facility, and then by their insurance carrier.

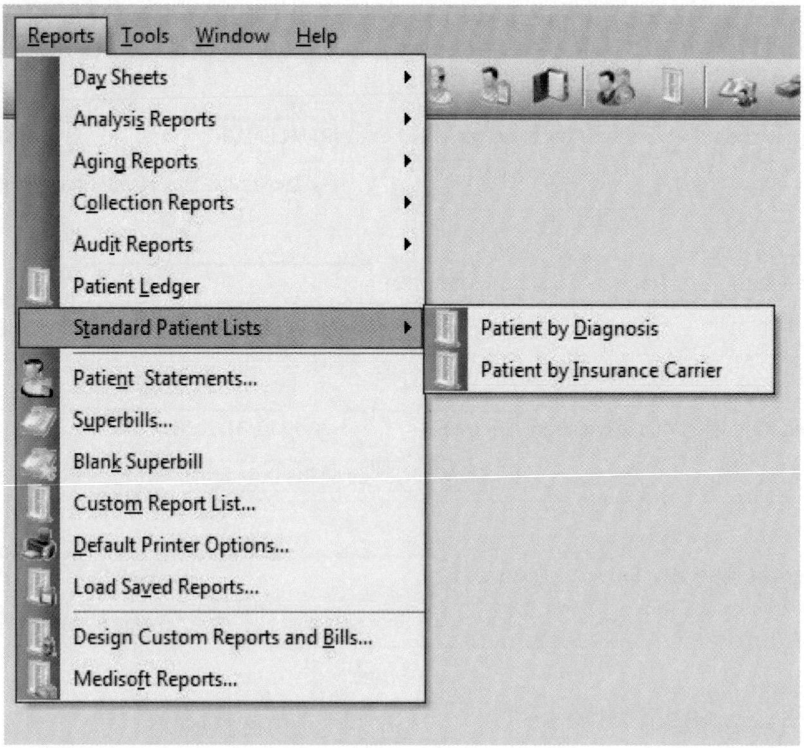

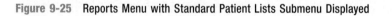

Reports
Tools
Window
Help
Day Sheets
Analysis Reports
Aging Reports
Collection Reports
Audit Reports
Patient Ledger
Standard Patient Lists
Patient Statements...
Superbills...
Blank Superbill
Custom Report List...
Default Printer Options...
Load Saved Reports...
Design Custom Reports and Bills...
Medisoft Reports...
Patient by Diagnosis
Patient by Insurance Carrier

Figure 9-25 Reports Menu with Standard Patient Lists Submenu Displayed

EXERCISE 9-4 PRINTING A PATIENT BY INSURANCE CARRIER LIST

Connect users: go to http://connect.mheducation.com to complete this exercise! Some steps may differ from what is listed here, so be sure to refer to the steps listed in Demo and Practice Modes for guidance.

connect

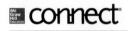

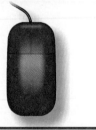

Print a Patient by Insurance Carrier list for all patients in the practice.

Date: October 31, 2018

1. On the Reports menu, click Standard Patient Lists and then Patient by Insurance Carrier. The Print Report Where? dialog box is displayed. Make the selection to send the report to the printer and then click the Start button.
2. Accept the Show all values of the Code field entry in the Search box. Click the OK button.
3. The Print dialog box for your printer appears. Click OK.
4. The report is sent to the printer.

✓ **You have completed Exercise 9-4.**

9.7 NAVIGATING IN MEDISOFT REPORTS

In addition to the standard reports already discussed, Medisoft also contains more than one hundred other reports. To access these additional reports, select Medisoft Reports on the Reports menu (see Figure 9-26) or click the shortcut button on the toolbar (see Figure 9-27).

The Medisoft Reports application features its own main window that contains menu items and a toolbar with shortcut buttons (see Figure 9-28).

The window is divided into two sections: an All Folders area and a Contents of 'All Folders' area. The All Folders section displays the reports directory and the subfolders in the directory. The Contents of 'All Folders' section lists the individual reports included in the folder that is selected in the All Folders list. In Figure 9-29, the Aging Power Pack folder is selected in All Folders, and the reports within the Aging Power Pack folder are listed in Contents of 'Aging Power Pack'.

Above the All Folders and Contents of 'All Folders' area, the Medisoft Reports window has its own menu bar, toolbar, and search area.

THE MEDISOFT REPORTS MENUS

The Medisoft Reports menus include File, View, and Help. The File menu, displayed in Figure 9-30, contains commands for creating a new folder, deleting a report, renaming a report, printing a report, previewing a report, importing a report from a file, exporting a report to a file, and closing the Medisoft Reports feature.

| Reports | Tools | Window | Help |

Day Sheets
Analysis Reports
Aging Reports
Collection Reports
Audit Reports
Patient Ledger
Standard Patient Lists
Patient Statements...
Superbills...
Blank Superbill
Custom Report List...
Default Printer Options...
Load Saved Reports...
Design Custom Reports and Bills...
Medisoft Reports...

Figure 9-26 The Medisoft Reports Option on the Reports Menu

Figure 9-27 Medisoft Reports Shortcut Button

Medisoft Reports - Family Care Center

File   View   Help

Find Report: [Find Now] [Favorites]

All Folders

- All Folders
  - Aging Power Pack
  - Data Analysis
  - Dymo LabelWriter
  - Facility Financials
  - Focus On Chiropractic
  - Focus On Collections
  - Focus On Data
  - Focus On Financials
  - Focus On Managed Care
  - Focus On Marketing and I
  - Insurance Data Analysis
  - MediSoft Reports
  - Plus Pack
- Recycle Bin

Contents of 'All Folders'

- Aging Power Pack
- Data Analysis
- Dymo LabelWriter
- Facility Financials
- Focus On Chiropractic
- Focus On Collections
- Focus On Data
- Focus On Financials
- Focus On Managed Care
- Focus On Marketing and Promotion
- Insurance Data Analysis
- MediSoft Reports
- Plus Pack

0 item(s) selected

Figure 9-28 Medisoft Reports Window

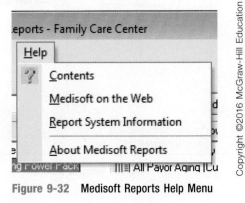

Figure 9-29 showing Medisoft Reports Window

Medisoft Reports - Family Care Center

File   View   Help

Find Report: [   ]   [Find Now]   [Favorites]

All Folders

- All Folders
  - Aging Power Pack
  - Data Analysis
  - Dymo LabelWriter
  - Facility Financials
  - Focus On Chiropractic
  - Focus On Collections
  - Focus On Data
  - Focus On Financials
  - Focus On Managed Care
  - Focus On Marketing and I
  - Insurance Data Analysis
  - MediSoft Reports
  - Plus Pack
- Recycle Bin

Contents of 'Aging Power Pack'

- Aging Summary by Billing Code
- All Payor Aging (Currently Responsible)
- Date Accurate Patient Aging by Date of Service
- Date Accurate Patient Aging by Statement Date
- Patient Aging by Allowed Amount
- Patient Aging by Date of Service (30 Days and Over)
- Patient Aging by Date of Service (60 Days and Over)
- Patient Aging by Date of Service (90 Days and Over)
- Patient Aging by Date of Service (Extended 180+)
- Patient Aging by Date of Service - Sorted by Account Balance
- Patient Aging by Statement Date (Extended 180+)
- Patient Remainder Aging (Extended 180+)
- Patient Remainder Aging (Extended 180+) Medisoft 12+
- Patient Remainder Aging Detail - Sort by Acct Balance (v12+)
- Primary Insurance Aging Detail (Extended 180+)
- Primary Insurance Aging Summary (Extended 180+)
- Primary Insurance Class Aging
- Procedure Code Aging (Extended 150+)
- Secondary Insurance Aging (Extended 180+)
- Secondary Insurance Aging Summary (180+)
- Tertiary Insurance Aging Detail (Extended 180+)
- Tertiary Insurance Aging Summary (Extended 180+)

22 items

List of folders with Aging Power Pack selected

List of reports contained within selected folder

Figure 9-29   Medisoft Reports Window with the Aging Power Pack Folder Selected

Commands on the View menu include options for displaying the toolbar and status bar, and whether to display the Contents of All Folders list of reports in List view or in Detail view (see Figure 9-31).

The Help menu contains entries for viewing help contents, navigating to Medisoft's website, viewing Medisoft Reports file location and path, and displaying the version of Medisoft Reports you are using. The Help menu is pictured in Figure 9-32.

Medisoft Reports - Family Care C

File   View   Help

- New Folder
- Delete   Del
- Rename   F2
- Print Report   Ctrl+P
- Preview Report
- Import Report...
- Export Report...
- Close   Ctrl+F4
- Focus On Financials

Figure 9-30   Medisoft Reports File Menu

edisoft Reports - Family C

View   Help

- ✓ Toolbar
- ✓ Status Bar
- List
- Detail

Aging Power Pack

Figure 9-31   Medisoft Reports View Menu

eports - Family Care Center

Help

- Contents
- Medisoft on the Web
- Report System Information
- About Medisoft Reports

g Power Pack   All Payor Aging (Cu

Figure 9-32   Medisoft Reports Help Menu

THE MEDISOFT REPORTS TOOLBAR

Below the menu bar is a toolbar featuring shortcut buttons (see Figure 9-33). From left to right, these buttons are used for:

Figure 9-33　Medisoft Reports Toolbar

- Moving up a folder level
- Creating a new folder
- Previewing a report
- Printing a report
- Displaying reports in a list
- Displaying report details
- Exiting the application

Figure 9-34　Medisoft Reports Find Report box

THE MEDISOFT REPORTS FIND REPORT BOX

Below the toolbar are the Find Report box and the Find Now button, which are used for searching for specific reports, and the Favorites button, which displays reports marked as favorites (see Figure 9-34).

THE MEDISOFT REPORTS HELP FEATURE

To view descriptions of all the reports available in Medisoft Reports, select Contents on the Medisoft Reports Help menu. The Medisoft Reports window appears. In the left side of the window, under the Contents tab, click Reports Available from the Medisoft Reports window (see Figure 9-35). Scroll down the window for a full listing of the reports and their descriptions.

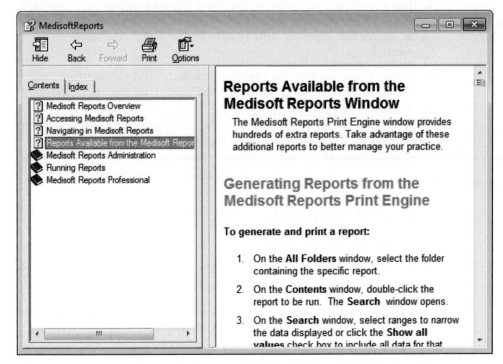

Figure 9-35　Contents of the Medisoft Reports Help File with Reports Available from the Medisoft Reports Window Selected

9.8 CREATING AGING REPORTS

In Medisoft, standard aging reports are contained on the Reports menu under the Aging Reports submenu. Additional aging reports are also contained in the Medisoft Reports feature. Refer back to Figure 9-29 to see the list of aging reports available in the Aging Power Pack folder of the Medisoft Reports feature. The exercise that follows provides practice in creating a patient aging report using the Medisoft Reports feature.

EXERCISE 9-5	PRINTING A PATIENT AGING REPORT

Print a patient aging report for the period ending September 30, 2018, using the Medisoft Reports feature.

Date: September 30, 2018

1. On the Reports menu, click Medisoft Reports. The Medisoft Reports window is displayed.

2. In the All Folders list on the left side of the window, click the Aging Power Pack folder to display its contents. The contents are listed in the area of the window to the right of the All Folders column.

3. Locate the Date Accurate Patient Aging by Date of Service report and double-click it. After several seconds, a Search box appears.

4. In the Charges/Payments/Adj is on or before box, enter **09302018**. Then click OK.

5. The report is displayed in the Print Preview window. From here, you can either print the report or close the window. Click Close to close the window and return to the main Medisoft Reports window.

6. Select Close on the File menu, or click the red Close box to close the Medisoft Reports window, and return to the main Medisoft window. **CiMO**

☑ **You have completed Exercise 9-5.**

9.9 CREATING CUSTOM REPORTS

In addition to its standard reports on the Reports menu and the reports in the Medisoft Reports feature, Medisoft has a number of built-in custom reports, including:

- Lists of addresses, billing codes, EDI receivers, patients, patient recalls, procedure codes, providers, and referring providers.
- The CMS-1500 and Medicare CMS-1500 forms in a variety of printer formats.

- Patient statements and walkout receipts.
- Superbills (encounter forms).

The built-in custom reports, which were created in Medisoft using the Report Designer, are accessed via the Custom Report List option on the Reports menu (see Figure 9-36). When Custom Report List is clicked on the Reports menu, the Open Report dialog box is displayed (see Figure 9-37). When a new custom report is created, it is added to the list of custom reports displayed on the screen.

Listed under the heading Show Report Style, the Open Report dialog box contains eleven radio buttons that are used to control the list of reports displayed in the dialog box. When the All radio button is clicked, all types of custom reports are listed in the dialog box. When one of the other radio buttons is clicked, only reports of that style are listed. For example, if the Insurance Form radio button is clicked, only reports that are insurance forms are listed.

To print a custom report, highlight the title of the report by clicking it and then click the OK button. The same options that are available with standard reports for previewing the report on the screen, sending it directly to the printer, or exporting it to a file are available with reports created through the Custom Report List option.

Figure 9-36   Custom Report List Option on the Reports Menu

PRINTING A CUSTOM REPORT

To print a custom report, double-click the report title.

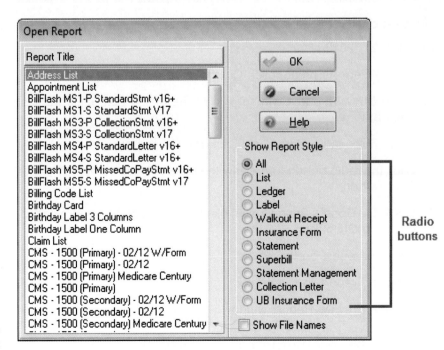

Figure 9-37   Open Report Dialog Box

EXERCISE 9-6 PRINTING A LIST OF PATIENTS

Print a list of all patients.

Date: July 31, 2018

1. On the Reports menu, click Custom Report List.

2. In the Show Report Style list, click the List radio button. Only list reports are displayed in the Open Report dialog box.

3. Select the Patient List report and click the OK button.

4. Accept the option to preview the report on the screen and click the Start button. The Data Selection Questions dialog box appears.

5. Leave the Chart Number Range boxes blank to select all patients.

6. Click the OK button.

7. View the report on the screen. Notice that the computer's system date—the date you are doing the exercise—is displayed at the top of the report by default.

8. Send the report to the printer.

9. Exit the Preview Report window. **CiMO**

✓ **You have completed Exercise 9-6.**

EXERCISE 9-7 PRINTING A LIST OF PROCEDURE CODES

Print a list of all procedure codes in the database.

Date: July 31, 2018

1. On the Reports menu, click Custom Report List.

2. In the Show Report Style section of the dialog box, click the List radio button.

3. Select Procedure Code List. Click the OK button.

4. Click the radio button to preview the report on the screen. Click the Start button.

5. Leave the Code 1 Range boxes blank to select all procedure codes. Click the OK button.

6. View the report on the screen.

7. Send the report to the printer.

8. Exit the Preview Report window. **CiMO**

 You have completed Exercise 9-7.

9.10 USING REPORT DESIGNER

Medisoft comes with a built-in program, called the Medisoft Report Designer, which allows users to modify existing reports or create new reports to add to the custom report list. The program provides maximum flexibility and control over data in the report and over how the data are displayed. Formatting styles include list, ledger, statement, and insurance. A report can be created from scratch or an existing report can be used as a starting point. Although the details of how to create new custom reports with the Report Designer are beyond the coverage of this text/workbook, Exercise 9-8 offers practice using the Report Designer to modify an existing report.

The Report Designer is accessed by clicking Design Custom Reports and Bills on the Reports menu (see Figure 9-38). This action displays the Medisoft Report Designer window (see Figure 9-39).

Figure 9-38 Reports Menu with Design Custom Reports and Bills Selected

Figure 9-39 Report Designer Window

Using the Medisoft Report Designer, modify the Patient List report so that a work telephone number replaces a home telephone number in the report.

Date: July 31, 2018

1. On the Reports menu, click Design Custom Reports and Bills. The Report Designer window is displayed.

2. Click Open Report on the File menu. The Open Report dialog box is displayed.

3. Double-click Patient List in the list. The Patient List report is displayed (see Figure 9-40).

4. Double-click Phone, which appears between the two horizontal black lines near the top of the report, to select it. Then, double-click Phone again to edit it. The Text Properties dialog box is displayed (see Figure 9-41).

5. Enter **Work Phone** in the Text box that currently reads "Phone." Be sure that the Auto Size button is checked so the program will automatically resize the text box to accommodate the longer title.

Figure 9-40 Patient List Report Open in Medisoft Report Designer

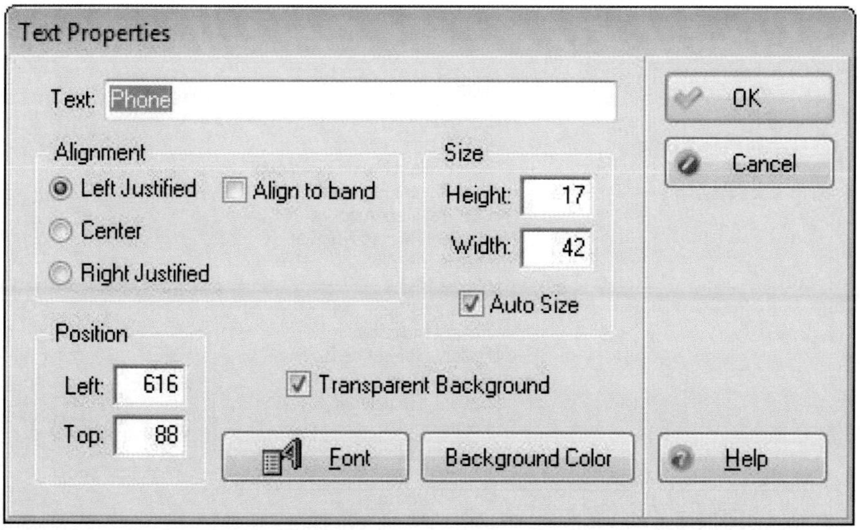

Text Properties

Text: Phone

Alignment
- ◉ Left Justified
- ☐ Align to band
- ○ Center
- ○ Right Justified

Size
Height: 17
Width: 42
☑ Auto Size

Position
Left: 616
Top: 88

☑ Transparent Background

[Font] [Background Color]

[✓ OK] [⊘ Cancel] [? Help]

Figure 9-41 Text Properties Dialog Box

6. Click the OK button. Work Phone is displayed in the band where Phone used to be.

7. In the green band below the band in which Work Phone appears, click the Phone 1 box to select it. Then double-click the Phone 1 box again to edit its contents. The Data Field Properties dialog box is displayed (see Figure 9-42).

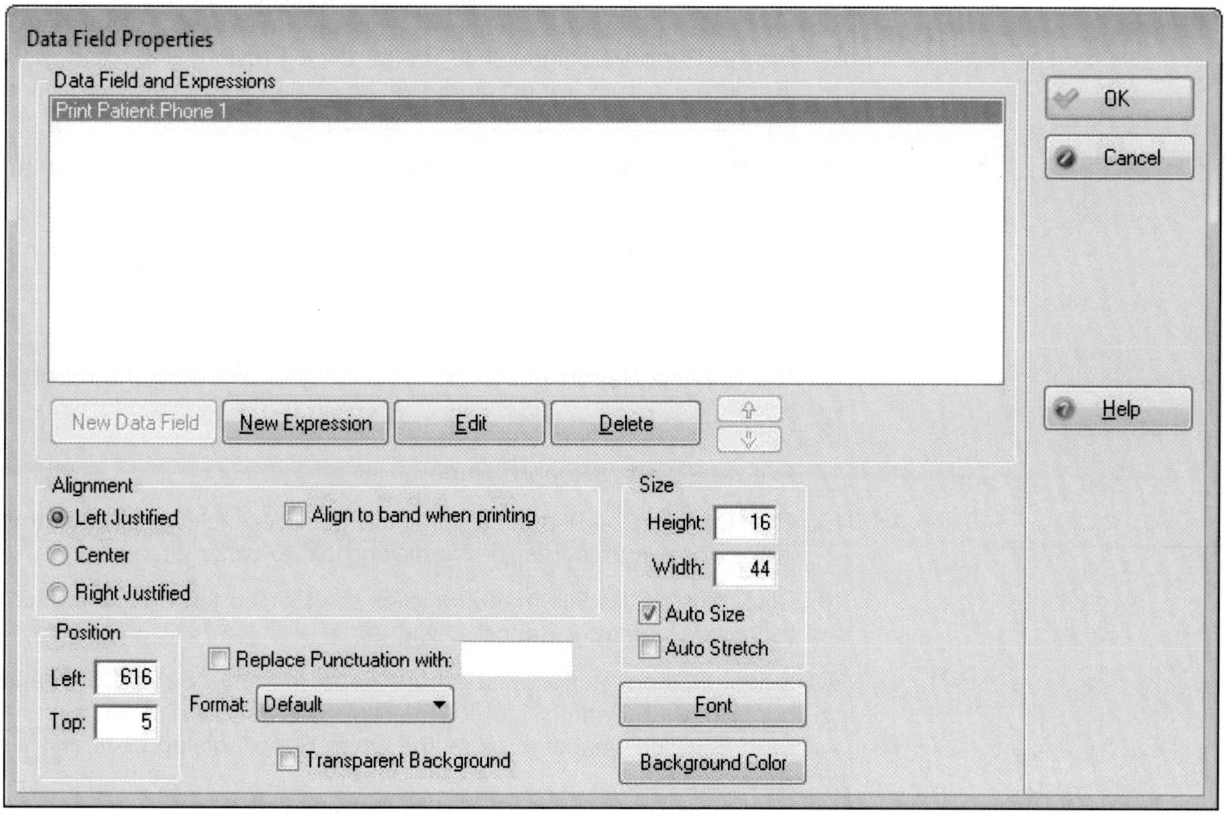

Data Field Properties

Data Field and Expressions

Print Patient.Phone 1

[New Data Field] [New Expression] [Edit] [Delete] [↑] [↓]

Alignment
- ◉ Left Justified
- ☐ Align to band when printing
- ○ Center
- ○ Right Justified

Size
Height: 16
Width: 44
☑ Auto Size
☐ Auto Stretch

Position
Left: 616
Top: 5

☐ Replace Punctuation with: [   ]
Format: Default ▼
☐ Transparent Background

[Font]
[Background Color]

[✓ OK] [⊘ Cancel] [? Help]

Figure 9-42 Data Field Properties Dialog Box

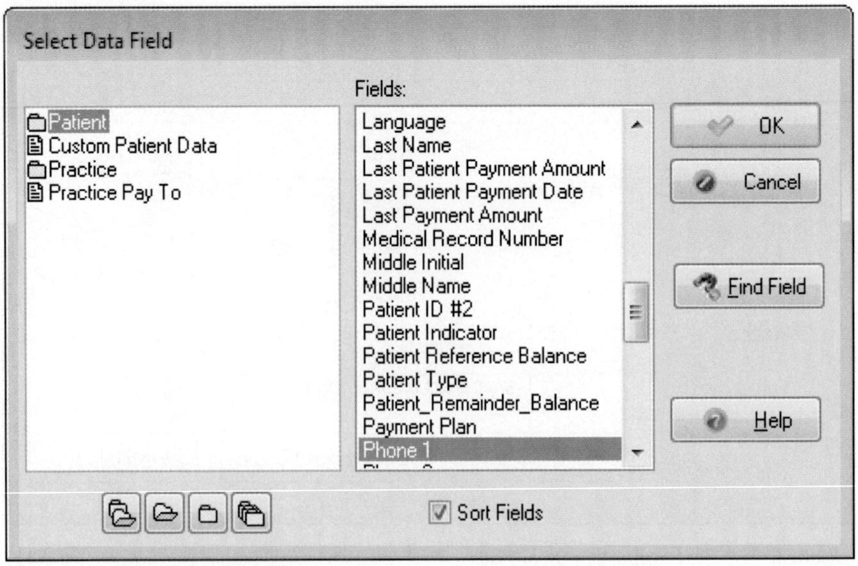

Figure 9-43 Select Data Field Dialog Box

8. The current data box, Print Patient.Phone 1, is active in the Data Field and Expressions box. Click the Edit button to change this box. The Select Data Field dialog box is displayed (see Figure 9-43).

9. In the Fields column, scroll down, highlight Work Phone, and click OK. The Data Field and Expressions box now lists Print Patient.Work Phone.

10. Be sure the Auto Size box is checked and click the OK button. Work Phone is displayed where Phone 1 used to be.

11. On the Report Designer File menu, click Preview Report to save the file as a new report and see how the report will look when printed. The Save Report As. . . dialog box is displayed.

12. Key **Patient List—Work** in the Report Title box. Click the OK button. The Search dialog box is displayed.

13. Leave the Chart Number Range boxes blank to select all patients for the report.

14. Click the OK button.

15. The Preview Report dialog box is displayed, showing the report.

16. Click the Print button to print the report.

17. Exit the Preview Report window.

18. Click Close on the Report Designer File menu, or click the Close button in the upper-right corner of the dialog box, to close the report file.

19. Click Exit on the File menu, or click the Exit button on the toolbar, to leave Medisoft's Report Designer.

20. Select Custom Report List on the Reports menu. Scroll down and confirm that Patient List—Work appears in the list of custom reports. Click Cancel to close the Open Report dialog box. **çiMc**

✓ **You have completed Exercise 9-8.**

APPLYING YOUR SKILLS

10: PRINT A PATIENT DAY SHEET

September 4, 2018
Using Medisoft standard reports, print a patient day sheet for September 4, 2018. **Check to be sure the box labeled *Show all values of the Date Created* is checked and enter the exercise dates in the *Date From* fields.**

APPLYING YOUR SKILLS

11: PRINT AN INSURANCE PAYMENT BY TYPE REPORT

September 1–September 30, 2018
Using Medisoft Reports, open the Plus Pack folder and locate the Insurance Payment by Type report to create a report for September 2018.

Remember to create a backup of your work before exiting Medisoft! To help you keep track of your work, name the backup file after the chapter you are working on; for example, StudentID-c9.mbk.

ELECTRONIC HEALTH RECORD EXCHANGE

Viewing Electronic Record Logs

In addition to the many standard reports available in Medisoft, the McKesson Practice Interface Center (MPIC) program provides logs of inbound and outbound data transfers to and from an electronic health record, and to outside organizations, such as laboratories. MPIC is the program that makes it possible for Medisoft and an electronic health record to exchange information.

20180903_10:20:10:90115FLSTRDReceived messageStringMSH | ^~\& | Medisoft | Family Care Center | Medisoft Clinical | Stephenson OH | 20180903102009+0000^S \ NO SECURITY | ADT^A04 | 20 | D | 2.5.1 | | | | EVN | A04 | 20180903102009+0000^S | | 01 | | PID | 1 | ARLENSU0 | ARLENSU0 | ARLENSU0 | Arlen_Susan | 309620422 | F | A | 310 Oneida Lane^^Stephenson^OH^60089 | | (614-315-2233^(614) 325-0011^^sarlen@abc.com | (614)202-0000 | English | F | ARLENSU0 | 309-62-0422 | N | | | | | | | | |PV1 | 1 |O | | R | | | Beach^Robert^MD^^ | | | | | | | | | | | | | | | | | | | | | | | | | | | IN1 | 1 | ID1234 | EastOhio PPO | Arlen^Susan | Self | | ^ ^ ^ ^ | | | | | | | | | | | | | | | | | | DB1234 | | | | | | | | | | | | | U | | | | | | | | | | | | IN1 | 3 | | | | | | | | | | | | | | | ^ ^ ^ ^ | | | | | | | | | | | | | | | | | | | | | | | | | | |

BE THE DETECTIVE!

If assigned by your instructor, complete the Missing Charges Video Case in Connect. Put your skills to use identifying mistakes made in Medisoft and enhance your knowledge by determining the impact of those mistakes.

chapter 9 worksheet

[Note: These questions are designed for students using the live Medisoft CD software, since students may need to refer back to specific screens in the software to answer the questions.]

1. *[LO 9.3]* In the patient day sheet created in Exercise 9-1, what is the total of the adjustments to Jonathan Bell's account?

2. *[LO 9.3]* In the patient day sheet created in Exercise 9-1, what is the patient's balance on John Fitzwilliams's account?

3. *[LO 9.4]* In the practice analysis report created in Exercise 9-2, what were the total procedure charges?

4. *[LO 9.5]* In the patient account ledger created in Exercise 9-3, what is Jill Simmons's patient total at the end of October?

5. *[LO 9.8]* In the Patient by Insurance Carrier report created in Exercise 9-4, how many patients are listed under Medicare?

6. *[LO 9.6]* In the Patient List report created in Exercise 9-6, what are the four columns of information displayed?

7. *[LO 9.9]* In the Procedure Code List created in Exercise 9-7, what is the description and charge for procedure code 99214?

8. *[LO 9.10]* According to the patient day sheet created in Applying Your Skills 10, how many procedures were performed on September 4, 2018?

9. *[LO 9.10]* According to the Insurance Payment by Type report created in Applying Your Skills 11, which type of insurance carrier plan paid the greatest amount to the Family Care Center?

10. *[LO 9.10]* According to the Insurance Payment by Type report created in Applying Your Skills 11, what percentage of the Family Care Center's payments came from Medicare during September 2018?

LEARNING OUTCOMES	CONCEPTS TO REVIEW
9.1 List the three types of reports available in Medisoft.	1. Standard reports 2. Medisoft Reports 3. Custom reports
9.2 Explain why accounts receivable reports are critical to a practice's financial success.	Accounts receivable reports track money that is owed to the practice and detail how successful the practice is in collecting the amounts owed. With this information, practices are able to focus on collecting these amounts from patients and third-party payers.
9.3 Distinguish between patient, procedure, and payment day sheets.	– A patient day sheet lists patient transactions for a day, organized alphabetically by chart number. – A procedure day sheet lists patient transactions by procedure code and is sorted numerically, then alphabetically (for codes that begin with letters). – A payment day sheet lists patient transactions by provider, ordered numerically by the code assigned to the provider in Medisoft.
9.4 Demonstrate how to create a practice analysis report.	1. On the Reports menu, click Analysis Reports and then Practice Analysis. The Print Report Where? dialog box appears. 2. Select the desired option in the Print Report Where? dialog box. 3. Click the Start button. The Search dialog box is displayed. 4. Make the necessary entries in the following selection boxes: Code 1 Date Created Date From Attending Provider Place of Service 5. Click the OK button. If you elected to preview the report, the report will open in the Print Preview window. If you chose to print the report, the Print dialog box for your printer appears. Click OK to print the report.

LEARNING OUTCOMES	CONCEPTS TO REVIEW
9.5 Demonstrate how to create a patient ledger report.	1. On the Reports menu, click Patient Ledger. The Print Report Where? dialog box appears. 2. Select the desired option in the Print Report Where? dialog box. 3. Click the Start button. The Search dialog box is displayed. 4. Make the necessary entries in the following selection boxes: Chart Number Patient Reference Balance Date From Attending Provider Billing Code Patient Indicator 5. Click the OK button. If you elected to preview the report, the report will open in the Print Preview window. If you chose to print the report, the Print dialog box for your printer appears. Click OK to print the report.
9.6 Demonstrate how to create a standard patient list report.	1. On the Reports menu, click Standard Patient Lists. Select Patient by Diagnosis or Patient by Insurance Carrier from the submenu. The Print Report Where? dialog box appears. 2. Select the desired option in the Print Report Where? dialog box. 3. Click the Start button. The Search dialog box is displayed. 4. For a Patient by Diagnosis report, make the necessary entries in the Diagnosis Code 1 selection box. For a Patient by Insurance Carrier report, make the necessary entry in the Code selection box. 5. Click the OK button. If you elected to preview the report, the report will open in the Print Preview window. If you chose to print the report, the Print dialog box for your printer appears. Click OK to print the report.
9.7 Describe how to use Medisoft Reports to create a report.	1. Select Medisoft Reports on the Reports menu. The Medisoft Reports window opens. 2. Locate the folder in the All Folders column that contains the report you want to create. 3. Double-click the folder to see its contents. 4. In the list of reports that appears in the window to the right of the All Folders list, locate the report. 5. Double-click the report. After several seconds, the Search dialog box appears. 6. Make the necessary entries in the selection boxes and then click the OK button. 7. The report appears in the Print Preview window. 8. To send the report to the printer, click the Print button.

LEARNING OUTCOMES	CONCEPTS TO REVIEW
9.8 Demonstrate how to create a patient aging report.	1. Select Medisoft Reports on the Reports menu. The Medisoft Reports window opens. 2. In the All Folders list on the left side of the window, click the Aging Power Pack folder to display its contents. The contents are listed in the area of the window to the right of the All Folders column. 3. Locate the Date Accurate Patient Aging by Date of Service report and double-click it. After several seconds, a Search box appears. 4. Make the necessary entries in the selection boxes and then click the OK button. 5. The report appears in the Print Preview window. 6. To send the report to the printer, click the Print button.
9.9 Explain how to access Medisoft's built-in custom reports.	1. Click Custom Report List on the Reports menu. The Open Report dialog box appears. 2. Select the desired report from the list of reports and click the OK button. 3. Select the option to preview or print the report and then click the Start button. 4. Make the necessary entries in the Data Selection Questions dialog box and click OK. 5. The report appears in the Print Preview window or is sent to the printer.
9.10 Demonstrate how to open a report for editing in Medisoft's Report Designer.	1. On the Reports menu, click Design Custom Reports and Bills. The Medisoft Report Designer window is displayed. 2. Click Open Report on the File menu. The Open Report dialog box is displayed. 3. Click to select a report in the list and click the OK button, or simply double-click the report title. 4. The report opens in Report Designer for editing. 5. Once the desired changes have been made, click Save or Save As on the File menu.

USING TERMINOLOGY

Match the terms on the left with the definitions on the right.

1. *[LO 9.2]* accounts receivable

2. *[LO 9.2]* aging report

3. *[LO 9.2]* day sheet

4. *[LO 9.2]* insurance aging report

5. *[LO 9.2]* patient aging report

6. *[LO 9.3]* patient day sheet

7. *[LO 9.5]* patient ledger

8. *[LO 9.3]* payment day sheet

9. *[LO 9.4]* practice analysis report

10. *[LO 9.3]* procedure day sheet

a. A summary of the patient activity on a given day.

b. A report that lists the amount of money owed the practice, organized by the length of time the money has been owed.

c. A report that provides information on practice activities for a twenty-four-hour period.

d. A report that lists the financial activity in each patient's account, including charges, payments, and adjustments.

e. A report that lists a patient's balance by age, date, and amount of the last payment.

f. A report that lists payments received on a given day, organized by provider.

g. A report that analyzes the revenue of a practice for a specified period of time, usually a month or a year.

h. A report that lists the procedures performed on a given day, listed in numerical order.

i. A report that lists how long a payer has taken to respond to insurance claims.

j. Monies that are coming into the practice.

connect Enhance your learning by completing these exercises and more at http://connect.mheducation.com

chapter 9 review

CHECKING YOUR UNDERSTANDING

11. *[LO 9.3]* What is the difference between a patient day sheet and a procedure day sheet?

12. *[LO 9.1]* What is the name of the dialog box that provides options for selecting data to be included on a report?

13. *[LO 9.7]* How do you select a report in the Medisoft Reports program?

14. *[LO 9.1]* What are the three options in the Print Report Where? dialog box?

15. *[LO 9.2]* What type of report is used to confirm that all patients seen in the office on a given day also have charges?

16. *[LO 9.4]* Which report analyzes the revenue of a practice for a specified period of time (typically a month or a year)?

17. *[LO 9.5]* To create a patient ledger report for a specific group of patients, click the _____ button to select the patients.

18. *[LO 9.6]* The Standard Patient Lists option on the Reports menu provides access to a report that lists patients by insurance carrier or _____.

19. *[LO 9.8]* Patient aging reports are located in the _____ folder in Medisoft Reports.

20. *[LO 9.9]* The built-in custom reports in Medisoft are listed in the _____ dialog box.

21. *[LO 9.10]* In Medisoft's Report Designer, changing the name of the Phone field to Work Phone takes place in the _____ dialog box.

APPLYING YOUR KNOWLEDGE

22. *[LO 9.3]* One of the providers in a practice asks for a report of yesterday's transactions. How would this report be created?

23. *[LO 9.5]* A patient is unsure whether she mailed a check last month to pay an outstanding balance on her account. What standard report would you use to help answer her question?

24. *[LO 9.3]* If the office manager asked you for a list of procedure codes representing services performed on a particular day, what report would you create in Medisoft?

25. *[LO 9.2, 9.8]* What would the consequences be if a medical practice did not produce patient aging reports on a regular basis?

---

connect Enhance your learning by completing these exercises and more at http://connect.mheducation.com

COLLECTIONS IN THE MEDICAL OFFICE

key terms

collection agency
collection list
collection tracer report
payment plan
prompt payment laws
tickler
timely filing
uncollectible account
write-off

learning outcomes

When you finish this chapter, you will be able to:

10.1 Explain the importance of prompt follow-up on insurance claims.

10.2 Summarize the importance of a financial policy in a medical office.

10.3 Identify the laws that regulate collections from patients.

10.4 Demonstrate how to create a payment plan and assign a patient account to a payment plan.

10.5 Demonstrate how to post a payment from a collection agency.

10.6 Discuss the process of writing off uncollectible accounts.

10.7 Explain how to use a patient aging report to identify past-due accounts.

10.8 Demonstrate how to add an account to the collection list.

10.9 Demonstrate how to create a collection letter.

10.10 Demonstrate how to create a collection tracer report.

what you need to know

To use this chapter, you need to know how to:

- Start Medisoft, use menus, and enter and edit text.
- Work with chart numbers and codes.
- Create an aging report.

Receiving prompt payment for services is key to the financial success of a medical practice. While most patients and health plans pay on time, there are some that do not. Members of the billing staff may be asked to work with patients and representatives of health plans to follow up on overdue accounts and unpaid claims.

10.1 FOLLOWING UP ON INSURANCE CLAIMS

Once claims are submitted to a clearinghouse, it is essential to follow up on the claims until the practice receives payment. This requires the review of electronic reports received from the clearinghouse as well as regular monitoring of claim status.

Once a clearinghouse receives claims from a physician office, the claims are "scrubbed" against a series of edits. Claims that pass the edits are reported as accepted and sent on to the appropriate payers and claims that fail the edits are listed as rejected. The clearinghouse sends an acknowledgment report to the practice, indicating whether each claim was accepted or rejected. This report should be reviewed daily so that rejected claims can be researched and resubmitted.

In addition, to ensure that all sent claims have been received by the clearinghouse, staff should compare claims listed on the acknowledgment report with claims listed in the practice management program. Any claims not found on the report should be investigated for transmission errors.

PROMPT PAYMENT LAWS

prompt payment laws state laws that mandate a time period within which clean claims must be paid; if they are not, financial penalties are levied against the payer.

Once claims reach the payer, they are again reviewed and scrubbed against a series of edits. Payers check claims against common edits, but most also have their own specific set of edits. The time it takes a payer to adjudicate a claim varies. However, most states have enacted prompt payment laws to ensure that claims are paid in a timely manner. **Prompt payment laws** are state laws that mandate a time period within which clean claims must be paid and call for financial penalties to be levied against late payers. (Clean claims are error-free claims that do not require additional documentation.) For example, under the New York Prompt Payment Law, when a managed care organization or insurance company fails to make payment on a clean claim within forty-five days of submission, the physician is entitled to receive interest on the late payment at the rate of 12 percent per year.

Most practice management programs can be set up to automatically track how many days' claims have been unpaid and to send a claim status inquiry after a certain number of days. For example, if a particular payer usually pays claims on the fourteenth day after receiving the claim, the program transmits a request for a status report on the fifteenth day.

If a clean claim is not paid within the allotted time frame, the payer should be notified in writing that payment has not been received according to applicable prompt payment laws. Practices should also request written explanations for all claim delays, partial payments, and denials. If satisfaction is not achieved, the applicable state or federal regulatory agency may be notified of the violation.

WORKING CLAIM DENIALS

Following adjudication, a report is sent to the clearinghouse, or directly to the practice, listing claims that have been paid or denied. While most claims are paid, there are numerous reasons that a claim may be fully or partially denied. For example, the patient may not have been eligible for coverage on the date of service or the service provided may not have been covered under the terms of the policy. Table 10-1 lists common reasons that claims are rejected by payers.

All denied claims should be investigated in a timely manner. Most practices keep a claim denial tracking log that lists the reason for the denial, the action taken to correct the problem, and the status of the resubmission. Some claims are denied because more information is needed. When further documentation is requested, the additional information should be sent as quickly as possible, since claims must be submitted within a specific number of days from the date of service. This requirement is known as **timely filing** and the number of days allowed varies from payer to payer. Some payers, such as Medicare, allow practices up to one year to file claims; other payers allow as little as sixty days. Medical biller or insurance specialists may be asked to provide proof of timely filing. Most times, this can be accomplished by providing the payer with copies of clearinghouse reports that show the time and date of the filing. Claims rejected because they do not meet timely filing requirements are the responsibility of the provider and cannot be billed to the patient. This is one of the reasons why practices prefer that claims be submitted on the date of service.

timely filing the requirement that claims must be submitted to payers within a specific number of days from the date of service.

TABLE 10-1	Common Reasons for Claim Denials

No coverage based on date of service
Noncovered/non-network benefit or service
Not reasonable and necessary (medical necessity)
Service provided not covered
Preauthorization not obtained
Duplicate claim submitted
Lack of necessary information
Unbundled code
Modifier not provided
Diagnosis procedure code does not match service provided
Procedure code does not match patient sex
Procedure code inconsistent with modifier used
Procedure code inconsistent with place of service
Diagnosis is inconsistent with age, sex, and procedure

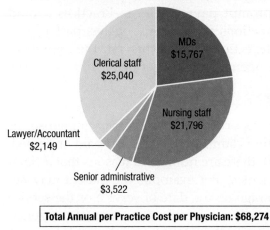

Mean Dollar Value of Hours Spent per Physician per Year on All Interactions with Health Plans

- MDs $15,767
- Clerical staff $25,040
- Nursing staff $21,796
- Lawyer/Accountant $2,149
- Senior administrative $3,522

Total Annual per Practice Cost per Physician: $68,274

Figure 10-1 Annual Cost to Physician Practices for Interactions with Health Plans

(*Source: Commonwealth Fund*, How Health Care Reform Can Lower the Costs of Insurance Administration (*2009*).)

AGING INSURANCE CLAIMS

To track unpaid claims, practice management programs generate an insurance aging report, which lists the claims transmitted on each day, the date of service, and how long they have been in process with the payer. It is important to work on the oldest claims first, to ensure resolution within timely filing limitations.

RESUBMITTING CLAIMS

Claims that were rejected must be resubmitted once the error has been corrected. Resubmitting rejected claims is a time-consuming process, resulting in increased practice expenses and more delay in payment. Researching and resubmitting claims also costs the practice money. A study conducted in 2009 revealed that physician practices spend about $31 billion a year interacting with insurance carriers (see Figure 10-1). For this reason, practices emphasize the importance of submitting clean claims that are approved the first time they are submitted.

10.2 THE IMPORTANCE OF A FINANCIAL POLICY

For many years, medical-practice collections activities focused primarily on insurance payers. As high-deductible health plans, health savings accounts, and the number of uninsured patients have increased in recent years, practices are now adding patient accounts to their collections efforts. According to the Medical Group Management Association (MGMA), practices surveyed reported that $1 of every $4 in practice revenue comes directly from patients.

Millions of Adults Continue to Report Problems Paying Medical Bills or Medical Debt

Percent of adults ages 19–64	2005	2010	2012
In the past 12 months:			
Had problems paying or unable to pay medical bills	23% 39 million	29% 53 million	30% 55 million
Contacted by a collection agency about medical bills*	21% 36 million	23% 42 million	22% 41 million
Contacted by collection agency for unpaid medical bills	13% 22 million	16% 30 million	10% 32 million
Contacted by a collection agency because of billing mistake	7% 11 million	5% 9 million	4% 7 million
Had to change way of life to pay bills	14% 24 million	17% 31 million	16% 29 million
Any of three bill problems (does not include billing mistake)	28% 48 million	34% 62 million	34% 63 million
Medical bills being paid off over time	21% 37 million	24% 44 million	26% 48 million
Any of three bill problems or medical debt	34% 58 million	40% 73 million	41% 75 million

* Subtotals may not sum to total: respondents who answered "don't know" or refused are included in the distribution but not reported.
Source: The Commonwealth Fund Biennial Health Insurance Surveys (2005, 2010, and 2012).

Figure 10-2 Medical Bill Problems or Medical Debt

(*Source*: http://www.commonwealthfund.org/publications/surveys/2013/biennial-health-insurance-survey)

(Source: Medical Group Management Association (MGMA), *Practice Perspectives on Patient Payments* (2009).)

While most patients pay their bills on time, every practice has some patients who do not. Patients' reasons for not paying include:

- Lack of insurance.
- Lack of financial resources.
- Significant medical costs.
- Consumer-directed health plans with high out-of-pocket costs.
- Lack of understanding that payment is their responsibility.

According to a 2013 study by the Commonwealth Fund, 30 percent of Americans ages nineteen to sixty-four had problems paying or were unable to pay medical bills in 2012, up from 23 percent in 2005 (see Figure 10-2).

The patient collection process begins with a clear financial policy and effective communications with patients about their financial responsibilities. When patients understand the charges and the practice's financial policy in advance, collecting payments is not usually problematic. As a result, it is important to have a written financial policy that spells out patients' responsibilities.

The financial policy of a medical practice explains how the practice handles financial matters. When new patients register, they should be given copies of the financial policy along with the practice's

**Financial Policy of
Any Medical Practice
Any Town, USA**

Thank you for choosing Any Medical Practice for your healthcare needs. The following information is being provided to assist you in understanding our financial policies and to address the questions most frequently asked by our patients.

Account Responsibility

You are responsible for all charges incurred on your account. It is also your responsibility to make sure all information on your account is current and accurate. Incorrect information can cause payment delays, which may result in late fees being applied to your account. Many people are under the impression that it is up to the physician and staff to make sure that all charges are paid or covered by insurance. This is not the case. Please remember that the insurance contract is between you and the insurance company, not the physician. It is your responsibility to know what your contract covers and pays and to communicate this to physicians and staff. Therefore, you are responsible for charges incurred regardless of insurance coverage.

Insurance Billing

If you have medical insurance, we will be happy to bill your insurance carrier for you. As a courtesy we will also bill the carrier of any secondary insurance coverage that you may have. Any Medical Practice contracts with many insurance companies, but due to the fact that these companies have many different plans available, it is impossible for us to know if your specific plan is included. You will need to check with your insurance company in advance. Please remember that your insurance may not cover or pay all charges incurred. Any unpaid balance after insurance is your responsibility.

Copays

All copays are due at time of service. A $5.00 billing fee is assessed if your copay is not paid at time of service. This fee will not be waived. It is your responsibility to know whether your insurance requires you to pay a copay.

No Insurance

If you have no insurance, payment in full is expected at time of service, unless payment arrangements have been made prior to your visit.

Late Fees

All patient balances are to be paid in full within 60 days. This refers to balances after your insurance has paid. If you are unable to pay your balance in full within 60 days, please contact the business office to set up a payment plan. A late fee of $20.00 per month will be assessed on patient balances over 60 days.

Cash Only

If your account has been turned over to collection, it will also be changed to a cash-only account. This means that all services will need to be paid in full at time of service. A letter will be sent to inform you if your account has been changed to a cash-only basis.

Dishonored Checks

A $25.00 service charge will be assessed on all dishonored checks.

Payment Methods

Any Medical Practice accepts cash, personal checks, and the following credit cards: Visa, MasterCard, American Express, and Discover. Payments can be made at any reception area. For your convenience, an ATM machine is located in the lobby of the building.

Figure 10-3   A Sample Medical Practice Financial Policy

TABLE 10-2	Patient Collection Timeline
Amount Past Due	**Action**
30 days	Bill patient
45 days	Call patient regarding bill
60 days	Letter 1
75 days	Letter 2 and call
80 days	Letter 3
90 days	Turn over to collections

HIPAA privacy policies and patient registration material. The policy should tell patients how the practice handles:

- Collecting copayments and past-due balances.
- Setting up financial arrangements for unpaid balances.
- Providing charity care or using a sliding scale for patients with low incomes.
- Collecting payments for services not covered by insurance.
- Collecting prepayment for services.
- Accepting cash, checks, money orders, and credit cards.

Figure 10-3 shows a sample financial policy of a medical practice.

Despite the practice's efforts to communicate the financial policy to all patients, some individuals still do not pay in full and on time. Medical insurance specialists are often responsible for some aspect of the collection process. Each practice sets its own procedures. Large bills have priority over smaller ones. Usually, an automatic reminder notice and a second statement are mailed when a bill has not been paid within thirty days after it was issued. Some practices phone a patient whose account is thirty days overdue. If the bill is not paid then, a series of collection letters are generated at intervals, each more stringent in tone and more direct in approach. Table 10-2 provides an example of one practice's collection timeline; different approaches are used in other practices. Some practices send all accounts that are past thirty days to an outside agency.

10.3 LAWS GOVERNING PATIENT COLLECTIONS

Collections from insurance carriers are considered business collections. Collections from patients, on the other hand, are consumer collections and are regulated by federal and state laws. The Fair

Debt Collection Practices Act of 1977 and the Telephone Consumer Protection Act of 1991 regulate debt collections, forbidding unfair practices. General guidelines include the following:

- Do not call a patient before 8 a.m. or after 9 p.m.
- Do not make threats or use profane language.
- Do not discuss the patient's debt with anyone except the person who is responsible for payment. If the patient has a lawyer, discuss the problem only with the lawyer, unless the lawyer gives permission to talk with the patient.
- Do not use any form of deception or violence to collect a debt. For example, do not impersonate a law officer to try to force a patient to pay.

If the practice's printed or displayed payment policy covers adding finance charges on late accounts, it is acceptable to do so. The amount of the finance charge must comply with federal and state law.

10.4 CREATING AND ASSIGNING PAYMENT PLANS

payment plan an agreement between a patient and a practice in which the patient agrees to make regular monthly payments over a specified period of time.

For large bills or special situations, some practices may offer payment plans to patients. A **payment plan** is an agreement between a patient and a practice in which the patient agrees to make regular monthly payments over a specified period of time. If no finance charges are applied to unpaid balances, this type of arrangement is between the practice and the patient, and no legal regulations apply. If, however, the practice adds finance charges and the payments are to be made in more than four installments, the arrangement is subject to the Truth in Lending Act, which is part of the Consumer Credit Protection Act. In this case, the practice notifies the patient in writing about the total amount, the finance charges (stated as a percentage), when each payment is due and the amount, and the date the last payment is due. The agreement must be signed by the practice manager and the patient.

In Medisoft, before a patient account can be assigned to a payment plan, a plan must be created. Patient payment plans are viewed and created by selecting Patient Payment Plan on the Lists menu (see Figure 10-4). Once this menu option is selected, the Patient Payment Plan List dialog box is displayed.

The Patient Payment Plan List dialog box displays a list of existing payment plans. The first step in creating a payment plan is clicking the New button in the Patient Payment Plan List dialog box. The Patient Payment Plan dialog box contains the following data fields (see Figure 10-5):

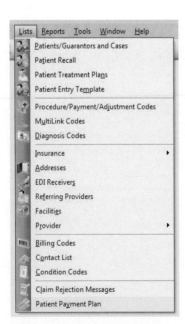

Figure 10-4 Lists Menu with Patient Payment Plan Highlighted

Code Payment plans are assigned a three-character alphanumeric code.

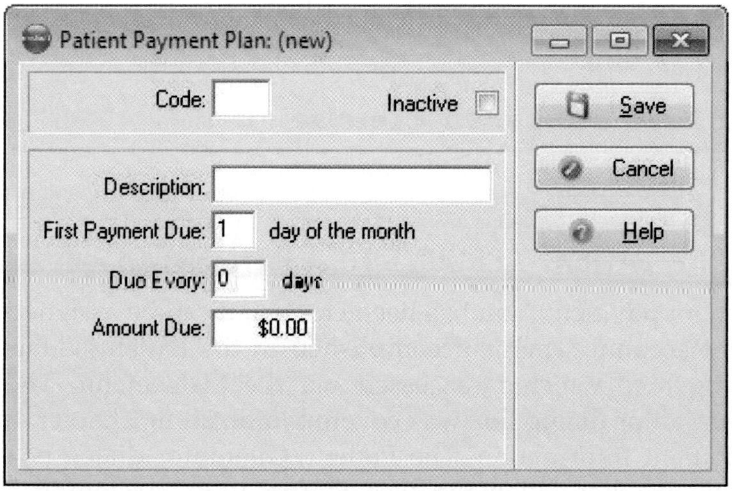

Figure 10-5 Patient Payment Plan (new) Dialog Box

Inactive   If the plan is no longer in use, the inactive box is checked.

Description   Contains a description of the plan.

First Payment Due _1_ Day of the Month   Specifies the day of the month when the first payment is due, and when each successive payment will be due.

Due Every _0_ Days   Specifies how often a payment is due, such as every 30 days, every 14 days, etc.

Amount Due   Specifies the amount of each payment.

If a patient is on a payment plan and pays the amount due by the due date specified in the plan, a collection letter is not created.

CREATING A PATIENT PAYMENT PLAN   EXERCISE 10-1

Date: July 31, 2018

1. Start Medisoft and restore the data from your last work session.

2. Change the Medisoft Program Date to July 31, 2018.

3. Click the Lists menu and select Patient Payment Plan. The Patient Payment Plan List dialog box is displayeds.

4. Click the New button. The Patient Payment Plan: (new) dialog box appears.

5. Enter *$50* in the Code field. Press Tab twice.

6. Enter *$50 Every 30 Days* in the Description field. Press Tab.

7. Enter *15* in the First Payment Due field. Press Tab.

8. Enter *30* in the Due Every field. Press Tab.

9. Enter *50* in the Amount Due field. Press Tab.

10. Click the Save button. The payment plan is listed in the Patient Payment Plan List dialog box.

Connect users: go to http://connect.mheducation.com to complete this exercise! Some steps may differ from what is listed here, so be sure to refer to the steps listed in Demo and Practice Modes for guidance.

11. Click the Close button to close the Patient Payment Plan List dialog box.

☑ **You have completed Exercise 10-1.**

ASSIGNING A PATIENT ACCOUNT TO A PAYMENT PLAN

Once a patient payment plan has been created, it can be assigned to a patient account. This is accomplished in the Patient/Guarantor dialog box, which is accessed via the Lists menu. The Patient/Guarantor dialog box was covered in detail in Chapter 4, Entering Patient Information. The Patient/Guarantor dialog box contains the Payment Plan tab (see Figure 10-6). Assigning a

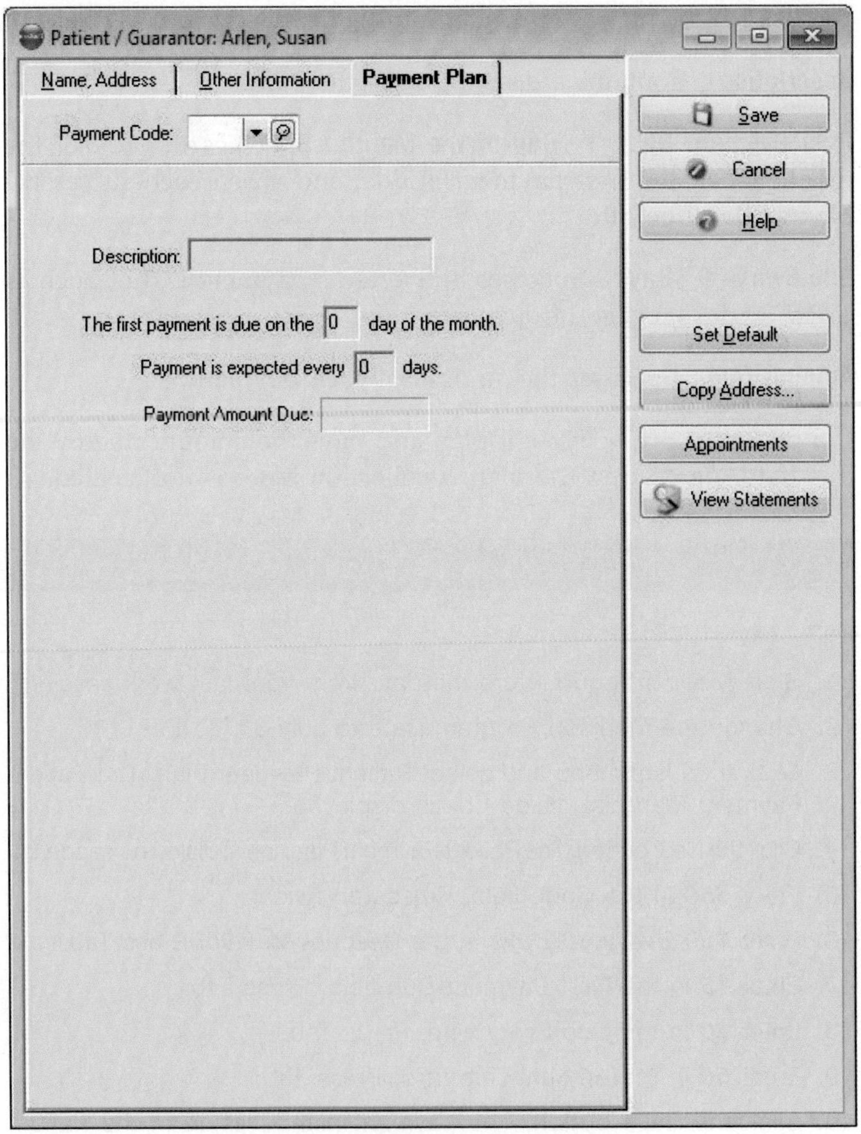

Figure 10-6 Payment Plan tab in the Patient/Guarantor dialog box

patient to a payment plan is a matter of selecting a payment plan from the Payment Code drop-down list and clicking the Save button.

| ASSIGNING A PATIENT ACCOUNT TO A PAYMENT PLAN | EXERCISE 10-2 |

Date: July 31, 2018

1. Click the Lists menu and select Patients/Guarantors and Cases. The Patient List dialog box is displayed.

2. Enter **GL** in the Search for field to select Olivia Glover.

3. Click the Edit Patient button. The Patient/Guarantor dialog box appears.

4. Click the Payment Plan tab.

5. Click in the Payment Code field and select code $50. The plan details are displayed in the other fields.

6. Click the Save button.

7. Click the Close button to close the Patient List dialog box.

✓ **You have completed Exercise 10-2.**

Connect users: go to http://connect.mheducation.com to complete this exercise! Some steps may differ from what is listed here, so be sure to refer to the steps listed in Demo and Practice Modes for guidance.

10.5 WORKING WITH COLLECTION AGENCIES

After a number of collection attempts that do not produce results, some practices use collection agencies to pursue large unpaid bills. A **collection agency** is an outside firm hired to collect on delinquent accounts. The agency that is selected should have a reputation for fair and ethical handling of collections.

When a patient's account is referred to an agency for collection, the medical insurance specialist no longer contacts the patient or sends statements. If a payment is received from a patient while the account is with the agency, the agency is notified. Collection agencies are often paid on the basis of the amount of money they collect. For example, a collection agency may keep 30 percent of the amount they collect.

When a payment is received from a collection agency, it must be posted to the patient's account. The agency provides a statement that shows which patient accounts have paid and the amounts of the payments.

collection agency an outside firm hired to collect on delinquent accounts.

POSTING A PAYMENT FROM A COLLECTION AGENCY

The practice has received a payment from a collection agency for Ali Mazloum's account. Per the Family Care Center's financial policy, the account was assigned to the agency once it was more than ninety days past due. The statement included with the payment indicates that the agency collected 50 percent of the amount owed, or $360.25, as payment in full. The agency then subtracted its fee of 25 percent ($90.06), leaving a payment to the provider of $270.19. Post this amount to the patient's account in Medisoft®.

Amount owed	$720.50
Amount collected	360.25
Fees	90.06
Net paid to provider	270.19

Date: October 31, 2018

1. Change the Medisoft Program Date to October 31, 2018.

2. On the Activities menu, click Enter Transactions. The Transaction Entry dialog box is displayed.

3. Key **M** in the Chart box and then press Tab to select Ali Mazloum.

4. Verify that Accident is active in the Case box.

5. In the Payments, Adjustments, And Comments section of the dialog box, click the New button.

6. Verify that the entry in the Date box is 10/31/2018.

7. Click in the Pay/Adj Code box, select the payment code 04—Collections payment from collections as the payment code, and then press Tab.

8. Verify that Mazloum, Ali—Guarantor is listed in the Who Paid box.

9. Enter **Collections payment** in the Description field.

10. Enter the amount of the payment, **270.19**, in the Amount box and then press Tab.

11. The Unapplied Amount box should read ($270.19).

12. Your screen should look like the dialog box in Figure 10-7.

13. Click the Apply button. The Apply Payment to Charges dialog box is displayed.

14. In the first line of charges, the amount owed is $178.00. Since the payment is for more than $178.00, you will enter $178.00 toward this charge and the remaining amount to the other charges. Enter **178.00** in the This Payment box for the first charge and press Enter.

15. Check the amount that is listed in the upper-right corner of the dialog box to see the amount of the payment that is still unapplied

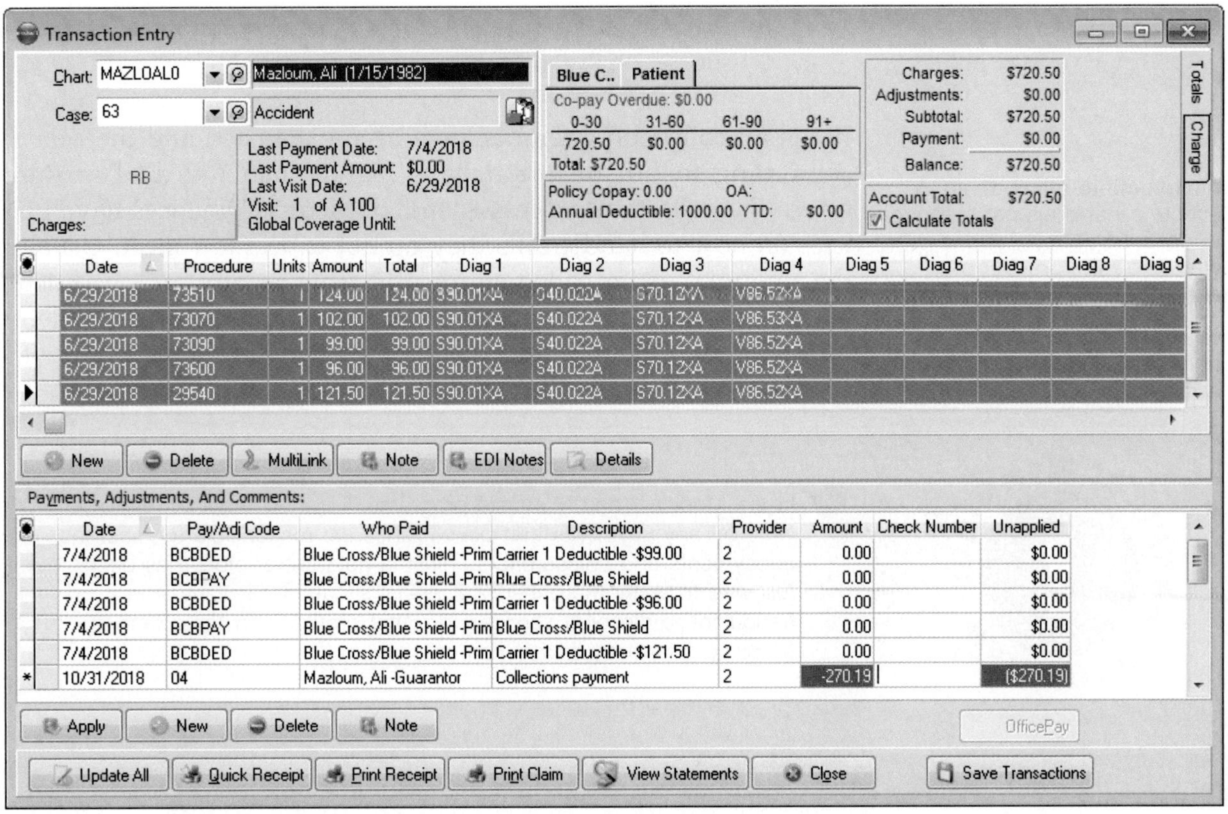

Figure 10-7 Transaction Entry Dialog Box After Collections Payment Is Entered

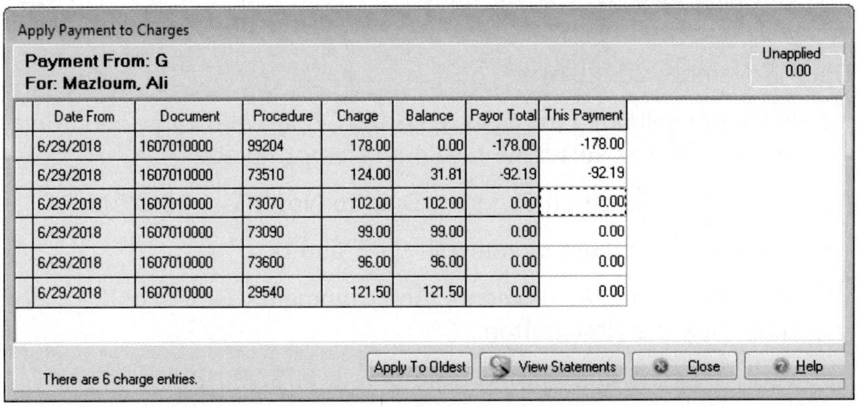

Figure 10-8 Apply Payment to Charges Dialog Box After Collections Payment Is Applied

(−92.19). Enter the remaining unapplied amount to the charge on the second line. Check your work against Figure 10-8.

16. Click the Close button.

17. Click the Save Transactions button.

18. When a Date of Service Validation message appears, click Yes to save the transaction. Leave the Transaction Entry dialog box open.

✓ **You have completed Exercise 10-3.**

10.6 WRITING OFF UNCOLLECTIBLE ACCOUNTS

uncollectible account an account that does not respond to collection efforts and is written off the practice's expected accounts receivable.

write-off a balance that has been removed from a patient's account.

When all collection attempts have been exhausted and the cost of continuing to pursue the debt is higher than the total amount owed, the collection process is ended. Medical practices have policies on how to handle bills they do not expect to collect. Usually, the amount owed is called an **uncollectible account** or a bad debt, and it is written off the practice's expected accounts receivable. A **write-off** is a balance that has been removed from a patient's account.

In the Medicare and Medicaid programs, it is fraudulent to forgive or write off any payments that beneficiaries are responsible for, such as copayments and coinsurance, unless a rigid set of steps has been followed to verify the patient's financial situation. Similarly, it is fraudulent to discount services for other providers or their families, which was formerly a common practice.

| EXERCISE 10-4 | WRITING OFF A PATIENT BALANCE |

Connect users: go to http://connect.mheducation.com to complete this exercise! Some steps may differ from what is listed here, so be sure to refer to the steps listed in Demo and Practice Modes for guidance.

The collection agency accepted 50 percent of the amount owed from Ali Mazloum as payment in full. The practice manager has informed you that the remaining balance is to be written off, even though it is a significant amount.

Date: November 30, 2018

1. If it is not still open from Exercise 10-3, open the Transaction Entry dialog box and select Ali Mazloum's chart number.

2. Change the Medisoft Program Date to November 30, 2018.

3. Verify that Accident is active in the Case box.

4. In the Payments, Adjustments, And Comments section of the dialog box, click the New button.

5. Verify that the entry in the Date box is 11/30/2018.

6. Click in the Pay/Adj Code box, select WRITEOFF—Write Off as the adjustment code and press Tab.

7. Select Mazloum, Ali—Guarantor in the Who Paid box.

8. Enter **Auth SMZ** in the Description box. These are the initials of the practice manager who approved the write-off.

9. Enter the amount to be written off, **450.31**, in the Amount box and press Tab.

10. The Unapplied Amount box should read ($450.31). Check your work against Figure 10-9.

11. Click the Apply button. The Apply Adjustment to Charges dialog box is displayed.

Transaction Entry

Chart: MAZLOAL0 ▼ 🔍 Mazloum, Ali (1/15/1982)

Case: 63 ▼ 🔍 Accident

RB

Charges:

Last Payment Date: 10/31/2018
Last Payment Amount: -$270.19
Last Visit Date: 6/29/2018
Visit: 1 of A 100
Global Coverage Until:

Blue C.. | Patient

Co-pay Overdue: $0.00

	0-30	31-60	61-90	91+
	450.31	$0.00	$0.00	$0.00

Total: $450.31

Policy Copay: 0.00   OA:
Annual Deductible: 1000.00 YTD: $0.00

Charges: $720.50
Adjustments: $0.00
Subtotal: $720.50
Payment: -$270.19
Balance: $450.31

Account Total: $450.31
☑ Calculate Totals

	Date	Procedure	Units	Amount	Total	Diag 1	Diag 2	Diag 3	Diag 4	Diag 5	Diag 6	Diag 7	Diag 8	Diag 9
	6/29/2018	73510	1	124.00	124.00	S90.01XA	S40.022A	S70.12XA	V86.52XA					
	6/29/2018	73070	1	102.00	102.00	S90.01XA	S40.022A	S70.12XA	V86.53XA					
	6/29/2018	73090	1	99.00	99.00	S90.01XA	S40.022A	S70.12XA	V86.52XA					
	6/29/2018	73600	1	96.00	96.00	S90.01XA	S40.022A	S70.12XA	V86.52XA					
▶	6/29/2018	29540	1	121.50	121.50	S90.01XA	S40.022A	S70.12XA	V86.52XA					

[New] [Delete] [MultiLink] [Note] [EDI Notes] [Details]

Payments, Adjustments, And Comments:

	Date	Pay/Adj Code	Who Paid	Description	Provider	Amount	Check Number	Unapplied
	7/4/2018	BCBPAY	Blue Cross/Blue Shield -Prim	Blue Cross/Blue Shield	2	0.00		$0.00
	7/4/2018	BCBDED	Blue Cross/Blue Shield -Prim	Carrier 1 Deductible -$96.00	2	0.00		$0.00
	7/4/2018	BCBPAY	Blue Cross/Blue Shield -Prim	Blue Cross/Blue Shield	2	0.00		$0.00
	7/4/2018	BCBDED	Blue Cross/Blue Shield -Prim	Carrier 1 Deductible -$121.50	2	0.00		$0.00
	10/31/2018	04	Mazloum, Ali -Guarantor	Collections payment	2	-270.19		$0.00
▶	11/30/2018	WRITEOFF	Mazloum, Ali -Guarantor	Auth SMZ	2	-450.31		($450.31)

[Apply] [New] [Delete] [Note]   [OfficePay]

[Update All] [Quick Receipt] [Print Receipt] [Print Claim] [View Statements] [Close] [Save Transactions]

Figure 10-9   Transaction Entry Dialog Box After Write-Off Is Entered

12. Locate the Balance column. In the This Adjust. column, enter an amount equal to the amount in the Balance column for each outstanding charge.

13. When all the charges have been adjusted, click the Close button.

14. Confirm that amount listed in Account Total is $0.00.

15. Click the Save Transactions button. When the Date of Service Validation box appears, click Yes to save the transaction.

16. Close the Transaction Entry dialog box. **CiMO**

✓ You have completed Exercise 10-4.

10.7 USING A PATIENT AGING REPORT FOR COLLECTIONS

Medical practices frequently use practice management software to monitor collection activities. While specific collection features vary from program to program, common features used for this purpose include aging reports, collection lists, collection letters, and collection reports.

The aging report, which shows the status of each account over time, is an important tool in the collections process. For each account, an

Patient Aging by Date of Service
Family Care Center
Show all data where the Charges/Payments/Adj is on or before 9/30/2018

Chart	Name	0-30	31-60	61-90	91-120	121+	Total
FITZWJO0	Fitzwilliams, John	50.00					50.00
GLOVEOL0	Glover, Olivia			224.00			224.00
JONESEL0	Jones, Elizabeth	21.17		7.47			28.64
WONGJO10	Wong, Jo	7.47		7.47			14.94
WONGLIY0	Wong, Li	4.14					4.14
Report Totals:		82.78	0.00	238.94	0.00	0.00	321.72

Figure 10-10   Sample Patient Aging Report

aging report shows the patient's chart number and name, and the amount of unpaid charges in each of these categories:

- Current: Up to 30 days
- Past: 31 to 60 days
- Past: 61 to 90 days
- Past: 91 to 120 days
- Past: More than 121 days

Figure 10-10 shows a sample patient aging report created in Medisoft Reports.

EXERCISE 10-5   IDENTIFYING OVERDUE ACCOUNTS

Connect users: go to
http://connect.mheducation.com to
complete this exercise! Some steps may
differ from what is listed here, so be sure
to refer to the steps listed in Demo and
Practice Modes for guidance.

Review the patient aging report displayed in Figure 10-10. Using the information contained in the report, locate the patient accounts that are 61–90 days overdue. List the chart number, patient name, past-due amounts, and account balance below. This information will be used later on in Exercise 10-6 to create a tickler item for the practice's collection list.

Chart #	Name	Past 31–60	Past 61–90	Past 91+	Total

ciMo

✓ You have completed Exercise 10-5.

10.8 ADDING AN ACCOUNT TO THE COLLECTION LIST

Once overdue accounts have been identified, the next step is to add collection items to a collection list. The **collection list** is designed to track activities that need to be completed as part of the collection process. Ticklers or collection reminders are displayed as collection list items. A **tickler** is a reminder to follow up on an account that is entered on the collection list.

collection list a tool for tracking activities that need to be completed as part of the collection process.

tickler a reminder to follow up on an account.

In Medisoft, the selections for the Collection List feature are located on the Activities menu (see Figure 10-11).

USING THE COLLECTION LIST WINDOW

The Collection List dialog box displays ticklers that have already been entered into the database (see Figure 10-12). The information displayed in the dialog box depends on the dates entered in the Date boxes at the top-left corner of the window. For example, if the date in both boxes is 9/30/2018, only ticklers marked for follow-up on September 30, 2018, will be listed.

Options for controlling what appears in the Collection List window are at the top of the dialog box and include the following:

Date Items can be displayed for the current date, for a range of dates, or for all dates. By default, the current date (the Windows System Date) is used as the range of dates and only those tickler items that are due on that date are displayed. To see all ticklers regardless of the date, click the Show All Ticklers box.

Show All Ticklers A check in this box results in the listing of all tickler items.

Show Deleted Only A check in this box displays only ticklers that have been deleted.

Exclude Deleted A check in this box indicates that deleted ticklers are not displayed.

The Collection List dialog box contains the following information about each tickler item:

Item This unique number identifying a tickler item is assigned automatically by the program.

Responsible Party This field contains the chart number (patient/guarantor) or insurance code (insurance carrier) that identifies the responsible party for this item. By clicking a plus sign (+) that appears to the left of an entry, the field can be expanded to view more information about the responsible party. *Note:* The plus sign is only visible when a tickler has been entered.

Figure 10-11 Collection List Options on the Activities Menu

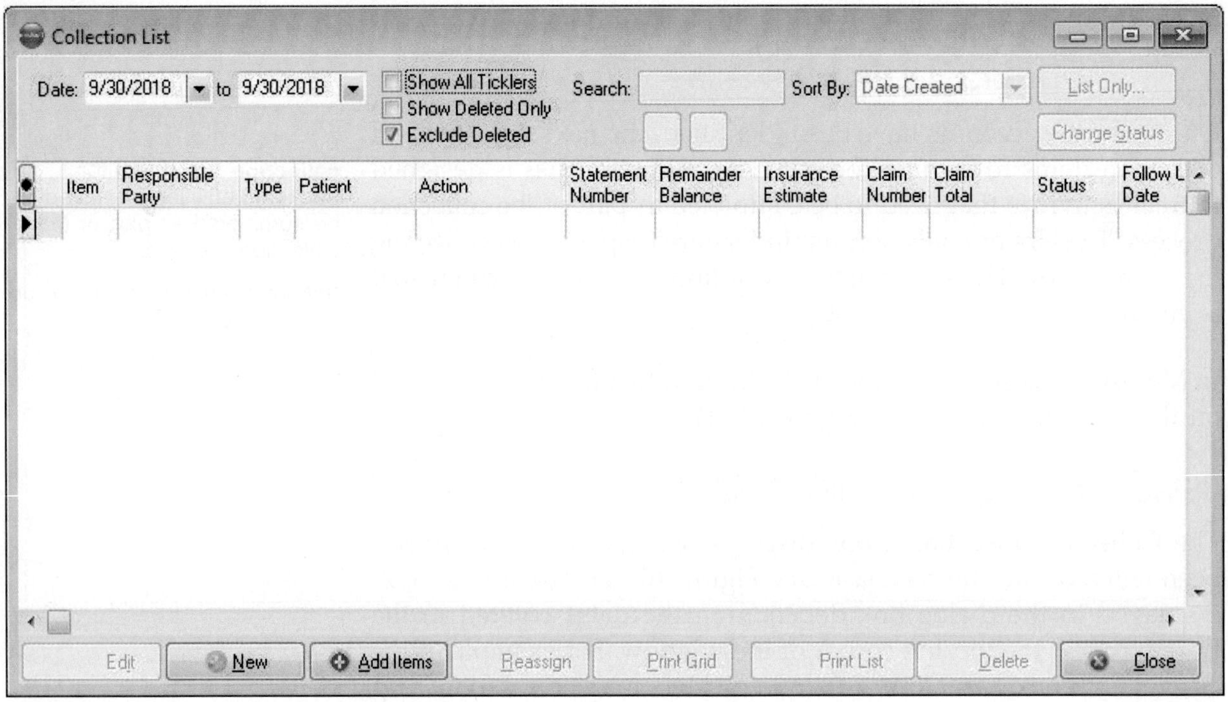

Figure 10-12 Collection List Dialog Box

When the responsible party is an insurance carrier, the following additional information appears (see Figure 10-13):

- Code
- Name
- Contact

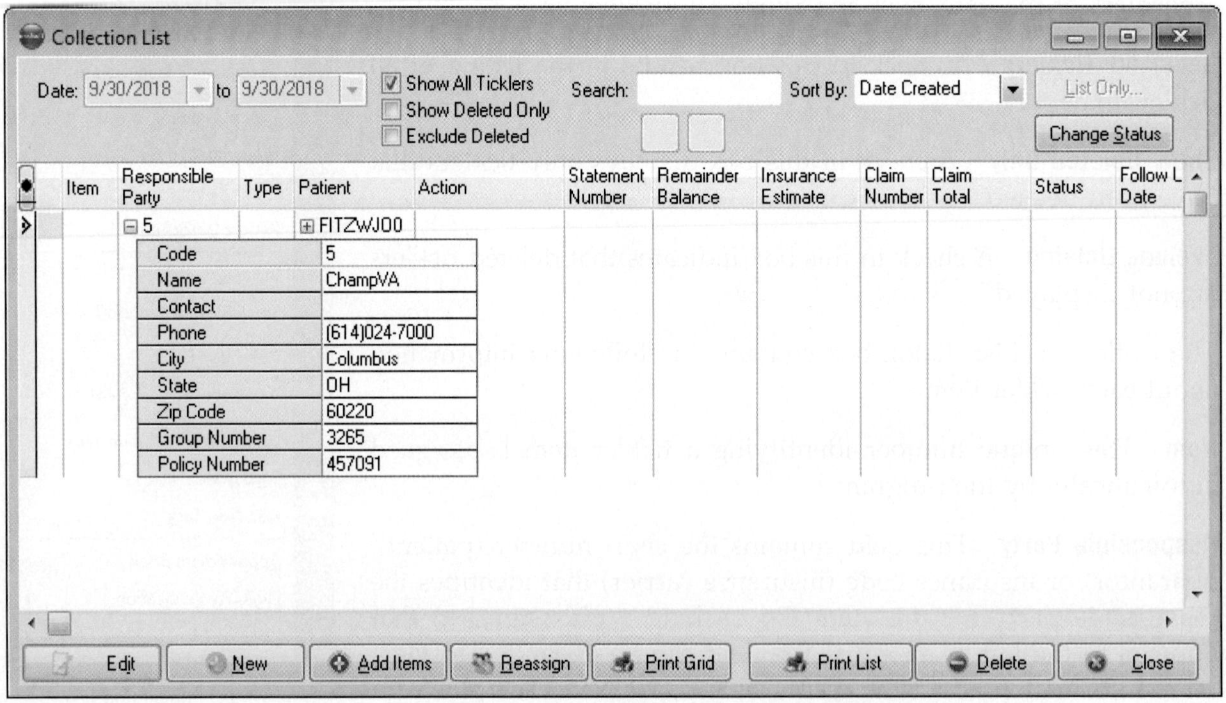

Figure 10-13 Additional Information Displayed When the Responsible Party Is an Insurance Carrier

- Phone
- City
- State
- Zip Code
- Group Number
- Policy Number

When the responsible party is a patient/guarantor, the following additional information is displayed (see Figure 10-14):

- Chart Number
- Name
- City
- Zip Code
- Phone 1
- Patient Reference Balance
- Payment Plan
- Plan Description
- Days in Cycle
- Amount Due

Type   The type is either *P* for Patient or *I* for Insurance. If the type is *P*, the responsible party is a patient. If the type is *I*, the responsible party is the insurance carrier.

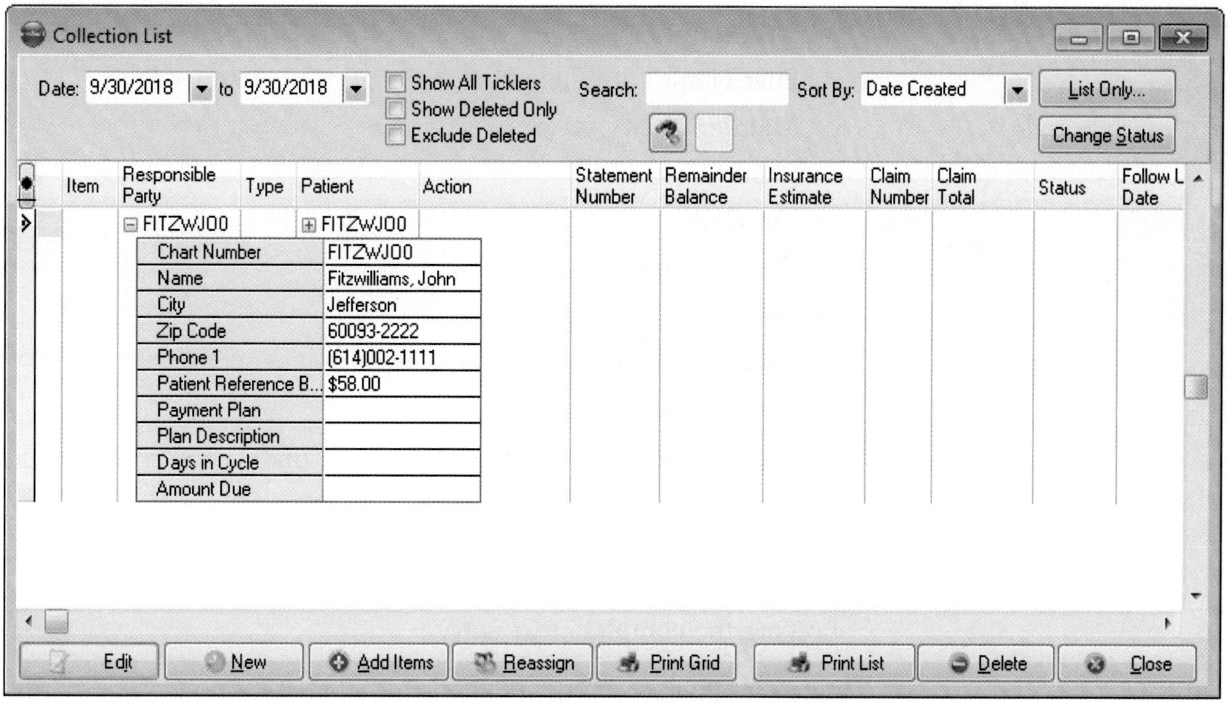

Item	Responsible Party	Type	Patient	Action	Statement Number	Remainder Balance	Insurance Estimate	Claim Number	Claim Total	Status	Follow L Date
	⊟ FITZWJ00		⊞ FITZWJ00								
	Chart Number		FITZWJ00								
	Name		Fitzwilliams, John								
	City		Jefferson								
	Zip Code		60093-2222								
	Phone 1		(614)002-1111								
	Patient Reference B...		$58.00								
	Payment Plan										
	Plan Description										
	Days in Cycle										
	Amount Due										

Figure 10-14   Additional Information Displayed When the Responsible Party Is a Patient/Guarantor

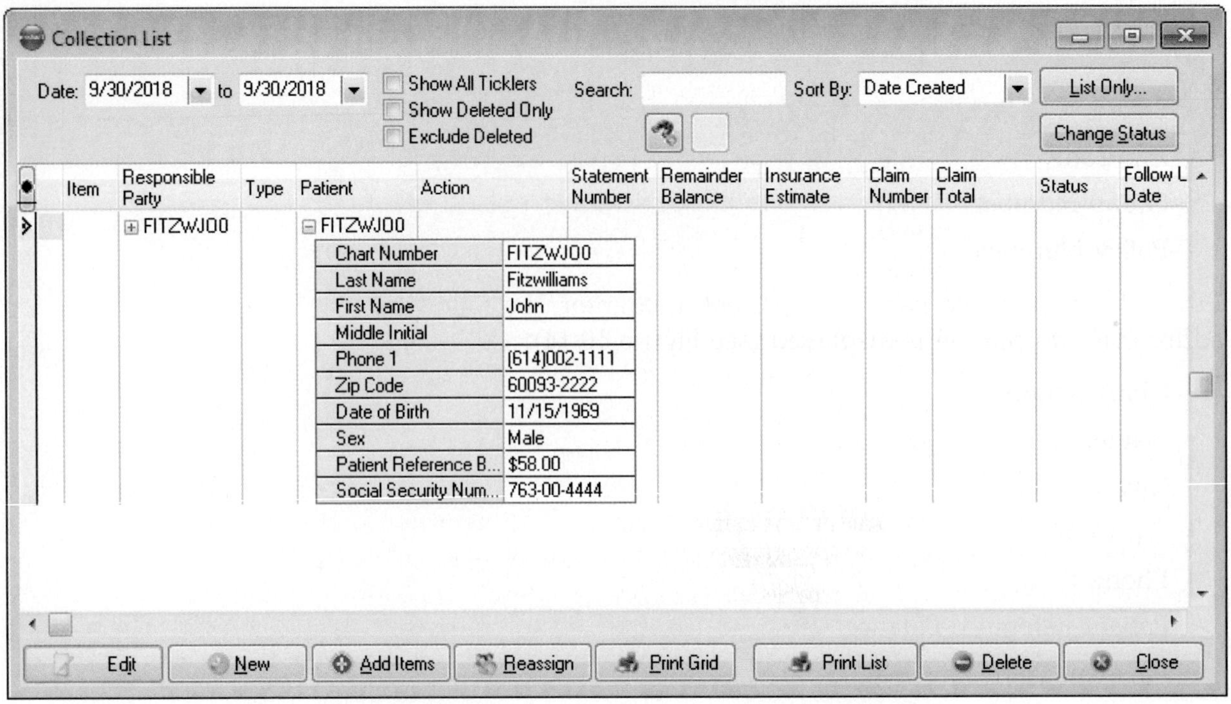

Figure 10-15 Additional Information Available in the Patient Field of the Collection List Dialog Box

Patient This field contains the patient chart number for this tickler. Clicking the plus sign (+) expands it to show more information on the patient (see Figure 10-15).

The additional information displayed includes:

- Chart Number
- Last Name
- First Name
- Middle Initial
- Phone 1
- Zip Code
- Date of Birth
- Sex
- Patient Reference Balance
- Social Security Number

Other information in the Collection List dialog box includes the following:

Action This field lists the action required. To see all of the text entered for this field, double-click in the field. This opens a window showing the complete text entry.

Statement Number If the tickler is for a patient, the statement number is listed.

Remainder Balance   If the responsible party type is Patient, the balance reported is the patient's balance as listed in Transaction Entry. If the responsible party type is Insurance, the balance reported is an estimated balance for the patient's specified carrier. This is the balance at the time the tickler is created. This balance does not refresh when payments are made to the patient's account. To manually update the amounts, the tickler must be edited and saved again.

Insurance Estimate   This field displays an estimate of the amount of payment expected from the insurance carrier.

Claim Number   If the tickler is for an insurance carrier, the claim number is listed in this column.

Claim Total   If the tickler is for an insurance carrier, the total amount of charges on the claim is listed here.

Status   The entries in the field are Open, Resolved, and Deleted.

Follow Up Date   This is the date the tickler will appear on the collection list.

Date Resolved   This is the date that the status of the item was changed to Resolved. Resolution is determined by the user.

User ID   The User ID identifies the user who is responsible for following up on the item. In an actual practice, users are assigned login names and passwords in the Security Setup area of the program.

ENTERING A TICKLER ITEM

A new tickler item is created by pressing the New button in the Collection List dialog box. This action opens the Tickler Item dialog box. The Tickler Item dialog box is displayed in Figure 10-16.

The Tickler Item dialog box contains two tabs for information: Tickler and Office Notes.

Tickler Tab

The following information is entered in the Tickler tab:

Action Required   The Action Required field specifies the action that is to be taken to remedy the problem. Up to eighty characters of text can be entered.

Responsible Party Type   The button selected in this field indicates whether the patient or the insurance carrier is responsible for the account balance. This entry also controls the contents of the drop-down lists for the Responsible Party field below.

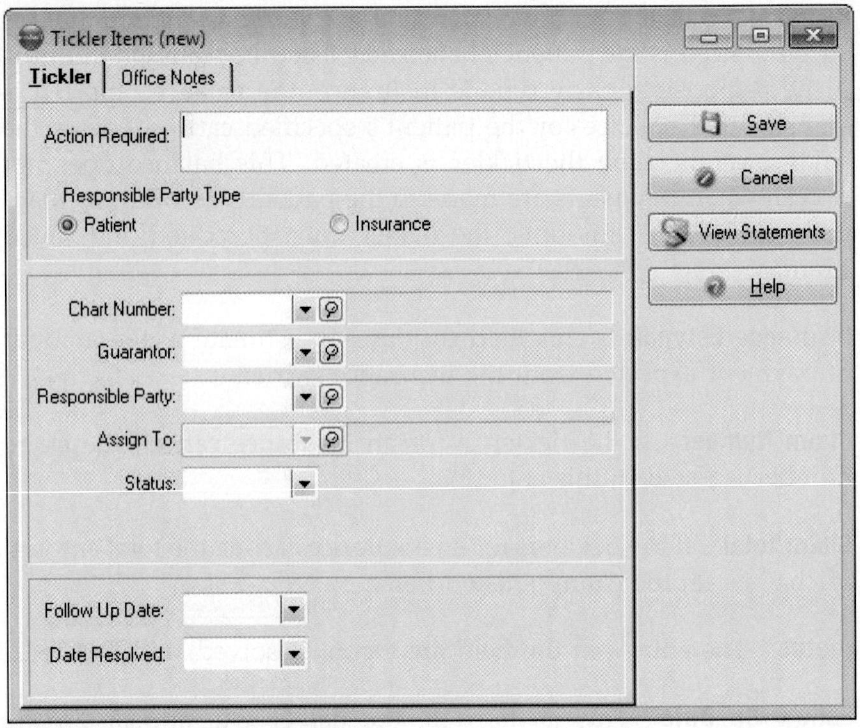

Figure 10-16   Tickler Item Dialog Box

Chart Number   The patient's chart number is selected from the list.

Guarantor   The Guarantor field lists the account guarantor chart number for this tickler item.

Responsible Party   If the responsible party type is Patient, a chart number is selected from the drop-down list. If the responsible party type is Insurance, the code for an insurance carrier is selected.

Assign To   The Assign To box lists the name of the individual responsible for following up on the tickler item. These names are set up by selecting Security Setup on the File menu. *Note:* This feature is not demonstrated in this text/workbook, so the field is grayed out and an entry cannot be made.

Status   The status of the tickler item is chosen from a drop-down list. The options are Open, Resolved, or Deleted.

Follow Up Date   This is the date the tickler will appear on the collection list if the Date range in the Collection List window is used. By default, Medisoft enters the current date—the Windows System Date—in this field.

Date Resolved   This field lists the date on which the status of the item was changed to Resolved. When the status is set to Resolved, the Date Resolved is set to the current date. Again, this is determined by the Windows System Date.

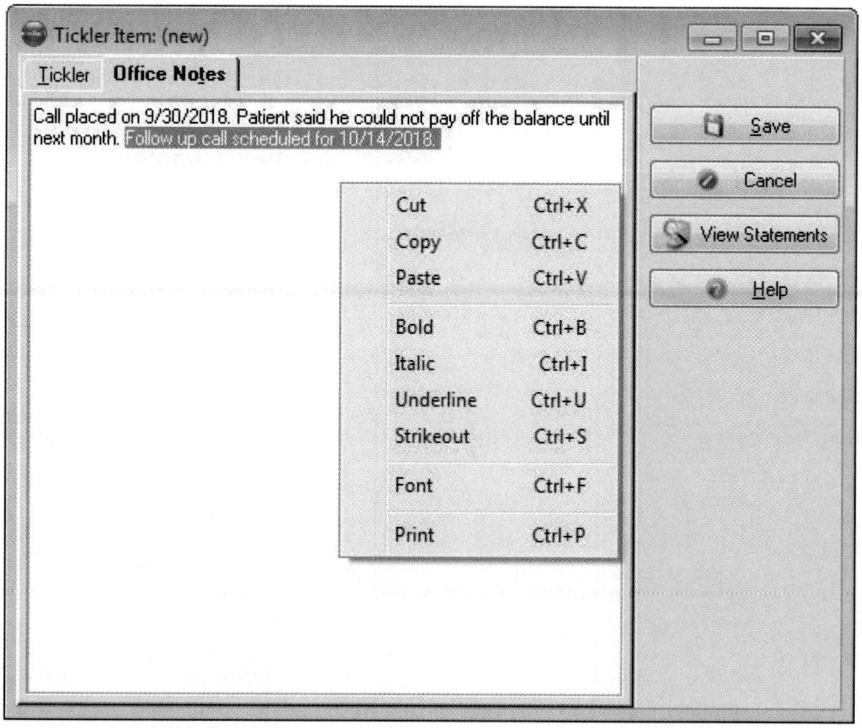

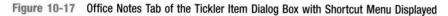

Figure 10-17   Office Notes Tab of the Tickler Item Dialog Box with Shortcut Menu Displayed

Office Notes Tab

The Office Notes tab consists of several buttons and a large area in which to enter notes. Notes that relate to the collection process of the selected tickler are entered in the large box.

When the right mouse button is clicked within the typing area, a shortcut menu is displayed (see Figure 10-17). Using this menu, notes can be edited, formatted, and printed from within the Office Notes tab.

Once a new tickler has been saved, the program automatically assigns a unique identifier code to the item.

CREATING A TICKLER   EXERCISE 10-6

Using the information in Exercise 10-5, create a tickler item for the patient who has an outstanding balance of more than $50.00 and whose account is more than sixty days overdue.

Date: September 30, 2018

1. Change the Medisoft Program Date to September 30, 2018.

2. Select Collection List on the Activities menu.

3. Enter **09302018** in both Date fields.

4. Click the New button to display the Tickler Item dialog box.

5. In the Action Required box, enter **Telephone call about overdue balance. See notes.**

6. Select Patient as the Responsible Party Type.

Connect users: go to http://connect.mheducation.com to complete this exercise! Some steps may differ from what is listed here, so be sure to refer to the steps listed in Demo and Practice Modes for guidance.

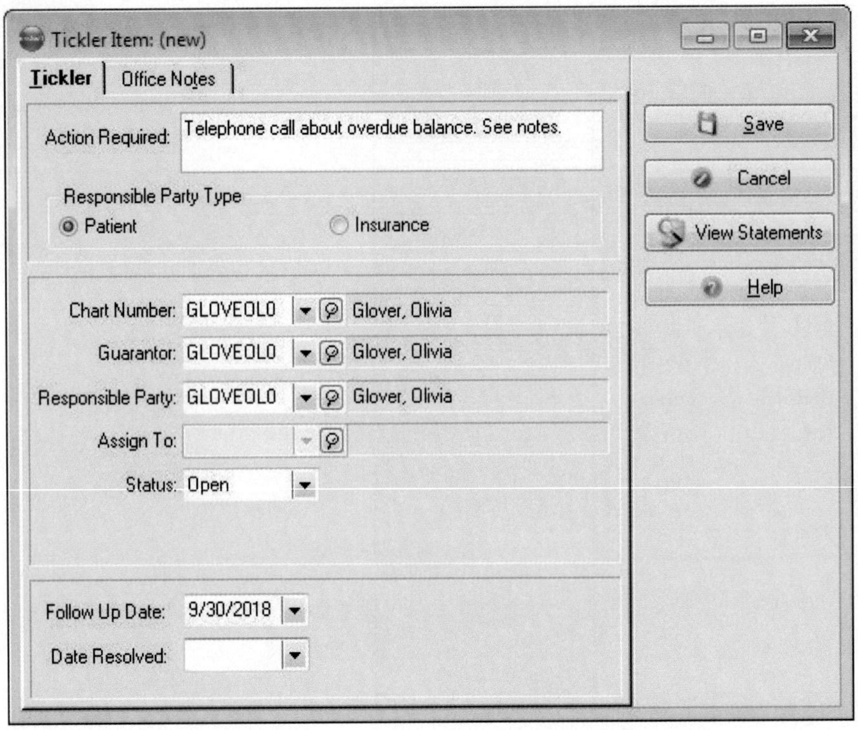

Figure 10-18 Completed Tickler Tab

7. Select the patient's chart number in the Chart Number field.

8. Select the guarantor in the Guarantor field.

9. Complete the Responsible Party field.

10. Leave the Assign To field blank. (In a real practice setting, this field would contain the name of the staff member who was assigned to follow up on this collection list item.)

11. Set the Status of the item to Open.

12. Change the entry in the Follow Up Date box to the current exercise date, 9/30/2018.

13. Leave the Date Resolved field blank. Check your work against Figure 10-18.

14. Click on the Office Notes tab and enter the following text: **Patient was assigned to a payment plan in July. So far no payments have been received.**

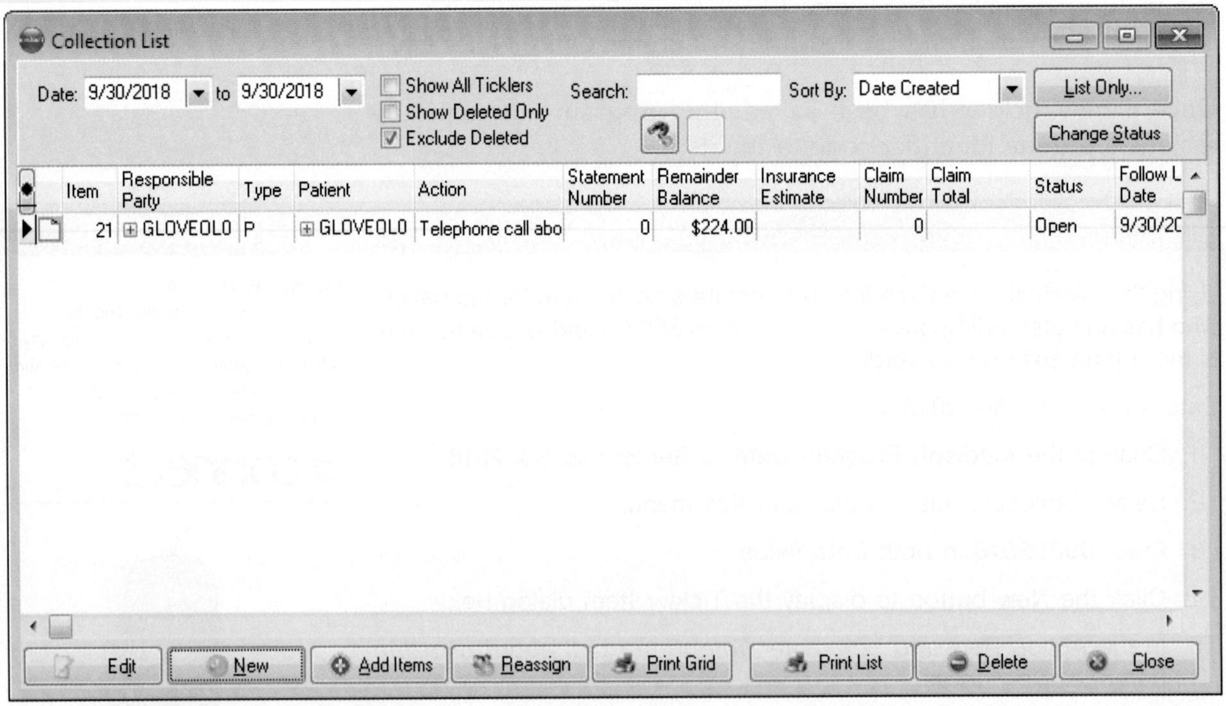

Figure 10-19 Tickler Added to Collection List

15. Click the Save button. The item is added to the collection list. Your screen should look like the window in Figure 10-19.

16. Click the Close button to close the Collection List dialog box.

✓ **You have completed Exercise 10-6.**

⚫ When an account is added to the collection list, the current balance for the tickler is determined. Once recorded in the tickler, it is not updated when new transactions are entered in the program.

For patient-responsible ticklers, the balance is the balance shown in the Transaction Entry window. It could also include insurance balances. For insurance-responsible ticklers, the balance is the estimated amount due from the assigned insurance carrier.

10.9 CREATING COLLECTION LETTERS

A number of actions must be taken within Medisoft before collection letters can be sent. A patient-responsible tickler item for the patient's account must be entered in the collection list. Also, a collection letter report must be created. This report is generated when the Patient Collection Letters option is selected on the Collection Reports submenu of the Reports menu (see Figure 10-20). The collection letter report lists patients with overdue accounts to whom statements have been mailed (see Figure 10-21).

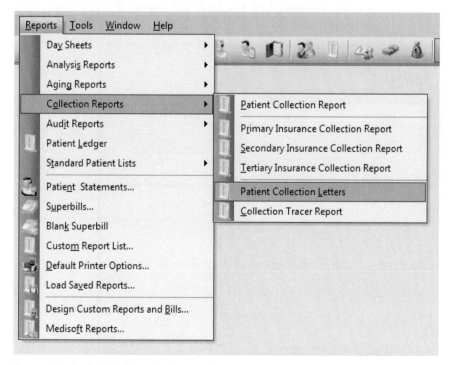

Figure 10-20 Patient Collection Letters Selected on the Collection Reports Submenu

Family Care Center
Collection Letter Report
10/31/2018

User ID:								
Item	Status	Responsible Party	Patient Chart	Date Created	Date Resolved	Follow Up Date	Balance	# Days Old
21	Open	Kristin Zapata	ZAPATKR0	10/31/2018		10/31/2018	$247.50	0
20	Open	Elizabeth Jones	JONESEL0	10/31/2018		10/31/2018	$28.64	0

Figure 10-21   Collection Letter Report

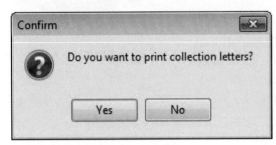

Figure 10-22   Confirm Dialog Box

After the patient collection report is printed (or the Preview window is closed), the program displays a Confirm dialog box that asks whether to print collection letters (see Figure 10-22).

If the Yes button is clicked, an Open Report dialog box appears (see Figure 10-23).

Once the OK button in the Open Report window is clicked, the program generates collection letters (see Figure 10-24).

After printing collection letters, an account alert appears in the Transaction Entry, Quick Ledger, and Appointment Entry windows and remains until the patient no longer has an open tickler in the collection list. There are three account alert abbreviations:

- **RB**   The patient has a remainder balance greater than the amount specified in the General tab in the Program Options window.

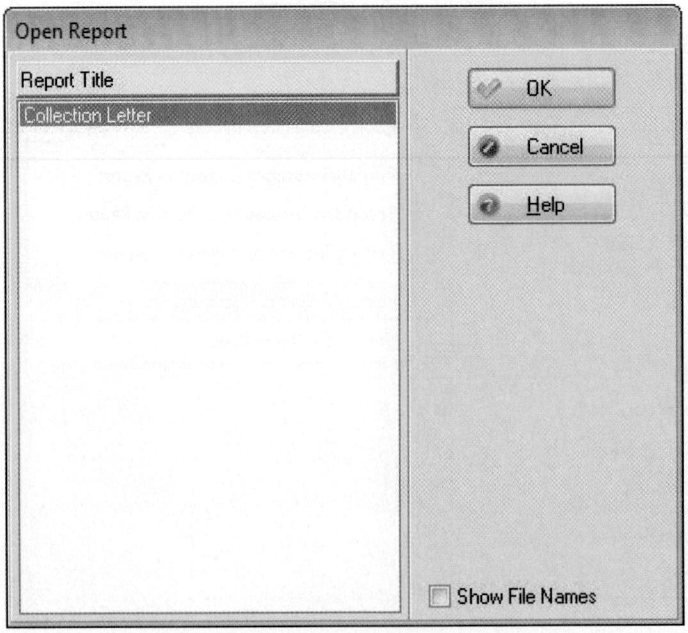

Figure 10-23   Open Report Window for Printing Collection Letters

Family Care Center
285 Stephenson Boulevard
Stephenson, OH 60089-1111
(614)555-0000

Kristin Zapata
109 East Milan Avenue
Stephenson, OH 60089-1111

10/31/2018
Patient Account: Zapata, Kristin

Dear Kristin Zapata

Our records indicate that your account with us is overdue. The total unpaid amount is *$ 282.50

If you have already forwarded your payment, please disregard this letter; otherwise, please forward
your payment immediately.

Please contact us at (614)555-0000 if you have any questions or concerns about your account.

Sincerely,

Katherine Yan

ZAPATKR0

*Balance does not reflect any outstanding insurance payments

Figure 10-24   Patient Collection Letter

Transaction Entry Dialog Box

Transaction Entry

Chart: ZAPATKR0 ▾ 🔍 Zapata, Kristin (1/16/1995)

Case: 60 ▾ 🔍 Preventive Exam

RB IC

Last Payment Date: 9/19/2018
Last Payment Amount: -$247.50
Last Visit Date: 10/1/2018
Visit: 2 of A 100
Charges: Global Coverage Until:

Blue C.. | Patient
Co-pay Overdue: $0.00

0-30	31-60	61-90	91+
282.50	$0.00	$0.00	$0.00

Total: $282.50

Policy Copay: 0.00 OA:
Annual Deductible: 1000.00 YTD: $0.00

Charges: $282.50
Adjustments: $247.50
Subtotal: $530.00
Payment: -$247.50
Balance: $282.50

Account Total: $282.50
☑ Calculate Totals

	Date	Procedure	Units	Amount	Total	Diag 1	Diag 2	Diag 3	Diag 4	Diag 5	Diag 6	Diag 7	Diag 8	Diag 9
	8/27/2018	9.385	1	247.50	247.50	Z00.00								
▶	10/1/2018	NSFEE	1	35.00	35.00	Z00.00								

account alert--
RB remainder balance
IC in collections

[New] [Delete] [MultiLink] [Note] [EDI Notes] [Details]

Payments, Adjustments, And Comments:

	Date	Pay/Adj Code	Who Paid	Description	Provider	Amount	Check Number	Unapplied
▶	9/8/2018	BCBPAY	Blue Cross/Blue Shield -Prim	#23451234 Blue Cross/Blue Shie	1	0.00	23451234	$0.00
	9/8/2018	BCBDED	Blue Cross/Blue Shield -Prim	Carrier 1 Deductible -$247.50	1	0.00		$0.00
	9/19/2018	02	Zapata, Kristin -Guarantor		1	-247.50	1078	$0.00
	10/1/2018	NSF		Returned Check	1	247.50	1033	$0.00

[Apply] [New] [Delete] [Note] OfficePay

[Update All] [Quick Receipt] [Print Receipt] [Print Claim] [View Statements] [Close] [Save Transactions]

Figure 10-25   Transaction Entry Dialog Box with Account Alert Message Displayed

- **DP**   The patient is delinquent on his or her payment plan.
- **IC**   The patient account is in collections. (For this message to appear, a collection letter must have been printed.)

A sample account alert in the Transaction Entry window is displayed in Figure 10-25.

EXERCISE 10-7   CREATING A COLLECTION LETTER

Create a collection letter for the patient you added to the collection list in Exercise 10-6.

Date: September 30, 2018

1. Select Collection Reports > Patient Collection Letters on the Reports menu. The Print Report Where? dialog box appears. Accept the default entry to preview the report and click the Start button. The Data Selection Questions dialog box appears.

2. Leave the Responsible Party Range and the Patient Range boxes blank. Enter **09302018** in both Follow Up Date Range boxes.

3. In the first Balance Range field, enter 50. Press Tab.

4. Leave the other boxes as they are, except for the check boxes at the bottom of the dialog box. Click the box Exclude items that follow Payment Plan. *Note: Even though Olivia Glover was assigned to a payment plan, she has not made any payments. As a result, she will be included in the Collection Letter Report.*

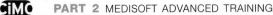

Collection Letter Report: Data Selection Questions

NOTE: A blank field indicates no limitation, all records will be included.

Responsible Party Range:		to	
Patient Range:		to	
Follow Up Date Range:	9/30/2018	to	9/30/2018
Date Created Range:		to	
Item Number Range:		to	
Balance Range:	50	to	99999
Status Match:	0		

☑ Exclude items that follow Payment Plan
☑ Generate Collection Letters
☑ Add To Collection Tracer

[✔ OK]   [⊘ Cancel]   [◉ Help]

Figure 10-26 Data Selection Questions Dialog Box Completed

5. Click the Generate Collection Letters box. The Add to Collection Tracer box will automatically be checked. Compare your screen to Figure 10-26.

6. Click the OK button. The collection letter report appears.

7. Click the Close button to exit the Preview window.

8. A Confirm dialog box is displayed, asking if collection letters should be printed. Click the Yes button. The Open Report window appears.

9. Select Collection Letter if it is not already selected and click OK.

10. The Print Report Where? dialog box appears. Select the option to send the report directly to the printer and click the Start button. (*Note:* If the letter is not actually printed, the account alert message feature will not work in the next step.)

11. Open the Transaction Entry dialog box and select Olivia Glover in the Chart field. Notice that the letters *RB DP IC* appear in red in the upper-left section of the window. This is an account alert message, indicating that the account has a remainder balance, is delinquent on a payment plan, and is in collections. Close the Transaction Entry dialog box.

Note: The date shown in the collection letter is the current date—the Windows System Date. In an actual office setting, this date would be the actual date the letter was created. **CiMO**

✔ **You have completed Exercise 10-7.**

10.10 CREATING A COLLECTION TRACER REPORT

A **collection tracer report** is used to keep track of collection letters that were sent. The report lists the tickler item number, the responsible party, the chart number, the account balance (as of the date

collection tracer report a tool for keeping track of collection letters that were sent.

Family Care Center
Collection Tracer Report
10/31/2018

Item #	Responsible Party	Patient Chart	Balance	Date Letter Sent	Reasons
Elizabeth Jones					
2	Elizabeth Jones	JONESEL0	28.64	10/31/2018	The outstanding balance is greater than 0.01.
				Total Letters Sent:	1
Kristin Zapata					
3	Kristin Zapata	ZAPATKR0	247.50	10/31/2018	The outstanding balance is greater than 0.01.
				Total Letters Sent:	1

Figure 10-27   Collection Tracer Report

the tickler was created), the date the collection letter was sent, and the reasons the account is in collections (see Figure 10-27).

EXERCISE 10-8   CREATING A COLLECTION TRACER REPORT

Connect users: go to http://connect.mheducation.com to complete this exercise! Some steps may differ from what is listed here, so be sure to refer to the steps listed in Demo and Practice Modes for guidance.

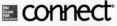

Create a collection tracer report.

Date: September 30, 2018

1. Select Collection Reports > Collection Tracer Report on the Reports menu.

2. In the Print Report Where? dialog box, click the Start button to preview the report on the screen.

3. In the Data Selection Questions dialog box, select Olivia Glover in both Responsible Party Range boxes.

4. Leave the Date Letter Sent Range boxes blank to include all dates.

5. Click the OK button.

6. The report appears in the Preview window. When you are finished viewing the report, close the Preview window. **CiMO**

✓ **You have completed Exercise 10-8.**

APPLYING YOUR SKILLS

12: PRINT A PATIENT AGING REPORT

December 31, 2018

Print a Date Accurate Patient Aging by Date of Service report for charges, payments, and adjustments on or before 12/31/2018. (This report is included in the Medisoft Reports feature, in the Aging Power Pack folder.) Review the status of Lisa Wright's account.

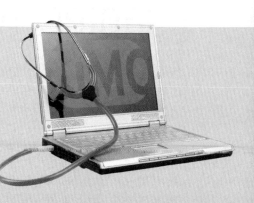

APPLYING YOUR SKILLS

13: ADD A PATIENT TO THE COLLECTION LIST

December 31, 2018

Add an item to the collection list for patient Lisa Wright. Notice that her account has an overdue balance. Add a tickler to the collection list indicating that her account is overdue. Enter **Call about overdue account** in the Action Required field. Enter **12312018** as the follow-up date. (Remember to change entries in the Date fields at the top of the Collection List to 12/31.)

APPLYING YOUR SKILLS

14: CREATE A COLLECTION LETTER

December 31, 2018

Create a collection letter for Lisa Wright. When setting up the collection letter report, be sure to enter Lisa Wright's chart number in the Responsible Party Range boxes; check the Exclude items that follow Payment Plan box and the Generate Collection Letters box. The Add to Collection Tracer box will be checked automatically.

Remember to create a backup of your work before exiting Medisoft! To help you keep track of your work, name the backup file after the chapter you are working on; for example, StudentID-c10.mbk.

BE THE DETECTIVE!

If assigned by your instructor, complete the Collections Payment Video Case in Connect. Put your skills to use identifying mistakes made in Medisoft and enhance your knowledge by determining the impact of those mistakes.

chapter 10 worksheet

[Note: These questions are designed for students using the live Medisoft CD software, since students may need to refer back to specific screens in the software to answer the questions.]

1. *[LO 10.4]* In Exercise 10-2, what is listed in the Description field in the Payment Plan tab of the Patient/Guarantor dialog box?

2. *[LO 10.5]* In Exercise 10-3, what is the amount of the payment entered on 10/31/2018?

3. *[LO 10.6]* In Exercise 10-4, what is entered in the Pay/Adj Code box for the entry on 11/30/2018?

4. *[LO 10.7]* In Exercise 10-6, who is listed in the Responsible Party field of the Tickler Item dialog box?

5. *[LO 10.8]* In Exercise 10-6, what is listed in the Status column of the Collection List dialog box?

6. *[LO 10.7]* In the collection letter printed in Exercise 10-7, what is listed as the total unpaid amount?

7. *[LO 10.9]* After completing Exercise 10-7, what six letters are displayed under the Case field in the Transaction Entry dialog box for Olivia Glover?

8. *[LO 10.10]* In the report created in Applying Your Skills 12, how many patients have accounts that are more than 121 days late?

9. *[LO 10.10]* What is listed in the Guarantor field in the Tickler Item dialog box in Applying Your Skills 13?

10. *[LO 10.10]* In Applying Your Skills 14, whose name appears after the closing "Sincerely,"?

11. *[LO 10.10]* In Applying Your Skills 14, what is listed as the total unpaid amount in the letter to Lisa Wright?

LEARNING OUTCOMES	CONCEPTS TO REVIEW
10.1 Explain the importance of prompt follow-up on insurance claims.	The financial well-being of a practice depends on timely payment from insurance carriers. If initial claims or resubmissions are not filed within a certain period of time, the insurance carrier will not pay the claim. In turn, the provider cannot bill the patient for the uncollected amount.
10.2 Summarize the importance of a financial policy in a medical office.	A financial policy is used to communicate how a practice handles financial matters, such as past-due balances and payments for services not covered by insurance. When patients are aware of and understand a practice's financial policy, they are more likely to pay their accounts on time.
10.3 Identify the laws that regulate collections from patients.	The Fair Debt Collection Practices Act of 1977 and the Telephone Consumer Protection Act of 1991 regulate debt collections.
10.4 Demonstrate how to create a payment plan and assign a patient account to a payment plan.	To create a new payment plan: 1. Click the Lists menu and select Patient Payment Plan. 2. Click the New button. 3. Enter a three-digit alphanumeric code in the Code field. 4. Enter a description of the plan in the Description field. 5. Enter the desired due date in the First Payment Due field. 6. Enter the desired number of days in the Due Every field. 7. Enter the desired amount in the Amount Due field. 8. Click the Save button. To assign a patient account to a payment plan: 1. Click the Lists menu and select Patients/Guarantors and Cases. 2. Enter the patient's chart number in the Search for field. 3. Click the Edit Patient button. 4. Click the Payment Plan tab. 5. Click in the Payment Code field and select the desired code. 6. Click the Save button.

LEARNING OUTCOMES	CONCEPTS TO REVIEW
10.5 Demonstrate how to post a payment from a collection agency.	1. On the Activities menu, click Enter Transactions. 2. Select the patient in the Chart box. 3. Verify that the correct case is active in the Case box. 4. In the Payments, Adjustments, And Comments section of the dialog box, click the New button. 5. Verify the entry in the Date box. 6. Click in the Pay/Adj Code box and select the payment code 04—Patient pymt via collections. 7. Verify that the guarantor is listed in the Who Paid box. 8. Enter *Collections payment* in the Description field. 9. Enter the amount of the payment in the Amount box. 10. Click the Apply button. 11. Enter the amount of the payment that is to be applied to each charge until the unapplied amount is zero. 12. Click the Close button. 13. Click the Save Transactions button.
10.6 Discuss the process of writing off uncollectible accounts.	1. Open the Transaction Entry dialog box. 2. Select the patient in the Chart box. 3. Verify that the correct case is active in the Case box. 4. In the Payments, Adjustments, And Comments section of the dialog box, click the New button. 5. Verify the entry in the Date box. 6. Click in the Pay/Adj Code box and select WRITEOFF—Write Off as the adjustment code. 7. Verify that the guarantor is listed in the Who Paid box. 8. Enter an authorization in the Description field, if appropriate. 9. Enter the amount to be written off in the Amount box. 10. Click the Apply button. 11. Locate the Balance column. In the This Adjust. Column, enter an amount equal to the amount in the Balance column for each outstanding charge. 12. When all the charges have been adjusted, click the Close button. 13. Click the Save Transactions button. 14. Close the Transaction Entry dialog box.

LEARNING OUTCOMES	CONCEPTS TO REVIEW
10.7 Explain how to use a patient aging report to identify past-due accounts.	The aging report shows the status of each patient's account over time. For each account, an aging report shows the patient's chart number and name and the amount of unpaid charges categorized by the number of days past due. Using this report, it is possible to identify patients who have the largest outstanding balance, as well as the most overdue balance.
10.8 Demonstrate how to add an account to the collection list.	1. Select Collection List on the Activities menu. 2. Make appropriate entries in the Date fields. 3. Click the New button to display the Tickler Item dialog box. 4. Make an appropriate entry in the Action Required box. 5. Select Patient as the Responsible Party Type. 6. Select the patient's chart number in the Chart Number field. 7. Select the guarantor in the Guarantor field. 8. Complete the Responsible Party field. 9. Leave the Assign To field blank. (In a real practice setting, this field would contain the name of the staff member who was assigned to follow up on this collection list item.) 10. Set the Status of the item to Open. 11. Enter a value in the Follow Up Date field. 12. Leave the Date Resolved field blank. 13. Click the Office Notes tab and enter any additional notes. 14. Click the Save button. 15. The account is added to the collection list. Close the Collection List dialog box.

LEARNING OUTCOMES	CONCEPTS TO REVIEW

10.9
Demonstrate how to create a collection letter.
	1. Select Collection Reports > Patient Collection Letters on the Reports menu.
	2. The Print Report Where? dialog box appears. Make an appropriate entry. The Data Selection Questions dialog box appears.
	3. If needed, make selections in the following boxes:
	    Responsible Party Range
	    Patient Range
	    Follow Up Date Range
	    Date Created Range
	    Item Number Range
	    Balance Range
	    Status Match
	4. Click in the Exclude items that follow Payment Plan box.
	5. Click in the Generate Collection Letters box. The Add to Collection Tracer box will automatically be checked.
	6. Click the OK button. The collection letter report appears.
	7. Click the Close button to exit the Preview window.
	8. A Confirm dialog box is displayed, asking if collection letters should be printed. Click the Yes button. The Open Report window appears.
	9. Select Collection Letter, if it is not already selected, and click OK.
	10. The Print Report Where? dialog box appears. Select the option to send the report directly to the printer and click the Start button. (*Note:* If the letter is not actually printed, the account alert message feature will not work.)

10.10 Demonstrate how to create a collection tracer report.	1. Select Collection Reports > Collection Tracer Report on the Reports menu. 2. In the Print Report Where? dialog box, click the Start button to preview the report on the screen. 3. In the Data Selection Questions dialog box, enter information as needed in the Responsible Party Range and Date Letter Sent Range boxes. 4. Click the OK button. 5. The report appears in the Preview window. When you are finished viewing the report, close the Preview window.

USING TERMINOGY

Match the terms on the left with the definitions on the right.

1. *[LO 10.5]* collection agency
2. *[LO 10.8]* collection list
3. *[LO 10.10]* collection tracer report
4. *[LO 10.4]* payment plan
5. *[LO 10.1]* prompt payment laws
6. *[LO 10.8]* tickler
7. *[LO 10.1]* timely filing
8. *[LO 10.6]* uncollectible account
9. *[LO 10.6]* write-off

a. An agreement between a patient and a practice in which the patient agrees to make regular monthly payments over a specified period of time.

b. A reminder to follow up on an account.

c. An outside firm hired to collect on delinquent accounts.

d. An account that does not respond to collection efforts and is written off the practice's expected accounts receivable.

e. A balance that is removed from a patient's account.

f. A time period within which claims must be filed with an insurance carrier.

g. Legislation that mandates a time period within which clean claims must be paid; if they are not, financial penalties are levied against the payer.

h. A tool for tracking activities that need to be completed as part of the collection process.

i. A tool for tracking collection letters that were sent.

CHECKING YOUR UNDERSTANDING

10. *[LO 10.1]* A claim denial tracking log lists the reason a claim was denied payment, the action taken to correct the problem, and the status of the _____.

11. *[LO 10.2]* According to the Commonwealth Fund, _____ percent of Americans ages 19–64 had problems paying or were unable to pay medical bills in 2012.

12. *[LO 10.3]* General guidelines for telephone collection practices recommend not calling before 8:00 a.m. or after _____ p.m.

13. *[LO 10.4]* A new payment plan is created by selecting Patient Payment Plan on the _____ menu.

14. *[LO 10.5]* What is the two-digit payment code used to enter a payment from a collection agency?

15. *[LO 10.6]* An account that must be written off the practice's expected accounts receivable is called a(n) _____.

16. *[LO 10.7]* On a patient aging report, what number of days is used to represent current accounts?

17. *[LO 10.8]* In the Collection List dialog box, the entry in the Type field, which describes the responsible party, is either *P* for patient or *I* for _____.

18. *[LO 10.9]* If a patient's account is in collections, what two-letter code appears in red in the Transaction Entry dialog box?

19. *[LO 10.10]* The report that tracks collection letters is called the _____ report.

20. *[LO 10.8]* A new tickler item is created by clicking the New button in the _____ dialog box

APPLYING YOUR KNOWLEDGE

21. *[LO 10.1]* Why is it important to review reports received from a clearinghouse?

22. *[LO 10.2]* What is the purpose of a medical practice's financial policy?

23. *[LO 10.2]* What is the first step in the collection process?

24. *[LO 10.7]* How is an aging report used to identify accounts for collection?

25. *[LO 10.9]* What two steps need to occur before a collection letter can be printed in Medisoft?

26. *[LO 10.1]* If a biller or insurance specialist finds that a number of claims are rejected for the same reason, what should he or she do?

27. *[LO 10.2]* Why is it important for a medical practice to share its financial policy with patients?

28. *[LO 10.5]* What are the positive and negative factors in using an outside collection agency to pursue overdue patient accounts?

 connect Enhance your learning by completing these exercises and more at http://connect.mheducation.com

part 3

APPLYING YOUR SKILLS

chapter 11

APPOINTMENTS AND REGISTRATION

an overview of chapters 11–14

Chapters 11–14 provide you with an opportunity to practice what you learned in Chapters 2–10. These last chapters differ from the others in several ways:

- The purpose of these chapters is to see how well you have mastered the Medisoft® skills taught in earlier chapters, rather than to cover new topics.

- Minimal instructions are provided for the exercises in Chapters 11, 12, and 13. In Chapter 14, you are on your own—no instructions are provided.

- Convenient cross-references are provided to pages in the earlier chapters that teach each Medisoft skill, in case you need to review a procedure or refresh your skills. These references are listed at the beginning of each chapter, under the heading What You Need to Know, for each Medisoft function.

- There are no objectives, key terms, or end-of-chapter exercises.

Additional practice is available in the companion text/workbook, *Case Studies for Use with Computers in the Medical Office, 9e. Case Studies* contains a realistic and extensive simulation covering two weeks of billing work in a medical office. Students use *Medisoft® Advanced Version 19* to complete the daily tasks. This capstone simulation gives students enhanced training that fosters superior qualifications for a variety of medical office jobs. Extensive hands-on practice with realistic source documents teaches students to input information; schedule appointments; and handle billing, reports, and other essential tasks. For students who have completed the study of Medisoft Advanced Version 19 using *Computers in the Medical Office, Case Studies* is the next step in learning practice management in a clear, logical progression—just like a real medical practice!

what you need to know

To complete the exercises in this chapter, you need to know how to:

- Schedule appointments. (Chapter 3, pages 89–98)
- Cancel or reschedule an appointment. (Chapter 3, pages 104–105)
- Print a provider schedule. (Chapter 3, pages 117–118)
- Enter a new patient. (Chapter 4, pages 130–144)
- Update information on an established patient. (Chapter 4, pages 149–150)
- Locate patient information. (Chapter 4, pages 144–149)

The Family Care Center uses Office Hours as the primary tool for recording appointments. For the simulations in this chapter, assume that you are the front-desk receptionist and are responsible for most of the center's scheduling tasks.

It is Tuesday, November 6, 2018. You are reviewing a call report from the answering service from last night. Several patients have requested appointments. As you return the phone calls, schedule appointments as appropriate.

SCHEDULING AN APPOINTMENT: LAWANA BROOKS — EXERCISE 11-1

Lawana Brooks is experiencing a cough and would like to make an appointment with Dr. McGrath.

Start Medisoft and restore the backup file from your last work session.

Schedule Ms. Brooks for a fifteen-minute appointment with Dr. McGrath on November 9, 2018, at 10:00 a.m.

✓ **You have completed Exercise 11-1.**

SCHEDULING AN APPOINTMENT: EDWIN HSU — EXERCISE 11-2

Edwin Hsu calls and says that he feels his head is congested and he has postnasal drip and a cough. He would like to come in to see Dr. McGrath.

Schedule Mr. Hsu for a fifteen-minute appointment with Dr. McGrath on November 9, 2018, at 11:15 a.m.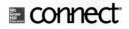

✓ **You have completed Exercise 11-2.**

EXERCISE 11-3

SCHEDULING AN APPOINTMENT: ANTHONY BATTISTUTA

Anthony Battistuta calls to request an appointment for his regular diabetes check-up. He is one of Dr. McGrath's patients. Before he hangs up, he states that he and Mrs. Battistuta have sold their house and moved to a condominium at 36 Grant Blvd., Grandville, OH, 60092-1111. Their phone number is the same. Since the visit is for an existing condition, a new case is not needed.

Schedule a thirty-minute appointment for Mr. Battistuta on November 9, 2018, with Dr. McGrath at 9:00 a.m. Change his address in the database and also change the address for his wife, Pauline. (*Hint:* Change this information in the Patient/Guarantor dialog box.) **ciMO**

✓ **You have completed Exercise 11-3.**

EXERCISE 11-4

SCHEDULING AN APPOINTMENT: STEWART ROBERTSON

For this exercise, you need Source Document 13.

Stewart Robertson calls to ask whether Dr. Beach is in the OhioCare HMO network and whether she could become his primary care provider. He says he is in good health but would like a physical since he has not had one for many years. Dr. Beach is in the OhioCare HMO network and is accepting new patients.

Since he is a new patient, create a chart number and enter his information in the Patient/Guarantor dialog box. Then schedule Mr. Robertson for a sixty-minute appointment with Dr. Beach at 3:00 p.m. on Monday, November 12, 2018. **ciMO**

✓ **You have completed Exercise 11-4.**

For this exercise, you need Source Document 14.

Debra Syzmanski has phoned to ask whether her daughter Hannah could be seen by Dr. Banu. Hannah is the daughter of Michael and Debra Syzmanski, who are both Dr. Banu's patients. Hannah's pediatrician, Dr. Harold Gearhart, has referred her to the Family Care Center.

Create a chart number for Hannah and enter her information in the Patient/Guarantor dialog box. Then schedule Hannah for a forty-five-minute routine physical examination with Dr. Banu on November 9, 2018, at 10:00 a.m.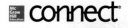

 You have completed Exercise 11-5.

Carlos Lopez has just called to say that he lost his appointment card and cannot remember the time of his November 28, 2018 appointment. He thinks he may have a scheduling conflict. If the appointment is in the morning, he wants it changed to 2:00 p.m. the same day. If the 2:00 slot is not available, he needs to make the appointment for the next day at the earliest possible time.

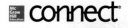

Find out who Lopez's doctor is by calling up the Patient/Guarantor dialog box in Medisoft. Then select Lopez's provider from the Provider drop-down list in Office Hours. Locate Mr. Lopez's appointment on November 28. Check to see whether the 2:00 p.m. time is available. If it is available, move his appointment to that time slot. If not, schedule him for the earliest possible appointment on November 29.

You have completed Exercise 11-6.

EXERCISE 11-7   JUGGLING SCHEDULES

Luther Jackson's sister is on the phone. She will be taking care of the Jackson twins, Darnell and Tyrone, on Saturday, December 8, 2018, and she needs to make appointments for both of them for tetanus shots at 9:00 a.m. or later with Dr. Banu.

Check Dr. Banu's schedule for December 8. If she is available, book the appointments at 9:00 a.m. and 9:15 a.m. If Dr. Banu is not available, check the schedules of Dr. McGrath and Dr. Beach and book the appointments as early in the day as possible, but not before 9:00 a.m. **CiMO**

✓ **You have completed Exercise 11-7.**

EXERCISE 11-8   SCHEDULING AN APPOINTMENT: MICHAEL SYZMANSKI

Michael Syzmanski calls and asks to speak with Dr. Banu. He sounds upset. Dr. Banu is not available, so you ask if you can take a message. He reports that he has had more than one incident lately of blood in his stools. Looking at Dr. Banu's schedule, you ask if he would like to make an appointment. He responds that he would like an appointment as soon as possible.

Schedule him for a sixty-minute appointment at 2:30 p.m. with Dr. Banu on November 12, 2018. **CiMO**

✓ **You have completed Exercise 11-8.**

Print Dr. Patricia McGrath's schedule for November 9, 2018.

Connect users: go to http://connect.mheducation.com to complete this exercise! Some steps may differ from what is listed here, so be sure to refer to the steps listed in Demo and Practice Modes for guidance.

✓ **You have completed Exercise 11-9.**

Remember to create a backup of your work before exiting Medisoft! To help you keep track of your work, name the backup file after the chapter you are working on; for example, StudentID-c11.mbk.

chapter 12

CASES, TRANSACTIONS, AND CLAIMS

To complete the exercises in this chapter, you need to know how to:

- Change the Medisoft Program Date. (Chapter 2, pages 62–64)
- Schedule appointments. (Chapter 3, pages 89–98)
- Locate patient information. (Chapter 4, pages 144–149)
- Enter a new patient. (Chapter 4, pages 130–144)
- Update information on an established patient. (Chapter 4, pages 149–150)
- Create a new case. (Chapter 5, pages 157–188)
- Copy and modify an existing case. (Chapter 5, pages 188–189)
- Enter procedures, charges, and diagnoses. (Chapter 6, pages 200–211)
- Record payments from patients. (Chapter 6, pages 211–220)
- Record payments from insurance carriers. (Chapter 8, pages 279–286)
- Create walkout receipts. (Chapter 6, pages 220–223)
- Create insurance claims. (Chapter 7, pages 249–252)
- Enter and apply a payment from an insurance carrier. (Chapter 8, pages 279–297)

All office personnel at the Family Care Center (FCC) know how to enter patient charges and payments in Medisoft. Whenever possible, patient transactions are entered into the computer the same day as their office visit. On busy days, however, or when the office is understaffed because one of the staff is sick or on vacation, input of transactions may be delayed.

The transactions in the chapter are entered on November 12, 2018. However, as you will learn in Exercise 12-1, not all transactions actually occurred on November 12. Be sure to change the Medisoft Program Date as needed to match the date of the patient's visit.

ENTERING TRANSACTIONS | EXERCISE 12-1

For this exercise, you need Source Documents 14–18.

Start Medisoft and restore the backup file from your last work session.

It is Monday morning, November 12, 2018. Since the staff was unable to enter all of Friday's office visits, you are responsible for entering transactions from Friday afternoon. First, you arrange the encounter forms alphabetically:

Anthony Battistuta

Lawana Brooks

Edwin Hsu

Hannah Syzmanski

First, determine if any patients need new cases. If they do, create the cases. Then enter the transactions. Walkout receipts should be created for patients who make a payment at the time of an office visit. (Remember to change the Medisoft Program Date to November 9, 2018.) **CiMO**

✓ **You have completed Exercise 12-1.**

Connect users: go to http://connect.mheducation.com to complete this exercise! Some steps may differ from what is listed here, so be sure to refer to the steps listed in Demo and Practice Modes for guidance.

AN UNSCHEDULED VISIT | EXERCISE 12-2

You will need Source Document 19 for this exercise.

It is still Monday morning, November 12. Carlos Lopez came in to see Dr. McGrath without an appointment. He said he felt like his heart was beating too fast, and he was clearly concerned. Dr. McGrath fit Mr. Lopez into her schedule at 10:30 a.m. She examined him and determined that he was suffering from heart palpitations. First, you need to enter the appointment and check-in the patient. Then, create a new case by copying an existing case and changing the necessary information. Finally, enter the procedure charges, accept Mr. Lopez's payment, and create a walkout receipt. Make sure all transaction information is properly recorded. **CiMO**

Connect users: go to http://connect.mheducation.com to complete this exercise! Some steps may differ from what is listed here, so be sure to refer to the steps listed in Demo and Practice Modes for guidance.

✓ **You have completed Exercise 12-2.**

EXERCISE 12-3 — CHANGING A TRANSACTION RECORD

You need Source Document 17 for this exercise.

Just as you finish entering Mr. Lopez's visit, Dr. McGrath comes to the desk to say that she thinks she forgot to check off the chest X-ray (single view) she performed on Edwin Hsu on November 9, 2018, on the encounter form. She asks you to check and to add the charge if necessary.

Look at Mr. Hsu's encounter form to find out if the box was checked. If it was, check that the transaction was entered in Medisoft. If it was not, enter the transaction now. (*Hint:* Before you enter the charge, remember to change the date entry in the Date box to November 9, 2018.)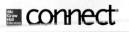

✓ **You have completed Exercise 12-3.**

EXERCISE 12-4 — SCHEDULING AN APPOINTMENT: DIANE HSU

Diane Hsu, the wife of Edwin Hsu, calls to request an appointment, today if possible, with Dr. McGrath. She has a fever of 101 degrees, body aches, and chills.

Schedule her for a thirty-minute appointment at 4:30 p.m. today with Dr. McGrath. (*Hint:* Remember to change the date back to today, November 12, 2018 before entering the appointment.)

✓ **You have completed Exercise 12-4.**

ENTERING CHARGES AND PAYMENTS: STEWART ROBERTSON

EXERCISE 12-5

For this exercise, you need Source Documents 13 and 20.

Stewart Robertson, a new patient, has arrived in the office for his exam. First, open the Patient/Guarantor dialog box and check the Signature on File box in the Other Information tab. Enter November 12, 2018 in the Signature Date field and save your work. Create a case and enter the charges and the copayment for his visit. Add him to the Recall List for a physical examination one year from today.

Connect users: go to http://connect.mheducation.com to complete this exercise! Some steps may differ from what is listed here, so be sure to refer to the steps listed in Demo and Practice Modes for guidance.

✓ **You have completed Exercise 12-5.**

ENTERING CHARGES AND PAYMENTS: DIANE HSU

EXERCISE 12-6

For this exercise, you need Source Document 21.

Dr. McGrath has just finished examining Diane Hsu. She has diagnosed her condition as influenza. After checking her records in Medisoft, you determine that a new case is required.

Create a new case for Mrs. Hsu by copying an existing case and modifying the relevant information. Then enter the charges and payments for today's visit in Medisoft. Create a walkout receipt for Mrs. Hsu.

Connect users: go to http://connect.mheducation.com to complete this exercise! Some steps may differ from what is listed here, so be sure to refer to the steps listed in Demo and Practice Modes for guidance.

✓ **You have completed Exercise 12-6.**

EXERCISE 12-7

ENTERING CHARGES AND PAYMENTS: MICHAEL SYZMANSKI

For this exercise, you need Source Document 22.

Michael Syzmanski is at the checkout desk. He was just seen by Dr. Banu because he had several episodes of bright red blood in his stool. Dr. Banu examined Mr. Syzmanski and asked him to complete a fecal occult blood test at home and return for a follow-up visit in one week.

Since this appointment is for a new condition, a new case is needed. Create the case by copying and modifying an existing case and then enter the charges and payments from today's visit. Create a walkout receipt for Mr. Syzmanski. Finally, schedule him for a fifteen-minute follow-up visit one week from today (at 4:00 p.m. or later, if possible). **ciMO**

✓ **You have completed Exercise 12-7.**

EXERCISE 12-8

ENTERING AND APPLYING AN INSURANCE CARRIER PAYMENT

For this exercise, you need Source Document 23.

It is still November 12, 2018. A remittance advice and electronic funds transfer (EFT) have been received from East Ohio PPO. Enter the deposit in Medisoft and apply the payment to the appropriate patient accounts.

Follow the procedures that you practiced in Chapter 8 for entering and applying insurance payments. **ciMO**

✓ **You have completed Exercise 12-8.**

Today you entered charges and copayments for a number of patients. Before you go home, you need to create insurance claims for these patients. Using the procedure that you learned in Chapter 7, create insurance claims for these patients. Then, for the claims just created, change the claim status from Ready to Send to Sent. **CiMO**

 You have completed Exercise 12-9.

Anthony Battistuta is on the phone. He would like to know the amount of the charges from November 9 that he is responsible for, assuming that Medicare pays its portion (80 percent) of the total charges.

To find the amount he is responsible for, begin by locating the charges for his visit in the Entering Transactions dialog box. Verify that the Diabetes case is active in the Case box. Look at the Allowed column in the Charges section for the three procedures on 11/9/2018. Add up the amounts in the Allowed column to determine how much Medicare is likely to pay. Since you know that Medicare pays 80 percent of the allowed amount and the patient is responsible for the remaining 20 percent, calculate how much the patient is likely to owe for the visit. **CiMO**

You have completed Exercise 12-10.

EXERCISE 12-11 CREATING PATIENT STATEMENTS

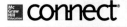

Today is November 30, 2018. Create Remainder Statements for all patients. **ciMO**

☑ **You have completed Exercise 12-11.**

Remember to create a backup of your work before exiting Medisoft! To help you keep track of your work, name the backup file after the chapter you are working on; for example, StudentID-c12.mbk.

chapter 13

REPORTS AND COLLECTIONS

what you need to know

To complete the exercises in this chapter, you need to know how to:

- Change the Medisoft Program Date. (Chapter 2, pages 62–64)
- Create a day sheet report. (Chapter 9, pages 336–342)
- Create a patient aging report. (Chapter 9, page 356)
- Create a practice analysis report. (Chapter 9, pages 342–347)
- Add an item to the collection list. (Chapter 10, pages 387–395)
- Create collection letters. (Chapter 10, pages 395–399)

Because Medisoft® is a medical billing program, its most powerful features involve computerized manipulation of account data. Medisoft uses information in the system to produce reports on any facet of patients' or insurers' accounts and to generate claims for insurance companies and statements for patients. As long as the office personnel in the Family Care Center have entered transactions correctly, Medisoft can be used to print reports on the center's finances.

EXERCISE 13-1   CREATING A PATIENT DAY SHEET REPORT

Connect users: go to http://connect.mheducation.com to complete this exercise! Some steps may differ from what is listed here, so be sure to refer to the steps listed in Demo and Practice Modes for guidance.

Start Medisoft and restore the backup file from your last work session.

Create a patient day sheet report for November 12, 2018. Apply the procedure that you learned in Chapter 9 to create the report.

Medisoft Program Date: November 12, 2018 ciMO

☑ **You have completed Exercise 13-1.**

EXERCISE 13-2   CREATING A PATIENT AGING REPORT

Connect users: go to http://connect.mheducation.com to complete this exercise! Some steps may differ from what is listed here, so be sure to refer to the steps listed in Demo and Practice Modes for guidance.

Create a Date Accurate Patient Aging by Date of Service report, as of November 30, 2018. The report shows which accounts are overdue and how long they have been overdue.

Medisoft Program Date: November 30, 2018 ciMO

☑ **You have completed Exercise 13-2.**

Print a practice analysis report for the month of November 2018.

Medisoft Program Date: November 30, 2018

 You have completed Exercise 13-3.

Study the Date Accurate Patient Aging by Date of Service report created in Exercise 13-2. Determine which patients have outstanding balances of greater than $5.00 that are more than ninety days past due.

Be sure to enter *11302018* in both Dates fields in the Collection List dialog box.

Add these patient accounts to the collection list. In the Action Required box, enter **Call about overdue account**. (Note: Do not include Olivia Glover's account since you added it to the list in Chapter 10.)

Medisoft Program Date: November 30, 2018

You have completed Exercise 13-4.

EXERCISE 13-5 CREATING COLLECTION LETTERS

Create collection letters for the patient(s) you just added to the collection list.

Medisoft Program Date: November 30, 2018

✓ **You have completed Exercise 13-5.**

Remember to create a backup of your work before exiting Medisoft! To help you keep track of your work, name the backup file after the chapter you are working on; for example, StudentID-c13.mbk.

PUTTING IT ALL TOGETHER

chapter 14

what you need to know

To complete the exercises in this chapter, you need to know how to:

- Change the Medisoft Program Date. (Chapter 2, pages 62–64)
- Schedule appointments. (Chapter 3, pages 89–98)
- Enter a new patient. (Chapter 4, pages 130–144)
- Create a new case. (Chapter 5, pages 157–188)
- Copy and modify an existing case. (Chapter 5, pages 189–189)
- Enter procedures, charges, and diagnoses. (Chapter 6, pages 200–211)
- Record payments from patients. (Chapter 6, pages 211–220)
- Record payments from insurance carriers. (Chapter 8, pages 279–286)
- Create walkout receipts. (Chapter 6, pages 220–223)
- Create insurance claims. (Chapter 7, pages 249–252)
- Enter and apply a payment from an insurance carrier. (Chapter 8, pages 279–297)
- Enter a capitation payment and adjust capitated accounts. (Chapter 8, pages 299–306)
- Create patient statements. (Chapter 8, pages 307–311)
- Print reports. (Chapter 9, pages 336–358)
- Add items to the collection list. (Chapter 10, pages 387–395)
- Create collection letters. (Chapter 10, pages 395–399)

In this chapter, you need to use almost all the skills you have practiced throughout the exercises in the book. If you have any problems, refer back to the chapters in the book that cover the material.

EXERCISE 14-1   SCHEDULING APPOINTMENTS

Start Medisoft and restore the backup file from your last work session.

Schedule appointments for January 2, 2019, for the following patients. Make sure they are scheduled for the appropriate providers.

Jackson, Luther	30 minutes	9:00 a.m.
Hsu, Edwin	15 minutes	9:15 a.m.
Simmons, Jill	15 minutes	10:15 a.m.
Stern, Nancy	1 hour	9:30 a.m.
Syzmanski, Debra	30 minutes	9:30 a.m.
Giles, Sheila	15 minutes	9:00 a.m.
Battistuta, Pauline	30 minutes	10:30 a.m.
Palmer, Christopher	30 minutes	4:00 p.m.

Note: Mr. Palmer is a new patient. Create a chart number and register him in Medisoft and then enter his appointment with Dr. Beach. Refer to Source Document 24 for the information you need. **CiMO**

 You have completed Exercise 14-1.

EXERCISE 14-2   RESCHEDULING AND CANCELING APPOINTMENTS

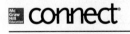

Ms. Giles just called to say she is running late for her 9:00 a.m. appointment. Jill Simmons has arrived for her 10:15 appointment, hoping she can see the doctor early. Switch the appointment times for Giles and Simmons. Also, Edwin Hsu just called and cannot make his 9:15 a.m. appointment with Dr. McGrath. Cancel the appointment for Edwin Hsu. **CiMO**

You have completed Exercise 14-2.

Print the appointment lists for January 2, 2019, for Dr. Banu, Dr. Beach, and Dr. McGrath. **CiMO**

Connect users: go to http://connect.mheducation.com to complete this exercise! Some steps may differ from what is listed here, so be sure to refer to the steps listed in Demo and Practice Modes for guidance.

☑ **You have completed Exercise 14-3.**

Check to determine whether new cases are needed for the patients with appointments on January 2, 2019. When appropriate, create new cases using the information found on Source Documents 24–31. **CiMO**

Connect users: go to http://connect.mheducation.com to complete this exercise! Some steps may differ from what is listed here, so be sure to refer to the steps listed in Demo and Practice Modes for guidance.

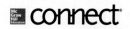

☑ **You have completed Exercise 14-4.**

EXERCISE 14-5 ENTERING TRANSACTIONS

Using Source Documents 25–31, record the charge and payment transactions for all of the patients who had appointments. Print walkout receipts for all patients who made payments. **CiMO**

✓ **You have completed Exercise 14-5.**

EXERCISE 14-6 CREATING CLAIMS

Create insurance claims for all transactions that have not already been placed on claims. Change the status of the newly created claims from Ready to Send to Sent. **CiMO**

✓ **You have completed Exercise 14-6.**

ENTERING INSURANCE PAYMENTS EXERCISE 14-7

Change the Medisoft Program Date to December 31, 2018.

Enter the insurance payments listed on Source Documents 32–35 and apply the payments to patient charges. For capitated payments, remember to identify patients covered by this plan who had visited the practice during the month of November 2018, using the List Only . . . button in the Claim Management window, then enter a zero insurance deposit to adjust capitated patient accounts to a zero balance.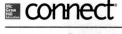

Connect users: go to http://connect.mheducation.com to complete this exercise! Some steps may differ from what is listed here, so be sure to refer to the steps listed in Demo and Practice Modes for guidance.

 You have completed Exercise 14-7.

CREATING PATIENT STATEMENTS EXERCISE 14-8

Create remainder statements as of December 31, 2018, for patients whose last names begin with the letters *J* through *Z*. Print any statements that were created.

Connect users: go to http://connect.mheducation.com to complete this exercise! Some steps may differ from what is listed here, so be sure to refer to the steps listed in Demo and Practice Modes for guidance.

You have completed Exercise 14-8.

EXERCISE 14-9 | PRINTING REPORTS

First, print a patient day sheet for December 31, 2018. Then print a patient day sheet for January 2, 2019. Finally, print a practice analysis report for the period of October 1, 2018, to December 31, 2018. **CiMO**

 You have completed Exercise 14-9.

EXERCISE 14-10 | ENTERING COLLECTION AGENCY AND PATIENT PAYMENTS

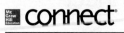

Date: December 31, 2018

COLLECTION AGENCY PAYMENT

A notice of an electronic payment from a collection agency has come in for Kristin Zapata's account. The agency collected the full amount owed to the practice, $282.50. The payment to the practice is the full amount minus the 25 percent fee charged by the agency. Calculate the net amount of the payment and enter it in Medisoft. Write off the remaining balance. Enter **SMZ**, the initials of the manager who approved the write off in the Description field.

PATIENT PAYMENT

A check has been received from Lisa Wright in the amount of $46.40. Enter the payment. The check number is 4629. **CiMO**

You have completed Exercise 14-10.

Date: December 31, 2018

PATIENT AGING REPORT

Print a Date Accurate Patient Aging by Date of Service report for transactions through December 31, 2018.

✓ **You have completed Exercise 14-11.**

Date: December 31, 2018

COLLECTION LIST

Study the patient aging report you created in Exercise 14-11. Determine which patient(s) have account balances of greater than $50.00 whose accounts are more than sixty days late. These patient(s) must be added to the collection list and sent collection letters. *Note:* If a patient is already on the collection list, they do not need to be added. *Hint:* To view all items on the collection list, be sure to check the box Show All Ticklers in the Collection List dialog box.

When completing the Tickler Item dialog box, enter **Call about overdue account** in the Action Required box and **12312018** in the Follow Up Date box. Complete the other fields as appropriate.

COLLECTION LETTERS

Create collection letters for the patient(s) you just added to the collection list. *Hint:* In the Collection Letter Report dialog box, enter **12312018** in both Follow Up Date Range boxes. Don't forget to check the Exclude Items that follow Payment Plan box and the Generate Collection Letters box.

✓ **You have completed Exercise 14-12.**

Remember to create a backup of your work before exiting Medisoft! To help you keep track of your work, name the backup file after the chapter you are working on; for example, StudentID-c14.mbk.

SOURCE
DOCUMENTS

1 source document

FAMILY CARE CENTER

PATIENT INFORMATION FORM

Patient

Last Name	First Name	MI	Sex	Date of Birth
Tanaka	Hiro		__ M X F	2 / 20 / 1983

Address	City	State	Zip
80 Cedar Lane	Stephenson	OH	60089

Home Ph # (614) 555-7373 Cell Ph # (614) 555-0162	Marital Status Single	Student Status

Race	Ethnicity	Language
__ American Indian or Alaska Native X Asian __ Black or African American __ White __ Other __ Native Hawaiian or Other Pacific Islander __ Declined	__ Hispanic or Latino X Non-Hispanic or Latino __ Declined	English

SS# Email	Allergies:
812-73-6000 htanaka@abc.com	penicillin

Employment Status	Employer Name	Work Ph #	Primary Insurance ID#
Full-time	McCray Manufacturing Inc.	(614) 555-1001	812736000 Group HJ31

Employer Address	City	State	Zip
1311 Kings Highway	Stephenson	OH	60089

Referred By	Ph # of Referral (614) 567-7896
Dr. Bertram Brown	

Responsible Party (Complete this section if the person responsible for the bill is not the patient)

Last Name	First Name	MI	Sex	Date of Birth
			__ M __ F	/ /

Address	City	State	Zip	SS#

Relation to Patient	Employer Name	Work Phone #
__ Spouse __ Parent __ Other		( )

Spouse, or Parent (if minor):	Home Phone # ( )

Insurance (If you have multiple coverage, supply information from both carriers)

Primary Carrier Name	Secondary Carrier Name
OhioCare HMO	
Name of the Insured (Name on ID Card)	Name of the Insured (Name on ID Card)
Hiro Tanaka	
Patient's relationship to the insured	Patient's relationship to the insured
X Self __ Spouse __ Child	__ Self __ Spouse __ Child
Insured ID #	Insured ID #
812736000	
Group # or Company Name	Group # or Company Name
HJ31	
Insurance Address	Insurance Address
147 Central Ave., Haleville, OH 60890	

Phone # 614-555-0101	Copay $ 20	Phone #	Copay $
	Deductible $		Deductible $

Other Information

Is patient's condition related to:	Reason for visit: back pain
__ Employment __ Auto Accident (if yes, state in which accident occurred: ___) __ Other Accident	

Date of Accident: / /   Date of First Symptom of Illness: 9 /23/2018

Financial Agreement and Authorization for Treatment

I authorize treatment and agree to pay all fees and charges for the person named above. I agree to pay all charges shown by statements, promptly upon their presentation, unless credit arrangements are agreed upon in writing.

I authorize payment directly to FAMILY CARE CENTER of insurance benefits otherwise payable to me. I hereby authorize the release of any medical information necessary in order to process a claim for payment in my behalf.

Signed: Hiro Tanaka

Date: 10/1/2018

FAMILY CARE CENTER **PATIENT INFORMATION FORM**

Patient

Last Name	First Name	MI	Sex	Date of Birth
Wright	Lisa		__ M X F	3 / 15 / 1978

Address	City	State	Zip
39 Woodlake Rd.	Stephenson	OH	60089

Home Ph # (614) 555-7059   Cell Ph # (614) 505-1397   Marital Status Divorced   Student Status

Race	Ethnicity	Language
__ American Indian or Alaska Native __ Asian X Black or African American __ White __ Other __ Native Hawaiian or Other Pacific Islander __ Declined	__ Hispanic or Latino X Non-Hispanic or Latino __ Declined	English

SS# Email	Allergies:
333-46-7904 lwright@abc.com	none

Employment Status	Employer Name	Work Ph #	Primary Insurance ID#
Full-time	Wheeler, Sampson, & Hull	(614) 086-9000	0032697 Group A4

Employer Address	City	State	Zip
100 Central Ave.	Stephenson	OH	60089

Referred By	Ph # of Referral (614) 444-3200
Dr. Marion Davis	

Responsible Party (Complete this section if the person responsible for the bill is not the patient)

Last Name	First Name	MI	Sex	Date of Birth
			__ M __ F	/ /

Address	City	State	Zip	SS#

Relation to Patient	Employer Name	Work Phone #
__ Spouse __ Parent __ Other		( )

Spouse, or Parent (if minor):	Home Phone # ( )

Insurance (If you have multiple coverage, supply information from both carriers)

Primary Carrier Name	Secondary Carrier Name
Blue Cross Blue Shield	
Name of the Insured (Name on ID Card)	Name of the Insured (Name on ID Card)
Lisa Wright	
Patient's relationship to the insured	Patient's relationship to the insured
X Self __ Spouse __ Child	__ Self __ Spouse __ Child
Insured ID #	Insured ID #
0032697	
Group # or Company Name	Group # or Company Name
Group A4	
Insurance Address	Insurance Address
340 Boulevard, Columbus, OH 60220	

Phone # 614-024-9000	Copay $	Phone #	Copay $
	Deductible $ $500 (met)		Deductible $

Other Information

Is patient's condition related to: Reason for visit: cough

__ Employment   __ Auto Accident (if yes, state in which accident occurred: ___)   __ Other Accident

Date of Accident: /   /   Date of First Symptom of Illness: /   /

Financial Agreement and Authorization for Treatment

I authorize treatment and agree to pay all fees and charges for the person named above. I agree to pay all charges shown by statements, promptly upon their presentation, unless credit arrangements are agreed upon in writing.

I authorize payment directly to FAMILY CARE CENTER of insurance benefits otherwise payable to me. I hereby authorize the release of any medical information necessary in order to process a claim for payment in my behalf.

Signed: Lisa Wright   Date: 10/1/2018

ENCOUNTER FORM

10/1/2018	**3:00 pm**
DATE	TIME
Hiro Tanaka	**TANAKHI0**
PATIENT NAME	CHART #

OFFICE VISITS - SYMPTOMATIC			
NEW			
99201	OF--New Patient Minimal		
99202	OF--New Patient Low	X	
99203	OF--New Patient Detailed		
99204	OF--New Patient Moderate		
99205	OF--New Patient High		
ESTABLISHED			
99211	OF--Established Patient Minimal		
99212	OF--Established Patient Low		
99213	OF--Established Patient Detailed		
99214	OF--Established Patient Moderate		
99215	OF--Established Patient High		
PREVENTIVE VISITS			
NEW			
99381	Under 1 Year		
99382	1 - 4 Years		
99383	5 - 11 Years		
99384	12 - 17 Years		
99385	18 - 39 Years		
99386	40 - 64 Years		
99387	65 Years & Up		
ESTABLISHED			
99391	Under 1 Year		
99392	1 - 4 Years		
99393	5 - 11 Years		
99394	12 - 17 Years		
99395	18 - 39 Years		
99396	40 - 64 Years		
99397	65 Years & Up		
PROCEDURES			
12011	Simple suture--face--local anes.		
29125	App. of short arm splint; static		
29425	Application of short leg cast, walking		
29540	Strapping, ankle		
50390	Aspiration of renal cyst by needle		
71010	Chest x-ray, single view, frontal		
71020	Chest x-ray, two views, frontal & lateral		

PROCEDURES		
71030	Chest x-ray, complete, four views	
73070	Elbow x-ray, AP & lateral views	
73090	Forearm x-ray, AP & lateral views	
73100	Wrist x-ray, AP & lateral views	
73510	Hip x-ray, complete, two views	
73600	Ankle x-ray, AP & lateral views	
LABORATORY		
80048	Basic metabolic panel	
80061	Lipid panel	
82270	Blood screening, occult; feces	
82947	Glucose screening--quantitative	
82951	Glucose tolerance test, three specimens	
83718	HDL cholesterol	
84478	Triglycerides test	
85007	Manual differential WBC	
85018	Hemoglobin	
85025	Complete CBC w/auto diff WBC	
85651	Erythrocyte sedimentation rate--non-auto	
86580	TB Mantoux test	
87040	Culture, bacterial; blood	
87076	Culture, anerobic isolate	
87077	Bacterial culture, aerobic isolate	
87086	Urine culture and colony count	
87430	Strep test	
87880	Direct streptococcus screen	
INJECTIONS AND OTHERS		
90471	Immunization administration	
90656	Influenza virus vaccine, 3+	
90662	Influenza virus vaccine, 65+	
90703	Tetanus injection	
92516	Facial nerve function studies	
93000	Electrocardiogram--ECG with interpretation	
93015	Treadmill stress test, with physician...	
96372	Injection	
96900	Ultraviolet light treatment	
99070	Supplies and materials provided	

FAMILY CARE CENTER
285 Stephenson Blvd.
Stephenson, OH 60089
614-555-0000

☐ DANA BANU, M.D.
☐ ROBERT BEACH, M.D.
☐ PATRICIA MCGRATH, M.D.

☐ JESSICA RUDNER, M.D.
☐ JOHN RUDNER, M.D.
☒ KATHERINE YAN, M.D.

NOTES

REFERRING PHYSICIAN
Bertram Brown, MD

NPI
1234567890

AUTHORIZATION #

DIAGNOSIS
M54.5, W11XXXD

PAYMENT AMOUNT
$20, check #123

source document 4

FAMILY CARE CENTER
285 Stephenson Boulevard
Stephenson, OH 60089
614-555-0000

KATHERINE YAN, M.D.
PHYSICIAN'S NOTES

PATIENT NAME	Hiro Tanaka
CHART NUMBER	TANAKHI0
DATE	10/1/2018
CASE	Back Pain

NOTES

Patient is here on referral from Dr. Bertram Brown, who assessed her in the ER for pain relating to a fall from a ladder at home on 9/23/2018. She has been attending physical therapy sessions daily and takes ibuprofen, 800 mg t.i.d. for pain as prescribed.

She is still experiencing stiffness and pain in the lower back.

Patient is to continue with ibuprofen as needed.

ENCOUNTER FORM

10/1/2018	9:45 am
DATE	TIME
Elizabeth Jones	**JONESEL0**
PATIENT NAME	CHART #

OFFICE VISITS - SYMPTOMATIC

NEW

99201	OF--New Patient Minimal	
99202	OF--New Patient Low	
99203	OF--New Patient Detailed	
99204	OF--New Patient Moderate	
99205	OF--New Patient High	

ESTABLISHED

99211	OF--Established Patient Minimal	
99212	OF--Established Patient Low	
99213	OF--Established Patient Detailed	X
99214	OF--Established Patient Moderate	
99215	OF--Established Patient High	

PREVENTIVE VISITS

NEW

99381	Under 1 Year	
99382	1 - 4 Years	
99383	5 - 11 Years	
99384	12 - 17 Years	
99385	18 - 39 Years	
99386	40 - 64 Years	
99387	65 Years & Up	

ESTABLISHED

99391	Under 1 Year	
99392	1 - 4 Years	
99393	5 - 11 Years	
99394	12 - 17 Years	
99395	18 - 39 Years	
99396	40 - 64 Years	
99397	65 Years & Up	

PROCEDURES

12011	Simple suture--face--local anes.	
29125	App. of short arm splint; static	
29425	Application of short leg cast, walking	
29540	Strapping, ankle	
50390	Aspiration of renal cyst by needle	
71010	Chest x-ray, single view, frontal	
71020	Chest x-ray, two views, frontal & lateral	

PROCEDURES

71030	Chest x-ray, complete, four views	
73070	Elbow x-ray, AP & lateral views	
73090	Forearm x-ray, AP & lateral views	
73100	Wrist x-ray, AP & lateral views	
73510	Hip x-ray, complete, two views	
73600	Ankle x-ray, AP & lateral views	

LABORATORY

80048	Basic metabolic panel	
80061	Lipid panel	
82270	Blood screening, occult; feces	
82947	Glucose screening--quantitative	
82951	Glucose tolerance test, three specimens	
83718	HDL cholesterol	
84478	Triglycerides test	
85007	Manual differential WBC	
85018	Hemoglobin	
85025	Complete CBC w/auto diff WBC	
85651	Erythrocyte sedimentation rate--non-auto	
86580	TB Mantoux test	
87040	Culture, bacterial; blood	
87076	Culture, anaerobic isolate	
87077	Bacterial culture, aerobic isolate	
87086	Urine culture and colony count	
87430	Strep test	
87880	Direct streptococcus screen	

INJECTIONS AND OTHERS

90471	Immunization administration	
90656	Influenza virus vaccine, 3+	
90662	Influenza virus vaccine, 65+	
90703	Tetanus injection	
92516	Facial nerve function studies	
93000	Electrocardiogram--ECG with interpretation	
93015	Treadmill stress test, with physician...	
96372	Injection	
96900	Ultraviolet light treatment	
99070	Supplies and materials provided	

FAMILY CARE CENTER
285 Stephenson Blvd.
Stephenson, OH 60089
614-555-0000

☐ DANA BANU, M.D.
☐ ROBERT BEACH, M.D.
☐ PATRICIA MCGRATH, M.D.
☐ JESSICA RUDNER, M.D.
☐ JOHN RUDNER, M.D.
☒ KATHERINE YAN, M.D.

NOTES

REFERRING PHYSICIAN	NPI	AUTHORIZATION #

DIAGNOSIS
E11.9

PAYMENT AMOUNT

ENCOUNTER FORM

10/1/2018		11:00 am	
DATE		TIMF	
John Fitzwilliams		FITZWJO0	
PATIENT NAME		CHART #	

OFFICE VISITS - SYMPTOMATIC
NEW

99201	OF--New Patient Minimal	
99202	OF--New Patient Low	
99203	OF--New Patient Detailed	
99204	OF--Ncw Patient Moderate	
99205	OF--New Patient High	

ESTABLISHED

99211	OF--Established Patient Minimal	
99212	OF--Established Patient Low	X
99213	OF--Established Patient Detailed	
99214	OF--Established Patient Moderate	
99215	OF--Established Patient High	

PREVENTIVE VISITS
NEW

99381	Under 1 Year	
99382	1 - 4 Years	
99383	5 - 11 Years	
99384	12 - 17 Years	
99385	18 - 39 Years	
99386	40 - 64 Years	
99387	65 Years & Up	

ESTABLISHED

99391	Under 1 Year	
99392	1 - 4 Years	
99393	5 - 11 Years	
99394	12 - 17 Years	
99395	18 - 39 Years	
99396	40 - 64 Years	
99397	65 Years & Up	

PROCEDURES

12011	Simple suture--face--local anes.	
29125	App. of short arm splint; static	
29425	Application of short leg cast, walking	
29540	Strapping, ankle	
50390	Aspiration of renal cyst by needle	
71010	Chest x-ray, single view, frontal	
71020	Chest x-ray, two views, frontal & lateral	

PROCEDURES

71030	Chest x-ray, complete, four views	
73070	Elbow x-ray, AP & lateral views	
73090	Forearm x-ray, AP & lateral views	
73100	Wrist x-ray, AP & lateral views	
73510	Hip x-ray, complete, two views	
73600	Ankle x-ray, AP & lateral views	

LABORATORY

80048	Basic metabolic panel	
80061	Lipid panel	
82270	Blood screening, occult; feces	X
82947	Glucose screening--quantitative	
82951	Glucose tolerance test, three specimens	
83718	HDL cholesterol	
84478	Triglycerides test	
85007	Manual differential WBC	
85018	Hemoglobin	
85025	Complete CBC w/auto diff WBC	
85651	Erythrocyte sedimentation rate--non-auto	
86580	TB Mantoux test	
87040	Culture, bacterial; blood	
87076	Culture, anerobic isolate	
87077	Bacterial culture, aerobic isolate	
87086	Urine culture and colony count	
87430	Strep test	
87880	Direct streptococcus screen	

INJECTIONS AND OTHERS

90471	Immunization administration	
90656	Influenza virus vaccine, 3+	
90662	Influenza virus vaccine, 65+	
90703	Tetanus injection	
92516	Facial nerve function studies	
93000	Electrocardiogram--ECG with interpretation	
93015	Treadmill stress test, with physician...	
96372	Injection	
96900	Ultraviolet light treatment	
99070	Supplies and materials provided	

FAMILY CARE CENTER
285 Stephenson Blvd.
Stephenson, OH 60089
614-555-0000

☐ DANA BANU, M.D.
☐ ROBERT BEACH, M.D.
☐ PATRICIA MCGRATH, M.D.

☐ JESSICA RUDNER, M.D.
☒ JOHN RUDNER, M.D.
☐ KATHERINE YAN, M.D.

NOTES

REFERRING PHYSICIAN	NPI	AUTHORIZATION #

DIAGNOSIS
K25.3

PAYMENT AMOUNT
$15 copay, check #456

ENCOUNTER FORM

10/1/2018
DATE

1:00 pm
TIME

Lisa Wright
PATIENT NAME

WRIGHLI0
CHART #

OFFICE VISITS - SYMPTOMATIC		
NEW		
99201	OF--New Patient Minimal	
99202	OF--New Patient Low	
99203	OF--New Patient Detailed	X
99204	OF--New Patient Moderate	
99205	OF--New Patient High	
ESTABLISHED		
99211	OF--Established Patient Minimal	
99212	OF--Established Patient Low	
99213	OF--Established Patient Detailed	
99214	OF--Established Patient Moderate	
99215	OF--Established Patient High	
PREVENTIVE VISITS		
NEW		
99381	Under 1 Year	
99382	1 - 4 Years	
99383	5 - 11 Years	
99384	12 - 17 Years	
99385	18 - 39 Years	
99386	40 - 64 Years	
99387	65 Years & Up	
ESTABLISHED		
99391	Under 1 Year	
99392	1 - 4 Years	
99393	5 - 11 Years	
99394	12 - 17 Years	
99395	18 - 39 Years	
99396	40 - 64 Years	
99397	65 Years & Up	
PROCEDURES		
12011	Simple suture--face--local anes.	
29125	App. of short arm splint; static	
29425	Application of short leg cast, walking	
29540	Strapping, ankle	
50390	Aspiration of renal cyst by needle	
71010	Chest x-ray, single view, frontal	
71020	Chest x-ray, two views, frontal & lateral	X

PROCEDURES		
71030	Chest x-ray, complete, four views	
73070	Elbow x-ray, AP & lateral views	
73090	Forearm x-ray, AP & lateral views	
73100	Wrist x-ray, AP & lateral views	
73510	Hip x-ray, complete, two views	
73600	Ankle x-ray, AP & lateral views	
LABORATORY		
80048	Basic metabolic panel	
80061	Lipid panel	
82270	Blood screening, occult; feces	
82947	Glucose screening--quantitative	
82951	Glucose tolerance test, three specimens	
83718	HDL cholesterol	
84478	Triglycerides test	
85007	Manual differential WBC	
85018	Hemoglobin	
85025	Complete CBC w/auto diff WBC	
85651	Erythrocyte sedimentation rate--non-auto	
86580	TB Mantoux test	
87040	Culture, bacterial; blood	
87076	Culture, anerobic isolate	
87077	Bacterial culture, aerobic isolate	
87086	Urine culture and colony count	
87430	Strep toot	
87880	Direct streptococcus screen	
INJECTIONS AND OTHERS		
90471	Immunization administration	
90656	Influenza virus vaccine, 3+	
90662	Influenza virus vaccine, 65+	
90703	Tetanus injection	
92516	Facial nerve function studies	
93000	Electrocardiogram--ECG with interpretation	
93015	Treadmill stress test, with physician...	
96372	Injection	
96900	Ultraviolet light treatment	
99070	Supplies and materials provided	

FAMILY CARE CENTER
285 Stephenson Blvd.
Stephenson, OH 60089
614-555-0000

☐ DANA BANU, M.D.
☐ ROBERT BEACH, M.D.
☐ PATRICIA MCGRATH, M.D.

☒ JESSICA RUDNER, M.D.
☐ JOHN RUDNER, M.D.
☐ KATHERINE YAN, M.D.

NOTES

REFERRING PHYSICIAN

NPI

AUTHORIZATION #

DIAGNOSIS
J40

PAYMENT AMOUNT

CHAMPVA
240 CENTER ST.
COLUMBUS, OH 60220

PROVIDER REMITTANCE
THIS IS NOT A BILL
A PAYMENT SUMMARY AND AN EXPLANATION OF
CODES ARE AT THE END OF THIS STATEMENT

FAMILY CARE CENTER
285 STEPHENSON BLVD.
STEPHENSON, OH 60089-4000

PAGE:	1 OF 1
DATE:	10/01/2018
ID NUMBER:	214778924

PROVIDER: JOHN RUDNER, M.D.

PATIENT: FITZWILLIAMS JOHN   CLAIM: 123456789

FROM DATE	THRU DATE	PROC CODE	UNITS	AMOUNT BILLED	AMOUNT ALLOWED	DEDUCT	COPAY/ COINS	PROV PAID	REASON CODE
09/04/18	09/04/18	99211	1	36.00	20.68	.00	15.00	5.68	
09/04/18	09/04/18	84478	1	29.00	8.04	.00	.00	8.04	
	CLAIM TOTALS			64.00	28.72	.00	15.00	13.72	

PROVIDER: KATHERINE YAN, M.D.

PATIENT: FITZWILLIAMS SARAH   CLAIM: 234567891

FROM DATE	THRU DATE	PROC CODE	UNITS	AMOUNT BILLED	AMOUNT ALLOWED	DEDUCT	COPAY/ COINS	PROV PAID	REASON CODE
09/04/18	09/04/18	90471	1	15.00	15.00	.00	15.00	.00	
09/04/18	09/04/18	90703	1	29.00	14.30	.00	.00	14.30	
	CLAIM TOTALS			44.00	29.30	.00	15.00	14.30	

******************** CHECK #214778924 IN THE AMOUNT OF $28.02 IS ATTACHED ********************

PAYMENT SUMMARY

		TOTAL ALL CLAIMS	
TOTAL AMOUNT PAID	28.02	AMOUNT CHARGED	108.00
PRIOR CREDIT BALANCE	.00	AMOUNT ALLOWED	58.02
CURRENT CREDIT DEFERRED	.00	DEDUCTIBLE	.00
PRIOR CREDIT APPLIED	.00	COPAY	30.00
NEW CREDIT BALANCE	.00	OTHER REDUCTION	.00
NET DISBURSED	28.02		

STATUS CODES:
A - APPROVED   AJ - ADJUSTMENT   IP - IN PROCESS   R - REJECTED   V - VOID

EAST OHIO PPO
10 CENTRAL AVENUE
HALEVILLE, OH 60890

PROVIDER REMITTANCE
THIS IS NOT A BILL
A PAYMENT SUMMARY AND AN EXPLANATION OF
CODES ARE AT THE END OF THIS STATEMENT

FAMILY CARE CENTER
285 STEPHENSON BLVD.
STEPHENSON, OH 60089-4000

PAGE:	1 OF 2
DATE:	10/01/2018
ID NUMBER:	00146972

PROVIDER: ROBERT BEACH, M.D.

PATIENT: ARLEN SUSAN   CLAIM: 123456789

FROM DATE	THRU DATE	PROC CODE	UNITS	AMOUNT BILLED	AMOUNT ALLOWED	DEDUCT	COPAY/ COINS	PROV PAID	REASON CODE
09/03/18	09/03/18	99212	1	54.00	48.60	.00	20.00	28.60	
	CLAIM TOTALS			54.00	48.60	.00	20.00	28.60	

PROVIDER: JOHN RUDNER, M.D.

PATIENT: BELL HERBERT   CLAIM: 234567891

FROM DATE	THRU DATE	PROC CODE	UNITS	AMOUNT BILLED	AMOUNT ALLOWED	DEDUCT	COPAY/ COINS	PROV PAID	REASON CODE
09/03/18	09/03/18	99211	1	36.00	32.40	.00	20.00	12.40	
	CLAIM TOTALS			36.00	32.40	.00	20.00	12.40	

PATIENT: BELL SAMUEL   CLAIM: 34567891

FROM DATE	THRU DATE	PROC CODE	UNITS	AMOUNT BILLED	AMOUNT ALLOWED	DEDUCT	COPAY/ COINS	PROV PAID	REASON CODE
09/03/18	09/03/18	99212	1	54.00	48.60	.00	20.00	28.60	
	CLAIM TOTALS			54.00	48.60	.00	20.00	28.60	

PROVIDER: JESSICA RUDNER, M.D.

PATIENT: BELL JANINE   CLAIM: 45678912

FROM DATE	THRU DATE	PROC CODE	UNITS	AMOUNT BILLED	AMOUNT ALLOWED	DEDUCT	COPAY/ COINS	PROV PAID	REASON CODE
09/03/18	09/03/18	99213	1	72.00	64.80	.00	20.00	44.80	
09/03/18	09/03/18	73510	1	124.00	111.60	.00	.00	111.60	
	CLAIM TOTALS			196.00	176.40	.00	20.00	156.40	

PATIENT: BELL SARINA   CLAIM: 56789123

FROM DATE	THRU DATE	PROC CODE	UNITS	AMOUNT BILLED	AMOUNT ALLOWED	DEDUCT	COPAY/ COINS	PROV PAID	REASON CODE
09/03/18	09/03/18	99213	1	72.00	64.80	.00	20.00	44.80	
	CLAIM TOTALS			72.00	64.80	.00	20.00	44.80	

STATUS CODES:
A - APPROVED   AJ - ADJUSTMENT   IP - IN PROCESS   R - REJECTED   V - VOID

EAST OHIO PPO
10 CENTRAL AVENUE
HALEVILLE, OH 60890

PROVIDER REMITTANCE
THIS IS NOT A BILL
A PAYMENT SUMMARY AND AN EXPLANATION OF
CODES ARE AT THE END OF THIS STATEMENT

FAMILY CARE CENTER
285 STEPHENSON BLVD.
STEPHENSON, OH 60089-4000

PAGE: 2 OF 2
DATE: 10/01/2018
ID NUMBER: 00146972

PROVIDER: KATHERINE YAN, M.D.

PATIENT: BELL JONATHAN   CLAIM: 56789123

FROM DATE	THRU DATE	PROC CODE	UNITS	AMOUNT BILLED	AMOUNT ALLOWED	DEDUCT	COPAY/ COINS	PROV PAID	REASON CODE
09/03/18	09/03/18	99394	1	222.00	199.80	.00	20.00	179.80	
	CLAIM TOTALS			222.00	199.80	.00	20.00	179.80	

PAYMENT SUMMARY

TOTAL AMOUNT PAID	450.60
PRIOR CREDIT BALANCE	.00
CURRENT CREDIT DEFERRED	.00
PRIOR CREDIT APPLIED	.00
NEW CREDIT BALANCE	.00
NET DISBURSED	450.60

TOTAL ALL CLAIMS

AMOUNT CHARGED	634.00
AMOUNT ALLOWED	570.60
DEDUCTIBLE	.00
COPAY	120.00
OTHER REDUCTION	.00
AMOUNT APPROVED	450.60

EFT INFORMATION

NUMBER	00146972
DATE	10/01/18
AMOUNT	450.60

STATUS CODES:
A - APPROVED   AJ - ADJUSTMENT   IP - IN PROCESS   R - REJECTED   V - VOID

BLUE CROSS/BLUE SHIELD
340 BOULEVARD
COLUMBUS, OH 60220

PROVIDER REMITTANCE
THIS IS NOT A BILL
A PAYMENT SUMMARY AND AN EXPLANATION OF
CODES ARE AT THE END OF THIS STATEMENT

FAMILY CARE CENTER
285 STEPHENSON BLVD.
STEPHENSON, OH 60089-4000

PAGE: 1 OF 1
DATE: 11/01/2018
ID NUMBER: 001234

PROVIDER: ROBERT BEACH, M.D.

PATIENT: GILES SHEILA   CLAIM: 123456789

FROM DATE	THRU DATE	PROC CODE	UNITS	AMOUNT BILLED	AMOUNT ALLOWED	DEDUCT	COPAY/ COINS	PROV PAID	REASON CODE
10/26/18	10/26/18	99213	1	72.00	72.00	.00	.00	57.60	
10/26/18	10/26/18	71010	1	91.00	91.00	.00	.00	72.80	
10/26/18	10/26/18	87430	1	29.00	.00	.00	.00	.00	R
	CLAIM TOTALS			192.00	163.00	.00	.00	130.40	

R* OUTSIDE LAB WORK NOT BILLABLE BY PROVIDER

PATIENT: SIMMONS JILL   CLAIM: 234567891

FROM DATE	THRU DATE	PROC CODE	UNITS	AMOUNT BILLED	AMOUNT ALLOWED	DEDUCT	COPAY/ COINS	PROV PAID	REASON CODE
10/26/18	10/26/18	99212	1	54.00	54.00	.00	.00	43.20	
10/26/18	10/26/18	87086	1	51.00	51.00	.00	.00	40.80	
	CLAIM TOTALS			105.00	105.00	.00	.00	84.00	

PAYMENT SUMMARY		TOTAL ALL CLAIMS		EFT INFORMATION	
TOTAL AMOUNT PAID	214.40	AMOUNT CHARGED	297.00	NUMBER	001234
PRIOR CREDIT BALANCE	.00	AMOUNT ALLOWED	268.00	DATE	11/01/18
CURRENT CREDIT DEFERRED	.00	DEDUCTIBLE	.00	AMOUNT	214.40
PRIOR CREDIT APPLIED	.00	COINSURANCE	.00		
NEW CREDIT BALANCE	.00	OTHER REDUCTION	.00		
NET DISBURSED	214.40	AMOUNT APPROVED	214.40		

STATUS CODES:
A - APPROVED   AJ - ADJUSTMENT   IP - IN PROCESS   R - REJECTED   V - VOID

OHIOCARE HMO
147 CENTRAL AVENUE
HALEVILLE, OH 60890

FAMILY CARE CENTER
285 STEPHENSON BLVD.
STEPHENSON, OH 60089-4000

PAGE:	1 OF 1
DATE:	10/28/2018
ID NUMBER:	001006003

OHIOCARE HMO CAPITATION STATEMENT
MONTH OF OCTOBER 2018

PROVIDERS
BANU DANA
BEACH ROBERT
MCGRATH PATRICIA
RUDNER JESSICA
RUDNER JOHN
YAN KATHERINE

MEMBER NUMBER	MEMBER NAME	CONTRACT NUMBER	CONTRACT STATUS
0003602149	FAMILY CARE CENTER	YG34906	APPROVED

AMOUNT OF PAYMENT $2,500.00
EFT STATUS: SENT 10/28/18 8:46AM
TRANSACTION #343434

BLUE CROSS/BLUE SHIELD
340 BOULEVARD
COLUMBUS, OH 60220

PROVIDER REMITTANCE
THIS IS NOT A BILL
A PAYMENT SUMMARY AND AN EXPLANATION OF
CODES ARE AT THE END OF THIS STATEMENT

FAMILY CARE CENTER
285 STEPHENSON BLVD.
STEPHENSON, OH 60089-4000

PAGE: 1 OF 1
DATE: 10/26/2018
ID NUMBER: 2000000

PROVIDER: JESSICA RUDNER, M.D.

PATIENT: WRIGHT LISA   CLAIM: 345678901

FROM DATE	THRU DATE	PROC CODE	UNITS	AMOUNT BILLED	AMOUNT ALLOWED	DEDUCT	COPAY/ COINS	PROV PAID	REASON CODE
10/01/18	10/01/18	99203	1	120.00	120.00	.00	.00	96.00	
10/01/18	10/01/18	71020	1	112.00	112.00	.00	.00	89.60	
	CLAIM TOTALS			232.00	232.00	.00	.00	185.60	

PAYMENT SUMMARY		TOTAL ALL CLAIMS		EFT INFORMATION	
TOTAL AMOUNT PAID	185.60	AMOUNT CHARGED	232.00	NUMBER	2000000
PRIOR CREDIT BALANCE	.00	AMOUNT ALLOWED	232.00	DATE	10/26/18
CURRENT CREDIT DEFERRED	.00	DEDUCTIBLE	.00	AMOUNT	185.60
PRIOR CREDIT APPLIED	.00	COINSURANCE	.00		
NEW CREDIT BALANCE	.00	OTHER REDUCTION	.00		
NET DISBURSED	185.60	AMOUNT APPROVED	185.60		

STATUS CODES:
A - APPROVED   AJ - ADJUSTMENT   IP - IN PROCESS   R - REJECTED   V - VOID

FAMILY CARE CENTER   **PATIENT INFORMATION FORM**

Patient				
Last Name Robertson	First Name Stewart	MI	Sex X M __ F	Date of Birth 12/ 21 /1977
Address 109 West Central Ave.	City Stephenson	State OH		Zip 60089

Home Ph # (614) 022-3111   Cell Ph # (614) 022-3279   Marital Status Divorced   Student Status

Race __ American Indian or Alaska Native __ Asian __ Black or African American X White __ Other __ Native Hawaiian or Other Pacific Islander __ Declined	Ethnicity __ Hispanic or Latino X Non-Hispanic or Latino __ Declined	Language English

SS# Email	Allergies
920-39-4567 srobertson@abc.com	

Employment Status Full-time	Employer Name Nichols Hardware	Work Ph # (614) 789-0200	Primary Insurance ID# 920394567 Group 63W
Employer Address 12 Central Ave.	City Stephenson	State OH	Zip 60089-1111

Referred By Dr. Janet Wood	Ph # of Referral (614) 459-3700

Responsible Party (Complete this section if the person responsible for the bill is not the patient)

Last Name	First Name	MI	Sex __ M __ F	Date of Birth / /
Address	City	State Zip	SS#	

Relation to Patient __ Spouse __ Parent __ Other	Employer Name	Work Phone # ( )
Spouse, or Parent (if minor):		Home Phone # ( )

Insurance (If you have multiple coverage, supply information from both carriers)

Primary Carrier Name OhioCare HMO	Secondary Carrier Name
Name of the Insured (Name on ID Card) Stewart Robertson	Name of the Insured (Name on ID Card)
Patient's relationship to the insured X Self __ Spouse __ Child	Patient's relationship to the insured __ Self __ Spouse __ Child
Insured ID # 920394567	Insured ID #
Group # or Company Name Group 63W	Group # or Company Name
Insurance Address 147 Central Ave., Haleville, OH 60890	Insurance Address
Phone # 614-555-0101	Copay $ 20 Deductible $	Phone #	Copay $ Deductible $

Other Information

Is patient's condition related to: __ Employment __ Auto Accident (if yes, state in which accident occurred: ___) __ Other Accident	Reason for visit: routine physical

Date of Accident: / /   Date of First Symptom of Illness: / /

Financial Agreement and Authorization for Treatment

I authorize treatment and agree to pay all fees and charges for the person named above. I agree to pay all charges shown by statements, promptly upon their presentation, unless credit arrangements are agreed upon in writing.

I authorize payment directly to FAMILY CARE CENTER of insurance benefits otherwise payable to me. I hereby authorize the release of any medical information necessary in order to process a claim for payment in my behalf.

Signed: Stewart Robertson _____   Date: ___11/12/2018____

FAMILY CARE CENTER   **PATIENT INFORMATION FORM**

Patient				
Last Name Syzmanski	First Name Hannah	MI	Sex __ M _X_ F	Date of Birth 2 / 26 / 2008
Address 3 Broadbrook Lane	City Stephenson		State OH	Zip 60089-1111
Home Ph # (614) 086-4444 Cell Ph # ( )		Marital Status Single		Student Status Full-time

Race	Ethnicity	Language
__ American Indian or Alaska Native __ Asian __ Black or African American _X_ White __ Other __ Native Hawaiian or Other Pacific Islander __ Declined	__ Hispanic or Latino _X_ Non-Hispanic or Latino __ Declined	English

SS# Email 907-66-0003	Allergies Bee stings

Employment Status	Employer Name	Work Ph # ( )	Primary Insurance ID#
Employer Address	City	State	Zip

Referred By Harold Gearhart, MD	Ph # of Referral (614) 556-2450

Responsible Party (Complete this section if the person responsible for the bill is not the patient)

Last Name Syzmanski	First Name Michael	MI	Sex _X_ M __ F	Date of Birth 6 / 5 / 1986
Address 3 Broadbrook Lane	City Stephenson	State OH	Zip 60089-1111	SS# 022-45-6789
Relation to Patient __ Spouse _X_ Parent __ Other	Employer Name Nichols Hardware		Work Phone # ( )	
Spouse, or Parent (if minor):			Home Phone # (614) 086-4444	

Insurance (If you have multiple coverage, supply information from both carriers)

Primary Carrier Name East Ohio PPO	Secondary Carrier Name
Name of the Insured (Name on ID Card) Michael Syzmanski	Name of the Insured (Name on ID Card)
Patient's relationship to the insured __ Self __ Spouse _X_ Child	Patient's relationship to the insured __ Self __ Spouse __ Child
Insured ID # 996782	Insured ID #
Group # or Company Name 8463	Group # or Company Name
Insurance Address 147 Central Ave., Haleville, OH	Insurance Address

Phone # 614-555-2229	Copay $ 20	Phone #	Copay $
	Deductible $		Deductible $

Other Information

Is patient's condition related to: Reason for visit: general check up

__ Employment   __ Auto Accident (if yes, state in which accident occurred: ___)   __ Other Accident

Date of Accident: /   /   Date of First Symptom of Illness: /   /

Financial Agreement and Authorization for Treatment

I authorize treatment and agree to pay all fees and charges for the person named above. I agree to pay all charges shown by statements, promptly upon their presentation, unless credit arrangements are agreed upon in writing.

I authorize payment directly to FAMILY CARE CENTER of insurance benefits otherwise payable to me. I hereby authorize the release of any medical information necessary in order to process a claim for payment in my behalf.

Signed: Michael Syzmanski _____   Date: 11/9/2018

ENCOUNTER FORM

11/9/2018
DATE

9:00 am
TIME

Anthony Battistuta
PATIENT NAME

BATTIAN0
CHART #

OFFICE VISITS - SYMPTOMATIC

NEW

99201	OF--New Patient Minimal	
99202	OF--New Patient Low	
99203	OF--New Patient Detailed	
99204	OF--New Patient Moderate	
99205	OF--New Patient High	

ESTABLISHED

99211	OF--Established Patient Minimal	
99212	OF--Established Patient Low	X
99213	OF--Established Patient Detailed	
99214	OF--Established Patient Moderate	
99215	OF--Established Patient High	

PREVENTIVE VISITS

NEW

99381	Under 1 Year	
99382	1 - 4 Years	
99383	5 - 11 Years	
99384	12 - 17 Years	
99385	18 - 39 Years	
99386	40 - 64 Years	
99387	65 Years & Up	

ESTABLISHED

99391	Under 1 Year	
99392	1 - 4 Years	
99393	5 - 11 Years	
99394	12 - 17 Years	
99395	18 - 39 Years	
99396	40 - 64 Years	
99397	65 Years & Up	

PROCEDURES

12011	Simple suture--face--local anes.	
29125	App. of short arm splint; static	
29425	Application of short leg cast, walking	
29540	Strapping, ankle	
50390	Aspiration of renal cyst by needle	
71010	Chest x-ray, single view, frontal	
71020	Chest x-ray, two views, frontal & lateral	

PROCEDURES

71030	Chest x-ray, complete, four views	
73070	Elbow x-ray, AP & lateral views	
73090	Forearm x-ray, AP & lateral views	
73100	Wrist x-ray, AP & lateral views	
73510	Hip x-ray, complete, two views	
73600	Ankle x-ray, AP & lateral views	

LABORATORY

80048	Basic metabolic panel	
80061	Lipid panel	
82270	Blood screening, occult; feces	
82947	Glucose screening--quantitative	
82951	Glucose tolerance test, three specimens	X
83718	HDL cholesterol	
84478	Triglycerides test	
85007	Manual differential WBC	
85018	Hemoglobin	
85025	Complete CBC w/auto diff WBC	
85651	Erythrocyte sedimentation rate--non-auto	
86580	TB Mantoux test	
87040	Culture, bacterial; blood	
87076	Culture, anaerobic isolate	
87077	Bacterial culture, aerobic isolate	
87086	Urine culture and colony count	X
87430	Strep test	
87880	Direct streptococcus screen	

INJECTIONS AND OTHERS

90471	Immunization administration	
90656	Influenza virus vaccine, 3+	
90662	Influenza virus vaccine, 65+	
90703	Tetanus injection	
92516	Facial nerve function studies	
93000	Electrocardiogram--ECG with interpretation	
93015	Treadmill stress test, with physician...	
96372	Injection	
96900	Ultraviolet light treatment	
99070	Supplies and materials provided	

FAMILY CARE CENTER
285 Stephenson Blvd.
Stephenson, OH 60089
614-555-0000

☐ DANA BANU, M.D.
☐ ROBERT BEACH, M.D.
☒ PATRICIA MCGRATH, M.D.

☐ JESSICA RUDNER, M.D.
☐ JOHN RUDNER, M.D.
☐ KATHERINE YAN, M.D.

NOTES

**New address:
36 Grant Blvd.
Grandville, OH
60092**

REFERRING PHYSICIAN | NPI | AUTHORIZATION #

DIAGNOSIS
E11.9, type 2 diabetes without complications
PAYMENT AMOUNT

ENCOUNTER FORM

11/9/2018	10:00 am
DATE	TIME
Lawana Brooks	BROOKLA0
PATIENT NAME	CHART #

OFFICE VISITS - SYMPTOMATIC

NEW

99201	OF--New Patient Minimal	
99202	OF--New Patient Low	
99203	OF--New Patient Detailed	
99204	OF--New Patient Moderate	
99205	OF--New Patient High	

ESTABLISHED

99211	OF--Established Patient Minimal	
99212	OF--Established Patient Low	X
99213	OF--Established Patient Detailed	
99214	OF--Established Patient Moderate	
99215	OF--Established Patient High	

PREVENTIVE VISITS

NEW

99381	Under 1 Year	
99382	1 - 4 Years	
99383	5 - 11 Years	
99384	12 - 17 Years	
99385	18 - 39 Years	
99386	40 - 64 Years	
99387	65 Years & Up	

ESTABLISHED

99391	Under 1 Year	
99392	1 - 4 Years	
99393	5 - 11 Years	
99394	12 - 17 Years	
99395	18 - 39 Years	
99396	40 - 64 Years	
99397	65 Years & Up	

PROCEDURES

12011	Simple suture--face--local anes.	
29125	App. of short arm splint; static	
29425	Application of short leg cast, walking	
29540	Strapping, ankle	
50390	Aspiration of renal cyst by needle	
71010	Chest x-ray, single view, frontal	
71020	Chest x-ray, two views, frontal & lateral	

PROCEDURES

71030	Chest x-ray, complete, four views	
73070	Elbow x-ray, AP & lateral views	
73090	Forearm x-ray, AP & lateral views	
73100	Wrist x-ray, AP & lateral views	
73510	Hip x-ray, complete, two views	
73600	Ankle x-ray, AP & lateral views	

LABORATORY

80048	Basic metabolic panel	
80061	Lipid panel	
82270	Blood screening, occult; feces	
82947	Glucose screening--quantitative	
82951	Glucose tolerance test, three specimens	
83718	HDL cholesterol	
84478	Triglycerides test	
85007	Manual differential WBC	
85018	Hemoglobin	
85025	Complete CBC w/auto diff WBC	
85651	Erythrocyte sedimentation rate--non-auto	
86580	TB Mantoux test	
87040	Culture, bacterial; blood	
87076	Culture, anerobic isolate	
87077	Bacterial culture, aerobic isolate	
87086	Urine culture and colony count	
87430	Strep test	
87880	Direct streptococcus screen	

INJECTIONS AND OTHERS

90471	Immunization administration	
90656	Influenza virus vaccine, 3+	
90662	Influenza virus vaccine, 65+	
90703	Tetanus injection	
92516	Facial nerve function studies	
93000	Electrocardiogram--ECG with interpretation	
93015	Treadmill stress test, with physician...	
96372	Injection	
96900	Ultraviolet light treatment	
99070	Supplies and materials provided	

FAMILY CARE CENTER
285 Stephenson Blvd.
Stephenson, OH 60089
614-555-0000

☐ DANA BANU, M.D.
☐ ROBERT BEACH, M.D.
☒ PATRICIA MCGRATH, M.D.

☐ JESSICA RUDNER, M.D.
☐ JOHN RUDNER, M.D.
☐ KATHERINE YAN, M.D.

NOTES

REFERRING PHYSICIAN	NPI	AUTHORIZATION #

DIAGNOSIS
J40, bronchitis

PAYMENT AMOUNT
copay $20, check #789

ENCOUNTER FORM

11/9/2018	11:15 am
DATE	TIME
Edwin Hsu	HSUEDWI0
PATIENT NAME	CHART #

OFFICE VISITS - SYMPTOMATIC

NEW

99201	OF--New Patient Minimal	
99202	OF--New Patient Low	
99203	OF--New Patient Detailed	
99204	OF--New Patient Moderate	
99205	OF--New Patient High	

ESTABLISHED

99211	OF--Established Patient Minimal	
99212	OF--Established Patient Low	X
99213	OF--Established Patient Detailed	
99214	OF--Established Patient Moderate	
99215	OF--Established Patient High	

PREVENTIVE VISITS

NEW

99381	Under 1 Year	
99382	1 - 4 Years	
99383	5 - 11 Years	
99384	12 - 17 Years	
99385	18 - 39 Years	
99386	40 - 64 Years	
99387	65 Years & Up	

ESTABLISHED

99391	Under 1 Year	
99392	1 - 4 Years	
99393	5 - 11 Years	
99394	12 - 17 Years	
99395	18 - 39 Years	
99396	40 - 64 Years	
99397	65 Years & Up	

PROCEDURES

12011	Simple suture--face--local anes.	
29125	App. of short arm splint; static	
29425	Application of short leg cast, walking	
29540	Strapping, ankle	
50390	Aspiration of renal cyst by needle	
71010	Chest x-ray, single view, frontal	
71020	Chest x-ray, two views, frontal & lateral	

PROCEDURES

71030	Chest x-ray, complete, four views	
73070	Elbow x-ray, AP & lateral views	
73090	Forearm x-ray, AP & lateral views	
73100	Wrist x-ray, AP & lateral views	
73510	Hip x-ray, complete, two views	
73600	Ankle x-ray, AP & lateral views	

LABORATORY

80048	Basic metabolic panel	
80061	Lipid panel	
82270	Blood screening, occult; feces	
82947	Glucose screening--quantitative	
82951	Glucose tolerance test, three specimens	
83718	HDL cholesterol	
84478	Triglycerides test	
85007	Manual differential WBC	
85018	Hemoglobin	
85025	Complete CBC w/auto diff WBC	
85651	Erythrocyte sedimentation rate--non-auto	
86580	TB Mantoux test	
87040	Culture, bacterial; blood	
87076	Culture, anerobic isolate	
87077	Bacterial culture, aerobic isolate	
87086	Urine culture and colony count	
87430	Strep test	
87880	Direct streptococcus screen	

INJECTIONS AND OTHERS

90471	Immunization administration	
90656	Influenza virus vaccine, 3+	
90662	Influenza virus vaccine, 65+	
90703	Tetanus injection	
92516	Facial nerve function studies	
93000	Electrocardiogram--ECG with interpretation	
93015	Treadmill stress test, with physician...	
96372	Injection	
96900	Ultraviolet light treatment	
99070	Supplies and materials provided	

FAMILY CARE CENTER
285 Stephenson Blvd.
Stephenson, OH 60089
614-555-0000

☐ DANA BANU, M.D.
☐ ROBERT BEACH, M.D.
☒ PATRICIA MCGRATH, M.D.

☐ JESSICA RUDNER, M.D.
☐ JOHN RUDNER, M.D.
☐ KATHERINE YAN, M.D.

NOTES

REFERRING PHYSICIAN	NPI	AUTHORIZATION #

DIAGNOSIS
J06.9, Acute URI

PAYMENT AMOUNT
$20 copay, check #1066

ENCOUNTER FORM

11/9/2018	10:00 am
DATE	TIME
Hannah Syzmanski	SYZMAHA0
PATIENT NAME	CHART #

OFFICE VISITS - SYMPTOMATIC
NEW

99201	OF--New Patient Minimal	
99202	OF--New Patient Low	
99203	OF--New Patient Detailed	
99204	OF--New Patient Moderate	
99205	OF--New Patient High	

ESTABLISHED

99211	OF--Established Patient Minimal	
99212	OF--Established Patient Low	
99213	OF--Established Patient Detailed	
99214	OF--Established Patient Moderate	
99215	OF--Established Patient High	

PREVENTIVE VISITS
NEW

99381	Under 1 Year	
99382	1 - 4 Years	
99383	5 - 11 Years	X
99384	12 - 17 Years	
99385	18 - 39 Years	
99386	40 - 64 Years	
99387	65 Years & Up	

ESTABLISHED

99391	Under 1 Year	
99392	1 - 4 Years	
99393	5 - 11 Years	
00094	12 - 17 Years	
99395	18 - 39 Years	
99396	40 - 64 Years	
99397	65 Years & Up	

PROCEDURES

12011	Simple suture--face--local anes.	
29125	App. of short arm splint; static	
29425	Application of short leg cast, walking	
29540	Strapping, ankle	
50390	Aspiration of renal cyst by needle	
71010	Chest x-ray, single view, frontal	
71020	Chest x-ray, two views, frontal & lateral	

PROCEDURES

71030	Chest x-ray, complete, four views	
73070	Elbow x-ray, AP & lateral views	
73090	Forearm x-ray, AP & lateral views	
73100	Wrist x-ray, AP & lateral views	
73510	Hip x-ray, complete, two views	
73600	Ankle x-ray, AP & lateral views	

LABORATORY

80048	Basic metabolic panel	
80061	Lipid panel	
82270	Blood screening, occult; feces	
82947	Glucose screening--quantitative	
82951	Glucose tolerance test, three specimens	
83718	HDL cholesterol	
84478	Triglycerides test	
85007	Manual differential WBC	
85018	Hemoglobin	
85025	Complete CBC w/auto diff WBC	
85651	Erythrocyte sedimentation rate--non-auto	
86580	TB Mantoux test	
87040	Culture, bacterial; blood	
87076	Culture, anaerobic isolate	
87077	Bacterial culture, aerobic isolate	
87086	Urine culture and colony count	
87430	Strep test	
87880	Direct streptococcus screen	

INJECTIONS AND OTHERS

90471	Immunization administration	
90656	Influenza virus vaccine, 3+	
90662	Influenza virus vaccine, 65+	
90703	Tetanus injection	
92516	Facial nerve function studies	
93000	Electrocardiogram--ECG with interpretation	
93015	Treadmill stress test, with physician...	
96372	Injection	
96900	Ultraviolet light treatment	
99070	Supplies and materials provided	

FAMILY CARE CENTER
285 Stephenson Blvd.
Stephenson, OH 60089
614-555-0000

- ☒ DANA BANU, M.D.
- ☐ ROBERT BEACH, M.D.
- ☐ PATRICIA MCGRATH, M.D.
- ☐ JESSICA RUDNER, M.D.
- ☐ JOHN RUDNER, M.D.
- ☐ KATHERINE YAN, M.D.

NOTES

REFERRING PHYSICIAN	NPI	AUTHORIZATION #
Harold Gearhart, M.D.		

DIAGNOSIS
Z00.129 routine physical exam

PAYMENT AMOUNT
$20 copay, check #3019

ENCOUNTER FORM

11/12/2018	**10:30 am**
DATE	TIME
Carlos Lopez	**LOPEZCA0**
PATIENT NAME	CHART #

OFFICE VISITS - SYMPTOMATIC		
NEW		
99201	OF--New Patient Minimal	
99202	OF--New Patient Low	
99203	OF--New Patient Detailed	
99204	OF--New Patient Moderate	
99205	OF--New Patient High	
ESTABLISHED		
99211	OF--Established Patient Minimal	
99212	OF--Established Patient Low	X
99213	OF--Established Patient Detailed	
99214	OF--Established Patient Moderate	
99215	OF--Established Patient High	
PREVENTIVE VISITS		
NEW		
99381	Under 1 Year	
99382	1 - 4 Years	
99383	5 - 11 Years	
99384	12 - 17 Years	
99385	18 - 39 Years	
99386	40 - 64 Years	
99387	65 Years & Up	
ESTABLISHED		
99391	Under 1 Year	
99392	1 - 4 Years	
99393	5 - 11 Years	
99394	12 - 17 Years	
99395	18 - 39 Years	
99396	40 - 64 Years	
99397	65 Years & Up	
PROCEDURES		
12011	Simple suture--face--local anes.	
29125	App. of short arm splint; static	
29425	Application of short leg cast, walking	
29540	Strapping, ankle	
50390	Aspiration of renal cyst by needle	
71010	Chest x-ray, single view, frontal	
71020	Chest x-ray, two views, frontal & lateral	

PROCEDURES		
71030	Chest x-ray, complete, four views	
73070	Elbow x-ray, AP & lateral views	
73090	Forearm x-ray, AP & lateral views	
73100	Wrist x-ray, AP & lateral views	
73510	Hip x-ray, complete, two views	
73600	Ankle x-ray, AP & lateral views	
LABORATORY		
80048	Basic metabolic panel	
80061	Lipid panel	
82270	Blood screening, occult; feces	
82947	Glucose screening--quantitative	
82951	Glucose tolerance test, three specimens	
83718	HDL cholesterol	
84478	Triglycerides test	
85007	Manual differential WBC	
85018	Hemoglobin	
85025	Complete CBC w/auto diff WBC	
85651	Erythrocyte sedimentation rate--non-auto	
86580	TB Mantoux test	
87040	Culture, bacterial; blood	
87076	Culture, anerobic isolate	
87077	Bacterial culture, aerobic isolate	
87086	Urine culture and colony count	
87430	Strep test	
87880	Direct streptococcus screen	
INJECTIONS AND OTHERS		
90471	Immunization administration	
90656	Influenza virus vaccine, 3+	
90662	Influenza virus vaccine, 65+	
90703	Tetanus injection	
92516	Facial nerve function studies	
93000	Electrocardiogram--ECG with interpretation	
93015	Treadmill stress test, with physician...	
96372	Injection	
96900	Ultraviolet light treatment	
99070	Supplies and materials provided	

FAMILY CARE CENTER
285 Stephenson Blvd.
Stephenson, OH 60089
614-555-0000

☐ DANA BANU, M.D.
☐ ROBERT BEACH, M.D.
☒ PATRICIA MCGRATH, M.D.

☐ JESSICA RUDNER, M.D.
☐ JOHN RUDNER, M.D.
☐ KATHERINE YAN, M.D.

NOTES

REFERRING PHYSICIAN	NPI	AUTHORIZATION #

DIAGNOSIS
Z71.1

PAYMENT AMOUNT
$20 copay, check #1001

ENCOUNTER FORM

11/12/2018
DATE

11:00 am
TIME

Stewart Robertson
PATIENT NAME

ROBERST0
CHART #

OFFICE VISITS - SYMPTOMATIC		
NEW		
99201	OF--New Patient Minimal	
99202	OF--New Patient Low	
99203	OF--New Patient Detailed	
99204	OF--New Patient Moderate	
99205	OF--New Patient High	
ESTABLISHED		
99211	OF--Established Patient Minimal	
99212	OF--Established Patient Low	
99213	OF--Established Patient Detailed	
99214	OF--Established Patient Moderate	
99215	OF--Established Patient High	
PREVENTIVE VISITS		
NEW		
99381	Under 1 Year	
99382	1 - 4 Years	
99383	5 - 11 Years	
99384	12 - 17 Years	
99385	18 - 39 Years	
99386	40 - 64 Years	X
99387	65 Years & Up	
ESTABLISHED		
99391	Under 1 Year	
99392	1 - 4 Years	
99393	5 - 11 Years	
99394	12 - 17 Years	
99395	18 - 39 Years	
99396	40 - 64 Years	
99397	65 Years & Up	
PROCEDURES		
12011	Simple suture--face--local anes.	
29125	App. of short arm splint; static	
29425	Application of short leg cast, walking	
29540	Strapping, ankle	
50390	Aspiration of renal cyst by needle	
71010	Chest x-ray, single view, frontal	
71020	Chest x-ray, two views, frontal & lateral	

PROCEDURES		
71030	Chest x-ray, complete, four views	
73070	Elbow x-ray, AP & lateral views	
73090	Forearm x-ray, AP & lateral views	
73100	Wrist x-ray, AP & lateral views	
73510	Hip x-ray, complete, two views	
73600	Ankle x-ray, AP & lateral views	
LABORATORY		
80048	Basic metabolic panel	
80061	Lipid panel	
82270	Blood screening, occult; feces	
82947	Glucose screening--quantitative	
82951	Glucose tolerance test, three specimens	
83718	HDL cholesterol	
84478	Triglycerides test	
85007	Manual differential WBC	
85018	Hemoglobin	
85025	Complete CBC w/auto diff WBC	
85651	Erythrocyte sedimentation rate--non-auto	
86580	TB Mantoux test	
87040	Culture, bacterial; blood	
87076	Culture, anerobic isolate	
87077	Bacterial culture, aerobic isolate	
87086	Urine culture and colony count	
87430	Strep toot	
87880	Direct streptococcus screen	
INJECTIONS AND OTHERS		
90471	Immunization administration	
90656	Influenza virus vaccine, 3+	
90662	Influenza virus vaccine, 65+	
90703	Tetanus injection	
92516	Facial nerve function studies	
93000	Electrocardiogram--ECG with interpretation	X
93015	Treadmill stress test, with physician...	
96372	Injection	
96900	Ultraviolet light treatment	
99070	Supplies and materials provided	

FAMILY CARE CENTER
285 Stephenson Blvd.
Stephenson, OH 60089
614-555-0000

☐ DANA BANU, M.D.
☒ ROBERT BEACH, M.D.
☐ PATRICIA MCGRATH, M.D.

☐ JESSICA RUDNER, M.D.
☐ JOHN RUDNER, M.D.
☐ KATHERINE YAN, M.D.

NOTES

REFERRING PHYSICIAN
Janet Wood, M.D.

NPI

AUTHORIZATION #

DIAGNOSIS
Z00.00

PAYMENT AMOUNT
$20 copay, check #416

ENCOUNTER FORM

11/12/2018	**11:30 am**
DATE	TIME
Diane Hsu	**HSUDIAN0**
PATIENT NAME	CHART #

OFFICE VISITS - SYMPTOMATIC

NEW

99201	OF--New Patient Minimal	
99202	OF--New Patient Low	
99203	OF--New Patient Detailed	
99204	OF--New Patient Moderate	
99205	OF--New Patient High	

ESTABLISHED

99211	OF--Established Patient Minimal	
99212	OF--Established Patient Low	X
99213	OF--Established Patient Detailed	
99214	OF--Established Patient Moderate	
99215	OF--Established Patient High	

PREVENTIVE VISITS

NEW

99381	Under 1 Year	
99382	1 - 4 Years	
99383	5 - 11 Years	
99384	12 - 17 Years	
99385	18 - 39 Years	
99386	40 - 64 Years	
99387	65 Years & Up	

ESTABLISHED

99391	Under 1 Year	
99392	1 - 4 Years	
99393	5 - 11 Years	
99394	12 - 17 Years	
99395	18 - 39 Years	
99396	40 - 64 Years	
99397	65 Years & Up	

PROCEDURES

12011	Simple suture--face--local anes.	
29125	App. of short arm splint; static	
29425	Application of short leg cast, walking	
29540	Strapping, ankle	
50390	Aspiration of renal cyst by needle	
71010	Chest x-ray, single view, frontal	
71020	Chest x-ray, two views, frontal & lateral	

PROCEDURES

71030	Chest x-ray, complete, four views	
73070	Elbow x-ray, AP & lateral views	
73090	Forearm x-ray, AP & lateral views	
73100	Wrist x-ray, AP & lateral views	
73510	Hip x-ray, complete, two views	
73600	Ankle x-ray, AP & lateral views	

LABORATORY

80048	Basic metabolic panel	
80061	Lipid panel	
82270	Blood screening, occult; feces	
82947	Glucose screening--quantitative	
82951	Glucose tolerance test, three specimens	
83718	HDL cholesterol	
84478	Triglycerides test	
85007	Manual differential WBC	
85018	Hemoglobin	
85025	Complete CBC w/auto diff WBC	
85651	Erythrocyte sedimentation rate--non-auto	
86580	TB Mantoux test	
87040	Culture, bacterial; blood	
87076	Culture, anerobic isolate	
87077	Bacterial culture, aerobic isolate	
87086	Urine culture and colony count	
87430	Strep test	X
87880	Direct streptococcus screen	

INJECTIONS AND OTHERS

90471	Immunization administration	
90656	Influenza virus vaccine, 3+	
90662	Influenza virus vaccine, 65+	
90703	Tetanus injection	
92516	Facial nerve function studies	
93000	Electrocardiogram--ECG with interpretation	
93015	Treadmill stress test, with physician...	
96372	Injection	
96900	Ultraviolet light treatment	
99070	Supplies and materials provided	

FAMILY CARE CENTER
285 Stephenson Blvd.
Stephenson, OH 60089
614-555-0000

- ☐ DANA BANU, M.D.
- ☐ ROBERT BEACH, M.D.
- ☒ PATRICIA MCGRATH, M.D.
- ☐ JESSICA RUDNER, M.D.
- ☐ JOHN RUDNER, M.D.
- ☐ KATHERINE YAN, M.D.

NOTES

REFERRING PHYSICIAN	NPI	AUTHORIZATION #

DIAGNOSIS
J11.1 influenza

PAYMENT AMOUNT
$20 copay, check #3419

ENCOUNTER FORM

11/12/2018	2:30 pm
DATE	TIME
Michael Syzmanski	SYZMAMI0
PATIENT NAME	CHART #

OFFICE VISITS - SYMPTOMATIC

NEW		
99201	OF--New Patient Minimal	
99202	OF--New Patient Low	
99203	OF--New Patient Detailed	
99204	OF--New Patient Moderate	
99205	OF--New Patient High	

ESTABLISHED		
99211	OF--Established Patient Minimal	
99212	OF--Established Patient Low	
99213	OF--Established Patient Detailed	
99214	OF--Established Patient Moderate	
99215	OF--Established Patient High	X

PREVENTIVE VISITS

NEW		
99381	Under 1 Year	
99382	1 - 4 Years	
99383	5 - 11 Years	
99384	12 - 17 Years	
99385	18 - 39 Years	
99386	40 - 64 Years	
99387	65 Years & Up	

ESTABLISHED		
99391	Under 1 Year	
99392	1 - 4 Years	
99393	5 - 11 Years	
99394	12 - 17 Years	
99395	18 - 39 Years	
99396	40 - 64 Years	
99397	65 Years & Up	

PROCEDURES		
12011	Simple suture--face--local anes.	
29125	App. of short arm splint; static	
29425	Application of short leg cast, walking	
29540	Strapping, ankle	
50390	Aspiration of renal cyst by needle	
71010	Chest x-ray, single view, frontal	
71020	Chest x-ray, two views, frontal & lateral	

PROCEDURES		
71030	Chest x-ray, complete, four views	
73070	Elbow x-ray, AP & lateral views	
73090	Forearm x-ray, AP & lateral views	
73100	Wrist x-ray, AP & lateral views	
73510	Hip x-ray, complete, two views	
73600	Ankle x-ray, AP & lateral views	

LABORATORY		
80048	Basic metabolic panel	
80061	Lipid panel	
82270	Blood screening, occult; feces	X
82947	Glucose screening--quantitative	
82951	Glucose tolerance test, three specimens	
83718	HDL cholesterol	
84478	Triglycerides test	
85007	Manual differential WBC	
85018	Hemoglobin	
85025	Complete CBC w/auto diff WBC	
85651	Erythrocyte sedimentation rate--non-auto	
86580	TB Mantoux test	
87040	Culture, bacterial; blood	
87076	Culture, anerobic isolate	
87077	Bacterial culture, aerobic isolate	
87086	Urine culture and colony count	
87430	Strep test	
87880	Direct streptococcus screen	

INJECTIONS AND OTHERS		
90471	Immunization administration	
90656	Influenza virus vaccine, 3+	
90662	Influenza virus vaccine, 65+	
90703	Tetanus injection	
92516	Facial nerve function studies	
93000	Electrocardiogram--ECG with interpretation	
93015	Treadmill stress test, with physician...	
96372	Injection	
96900	Ultraviolet light treatment	
99070	Supplies and materials provided	

FAMILY CARE CENTER
285 Stephenson Blvd.
Stephenson, OH 60089
614-555-0000

- [X] DANA BANU, M.D.
- [ ] ROBERT BEACH, M.D.
- [ ] PATRICIA MCGRATH, M.D.
- [ ] JESSICA RUDNER, M.D.
- [ ] JOHN RUDNER, M.D.
- [ ] KATHERINE YAN, M.D.

NOTES

Next appt. one week from today, 15 min.

REFERRING PHYSICIAN	NPI	AUTHORIZATION #

DIAGNOSIS
K64.9

PAYMENT AMOUNT
$20 copay, check #3119

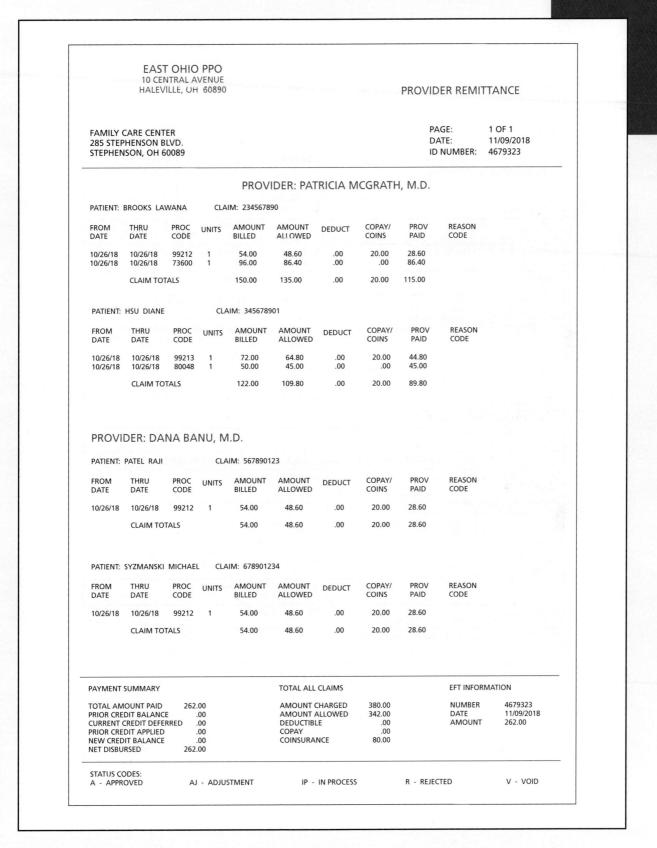

EAST OHIO PPO
10 CENTRAL AVENUE
HALEVILLE, OH 60890

PROVIDER REMITTANCE

FAMILY CARE CENTER
285 STEPHENSON BLVD.
STEPHENSON, OH 60089

PAGE: 1 OF 1
DATE: 11/09/2018
ID NUMBER: 4679323

PROVIDER: PATRICIA MCGRATH, M.D.

PATIENT: BROOKS LAWANA   CLAIM: 234567890

FROM DATE	THRU DATE	PROC CODE	UNITS	AMOUNT BILLED	AMOUNT ALLOWED	DEDUCT	COPAY/ COINS	PROV PAID	REASON CODE
10/26/18	10/26/18	99212	1	54.00	48.60	.00	20.00	28.60	
10/26/18	10/26/18	73600	1	96.00	86.40	.00	.00	86.40	
	CLAIM TOTALS			150.00	135.00	.00	20.00	115.00	

PATIENT: HSU DIANE   CLAIM: 345678901

FROM DATE	THRU DATE	PROC CODE	UNITS	AMOUNT BILLED	AMOUNT ALLOWED	DEDUCT	COPAY/ COINS	PROV PAID	REASON CODE
10/26/18	10/26/18	99213	1	72.00	64.80	.00	20.00	44.80	
10/26/18	10/26/18	80048	1	50.00	45.00	.00	.00	45.00	
	CLAIM TOTALS			122.00	109.80	.00	20.00	89.80	

PROVIDER: DANA BANU, M.D.

PATIENT: PATEL RAJI   CLAIM: 567890123

FROM DATE	THRU DATE	PROC CODE	UNITS	AMOUNT BILLED	AMOUNT ALLOWED	DEDUCT	COPAY/ COINS	PROV PAID	REASON CODE
10/26/18	10/26/18	99212	1	54.00	48.60	.00	20.00	28.60	
	CLAIM TOTALS			54.00	48.60	.00	20.00	28.60	

PATIENT: SYZMANSKI MICHAEL   CLAIM: 678901234

FROM DATE	THRU DATE	PROC CODE	UNITS	AMOUNT BILLED	AMOUNT ALLOWED	DEDUCT	COPAY/ COINS	PROV PAID	REASON CODE
10/26/18	10/26/18	99212	1	54.00	48.60	.00	20.00	28.60	
	CLAIM TOTALS			54.00	48.60	.00	20.00	28.60	

PAYMENT SUMMARY		TOTAL ALL CLAIMS		EFT INFORMATION	
TOTAL AMOUNT PAID	262.00	AMOUNT CHARGED	380.00	NUMBER	4679323
PRIOR CREDIT BALANCE	.00	AMOUNT ALLOWED	342.00	DATE	11/09/2018
CURRENT CREDIT DEFERRED	.00	DEDUCTIBLE	.00	AMOUNT	262.00
PRIOR CREDIT APPLIED	.00	COPAY	.00		
NEW CREDIT BALANCE	.00	COINSURANCE	80.00		
NET DISBURSED	262.00				

STATUS CODES:
A - APPROVED   AJ - ADJUSTMENT   IP - IN PROCESS   R - REJECTED   V - VOID

FAMILY CARE CENTER   **PATIENT INFORMATION FORM**

Patient				

Last Name	First Name	MI	Sex	Date of Birth
Palmer	Christopher		X M __ F	1 / 5 / 1962

Address	City	State	Zip
17 Red Oak Lane	Jefferson	OH	60093

Home Ph # (614) 077-2249 Cell Ph # (614) 077-2250   Marital Status Single   Student Status

Race	Ethnicity	Language
__ American Indian or Alaska Native __ Asian __ Black or African American X White __ Other __ Native Hawaiian or Other Pacific Islander __ Declined	__ Hispanic or Latino X Non-Hispanic or Latino __ Declined	English

SS# Email	Allergies
607-50-7620 cpalmer@abc.com	

Employment Status	Employer Name	Work Ph #	Primary Insurance ID#
Not employed		( )	607507620

Employer Address	City	State	Zip

Referred By	Ph # of Referral (614) 444-3200
Dr. Marion Davis	

Responsible Party (Complete this section if the person responsible for the bill is not the patient)

Last Name	First Name	MI	Sex	Date of Birth
			__ M __ F	/ /

Address	City	State	Zip	SS#

Relation to Patient	Employer Name	Work Phone #
__ Spouse __ Parent __ Other		( )

Spouse, or Parent (if minor):	Home Phone # ( )

Insurance (If you have multiple coverage, supply information from both carriers)

Primary Carrier Name	Secondary Carrier Name
Medicaid	
Name of the Insured (Name on ID Card)	Name of the Insured (Name on ID Card)
Christopher Palmer	
Patient's relationship to the insured	Patient's relationship to the insured
X Self __ Spouse __ Child	__ Self __ Spouse __ Child
Insured ID #	Insured ID #
607507620	
Group # or Company Name	Group # or Company Name
Insurance Address	Insurance Address
248 West Main St., Cleveland, OH 60120	

Phone # 614-599-6000	Copay $ 10	Phone #	Copay $
	Deductible $		Deductible $

Other Information

Is patient's condition related to:	Reason for visit: **difficulty breathing**

__ Employment   __ Auto Accident (if yes, state in which accident occurred: ___)   __ Other Accident

Date of Accident: / /   Date of First Symptom of Illness: / /

Financial Agreement and Authorization for Treatment

I authorize treatment and agree to pay all fees and charges for the person named above. I agree to pay all charges shown by statements, promptly upon their presentation, unless credit arrangements are agreed upon in writing.	I authorize payment directly to FAMILY CARE CENTER of insurance benefits otherwise payable to me. I hereby authorize the release of any medical information necessary in order to process a claim for payment in my behalf.

Signed: Christopher Palmer   Date: 1/2/2019

ENCOUNTER FORM

1/2/2019
DATE

9:00 am
TIME

Luther Jackson
PATIENT NAME

JACKSLU0
CHART #

OFFICE VISITS - SYMPTOMATIC
NEW

99201	OF--New Patient Minimal	
99202	OF--New Patient Low	
99203	OF--New Patient Detailed	
99204	OF--New Patient Moderate	
99205	OF--New Patient High	

ESTABLISHED

99211	OF--Established Patient Minimal	
99212	OF--Established Patient Low	X
99213	OF--Established Patient Detailed	
99214	OF--Established Patient Moderate	
99215	OF--Established Patient High	

PREVENTIVE VISITS
NEW

99381	Under 1 Year	
99382	1 - 4 Years	
99383	5 - 11 Years	
99384	12 - 17 Years	
99385	18 - 39 Years	
99386	40 - 64 Years	
99387	65 Years & Up	

ESTABLISHED

99391	Under 1 Year	
99392	1 - 4 Years	
99393	5 - 11 Years	
99394	12 - 17 Years	
99395	18 - 39 Years	
99396	40 - 64 Years	
99397	65 Years & Up	

PROCEDURES

12011	Simple suture--face--local anes.	
29125	App. of short arm splint; static	
29425	Application of short leg cast, walking	
29540	Strapping, ankle	
50390	Aspiration of renal cyst by needle	
71010	Chest x-ray, single view, frontal	
71020	Chest x-ray, two views, frontal & lateral	

PROCEDURES

71030	Chest x-ray, complete, four views	
73070	Elbow x-ray, AP & lateral views	
73090	Forearm x-ray, AP & lateral views	
73100	Wrist x-ray, AP & lateral views	
73510	Hip x-ray, complete, two views	
73600	Ankle x-ray, AP & lateral views	

LABORATORY

80048	Basic metabolic panel	
80061	Lipid panel	
82270	Blood screening, occult; feces	
82947	Glucose screening--quantitative	
82951	Glucose tolerance test, three specimens	
83718	HDL cholesterol	
84478	Triglycerides test	
85007	Manual differential WBC	
85018	Hemoglobin	
85025	Complete CBC w/auto diff WBC	
85651	Erythrocyte sedimentation rate--non-auto	
86580	TB Mantoux test	
87040	Culture, bacterial; blood	
87076	Culture, anaerobic isolate	
87077	Bacterial culture, aerobic isolate	
87086	Urine culture and colony count	
87430	Strep test	
87880	Direct streptococcus screen	

INJECTIONS AND OTHERS

90471	Immunization administration	
90656	Influenza virus vaccine, 3+	
90662	Influenza virus vaccine, 65+	
90703	Tetanus injection	
92516	Facial nerve function studies	
93000	Electrocardiogram--ECG with interpretation	
93015	Treadmill stress test, with physician...	
96372	Injection	
96900	Ultraviolet light treatment	
99070	Supplies and materials provided	

FAMILY CARE CENTER
285 Stephenson Blvd.
Stephenson, OH 60089
614-555-0000

☒ DANA BANU, M.D.
☐ ROBERT BEACH, M.D.
☐ PATRICIA MCGRATH, M.D.

☐ JESSICA RUDNER, M.D.
☐ JOHN RUDNER, M.D.
☐ KATHERINE YAN, M.D.

NOTES

REFERRING PHYSICIAN	NPI	AUTHORIZATION #

DIAGNOSIS
J11.1, influenza

PAYMENT AMOUNT
$20 copay, check #1291

ENCOUNTER FORM

1/2/2019
DATE

9:00 am
TIME

Jill Simmons
PATIENT NAME

SIMMOJI0
CHART #

OFFICE VISITS - SYMPTOMATIC
NEW

99201	OF--New Patient Minimal	
99202	OF--New Patient Low	
99203	OF--New Patient Detailed	
99204	OF--New Patient Moderate	
99205	OF--New Patient High	

ESTABLISHED

99211	OF--Established Patient Minimal	X
99212	OF--Established Patient Low	
99213	OF--Established Patient Detailed	
99214	OF--Established Patient Moderate	
99215	OF--Established Patient High	

PREVENTIVE VISITS
NEW

99381	Under 1 Year	
99382	1 - 4 Years	
99383	5 - 11 Years	
99384	12 - 17 Years	
99385	18 - 39 Years	
99386	40 - 64 Years	
99387	65 Years & Up	

ESTABLISHED

99391	Under 1 Year	
99392	1 - 4 Years	
99393	5 - 11 Years	
99394	12 - 17 Years	
99395	18 - 39 Years	
99396	40 - 64 Years	
99397	65 Years & Up	

PROCEDURES

12011	Simple suture--face--local anes.	
29125	App. of short arm splint; static	
29425	Application of short leg cast, walking	
29540	Strapping, ankle	
50390	Aspiration of renal cyst by needle	
71010	Chest x-ray, single view, frontal	
71020	Chest x-ray, two views, frontal & lateral	

PROCEDURES

71030	Chest x-ray, complete, four views	
73070	Elbow x-ray, AP & lateral views	
73090	Forearm x-ray, AP & lateral views	
73100	Wrist x-ray, AP & lateral views	
73510	Hip x-ray, complete, two views	
73600	Ankle x-ray, AP & lateral views	

LABORATORY

80048	Basic metabolic panel	
80061	Lipid panel	
82270	Blood screening, occult; feces	
82947	Glucose screening--quantitative	
82951	Glucose tolerance test, three specimens	
83718	HDL cholesterol	
84478	Triglycerides test	
85007	Manual differential WBC	
85018	Hemoglobin	
85025	Complete CBC w/auto diff WBC	
85651	Erythrocyte sedimentation rate--non-auto	
86580	TB Mantoux test	
87040	Culture, bacterial; blood	
87076	Culture, anerobic isolate	
87077	Bacterial culture, aerobic isolate	
87086	Urine culture and colony count	
87430	Strep test	X
87880	Direct streptococcus screen	

INJECTIONS AND OTHERS

90471	Immunization administration	
90656	Influenza virus vaccine, 3+	
90662	Influenza virus vaccine, 65+	
90703	Tetanus injection	
92516	Facial nerve function studies	
93000	Electrocardiogram--ECG with interpretation	
93015	Treadmill stress test, with physician...	
96372	Injection	
96900	Ultraviolet light treatment	
99070	Supplies and materials provided	

FAMILY CARE CENTER
285 Stephenson Blvd.
Stephenson, OH 60089
614-555-0000

☐ DANA BANU, M.D.
☒ ROBERT BEACH, M.D.
☐ PATRICIA MCGRATH, M.D.

☐ JESSICA RUDNER, M.D.
☐ JOHN RUDNER, M.D.
☐ KATHERINE YAN, M.D.

NOTES

REFERRING PHYSICIAN

NPI

AUTHORIZATION #

DIAGNOSIS

J02.0 strep sore throat

PAYMENT AMOUNT

ENCOUNTER FORM

1/2/2019
DATE

9:30 am
TIME

Nancy Stern
PATIENT NAME

STERNNA0
CHART #

OFFICE VISITS - SYMPTOMATIC

NEW

99201	OF--New Patient Minimal	
99202	OF--New Patient Low	
99203	OF--New Patient Detailed	
99204	OF--New Patient Moderate	
99205	OF--New Patient High	

ESTABLISHED

99211	OF--Established Patient Minimal	
99212	OF--Established Patient Low	
99213	OF--Established Patient Detailed	
99214	OF--Established Patient Moderate	
99215	OF--Established Patient High	

PREVENTIVE VISITS

NEW

99381	Under 1 Year	
99382	1 - 4 Years	
99383	5 - 11 Years	
99384	12 - 17 Years	
99385	18 - 39 Years	
99386	40 - 64 Years	
99387	65 Years & Up	

ESTABLISHED

99391	Under 1 Year	
99392	1 - 4 Years	
99393	5 - 11 Years	
99394	12 - 17 Years	
99395	18 - 39 Years	
99396	40 - 64 Years	X
99397	65 Years & Up	

PROCEDURES

12011	Simple suture--face--local anes.	
29125	App. of short arm splint; static	
29425	Application of short leg cast, walking	
29540	Strapping, ankle	
50390	Aspiration of renal cyst by needle	
71010	Chest x-ray, single view, frontal	
71020	Chest x-ray, two views, frontal & lateral	

PROCEDURES

71030	Chest x-ray, complete, four views	
73070	Elbow x-ray, AP & lateral views	
73090	Forearm x-ray, AP & lateral views	
73100	Wrist x-ray, AP & lateral views	
73510	Hip x-ray, complete, two views	
73600	Ankle x-ray, AP & lateral views	

LABORATORY

80048	Basic metabolic panel	
80061	Lipid panel	
82270	Blood screening, occult; feces	
82947	Glucose screening--quantitative	
82951	Glucose tolerance test, three specimens	
83718	HDL cholesterol	X
84478	Triglycerides test	
85007	Manual differential WBC	X
85018	Hemoglobin	
85025	Complete CBC w/auto diff WBC	
85651	Erythrocyte sedimentation rate--non-auto	
86580	TB Mantoux test	
87040	Culture, bacterial; blood	
87076	Culture, anerobic isolate	
87077	Bacterial culture, aerobic isolate	
87086	Urine culture and colony count	X
87430	Strep test	
87880	Direct streptococcus screen	

INJECTIONS AND OTHERS

90471	Immunization administration	
90656	Influenza virus vaccine, 3+	
90662	Influenza virus vaccine, 65+	
90703	Tetanus injection	
92516	Facial nerve function studies	
93000	Electrocardiogram--ECG with interpretation	X
93015	Treadmill stress test, with physician...	
96372	Injection	
96900	Ultraviolet light treatment	
99070	Supplies and materials provided	

FAMILY CARE CENTER
285 Stephenson Blvd.
Stephenson, OH 60089
614-555-0000

- ☐ DANA BANU, M.D.
- ☐ ROBERT BEACH, M.D.
- ☒ PATRICIA MCGRATH, M.D.
- ☐ JESSICA RUDNER, M.D.
- ☐ JOHN RUDNER, M.D.
- ☐ KATHERINE YAN, M.D.

NOTES

REFERRING PHYSICIAN	NPI	AUTHORIZATION #

DIAGNOSIS
Z00.00 routine physical examination

PAYMENT AMOUNT
$20 copay, check #1022

ENCOUNTER FORM

1/2/2019
DATE

9:30 am
TIME

Debra Syzmanski
PATIENT NAME

SYZMADE0
CHART #

OFFICE VISITS - SYMPTOMATIC		
NEW		
99201	OF--New Patient Minimal	
99202	OF--New Patient Low	
99203	OF--New Patient Detailed	
99204	OF--New Patient Moderate	
99205	OF--New Patient High	
ESTABLISHED		
99211	OF--Established Patient Minimal	
99212	OF--Established Patient Low	
99213	OF--Established Patient Detailed	
99214	OF--Established Patient Moderate	
99215	OF--Established Patient High	
PREVENTIVE VISITS		
NEW		
99381	Under 1 Year	
99382	1 - 4 Years	
99383	5 - 11 Years	
99384	12 - 17 Years	
99385	18 - 39 Years	
99386	40 - 64 Years	
99387	65 Years & Up	
ESTABLISHED		
99391	Under 1 Year	
99392	1 - 4 Years	
99393	5 - 11 Years	
99394	12 - 17 Years	
99395	18 - 39 Years	
99396	40 - 64 Years	X
99397	65 Years & Up	
PROCEDURES		
12011	Simple suture--face--local anes.	
29125	App. of short arm splint; static	
29425	Application of short leg cast, walking	
29540	Strapping, ankle	
50390	Aspiration of renal cyst by needle	
71010	Chest x-ray, single view, frontal	
71020	Chest x-ray, two views, frontal & lateral	

PROCEDURES		
71030	Chest x-ray, complete, four views	
73070	Elbow x-ray, AP & lateral views	
73090	Forearm x-ray, AP & lateral views	
73100	Wrist x-ray, AP & lateral views	
73510	Hip x-ray, complete, two views	
73600	Ankle x-ray, AP & lateral views	
LABORATORY		
80048	Basic metabolic panel	
80061	Lipid panel	
82270	Blood screening, occult; feces	
82947	Glucose screening--quantitative	
82951	Glucose tolerance test, three specimens	
83718	HDL cholesterol	X
84478	Triglycerides test	
85007	Manual differential WBC	X
85018	Hemoglobin	
85025	Complete CBC w/auto diff WBC	
85651	Erythrocyte sedimentation rate--non-auto	
86580	TB Mantoux test	
87040	Culture, bacterial; blood	
87076	Culture, anaerobic isolate	
87077	Bacterial culture, aerobic isolate	
87086	Urine culture and colony count	X
87430	Strep test	
87000	Direct streptococcus screen	
INJECTIONS AND OTHERS		
90471	Immunization administration	
90656	Influenza virus vaccine, 3+	
90662	Influenza virus vaccine, 65+	
90703	Tetanus injection	
92516	Facial nerve function studies	
93000	Electrocardiogram--ECG with interpretation	X
93015	Treadmill stress test, with physician...	
96372	Injection	
96900	Ultraviolet light treatment	
99070	Supplies and materials provided	

FAMILY CARE CENTER
285 Stephenson Blvd.
Stephenson, OH 60089
614-555-0000

- ☒ DANA BANU, M.D.
- ☐ ROBERT BEACH, M.D.
- ☐ PATRICIA MCGRATH, M.D.
- ☐ JESSICA RUDNER, M.D.
- ☐ JOHN RUDNER, M.D.
- ☐ KATHERINE YAN, M.D.

NOTES

REFERRING PHYSICIAN	NPI	AUTHORIZATION #

DIAGNOSIS
Z00.00 routine physical examination

PAYMENT AMOUNT
$20 copay, check #3219

ENCOUNTER FORM

1/2/2019	**10:15 am**
DATE	TIME
Sheila Giles	**GILESSH0**
PATIENT NAME	CHART #

OFFICE VISITS - SYMPTOMATIC

NEW

99201	OF--New Patient Minimal	
99202	OF--New Patient Low	
99203	OF--New Patient Detailed	
99204	OF--New Patient Moderate	
99205	OF--New Patient High	

ESTABLISHED

99211	OF--Established Patient Minimal	X
99212	OF--Established Patient Low	
99213	OF--Established Patient Detailed	
99214	OF--Established Patient Moderate	
99215	OF--Established Patient High	

PREVENTIVE VISITS

NEW

99381	Under 1 Year	
99382	1 - 4 Years	
99383	5 - 11 Years	
99384	12 - 17 Years	
99385	18 - 39 Years	
99386	40 - 64 Years	
99387	65 Years & Up	

ESTABLISHED

99391	Under 1 Year	
99392	1 - 4 Years	
99393	5 - 11 Years	
99394	12 - 17 Years	
99395	18 - 39 Years	
99396	40 - 64 Years	
99397	65 Years & Up	

PROCEDURES

12011	Simple suture--face--local anes.	
29125	App. of short arm splint; static	
29425	Application of short leg cast, walking	
29540	Strapping, ankle	
50390	Aspiration of renal cyst by needle	
71010	Chest x-ray, single view, frontal	
71020	Chest x-ray, two views, frontal & lateral	

PROCEDURES

71030	Chest x-ray, complete, four views	
73070	Elbow x-ray, AP & lateral views	
73090	Forearm x-ray, AP & lateral views	
73100	Wrist x-ray, AP & lateral views	
73510	Hip x-ray, complete, two views	
73600	Ankle x-ray, AP & lateral views	

LABORATORY

80048	Basic metabolic panel	
80061	Lipid panel	
82270	Blood screening, occult; feces	
82947	Glucose screening--quantitative	
82951	Glucose tolerance test, three specimens	
83718	HDL cholesterol	
84478	Triglycerides test	
85007	Manual differential WBC	
85018	Hemoglobin	
85025	Complete CBC w/auto diff WBC	
85651	Erythrocyte sedimentation rate--non-auto	
86580	TB Mantoux test	
87040	Culture, bacterial; blood	
87076	Culture, anaerobic isolate	
87077	Bacterial culture, aerobic isolate	
87086	Urine culture and colony count	
87430	Strep test	
87880	Direct streptococcus screen	

INJECTIONS AND OTHERS

90471	Immunization administration	X
90656	Influenza virus vaccine, 3+	
90662	Influenza virus vaccine, 65+	
90703	Tetanus injection	X
92516	Facial nerve function studies	
93000	Electrocardiogram--ECG with interpretation	
93015	Treadmill stress test, with physician...	
96372	Injection	
96900	Ultraviolet light treatment	
99070	Supplies and materials provided	

FAMILY CARE CENTER
285 Stephenson Blvd.
Stephenson, OH 60089
614-555-0000

☐ DANA BANU, M.D.
☒ ROBERT BEACH, M.D.
☐ PATRICIA MCGRATH, M.D.

☐ JESSICA RUDNER, M.D.
☐ JOHN RUDNER, M.D.
☐ KATHERINE YAN, M.D.

NOTES

REFERRING PHYSICIAN	NPI	AUTHORIZATION #

DIAGNOSIS

Z23 immunization

PAYMENT AMOUNT

ENCOUNTER FORM

1/2/2019	**10:30 am**
DATE	TIME
Pauline Battistuta	**BATTIPA0**
PATIENT NAME	CHART #

OFFICE VISITS - SYMPTOMATIC

NEW

99201	OF--New Patient Minimal	
99202	OF--New Patient Low	
99203	OF--New Patient Detailed	
99204	OF--New Patient Moderate	
99205	OF--New Patient High	

ESTABLISHED

99211	OF--Established Patient Minimal	X
99212	OF--Established Patient Low	
99213	OF--Established Patient Detailed	
99214	OF--Established Patient Moderate	
99215	OF--Established Patient High	

PREVENTIVE VISITS

NEW

99381	Under 1 Year	
99382	1 - 4 Years	
99383	5 - 11 Years	
99384	12 - 17 Years	
99385	18 - 39 Years	
99386	40 - 64 Years	
99387	65 Years & Up	

ESTABLISHED

99391	Under 1 Year	
99392	1 - 4 Years	
99393	5 - 11 Years	
99394	12 - 17 Years	
99395	18 - 39 Years	
99396	40 - 64 Years	
99397	65 Years & Up	

PROCEDURES

12011	Simple suture--face--local anes.	
29125	App. of short arm splint; static	
29425	Application of short leg cast, walking	
29540	Strapping, ankle	
50390	Aspiration of renal cyst by needle	
71010	Chest x-ray, single view, frontal	
71020	Chest x-ray, two views, frontal & lateral	

PROCEDURES

71030	Chest x-ray, complete, four views	
73070	Elbow x-ray, AP & lateral views	
73090	Forearm x-ray, AP & lateral views	
73100	Wrist x-ray, AP & lateral views	
73510	Hip x-ray, complete, two views	
73600	Ankle x-ray, AP & lateral views	

LABORATORY

80048	Basic metabolic panel	
80061	Lipid panel	
82270	Blood screening, occult; feces	
82947	Glucose screening--quantitative	
82951	Glucose tolerance test, three specimens	
83718	HDL cholesterol	
84478	Triglycerides test	
85007	Manual differential WBC	
85018	Hemoglobin	
85025	Complete CBC w/auto diff WBC	
85651	Erythrocyte sedimentation rate--non-auto	
86580	TB Mantoux test	
87040	Culture, bacterial; blood	
87076	Culture, anaerobic isolate	
87077	Bacterial culture, aerobic isolate	
87086	Urine culture and colony count	
87430	Strep test	
87880	Direct streptococcus screen	

INJECTIONS AND OTHERS

90471	Immunization administration	
90656	Influenza virus vaccine, 3+	
90662	Influenza virus vaccine, 65+	
90703	Tetanus injection	
92516	Facial nerve function studies	
93000	Electrocardiogram--ECG with interpretation	
93015	Treadmill stress test, with physician...	
96372	Injection	
96900	Ultraviolet light treatment	
99070	Supplies and materials provided	

FAMILY CARE CENTER
285 Stephenson Blvd.
Stephenson, OH 60089
614-555-0000

☐ DANA BANU, M.D.
☐ ROBERT BEACH, M.D.
☒ PATRICIA MCGRATH, M.D.

☐ JESSICA RUDNER, M.D.
☐ JOHN RUDNER, M.D.
☐ KATHERINE YAN, M.D.

NOTES

upper respiratory infection

REFERRING PHYSICIAN	NPI	AUTHORIZATION #

DIAGNOSIS
J06.9

PAYMENT AMOUNT

ENCOUNTER FORM

1/2/2019	**4:00 pm**
DATE	TIME
Christopher Palmer	**PALMECH0**
PATIENT NAME	CHART #

OFFICE VISITS - SYMPTOMATIC

NEW

99201	OF--New Patient Minimal	X
99202	OF--New Patient Low	
99203	OF--New Patient Detailed	
99204	OF--New Patient Moderate	
99205	OF--New Patient High	

ESTABLISHED

99211	OF--Established Patient Minimal	
99212	OF--Established Patient Low	
99213	OF--Established Patient Detailed	
99214	OF--Established Patient Moderate	
99215	OF--Established Patient High	

PREVENTIVE VISITS

NEW

99381	Under 1 Year	
99382	1 - 4 Years	
99383	5 - 11 Years	
99384	12 - 17 Years	
99385	18 - 39 Years	
99386	40 - 64 Years	
99387	65 Years & Up	

ESTABLISHED

99391	Under 1 Year	
99392	1 - 4 Years	
99393	5 - 11 Years	
99394	12 - 17 Years	
99395	18 - 39 Years	
99396	40 - 64 Years	
99397	65 Years & Up	

PROCEDURES

12011	Simple suture--face--local anes.	
29125	App. of short arm splint; static	
29425	Application of short leg cast, walking	
29540	Strapping, ankle	
50390	Aspiration of renal cyst by needle	
71010	Chest x-ray, single view, frontal	
71020	Chest x-ray, two views, frontal & lateral	

PROCEDURES

71030	Chest x-ray, complete, four views	
73070	Elbow x-ray, AP & lateral views	
73090	Forearm x-ray, AP & lateral views	
73100	Wrist x-ray, AP & lateral views	
73510	Hip x-ray, complete, two views	
73600	Ankle x-ray, AP & lateral views	

LABORATORY

80048	Basic metabolic panel	
80061	Lipid panel	
82270	Blood screening, occult; feces	
82947	Glucose screening--quantitative	
82951	Glucose tolerance test, three specimens	
83718	HDL cholesterol	
84478	Triglycerides test	
85007	Manual differential WBC	
85018	Hemoglobin	
85025	Complete CBC w/auto diff WBC	
85651	Erythrocyte sedimentation rate--non-auto	
86580	TB Mantoux test	
87040	Culture, bacterial; blood	
87076	Culture, anaerobic isolate	
87077	Bacterial culture, aerobic isolate	
87086	Urine culture and colony count	
87430	Strep test	
87880	Direct streptococcus screen	

INJECTIONS AND OTHERS

90471	Immunization administration	
90656	Influenza virus vaccine, 3+	
90662	Influenza virus vaccine, 65+	
90703	Tetanus injection	
92516	Facial nerve function studies	
93000	Electrocardiogram--ECG with interpretation	
93015	Treadmill stress test, with physician...	
96372	Injection	
96900	Ultraviolet light treatment	
99070	Supplies and materials provided	

FAMILY CARE CENTER
285 Stephenson Blvd.
Stephenson, OH 60089
614-555-0000

- ☐ DANA BANU, M.D.
- ☒ ROBERT BEACH, M.D.
- ☐ PATRICIA MCGRATH, M.D.
- ☐ JESSICA RUDNER, M.D.
- ☐ JOHN RUDNER, M.D.
- ☐ KATHERINE YAN, M.D.

NOTES

REFERRING PHYSICIAN	NPI	AUTHORIZATION #
Dr. Marion Davis		

DIAGNOSIS
J18.0 bronchopneumonia

PAYMENT AMOUNT
$10 copay, cash

MEDICARE
246 WEST MAIN ST.
CLEVELAND, OH 60120

PROVIDER REMITTANCE
THIS IS NOT A BILL
A PAYMENT SUMMARY AND AN EXPLANATION OF
CODES ARE AT THE END OF THIS STATEMENT

FAMILY CARE CENTER
285 STEPHENSON BLVD.
STEPHENSON, OH 60089-4000

PAGE: 1 OF 1
DATE: 12/30/2018
ID NUMBER: 3470629

PROVIDER: PATRICIA MCGRATH, M.D.

PATIENT: BATTISTUTA ANTHONY   CLAIM: 234567890

FROM DATE	THRU DATE	PROC CODE	UNITS	AMOUNT BILLED	AMOUNT ALLOWED	DEDUCT	COPAY/ COINS	PROV PAID	REASON CODE
10/25/18	10/25/18	99212	1	54.00	37.36	.00	.00	29.89	
10/25/18	10/25/18	82947	1	25.00	5.48	.00	.00	4.38	
	CLAIM TOTALS			79.00	42.84	.00	.00	34.27	

PATIENT: BATTISTUTA ANTHONY   CLAIM: 234567891

FROM DATE	THRU DATE	PROC CODE	UNITS	AMOUNT BILLED	AMOUNT ALLOWED	DEDUCT	COPAY/ COINS	PROV PAID	REASON CODE
11/09/18	11/09/18	99212	1	54.00	37.36	.00	.00	29.89	
11/09/18	11/09/18	82951	1	63.00	16.12	.00	.00	12.90	
11/09/18	11/09/18	87086	1	51.00	11.28	.00	.00	9.02	
	CLAIM TOTALS			168.00	64.76	.00	.00	51.81	

PROVIDER: KATHERINE YAN, M.D.

PATIENT: JONES ELIZABETH   CLAIM: 234567892

FROM DATE	THRU DATE	PROC CODE	UNITS	AMOUNT BILLED	AMOUNT ALLOWED	DEDUCT	COPAY/ COINS	PROV PAID	REASON CODE
10/01/18	10/01/18	99213	1	72.00	51.03	.00	.00	40.82	
	CLAIM TOTALS			72.00	51.03	.00	.00	40.82	

PAYMENT SUMMARY		TOTAL ALL CLAIMS		EFT INFORMATION	
TOTAL AMOUNT PAID	126.90	AMOUNT CHARGED	319.00	NUMBER	3470629
PRIOR CREDIT BALANCE	.00	AMOUNT ALLOWED	158.63	DATE	12/30/18
CURRENT CREDIT DEFERRED	.00	DEDUCTIBLE	.00	AMOUNT	126.90
PRIOR CREDIT APPLIED	.00	COPAY	.00		
NEW CREDIT BALANCE	.00	COINSURANCE	.00		
NET DISBURSED	126.90	AMOUNT APPROVED	158.63		

STATUS CODES:
A - APPROVED   AJ - ADJUSTMENT   IP - IN PROCESS   R - REJECTED   V - VOID

CHAMPVA
240 CENTER ST.
COLUMBUS, OH 60220

PROVIDER REMITTANCE
THIS IS NOT A BILL
A PAYMENT SUMMARY AND AN EXPLANATION OF
CODES ARE AT THE END OF THIS STATEMENT

FAMILY CARE CENTER
285 STEPHENSON BLVD.
STEPHENSON, OH 60089-4000

PAGE:	1 OF 1
DATE:	12/30/2018
ID NUMBER:	76374021

PROVIDER: JOHN RUDNER, M.D.

PATIENT: FITZWILLIAMS JOHN   CLAIM: 123456789

FROM DATE	THRU DATE	PROC CODE	UNITS	AMOUNT BILLED	AMOUNT ALLOWED	DEDUCT	COPAY/ COINS	PROV PAID	REASON CODE
10/01/18	10/01/18	99212	1	54.00	37.36	.00	15.00	22.36	
10/01/18	10/01/18	82270	1	19.00	4.54	.00	.00	4.54	
	CLAIM TOTALS			73.00	41.90	.00	15.00	26.90	

******************* CHECK #76374021 IN THE AMOUNT OF $26.90 IS ATTACHED *******************

PAYMENT SUMMARY

TOTAL AMOUNT PAID	26.90
PRIOR CREDIT BALANCE	.00
CURRENT CREDIT DEFERRED	.00
PRIOR CREDIT APPLIED	.00
NEW CREDIT BALANCE	.00
NET DISBURSED	26.90

TOTAL ALL CLAIMS

AMOUNT CHARGED	73.00
AMOUNT ALLOWED	41.90
DEDUCTIBLE	.00
COPAY	15.00
OTHER REDUCTION	.00

STATUS CODES:
AJ - ADJUSTMENT   IP - IN PROCESS   R - REJECTED   V - VOID

EAST OHIO PPO
10 CENTRAL AVENUE
HALEVILLE, OH 60890

PROVIDER REMITTANCE
THIS IS NOT A BILL
A PAYMENT SUMMARY AND AN EXPLANATION OF
CODES ARE AT THE END OF THIS STATEMENT

FAMILY CARE CENTER
285 STEPHENSON BLVD.
STEPHENSON, OH 60089-4000

PAGE:	1 OF 1
DATE:	12/30/2018
ID NUMBER:	376490713

PROVIDER: DANA BANU, M.D.

PATIENT: SYZMANSKI HANNAH   CLAIM: 78901234

FROM DATE	THRU DATE	PROC CODE	UNITS	AMOUNT BILLED	AMOUNT ALLOWED	DEDUCT	COPAY/ COINS	PROV PAID	REASON CODE
11/09/18	11/09/18	99383	1	224.00	201.60	.00	20.00	181.60	
	CLAIM TOTALS			224.00	201.60	.00	20.00	181.60	

PATIENT: SYZMANSKI MICHAEL   CLAIM: 89012345

FROM DATE	THRU DATE	PROC CODE	UNITS	AMOUNT BILLED	AMOUNT ALLOWED	DEDUCT	COPAY/ COINS	PROV PAID	REASON CODE
11/12/18	11/12/18	99215	1	163.00	146.70	.00	20.00	126.70	
11/12/18	11/12/18	82270	1	19.00	17.10	.00	.00	17.10	
	CLAIM TOTALS			182.00	163.80	.00	20.00	143.80	

PAYMENT SUMMARY		TOTAL ALL CLAIMS		EFT INFORMATION	
TOTAL AMOUNT PAID	325.40	AMOUNT CHARGED	406.00	NUMBER	376490713
PRIOR CREDIT BALANCE	.00	AMOUNT ALLOWED	365.40	DATE	12/30/18
CURRENT CREDIT DEFERRED	.00	DEDUCTIBLE	.00	AMOUNT	325.40
PRIOR CREDIT APPLIED	.00	COPAY	40.00		
NEW CREDIT BALANCE	.00	COINSURANCE	0.00		
NET DISBURSED	325.40				

REASON CODES:
AJ - ADJUSTMENT   IP - IN PROCESS   R - REJECTED   V - VOID

OHIOCARE HMO
147 CENTRAL AVENUE
HALFVILLE, OH 60890

FAMILY CARE CENTER
285 STEPHENSON BLVD.
STEPHENSON, OH 60089-4000

PAGE: 1 OF 1
DATE: 12/30/2018
ID NUMBER: 767729

OHIOCARE HMO CAPITATION STATEMENT
MONTH OF NOVEMBER 2018

PROVIDERS
RANU DANA
BEACH ROBERT
MCGRATH PATRICIA
RUDNER JESSICA
RUDNER JOHN
YAN KATHERINE

MEMBER NUMBER	MEMBER NAME	CONTRACT NUMBER	CONTRACT STATUS
0003602149	FAMILY CARE CENTER	YG34906	APPROVED

AMOUNT OF PAYMENT $2,500.00
EFT STATUS: SENT 12/30/18 2:46PM
TRANSACTION #767729

glossary

a

access rights   Security option that determines the areas of the program a user can access and whether the user has rights to enter or edit data.

accountable care organization (ACO)   A network of doctors and hospitals that share responsibility for managing the quality and cost of care provided to a group of patients.

accounts receivable (AR)   Monies that are coming into the practice.

adjudication   Series of steps that determine whether a claim should be paid.

adjustments   Changes to patients' accounts that alter the amounts charged or paid.

Affordable Care Act   Federal legislation passed in 2010 that includes a number of provisions designed to increase access to healthcare, improve the quality of healthcare, and explore new models of delivering and paying for healthcare.

after-visit summary (AVS)   A communication tool that provides the patient with relevant and actionable information and instructions.

aging report   A report that lists the amount of money owed to the practice, organized by the amount of time the money has been owed.

audit   A formal examination or review undertaken to determine whether a healthcare organization's staff members comply with regulations.

audit trail   A report that traces who has accessed electronic information, when information was accessed, and whether any information was changed.

Auto Log Off   Feature of Medisoft that automatically logs a user out of the program after a period of inactivity.

autoposting   The automatic posting of data in the remittance advice to a practice management program.

b

backup data   A copy of data files made at a specific point in time that can be used to restore data.

breach   The acquisition, access, use, or disclosure of unsecured PHI in a manner not permitted under the HIPAA Privacy Rule.

bundled payments   A model of reimbursement in which single payments to multiple providers involved in an episode of care, creating a sense of shared accountability among providers.

business associate   An individual or entity that creates, receives, maintains, or transmits PHI on behalf of a covered entity; may also include subcontractors of an entity.

c

capitated plan   An insurance plan in which prepayments made to a physician cover the physician's services to a plan member for a specified period of time.

capitation   Payment to a provider that covers each plan member's healthcare services for a certain period of time.

capitation payments   Payments made to physicians on a regular basis for providing services to patients in a managed care plan.

case   A grouping of transactions that share a common element.

charges   Amounts a provider bills for the services performed.

chart number   A unique number that identifies a patient.

clean claims   Claims with all the correct information necessary for payer processing.

clearinghouse   A company that receives claims from a provider, prepares them for processing, and transmits them to the payers in HIPAA-compliant format.

CMS-1500   The mandated paper insurance claim form.

coding   The process of translating a description of a diagnosis or procedure into a standardized code.

coinsurance   Percentage of charges that an insured person must pay for healthcare services after payment of the deductible amount.

collection agency   An outside firm hired to collect on delinquent accounts.

collection list   A tool for tracking activities that need to be completed as part of the collection process.

collection tracer report   A tool for keeping track of collection letters that were sent.

copayment   A fixed fee paid by the patient at the time of an office visit.

covered entity   A person or entity that furnishes, bills, or receives payment for healthcare in the normal course of business and conducts certain transactions in electronic form.

crossover claims Claims that are processed by Medicare and then transferred to Medicaid, or to a payer that provides supplemental insurance benefits to Medicare beneficiaries.

Current Procedural Terminology (CPT®) The standardized classification system for reporting medical procedures and services.

cycle billing A type of billing in which statement printing and mailing are staggered throughout the month.

d

database A collection of related bits of information.

day sheet A report that provides information on practice activities for a twenty-four-hour period.

deductible Amount due before benefits begin.

diagnosis Physician's opinion of the nature of the patient's illness or injury.

diagnosis code A standardized value that represents a patient's illness, signs, and symptoms.

documentation A record of healthcare encounters between the provider and the patient.

e

electronic data interchange (EDI) The exchange of routine business transactions from one computer to another using publicly available communications protocols.

electronic funds transfer (EFT) The electronic movement of money from one bank account to another.

electronic health record (EHR) A computerized lifelong healthcare record for an individual that incorporates data from all providers who treat the individual.

electronic prescribing The use of computers and handheld devices to transmit prescriptions in digital format.

electronic protected health information (ePHI) Protected health information (PHI) that is created, stored, transmitted, or received electronically.

electronic remittance advice (ERA) An electronic document that lists patients, dates of service, charges, and the amount paid or denied by the insurance carrier.

encounter form A list of the procedures and diagnoses for a patient's visit.

established patient A patient who has been seen by a provider in the practice in the same specialty or subspecialty within three years.

explanation of benefits (EOB) Paper document from a payer that shows how the amount of a benefit was determined.

f

fee-for-service A model of physician reimbursement in which payment is provided for specific, individual services provided to a patient.

fee schedule A document that specifies the amount the provider bills for provided services.

filter A condition that data must meet to be selected.

g

guarantor An individual who may not be a patient of the practice but who is financially responsible for a patient account.

h

HCPCS Codes used for supplies, equipment, and services not included in the CPT codes.

health information technology (HIT) Technology that is used to record, store, and manage patient healthcare information.

Health Information Technology for Economic and Clinical Health (HITECH) Act Part of the American Recovery and Reinvestment Act of 2009 that provides financial incentives to physicians and hospitals to adopt EHRs and strengthens HIPAA privacy and security regulations.

Health Insurance Portability and Accountability Act of 1996 (HIPAA) Federal act that sets forth guidelines for standardizing the electronic data interchange of administrative and financial transactions, exposing fraud and abuse in government programs, and protecting the security and privacy of health information.

health maintenance organization (HMO) A managed healthcare system in which providers agree to offer healthcare to the organization's members for fixed payments.

high-deductible health plan with savings option (HDHP/SO) A type of managed care insurance in which a high-deductible plan is combined with a pretax savings account to cover out-of-pocket medical expenses.

HIPAA Omnibus Rule Legislation passed in 2013 that made significant changes to the privacy, security, and enforcement provisions of the original HIPAA legislation.

HIPAA Privacy Rule Regulations for protecting individually identifiable information about a patient's health and payment for healthcare that is created or received by a healthcare provider.

HIPAA Security Rule Regulations outlining the minimum administrative, technical, and physical safeguards required to prevent unauthorized access to protected healthcare information.

i

ICD-9-CM Abbreviated title of *International Classification of Diseases*, Ninth Revision, *Clinical Modification*, the source of the codes used for reporting diagnoses until October 1, 2015.

ICD-10-CM Abbreviated title of *International Classification of Diseases*, Tenth Revision, *Clinical Modification*, the source of the codes used for reporting diagnoses.

indemnity plan Also known as a *fee-for-service plan;* a health plan that repays the policyholder for covered medical expenses.

insurance aging report A report that lists how long a payer has taken to respond to insurance claims.

m

managed care A type of insurance in which the carrier is responsible for both the financing and the delivery of healthcare.

meaningful use The utilization of certified EHR technology to improve quality, efficiency, and patient safety in the healthcare system.

medical documentation and billing cycle A ten-step process that results in timely payment for medical services.

medical necessity Treatment provided by a physician to a patient for the purpose of preventing, diagnosing, or treating an illness, injury, or its symptoms in a manner that is appropriate and is provided in accordance with generally accepted standards of medical practice.

Medisoft Program Date Date the program uses to record when a transaction occurred.

MMDDCCYY format The way dates must be keyed in Medisoft, in which *MM* stands for the month, *DD* stands for the day, *CC* represents the century, and *YY* stands for the year.

MultiLink codes Groups of procedure code entries that relate to a single activity.

n

National Health Information Network (NHIN) A common platform for health information exchange across the country.

National Provider Identifier (NPI) A standard identifier for healthcare providers consisting of ten numbers.

navigator buttons Buttons that simplify the task of moving from one entry to another.

new patient A patient who has not received services from the same provider or a provider of the same specialty or subspecialty within the same practice for a period of three years.

NSF check A check that is not honored by a bank because the account it was written on does not have sufficient funds to cover it.

o

Office Hours break A block of time when a physician is unavailable for appointments with patients.

Office Hours calendar An interactive calendar that is used to select or change dates in Office Hours.

Office Hours patient information The area of the Office Hours window that displays information about the patient who is selected in the provider's daily schedule.

once-a-month billing A type of billing in which statements are mailed to all patients at the same time each month.

p

packing data The deletion of vacant slots from the database.

patient aging report A report that lists a patient's balance by age, date, and amount of the last payment.

patient-centered medical home (PCMH) A model of primary care that provides comprehensive and timely care to patients, while emphasizing teamwork and patient involvement.

patient day sheet A summary of patient activity on a given day.

patient information form A form that includes a patient's personal, employment, and insurance data needed to complete an insurance claim.

patient ledger A report that lists the financial activity in each patient's account.

patient portal A secure online website which provides patients with the ability to communicate with their provider and access their health information at any time.

patient statement A list of the amount of money a patient owes, the procedures performed, and the dates the procedures were performed.

payer Private or government organization that insures or pays for healthcare on behalf of beneficiaries.

payment day sheet A report that lists all payments received on a particular day, organized by provider.

payment plan An agreement between a patient and a practice in which the patient agrees to make regular monthly payments over a specified period of time.

payments Monies received from patients and insurance carriers.

payment schedule   A document that specifies the amount the payer agrees to reimburse the provider for a service.

point-of-service (POS) plan   A plan, combining features of an HMO and a PPO, in which members may choose from providers in a primary or secondary network.

policyholder   A person or entity who buys an insurance plan; the insured.

practice analysis report   A report that analyzes the revenue of a practice for a specified period of time.

practice management programs (PMPs)   Software programs that automate many of the administrative and financial tasks in a medical practice.

preferred provider organization (PPO)   Managed care network of healthcare providers who agree to perform services for plan members at discounted fees.

premium   The periodic amount of money the insured pays to a health plan for insurance coverage.

primary insurance carrier   The first carrier to whom claims are submitted.

procedure   Medical treatment provided by a physician or other healthcare provider.

procedure code   A code that identifies a medical service.

procedure day sheet   A report that lists all the procedures performed on a particular day, in numerical order.

progress notes   A physician's notes about a patient's condition and diagnosis.

prompt payment laws   State laws that mandate a time period within which clean claims must be paid; if they are not, financial penalties are levied against the payer.

protected health information (PHI)   Information about a patient's health or payment for healthcare that can be used to identify the person.

provider's daily schedule   A listing of time slots for a particular day for a specific provider that corresponds to the date selected in the calendar.

provider selection box   A selection box that determines which provider's schedule is displayed in the provider's daily schedule.

purging data   The process of deleting files of patients who are no longer seen by a provider in a practice.

r

rebuilding indexes   A process that checks and verifies data and corrects any internal problems with the data.

recalculating balances   The process of updating balances to reflect the most recent changes made to the data.

recall list   A list of patients who need to be contacted for future appointments.

referring provider   A physician who recommends that a patient see a specific other physician.

remainder statements   Statements that list only those charges that are not paid in full after all insurance carrier payments have been received.

remittance advice (RA)   A document that lists the amount that has been paid on each claim as well as the reasons for nonpayment or partial payment.

restoring data   The process of retrieving data from backup storage devices.

revenue cycle management   Managing the activities associated with a patient encounter to ensure that the provider receives full payment for services.

S

sponsor   In TRICARE, the active-duty service member.

standard statements   Statements that show all charges regardless of whether the insurance has paid on the transactions.

t

tickler   A reminder to follow up on an account.

timely filing   The requirement that claims must be submitted to payers within a specific number of days from the date of service.

u

uncollectible account   An account that does not respond to collection efforts and is written off the practice's expected accounts receivable.

W

walkout receipt   A receipt given to the patient after a payment is made that lists the procedures, diagnosis, charges, and payment.

write-off   A balance that has been removed from a patient's account.

X

X12 837 Health Care Claim or Equivalent Encounter Information (837P)   HIPAA standard format for electronic transmission of a professional claim from a provider to a health plan.

d

Daily reports, 334–335
Data
  backup, 66
  deleting, 61–62
  editing, 58–61
  entering, 58
  packing, 72–73
  purging, 74–75
  for reports, 329–334
  restoring, 69–70
  saving, 61, 66
Databases
  defined, 8, 49
  Medisoft, 49–50
  restoration of, 69–70
Dates, in Medisoft, 62–64, 249–251,
  331–333
Day sheets
  defined, 334–335
  patient, 336–340
  payment, 341–342
  procedure, 340–341
Debt collections. *See* Collection
  issues
Deductible, 105, 170, 239
Delete button, 204
Delete Case button, 159–160
Deposit dialog box, 282–286, 299
Deposit List dialog box, 211,
  279–282, 285, 286
Detail button, 205, 280
Diagnosis, 19
Diagnosis Code List button, 56
Diagnosis codes, 19–20
Diagnosis tab, 176–178, 265, 266
Diagnostic code database, 49–50
Diagnostic codes, HCPCS, 21
Documentation, 10. *See also* Medical
  documentation and billing cycle

e

EDI. *See* Electronic data interchange
  (EDI)
EDI Notes button, 205, 266, 267
EDI Note tab, 259
EDI Report, 177, 265, 266
EDI Tab, 185–188
Edit Case button, 159
Edit feature
  for case information, 188–189
  for claims, 256–259
  for data in Medisoft, 58–61
  for insurance claims, 256–260
  for patient information, 149–150
  for patient statements, 311–313
  for transactions, 208

Edit menu, 51, 52
Edit Patient Notes in Final Draft
  button, 57, 87
Edits, 25
Edit Templates button, 87
EFT (electronic funds transfer). *See*
  Electronic funds transfer (EFT)
EHRs. *See* Electronic health records
  (EHRs)
Electronic claims. *See also* Claims
  (insurance)
  clearinghouse for, 262–263
  creating, 262
  performing edit check for, 263–265
  sending attachments with, 265–267
  transmission of, 242
Electronic claims analysis—detail
  and summary, 347
Electronic data interchange (EDI),
  28–29
Electronic funds transfer (EFT), 25,
  29, 278–279
Electronic health records (EHRs)
  administrative processes and, 13–14
  charge transactions imported
    from, 229–230
  creating cases for imported
    transactions, 190
  decision support and, 13
  defined, 4, 10
  electronic communication and
    connectivity and, 13
  health information and data
    elements of, 10–11
  McKesson Practice Interface
    Center program and, 363
  order management and, 12
  patient support and, 13
  reporting and population
    management and, 14
  results management and, 11–12
  transferring appointment
    information to, 120
  transferring patient information
    to, 120, 151–152
Electronic patient records (EPRs). *See*
  Electronic health records (EHRs)
Electronic prescribing, 12
Electronic protected health
  information (ePHI), 31
Electronic remittance advice (ERA),
  25, 276
Eligibility verification, 106–109
Employer identification number
  (EIN), 30
Employer information, 141–144
Encounter forms, 21–23, 161
Enter Deposits and Apply Payments
  button, 57
Entering data in Medisoft, 58

EPSDT (Early and Periodic Screen-
  ing, Diagnosis, and Treatment),
  173, 175
Established patients, 130. *See also*
  Patients
Exit button, 87
Exiting Medisoft, creating backup
  file while, 66–68
Exit Program button, 57
Explanation of benefits (EOB), 25

f

Fair Debt Collection Practices Act of
  1977, 377–378
Fee for service, 6
Fee-for-service plans. *See* Indemnity
  plans
Fee schedule, 274
Field options, 146
Fields box, 145–148
File Maintenance dialog box, 71, 75
File maintenance utilities
  creating backup files in, 66–69
  packing data in, 72–73
  purging data in, 74–75
  rebuilding indexes in, 72
  recalculating patient balances in,
    75, 76
  restoring backup files in, 69–70
File menu, 50–51
Filters, 249
Financial policy
  importance of, 374–377
  of medical practice, 17
Find Open Time dialog box, 100
First Claim button, 248
Flash drives, saving data on, 66
Follow-up appointments, 98–99. *See
  also* Appointment scheduling
Forms. *See also* Reports
  CMS-1500, 243
  encounter, 21–23, 161

g

General tab, 311–312
Go to a Date button, 87
Go to Today button, 87
Guarantor, 134–135

h

HCPCS codes, 21
Healthcare spending, 3
Healthcare system
  Affordable Care Act and, 4–5
  electronic health record programs
    and, 10–14

Medicare
  explanation of, 238
  fee schedules for, 275–276
  filing claims under, 373
Medicare Physician Fee Schedule
    (MPFS), 275–276
Medisoft
  appointment scheduling in,
      75–105 (*See also* Appointment
      scheduling)
  auto log off and unapproved
      codes in, 78–79
  changing program date in, 62–64
  claim management in, 248–249,
      262
  CMS-1500 in, 242–248
  creating backup files while exit-
      ing, 66–68
  creating reports in, 327–329,
      359–362
  databases and, 49–50
  dates in, 62–64, 249–251, 331–333
  defined, 49
  deleting data in, 61–62
  editing data in, 58–61
  entering data in, 58
  entering insurance information in,
      168–175
  entering insurance payment in,
      279–287
  entering new patient information
      in, 130–144
  exiting, 66
  file maintenance utilities in,
      71–76
  installation of, 44–45
  navigating cases in Medisoft,
      159–162
  organization of patient informa-
      tion in, 129–130
  packing data in, 72–73
  privacy and security features of,
      76–79
  purging data in, 74–75
  rebuilding indexes in, 72
  recalculating patient balances in,
      75, 76
  restoring backup file in, 69–70
  saving data in, 61
  Security Setup option, 76
  toolbar in, 55–57
  transferring information to electronic
      health record from, 120
  user logins and audit controls
      in, 78
  using help feature in, 54, 64–66
Medisoft Help button, 57
Medisoft menus
  Activities menu, 51–52, 89, 106, 387
  defined, 50

Edit menu, 51, 52
File menu, 50–51
Help menu, 54, 64–66
Lists menu, 52–53, 378
Reports menu, 53, 327, 336, 337,
    352, 353, 395
Window menu, 53–54
Medisoft payment entry
  applying insurance payments to
      charges, 213–215, 287–293
  for capitation payments, 299–304
  for patient payments received in
      mail, 297–299
Medisoft printing. *See* Printing
    procedures
Medisoft Program Date, 62–64
Medisoft Report Designer, 327
Medisoft reports. *See also* Reports
  aging, 356
  custom, 356–358
  navigating in, 352–355
  Report Designer to create, 327,
      359–362
  standard, 351–352, 363
  types of, 327
Medisoft Reports menu, 352–354
Medisoft Reports toolbar, 355
Medisoft Security Permissions
    dialog box, 77
Medisoft utilities
  creating backup files and, 66–69
  file maintenance, 71–76
  packing data and, 72–73
  purging data and, 74–75
  rebuilding indexes and, 72
  recalculating patient balances
      and, 75, 76
  restoring backup files in, 69–70
Miscellaneous tab, 182–183
MMDDCCYY format, 64
Monthly reports, 335–336
MultiLink button, 204–205
MultiLink codes, 204–205

n

Name, Address tab, 131–133
National Council for Prescription
    Drug Programs (NCPDP), 29
National Provider Identifier
    (NPI), 30
National Uniform Claim Committee
    (NUCC) (American Medical
    Association), 242
Navigator buttons, 248–249
Need Referral, 94
New Appointment Entry dialog
    box, 91, 92, 94, 96, 97, 102, 103
New Break Entry dialog box, 116
New Case button, 159

New patients. *See also* Patients
  defined, 130
  entering information for,
      130–144
  scheduling appointments for,
      101–102
New York Prompt Payment Law,
    372
Next Claim button, 249
Nonsufficient funds (NSF) checks,
    227–228
Note button, 205
Notice of Privacy Practices, 31–35

O

Office for Civil Rights (OCR), 37, 38
Office Hours break, 115–117
Office Hours calendar, 88
Office Hours menu bar, 86, 87
Office Hours patient information, 88
Office Hours program. *See also*
    Appointment scheduling
  booking follow-up appointments
      in, 98–99
  checking patients in and out in,
      109–110
  creating overdue balance report
      for patients in, 111
  creating patient recall list in, 111–115
  creating provider breaks in, 115–117
  entering and exiting, 89
  functions of, 86–89
  looking up provider in, 97–98
  procedure to enter appointments
      in, 89–98
  program options in, 89
  rescheduling and canceling
      appointments in, 104–105
  scheduling appointments for new
      patients in, 101–102
  scheduling repeat appointments
      in, 102–104
  searching for available time slots
      in, 99–101
  toolbar in, 86, 87
  transferring appointment informa-
      tion in, 120
  verifying insurance eligibility in,
      105–109
  viewing and printing schedules
      in, 117–118
Office Hours toolbar, 86, 87
Office Hours window, 86, 88, 90, 95
Office Notes tab, 393
Office visits
  entering payments made during,
      211–216
  walkout statements/receipts for,
      207, 220–223

Copyright ©2016 McGraw-Hill Education